—Prologue—

What is a space of possibilities? Who or what appropriates these spaces, designs, produces, adapts, modifies, and programs them ...? How can I seize it? How can I grasp this space continuum that is so very disjointed, indeterminate, fleeting? How do I track it down? How do I find its trail? Which invisible tracks should I follow?

"The only viable slogan is to 'follow the actors themselves'; yes, one must follow them when they multiply entities and again when they rarefy entities[1]."   Latour 2005: 227

Following the actors, but where to?

"Just follow the flow. Yes, follow the actors themselves or rather that which makes them act, namely the circulating entities."   ibid.: 237

... flowing after flowing with flowing around flowing away flowing toward ...

"The more 'affluence', the better. It is counterintuitive to try and distinguish 'what comes from viewers' and 'what comes from the object' when the obvious response is to 'go with the flow'."   Latour 2005: 237

What happens to the objects?

"(...) 'when faced with an object, attend first to the associations out of which it's made and only later look at how it has renewed the repertoire of social ties'. (...) the more attachments the better. (...) The more influence, the better."   ibid.: 233ff

1
Bruno Latour talks of entities as:
"(...) beings, objects, things, perhaps refer to them as invisibles" (Latour 2005: 240).

That is why I observe the connecting lines between the human and / or non-human objects[2] ...

"No matter how hesitant the metaphor, it is such a shift in perspective that ANT [Actor-Network Theory] is looking for. Things, quasi-objects, and attachments are the real center of the social world, not the agent, person, member, or participant — nor is it society or its avatars. (...) What gets highlighted now are all the mediators whose proliferation generates, among many other entities, what could be called quasi-objects and quasi-subjects. (...) Society is the consequence of associations and not their cause. (...) To understand what I take to be the ultimate goal of ANT, we have to let out of their cages entities which had been strictly forbidden to enter the scene until now and allow them to roam in the world again." Latour 2005: 238 ff

But what does the ANT perspective allow me to do?

"I hope it's clear that this flattening does not mean that the world of the actors themselves has been flattened out. Quite the contrary, they have been given enough space to deploy their own contradictory gerunds: scaling, zooming, embedding, 'panoraming', individualizing, and so on. The metaphor of a flatland was simply a way for the ANT observers to clearly distinguish their job from the labor of those they follow around. If the analyst takes upon herself to decide in advance and a priori the scale in which all the actors are embedded, then most of the work they have to do to establish connections will simply vanish from view. It is only by making flatness the default position of the observer that the activity necessary to generate some difference in size can be detected and registered." ibid.: 220

That surely means that this default setting can in some ways be equated to setting the clock back to zero? By first forgetting everything I already know. "The known ever is therefore, because it is known not to be recognized" as Hegel has already formulated it. Hegel in: Dell 2009/10: 13

"[Or] in other words, how vast is the terra incognita we will have to leave blank on our maps? (...) What lies in between these connections?" Latour 2005: 221

2

Bruno Latour introduces non-human objects (actants) and human objects (actors) into his Actor-Network Theory (ANT): "Actor, Actant: The great interest of science studies is that it offers, through the study of laboratory practice, many cases of emergence of an actor. Instead of starting with entities that are already components of the world, science studies focuses on the complex and controversial nature of what it is for an actor to come into existence. The key is to define the actor by what it does — its performances — under laboratory trials. Later its competence is deduced and made part of an institution. Since in English 'actor' is often limited to humans, the word 'actant', borrowed from semiotics, is sometimes used

2

to include
non-humans in
the definition."
(Latour 1999: 303)

—Latour briefly leaves the stage/
Serres appears slowly on the screen—

3
Over several cen-
turies, as a result of
dike construction,
the Elbe Island
developed from
an archipelago of
islands into today's
urban Elbe Island
(No Dike, No Land).
Today's Elbe Island
is also shaped by
a whole host of
different realities in
everyday life, which
I explore island by
island. Consequent-
ly, from my per-
spective the Elbe
Island is (still) made
up of many islands,
which is why I refer
to it in the plural
as the Elbe Islands.

What lies between the (in)visible connections, what lies between the flowing currents? The curiosity that seizes me now leads me as a researcher into my field (cf. Girtler 2004: 6). Salut actants. Salut actors. I am on the Elbe Islands[3] of Wilhelmsburg, south of Hamburg. My uncharted field of research. How does everyday life on the islands look? Where do possibilities unfold? Where do I start? What awaits me? Here. Continuing to search for a way to gain access to the field (cf. Wolff 2008: 334f) that will allow me to encircle, delimit the space of possibilities, to make it tangible[4]. For if it really—as I suspect—is such an erratic, ephemeral being, I must approach it cautiously. But how, how I can track it down, pick up its trail?

"In the old French hunting lexicon, 'courir à randon' meant to force the game: for example, to ride in pursuit of a deer following its movements from the beginning of the case to the kill. Rapid and impetuous the animal must often have changed. (…) Randon (…) is equally divided between the Franch and English languages. In French, randonnée ended up meaning a quite long and difficult walk. In English, in memory of the irregular and unex-pected course of the quarry, random means chance."

Serres 2009/1998: 259

You think I should move via a cross country route, run zigzagging closer to the space of possibilities?

4
Drawing on Alexa
Färber's text, from
the perspective
of "tangibility," ques-
tions are raised
about the material-
ity and the potential
of various prac-
tices, such as partic-
ipation, integration,
appropriation,
and establishing
close links in
these aspects.
She writes in
"Tangibility of the
city. A consider-
ation of urban and
anthropological
scientific research
into the acquisition
of urban space."
"The movement
of searching would
then pursue the
traces that demon-
strate how the city
offers itself up to
understand, to pick
up on and the
kind of collectives
that are formed in
the process."
(Färber 2010: 103)

"A walk through the countryside is called randonnée,
a ramble."   Serres 2009/1998: 259

Randonnée, randonnée?

"I should like to use randonnée in a sense close to its
origin, but inflected here and there, as chance would have
it, according to the direction I take and how long I ramble.
Weather conditions, difficult terrain, and wayward currents often turn the Odyssey into a randonnée. Ulysses
eschews the best way because of a combination of
circumstances."   ibid.

To abandon the best way as a researcher?!
You really think I should have no plan at all?

"The Odyssean path is an exodus rather than a method.
(...) The exodus and deviations inflect the path itself, not
the stable places on the route. When you have a method,
you say: a methodical approach — a tautology. But when
you are speaking about an exodus, you can say: a discourse of exodus — equivalence. The discourse deviates
in relation to the path travelled, just as the exodus moves
away from the middle, from equilibrium and from the
extremity of method."   Serres 2009/1998: 261

You say the randonnée is a non-method? But it seems to
me that it is one. Because as a non-method it offers me the
access to my research field that I have hoped for.

"Method clearly traces a journey, a pathway through a
space. Knows where it comes from and where it is going.
Running between both these situations, the methodical line passes through the middle and is defined and of
course constrained, in terms of these extremes. (...)
The Odyssey traces pathways outside this order, waste-
ful paths."   ibid.

Extravagant wastefulness — good! But how am I sup-
posed to ever find a path leading out of there again?

"Ulysses must have had a thousand tricks in his bag, to
cope with the unexpected and the unscripted; you
have to make do with forethought, if you are not good at
making predictions. Prediction assumes the predicta-
bility of a global, homogeneous space on which the law

can be written; forethought involves the countryside, the intuition of a historiated space with circumstantial cells, a set of localities: the person with foresight does not know what the neighbouring cell has in store for him tomorrow, hence this bag of a hundred tricks, at his side or in his head. Now it so happens that Ulysses is caught short by events, an unusual set of circumstances leaving him ill-prepared and helpless — he is short of a trick. Does he deviate from the designated route? No, this route would have to be drawn like a law on smooth, global space, a straight line in the forest or rhumb line across the ocean. No, Ulysses adds braids or loops to his route, which will count as a new trick in his bag and will add a new element to the countryside." Serres 2009/1998: 269

I see, I see. I should abandon myself to the adventure and turbulences, endure the uncertainties and insecurities in the process.

"If you happen upon a fertile method, forge straight ahead with it. It will be productive. You will soon have a notion of the sort of questions it resolves. Then stop because you are heading rapidly towards boredom, rigidity, old age, and idiocy. (...) In the beginning, however, the wondrous idea promised life. Leap sideways. Keep the recogniz- able method or methods in reserve, in case of illness, misery, fatigue; go rambling again." ibid.: 271

Randonnez!

"Explore space, a flying insect, a stag at bay, a stroller always chased off his habitual path by guard dogs growling around familiar places. Observe your own elec- troencephalogram jumping all over the place and sweep- ing across the page. Wander as free as a cloud, cast your gaze in every direction, improvise. Improvisation is a source of wonder for the eye. Think of anxiety as good fortune, self-assurance as poverty. Lose your balance, leave the beaten track, chase birds out of the hedges. Debrouillez-vous ..." Serres 2009/1998: 271

Débrouillons-nous?

"... muddle through, a perfect popular expression mean- ing literally to unscramble yourself. It supposes a tangled skein, a certain disorder and that vital confidence in the impromptu event that characterizes healthy innocents, lovers, esthetes and the lonely."   ibid.

... Upstream downstream flow sideways in "Flatland"...
                                        Latour 2005: 220

"The randonnée is there for time and intelligence, the wellbeing of though, freedom, peace: the creation of un-expected places. But take both paths, condemn neither; those who love the countryside sometimes need expressways."   Serres 2009/1998: 271

— They set off together —

The dialogue with the field is opened. My inner curiosity grows restless. Finally, I turn in a circle with my eyes closed until left is right and up is down. I have lost my bearings; my randonnée begins. Now. I set off sideways. Full stop. Leave paths seemingly familiar to me for a moment. Aimlessly. My constant and trusty companion, the Japanese camera. First, we manually set flatness as default[5] and from this point on consider the field of research with its different actors and actants from the eye-level perspective[6]. During my randonnée I observe and communicate with mailboxes aviaries locks cars pedalos benches strollers carpets bal-conies halls shopping carts Western Union banks pawn-shops takeaways kiosks the bunker tractors vegetable fields dikes sheep large housing estates tracks allotments dogs backyards Africans store windows retirees curtains flowerpots parasols bell buttons shopping bags family homes bubbles cats dog owners supermarkets receipts garden hoses tea glasses dumpsters doors cocoa beans rose hedges playgrounds containers Turks excavators cafes weekly markets odors police officers security staff junk-yards garages hairdressers tearooms Muslims launderettes

5
"It is only by making flatness the de-fault position of the observer that the activity necessary to generate some difference in size can be detected and registered."
(Latour 2005: 220)

6
I explore the Elbe Islands from the user's perspective

or from the perspective of the everyday. That means that the focus is, from the native's point of view, on coming into the field as a "participant observer" (cf. Spradley 1980).

7
Space becomes legible not only through use or by the processes of appropriation that can emerge from an array of diverse social interactions, but—picking up on the ideas of French philosopher Henri Lefebvre—space is actually produced by these factors. In this context the important aspect is not the way that spaces are but rather how they are produced and what they do. In keeping with this, we are all "space producers." Lefebvre draws a distinction between various kinds of space in his theoretical conception of space: "espace conçu" (the conceived space), "espace vécu" (the lived space) and "espace perçu" (the experienced space) (Lefebvre 1974: 1–67; 33). Relational space is constructed via what is known as "spacing" of people and goods as well as by one's own "effort of synthesis" (Löw 2001: 158f).

clothes lines children mosques glasshouses front yards ports caravans bridges global call shops mothers seagulls Rotenhäuser Feld bottles with deposits windmills clothes racks sunflower seed pods Germans lost objects Yum-Yum soups men Bulgarians walkers families bus stops suburban trains warehouses satellite dishes … and follow, in the Latourian sense, their various stable or fragile associations (cf. Prologue). For "rather than placeholders that reinforce existing assumptions, things, whether they are human or non-human, have agency; they are actively 'doing something'.[7] (…) For instance, highways, the electrical grid or a computer are active non-human agents influencing the desires of social networks that reciprocally shape them"[8] (Easterling 2010: 26). In the interplay of human and non-human objects I recognize various site-specific everyday practices. They produce an "immense texturology"[9]

8
"If it is true, as ANT claims, that the social landscape possesses such a flat 'networky' topography and that the ingredients making up society travel inside tiny conduits, what is in between the meshes of such a circuitry? This is why, no matter its many defects, the net metaphor remains so powerful. Contrary to substance, surface, domain, and spheres that fill every centimeter of what they bind and delineate, nets, networks, and 'worknets' leave everything they don't connect simply unconnected. Is not a net made up, first and foremost, of empty spaces? " (Latour 2005: 242)

9
However the producers of this "texturology" cannot decipher it themselves from their perspective, as "the ordinary practitioners of the city live 'down below', below the threshold at which visibility begins. They walk —an elementary form of this experience of the city; they are walkers, Wandersmänner,

as Michel de Certeau described it in "Practice of the Everyday Life" (de Certeau 1988: 92). However, absence also references, in the form of ephemeral traces, its spatial producers (Lefebvre 1991/1974: 330f) and their spatial tactics, which I follow as well. In the process, at different scales and zoom levels, I explore relational-spatial structures, becoming increasingly familiar with the everyday patterns and phenomena contained within them. With the ongoing reception of spatial practice, the urban program becomes legible for me,[10] influenced by the multifaceted realities of the islands' inhabitants, and by continuing this in a dynamic process. The program is adapted, modified, by adding "quasi-objects" or "quasi-subjects" (Latour 2005: 238f) or establishing new connections between them ... This means a permanent programming of urbanity in the realm of the simultaneous.[11]

"It's never clear who and what is acting when we act since an actor on stage is never alone acting.[12] Play-acting puts us immediately into a thick imbroglio where the question of who is carrying out the action has become unfathomable."   Latour in: Easterling 2010: 30

Amidst this programmatic interaction of everyday actions, my camera photographed the various phenomena and associative scenes. Every now and then my phone takes on this function, especially if the presence of the camera disturbs the field too much, disturbing it more than anything. There are some situations in which being respectful entails not taking pictures. Whenever possible, I use photography as a performative act to enter into a direct dialogue with people. When I ask if I can photograph them polishing their car, outside their store, or in the front yard of their house, brief moments of exchange come into being. Every now and then I have to delete my material on the spot, when a photo was clearly unwelcome, but the shutter had already been released ⟨Stage Directions from the Field⟩. In these situations, I jot down the scenes in my field diary and subsequently develop a series of open-ended stories[13]. The text becomes the photograph[14], the photograph becomes text[15]. In addition, as time passes, I discover a technique that lets me photograph discreetly — almost in passing. I use this in particular when I find

whose bodies follow the thicks and thins of an urban 'text' they write without being able to read it. These practitioners make use of space that cannot be seen; their knowledge of them is as blind as that of lovers in each other's arms. The paths that correspond in this intertwining, unrecognized poem in which each body is an element signed by many others, elude legibility."
(de Certeau 1988 Cap. VII: 92)

10
I take the urban program to mean the interaction between human and/or non-human objects and the specific mode of production that is generated by their everyday practice.

11
Bruno Latour also describes the space between the

8

connections as "plasma," in other words "which is not yet formatted, not yet measured, not yet socialized, not yet engaged in metrological chains, and not yet covered, surveyed, mobilized, or subjectified" (Latour 2005: 244). The plasma is always there, even when it is still unknown. Its etymological characteristics "have a soft impalpable liquid quality" (ibid.: 245). The invisible, everyday, practices that are already inherent in plasma, could also be described as the program that has not yet been formatted and is not yet interconnected, and that can develop from this to form a program.

12
Bruno Latour comments at this point that "action is dislocated or indeterminate. It is borrowed, distributed, suggested, influence dominated, betrayed, translated." (Latour in: Easterling 2010: 30)

13
I introduce the open-ended stories by echoing the Japanese poetry form of the haiku. It is not so much the strict syllabic form that fascinates me about this kind of poetry, but rather the poetic description of seasonal phenomena with their recurring cycles. The short Japanese poems are open-ended.

During my randonnée I come across various scenes that reflect the everyday routines of the islands' inhabitants and the rhythm of the Elbe Islands. The actions and narratives are depicted in the text images of the open-ended stories but are not concluded as a process. These short texts pop up like spotlights in the catalog section of this book and interweave with the contemporary and historical reproductions on the program of the Elbe Islands from sections A–K.

14
I view these texts like the open-ended stories, the catalog texts from sections A–K, and the scanned newspaper articles all as typographic landscapes. The relief of their surfaces should be read as a picture.

15
I consider my photographs as information. They are not static data vectors but dynamic ongoing processes.

16
Equivalent to the format of full frame 35mm.

myself in an unusual situation, situations that I find important to continue my research and that call for immediate action. Quite often the rapid action creates some motion blur in the photographs. Subsequently I draw upon this effect, deliberately reinforcing this blurriness to give the individual a level of anonymity. At the beginning of my work, the camera's focal length[16] is set at 28–35mm. During my twelve-week randonnée the focus changes; I zoom in closer to certain objects, and so accordingly the focal length is set to 50–85mm or even 112mm. Until the very end, deciding how close to move in to the various realities remains a balancing act for me (cf. "The Ten Commandments of Field Study," Girtler 2004: 3f). Interior views from the Elbe Islands do not arise, until later with one exception. This is

mostly due to my background in landscape architecture. My profession takes me through the various landscapes, but not necessarily into (private) interiors. But even from external vantage points, I find out something about the inner worlds in which I look at contexts and transitions Window Messages Balcony Usages .
It is almost summer. May June July August. The days are long and bright. It is raining, the sun shines. Overcast. Changeable. I journey around at various times of day or on different days of the week, I walk, cycle, or travel at random on whatever transport is available, such as buses or passenger ferries. It is not only the typical tempo of specific modes of transport that change the kind of access I have or alter my perspective in vis-à-vis the research field, but also fluctuating moods such as exhaustion, fatigue, insecurity, hunger or thirst, indecision, apathy, or a drive to explore. References such as odors and symbols also have a significant impact on the lengths and movements of my path.
It is not so unusual for these currents to lead me away from the islands to other kinds of everyday life, other unknown places Links .
During my everyday, researching life, I take on different roles. These change (un)consciously, sometimes in a very rapid succession. From a bench, as "researcher acts as observer" (Gans 1962: 338f), I attentively observe the Sunday activities of families, children, and dog owners. Or I take a break behind a thick hedge and listen to the different voices, languages, and sounds from behind the allotments. Again and again I sit in cafes drinking coffee or wine, watching the hustle and bustle around me. Sometimes I deliberately intervene into the research field. By acting, as "researcher participates, but as a researcher," by means of the temporary Post-it note intervention 'Here and I' in my research field (Gans 1962: 339). While I am putting up colored Post-its on the park benches, a playful dialogue between human and non-human objects begins to emerge. Shortly afterwards, as a participating observer, I watch the various reactions to the intervention from a nearby bench Here and I . A large part of my everyday life is spent as a real islander. As "researcher participates" (ibid.) I buy a loaf of bread at the Kismet Bakery for lunch with my local people; or I sit with a glass of mineral water in the garden of my new friend (born in

Wilhelmsburg in 1926) and I reply to private emails in the kitchen at the University of the Neighborhoods (UdN).[17] Here and I.

The Elbe Islands react very differently to myself and to my companions. Sometimes the islands react carefully, sometimes they are confused, or happy and inviting, then maybe reticent, thus unapproachable and sad, and then sometimes they are curious, or happy to share information, friendly, and then withdrawn again. In certain situations the islands are even suspicious toward us. "(…) However, before the researcher is ever able to develop a role in the field that would make his activities there seem plausible to the locals, his entrance into the field has found its own plausibility vis-à-vis his objects of study. (…) In practice, all the authors were initially viewed by locals as some sort of spy" (Linder 1981: 53). It is no different for me. My inquisitive gaze as a landscape architect and urban designer seems to precede me. By the time I arrive, the guards are often already in position and they turn me away from the entrance of the seemingly abandoned industrial complexes of the port. Their instructions are loud and resolute, and always crystal clear ⸢Stage Directions from the Field⸥. Every now and then the field suddenly leaves me in the lurch. The path ends abruptly, apparently without giving any notice at all. I improvise, liberate myself from the tangle. Search intuitively for a new flow or track. A young Muslim woman gets onto the

17 During research work, the University of the Neighborhoods is my temporary residence and research station all in one. As further researchers, students, and lecturers are engaging here with a range of different research topics and questions, it offers me an inspiring space of possibility that influences my approach and my gaze with reference to my research question: what is the "program of spaces of possibilities." Whether I think of the events, such as seminars, workshops, or discussion panels, as what made it possible for me to enter into a theoretical discourse with other participants; the various options to withdraw quietly in order to reflect on the material I had collected from the research field immediately adjacent or indeed drop-in visits from neighbors. This disruption often made a welcome check to the routine of my everyday research and often ended up with us cooking and eating in the UdN kitchen. Right from the outset the UdN had been conceived as a temporary project, which in a sense implies a conversion and redesign of its building. The continuing transformation of the premises gives rise to new possibilities of interpretation, which we tracked down and tested out independently over and over again through our everyday practice. The University of the Neighborhoods (UdN) is in Wilhelmsburg on the Elbe Islands. From 2008 to 2014 it was a cooperation project between Urban Design of HafenCity University Hamburg (HCU), the Hamburg International Building Exhibition (IBA), and Kampnagel Hamburg.

bus with her child in a stroller. Shortly afterwards she leaves the bus in Wilhelmsburg Mitte. I follow her. Unwittingly she guides me through a residential neighborhood in the eastern part of the Elbe Islands. There I lose her again. Waiting for some new impetus, I walk on. The streets of the residential area are empty. Street by street I move through the realities of life in this part of the island. The camera takes associative photographs while I focus on the specific characteristics of concatenated copy+paste combinations with front yards Self-Construction-Modes . Then. The field hits the ball into my court. Several black-and-white photographs, three letters dated 1944 and a medley of newspaper cuttings from 1954 to 1991. A neatly tied bundle — addressed to me. The meeting with a "real Wilhelmsburg woman" (year of birth 1926) came about by chance. Or just because I followed particular flows? Shortly after I ask her if she can tell me something about the Elbe Islands, I receive an envelope with letters written at the end of the Second World War and various newspaper articles about Wilhelmsburg. Change of per-spective. My randonnée traces out still further, unexpected loops. Across the country my hike leads me to the twelfth century and from there I make my way back to the present. I come across further map material from 1071, 1600, 1789, 1867, 1903, 1967, and 1978 in the cartography archive. I can, inter alia, read the morphological changes of the Elbe Islands brought about by the construction of dikes No Dike, No Land . My temporal, zigzag course, gives rise to count-less more linkages. It is as if a spotlight were turned on different situations and life stories. It makes no difference if these are the letters written in the bunker (1944), the opening of the fence that once enclosed the free port (2011), the spring tide flood (1962), the life of dike builders (1333), the construction of the large housing estate in Kirchdorf (1972). The Elbe Islands are a palimpsest of their ongoing transformations and events. The randonnée between each of the pages — an adventure.

—Pause—

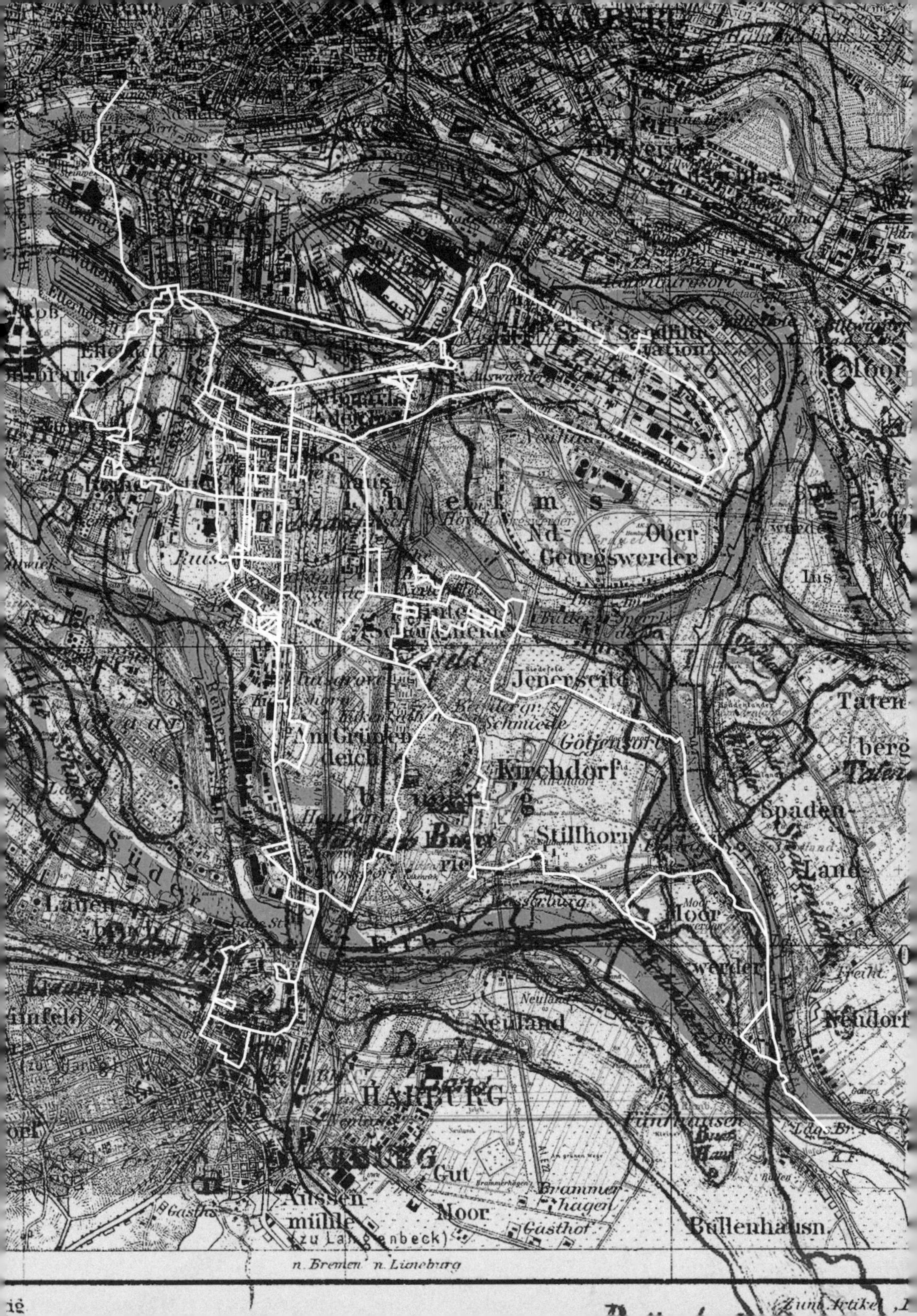

Ober-Georgswerder
Nd-Georgswerder
Jenerseite
Kirchdorf
Stillhorn
Götjensort
Tatenberg
Spaden-Land
Neuland
Neudorf
Moorwerder
HARBURG
Aussenmühle
(zu Langenbeck)
Brammerhagen
Gut
Moor
Gasthof
Bullenhausn.
n. Bremen   n. Lüneburg

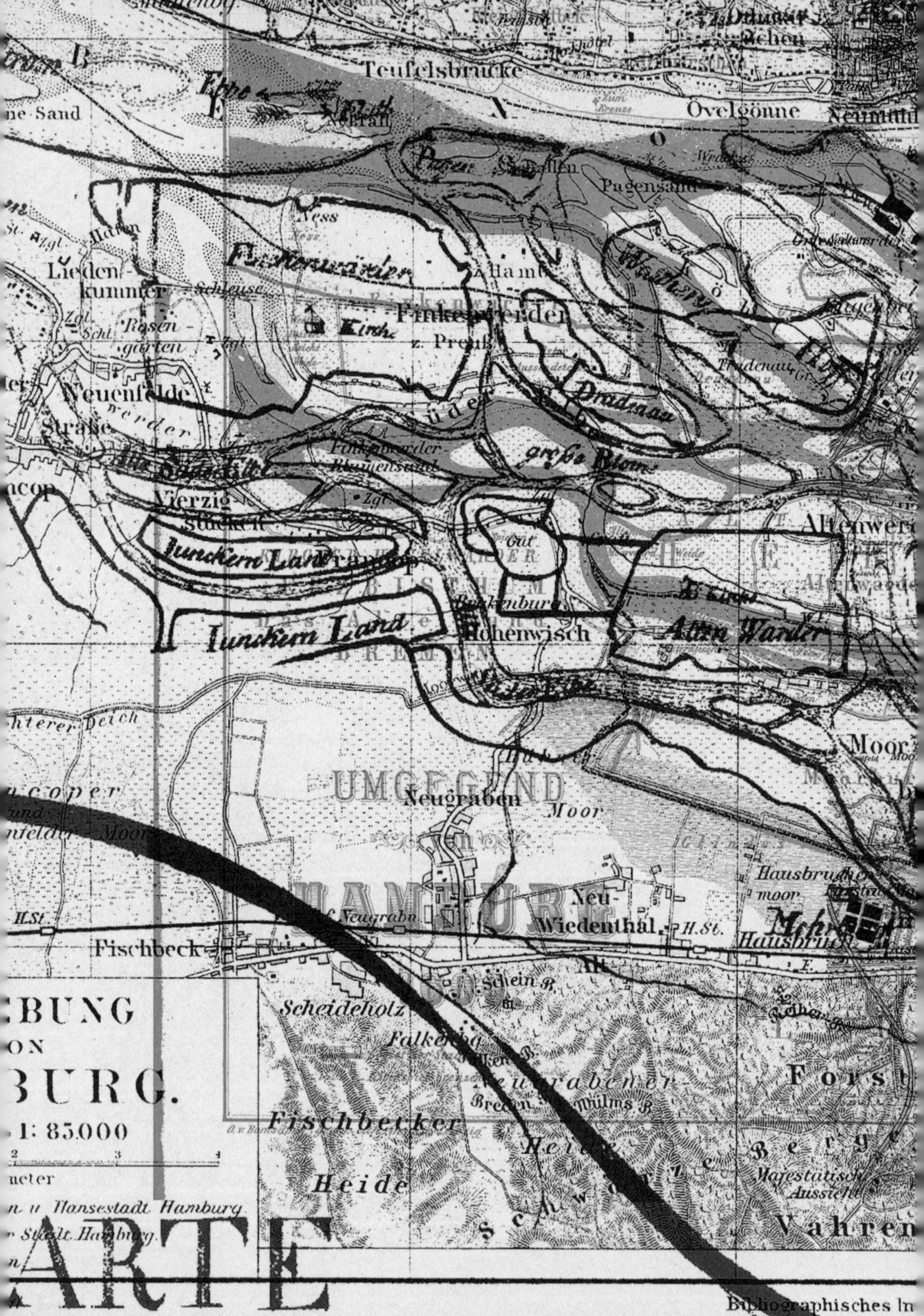

Teufelsbrücke
Ovelgönne
Neumühl
Pagensand
Schaffen
Ness
Finkenwärder
Hamb
Finkenwärder
z. Preuf.
Lieden-
kummer
Rosen-
garten
Neuenfelde
Straße
Dradenau
Finkenwärder
Rosensand
große Blom
Alte Süder
Vierzig
stücken
Gut
Altenwerder
Juncker Land
BISTHUM
HAMBURG
Altenwärder
Juncker Land
Buckenburg
Hohenwisch
Am Wärder
BREMEN
UMGEGEND
Moor
Neugraben
Moor
HAMBURG
Neu-
Wiedenthal
Hausbrucher
moor
Neugrabn
Hausbruch
Fischbeck
H.St.
Scheideholz
Schein B.
Falkenbg.
Neugrabener
Brecen
Wulms B.
Forst
Fischbecker
Heide
Berge
Heide
Majestätische
Aussicht
Vahren

EBUNG
ON
BURG.
1 : 85.000
Hansestadt Hamburg
Stadt Hamburg
ARTE
Bibliographisches In

In between, I always come back to my research station at University of the Neighborhoods. The UdN, formerly a hostel for single women, which was built after the Second World War, is a special kind of university. Especially because here, picking up on Martina Löw, "space is conceived performatively" (Löw in: Dell 2011: 152). Experiments and improvisations are carried out with the pre-existing structures found on the spot, giving rise to reciprocal interactions between the different actors and the UdN. These processes of appropriation and transformation continuously change the building on programmatic, substantive, and formal levels. Questions are developed based on the 1:1 model for urbanization processes in cities and tested out, used or discarded via a situational approach in interdisciplinary formats. That is particularly significant for me, as it becomes the initial situation and the starting point of my everyday research life and is an issue I can grapple with theoretically and practically through my research topic. "It is life, appropriation, the improvisation that is enabled that constitutes space as a particular quality (...)" (Dell 2011: 154). In this sense, I include my personal affairs in the university as "researcher participates" (Gans 1962: 339) and appropriate my own environment by ordinary, repetitive tasks such as washing up, doing laundry, cooking, sleeping, cleaning, gardening, writing, reading, and so on until my everyday life finally becomes part of the UdN-curriculum.[18] By mixing and superimposing,[19] an intense, and also lively, engagement with the context comes into being. Often a fleeting glimpse out of the window or a short trip to the bakery takes on an unexpected relevance for my work. The transitions between private and/or research-based participation in the intercultural life of the islands are fluid and sometimes difficult to distinguish from each other.

18
Social anthropologist Bronislaw Malinowski (1884–1942) shaped the terminology and method of "participant observation." Since then field research means that researchers also become part of the field in their everyday lives. However, in my situation this was not a private place of retreat in the research field, as described for example in "The Urban Villagers" by Herbert Gans (cf. Gans 1962), but the building is open to the public as it is a university.

19
This superposition of research and the everyday, along with the transformation of the former single women's hostel to its current utilization, is shown on the only four interior Elbe Islands photos that are included here.

—The doors at the UdN are open.—Kitchen. Foyer. Around me: high tide.—The coffee machine is full flow.—Living. Researching. Experimenting. Building. Back and forth.—In the rhythm of the UdN tides I search for a way.—There are no breaks. In between.—The field more or less lives with me.—
At my workplace, I am studying the descriptive field data and differences in primary and secondary data. The former include the numerous situations recorded with varying degrees of observational acuity in the form of field diary entries, my open-ended stories, or the photo catalog with a total of 3,000 photographs. However, it also encompasses the photographs, maps, newspaper articles, letters, and dialogues[20] that have pushed my way, as well as reflections on the one-off intervention 'Here and I.' The secondary material consists of various specialized literature and research studies. I move repeatedly through this topographic text and photograph landscape in the mode of an aimless randonnée. Jump between times, pages, and languages. Change from digital to analog media. Listen to the material. Write down, sketch, let my thoughts wander freely. After all. There are moments of being completely lost. Again and again I get lost, losing my paths among the countless stories, fragments, memories, questions, practices, moods, information, associations. Through this process, countless new associations come into being, spreading out before me a complex socio-material web of actors, places, objects, ideas, organizations, inequalities, sizes, orders of magnitude and geographic orderings (cf. Law 2009: 141f). It is obvious—the ANT produces. As an exploratory method, it generates a (huge) quantity of data. "Only by following, 'the making of …', 'the practice of …' can we describe the variable ontology of entities that are shaped in an intermediary, non-stabilized state of the world" (Yaneva 2013: 131f). The ANT produces a network of elements and attachments. In this process, each actor in the network in turn forms a network that does not fully recognize or understand the actor (cf. Law 2009: 147). Will I ever get out of there again? —It's a labyrinth.—Where is the exit?—The exit is called: "expressways" (Serres 2009/1998: 271)—Now I am remembering again.—"(…) those who love the countryside sometimes need expressways." (ibid.)—I am taking the next exit straight away.—Direction?—Direction: "Grounded Theory" (Glaser; Strauss: 2008)—Paragraph.—

20
The two narrative interviews, one with a native woman who has lived on the islands since 1926, and another with a representative of the Wilhelmsburg Citizens' House, became a part of my evaluation.

In further data evaluation, the focus is not on reducing, but on organizing the material collected in terms of my research topic. As I look at the space of possibility as a conceptual, analytical term, I engage with it in theoretical, object-related and reflexive terms. To continue to delimit it and render it tangible, I need a corresponding method to analyze my data. The signs at the 'expressway' exit lead me to Grounded Theory. It was developed as a social science research approach in the 1960s by American sociologists Anselm Strauss and Barney Glaser. It is a qualitative and object-anchored theory, derived from the study of the phenomenon. The important properties of Grounded Theory are its applicability to its respective field, being readily comprehensible to non-specialists from the field and enabling partial control of structures and processes for the user (cf. Glaser; Strauss 2008: 241ff). "The focus of the analysis is not only on collecting and ordering masses of data, but on organizing the multitude of associative thoughts that occur to the researcher while analyzing the data" (Strauss 1987: 22f). The cyclical, iterative process consists of three main research phases: data collection — coding — note-writing (cf. Oertzen 2006: 145f). At each stage it is possible to draw on preceding material, "(...) even when the last page of the research report is written" (Strauss 1987: 18). Data analysis is divided into the three steps of "open," "axial," and "selective" coding. This division should not be regarded as a strict rule; the transitions between the forms of codification are fluid" (Oertzen 2006: 148). Nevertheless, the method "(...) calls for a balance to be kept between the characteristics of creativity, rigor, perseverance and above all theoretical sensitivity" (Strauss; Corbin 1990: 58). "Because only theoretical sensitivity makes it possible to develop a theory that is rooted in objects, is conceptually dense and well-integrated" (ibid.: 42).

In my analysis, I use the first step[21] of the coding phase. But what is a code and what does "open or initial coding" mean? Codes are theoretical concepts, i.e., they provide conceptual designations or labels (cf. Strauss; Corbin 1990: 44) that can be used to categorize individual events, incidents or

[21] Grounded Theory is a complex methodological approach, which however, offers scope for individual steps of the method, such as "open coding" to be carried out independently. With my work I am therefore not aiming to generate an object-based theory together with the requisite application of all methodological steps of the "coding paradigm" but I am instead more interested in the possibility, with the method step of "open coding," in being able to analyze my data in a way that affords me scope to produce plausible conclusions about my research field and the terms "program" and "space of possibilities" at this time. As an object-based theory, Grounded Theory does call for a certain amount of time, something I only enjoyed to a limited degree due to structural circumstances when I was completing this research work. "Open coding" also calls for a certain level of concentration and stamina.

other examples of phenomena. This also produces so-called "natural in-vivo codes." These are terms and expressions from the field of research and they describe a phenomenon so well that they can be adopted directly from researchers (Oertzen 2006: 148).[22]

"Open coding" means unlimited coding. This step is about naming and not about paraphrasing these phenomena. Coding as a practice means translating or encrypting data, which produces an abstraction of the material. It is a process of breaking up, examining, comparing, and conceptualizing.[23] The basic analytical methods by which this is achieved are: asking questions of the data, comparing similarities and differences between each event, incident, and other examples of phenomena (cf. Strauss; Corbin 1990: 43). "What is actually said here?", "What is this about?", and "Which phenomenon is addressed?"; those are the initial questions when allocating every single word, sentence, paragraph or entire pages of text to a code or to several codes. With the help of questions like this, it becomes possible not just to clarify what the researcher is reading into with his or her material, but which phenomena may possibly be related to one another (cf. Strauss; Corbin 1990: 44). This process of analysis gives rise to codes that are not entirely determined or mandatory. Thit means that, depending on the coder other theoretical concepts can develop. Codes cannot be replicated and are not objective. Accordingly, they are never wrong, but must always be plausible and meaningful (i.e. abstract, content-rich, ordering, useful), and be comprehensible in inter-subjective terms (cf. Oertzen 2006: 151). As I search for the space of possibility, I code all my empirical material with a focus on the program, in other words on the interactions between actors and / or actants in the everyday specifically local life of the Elbe Islands. The program forms the principal core category and, as such, is of "central importance for the integration of the theory" (Strauss 1987: 21). Programs, actors, and actants are already categories,[24] no longer codes. That is because these concepts were determined at the beginning of my research, and they represent an important part of my research topic. In addition, I have taken the concepts of actors and actants from Bruno Latour's texts on Actor-Network Theory (cf. Latour 1999: 303) as "borrowed categories" (Strauss; Corbin 1990: 50).

22
For example from Low German usage I keep the code "Greunhöker," which comprises vegetable growers and traders.

23
Strauss and Corbin understand conceptualizing to mean picking out a specific observation from the empirical material to provide a designation — the label — for the phenomenon observed, describing what it symbolizes or best represents (Strauss; Corbin 1990: 44).

24
In the Grounded Theory sense, categories are classifications from concepts that should be viewed as non-

I develop my questions for open coding from the perspective of ANT: "Which specific human and non-human objects can I read from this? What kind of mutual interactions exist between them? What connects them? What is the nature of their connections—stable or fragile? Which tactical or strategic everyday practices do I recognize and which recur?" In this sense, I code the primary data and ascribe initial labels (cf. Strauss; Corbin 1990: 43) that occur to me as associations as I browse, read, and inspect my material more closely. The conceptual labels are modes of transport, spatial circulation, improvisation, routine, change, refuge, kitchen works, animal lovers, and so on. As I walk further, I start to systematically examine the still vague terms to check their plausibility, by juxtaposing and comparing them, guided by the generative questions as described above. Through the disjointed comparisons and repeated questions, ever-new connections come into being, pointing to unsuspected phenomena of everyday island life. In a further step, I differentiate the codes, searching for their affiliations or independent status, so that initial code families, the precursors of categories, are formed. Right up to the end of my research work, I go out into the field and target my examinations, through participatory observation, on the created codes and code families in the everyday life of the Elbe Islands. Back at the research station I sort, arrange, and compare all my material on the walls of my studio, over and over again, seeking to condense and saturate the various abstract concepts step by step.[25] In between, in various written memos I put into practice my associations and subjective observations, which are connected with the individual codes. In the process, the designations for the eleven code families crystallize: Self-Construction-Modes, Appropriations, Transformation-Rhythm, Island-Actors, Everyday Realities—Economic Survival Strategies, Mobile Actants, Performative Practices, Communication with, Poetical, Panoramas expanding up to and beyond the notion of Human—Machine—Space, which the program's "making of …" (Yaneva 2013: 7f) brings together in a diagrammatic catalog[26] from A–K.

The creative technique of Grounded Theory proves well suited to analyze the empirical material I collected from the ANT perspective. For through the coding, new phenomena and unexpected references in the material repeatedly come to light, enabling me to perceive the presence of fragile constellations in the hybrid immaterial structure of human and non-human connections Performative Practices . I can spot subtle changes in the pattern of current actions in my field of research more and more easily Appropriations . I pursue them with targeted focus until I can categorize their actions in the overall spatial context of the Elbe Islands Stage Directions from the Field . Such as the practice of parking vans near kiosks and tearooms Life and Business or in the immediate vicinity of pawnshops, Western Union banks and betting parlors Win and More . At various scales and in various media, contrasting opposites and dispositions of the Elbe Island Wilhelmsburg become apparent Panoramas . I can read off spatial, temporal and individual caesurae based on the increasingly dense concepts Self-Construction-Modes . Every now and then I discover the in-between on "terra incognita" (Latour 2005: 221). This happens especially when I superimpose current phenomena on past developments Transformation-Rhythm . Increasingly my sensory perception becomes more attuned to subtle disturbances, ephemeral traces, and currents. Sounds, smells and temporal changes are stored on my psycho-geographic[27] island map Communication with , this is so that my state is akin to a perpetual parallel reading, translation and discursive linking of the (in)visible everyday practices established in the program, its human and nonhuman producers Island-Actors (cf. Lefebvre 1991/1974: 330f). But not everything is or remains clear. Time after time, the complexity makes my eyes blur, so there are different degrees of out-of-focus[28] views.

stories, catalogue texts) as well as the individual sketches form the grammar of the Elbe Island program. In the catalog A–K, a certain code-sequence is ascribed to the data, although the linear arrangement in the mode of the randonnée—that is, in iterative switching between the pages—is suspended again, and consequently a mobile diagram comes into being.

27
"Psychogeography means the study of the precise effects of geographical setting, consciously managed or not, acting directly on the mood and behavior of the individual." (Situationist International, 2011/1958)

28
The out-of-focus runs as an experimental principle through my entire research work and at times

—The Elbe Islands slowly vanish behind a bend—

generates a certain inner, yet simulta-neously intriguing, uncertainty. It is only by recognizing and accepting the out-of-focus as a co-player that a more playful way of dealing with the complexity came into being and fostered my sensitivity to my research field. "Accepting the ineluctable existence and quality of blurriness— of data, statements, research results, and of actions too ...—is possibly most important and most groundbreaking in 'research with and through design' and in order to understand its particularity. (...) In the practical aspects of life, one constantly encounters blurriness. Nothing is simple and straightforward there. And above all in the contradiction-ridden tension between theory and practice, which is where design is always located, blurriness is experienced as constitutive and liberating. Consequently, an experience-based relaxed attitude toward blurriness also shapes an awareness of blurriness as a research principle." (Brandes et al. 2009: 98f)

—Has the concept of space of possibility changed?—Have I changed?—Has my way of looking changed?—Also. —"Thinking of the possible seems to favor a certain form of knowledge: the experiment" (Innhofer et al. 2011: 11).— But can 'the' space of possibility exist at all? Or does this analytical conceptual term shift depending on the perspective from which I view it and with whom or what I set it in relation?[29] Is it anyhow (im)possible to develop an universal or exhaustive definition for the 'possibilities' arising from my research work?[30] However, one thing that has, surprisingly, developed in the search for the space of possibility, is a distinct way of reading the relational space. During my randonnée, the program of everyday life unfurled before my eyes with a richness and wealth I had not anticipated beforehand. In this multi-layered complexity, I can decode various facets of what is possible through participant observation. The program of the Elbe Islands is the program of the space of possibility. Possibilities become visible through contrasts and opposites. Possibilities arise through use and specific appropriational tactics. Possibilities lie in the disposition of human and non-human objects. On the one hand engaging with "dispositional activity" (Easterling 2010: 30) opens up new perspectives and points of view; on the other hand it is only by taking into account the people actively involved in shaping a place that new design options or translations for urban areas become possible, writes Keller Easterling in

29
In this case, I juxtapose the space of possibilities and the specific program of the Elbe Islands and set myself in relation to these.

30
The space of possibilities in a sense forms a kind of framing for my research work that is not rigid or inflexible. Within this dynamic frame a lot is thinkable and conceivable. That is why I had to apply a suitable procedure: to smash through the Elbe Islands' programmatic structure via the randonnée.

"Action is the Form" (Easterling 2010: 30f). "Active forms are not at odds with, but rather propel, expand, (even rescue) form as object" (ibid.). That in turn requires a degree of perseverance and effort until, by entering into new connections, constellations arise that allow for leeway, extend space for maneuver. Possibilities cannot be planned for it is never clear who or what will act next. However, it is always necessary to define anew "who is acting, why it is necessary to act together, what are the boundaries of the collective, how responsibility should be allocated (...)"(Latour 1986: 276). Possibilities look for improvisation. Possibilities call for experimentation. Possibilities lie in the nature of their "materiality" (Färber 2010). Possibilities want to be discovered. And. Possibilities take shape through playful, open associations. Yes. It is only by connecting, comparing and contrasting different approaches that unsuspected cross-references in the relational space have been revealed. Possibilities come into being in spatial and temporal upheavals. Possibilities arise where order and disorder, the focused and the out-of-focus, certainty and uncertainty meet. But is the quintessence not to be found in precisely these indeterminate, unpredictable moments that tip the urban program out of balance for a brief moment? Only "in the possible the thought of change, of the future, of potential with the power for change, for intervention comes together (...)" (Innhofer et al. 2011: 9). There cannot be and there is no generally valid, definitive definition of 'the' space of possibility. That is because, by continuing to grapple with the complex program of the contemporary city, new facets of the possible will emerge. Unimagined associations unfold with disjointed leafing back and forth and these associations keep on shaping the program of the space of possibility in their own way. The randonnée of possibilities continues through the topographic landscape, page by page. It remains an "open book" (Serres 2009/1998: 244). Fragile. A trail to be discovered and pursued will always remain within it.

—Randonnez!—

Play the Game.—Endanger your work even more.—Don't
be the top dog.—Seek out the face-off.—But be unmindful.—
Have no thoughts in back of your head.—Keen nothing secret.
—Be soft and strong.—Be sly, enter the fray but hate to win.—
Don't observe, don't test, but be ready for signs.—Tremble,
quake, shatter, heal.—Show your eyes, wave the others on into
the depths,—care for spaces and behold each one in their
own picture.—Act only with enthusiasm.—Fail with ease.
—First of all, take time and the long way round.—Be addle-
brained.—Go on a holiday as it were.—Overhear no tree and
no water.—Enter where it pleases your heart and treat yourself to the sun.—Forget your kinfolk, strengthen the strangers,
spaces,—a hoot for the tragedy,—spit on misfortune,—
laugh conflicts to smithereens.—Move in your own colors,—
until you are in the right,—and the leaves' rustling turns sweet.
—Walk about the villages.—I will follow you.

Peter Handke

Self-Construction-Modes | Temporary Outside Rooms |

Temporary outside rooms can be discovered in very different places on the Elbe Islands: on the banks of the canals, on the water, in parks like Rotenhäuser Feld, on the roadside, in parking lots in the industrial and port area, in large family gardens or on housing estates. The spectrum ranges from temporary mini-cooking places on benches to ephemeral living rooms, which are large carpeted areas. The outside rooms vary both in their use, design, and materiality. Not infrequently, improvised structures are created by temporarily converting what is already there (park benches, trees, garbage cans, walls, abandoned shopping trolleys, etc.). Often an enormous effort is made to bring along everything required: dishes, cutlery, umbrellas, barbecues with cooking implements, firewood, coolers with food and drinks, chairs, toys, blankets, carpets, cushions, and so on. Some of these components are mobile (barbecue on wheels), very light (plastic chairs, carpets, blankets). Various transportation options are available (bikes, cars, shopping trolleys, and baby strollers), these are parked as close as possible to the outside rooms. Functions such as toilets, kitchens, and refrigerators are integrated into the campers and truck trailers. Depending on their configuration, the individual appropriations of space leave (in)visible traces. Often the usage patterns are ephemeral, manifesting for just a few hours, as they are very dependent on the weather. In some places, I was struck by a recurring rhythm to this phenomenon of transporting the home outside[1] | Territorial Stomping Grounds |. The reasons for outsourcing / expansion stem from a broad range of different lifestyles or circumstances. It is conceivable that there is often very limited space at home for a meal with a large family and / or friends. Itinerant and temporary workers who live in boarding houses, construction site containers, or in overcrowded basements certainly prefer to eat outdoors in the company of their ersatz families | Life and Business |. Truck drivers who need to rest before or after a tour stop at one of the designated, sometimes fee-paying, rest areas with the corresponding infrastructure (porta-potties, washing facilities, seating). Vacationers having a stopover in Hamburg with their campers or caravans | Mobile Homes |.

1
The German term "Veraushäusigung" refers to the temporary process of shifting domestic functions from inside the home to the exterior.

Other important aspects of transporting the home outside
may also be communicative, communitarian in addition to
the spatial advantages. Casually, spontaneously or by chance,
friends, family members, and colleagues meet. The rising
smoke announces their presence. The self-catering setups
in the temporary outdoor kitchens also provide an inexpensive
alternative to the fast food stands or restaurants in the neighborhood ⎣Life and Business⎦. I often had the impression
that all the numerous communities living on the Elbe Islands,
from Turkey, Poland, Macedonia, Bulgaria, Afghanistan, former
Serbia, Montenegro, Portugal, Ghana, Russia, and Italy,[2]
are thoroughly familiar with this practice. There seems to be
no clear demarcation line when it comes to outsourcing domestic features into outside space. The transitions between interior and exterior spaces merge one into another.
It is immaterial whether the activities conducted here relate
to personal hygiene ⎣Barbershops and Beauty Salons⎦, food
preparation, rest and sleep, or to cultural customs and festivals; by temporarily revealing various everyday practices,
the cultures on the islands come into contact. The urban
reality, the heterogeneity of the Elbe Islands is visible, tangible
in this simultaneous interaction, and experience. Here. Jetzt.
And now!

[2]
The Elbe Islands'
inhabitants have
links to 158 countries
in total. Here in
descending order
the 10 best-repre-
sented groups
in Wilhelmsburg
based on population
figures; Note:
Veddel deviates in
this respect; figures
as of 28.12.2011,
Statistik Amt Nord.

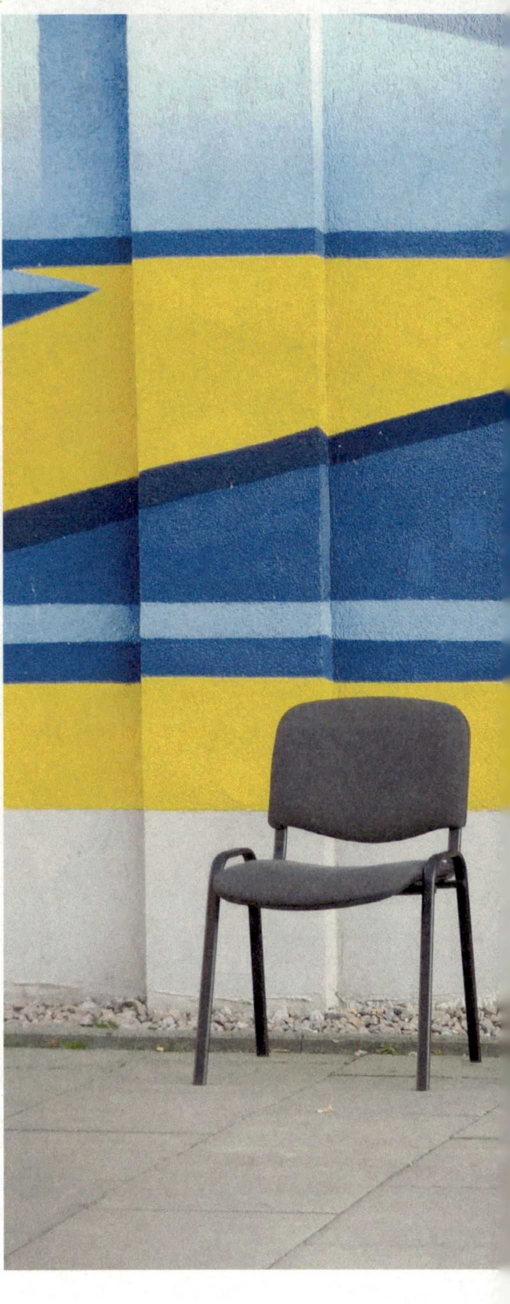

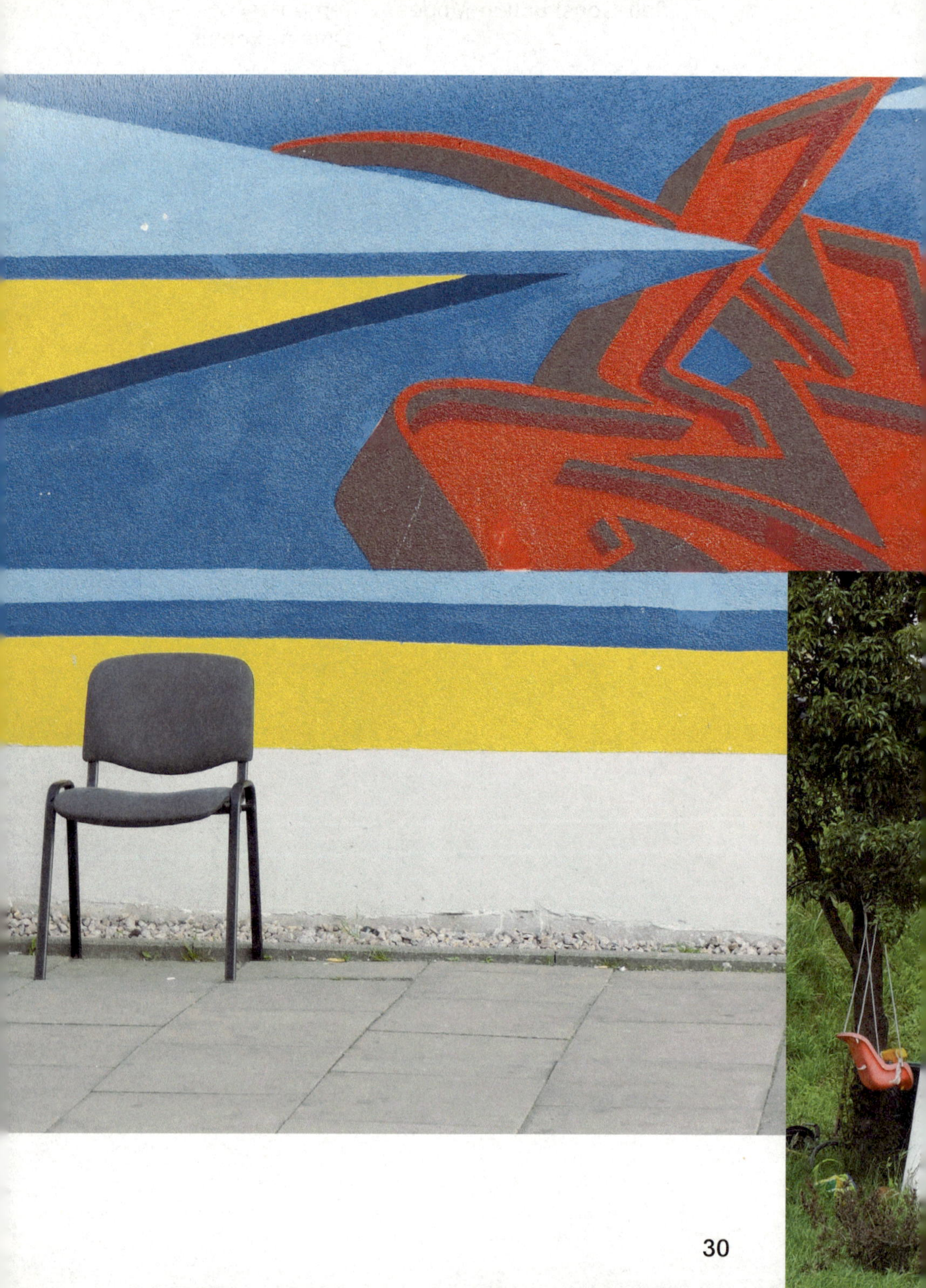

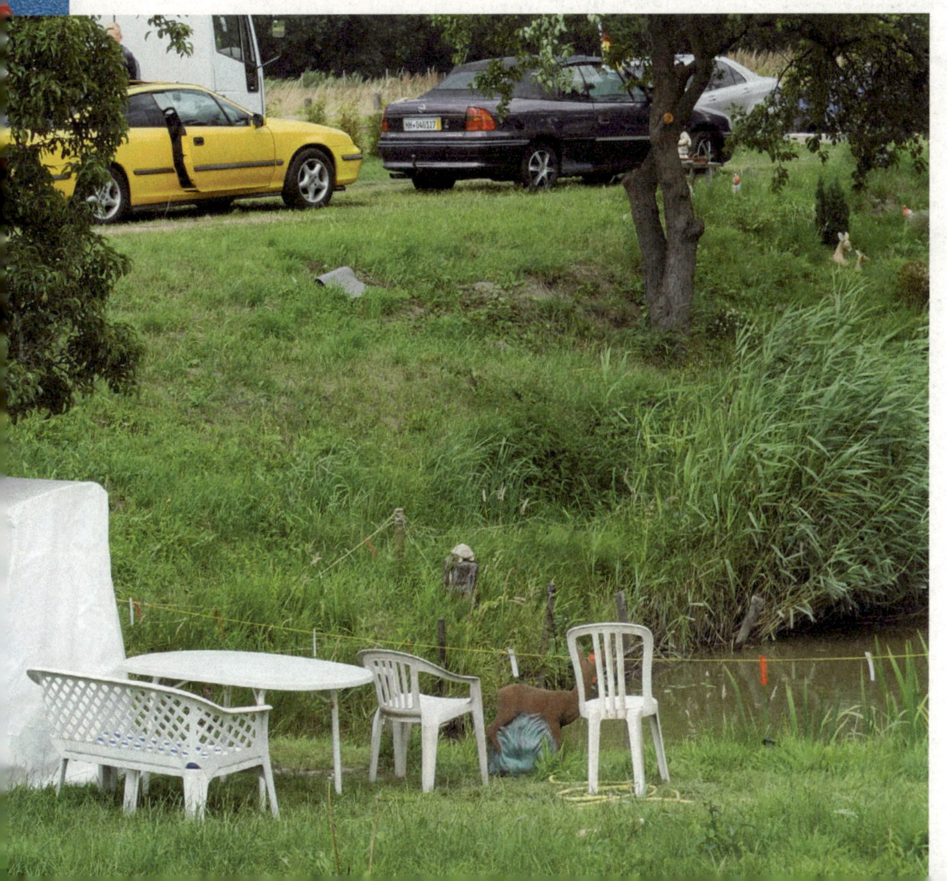

On the kitchen-bench in Rotenhäuser Feld is dinner. Vegetables,
possibly peppers, a little bread
too. The meat cooking on the
mobile grill. Five men stand or
kneel around it, talking. The local
radio station is playing in the
background—as usual.

Smoke drifts over on the high
dense hedge. Sounds penetrate
through the foliage. Here and
there clattering plates and glasses,
women and men all talking
at once. Voices mingle. Wood is
chopped. The smoke rises higher,
higher. Today. Baking yufka in
the small garden.

On the stone wall lie pale chicken
legs on shiny layers of foil. Next to
them, grilled meat piled on a black
wire grid. Round mamas bending
over it—Cooking Women. The children are playing, the men sit at
the table, drinking bottles of beer
until dinner is ready.

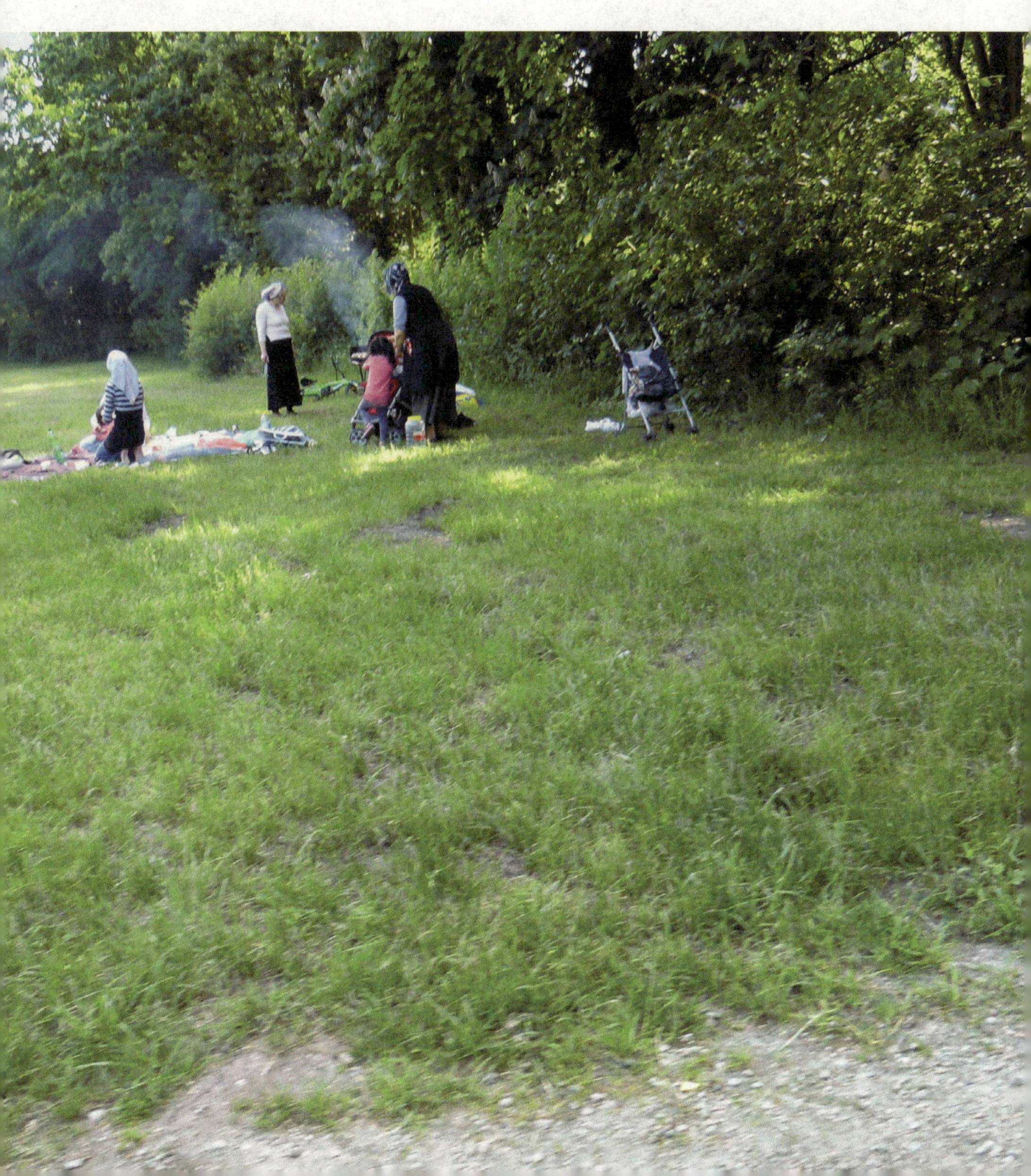

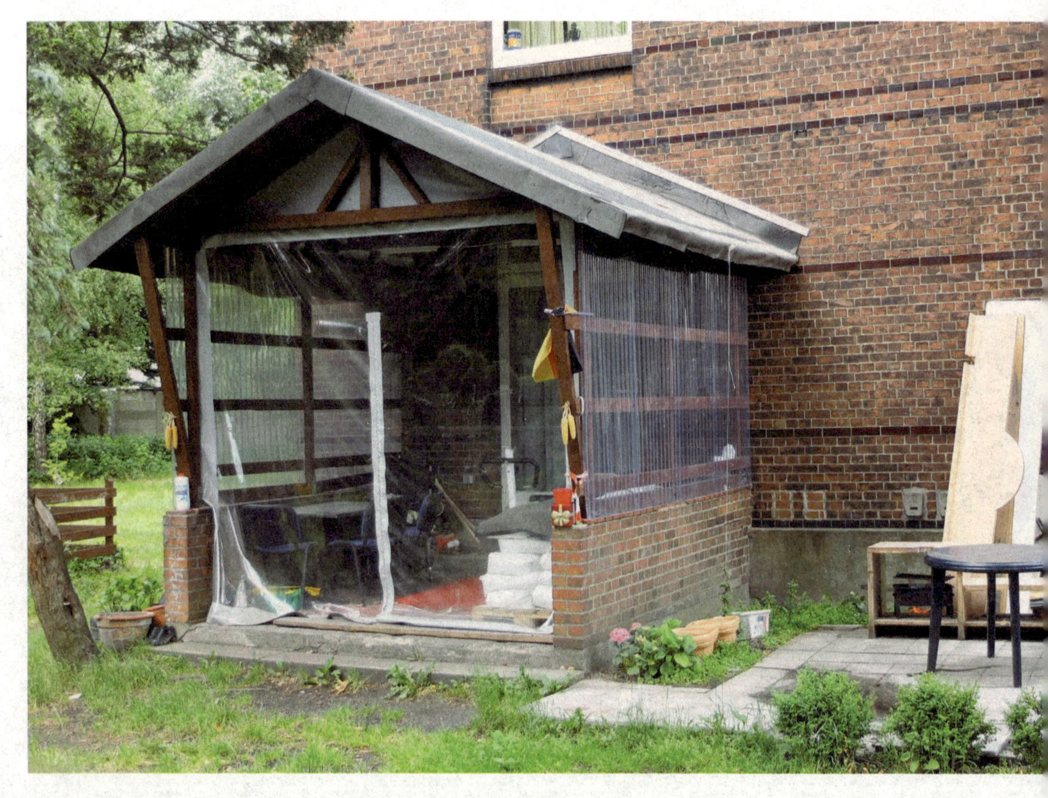

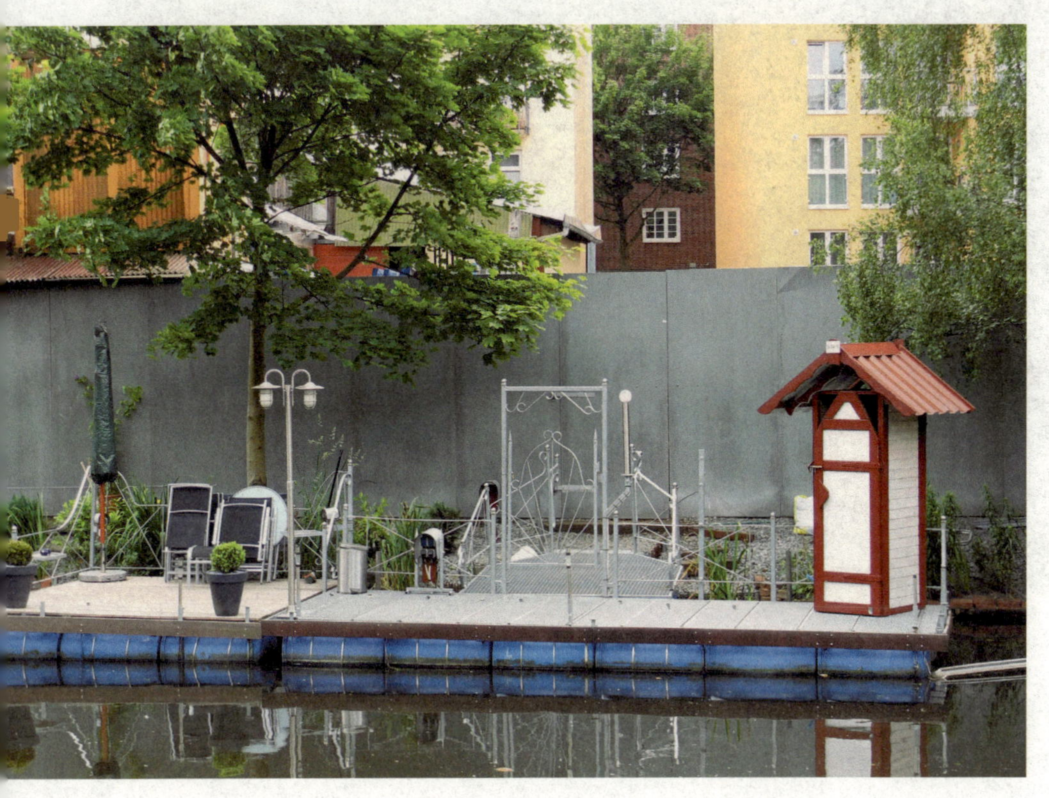

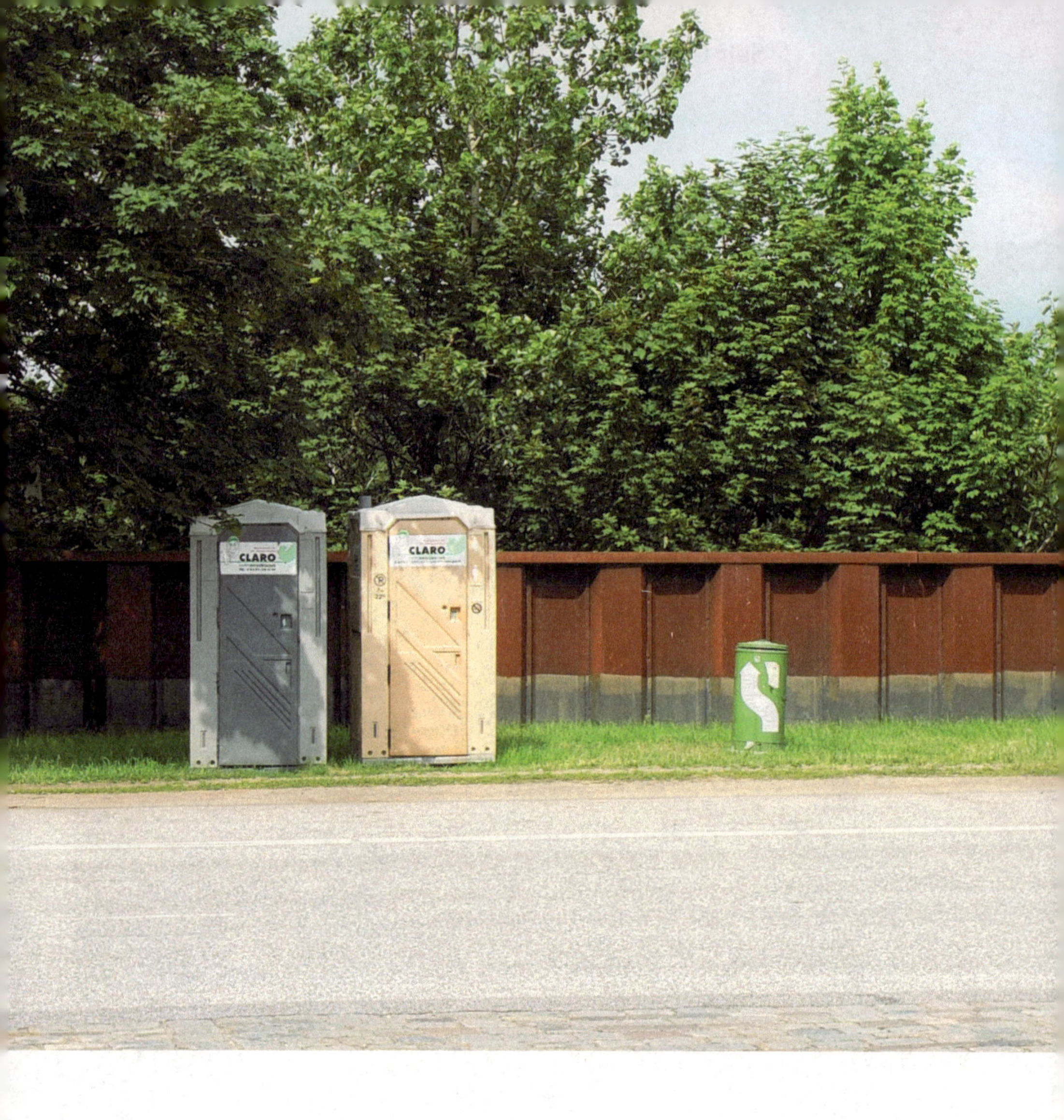

Self-Construction-Modes | Mobile Homes |

The Elbe Islands are dominated by water. This offers various means of transport or mobile modes of living on the Elbe, at the periphery of the Spreehafen (free port), or in Harburger Hafen. In addition to the modes of transportation | Movers and Transporters |, houseboats, ships, or freighters offer sometimes very generous living spaces. Some means of transport seem to be sitting out the winter here, while others are permanent residents or in transit. Another very frequently observed mobile residential practice is that of truck drivers. The traveling home has many different functions in a confined space. The cabin serves as a living room, dining room, and bedroom, as well as a changing room and office. The windows are decorated with many personal material artifacts such as cuddly toys, family photos, feathers, flags, or flashing badges. Everyday routines seem well coordinated, every last bit of the scant storage space is utilized. The infrastructure they are lacking, such as toilets, dumpsters, or food stands, are installed in parking lots or along the exit roads in the industrial and port areas for the people passing through | Breakfast and More |. Parked by the roadside, every now and then the mobilized dream of home ownership (clusters of travellers' homes) takes the form of revamped, self-converted and self-equipped fire engines, mail trucks, or police vans. Similarly to the scattered, makeshift, lightweight structures made from tents or tarpaulins in the undergrowth, the clusters of travellers' vans and caravans exist in an uncertain limbo. Fragile. The mobile living arrangements, which stem from very different motives or life circumstances often demand great improvisational talent. Especially when there is no electricity, water or other infrastructure. Living conditions change as a function of the context and environment. Again and again. Nevertheless, the temporality and mobility of this living practice seems to exert a fascination. Hints of this can be found in holidaymakers' campers and mobile homes that are huddled together around the port | Temporary Outside Rooms |, or the patiently waiting caravans of the Sinti family Weiss in Georgswerder, parked in the front garden between trips. It seems only a matter of time before their inhabitants will once again swap their permanent residence for their mobile home.

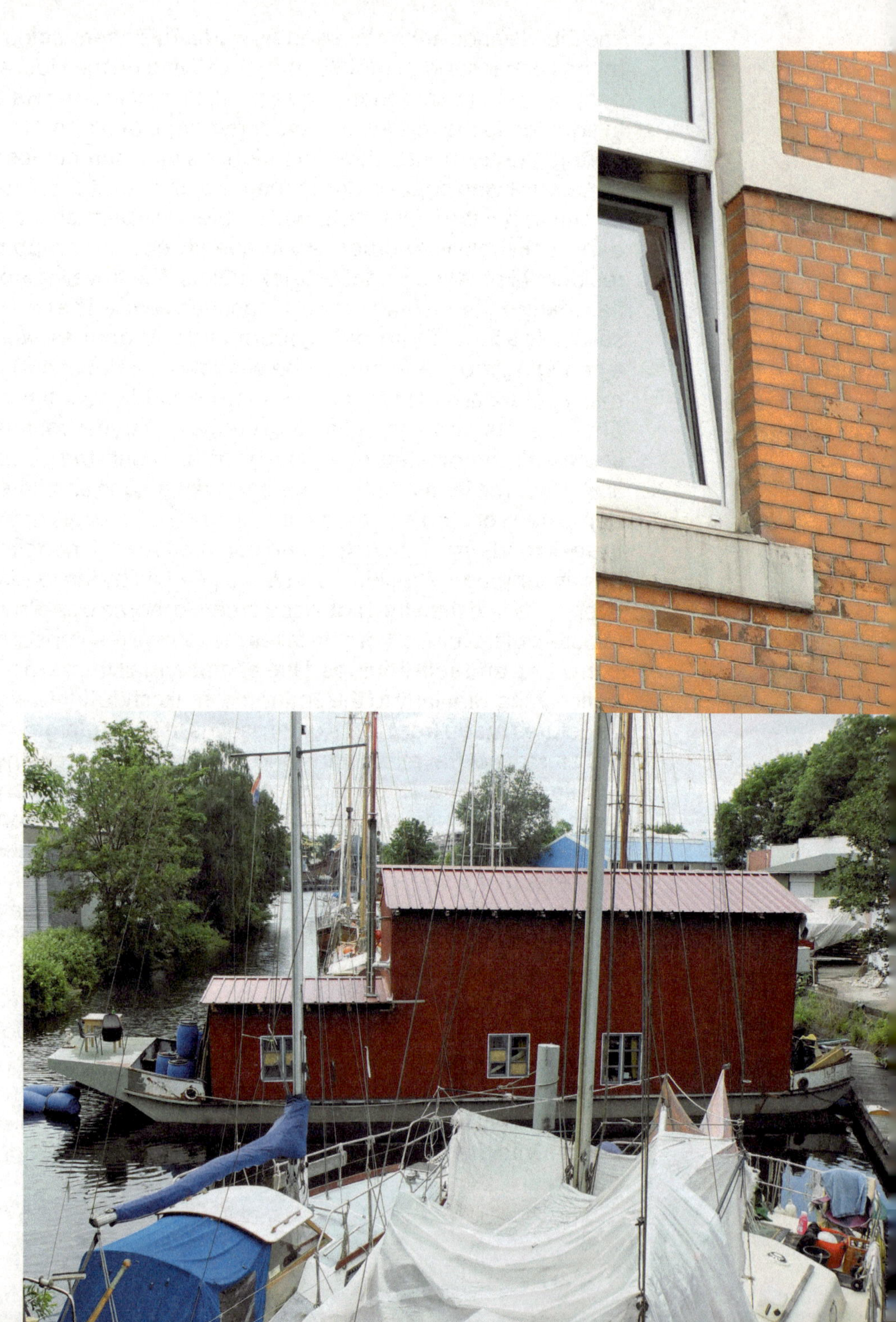

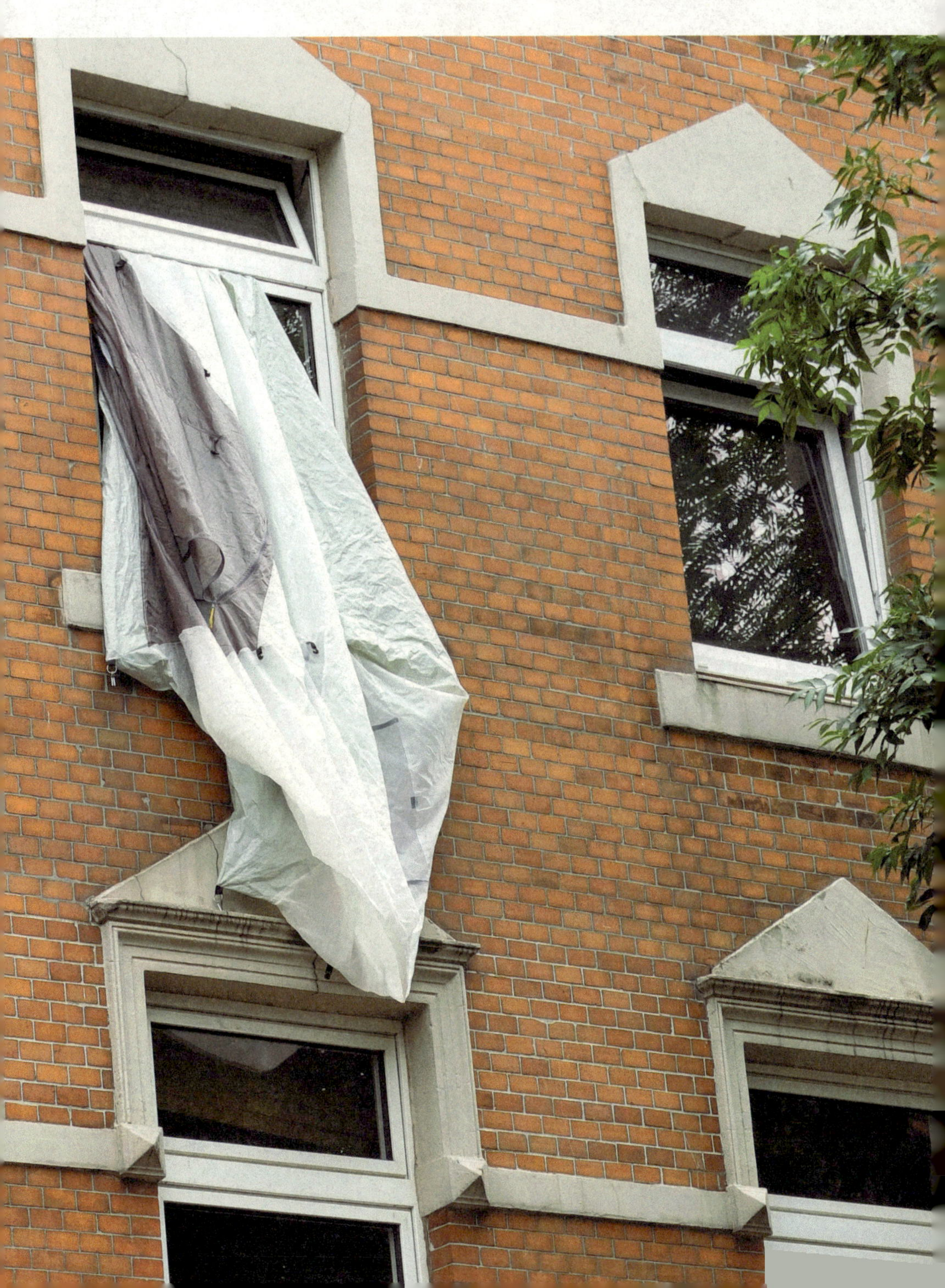

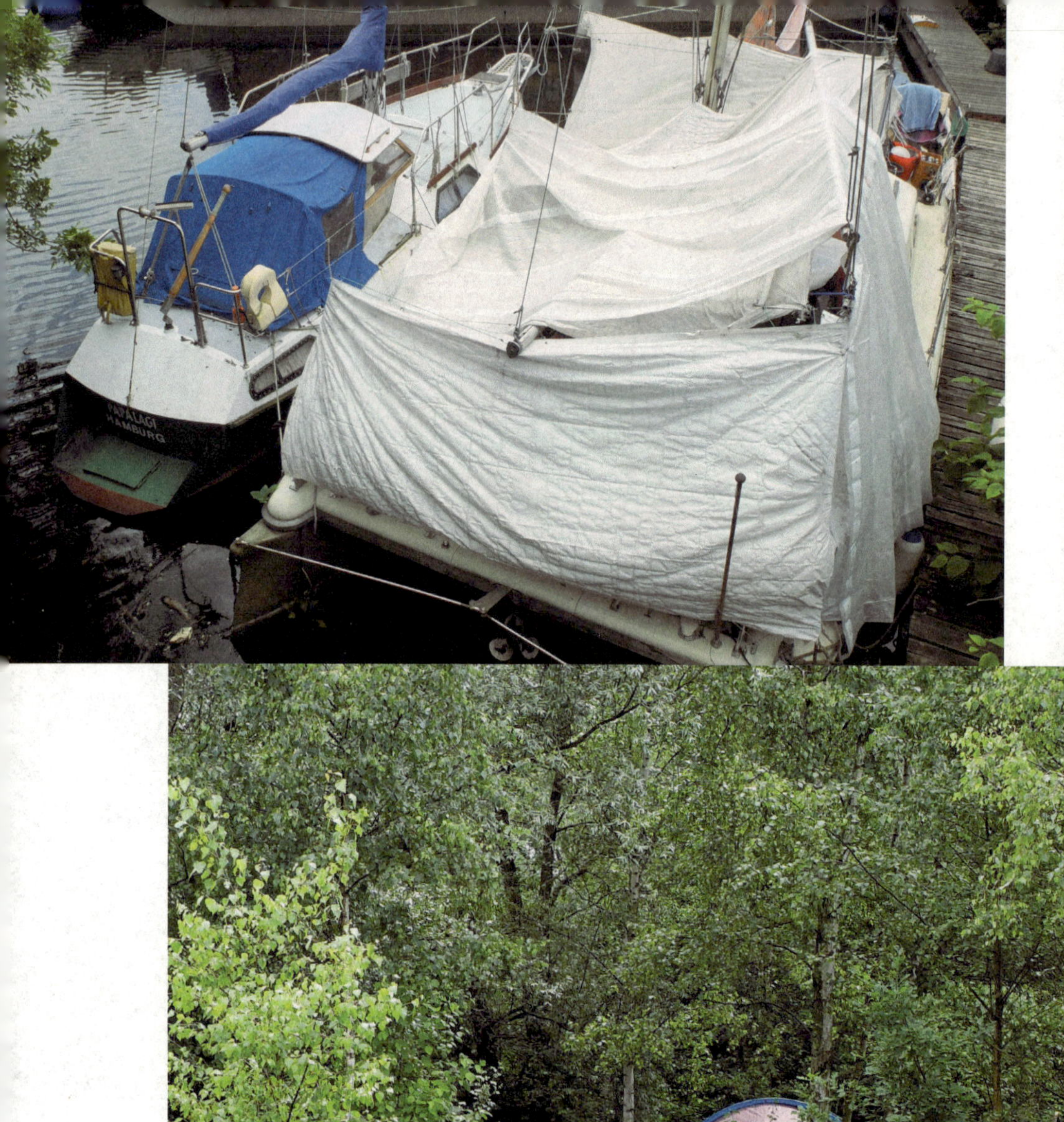

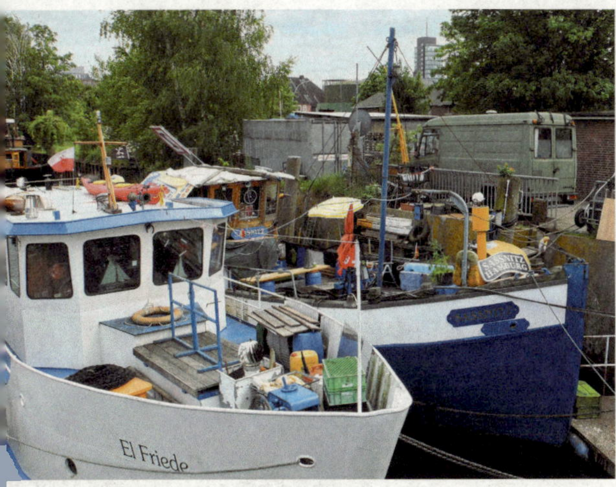

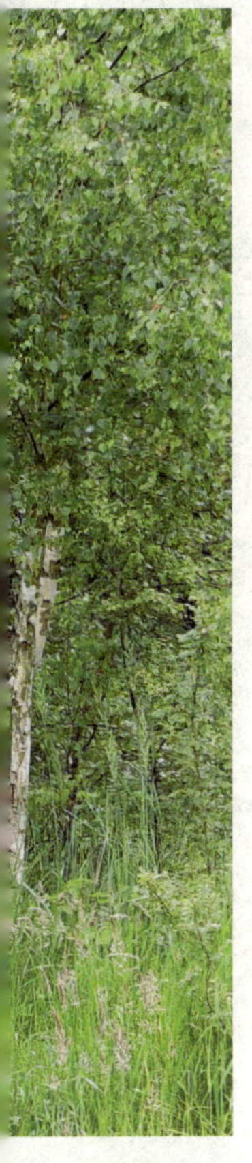

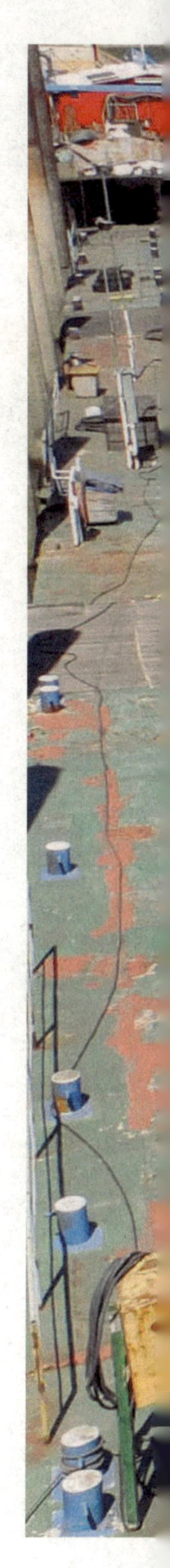

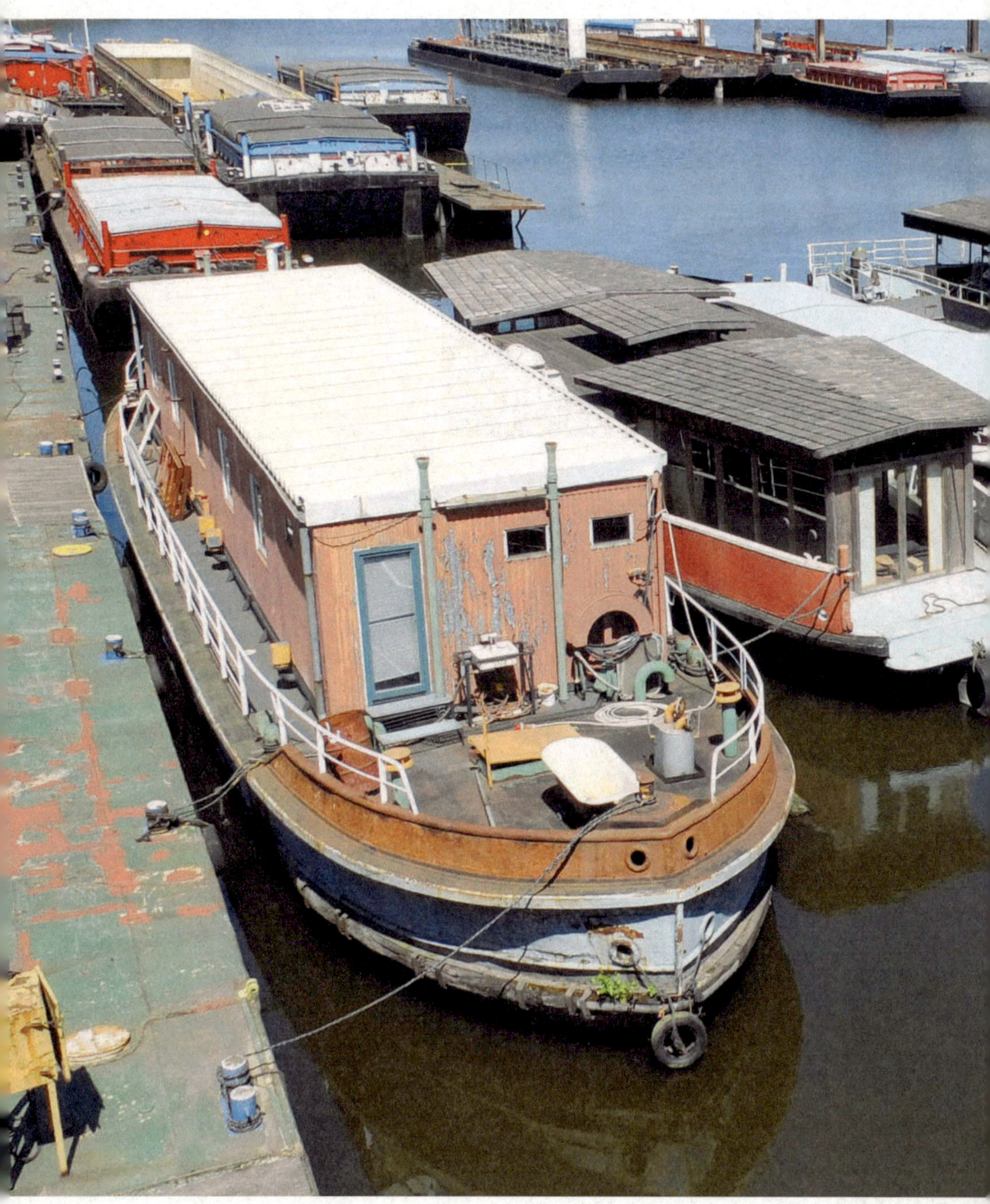

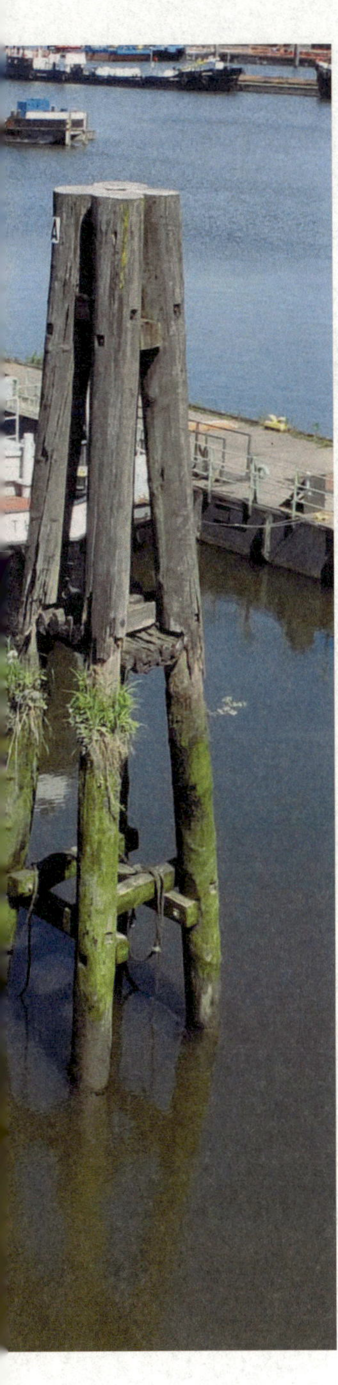

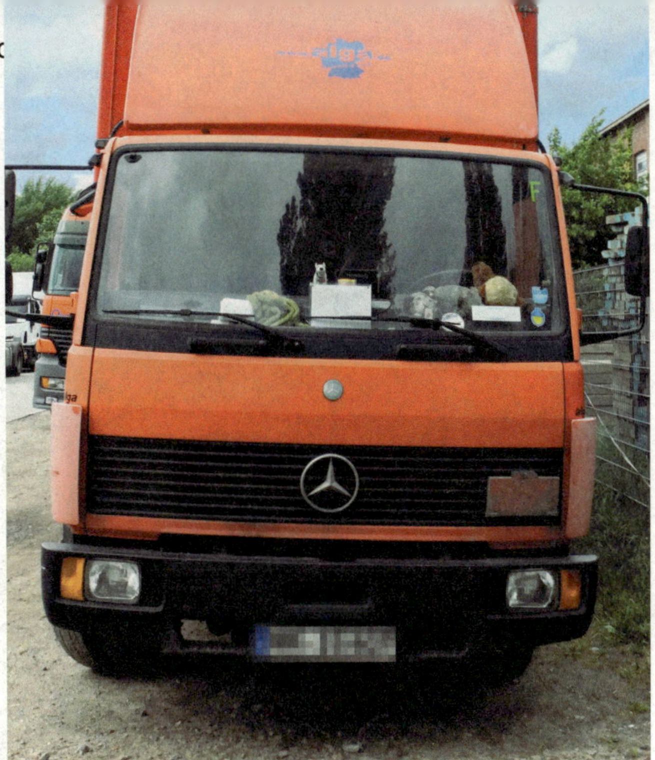

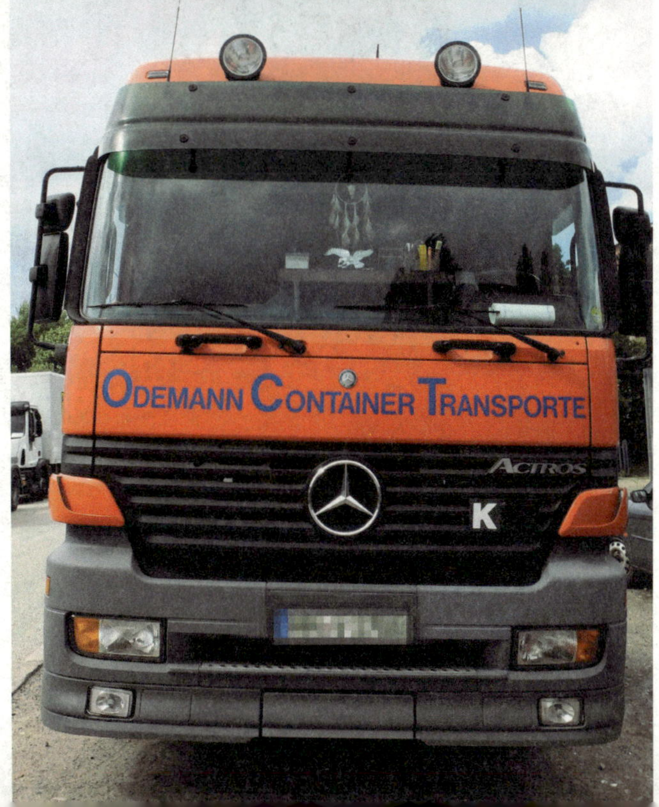
ODEMANN CONTAINER TRANSPORTE
ACTROS
K

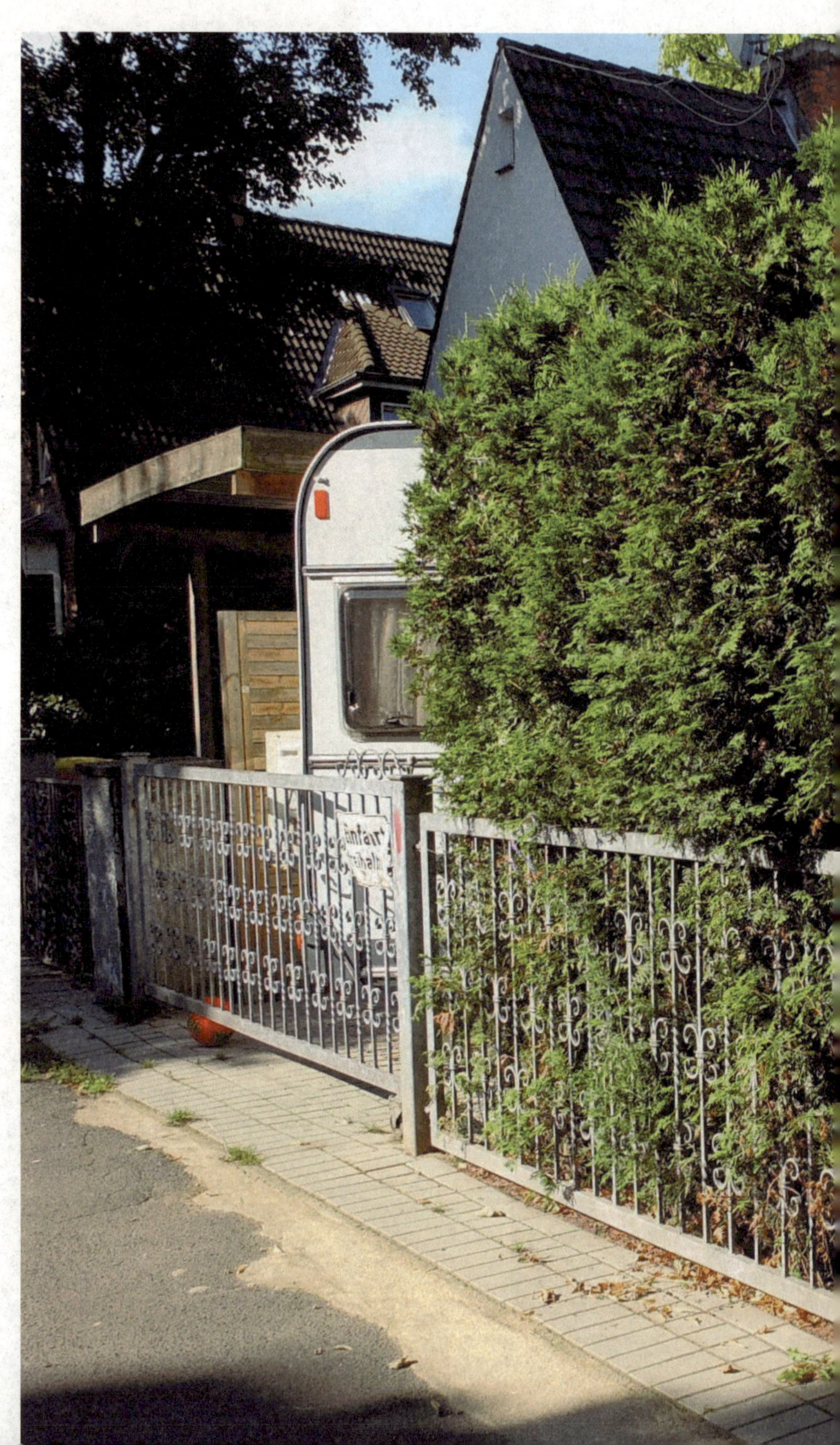

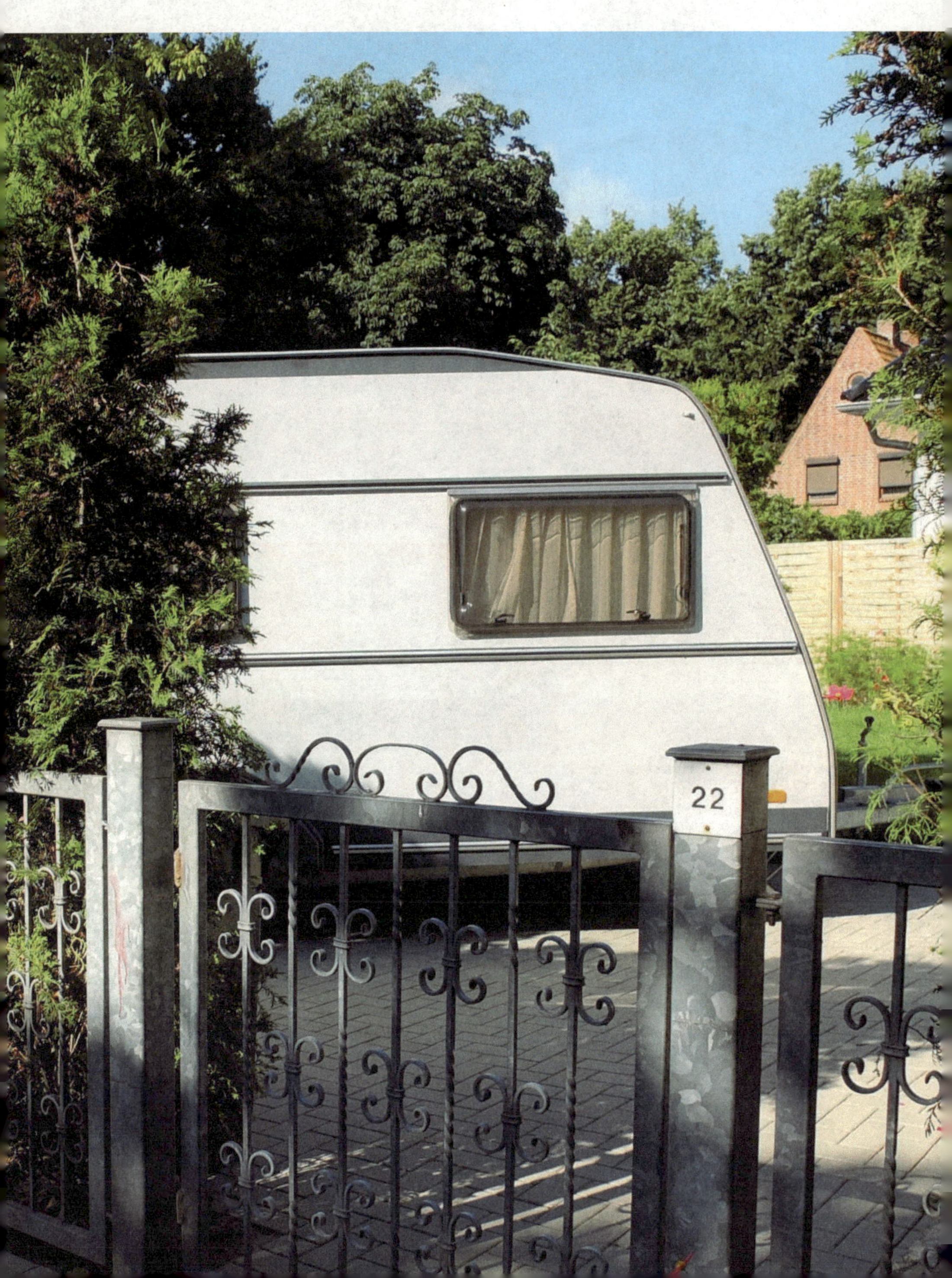

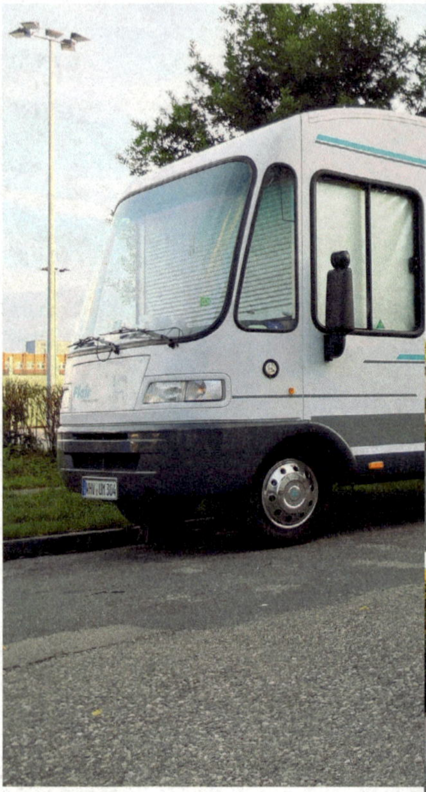

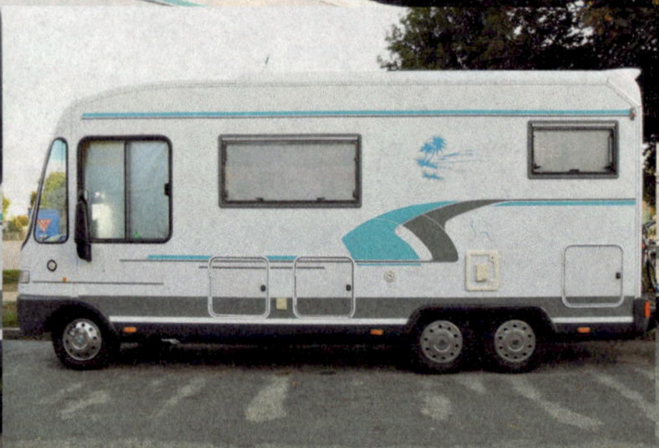

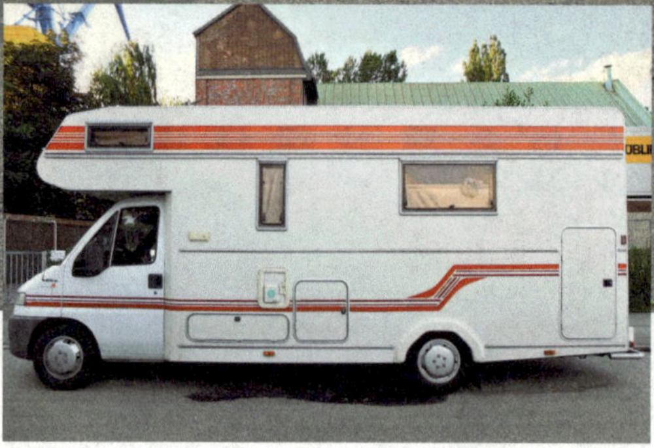

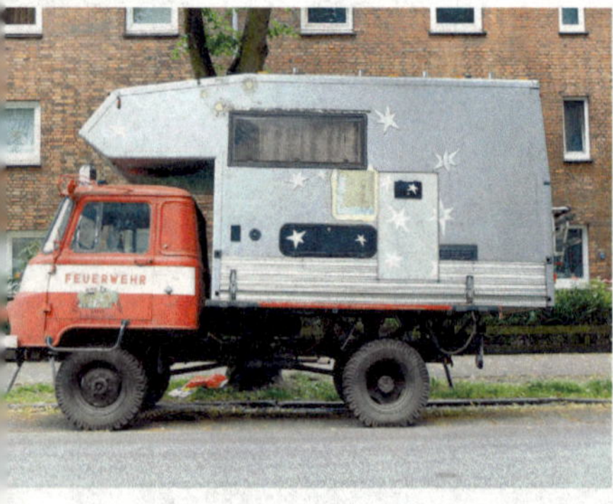
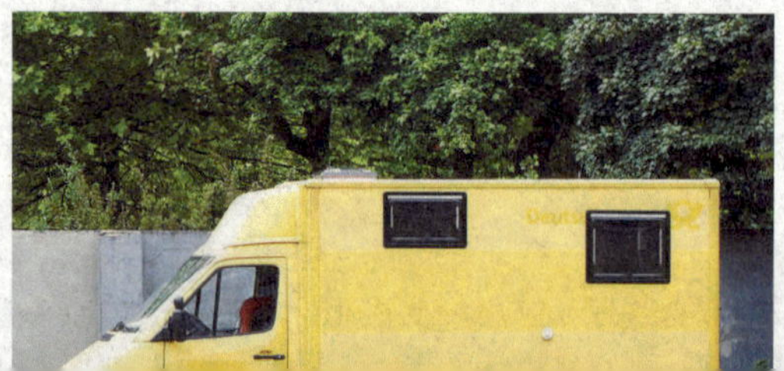

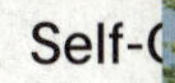

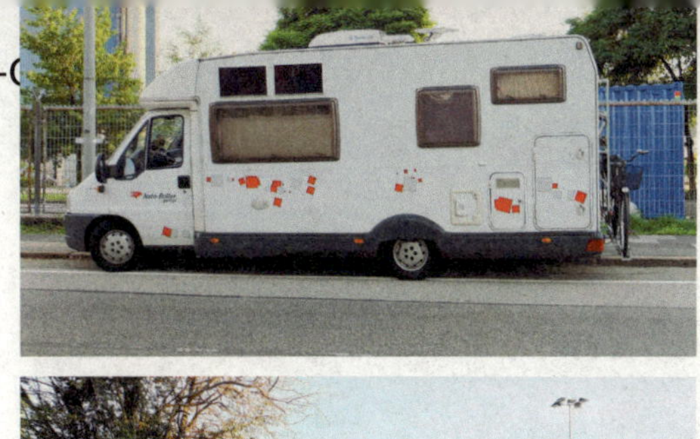

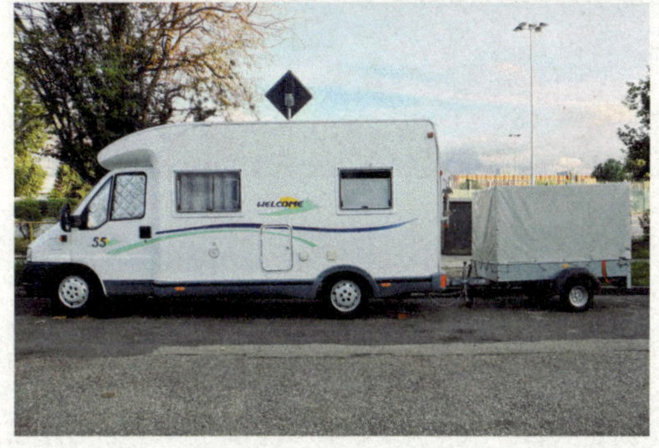

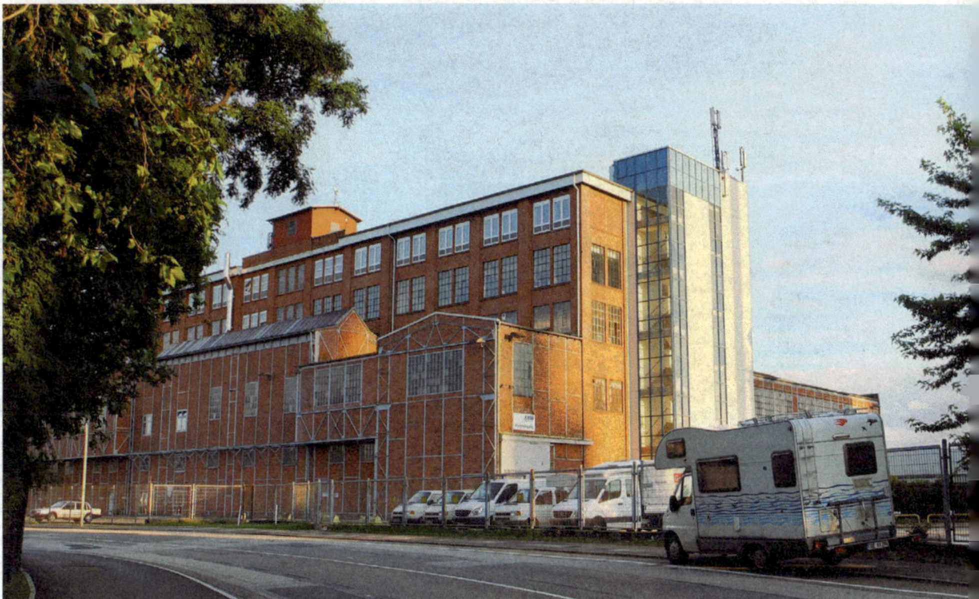

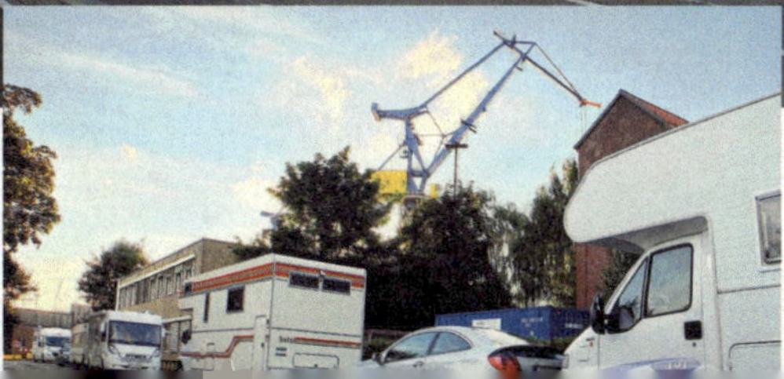

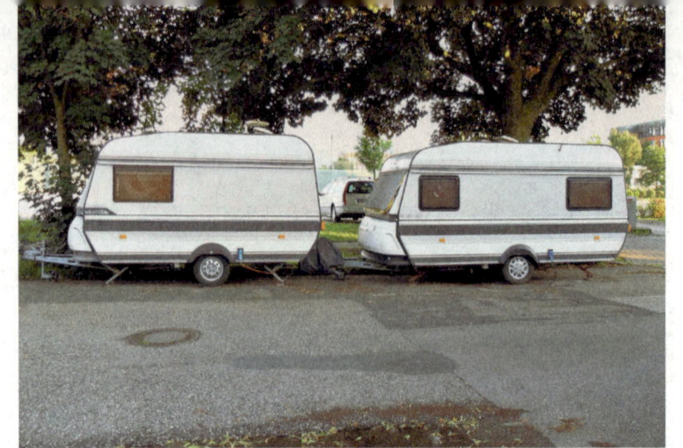

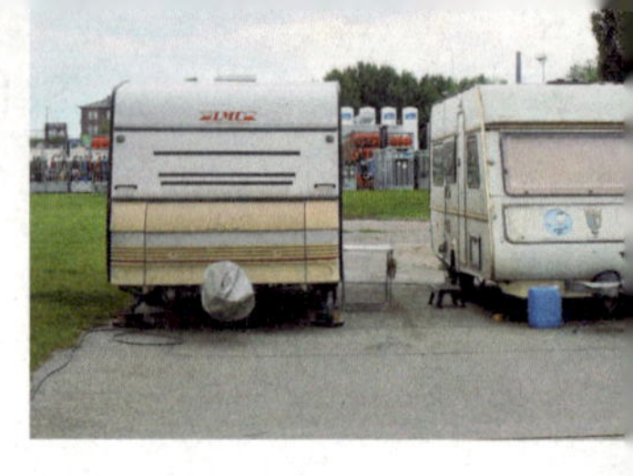

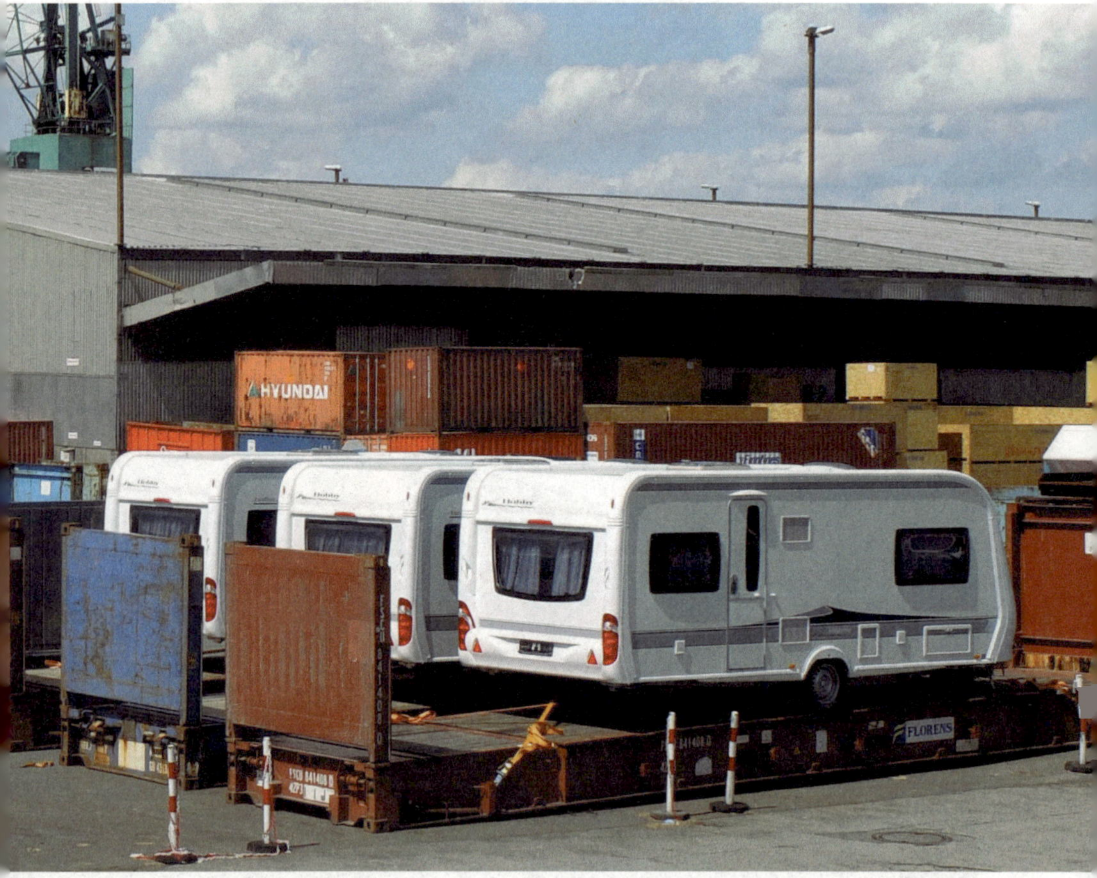

Balconies can be representative showcases and / or be used as additional storage space in very functional ways. Interior and exterior spaces flow into one another at this point, which are then connected to one another through utilization. Cleaning utensils are within easy reach of the kitchen, set on discarded furniture; outdated refrigerators await disposal; satellite dishes sit in the corner in receive mode; drying racks and clothes lines have their rightful place too; winter tires are stored for the season; expensive bicycles are kept safe; pots of herbs and the odd tomato plant or two are lined up alongside ornaments on a narrow ledge. It is only when you look more closely that you spot the occasional marijuana plant in a flower pot, along with small lanterns dangling on high, parasols and awnings to protect against the sun's rays and intrusive gazes; small homemade cages for pets fit in too. Empty bottles are packed into bags; carpets and bedding are aired in the private room open to the skies. Small tables with colorful plastic tablecloths invite you to enjoy a cup of coffee, mocha, or tea. There is just enough space to open up the weekly newspaper with the classified ads. Temporary mini gardens with fluttering flags of different nationalities hint at the tenants' diverse backgrounds. The pennants of favorite football clubs are displayed prominently on the parapets too. From these private grandstands, the hustle and bustle on the streets can be observed undisturbed. People call out loudly to acquaintances when they spot them or wave a greeting | Stands for Lingering |. Keys are thrown down several stories into the outstretched hands of friends or relatives who have dropped by. "Espace vécu" (cf. Lefebvre 1991/1974: 33). Lived space, appropriated by its inhabitants through intercultural use, shaped in highly nuanced ways, becomes a reality.

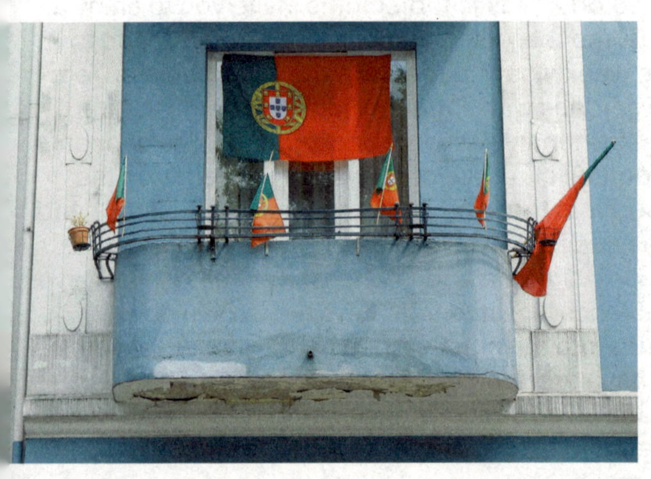

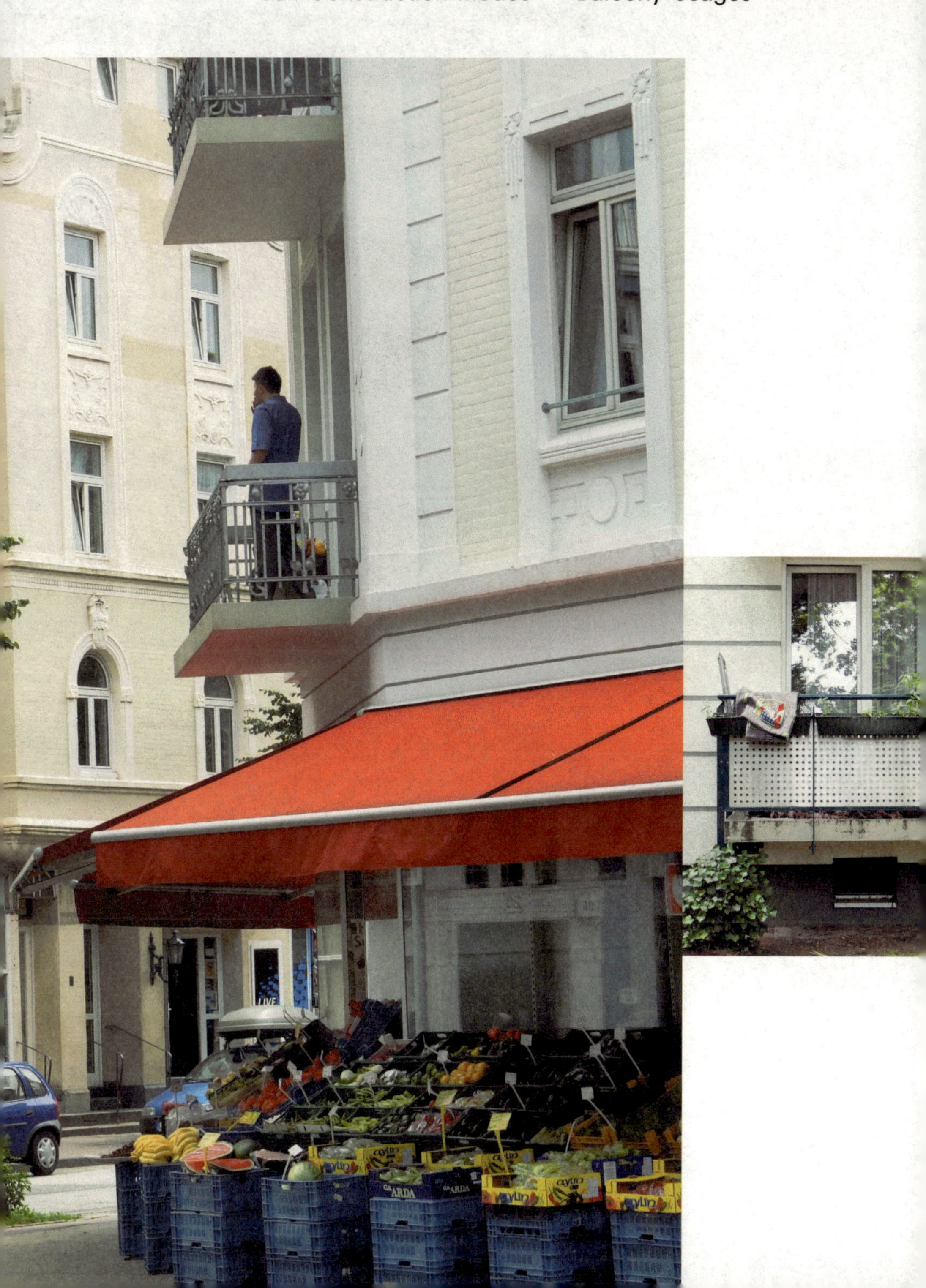

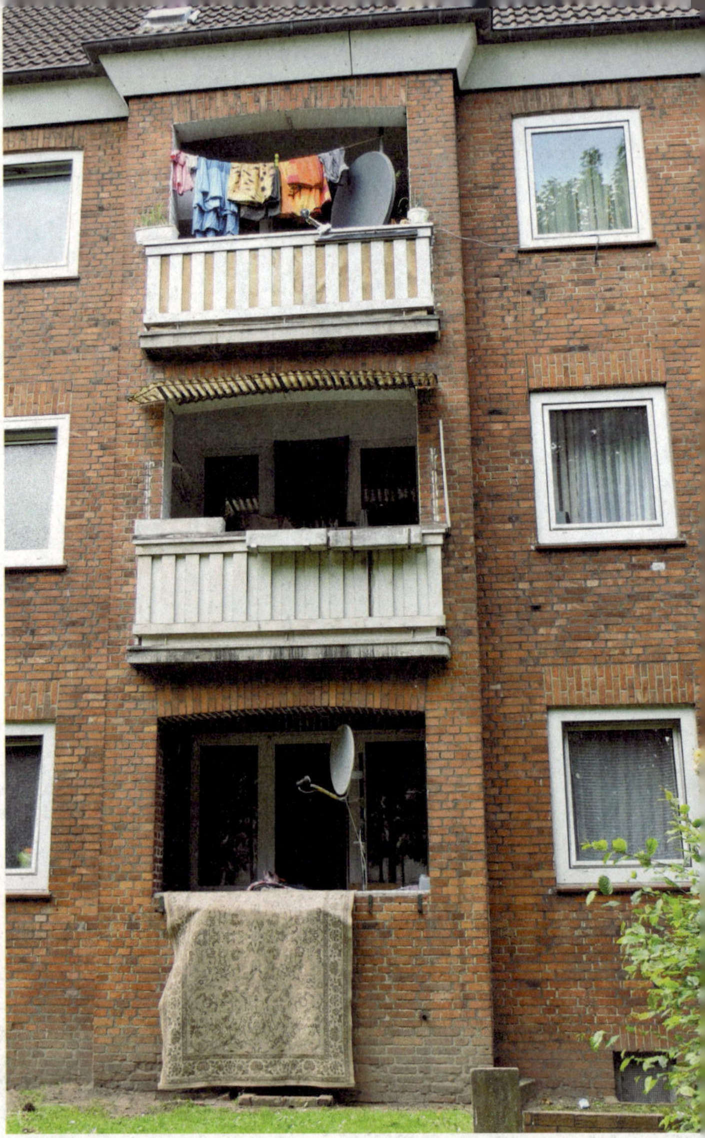

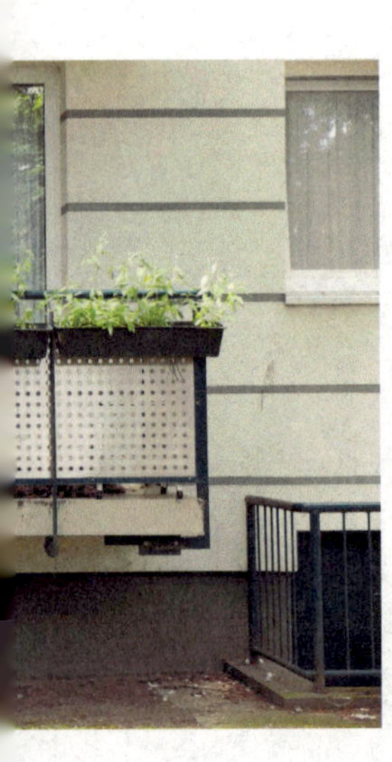

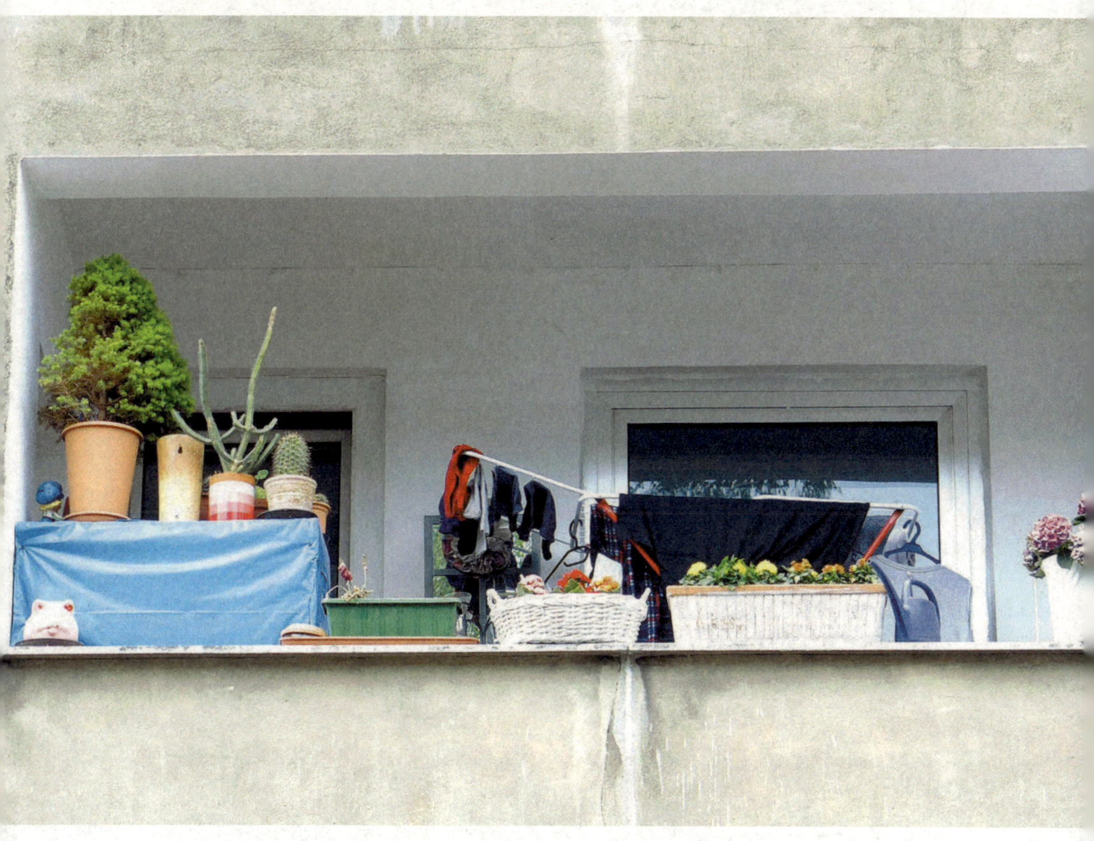

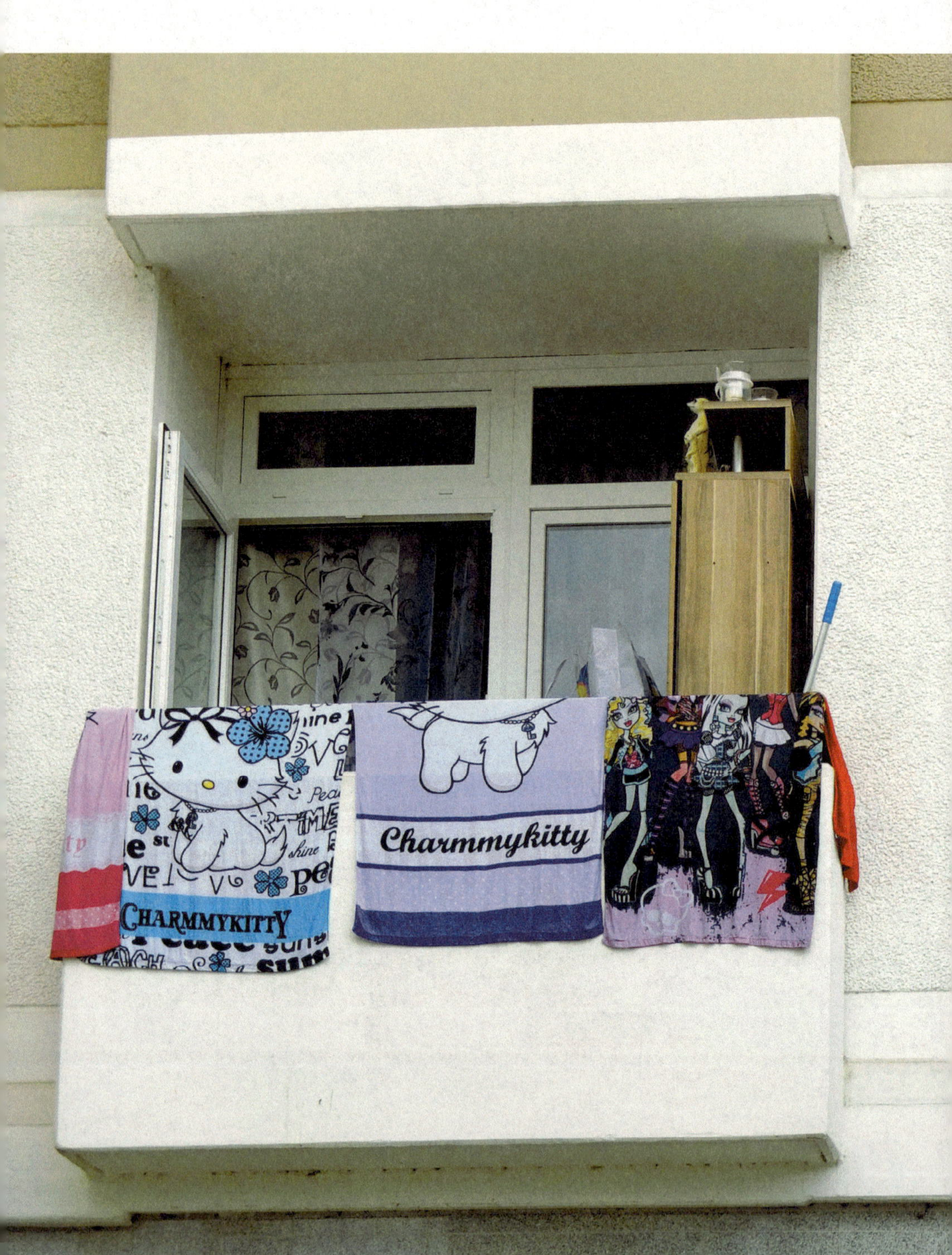
CHARMMYKITTY
Charmmykitty

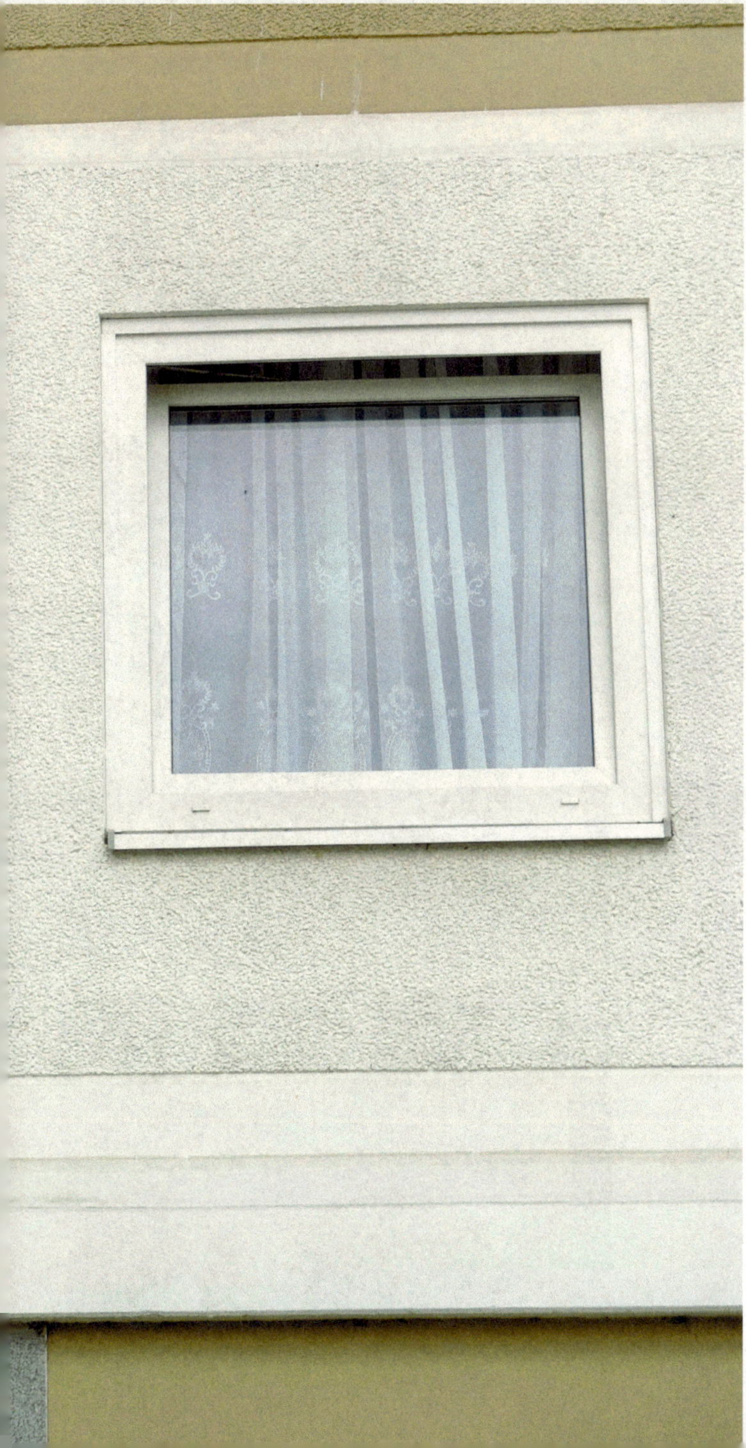

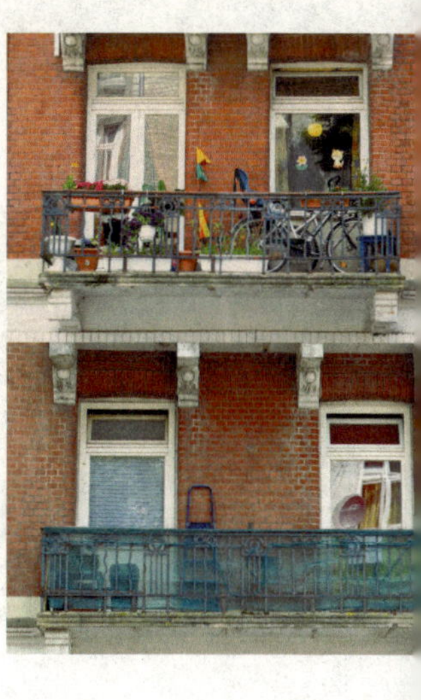

Self-Construction-Modes   Balcony-Usages

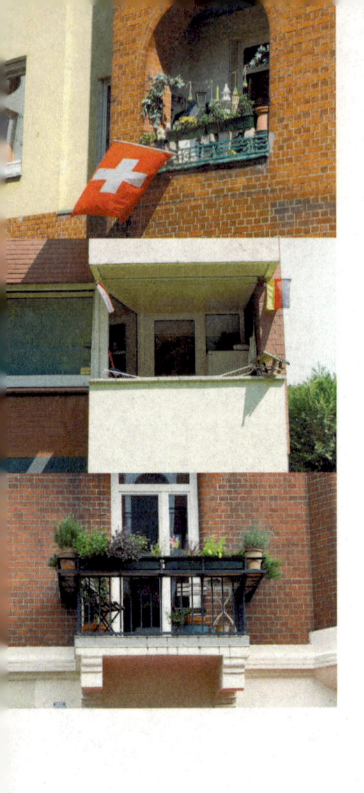
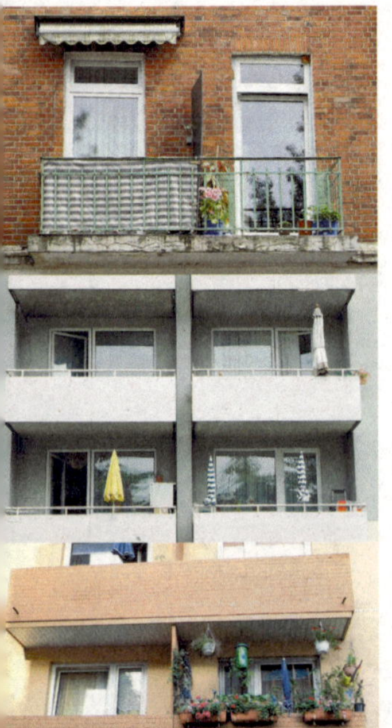

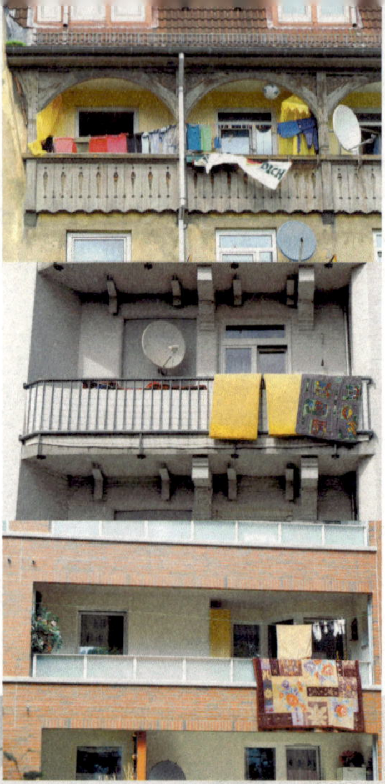

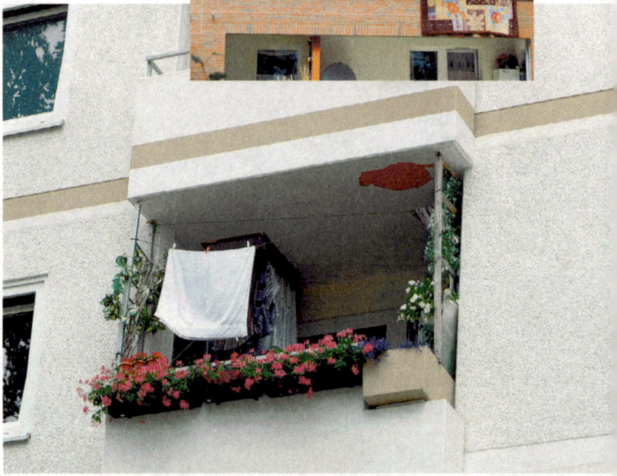

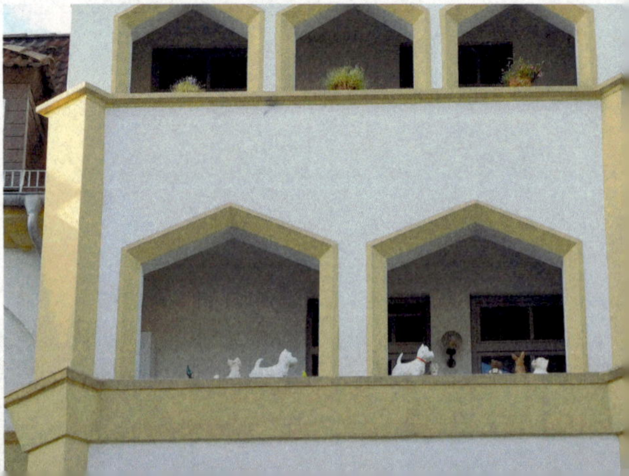

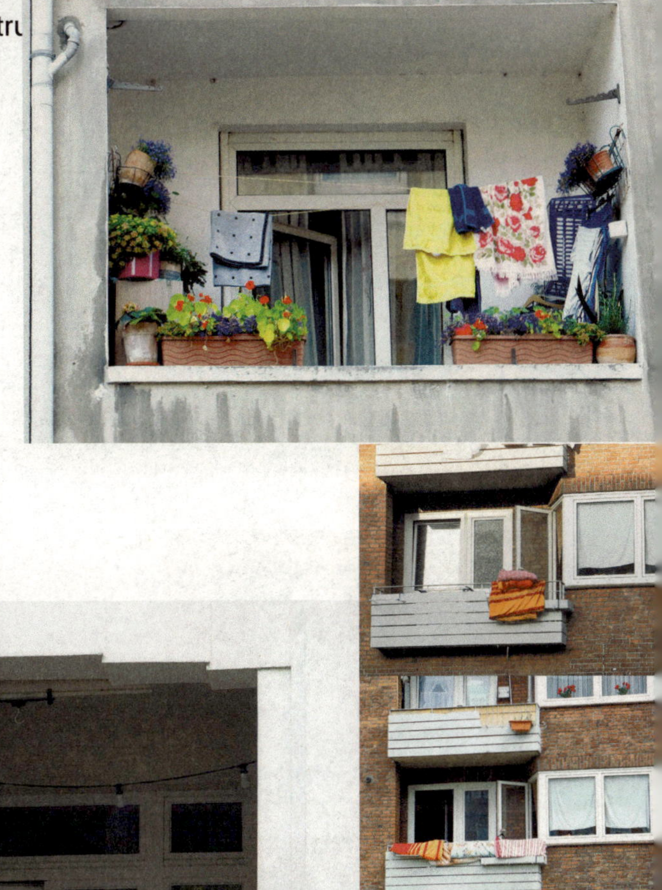

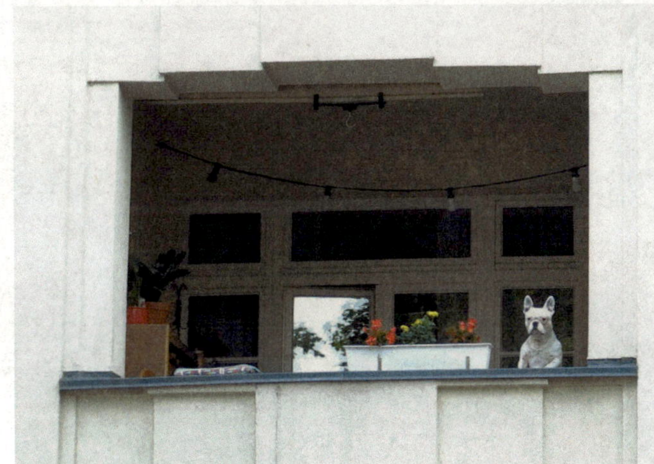

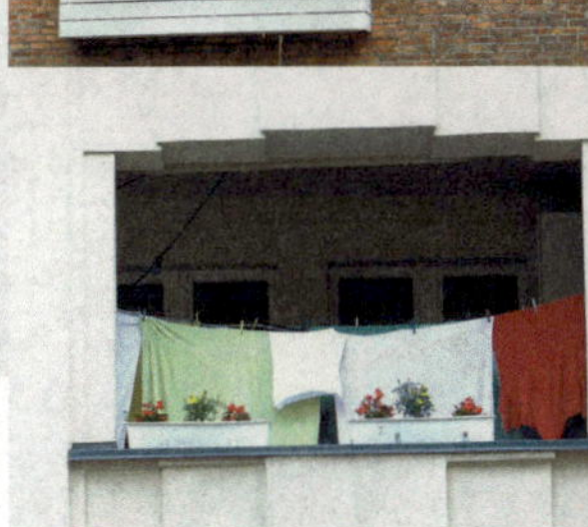

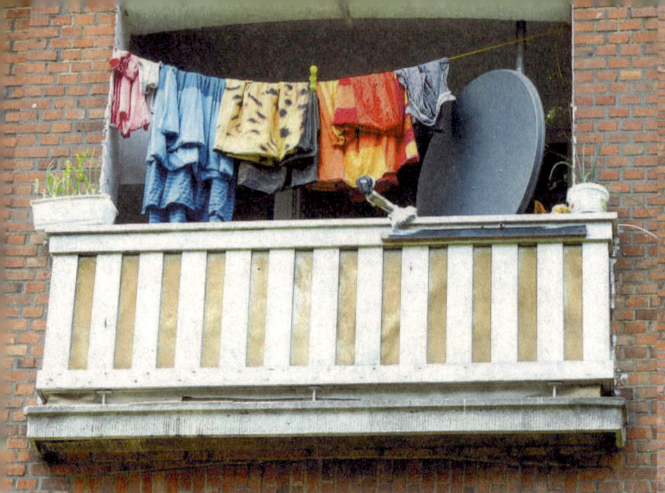

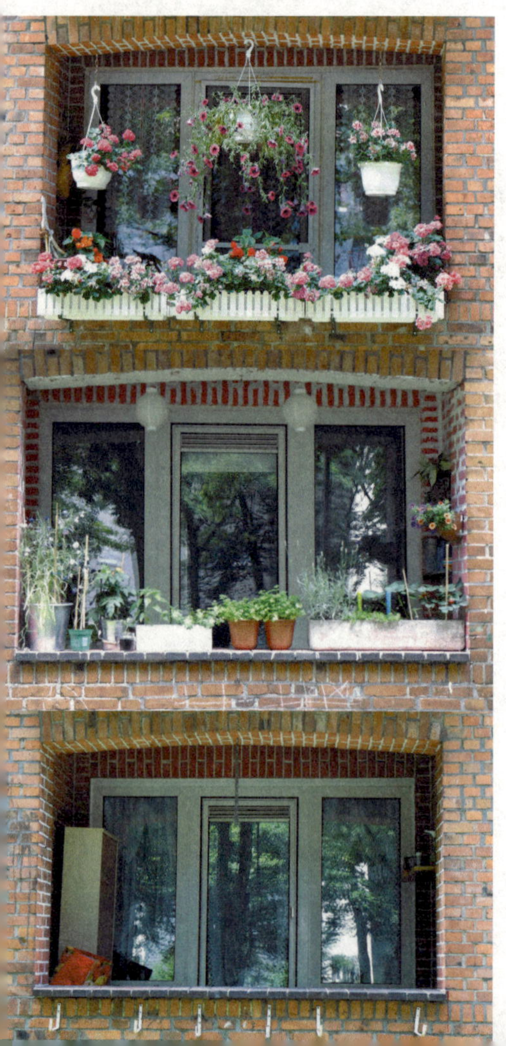

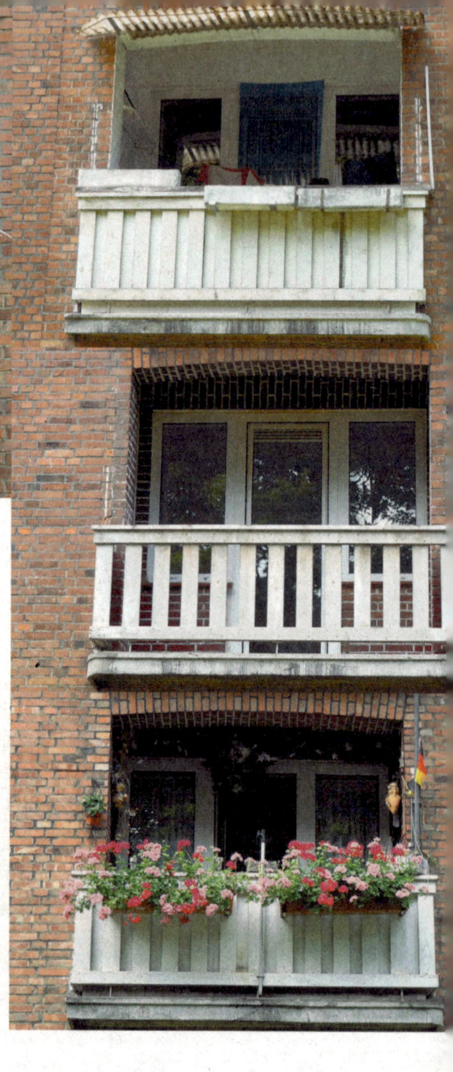

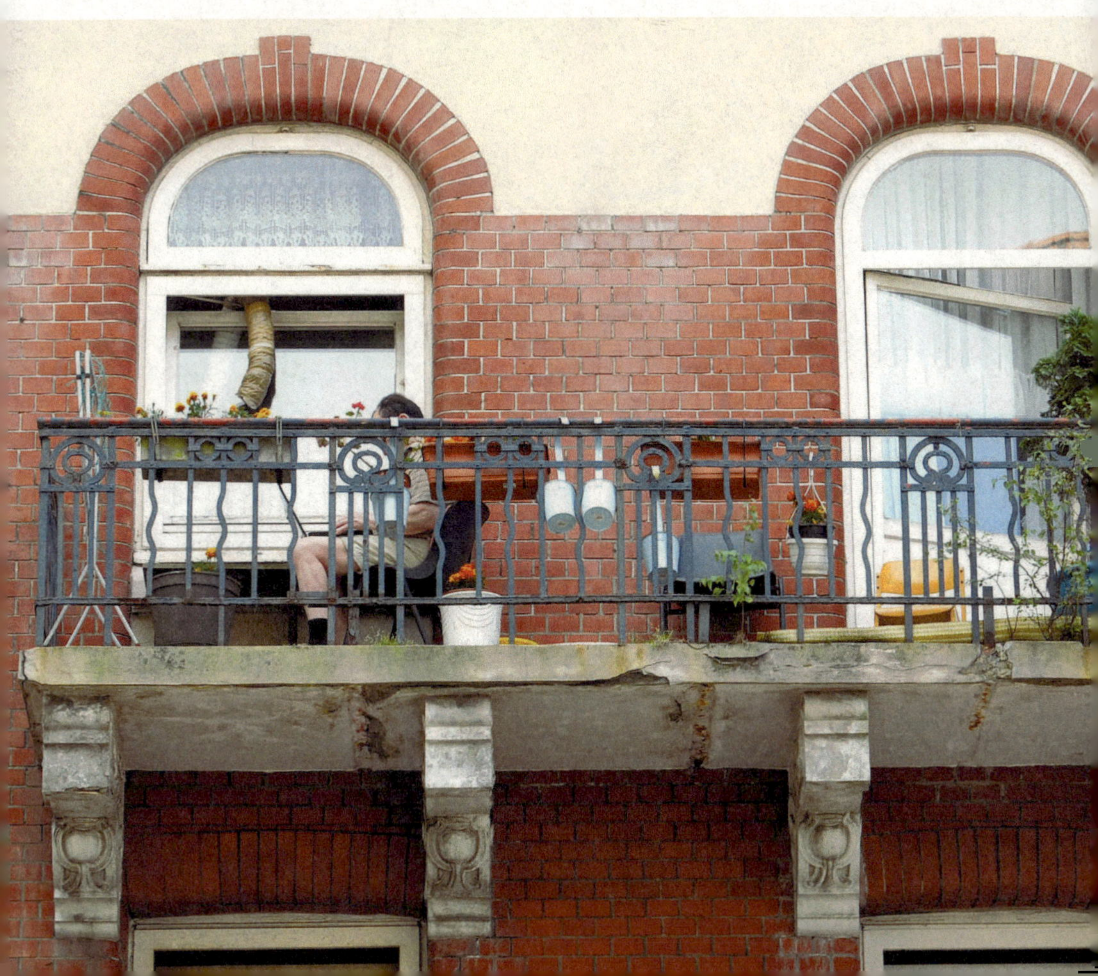

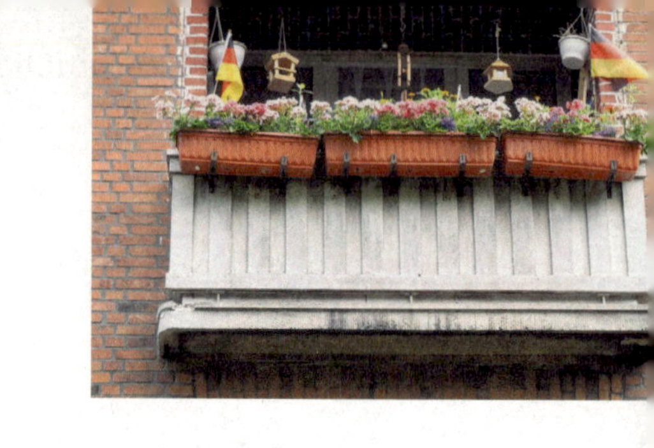

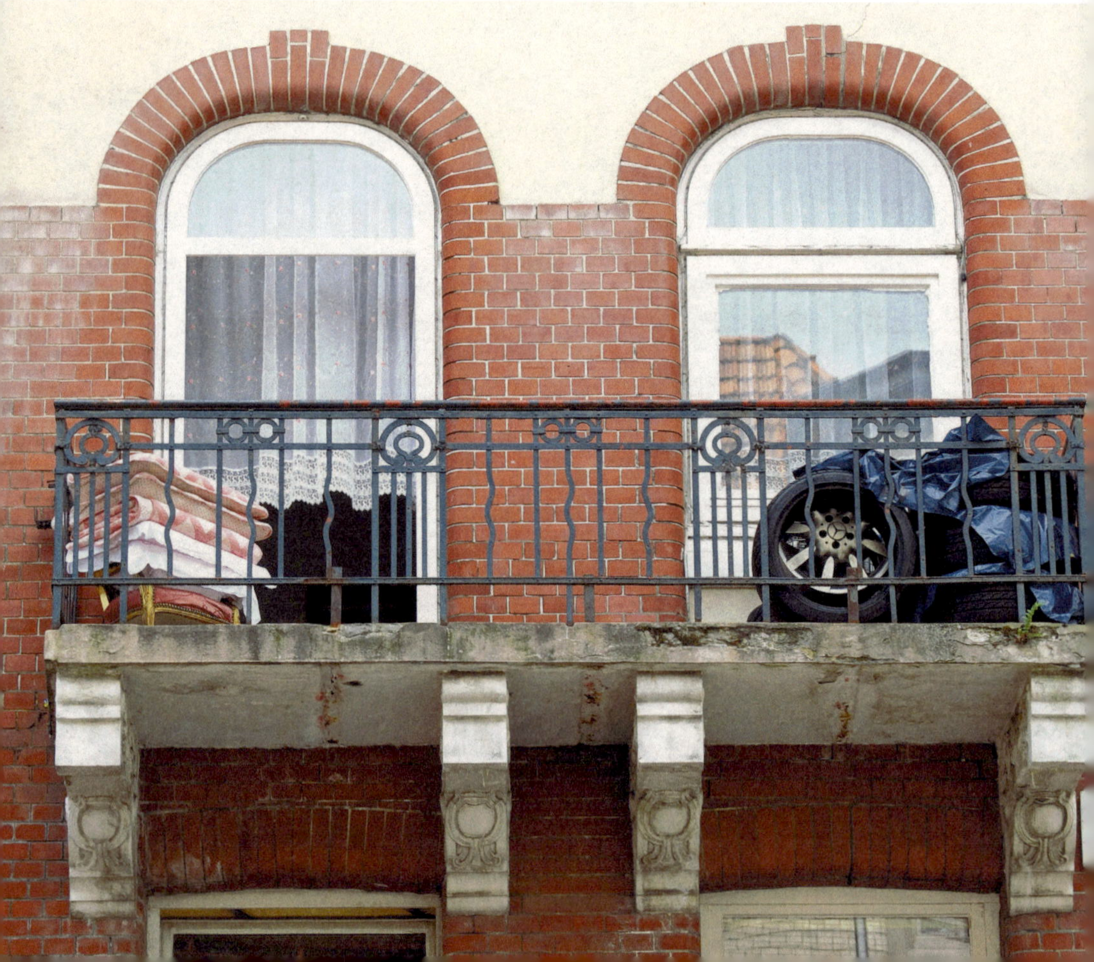

A copy+paste of various ways of building, styles, and traditions. Caesurae in the (un)planned combinatorics of individual modes of expression. (Un)conventional mixtures of serial modules and elements. Peculiar interconnections with organically developed structures. Serial repetitions of individual dreams. These ideas are articulated in the form of owner-occupied homes, housing estates, and family gardens. They are the built synthesis of craft, cultural practices, and narration Window Messages Balcony Usages . All in all, the Elbe Islands are a colorful catalog of houses, balconies, and windows: the inhabitants position, decorate, customize, hoard, sort, do DIY, live … There are lovingly constructed, kitsch, practical, functional, modest, befitting, improvised, (in)complete living environments with and without building instructions in the Italian, Russian, Ottoman, Muslim, Greek, English, North Frisian, Oriental, and Spanish … language.
It is a space of relationships, realization, appropriation. It is everyday life. It is a coming-and-going of new, old, familiar or foreign influences and flows Change-Comma-Pause .
A lived "open-ended urbanism" (Brands; Broekman 2010: 274f) that continues to be written, adapted, and implemented by the islands' inhabitants in the most different places at the same time: Elbe Islands Self-Construction-Modes.

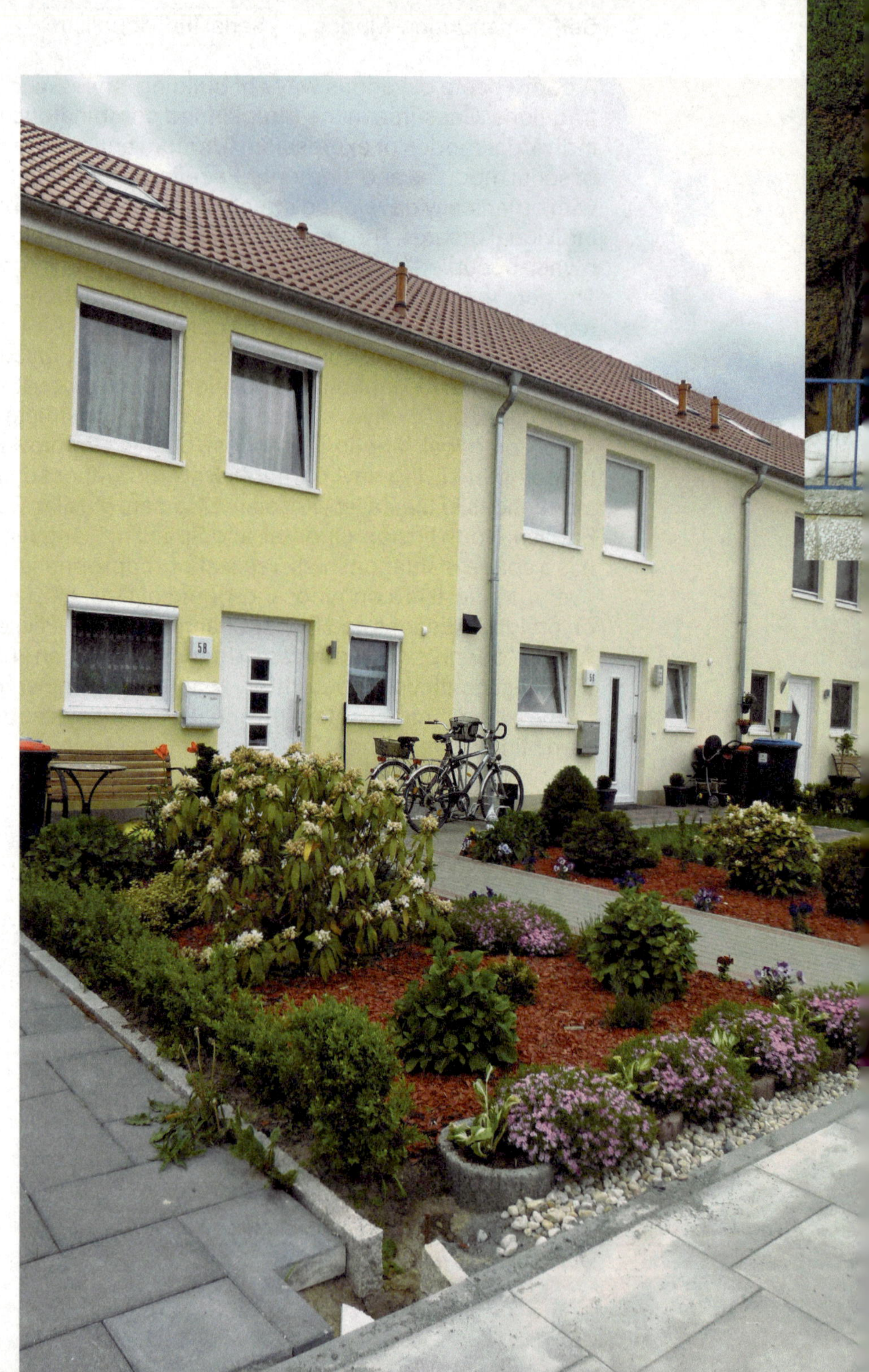

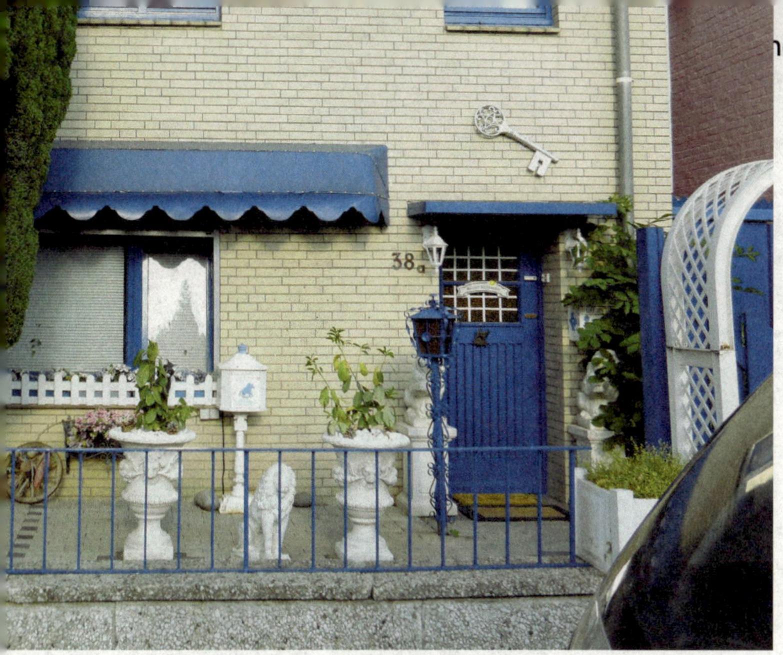

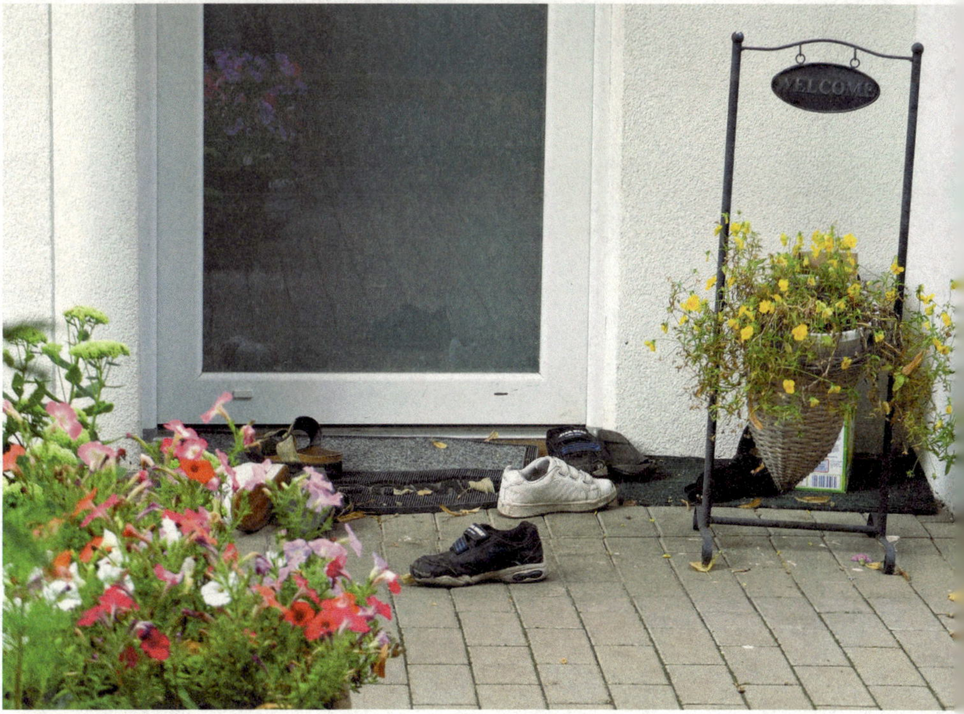

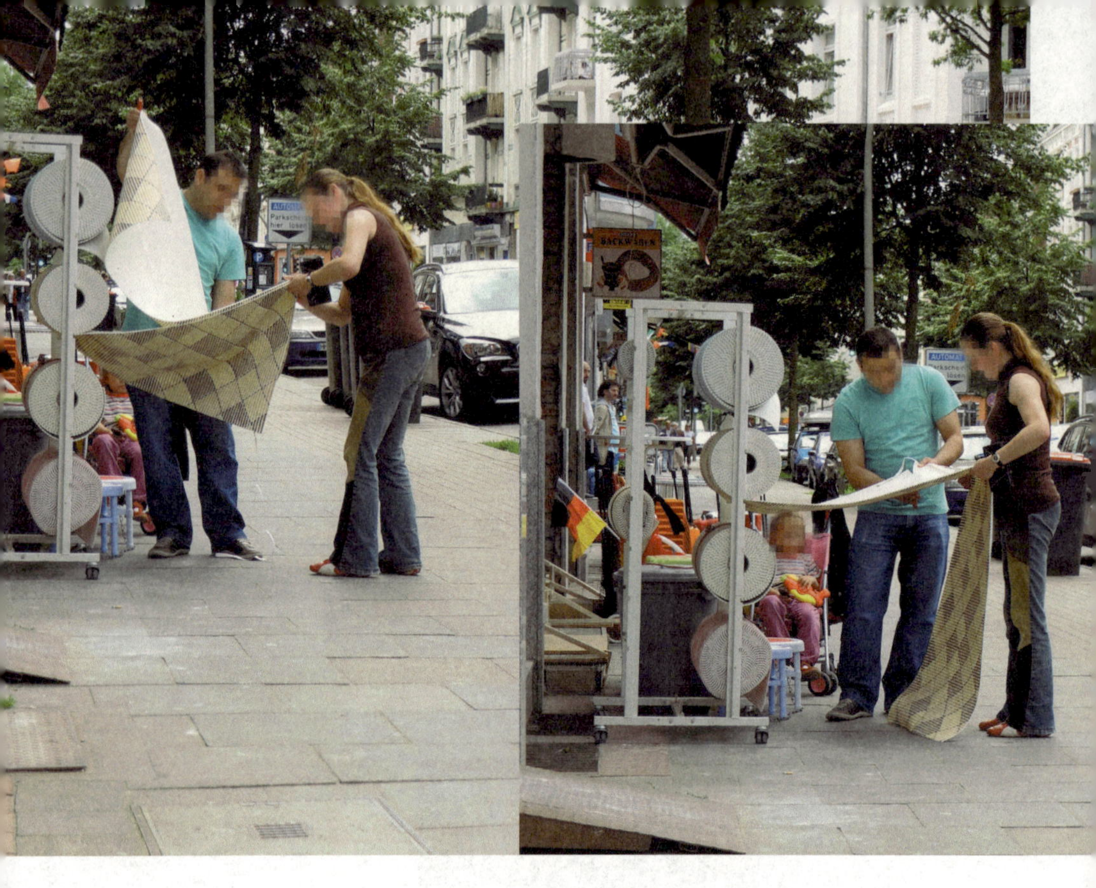

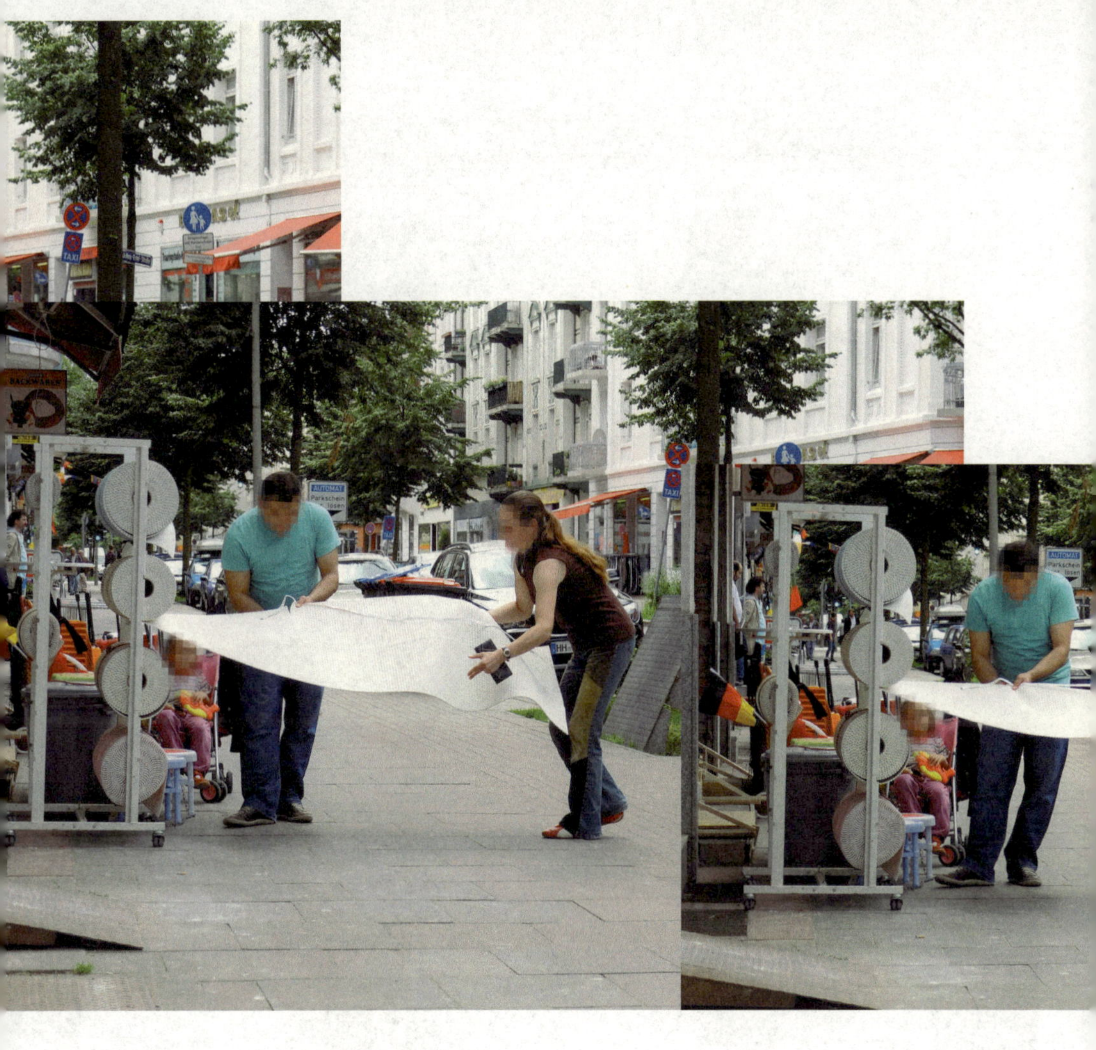

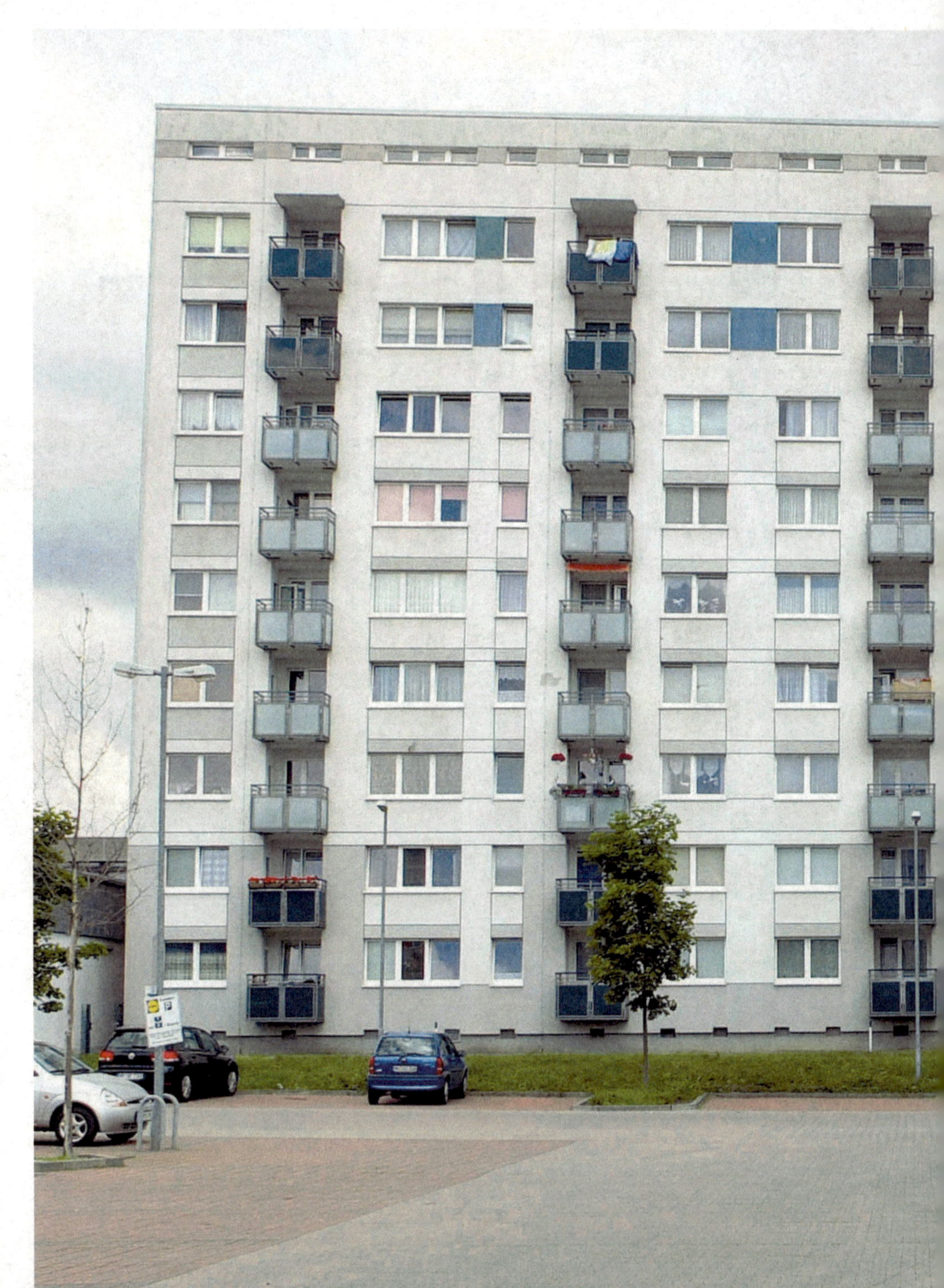

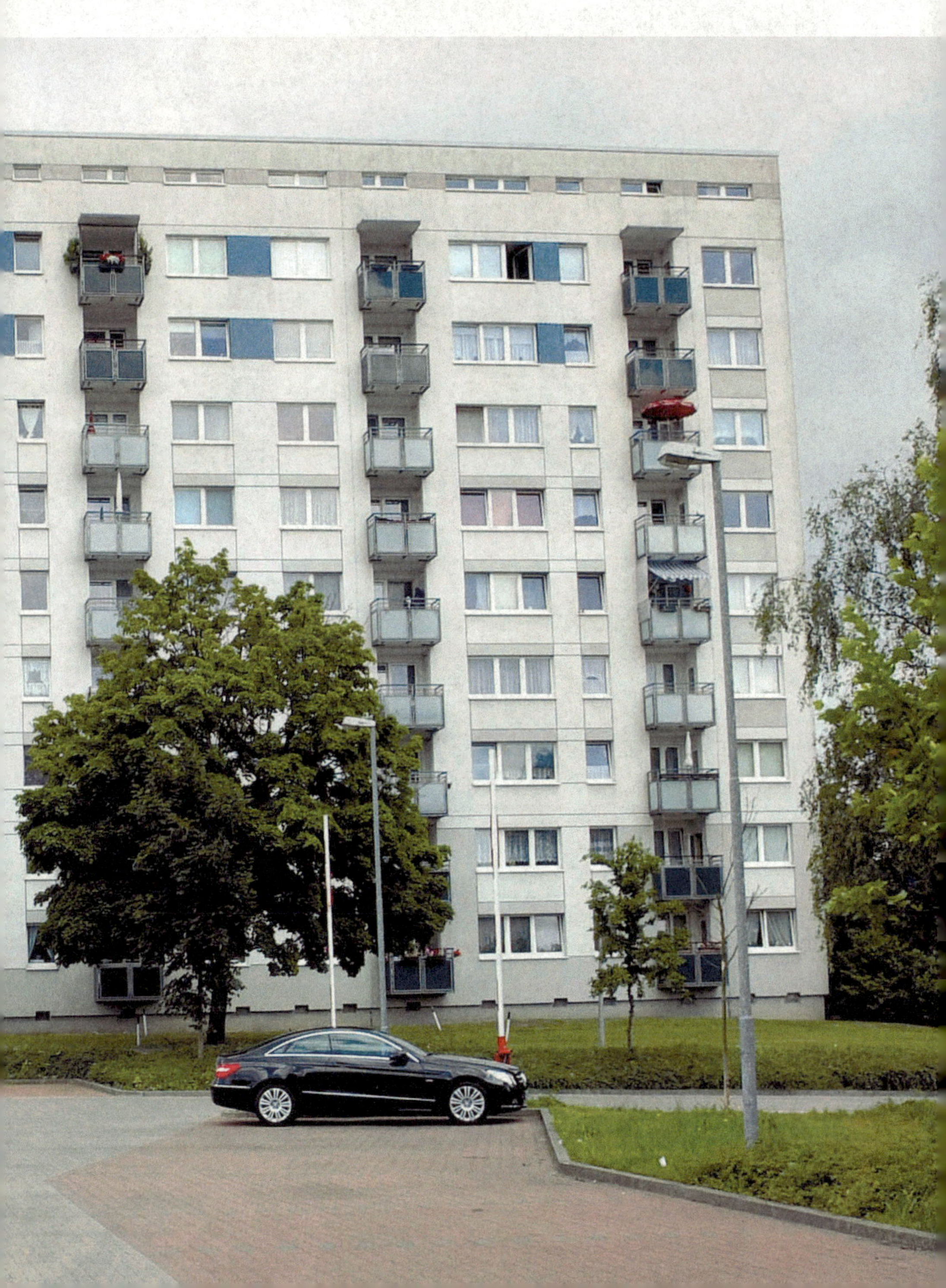

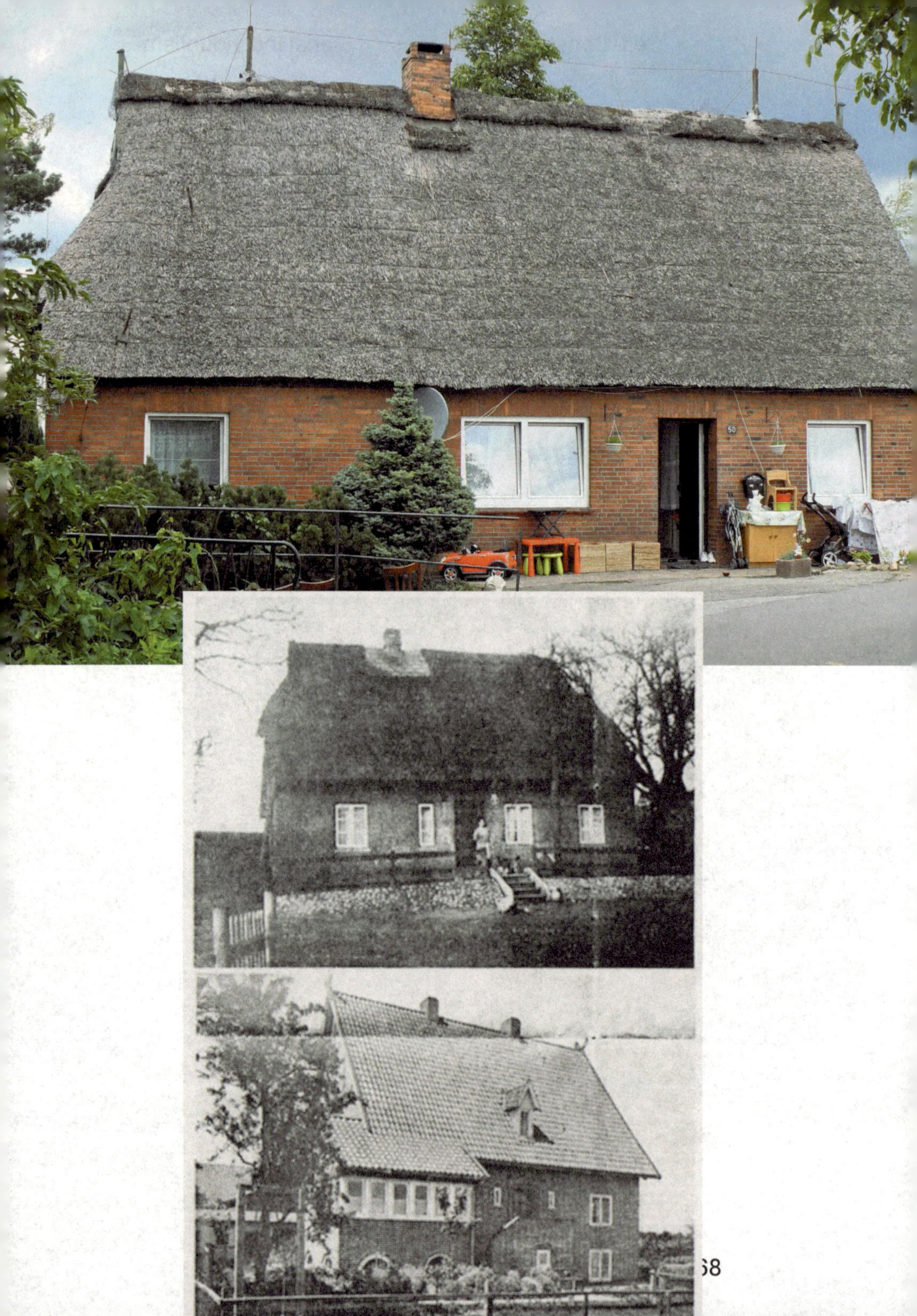

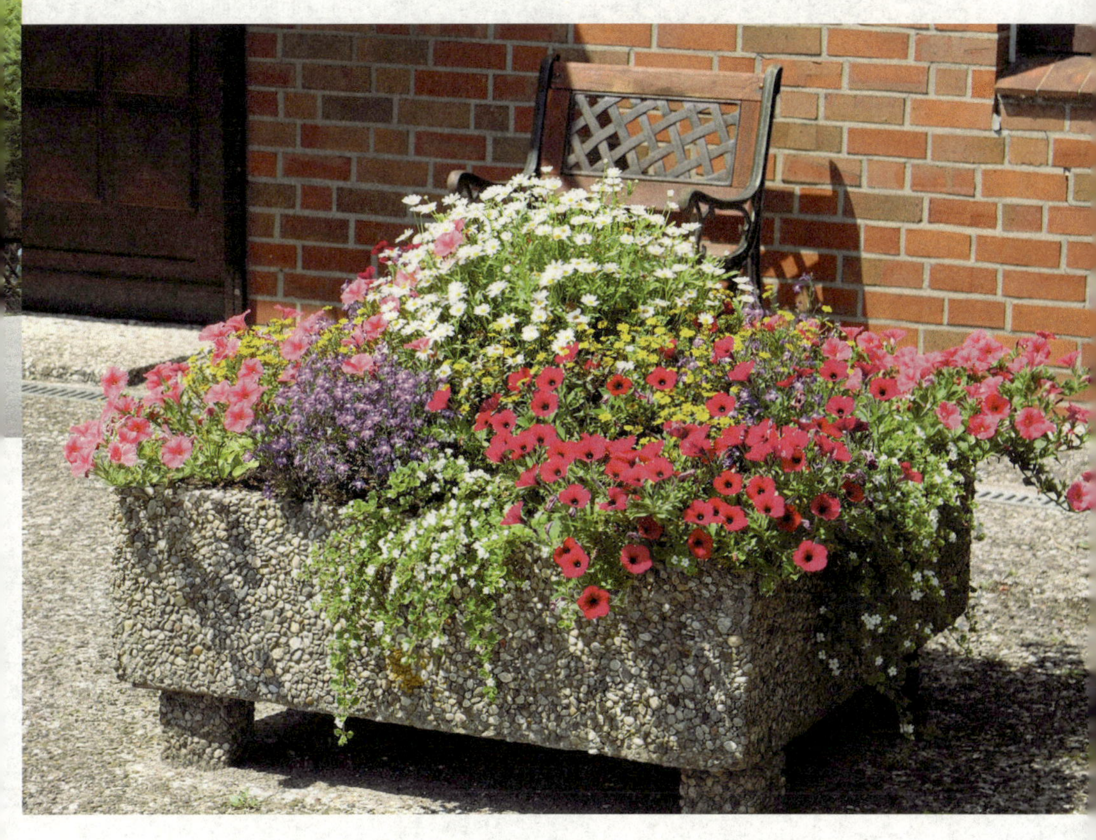

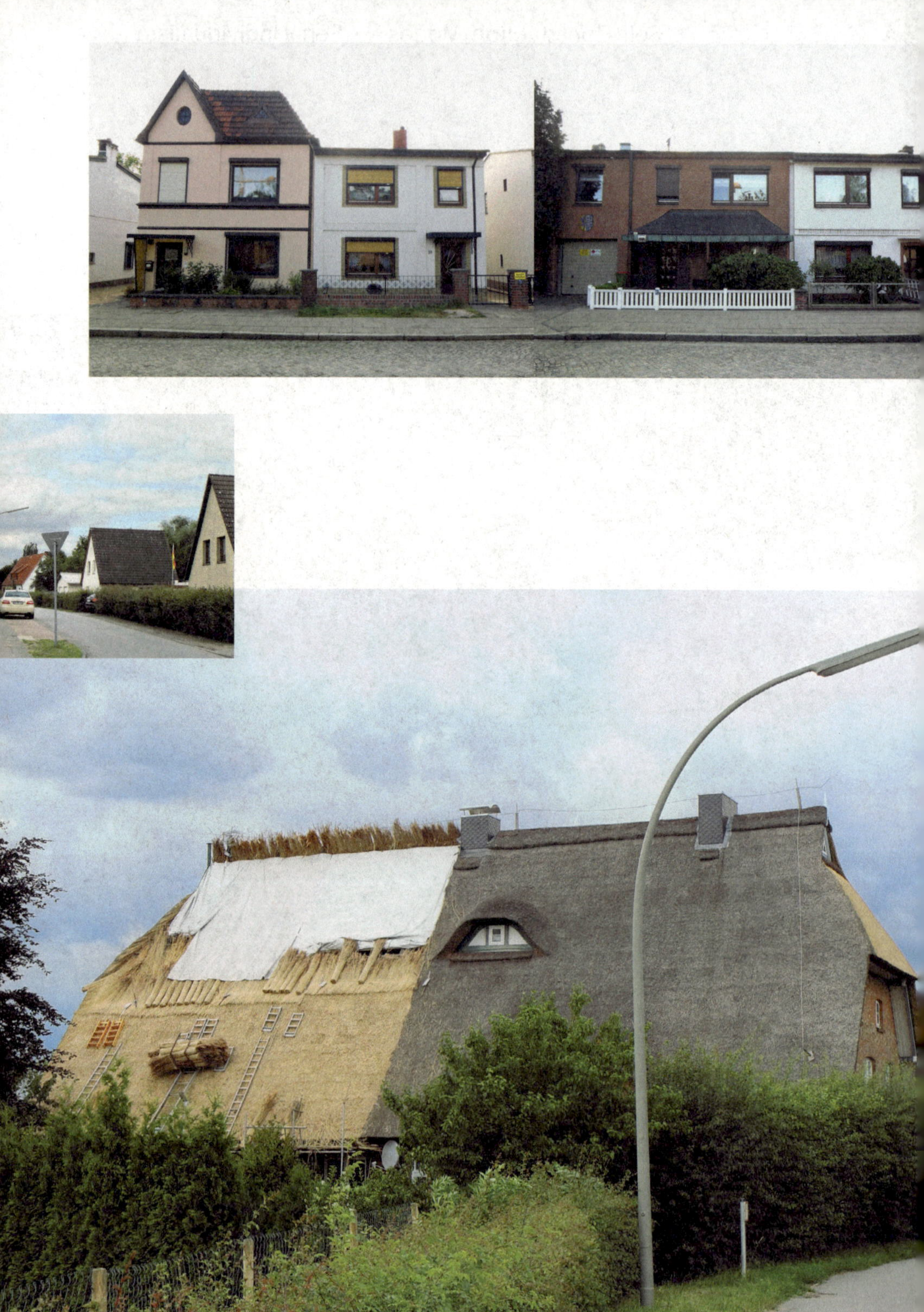

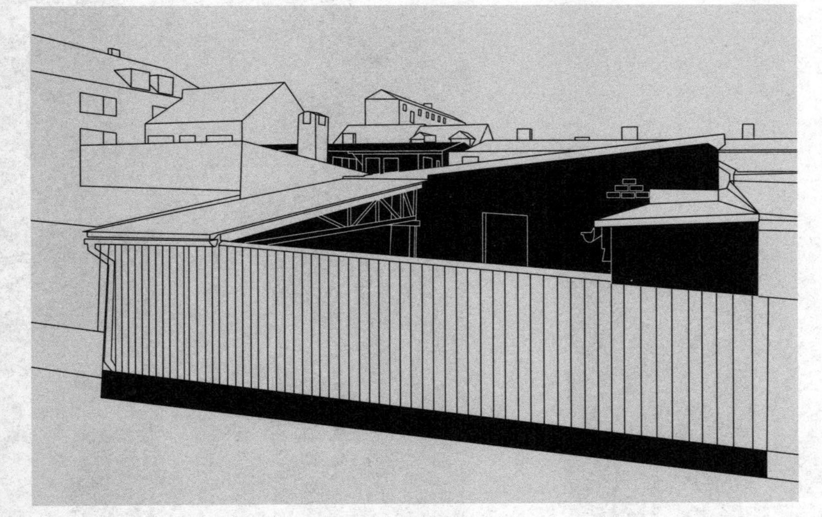

... sections keep being added onto, the writing is constantly updated, squeezed into a denser form later if need be. Restructured. Courtyard, niche, square. House. Out front, the narrow canal passes by ...

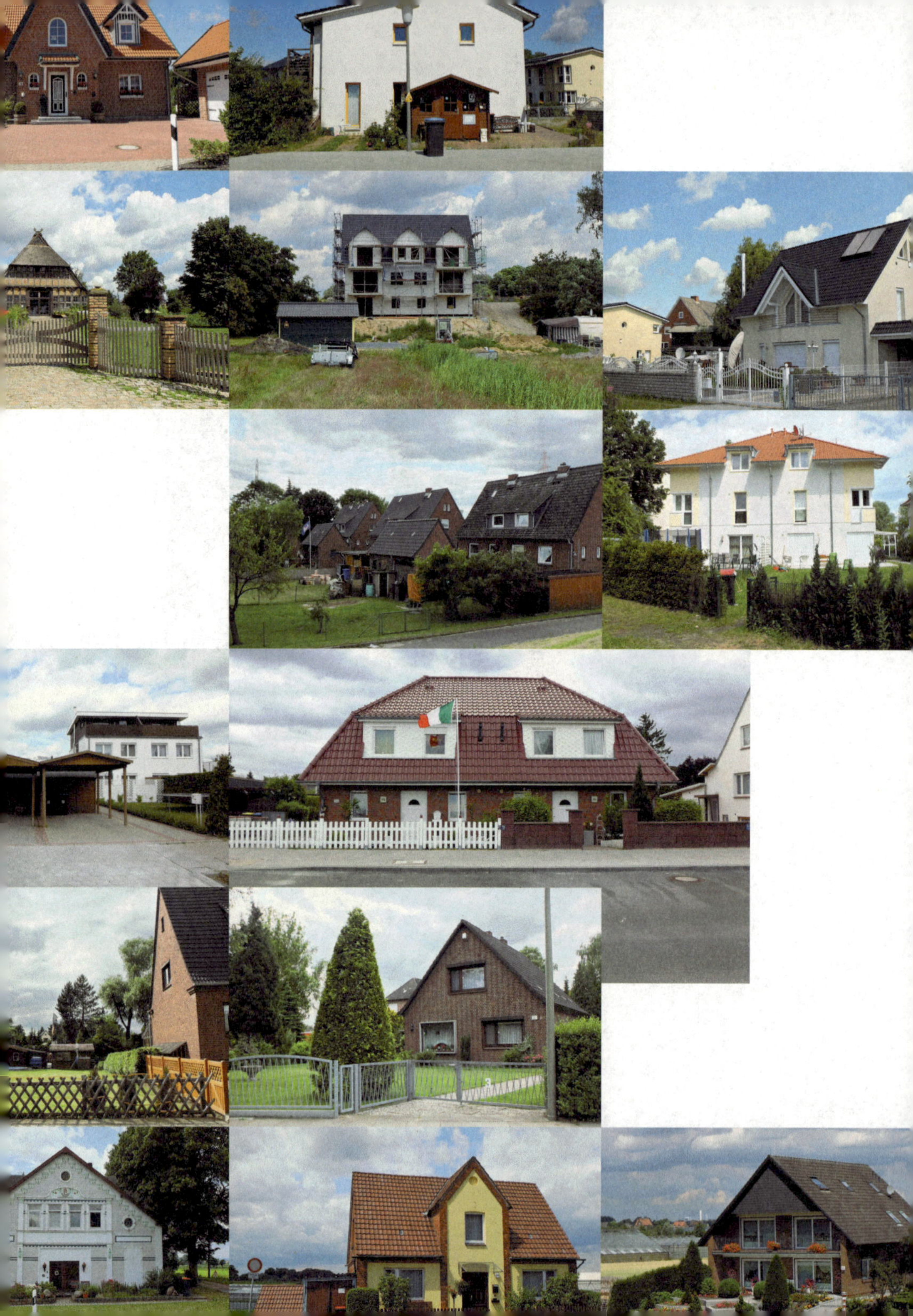

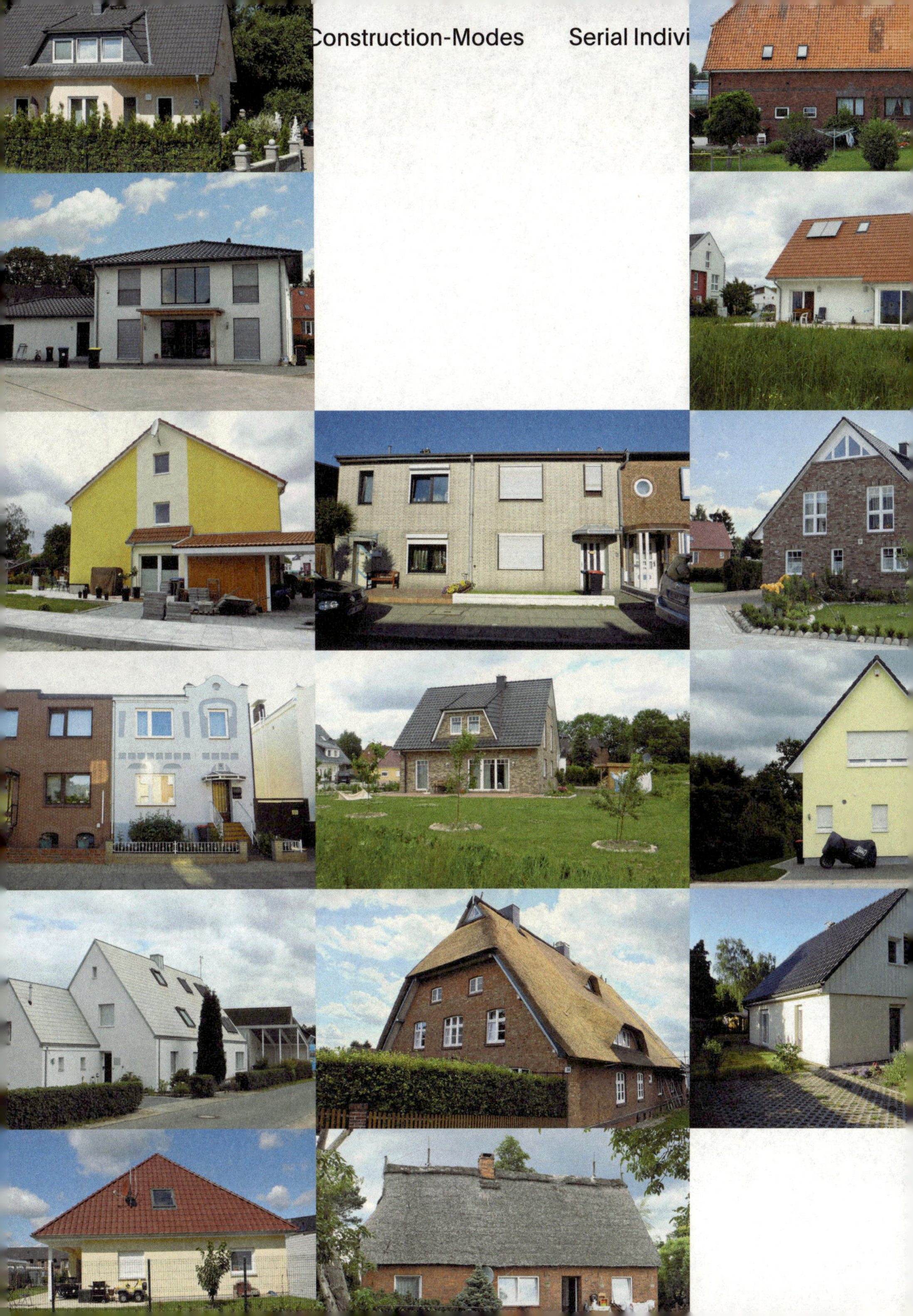
Construction-Modes
Serial Indivi

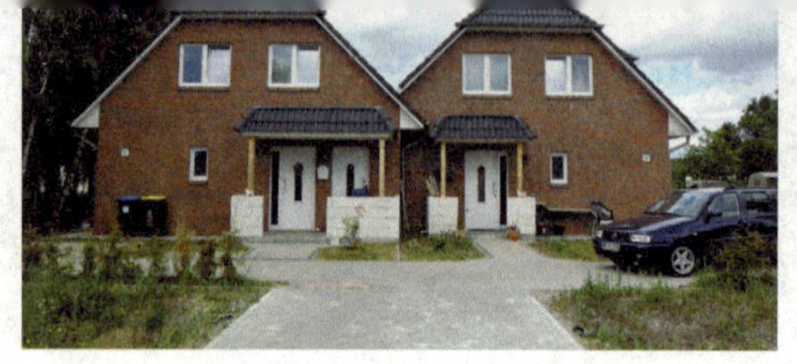

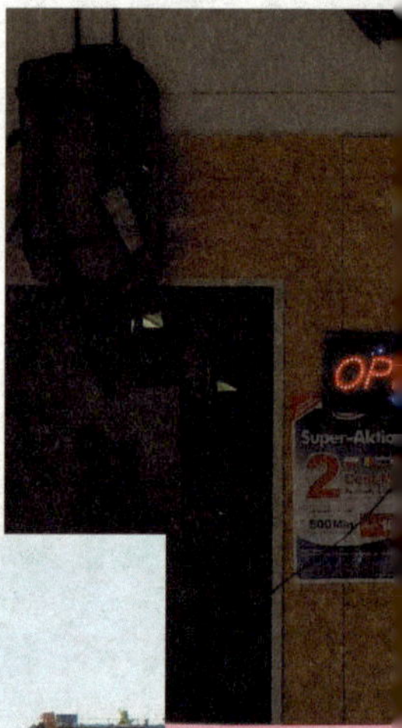

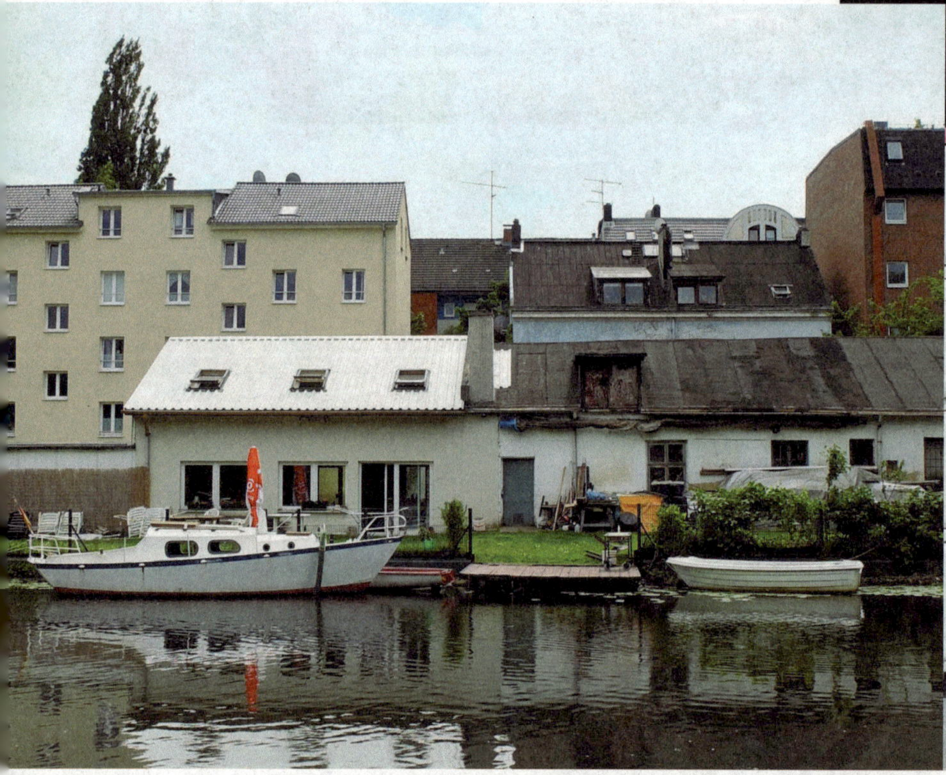

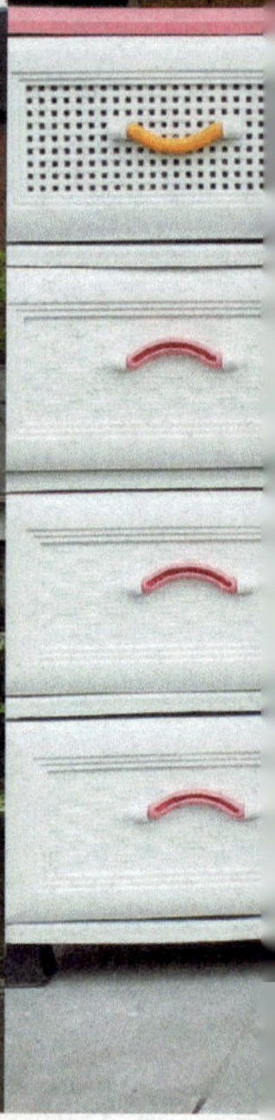

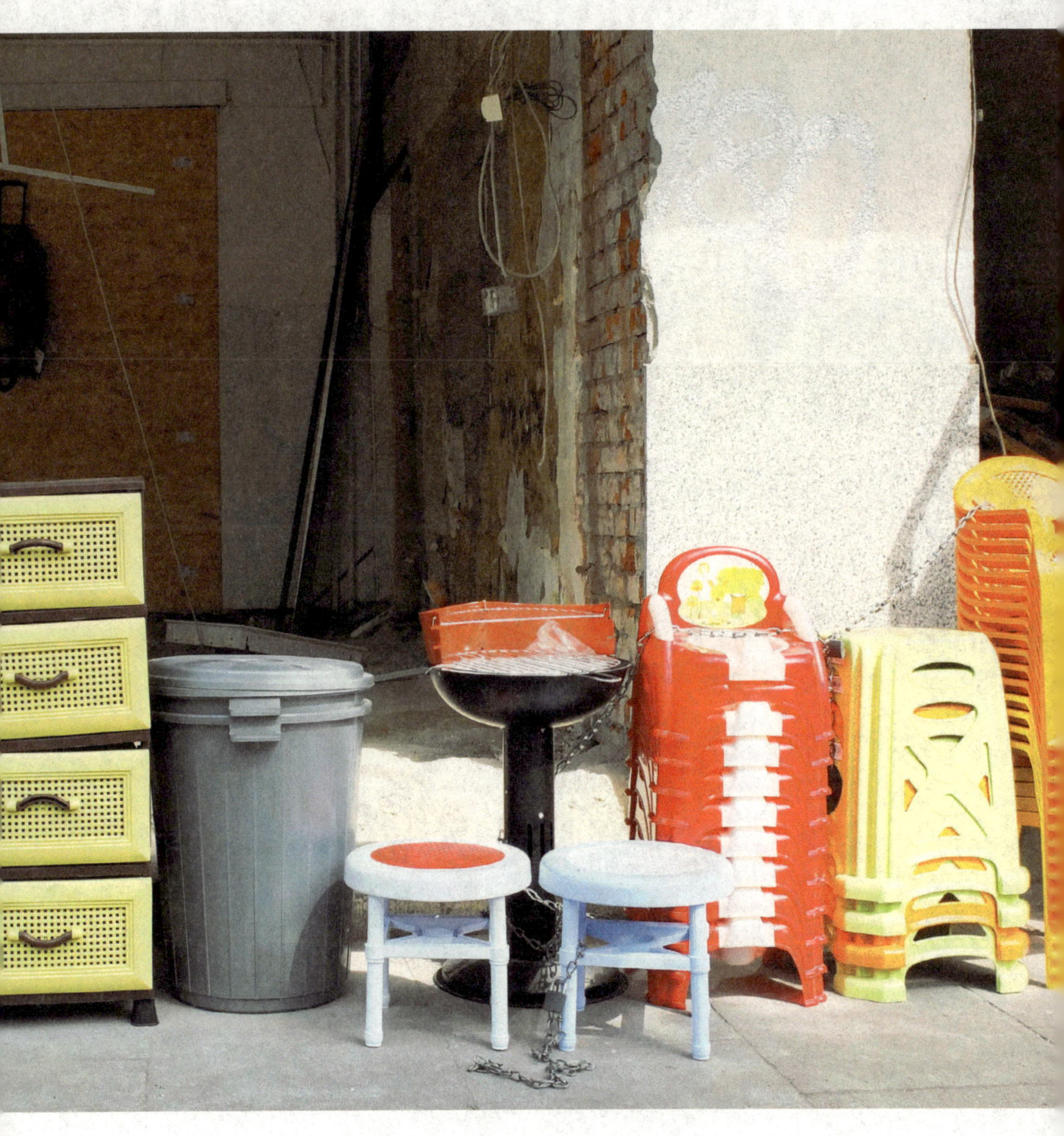

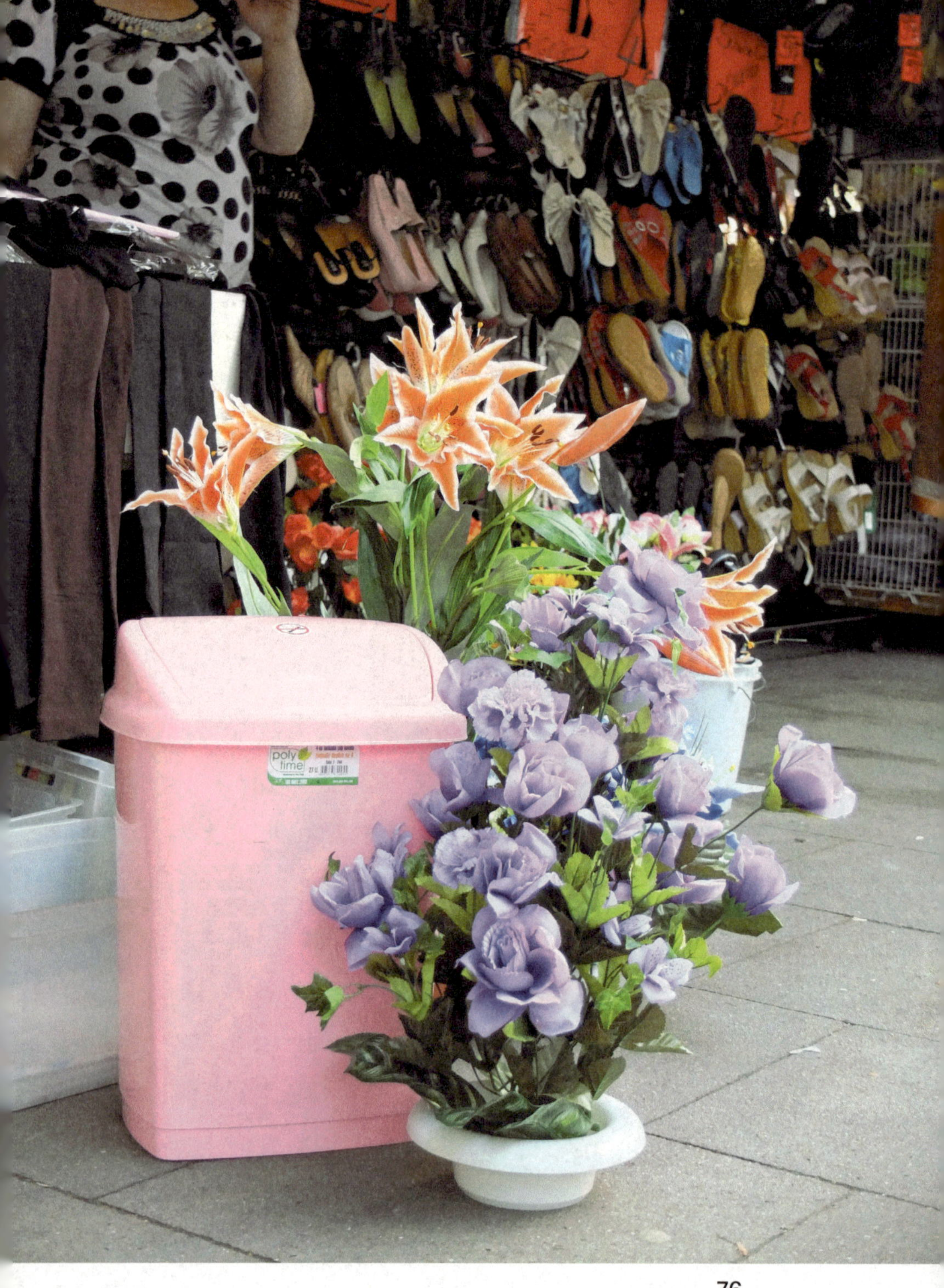

On the territorial stomping grounds, people endure, observe, make friends, fish, eat, laugh, cook, quarrel, smoke, talk, collect, sit, play, spit, meet, drink, practice, wait, throw, win, improvise, form teams, take breaks, participate, listen to the radio, store objects for a while, re-use, lose ... There are the spots well-trodden by anglers along the canals, mooring places and locks, certain benches like the kitchen-benches, the walker-bench or the gang-bench, and carpets spread out side by side at Rotenhäuser Feld ⌐Temporary Outside Rooms⌐. The bonfire and barbecue spots in the parks, various squares such as Stübenplatz, youth clubs, kiosks, pubs, fast food stands, betting shops, gaming arcades, billiard joints, sports clubs, playing fields, dog walking areas, sports fields, garbage containers ⌐Collectors and Sorters⌐ ...

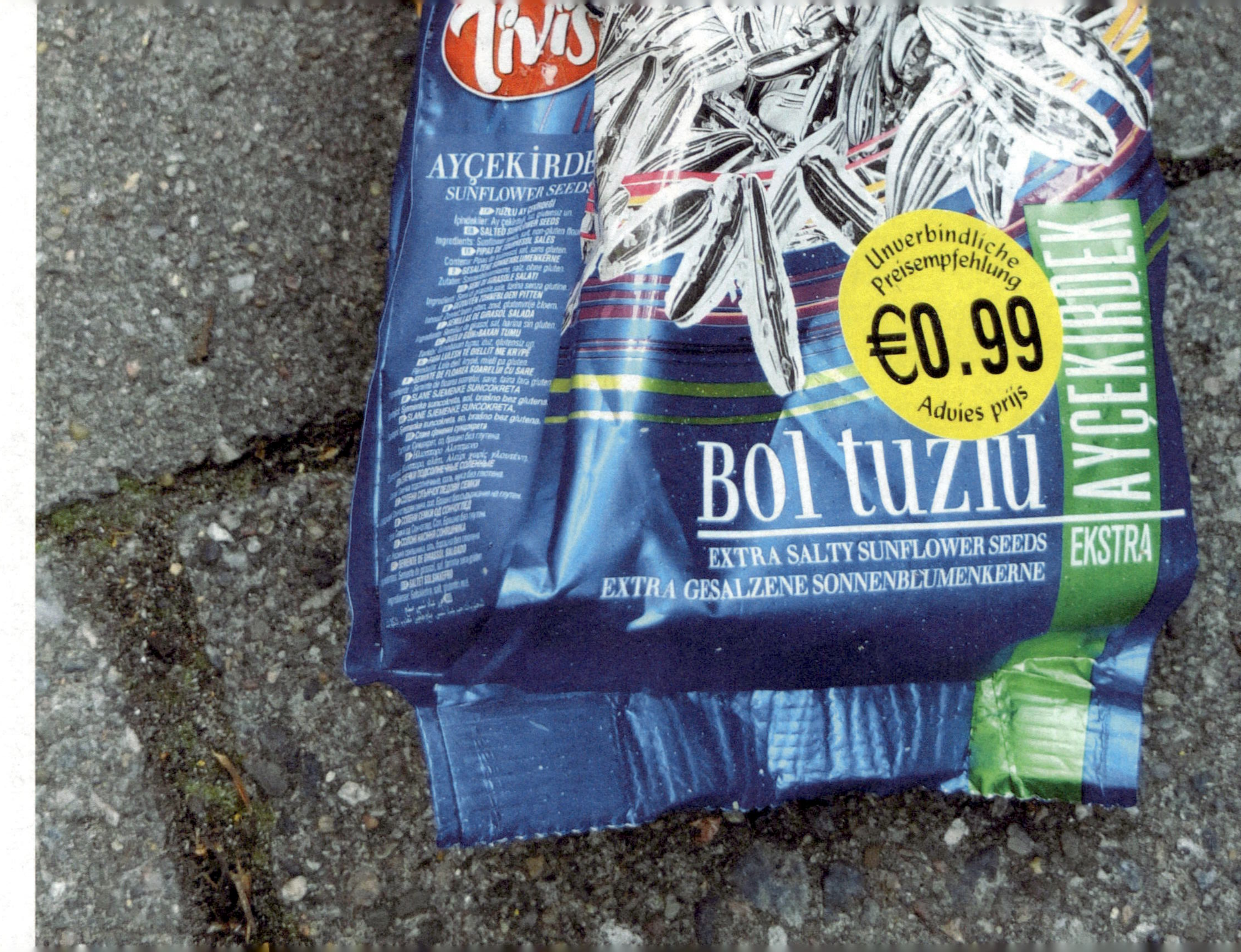

Tivis
AYÇEKİRDEK
SUNFLOWER SEEDS
Bol tuzlu
EXTRA SALTY SUNFLOWER SEEDS
EXTRA GESALZENE SONNENBLUMENKERNE
AYÇEKİRDEK
EKSTRA
Unverbindliche Preisempfehlung
€0.99
Advies prijs

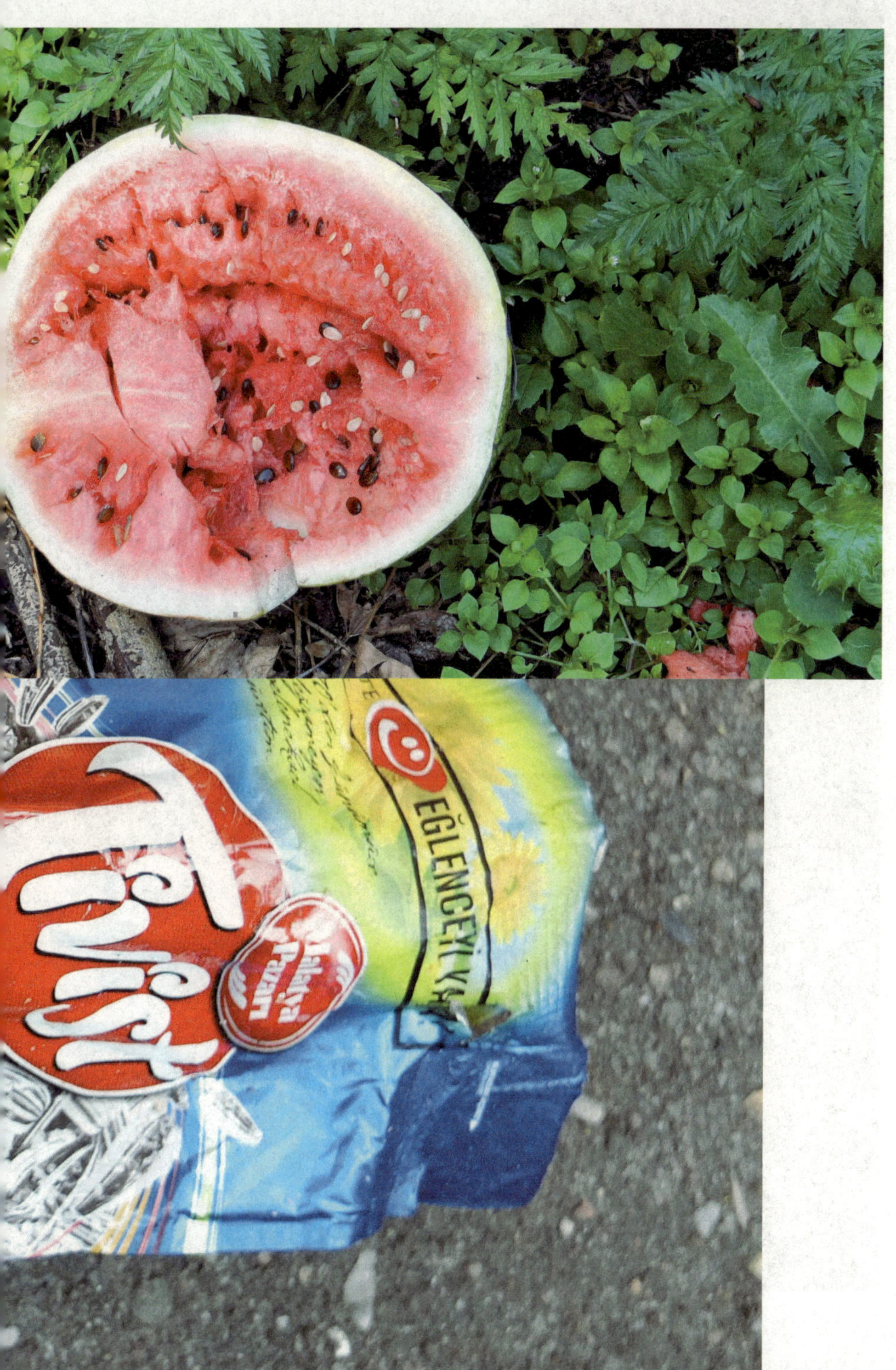
Twist
Talihya Pınar
EĞLENCEYLA

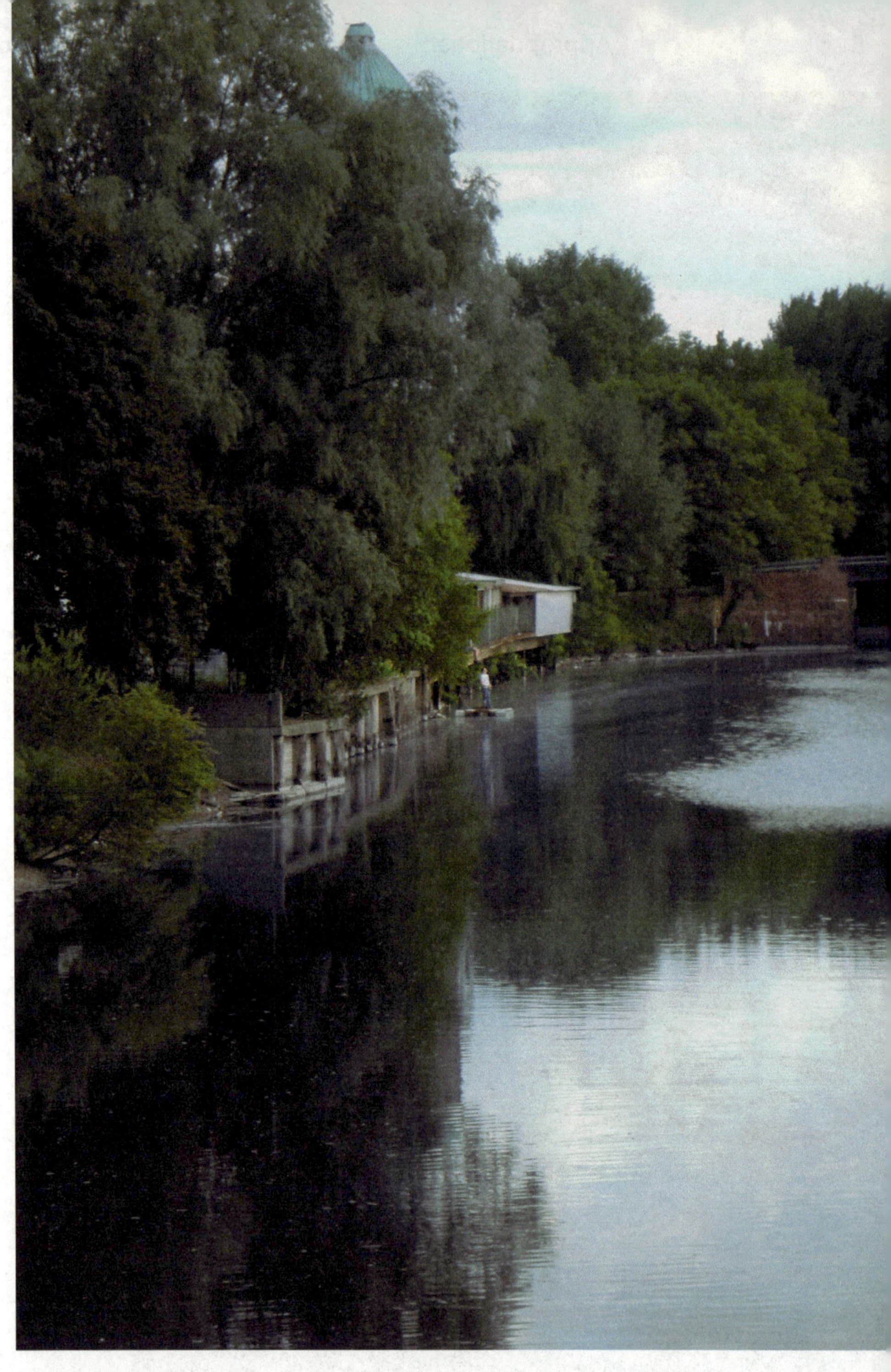

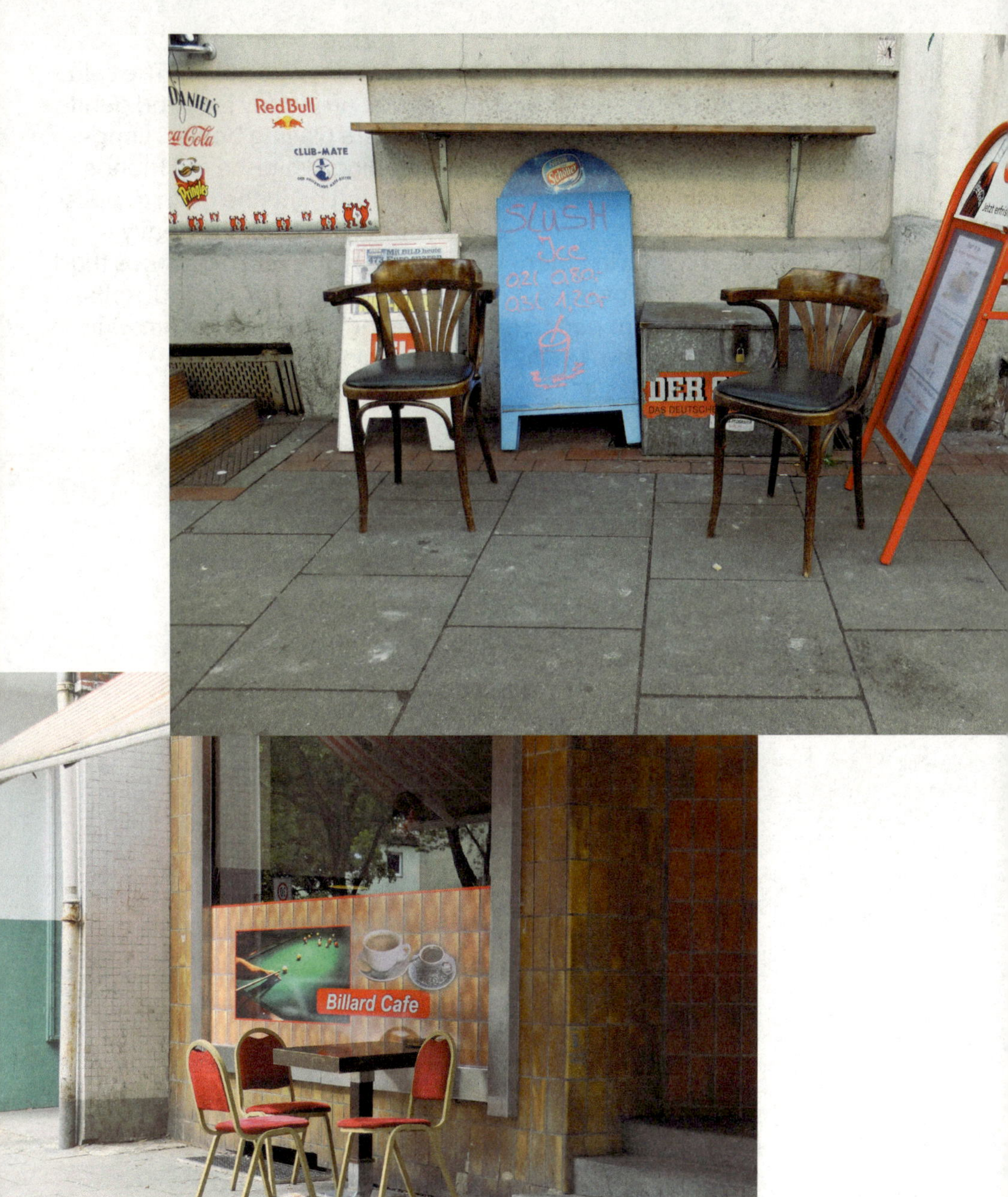
DANIEL'S
Red Bull
Coca'Cola
CLUB-MATE
Pringles
SLUSH
Ice
021 0,80
0,5L 1,30
DER
DAS DEUTSCHE
Billard Cafe

Under the bench next to the
bench, in front of the bench, and
on the bench, the empty shells
of sunflower seeds trace out long
dialogues. Again and again.

On an isolated bench in Rotenhäuser Feld sits a beige-clad
woman. The pink foam pad peeks
out on the side. Waiting. On the
lookout. Her walker has accompanied her here. Shortly thereafter,
two more walkers join it. The ladies
meet in the park every Saturday
and Sunday. On this very bench.

It is raining very quietly. The field
is wet. An elderly lady and gentle-
man are playing boules. Long-
standing, white-haired friends.
In his left hand the cloth to polish
with, in the other the heavy
ball. It lands with a vigorous thud
on the thin layer of sand. Rolls.
Waiting, taking turns throwing.
The rain grows louder. .

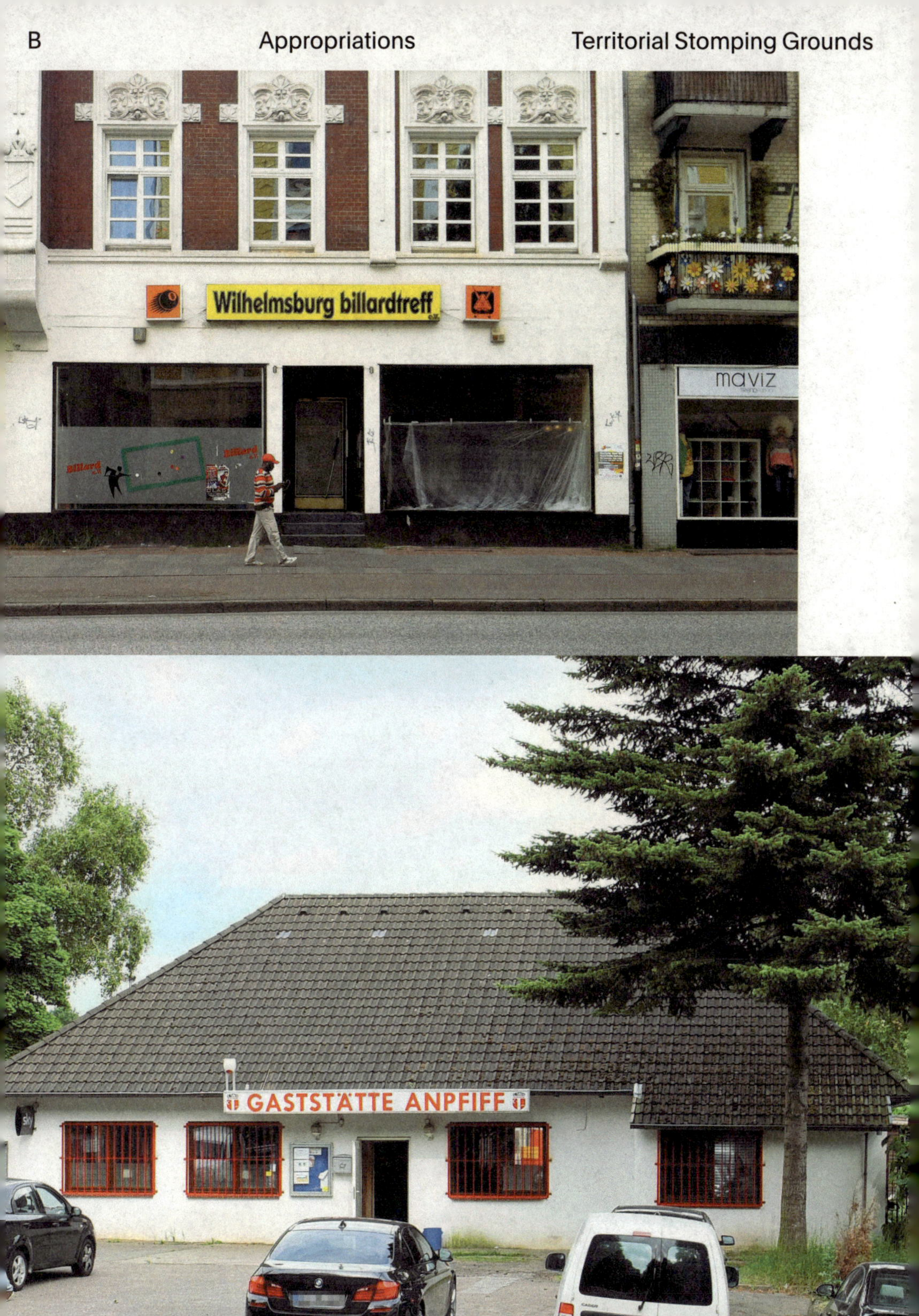
Wilhelmsburg billardtreff e.V.
Billard
Billard
maviz
GASTSTÄTTE ANPFIFF

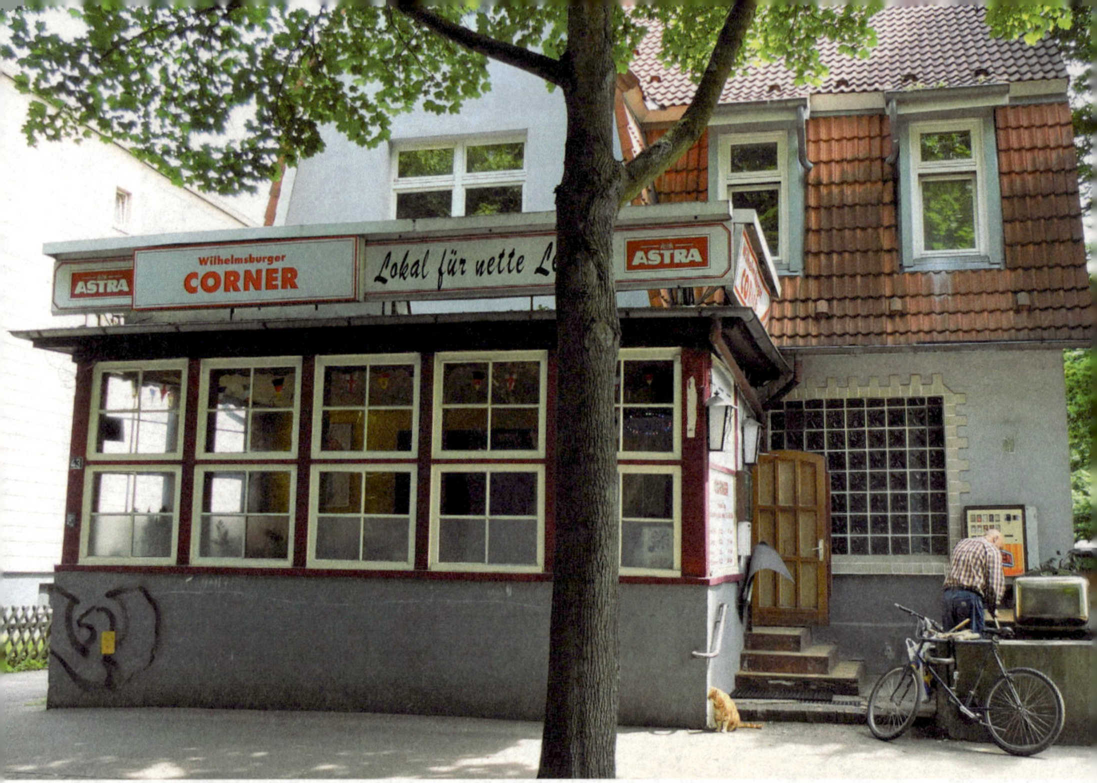

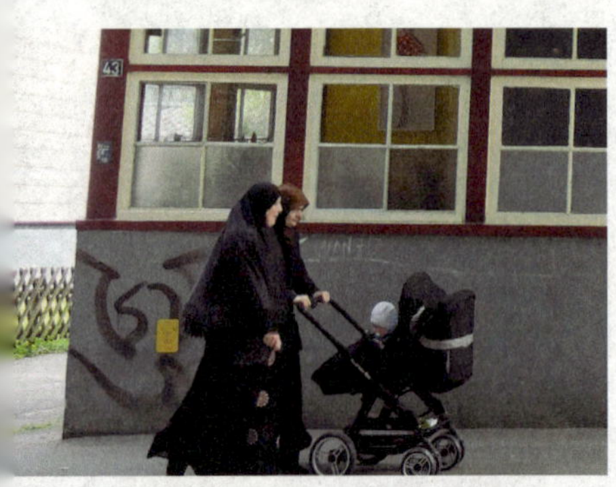

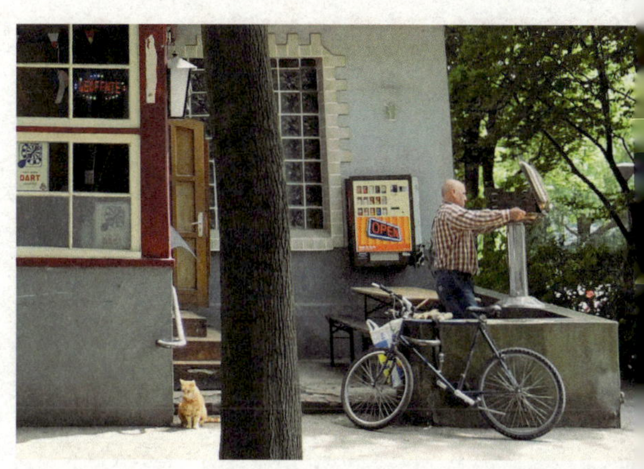

GEÖFFNET
DART
OPEN

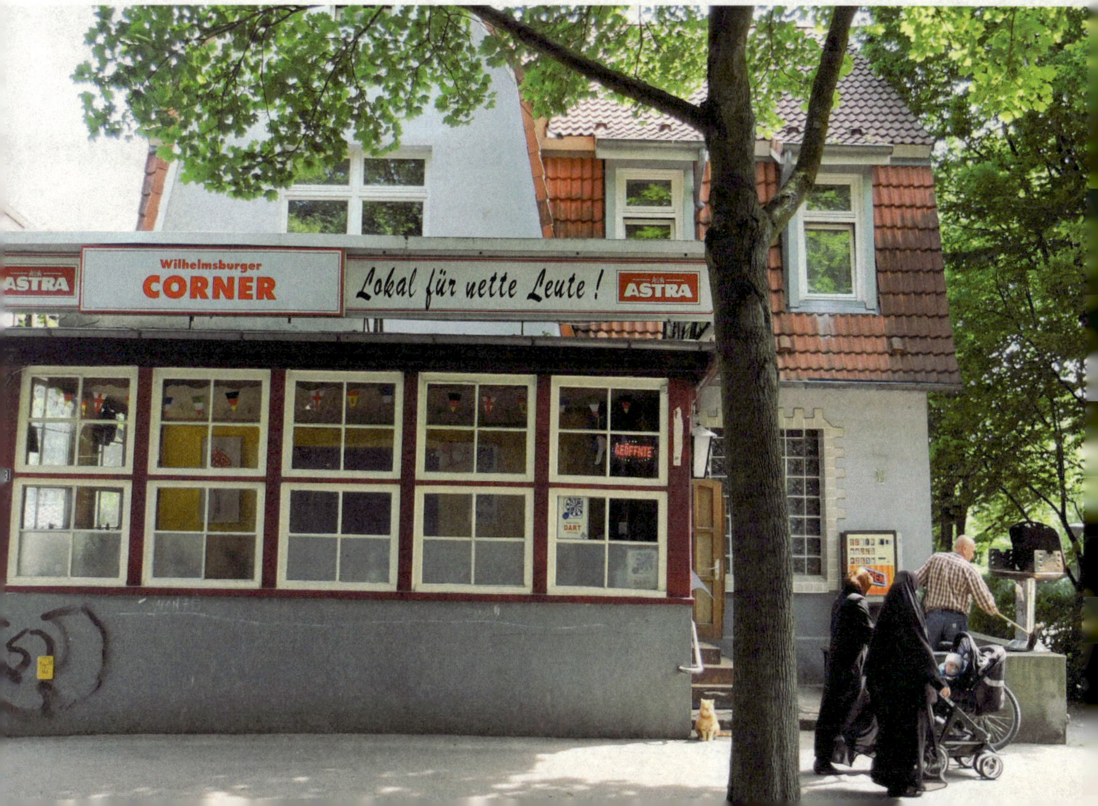

ASTRA
Wilhelmsburger
CORNER
Lokal für nette Leute!
ASTRA
GEÖFFNET
DART

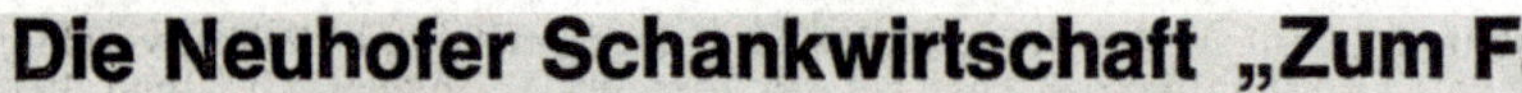

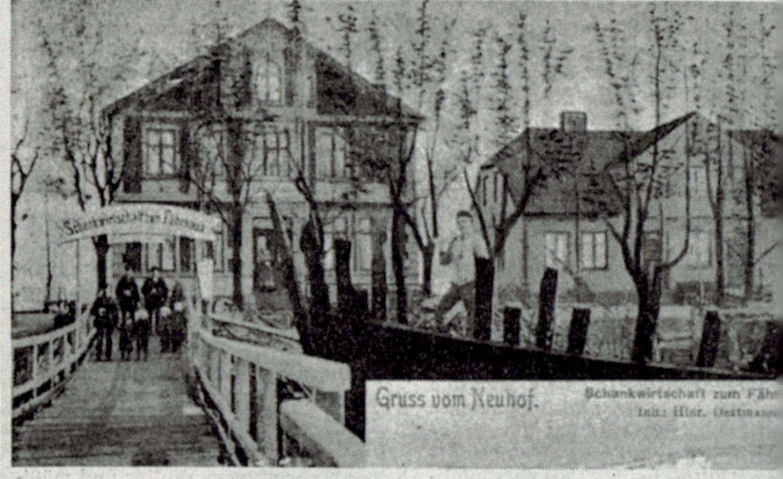

Die Neuhofer Schankwirtschaft „Zum Fä...

nnerungsfoto von 1904/1905.

 Wedigsche Haus, Vering-
ße 167. Zur damaligen Zeit
kaufte Marie Franke im ab-
ildeten Laden Zigarren und
votionalien   (Heiligenbilder
v.). Marie ist links im Bild.

 übrigen Damen sind Bewoh-
innen des Hauses mit ihren
dern.

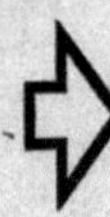

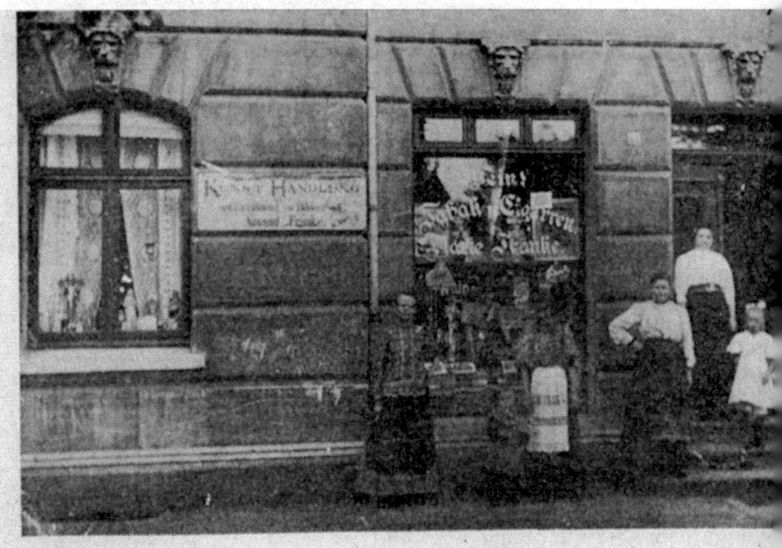

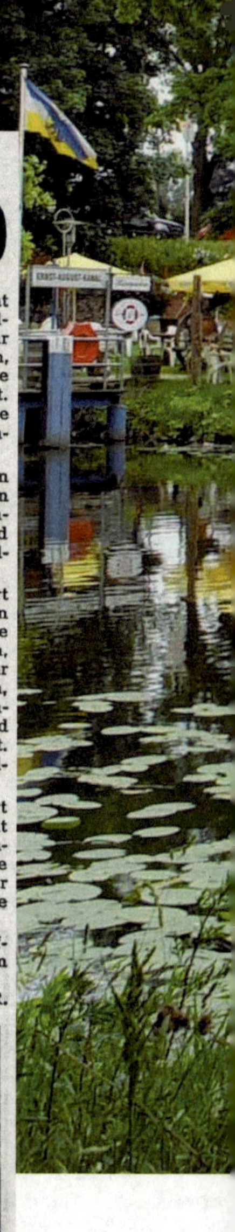

Vogelschießen schon 1680

Schützenvereine und Schützengilden sind vielerorts die ersten Sportgemeinschaften gewesen, das ist auch in jenem Fleckchen der Erde so, das seit nunmehr 300 Jahren Wilhelmsburg genannt wird.

Hier gibt es vor allem den Schützenverein Alt-Wilhelmsburg-Stillhorn, in dem man alle Spielarten des Schießsports betreiben kann. Ursprünglich waren die Schützenklubs privilegierte Gesellschaften, zu denen nicht jedermann gehören konnte. Der wehrfähige, damals durchaus noch nicht lächerliche „Spießbürger" übte dort Bogen-, Armbrust- und Pulverschießen. Schütze kann heute jeder werden, aber die Traditionen sind geblieben.

Die Schützenvereine verstehen sich heute durchaus als richtige Sportvereine. Die große Tradition dieser Sportart bringt jedoch manches Brauchtum mit sich, das von Außenstehenden nicht unbedingt mehr bejaht wird. Nichtsdestoweniger ist mancher alte Zopf gefallen, doch besteht nach Auffassung der Schützen kein Grund, von ihrem Brauchtum Abstand zu nehmen.

Gerade viele junge Leute gehören heute den Schützenvereinen an. Auch der König, der heute nur noch repräsentative Pflichten hat, hat große Tradition. Wie man aus alten Dokumenten entnehmen kann, war der Schützenkönig im Vogelschießen für ein Jahr aller Steuern ledig — eine beneidenswerte Einrichtung.

Zwar feiert man offiziell das Vogelschießen seit 1680, aber es besteht kein Zweifel, daß man seit dem Mittelalter auf den Vogel schoß. Das war einmal ein Papagei oder ein Hahn, seit 1680 ein Adler. Die Grafen Grote haben dabei eine große Rolle gespielt. Vor ihrer Burg stand vermutlich die Vogelstange, also etwa Ecke Kirchdorfer Straße — Neuenfelder Straße.

Die ersten Schützengesellschaften zur Pflege des Schießsports entstanden in Deutschland bereits im 11. Jahrhundert. Im Deutschen Schützenbund sind zur Zeit etwa 12 000 Schützengesellschaften zusammengeschlossen.

Der Deutsche Schützenbund gehört dem Deutschen Sportbund an. Schießen in mehreren Disziplinen ist olympische Sportart. Es gibt Kleinkaliberschießen, Freie Pistole, Schießen auf die Figur des laufenden Keilers, auf Tontauben, und neuerdings auch wieder Bogenschießen. Der Deutsche Schützenbund wurde schon 1861 in Gotha gegründet. Heute gibt es cirka 700 000 Einzelschützen.

Geschichtlich geht der Schießsport auf die Wurfgeschosse der Steinzeit zurück. Ihnen folgten Bögen und Armbrüste, bevor im 15. Jahrhundert die Feuerwaffen entwickelt wurden. Der weitere Fortgang der Geschichte dürfte weitgehend bekannt sein.

Seit 1890 gibt es Weltmeisterschaften im Schießen, seit 1896 wird um olympische Ehren gekämpft.

K. E. / W. R.

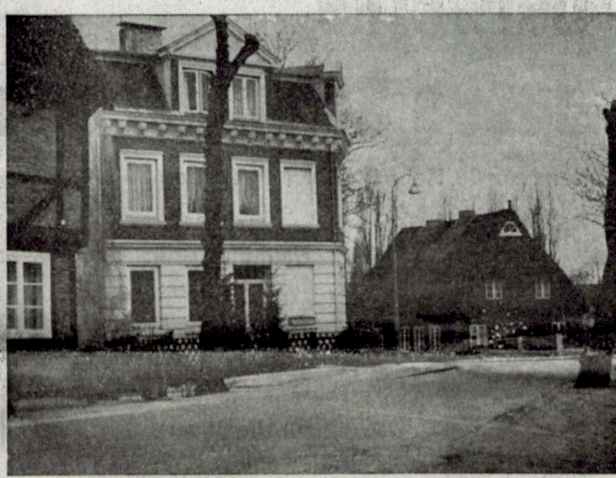

Bauernhaus und Jahrhundertwende-Haus — beide reizvoll.

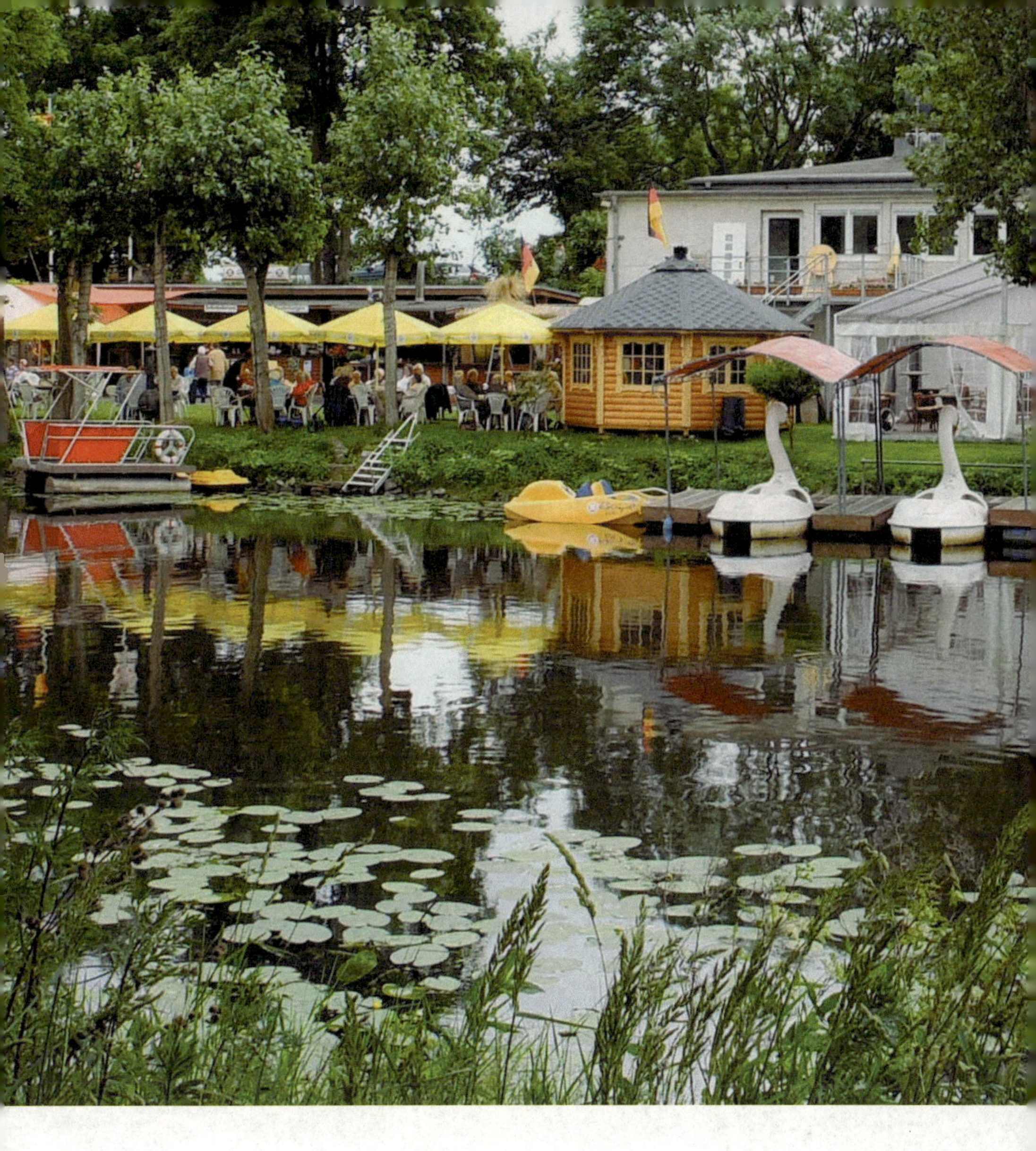

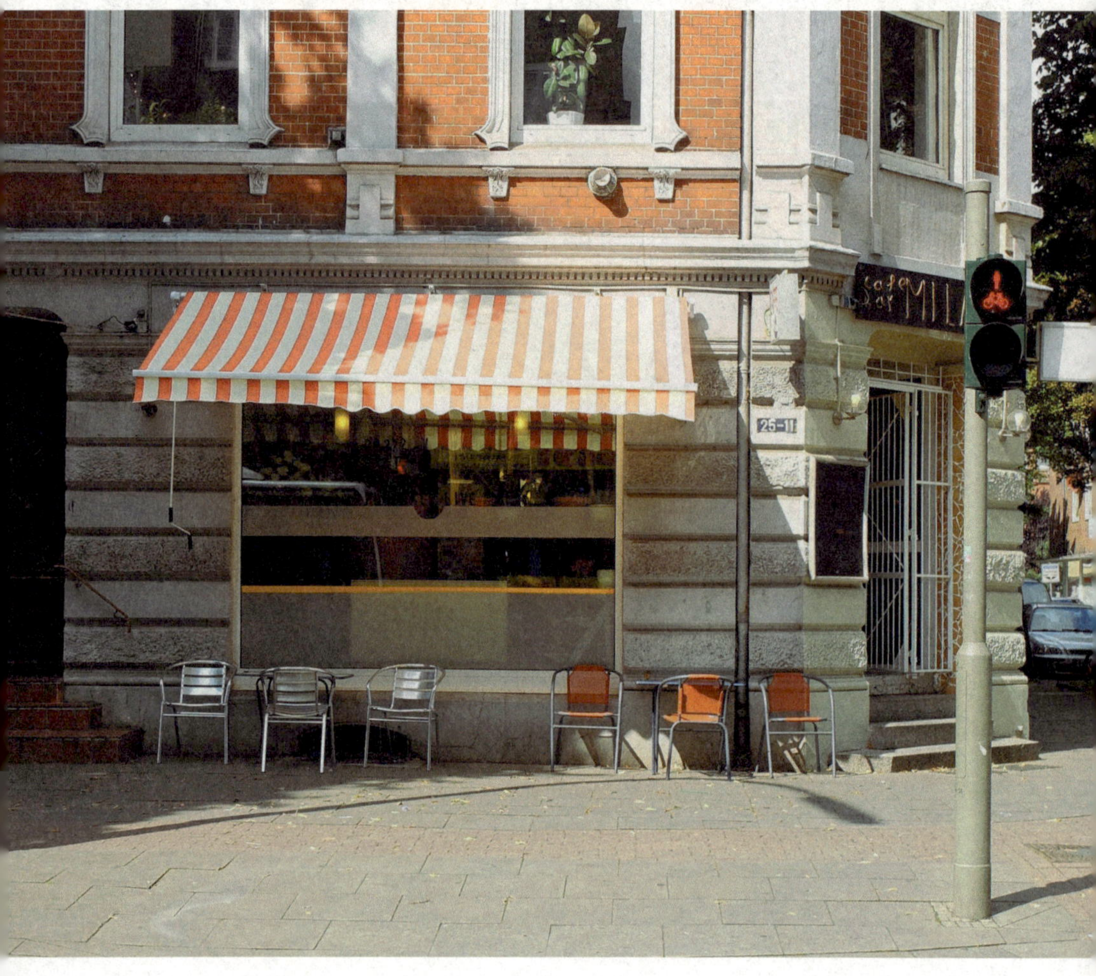

cafe
Bar MILA
25-1

In the cultural refuges people toe the line, take note, negotiate, exchange ideas, change their minds, present introductions, inaugurate, relax, allow, pray, confess, give thanks, fast, party, whisper, help, laugh, teach, preach, play, train, baptize, grieve, break up, sing, swear oaths, wash, consecrate, intervene, control, make music, organize, respect, repeat, set up rules, abide by rules, drink tea, chat, support, say farewell, ban, revere, negotiate, refrain, prepare, celebrate, listen ... There are a whole host of mosques, churches and free churches, cemeteries, memorials, the Wilhelmsburg Citizens' House, numerous tearooms and intercultural associations, some allotments, private living spaces, cultural holidays, festivals, traditions, customs, music ...

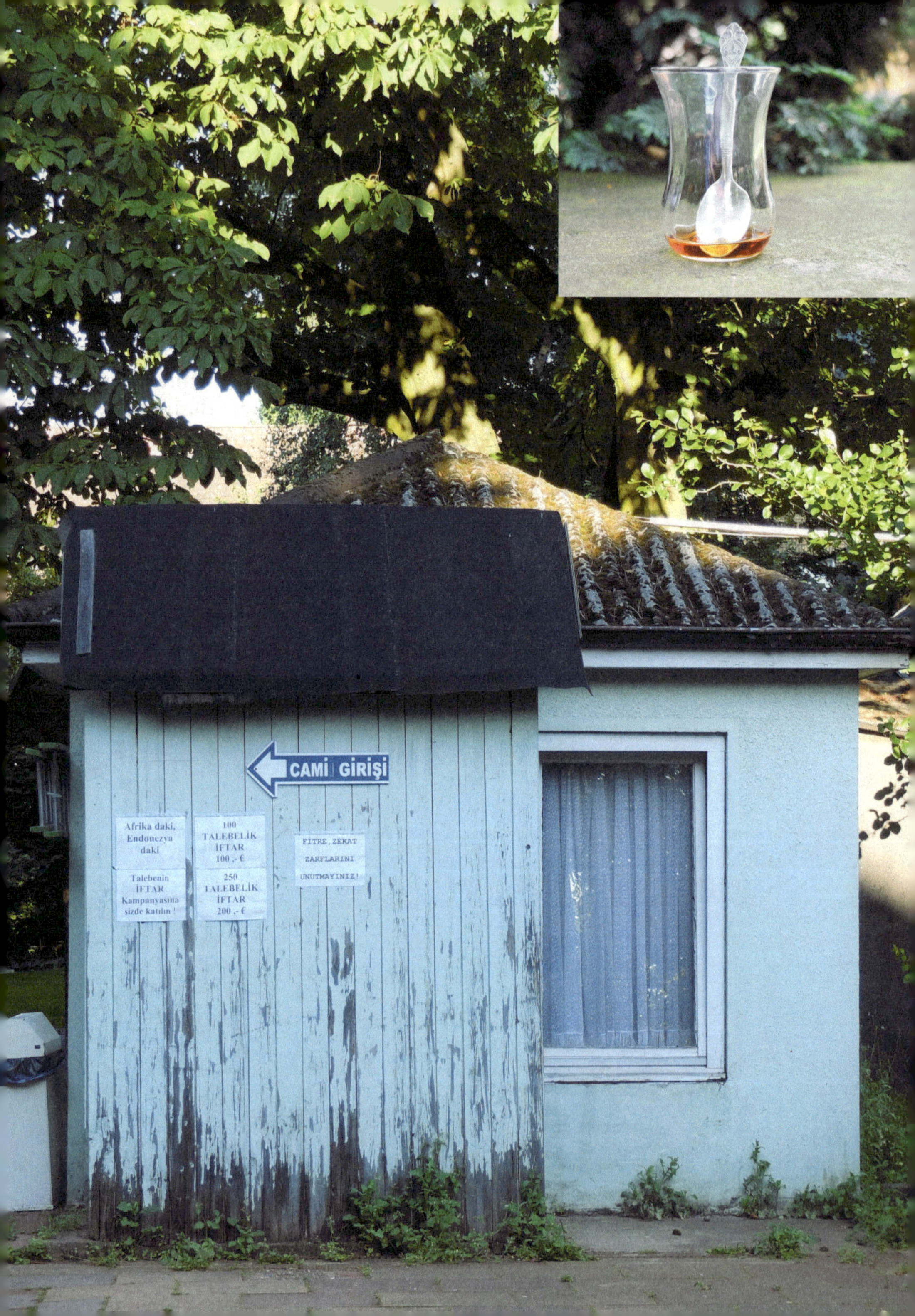

CAMİ GİRİŞİ
Afrika daki,
Endonezya
daki
100
TALEBELİK
İFTAR
100,- €
FİTRE, ZEKAT
ZARFLARINI
UNUTMAYINIZ!
Talebenin
İFTAR
Kampanyasına
sizde katılın !
250
TALEBELİK
İFTAR
200,- €

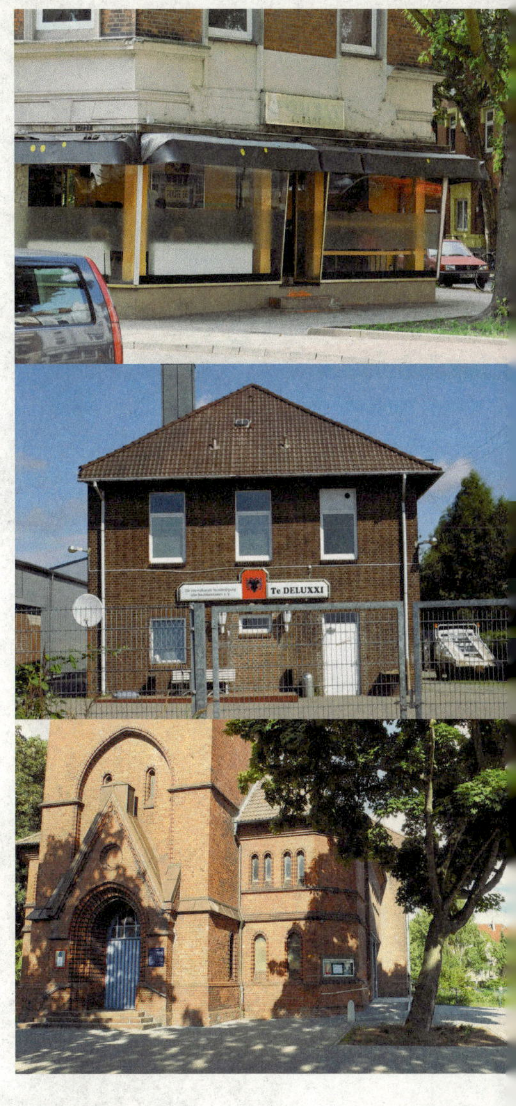

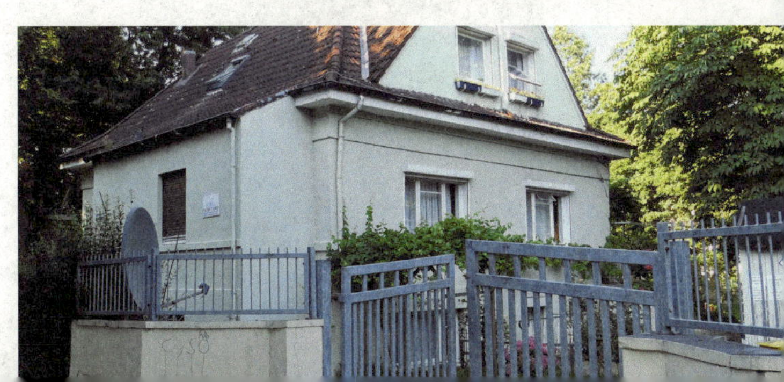

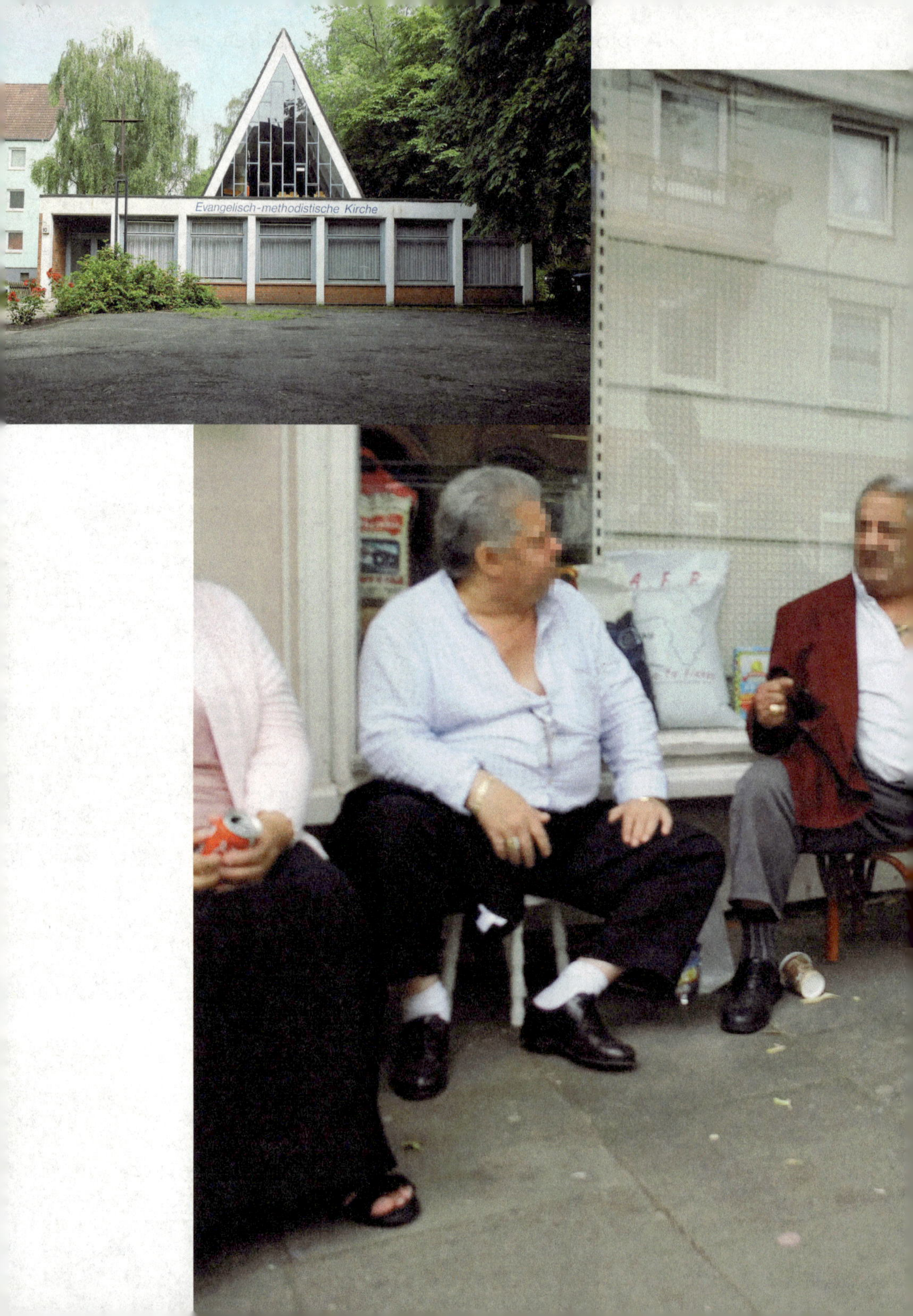
Evangelisch-methodistische Kirche

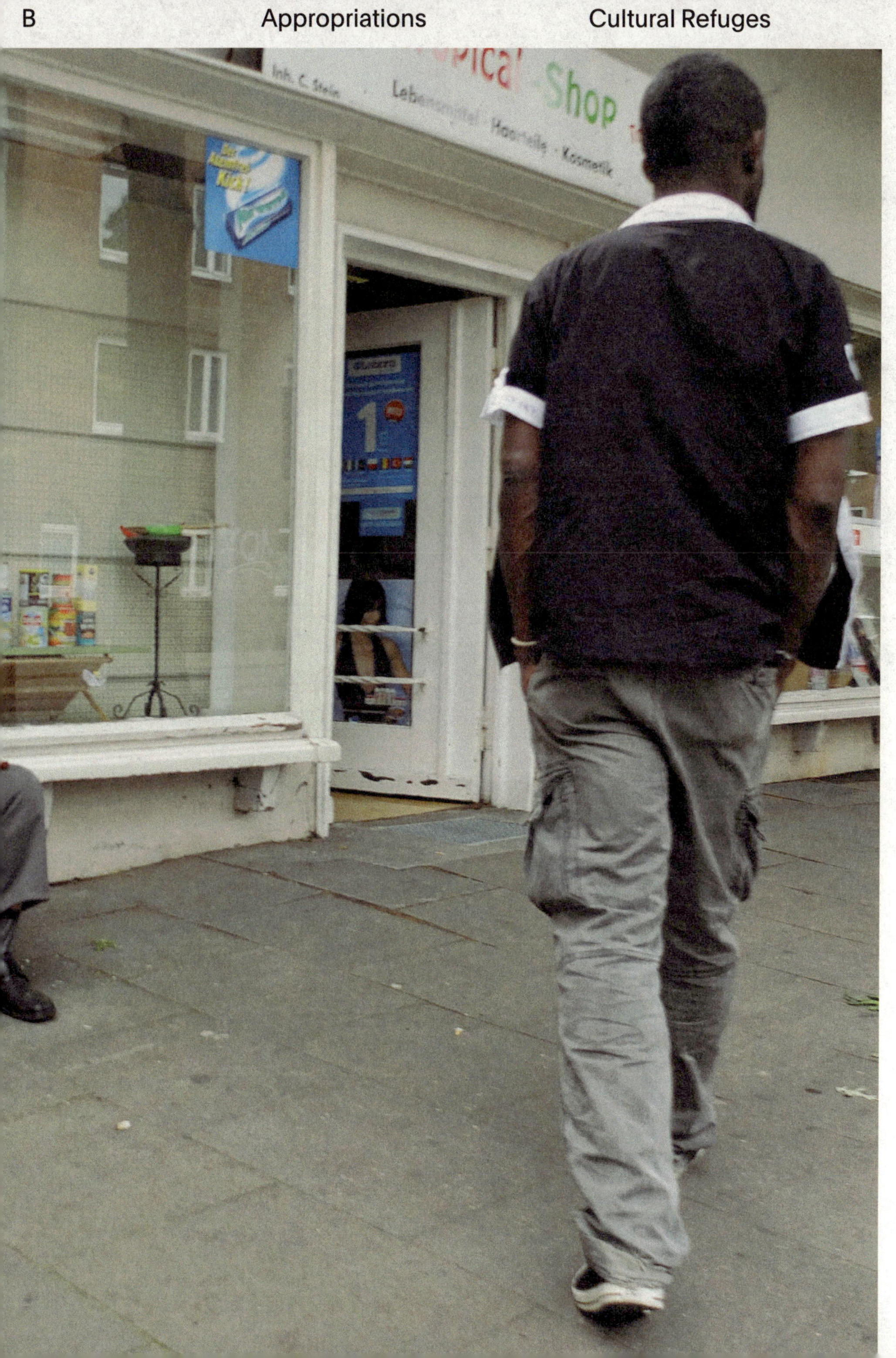
Inh. C. Stein
Lebensmittel · Haarteile · Kosmetik
Shop

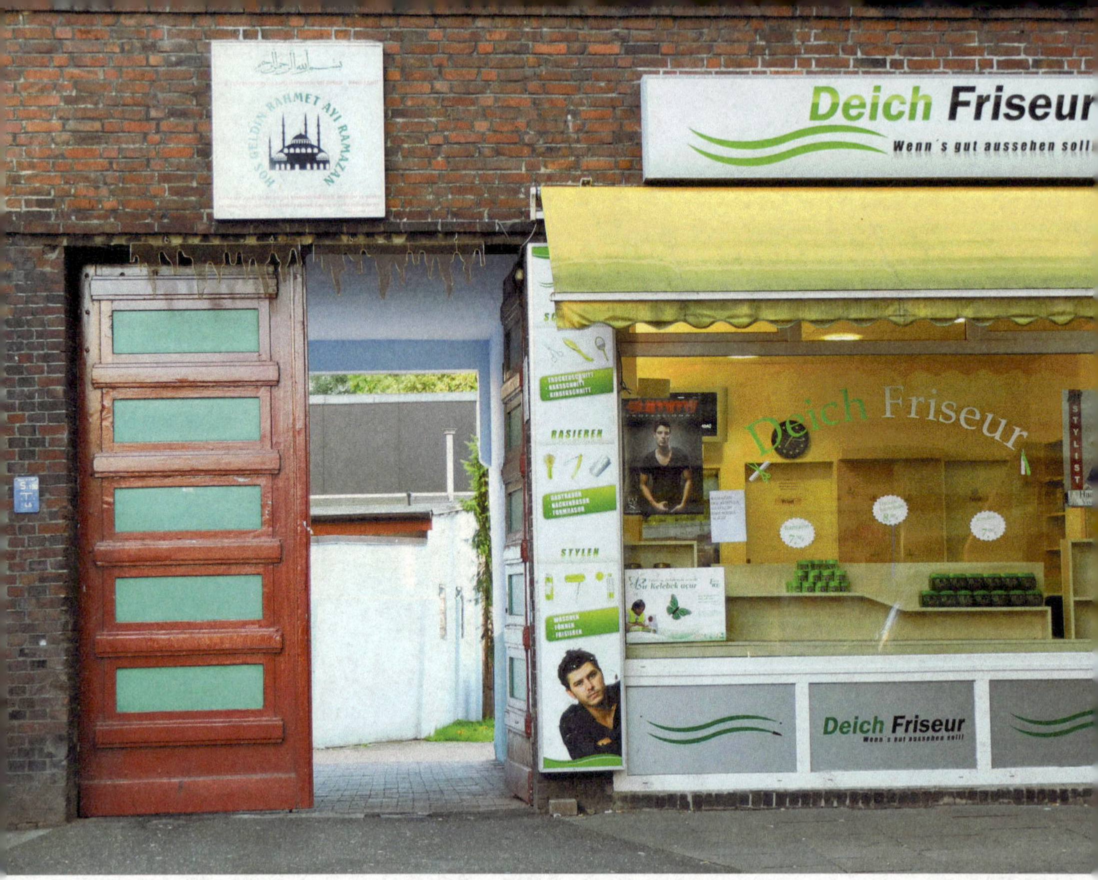

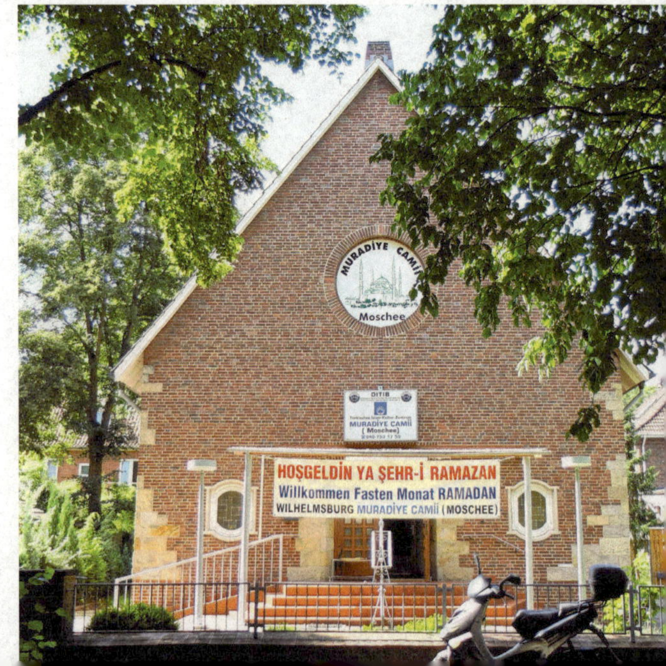
Deich Friseur
Wenn´s gut aussehen soll!
Deich Friseur
Deich Friseur
Wenn´s gut aussehen soll!
MURADİYE CAMİİ
Moschee
DİTİB
MURADİYE CAMİİ
(Moschee)
HOŞGELDİN YA ŞEHR-İ RAMAZAN
Willkommen Fasten Monat RAMADAN
WILHELMSBURG MURADİYE CAMİİ (MOSCHEE)

On the stands for lingering, people rest, keep a lookout, try things out, regret, observe, recover, feed, eat, hope, kiss, laugh, are bored, enjoy, puzzle, greet, sleep, sit, sunbathe, play, spit, wait, communicate, chew gum, meditate, make music, think, participate, phone, re-use, organize, forget, linger, misappropriate ... There are those 'other benches' $\boxed{\text{Territorial Stomping Grounds}}$, steps in front of the entrances, fountains, bus and local train stops, window-sills, front gardens, balconies, tree stumps on Stübenplatz, sofas and chairs dumped by the roadside, bridges, dikes and dike embankments, the observation tower at Bunthäuser-spitze ...

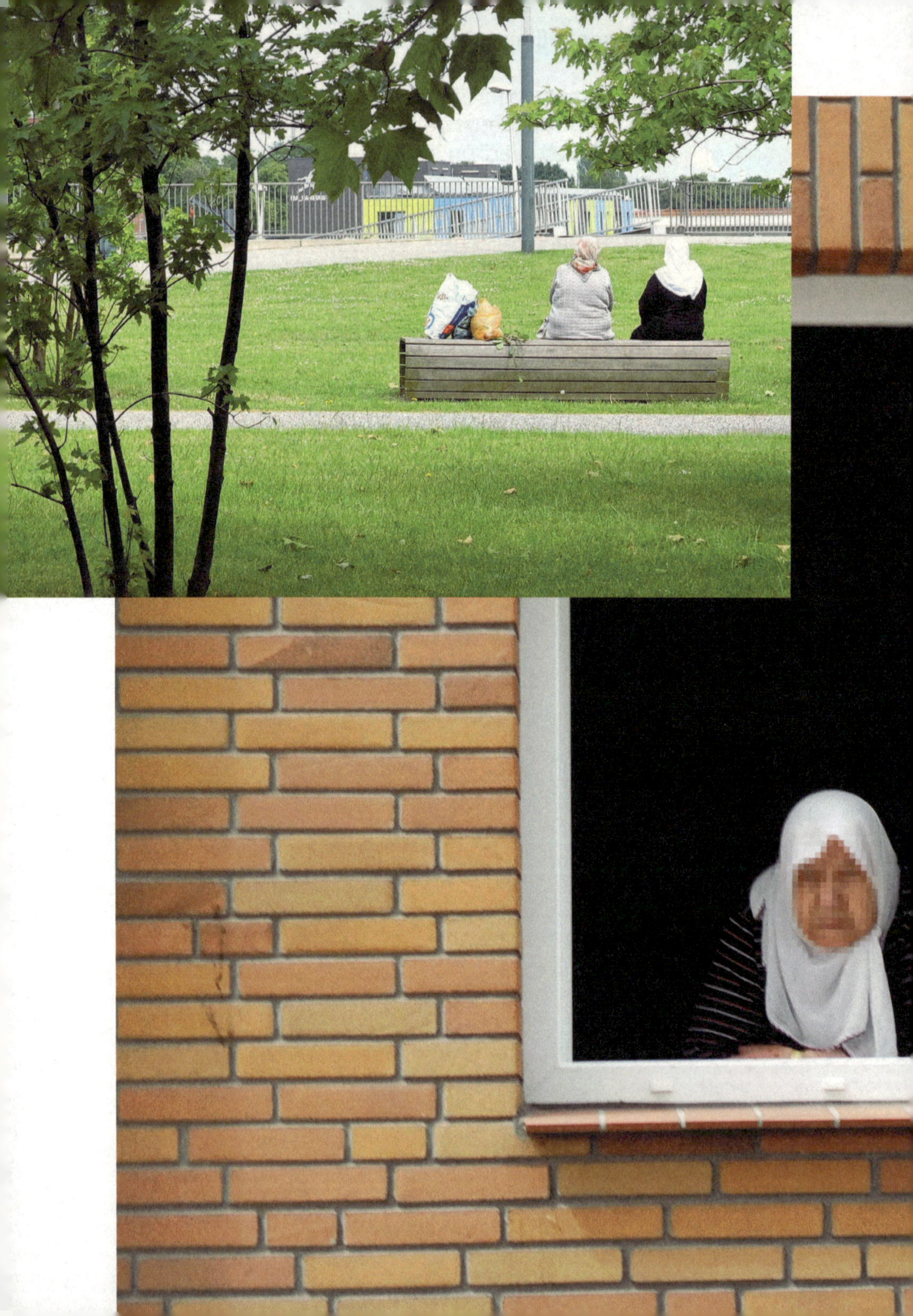

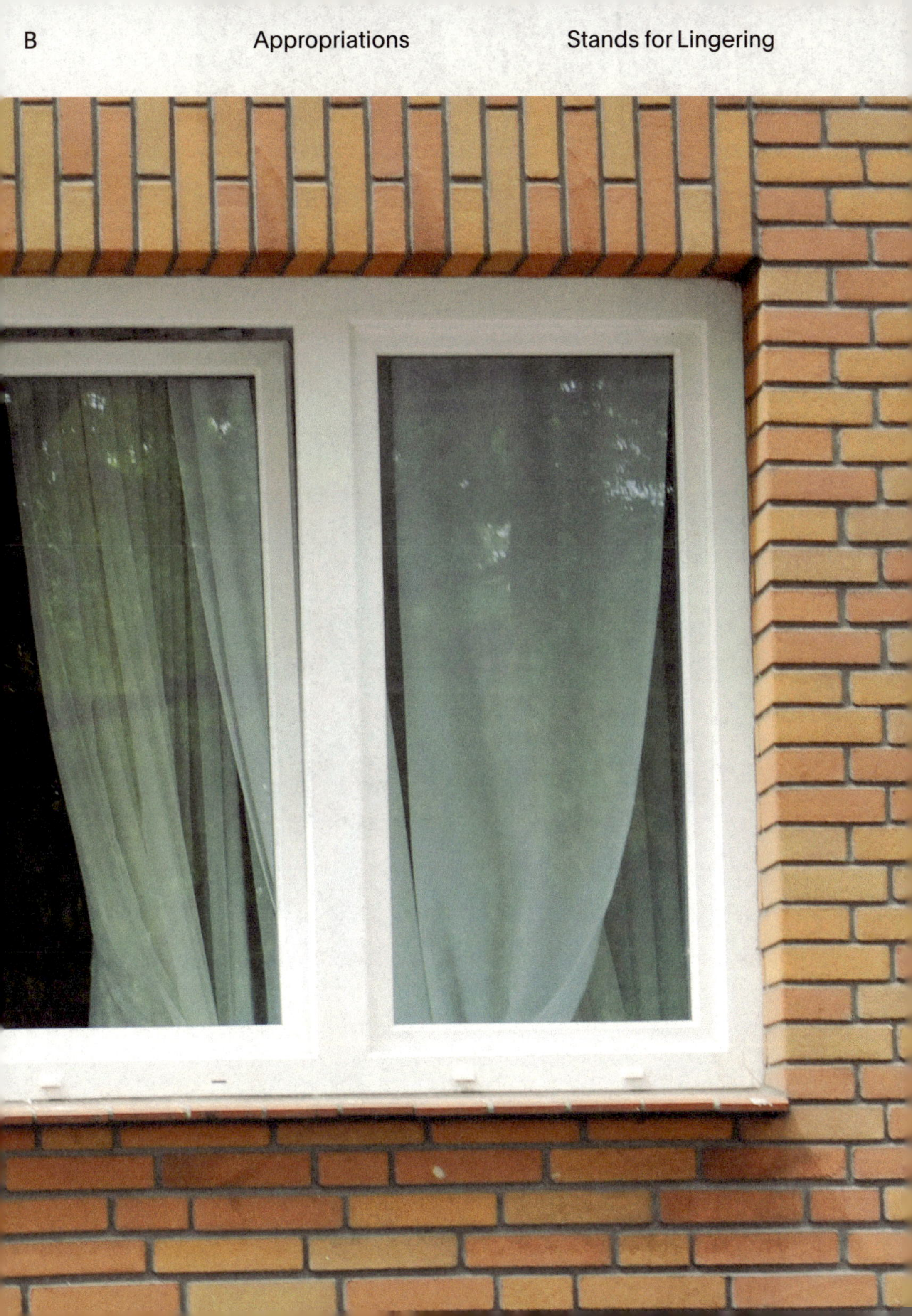

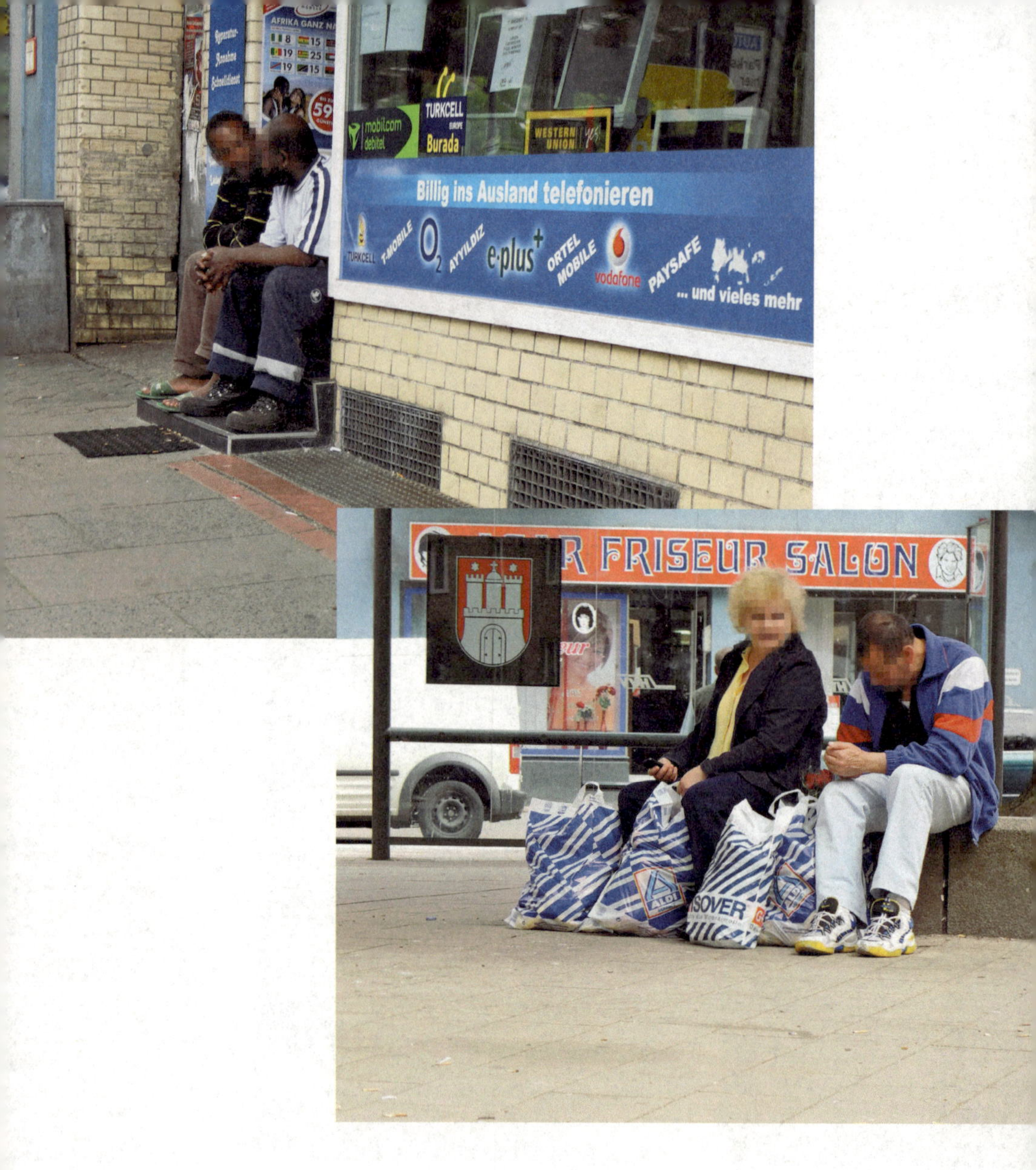
AFRIKA GANZ NA
mobilcom
debitel
TURKCELL
EUROPE
Burada
WESTERN
UNION
Billig ins Ausland telefonieren
TURKCELL
T-MOBILE
O₂
AYYILDIZ
e-plus⁺
ORTEL
MOBILE
vodafone
PAYSAFE
... und vieles mehr
FRISEUR SALON
ALDI

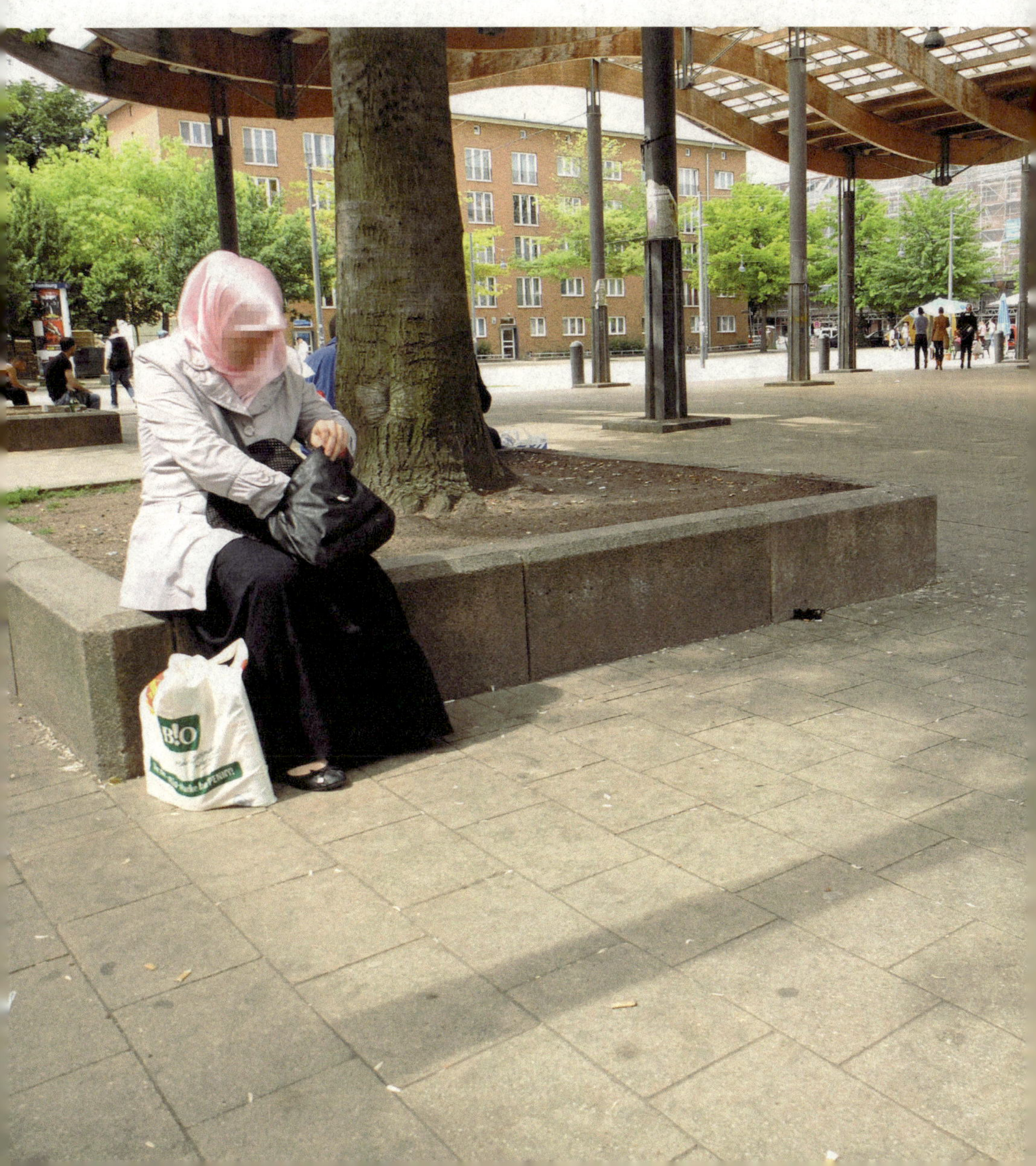

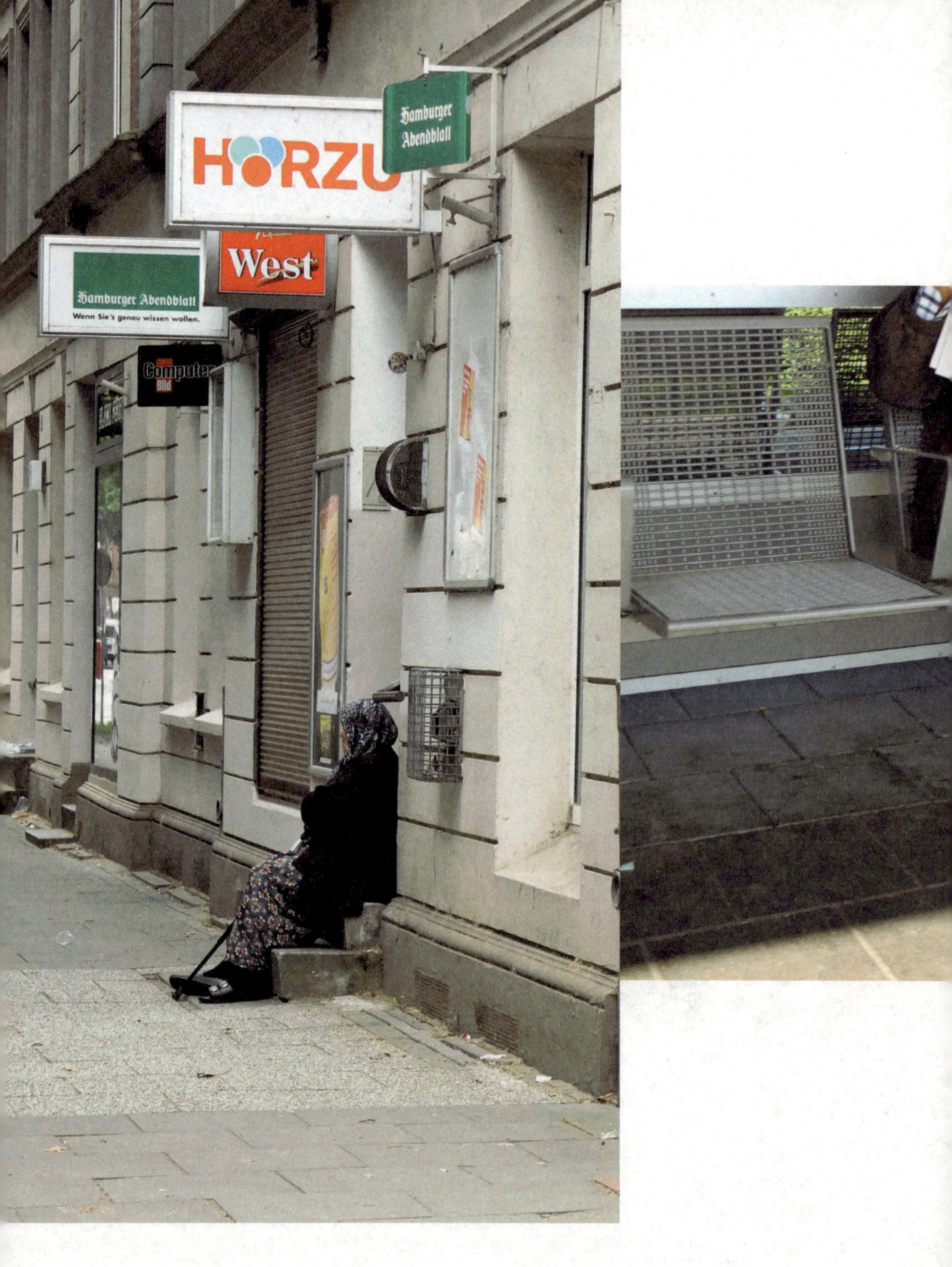

HÖRZU
Hamburger Abendblatt
West
Hamburger Abendblatt
Wenn Sie's genau wissen wollen.
Computer Bild

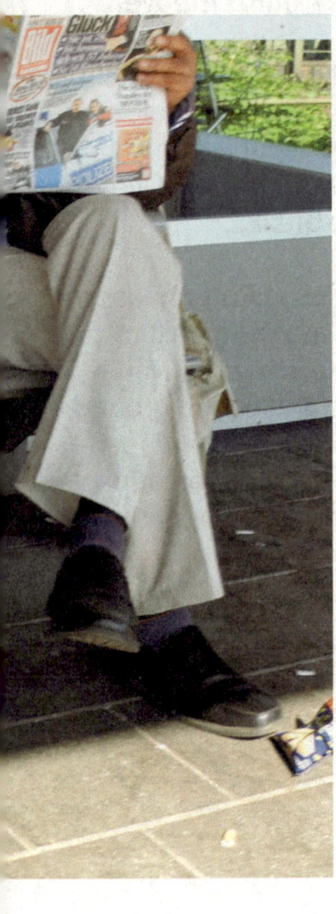

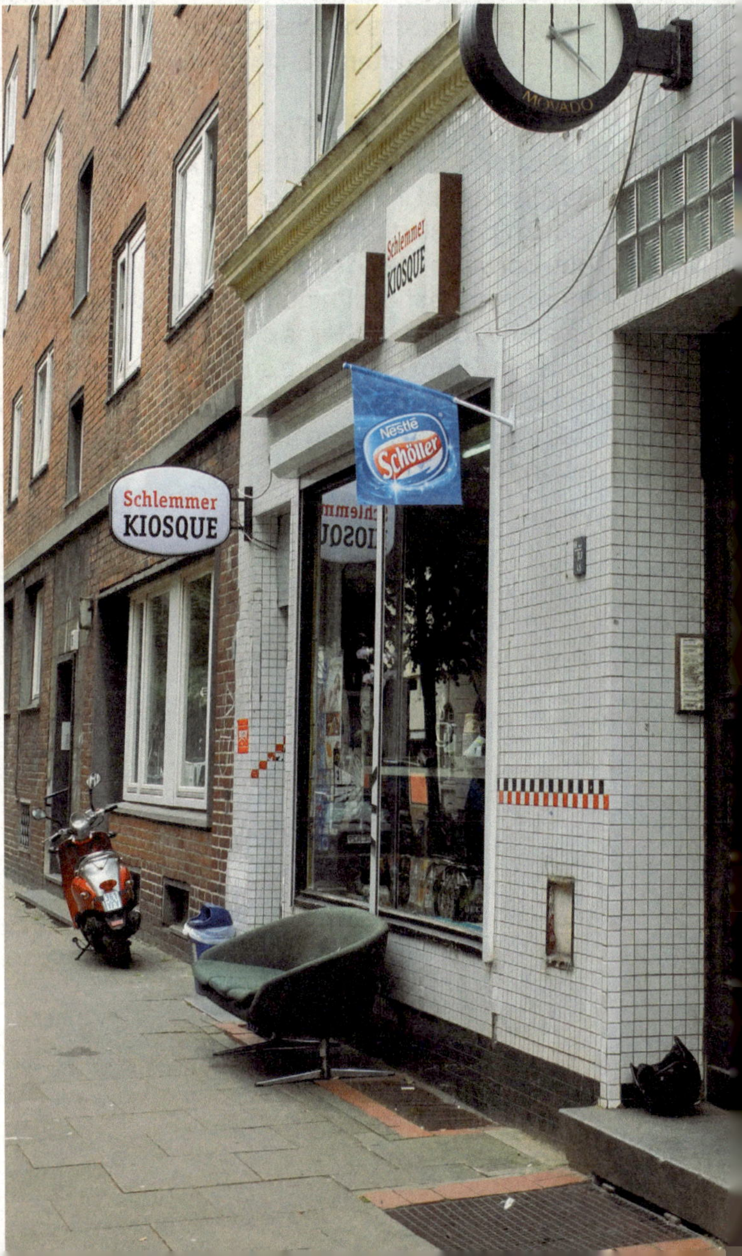

On a bench in Rotenhäuser Feld
there sits a very young and very
much in love Turkish-German/
German-Turkish couple. The time
is measured by chewing gum
being passed kiss by kiss in the
park in the late afternoon.

Sitting and waiting girls on the
front steps, not far from the Turkish
Bakery Kismet. From beneath
long ruffled skirts, ballerinas peep
out. Between, beside, and on
them, gymnastic, diminutive dogs.
Lively cuddly toys. Stems of pop-
sicles in bright colors are sucked
out of the transparent plastic
packaging. Girls sitting and waiting in Wilhelmsburg.

On a bench in the park sit two
roundish, Turkish women. Next to
them, their shopping bags are
slumped down upon themselves.
They talk, talk. A little stopover.

On a bench at the Georg-Wilhelm-
Straße intersection sit two elderly
ladies with headscarves and
open shoes. Under a roof of leaves.
Talking. A little break.

On two benches at Rotenhäuser
Feld a couple are lying on thin
mats they brought along. Water-
filled bottles stand on the ground,
these are lifted up now and
again. In between conversations.
Finally, a short nap in the park, in
the late afternoon.

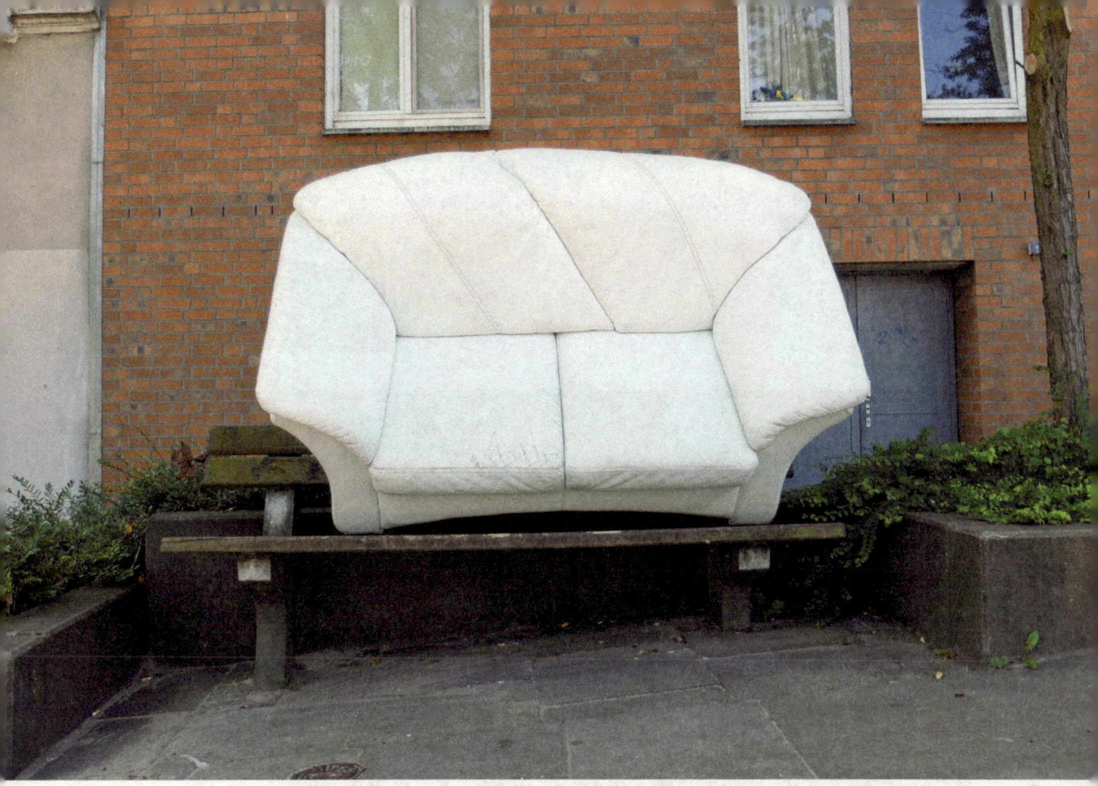

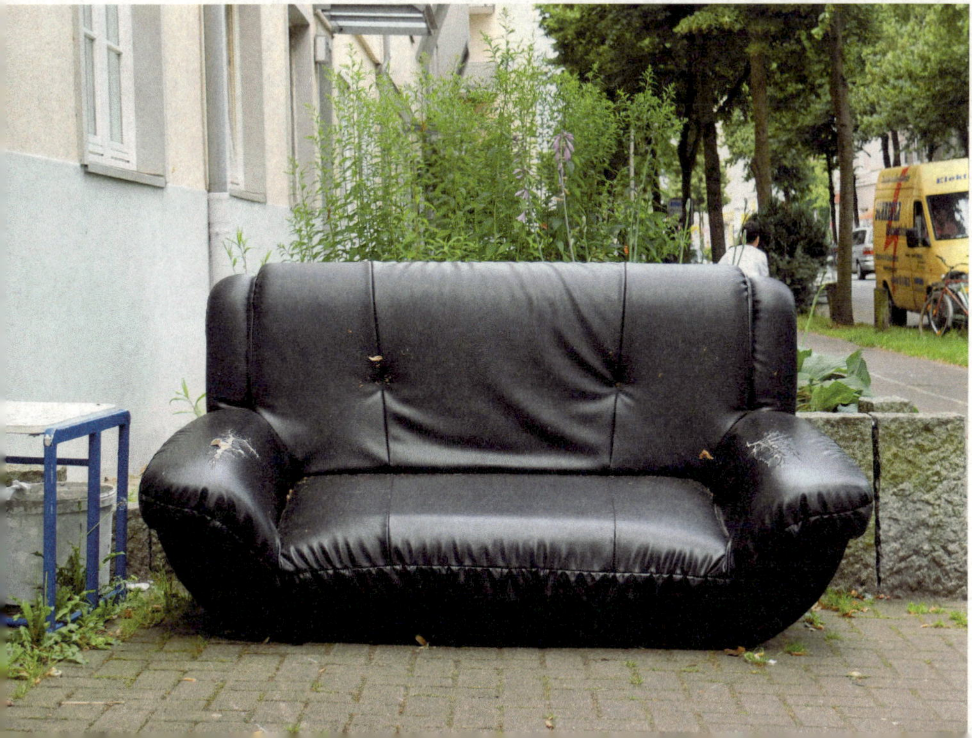

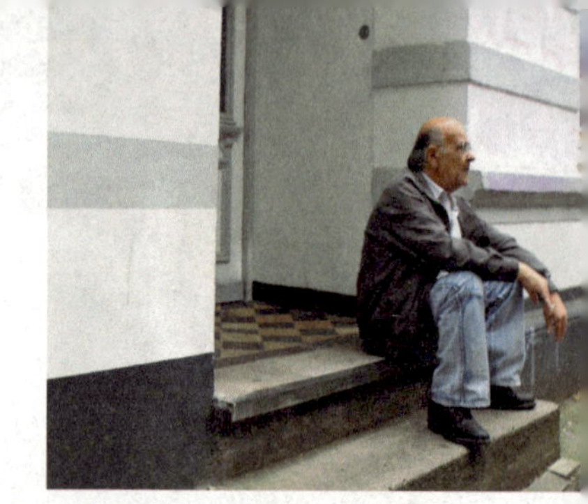

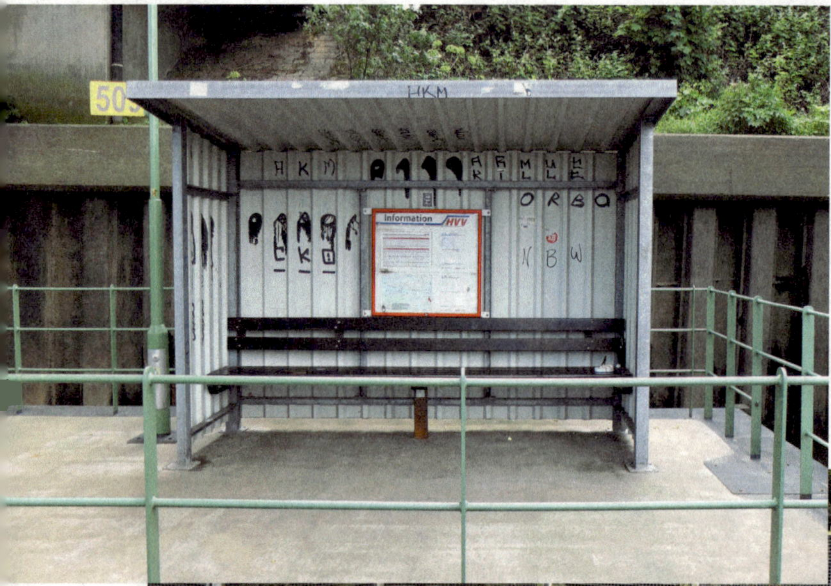

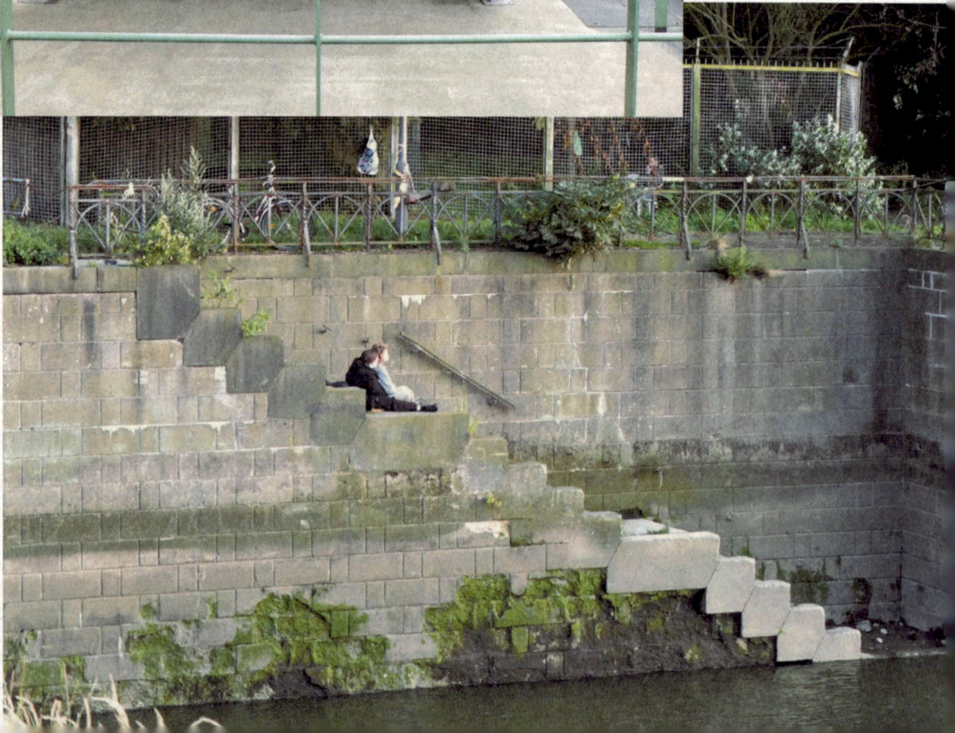

The Elbe Islands are in the throes of a constant change. Ever since the 12th century, they have been shaped by the different cultures, interests, and visions of their inhabitants Life and Business . The transformations happen sometimes more quietly, more subtly, loudly or radically. The numerous traces have been inscribed over time. The islands are the repository for their own process of Change-Comma-Pause. Formative interventions such as embankments are now legible from much more than just the topography No Dike, No Land . Even architectural eyewitnesses to different epochs and events (such as industrialization, World War II, the storm surge, free port) speak openly about past events. In these dialogues new spatial and temporal dimensions open up to me again and again, dimensions that touch me. Very much. The countless stories of the islands' inhabitants and their relations with the islands tie into the upheavals, departures, farewells, new beginnings, associations, turbulences, challenges, innovations, connections, breakthroughs, hopes, uncertainties, and declines. During my research work I encounter these personal voices very ephemerally, randomly, or particular friendships evolve with time Here and I . On the basis of eventful and shifting perspectives, I look at the multi-layered structures, the past and present facets and contrasts of the Elbe Islands. My gaze grows ever more acute, attuned to the wide range of scales on which subtle, quiet, loud, or radical developments unfurl on these still persistently heterogeneous and intercultural islands.

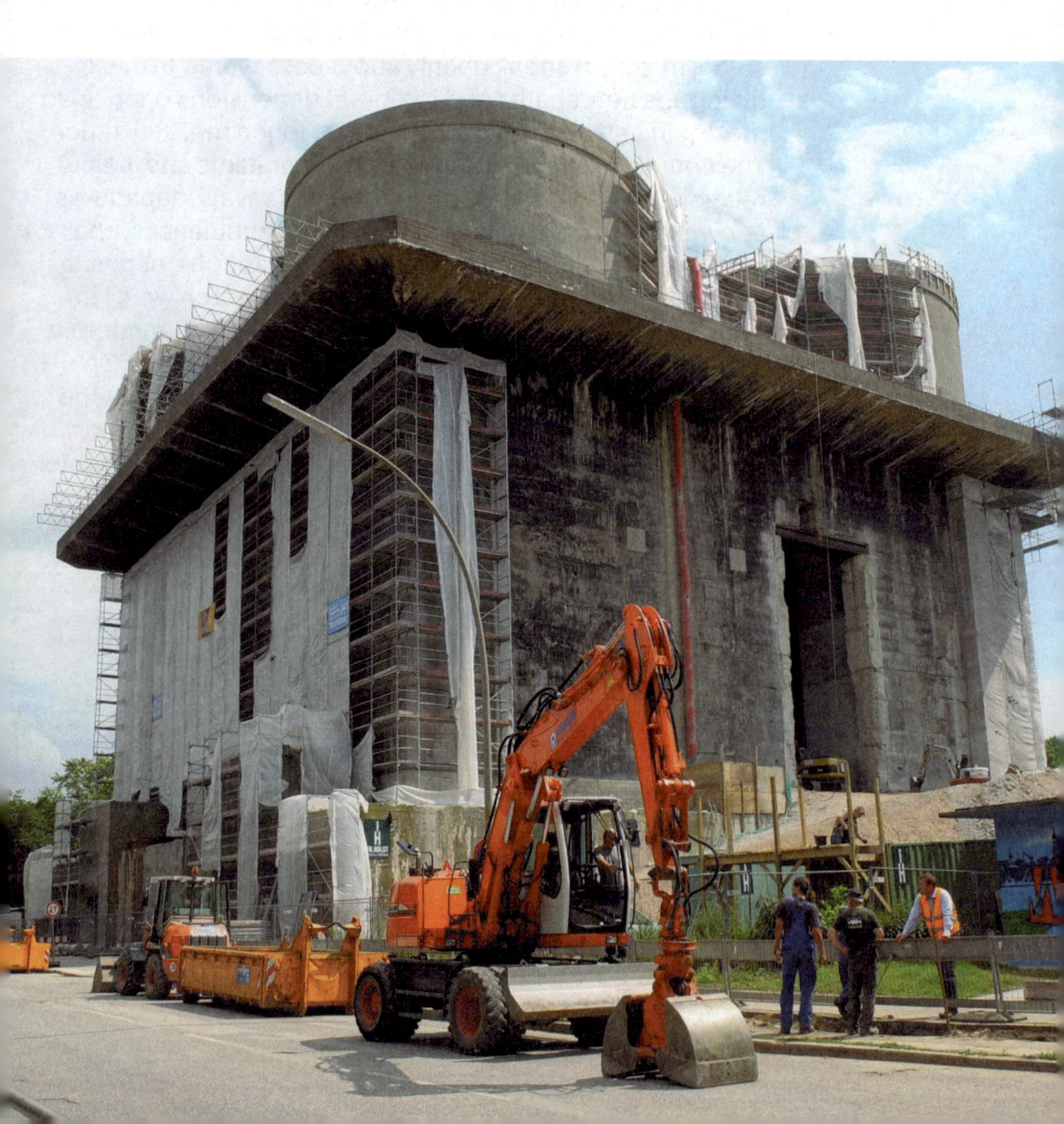

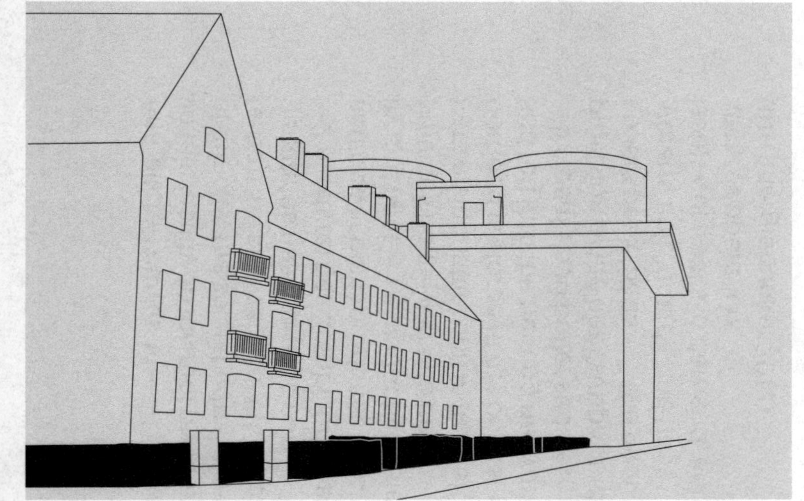

... her father owned the steel factory. They produced window frames for residential buildings, factories, and greenhouses. When they moved into their small terraced house in 1932 they could look directly across to the school, from there they could see the church too. The trees were very small back then. Her sister liked to play the accordion in the garden. She paid little or no attention to the construction of the anti-aircraft tower. She was stationed in Bavaria at the time—looking after children evacuated from crisis areas to safety. Now a Turkish family lives next door, the small gate to the neighbors' garden is always open ...

Anti-aircraft bunker VI—1 A photo-
voltaic facility on the roof generates
electricity; the solar thermal system on the south side of the facade
generates heat from the sun
—2 A natural gas combined heat
and power plant produces electricity and heat—3 A woodchip boiler
provides heat—4 Waste heat
from an industrial unit in the neighborhood is stored in the bunker
and fed into the heating network
—5 A peak-load boiler secures
provision of the heat supply and
covers peak loads—6 The heat
storage unit "hoards" the heat,
levels out peaks in demand, and
secures operation.
(IBA Energiebunker 2013)

Harburg, d. 14. 1. 44.

Meine liebe E.

Recht herzlichen Dank für Deinen langen schönen Brief. Hätte schon früher geantwortet, mußte aber mit'ner recht netten Grippe einige Tage zu Bett liegen. Jetzt geht's aber so ziemlich wieder. Ja, liebe E., mit dem Alarm, das ist eine böse Geschichte, nicht wahr? Dort in T. lebt Ihr ja bestimmt sicherer als wir hier, obgleich ich ja, trotz allem, am liebsten im Haus bin, auf unsern Keller gebe ich gar nichts, der ist nur splittersicher, aber wir müssen ja hier bleiben, weil wir keinen Bunker haben. Sonst Euch kann doch in dem 100 % ti=gen Bunker in der Schillerstraße gar nichts passieren, wenn wir solch Ding in der Nähe hätten, brächten mich keine zehn Pferde aus meiner Woh=nung. Aber wie gesagt, da kann man schlecht raten. H. geht fleißig zur Schule, bei Voralarm kommen die gleich nach Haus. Heute morgen brummten die Flieger schon wieder soviel, hoffentlich bleibt es ruhig, mein Mann hat die Ordnung von der Fachgruppe. Wo seid Ihr denn am 27. Jan. zu finden?

Mit den herzlichsten Grüßen Eure

Harburger v. R.

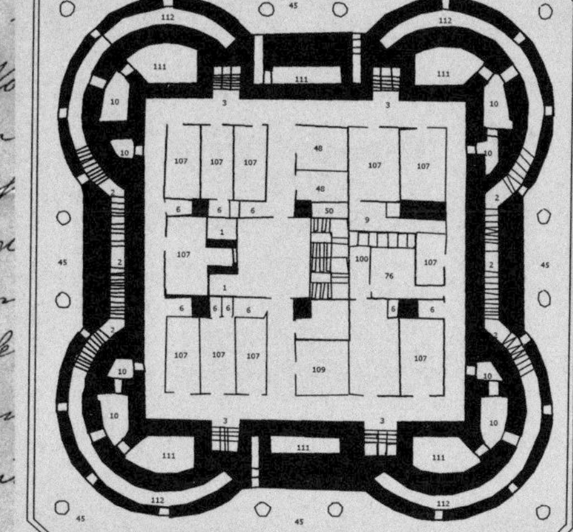

Harburg, d. 29. 5. 44.

Meine liebe E   !

Herzlich danke ich Dir für Deinen schönen
langen Brief. So nah wohnen wir beieinander
und müssen uns Briefe schreiben, wollen wir
mal was von einander wissen. Aber das
sind ja auch Zeiten, man wagt sich kaum
aus dem Hause heraus, geschweige denn nach
Wilhelmsburg zu fahren. Obgleich man sich
bei Euch doch wohl sicherer fühlen kann
als hier bei uns. Euer Bunker ist doch 100%ig.
Aber unser kleines Häuschen hier! Die goldene
Hochzeit haben wir gut überstanden. da
haben wir die mummelige Zeit mal ganz
vergessen und hatten ja auch Glück, der
Tag war alarmfrei. Unsere Mutter war so
vergnügt, unser Vater ist etwas stiller geworden. Weißt Du wieviel Blumen die beiden
hatten? 76 Töpfe, Sträuße und Buketts.
Es war eine Pracht. Fr.   hat auch geschrieben wir haben ihr auch schon geantwortet, aber nun hat sie die Post wohl
gar nicht erhalten inzwischen ist sie ja nach
Kiel versetzt worden. Was muß Du, meine liebe

E.   für eine Angst ausgestanden, haben beim
Terrorangriff auf Kiel! Ich freue mich mit Dir, daß
Fr   beschickt worden ist. Ich weiß, wie solche
Angst ermürbt. ich plage mich täglich, denn
He   fährt jeden Tag nach Lüneburg zur Schule.
Tü   wollte nicht, daß sie mit nach Teplitz ging,
weil dort Sperrgebiet ist. man käme auch, im Krank-
heitsfall nicht ohne Einreiseerlaubnis hin. Wäre es
hier in Deutschland gewesen, wäre wir die He
gern von hier losgewesen denn wer weiß, was
wir noch zu erwarten haben. So bin ich jeden Tag
froh wenn die Uhr nachmittags ½ 4 ist, und ich
sehe mein Mädel den U   raufkommen.
Daß He   nicht zur Schule geht, schadet meiner
Meinung nach gar nichts, sie kann alles nachho-
len und Du hast sie doch bestimmt lieber bei
Dir? Wie es mit dem Verreisen diesen Sommer
wird? Ich weiß es nicht ich habe keinen Mut zu
fahren, jetzt mit dem blöden Beschließen. Donner-
stag fährt Pe   wieder nach Berlin, bin ich gar
nicht mit einverstanden. aber ich sehe ein, daß es
sein muß, denn die Bombengeschädigten sind
noch längst nicht versorgt es kommen ja auch
immer Neue hinzu. Nun meine liebe E.   wollen
wir hoffen, daß das Schicksal uns hold gesinnt
bleibt und wir mal wieder sorglos vergnügt
sein können. Dir und den Deinen die herzlichsten
Grüße von Deiner U

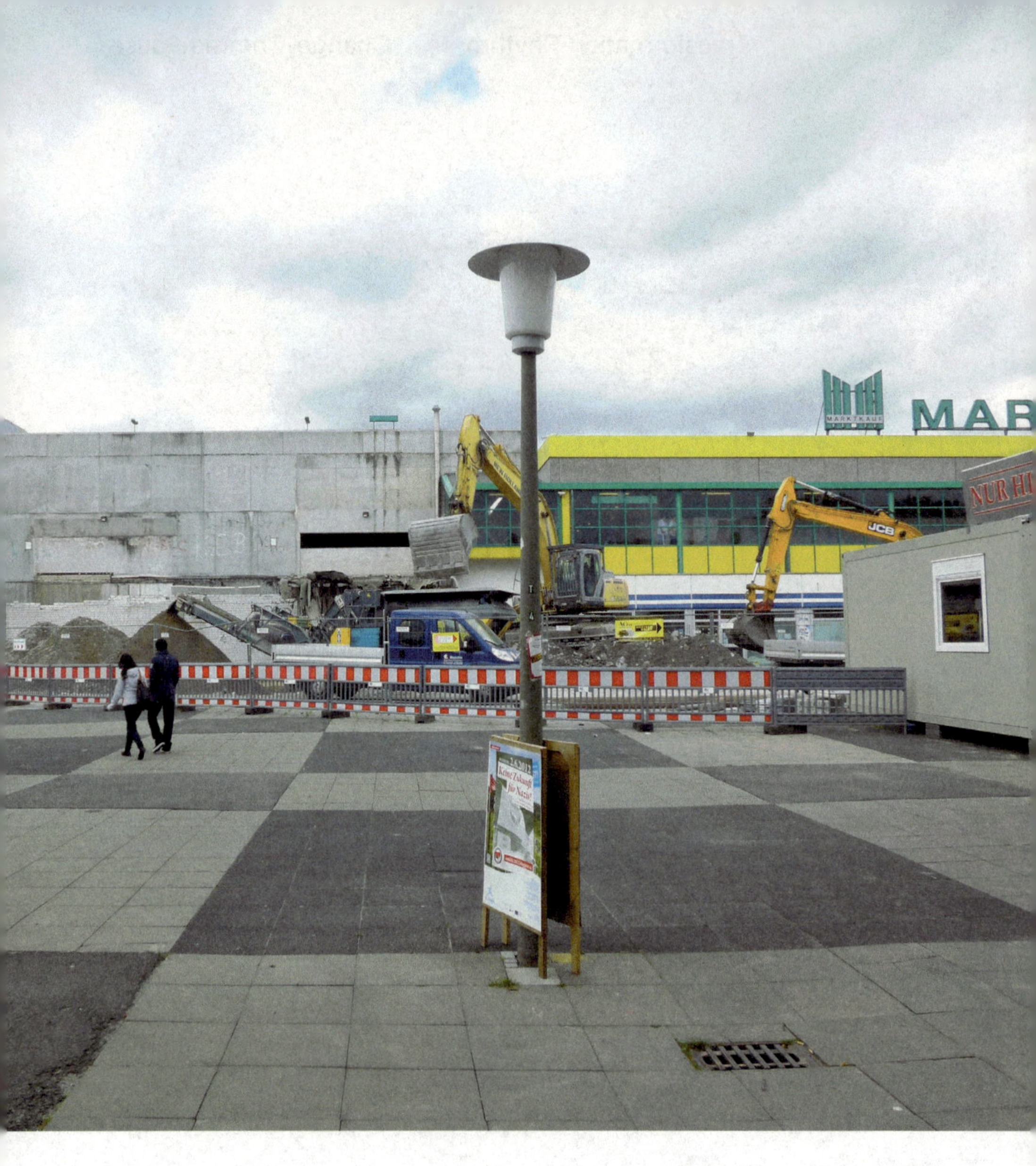

MARKTKAUF
MAR
NUR H
JCB
Keine Zukunft
für Nazis!

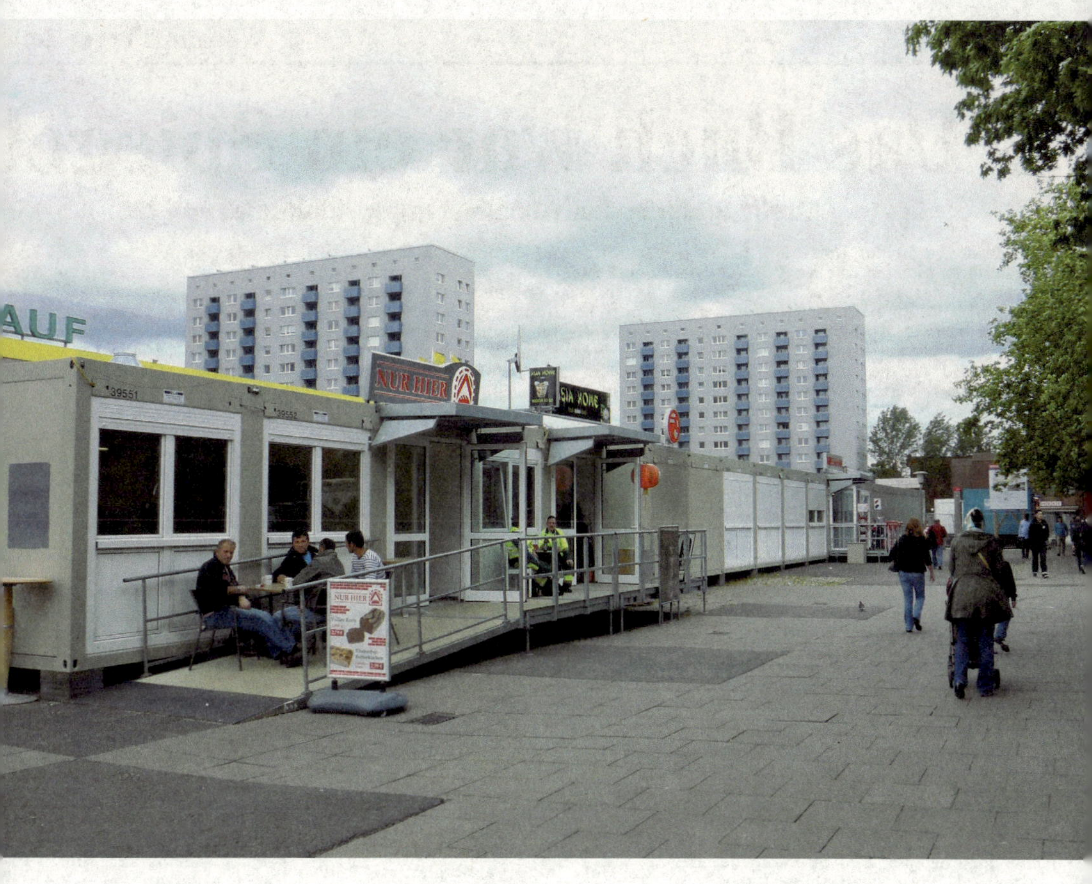
AUF
NUR HIER
NUR HIER

Das Buch war ein Spiegel

Streifzug durch das Wilhelmsburger Adreßbuch von 1931

Braunrot ist der Umschlag, eine Federzeichnung von der Kirchdorfer Kirche und der alten Schule ziert die Titelseite, darauf steht geschrieben „Wilhelmsburger Adreß-Buch — 1931". Anzeigen bedecken einen Teil der Vorder- und die gesamte Rückseite. Ein Adreßbuch der Harburg-Wilhelmsburger Zeit ist es, bearbeitet von Robert Böhme, verlegt von A. J. Schüthe, 20. Ausgabe. Die erste Ausgabe kam 1902 heraus. Bis 1914 erschien es alljährlich. Kriegs- und Nachkriegszeit unterbrachen die jährliche Reihenfolge. Erst 1925 gab es wieder ein alljährliches Adreßbuch für die Elbinsel Wilhelmsburg. Mir liegt die 20. Ausgabe vor, ein Geschenk der Tochter Robert Böhmes und mit Bemerkungen des Bearbeitesr versehen. Im Erscheinungsjahr 1931 kostete es 8 RM. Es macht Spaß, darin zu blättern. Da werden nicht nur Adressen geboten, o nein, da wird über sämtliche Vereine berichtet, da sind die Behörden aufgezählt. Das Buch gibt Aufschluß über die in den Reichstag und in den Landtag gewählten Volksvertreter, über Viehzählungen, Firmenjubiläen, Schulen und Genossenschaften.

Beginnen wir den Streifzug auf der Seite 1. Eine zweifarbige Karte von Wilhelmsburg ist abgedruckt. Wilhelmsburg, ein fast weißes Feld mit Hafenbecken und den vielen Verästelungen der Rangier- und Industriebahngleise. Ferner ist die Georg-Wilhelm-Straße eingezeichnet, damals noch Chaussee genannt, und die Straßenbahn. Auf der folgenden Seite steht Statistisches. Das Adreß-Buch gibt Aufschluß über die Einwohnerzahl. Genau 34 414 Wilhelmsburger wurden 1930 gezählt.

Tja, nun müßte doch eigentlich die Seite drei folgen. Nicht doch. Es beginnt wieder mit Seite 1 und zwar mit der „Ehrentafel aller seit 1905 und länger bestehenden Firmen und Geschäfte". Zwei Firmen sind unter der Überschrift „Über 100 Jahre" aufgeführt.

So erfährt man, daß die Lackfabrik J. D. Flügger die älteste Wilhelmsburger Firma ist, sie wurde 1783 gegründet. Die zweitälteste Firma ist die

Tran-Im- und -Export AG, J. F. Brückner Erben, Kanalstr. 107 und 113, die seit 1813 in Wilhelmsburg ansässig ist. Über 75 Jahre bestanden 1931 die Kartoffelgroßhandlung Peter Hiß, Am Jaffe-Kanal (1835); die Furnier- und Sägewerke Franz Schloßbach, Schlengendeich 13 (1846); die Deutsche Bohr- und Brunnenbaugesellschaft, Trettaustraße 34 (1851); und die Schiffswerft Röger Söhne, Kehrwieder 11 (1852). Es folgen die Aufzählungen der über 50jährigen Unternehmen, der 40jährigen und 25jährigen Unternehmungen auf Wilhelmsburg.

Viele Firmen existieren heute noch, andere sind erloschen oder mir schon nicht mehr bekannt. Eine Jugendstilkante schließt die Ehrentafel ab, und nun berichtet Albertus Gehrckens im Telegrammstil über die Ereignisse des Jahres 1930. Und gleich das erste Kapitel behandelt ein, leider noch immer hochaktuelles Problem Wilhelmsburgs, die Verkehrsverhältnisse. Auch 1930 gab es, wie man nachlesen kann, überfüllte Busse, keine Anhänger und zu lange Wartezeiten.

Weiter berichtet Albertus Gehrckens von lokalen Ereignissen, wie z. B. „Im Reformrealgymnasium bestanden am 25. März folgende Schüler die Reifeprüfung: Gustav Hensel (Philologie), Henry Hoffmann (Medizin), Jens-Jürgen Jensen (Finanz- und Postwesen), Heinrich Klippe (Eisenbahn), Elisabeth Lüdeke (Biologie), Johannes Lünzmann (Kaufmann), Herbert Riewe (Philologie), Bothilde Strodtmann (Medizin) und Roman Strubelt (Zahnarzt)".

„Am 25. Juni konnte die neue Feuerwache an der Rotenhäuser Straße durch einen Festakt eingeweiht werden. Das Gebäude ist mit allen Einrichtungen der Neuzeit eingerichtet."

„Am 1. Juli wurde das Schulgeld für die städtischen höheren Lehranstalten erhöht, und zwar für Einheimische von 200 auf 250 Reichsmark und für Auswärtige von 250 auf 312,50 Reichsmark."

„Die Straßen Vogelhüttendeich und Ernst-August-Deich wurden umgepflastert und mit neuen Gehstegplatten und besserer Beleuchtung versehen."

Das nächste Kapitel behandelt „Feuerauflüufe". 31 meist kleinere

Brände werden behandelt. Es die Unglücksfälle. Erwähnt werd Albertus Gehrckens 17 Tod Allein sieben Menschen erlitte nassen Tod, drei nahmen sich ö ben und die übrigen kamen durc kehrsunfälle oder Betriebsunfäl Leben.

Der Chronist geht jetzt zu de digen und heiteren Seiten des m lichen Lebens über, zu den Ju Gedächtnisfeiern und Ehrunge da mögen einige, ohne besonde sichtspunkte ausgewählte, für al hen, z. B.: „Die Maifeier verlie großer Beteiligung würdig und i und Ordnung." „Gelegentlich Hundeausstellung, die am 4. M früheren Hamburger Zoo stattfa hielten die Herren Henry Wiec für seinen Hund ,Arno' und Kl seinen Hund ,Brenno' Ehrenprei zwar für ,Arno' eine bronzene kette mit Diplom und für ,Bren silberne Plakette mit Diplom."

„Am 17. Mai feierten der He zirksvorsteher Albertus Gehrcke Frau Elisabeth geb. Eifels ihre g Hochzeit und am selben Tage di ste Tochter des Jubelpaares B geb. Gehrckens mit ihrem Ehe Herrn Ingenieur Louis Betz, ih berne Hochzeit."

„Zur Erinnerung an die Stun Verlesung der Augsburgischen fession vor 400 Jahren läuteten Juni, nachmittags 4 Uhr, die K glocken und am 29. Juni fander gottesdienste statt."

„Am 1. November wohnte He helm Busbas 40 Jahre in seiner nung Vogelhüttendeich 96. Eige des Hauses ist Herr Adolf Koop

Nach Albertus Gehrckens hab Statistiker das Wort. Da werde schließungen, Geburten und Ster registriert, die Haushaltungen g und die Wohnbevölkerung nad fessionen eingeteilt, was für d ser heute vielleicht ganz inter sein mag. Als Jahr wird 1925 a ben und da gab es 173 Refor 6030 Lutheraner, 16 666 Evang deskirche, 7162 kath. Kirche, dere Christen, 46 Israeliten un „Sonstige Religiöse".

8. September 1972

einen oder anderen Leser mö-
uch die Viehzählungen interes-
. Hier ist das Jahr 1929 maß-
d und zwar gab es in 4774
altungen 1343 Pferde und Foh-
Esel und Maulesel, 1054 Stück
ieh, 44 Schafe, 1519 Schweine,
iegen, 3802 Kaninchen, 51 709
Federvieh und 269 Bienenstöcke.
nächste Abhandlung gehört der
. Doch keine Wilhelmsburger
n Reichstag vertreten. Dafür aber
eußischen Landtag: die Sozial-
ratin Bertha Kröger.

neuer Abschnitt beginnt. Mit
Zeichnung von Wasserturm, Krä-
ndustrie und Schiffahrt wird ein
1931 schon sehr bedeutendes
lmsburger Kapitel angekündigt,
hilderung und Namensnennung
dustrie, des Handels, der Hand-
betriebe.

dann erst beginnt der Teil,
em Buch seinen Namen gegeben
er Adressenteil. Alphabetisch ge-
, mit Vornamen und Berufen
ie Wilhelmsburger eingetragen,
anchem Einwohner hat der Beer Robert Böhme Notizen ge-
z. B. bei Verstorbenen ein
Adressenänderungen und auch
tstage.

und dann werden die Einwoh-
och einmal aufgezählt, diesmal
net nach Ständen und Gewer-
Ein interessantes Kapitel, zeigt
h Stände, dei die Neuzeit weg-
vemmt hat und Einrichtungen,
Vilhelmsburg als Stadtteil der
und Hansestadt verloren hat.
einige Beispiele von Ständen
ewerben, die, wie ich meine, den
von heute ansprechen müßten,
etisch geordnet:

ufzeichnen von Handarbeiten
Weiß-Stickereien: Meyer, Frau,
r. 104; Rütsch, Frau, Chaussee
ktionatoren: Eddelbüttel, Peter,
lten Deich 17; Meyer, Gustav,
jstr. 37; Kruse, Wilhelmine, Frau,
hüttendeich 25.

armherzige Schwestern, Bonifa-
. 6, im kath. Gemeindehaus.

afé und Konditoreien: Kröger,
ch, Inh. Frau Emma, Wwe., Vo-
tendeich 40; Matthies, E., Chaus-
22; Schlichting, Robert, Alte
se 20; Stadt-Café, Jergolla,
Veringstr. 43.

scher: Meyer, Peter, Obergeorgs-
rdeich 148; Rübcke, Joh. sen.,
öhlbrand 76; Rübcke, Johs. jun.,

Am Köhlbrand 36; Six, Peter, Köhl-
brandstr. 215; Wehrenberg, Hinr., Kattwyk ohne Nr.

G Galanteriewaren: Bremer, Wilhelmine, Frau, Im Busch 38; Strufe, Frau,
Mary (Henrichsen, Chr. Nachf.), Vogelhüttendeich 24. Gardinen- und Bett-
decken-Spannerei: Plückhahn, Frau,
Magdalene, Vogelhüttendeich 56;
Wendt, Ludwig, und Sohn, Vogelhüttendeich 40.

H Hebammen: Drux, Klara, Wwe.,
Vogelhüttendeich 20; Grandowski,
Wanda, Frau, Kirchenallee 34; Knuth,
Martha, Freihafenstr. 154; Kraft, Elise,
Wwe., Freihafenstr. 172; Ollesch,
Maria, Frau, Fährstr. 79; Rave, Char-
lotte, Frau, Vogelhüttendeich 74;
Schipke, Berhardine, Frau, Eichenallee
49; Steinke, Frau Auguste, Fährstr. 86;
Wagenknecht, Olga, Frau, Wittestr. 1;
Wolff, Anna, Frau, Veringstr. 27.

K Kleinkinder-Bewahranstalten: Gemeindehaus der evangel.-lutherischen
Kirchengemeinde Reiherstieg, Kirchenallee 15; Gemeindehaus der katholi-
schen Kirchengemeinde, Bonifatius-
straße 6.

L Leichenfrauen: Kurbgeweit, Lina,
Wwe., Fährstr. 68; Nesemann, Anna,
Wwe., Steindamm 89.

M Milchproduzenten: Wegen der
Vielzahl der Milchproduzenten, es sind
72 an der Zahl, werden die Namen
nicht aufgeführt. Musiker: Auch der
Musiker gab es viele, daher werden
die Namen nicht aufgezählt.

T Trichinenschau: Ohl, Martin, Je-
nerseitedeich 6.

Z Zoologisches Spezialgeschäft:
Frank, Karl, Vogelhüttendeich 10.
Unter Z sind auch noch Zeitungen
aufgeführt. Doch damals wie heute
gab bzw. gibt es nur die Wilhelmsburger Zeitung.
Wer meint, nun sei das Buch abge-
schlossen, hat sich geirrt, es geht noch
weiter. Ein Anhang folgt. Über Polizei-
Hilfrufe, Städtische Feuerwehr, interne
Feuermelder, über die Sanitätskolonne
des Roten Kreuzes, über Postgebüh-
ren (ein Brief im Ortsverkehr kostete
8 Rpf), über Reichsbahn-Verkehr vom
Bahnhof Wilhelmsburg, Straßenbahn-
betrieb, Autobus-Fahrpläne, Fährdamp-
fer-Fahrpläne und abschließend über
die Wilhelmsburger Zeitung.
Hoffentlich hat Ihnen der Streifzug
Spaß gemacht. Mir ja!   ath

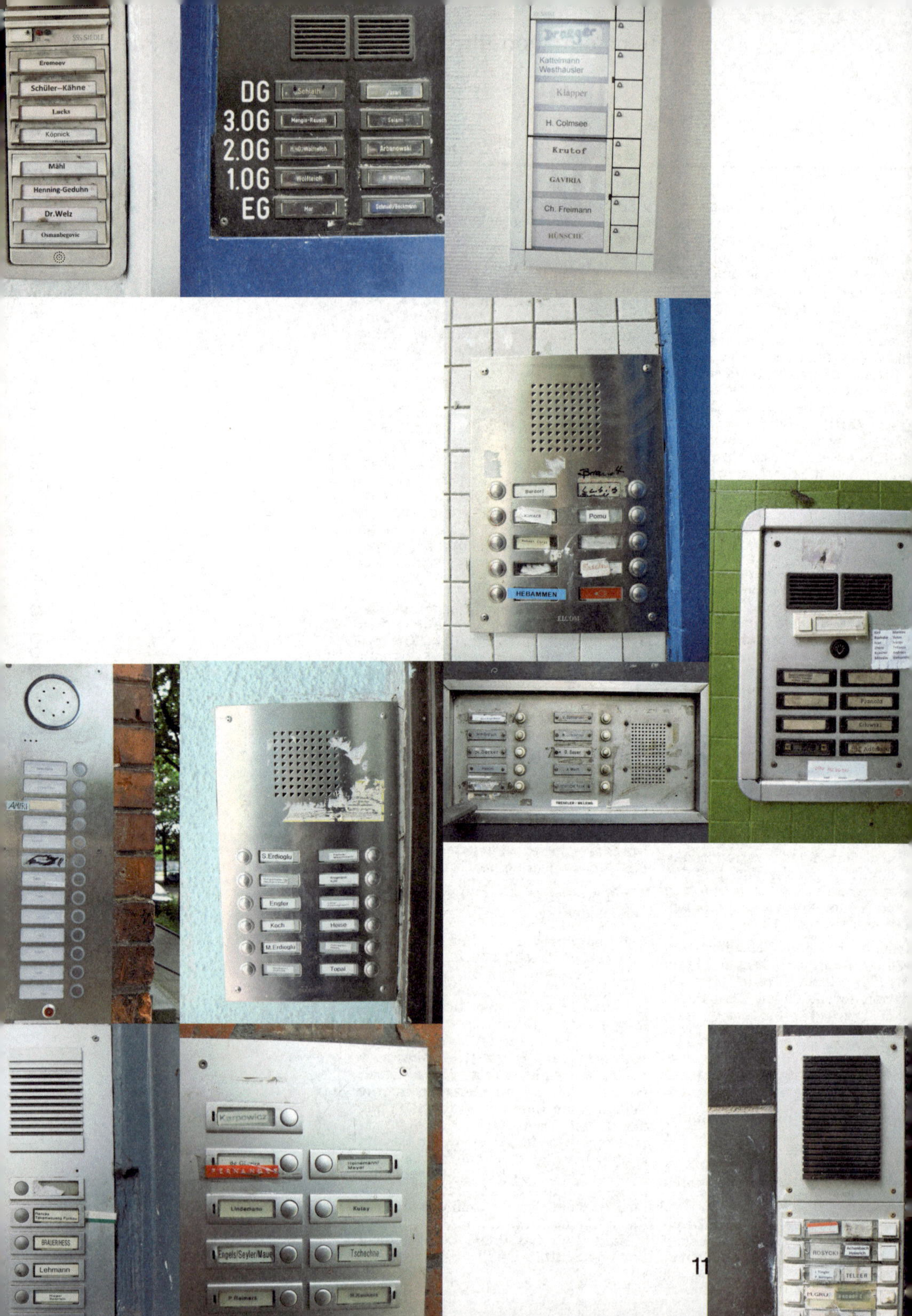

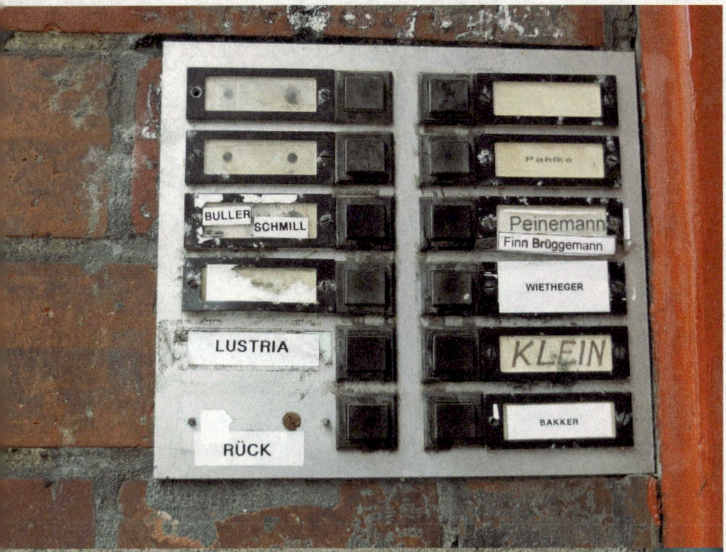

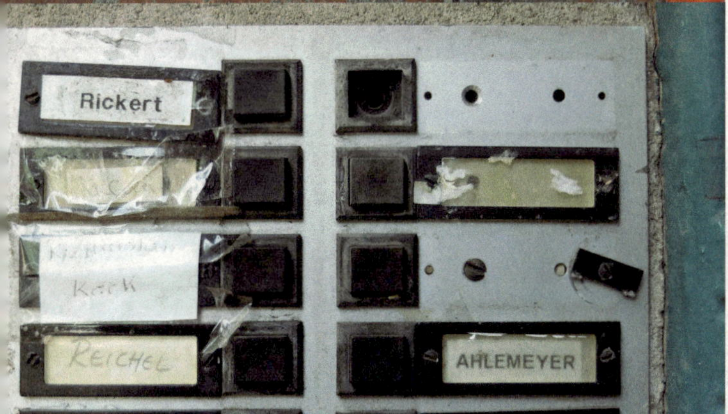

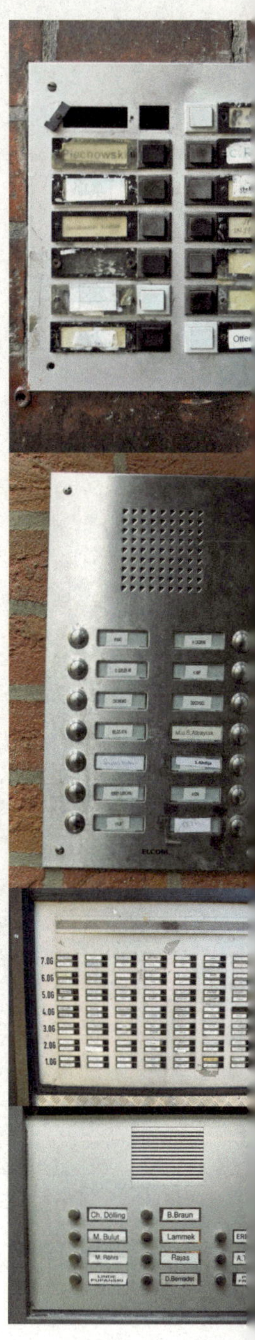

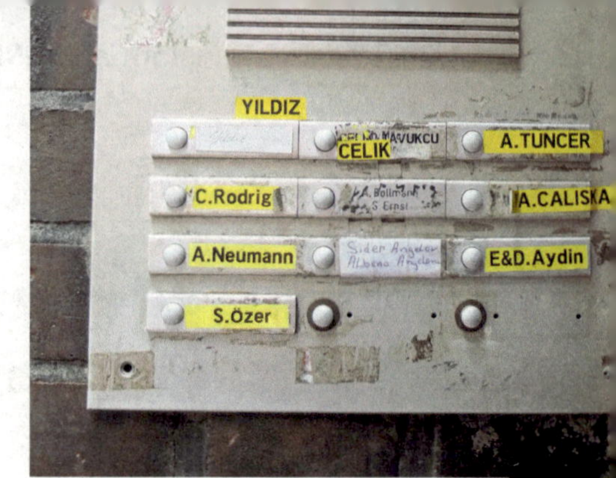

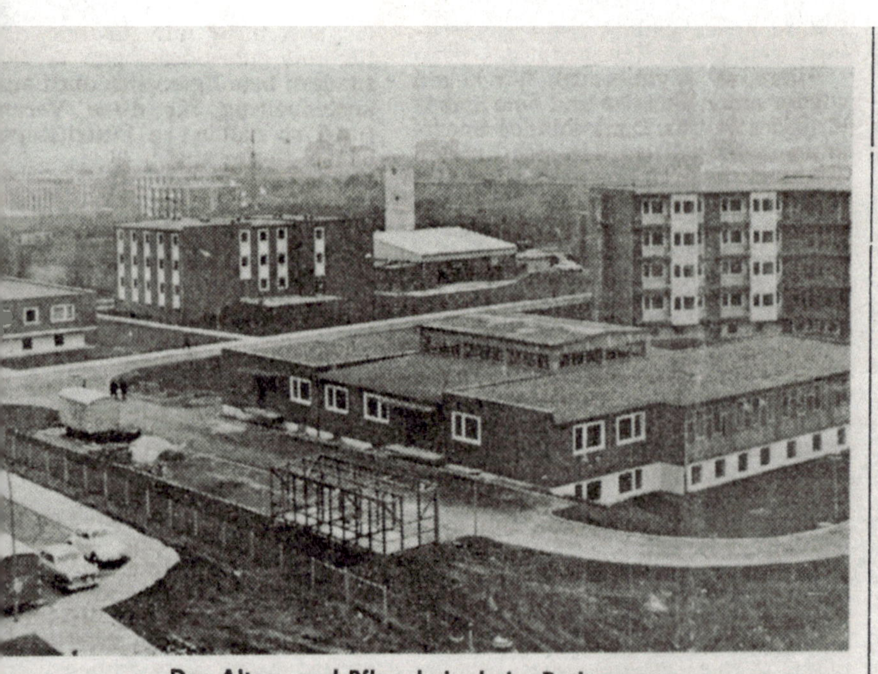

Das Alters- und Pflegeheim beim Rathaus

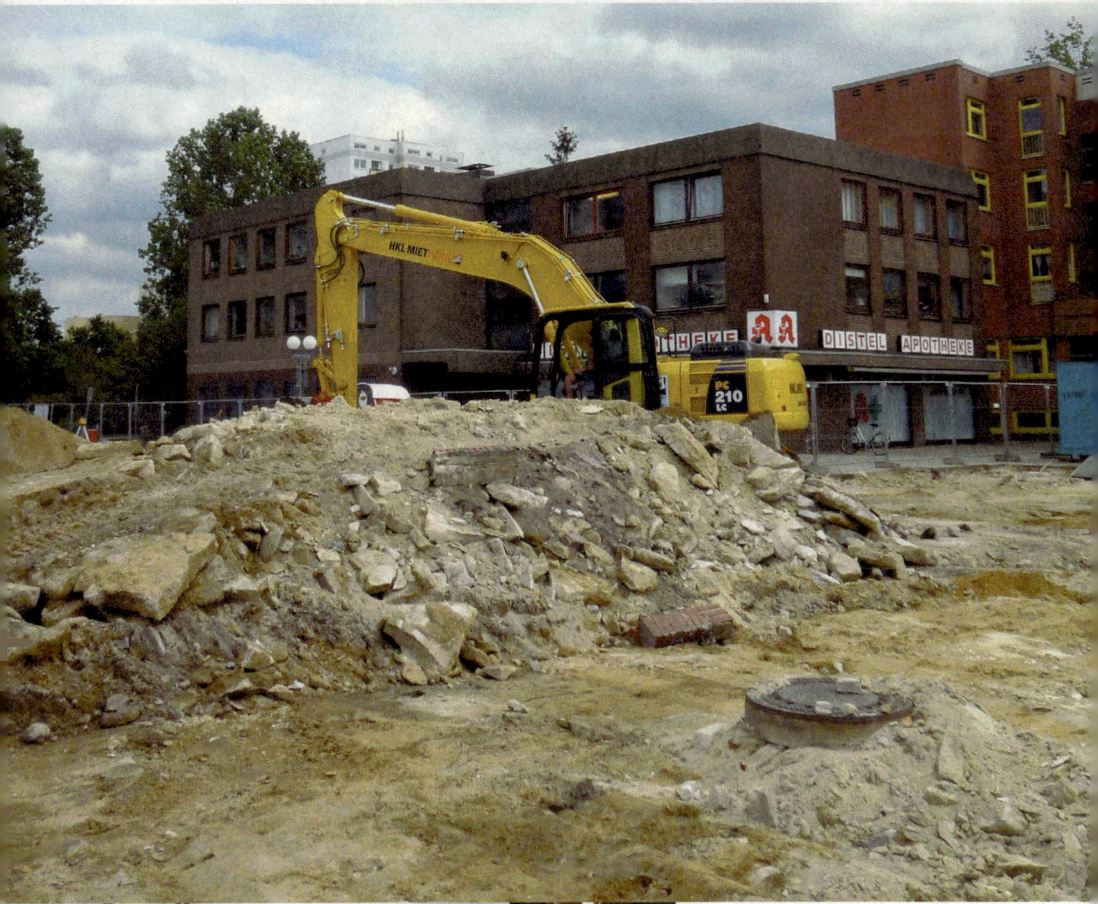

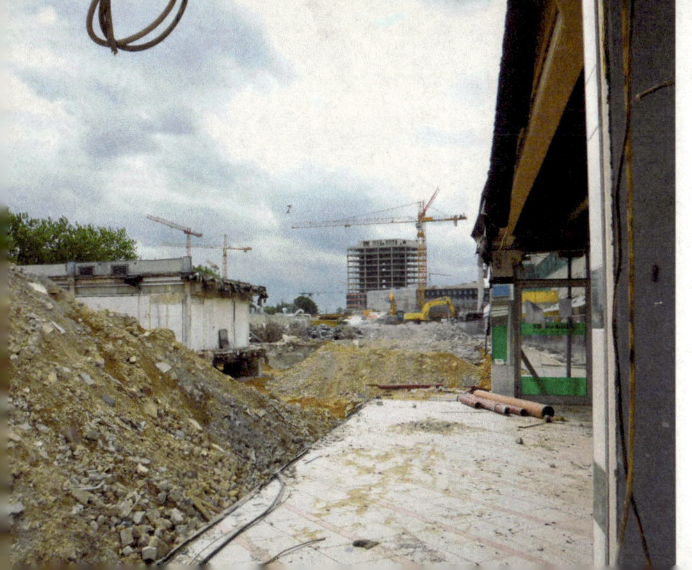

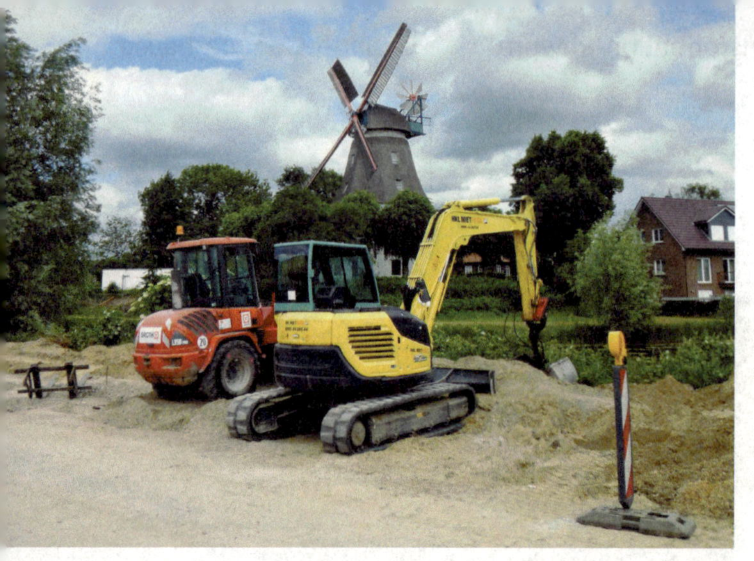

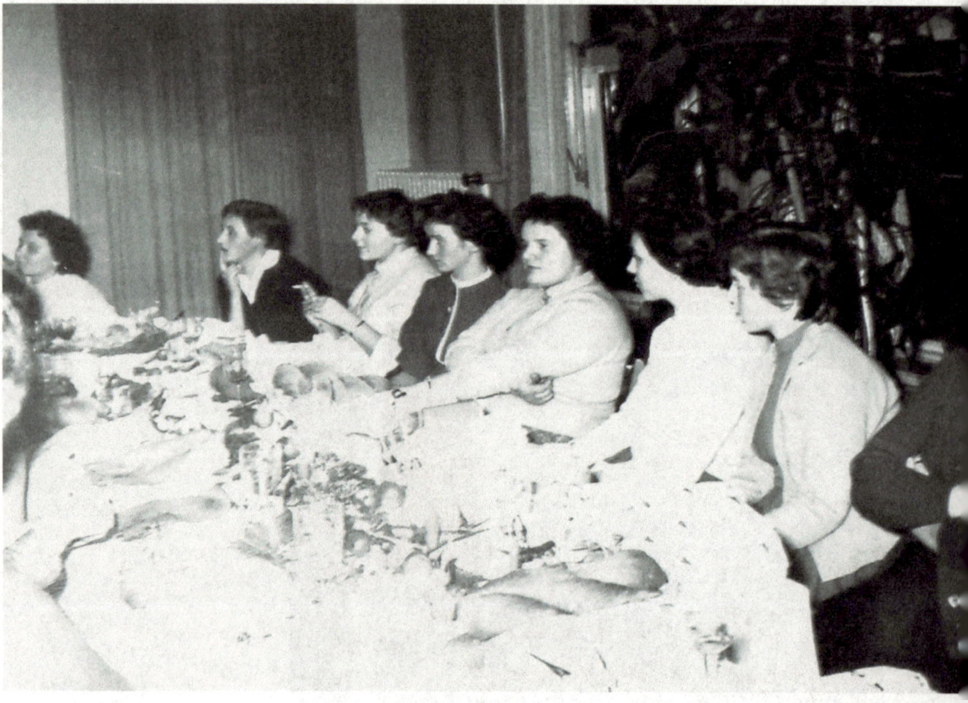

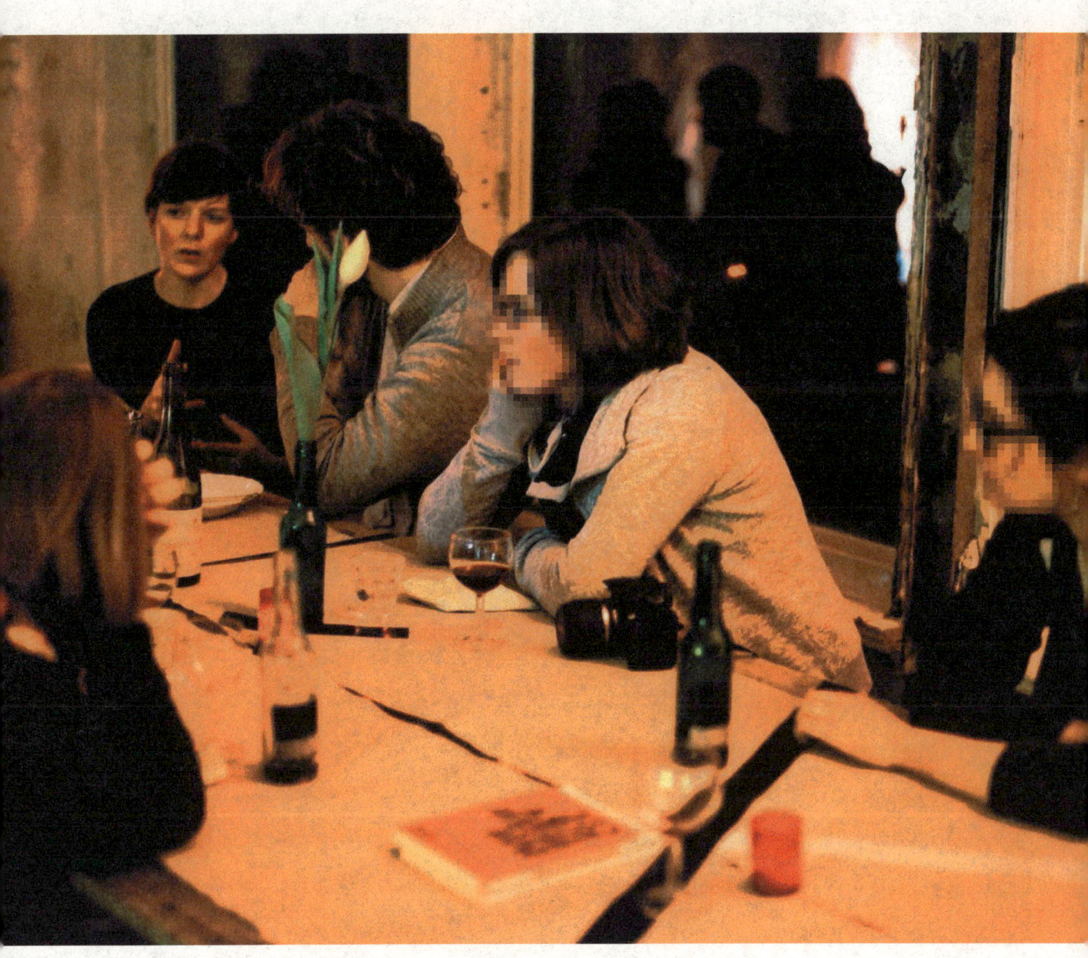

Harburg, d. 23. 6. 44.

Meine liebe E___!

Herzlichsten Dank für Deine l. Zeilen, einen Brief erhalten, im Bunker geschrieben, wer hätte das gedacht! Aber Ihr könnt froh sein, solch sichern Schutz in der Nähe zu haben. Wir sind ja leider vollkommen schutzlos; wer weiß, was noch alles kommt; kannst Du das Ganze verstehen? ich nicht. Wie kann der Haß zwischen Menschen so groß werden, daß sie sich mal eben gegenseitig tot werfen. Aber alles Klagen nützt nichts, wir müssen durch, und ich muß mich wundern, wie schnell man sich wieder aufrafft, einen Tag Ruhe und schon hat man wieder Mut. H___ ist heute wieder nach Lüneburg gefahren, dort sind die Mädel sehr nett aufgenommen worden; die ganze Woche haben sie ja nun versäumen müssen, aber die Lehrer und Lehrerinnen bringen ihnen viel Verständnis entgegen und sorgen in jeder Beziehung, so gut es geht, für Schutz; z. B. ist heute bekanntgegeben worden, daß sie erst nach der Vollentwarnung Lüneburg verlassen dürfen; sehr richtig finde ich das, denn immer aus dem Zuge raus und im Wald Deckung suchen, ist auch nicht schön. Und meine liebe E___ Ihr wollt es auch wagen und reisen? Wir wollten ja auch gern ein paar Tage raus, H___ und ich jedenfalls.

P. fährt ja leider in diesem Jahre nicht, weil
er ja schon durch seine notwendigen Geschäftsreisen
soviel unterwegs sein muß. Ich habe ja einen
Bammel, wenn ich an die Fahrt denke, von wegen
Tage beschießen oder was sich das Panzerzeug von
Amerikaner noch ausdenken. wir müssen unsern
Schutzengel mitnehmen. He würde 14 Tage
Erholung gut gebrauchen können, im nächsten
Jahr kommt dann der Arbeitsdienst, dann ist
wohl Schluß mit Urlaub, nicht wahr? Du weißt
ja schon damit Bescheid. Ob wir wohl noch
mal von Herzen vergnügt sein können? Ich mag
es doch immer noch so gern. Könnt Du und
Ke nicht mal am Nachmittag kommen? Bis
jetzt ist um die Zeit noch nichts gewesen. Wie wär's
mit Dienstag Nachmittag? Wir würden uns sehr
freuen. Sieht man mal zu, ob es sich nicht einrich-
ten läßt. Dann kann man sich mal richtig
ausklönen.
          Bis dahin mit den herzlichsten
          Grüßen Eure U

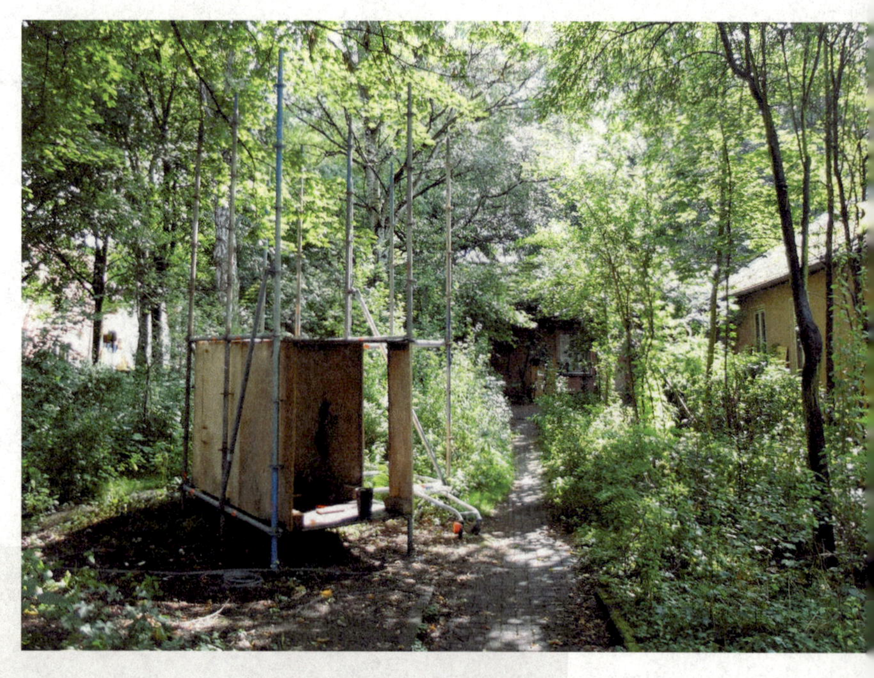

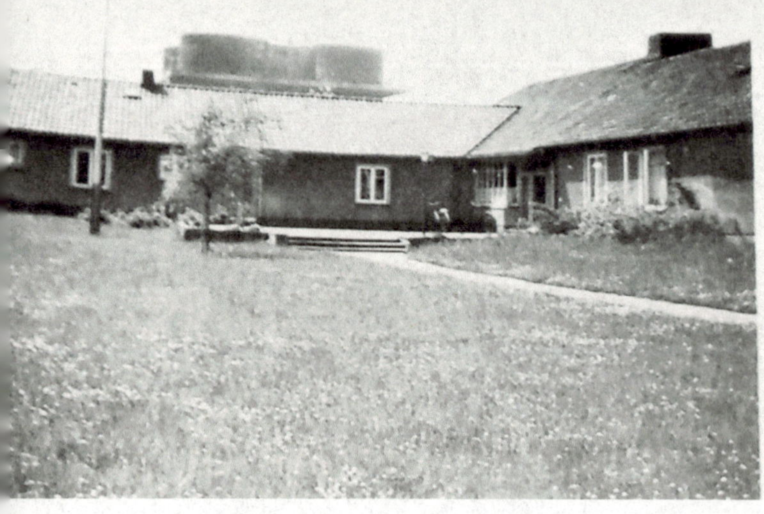

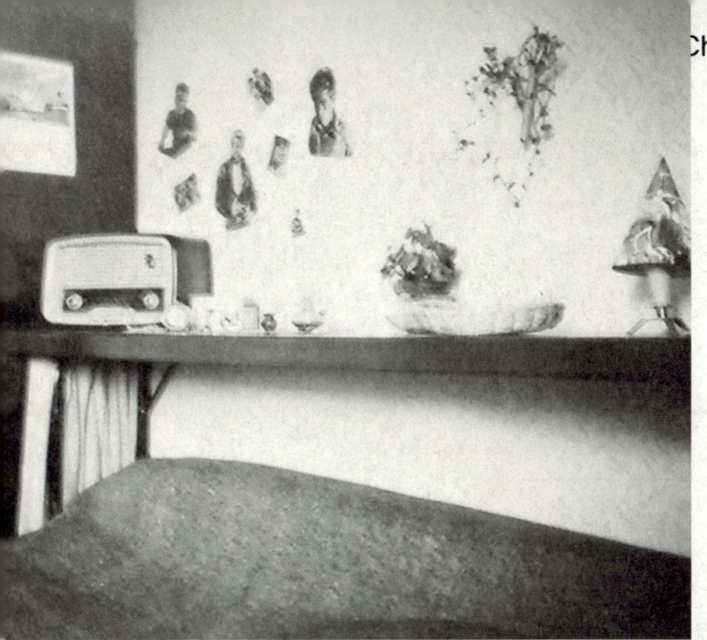

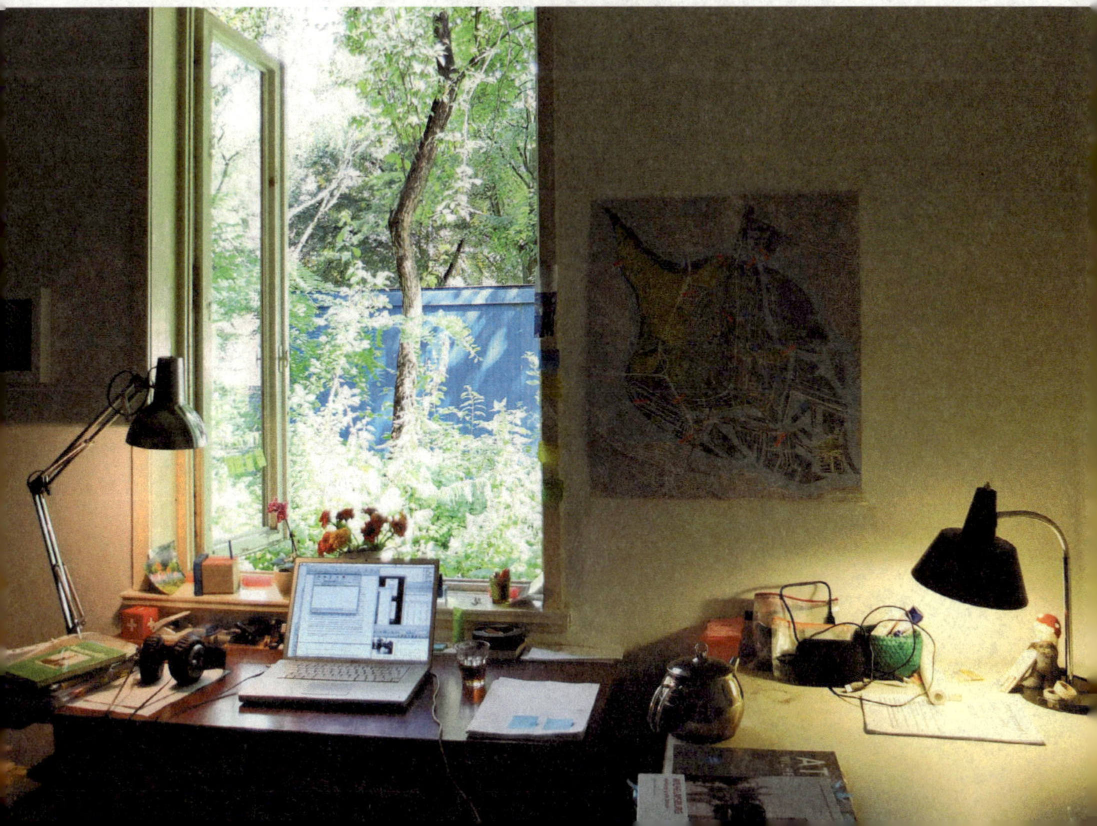

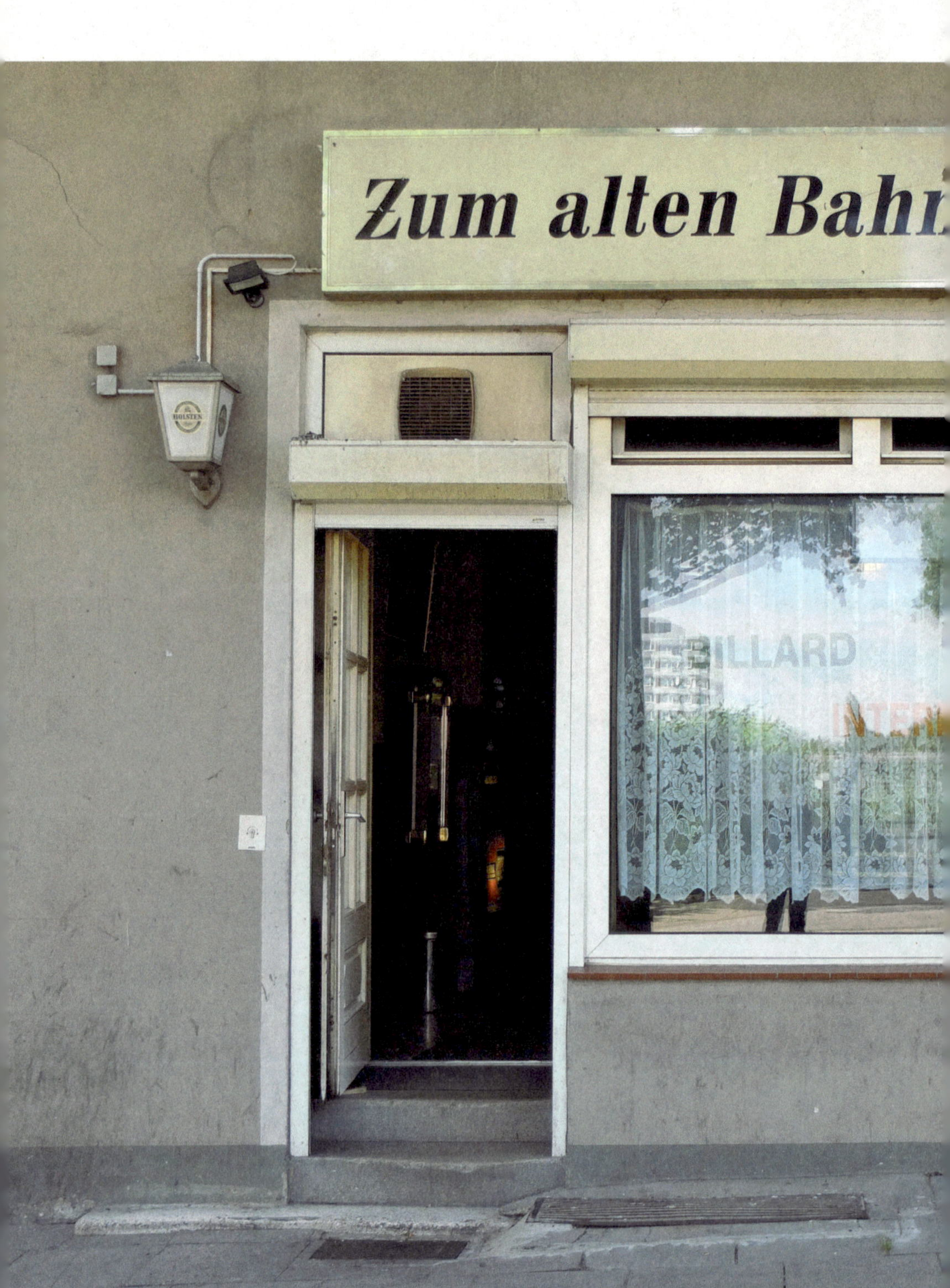

Zum alten Bahn
BILLARD
INTER
HOLSTEN

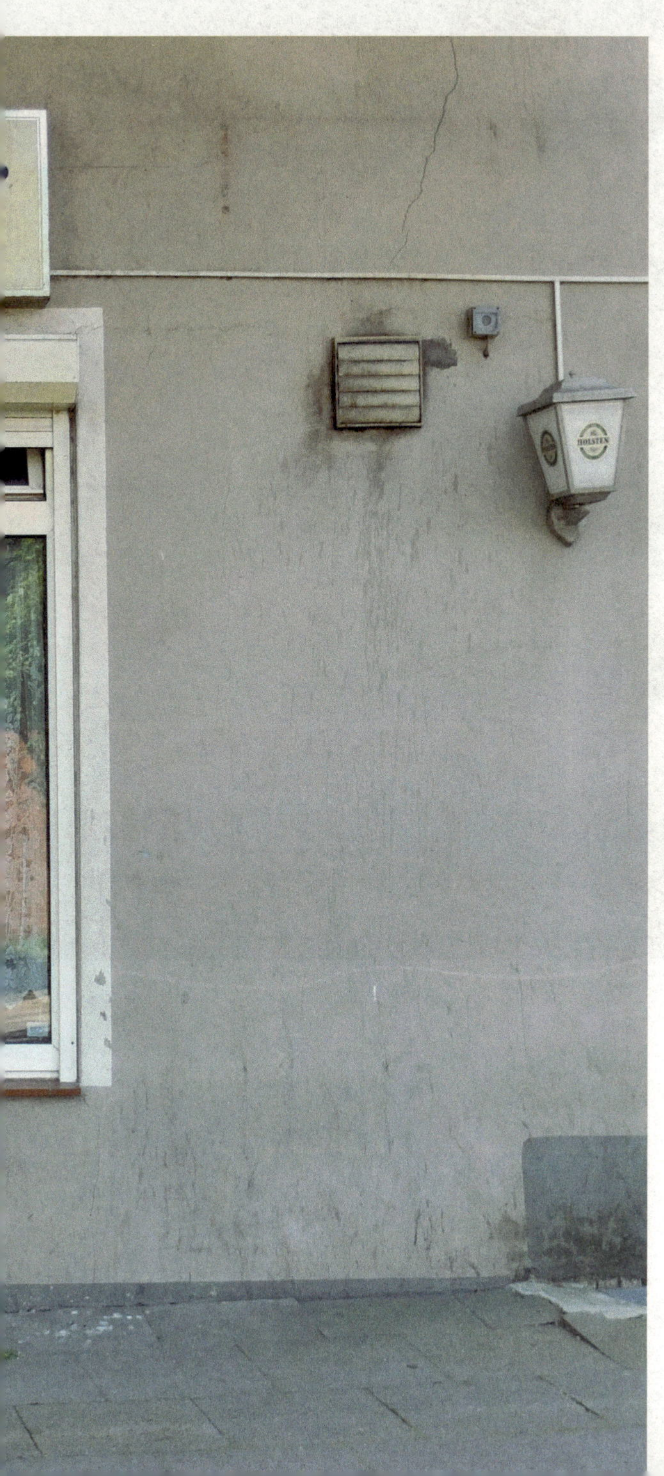

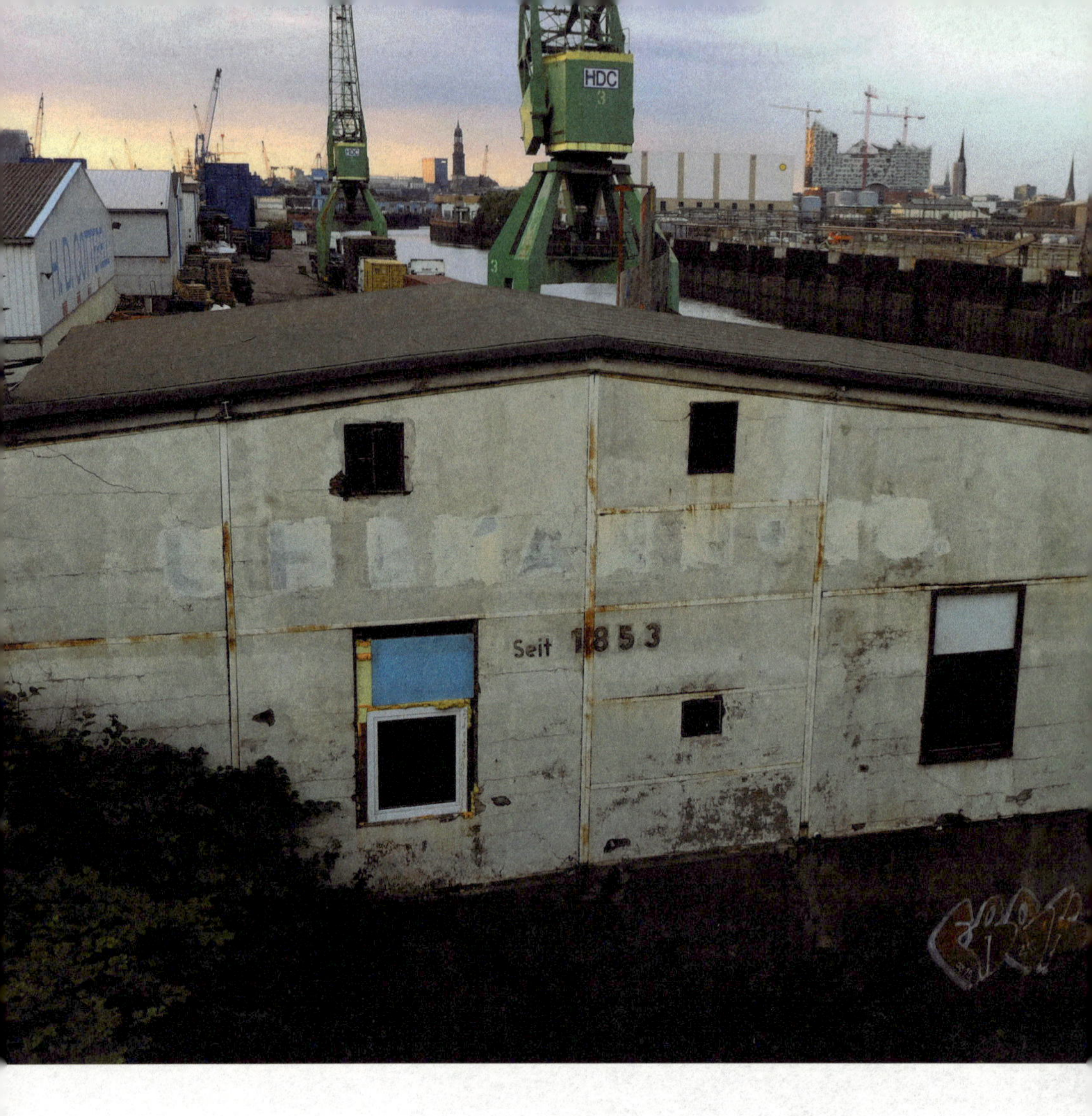

HDC
3
Seit 1853

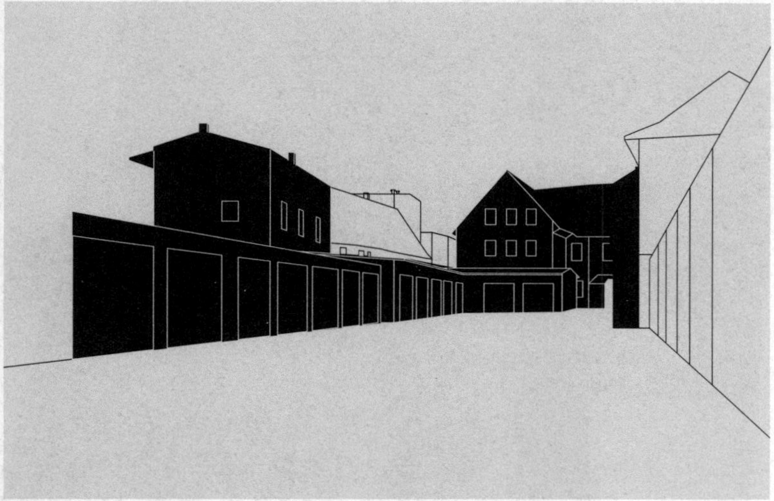

... I take a break here, interesting vistas of the back of things, diverse combinatorics. Look into the port. Into the new development zone. IBA is here too. They are revamping, converting the palace. Inconspicuously. The whole thing is a huge construction site, I cannot find a way out ...

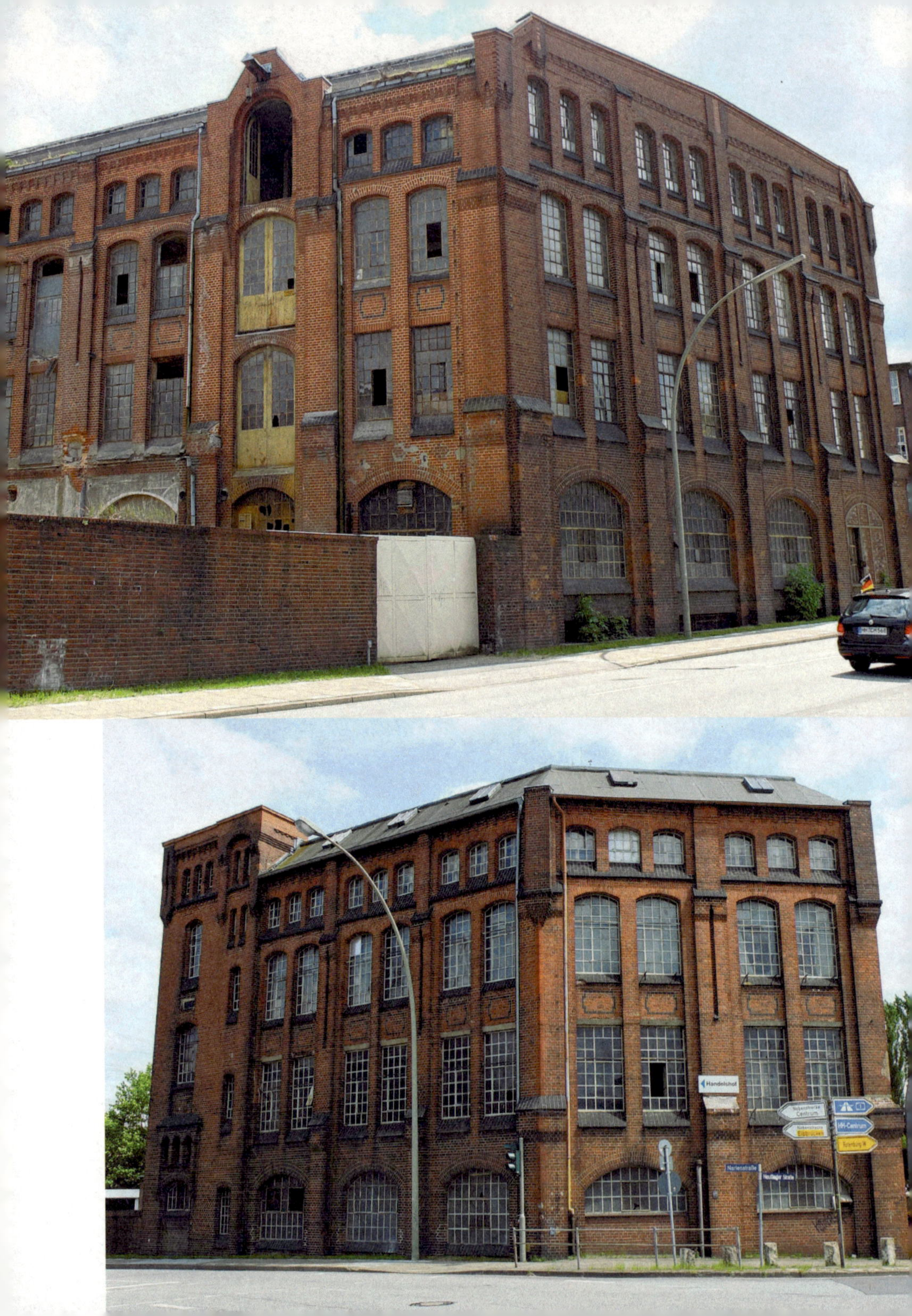

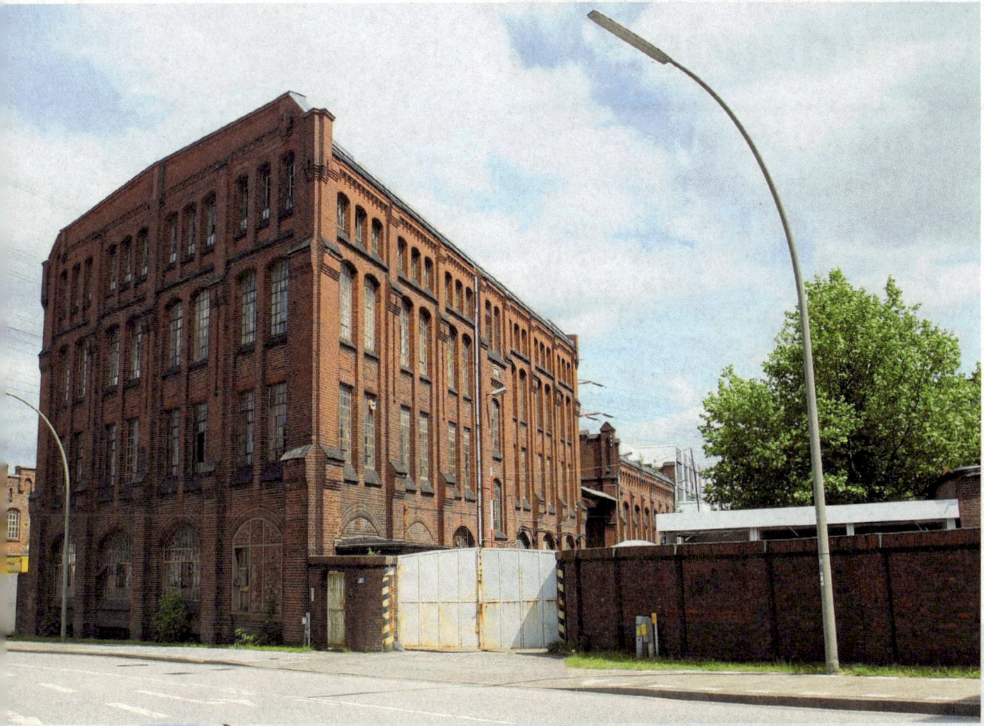

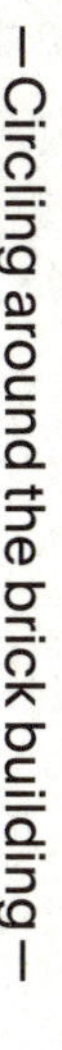
—Circling around the brick building—

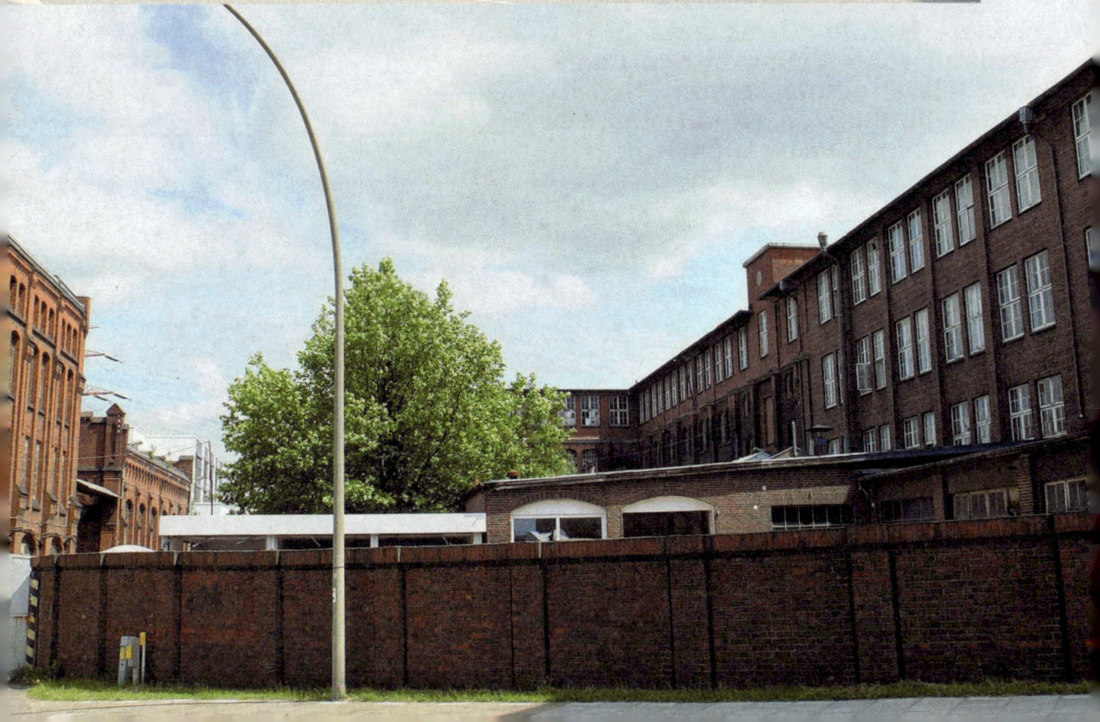

meldungen ●

Bald Ausländer im Ortsausschuß

An den Sitzungen des Wilhelmsburger Ortsausschusses werden bald Ausländer mit beratender Stimme teilnehmen. Das sieht ein Beschluß der Harburger Bezirksversammlung vor, der am Dienstag zu einem interfraktionellem Antrag gefällt wurde. Außerdem werden sie im Ausschuß für Schule und Kultur, im Sozial- und Jugendausschuß, im Wirtschafts- und im Bauausschuß vertreten sein. Von einem Zusatzantrag der CDU, auch für den Ortsausschuß Süderelbe Ausländer zu berufen, sahen sich SPD und FDP so überrascht, daß sie ihn ablehnten.

Der sozialdemokratische Abgeordnete Harald Muras sieht in der Ausländerbeteiligung in den Fachausschüssen einen ersten Schritt zum kommunalen Wahlrecht für steuerzahlende Ausländer. OK

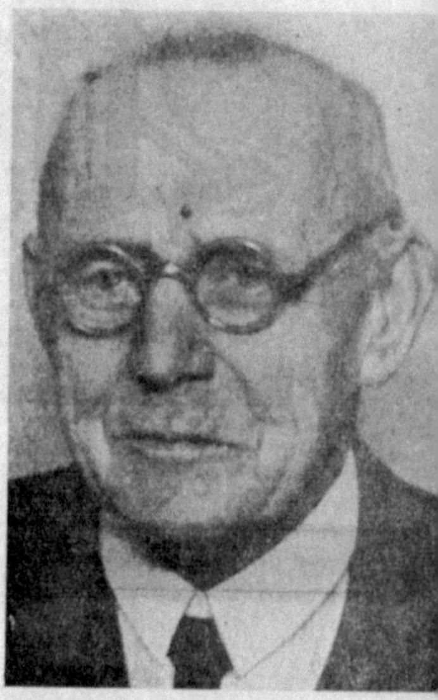

Dr. Reinhold Gräßner, wie ihn sehr viele noch kennen

Se

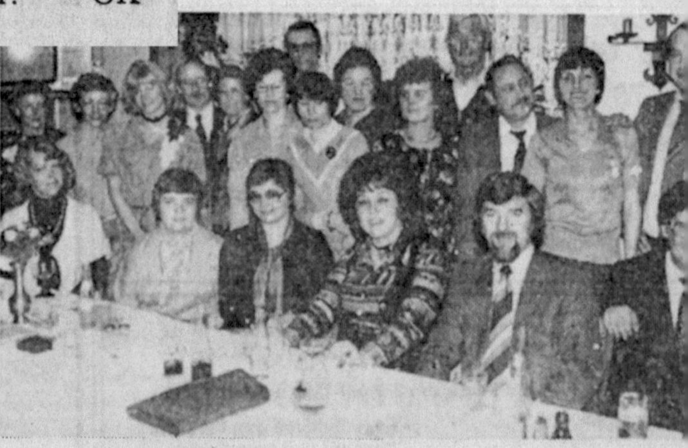

Wiedersehen nach 20 Jahre

Nach 20 Jahren trafen sich am 30. März 1979 die »Ehemaligen« der S
Neuhöfer Damm 95, Abgangsklasse 1959, wieder. Mit dabei waren: H

Resources are lying idle—waiting. Collectors and sorters track down the various recyclables on the island. They seem to know particular locations well and they are familiar with the area and are knowledgeable. Their gaze has become attuned to and specialized in valuable and recyclable material. They feel their way forward with a practiced eye, search and find—by the roadside, in the bushes, in the grassy part of the park, along the canals, in dumpsters, or in the port. Things that some people discard (carelessly and thoughtlessly) provide an important source of income for others. The practice of searching and collecting becomes a survival strategy Life and Business . Bags, Porsches at your heels, suitcases, bicycles, and other modes of transport Movers and Transporters carry away the various recyclable materials such as wooden planks, metal, tires, and other car parts, technical components, furniture or deposit bottles. On the one hand there are the professional sorters and collectors with special storage space for what they collect and who have large vans that load up the various resources available, process and then resell them. They advertise to their target audience with signs proclaiming "We buy cars" or "Cell phones purchased." Goods circulate, rotate, and change owners. In particular, various spare-parts warehouses can be found in the commercial and industrial areas. These are outdoor storage areas, surrounded by high fences and therefore not always easily visible. The doors have heavy locks. The goods are valuable. Often you can only guess at what is actually waiting there for better times or rates, certainly for months, years. Precipitation, heat, and the cold have an impact. Weathering processes often kick in at a very early stage. It is noisy and dusty, unreal and sometimes eerie Lost—Abandoned—Wait . I rarely see anyone else on foot in this area. The neighboring warehouse buildings look forbidding and closed. Often the facility operators live in two-storey houses on the premises. There are no flower beds in the front garden, but instead rows of tightly parked small and medium-sized cars, towers of car tires and unruly metal. Laundry flutters on the clothes line in some places in the midst of all this. Cars with missing doors or with doors open often are joined together with plastic chairs and small rickety tables where members of the collector-and-sorter family drink their coffee from thermos cans and smoke cigarettes. They take short breaks, then they climb into, onto, or under the vehicles, the cars, buses, and campers. Break them up into their components, reassemble them, sand down their paintwork, soup up their engines, and touch up their paintwork | Barbershops and Beauty Salons | | Machine-Space |. There are also various people collecting deposit bottles. They are mostly of retirement age or probably unemployed. Both women and men from different backgrounds (as their clothes suggest) make their rounds several times a day. They are not always lucky, for many of the containers get a lot of footfall. Gloves and a flashlight may help when collecting. With one hand, they deftly tip out any remaining liquid from the bottles before tucking them away in their bags or trolleys. Later they hand in the content of these receptacles, sometimes bulging, sometimes empty, depending on how the day has gone, at one of the automated recycling points in the various supermarket chains and claim the deposit. That at least provides a little additional income. Here and there, flowers, leaves, and roots of various herbs are gathered in the meadows or dike embankments by women in long skirts. However what they do with them or make out of them subsequently remains their secret.

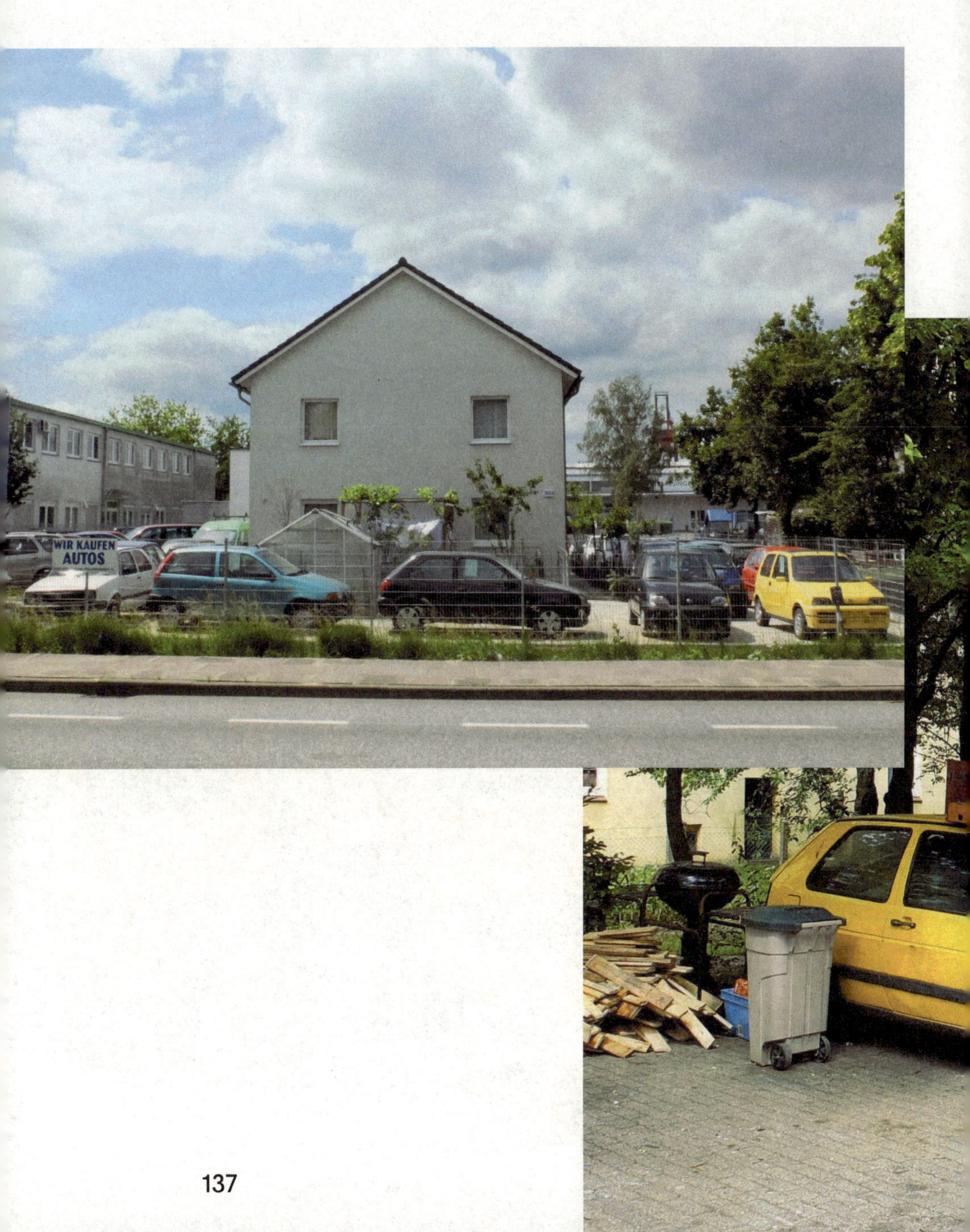
WIR KAUFEN
AUTOS

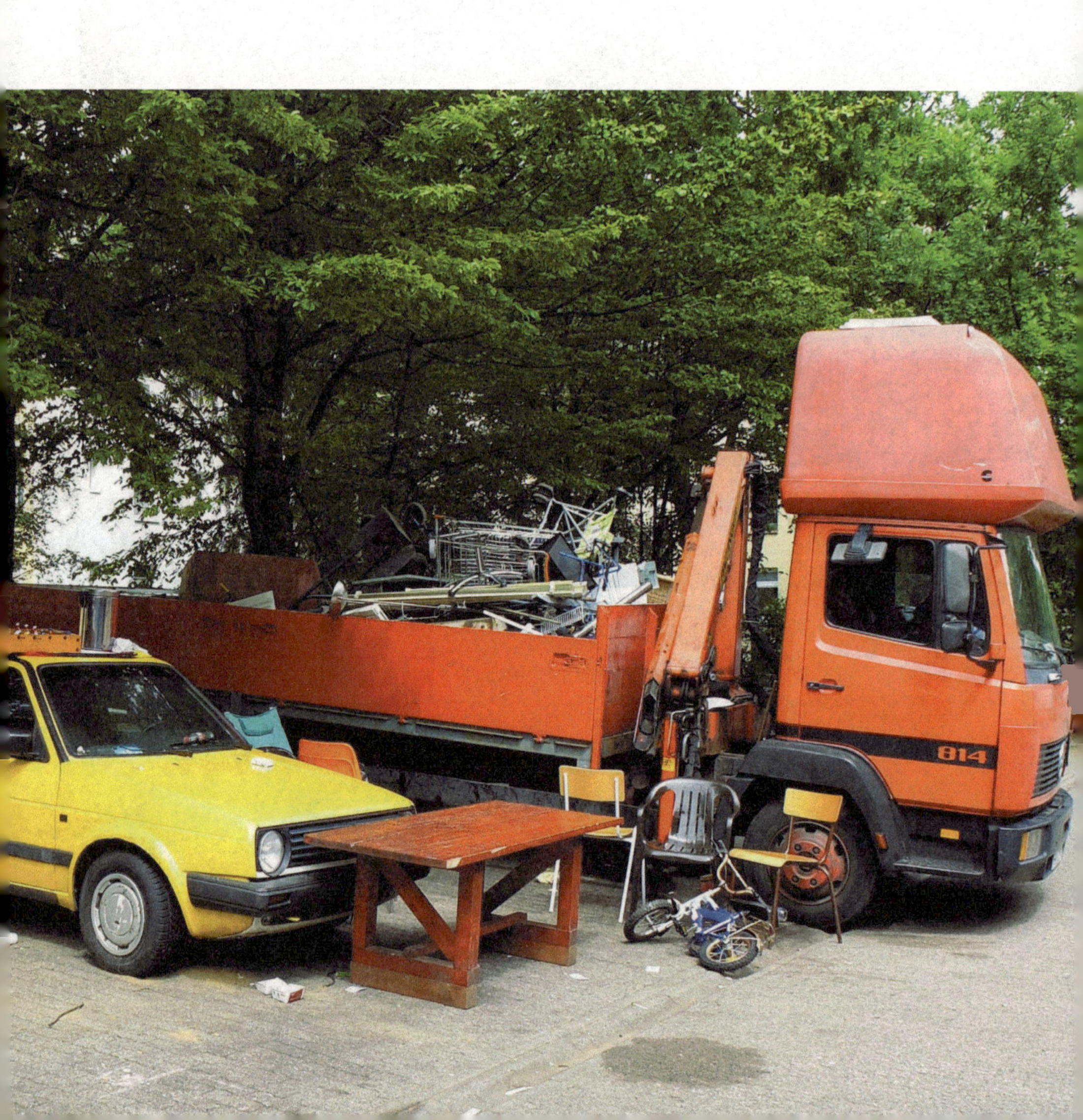

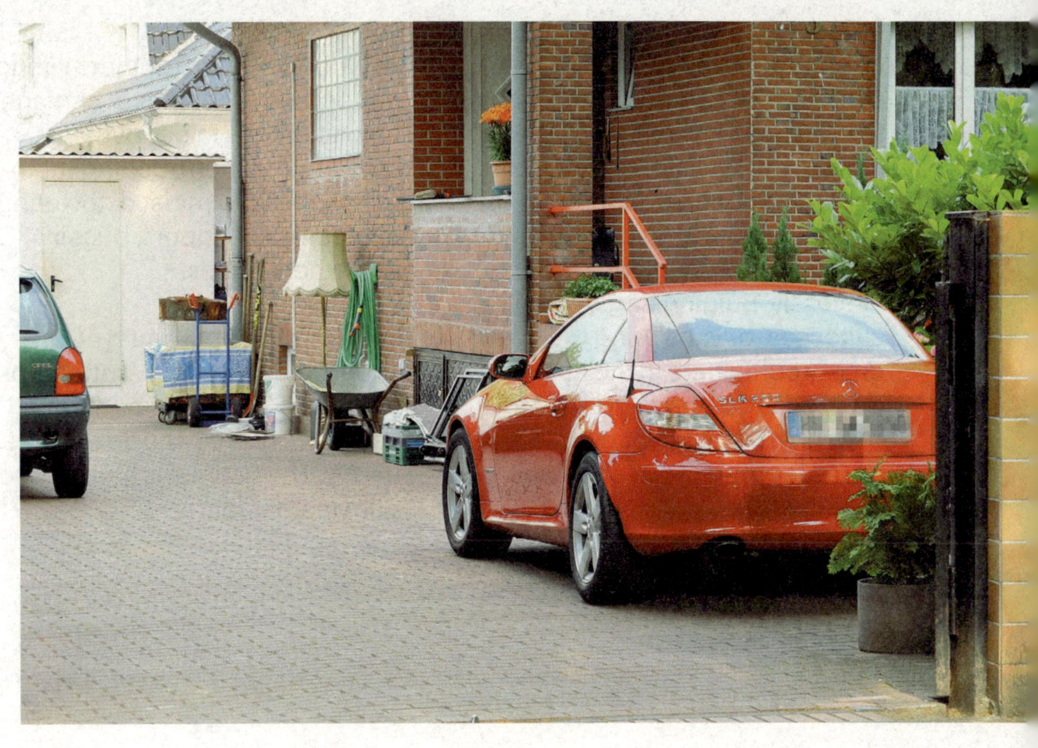

Beer bottles and tin cans stand or lie by the roadside. Stuck into the red trash containers in the park, at the bus stops. Collectors of different backgrounds and ages search and find. Again and again they pace out their routes. Tirelessly. Bulging bags, wheeled suitcases, or vans bring the empty containers to the automated exchange points in Lidl, Aldi, or Penny. Deposit vouchers are redeemed at the checkout.

Two young African mothers sitting on a ledge, their babies in carriages. Their husbands in oily overalls stand around them. Behind them the house in the midst of towering car tires and car doors, buses everywhere buses.

Three soft plump women are in a meadow dotted with buttercups in the Groß Sand allotments. They pluck leaves and flowers on Sunday. The harvest is tucked into a slim leather folder.

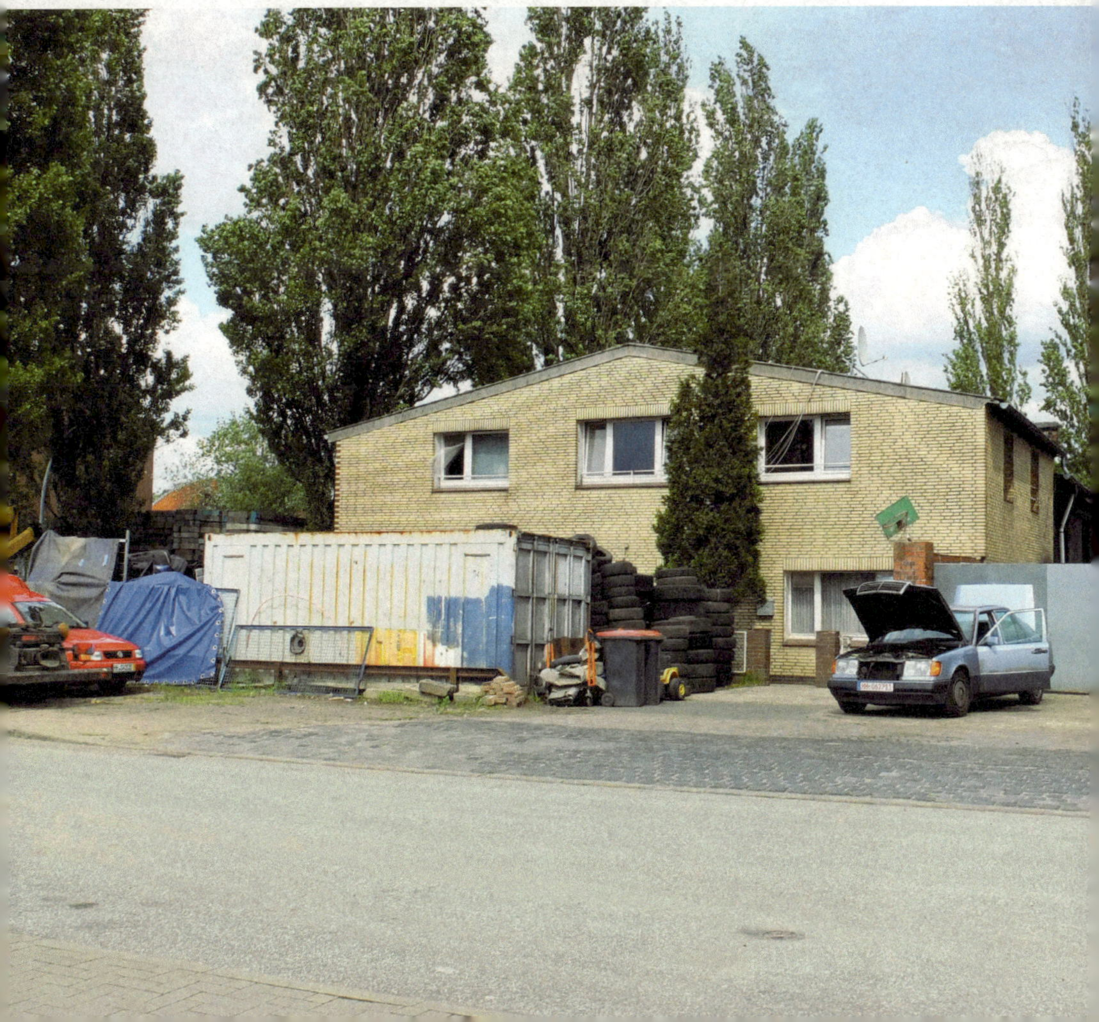

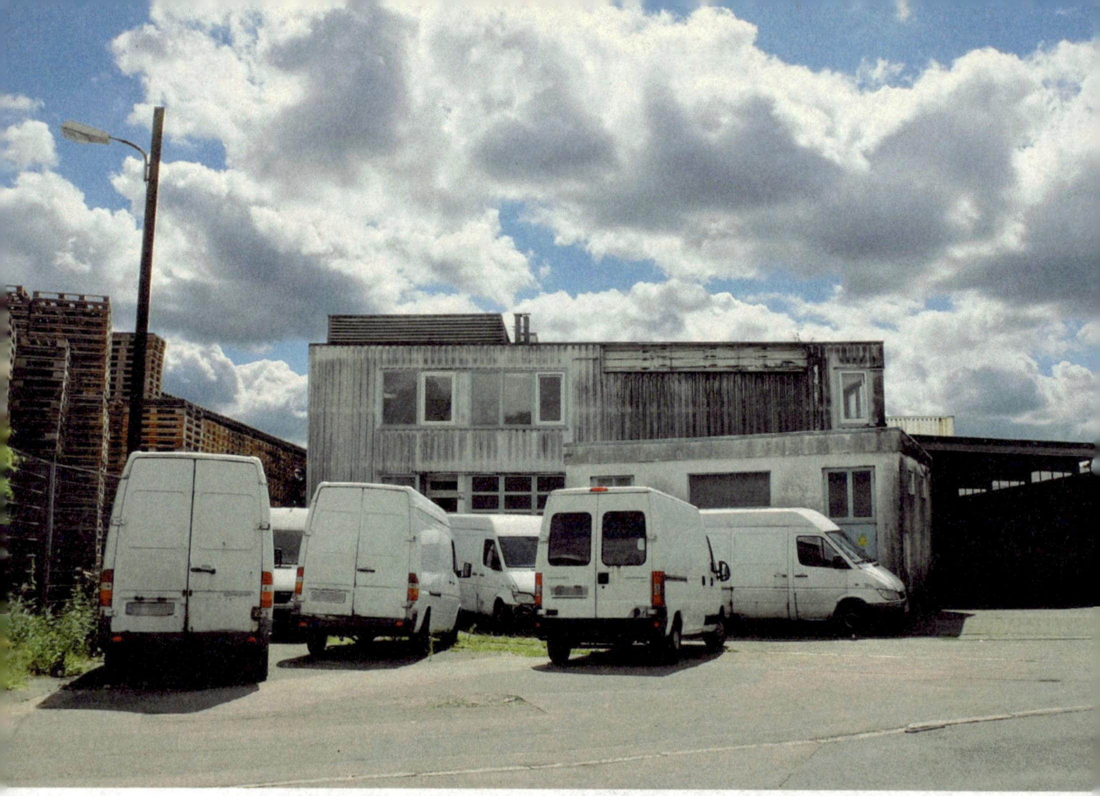

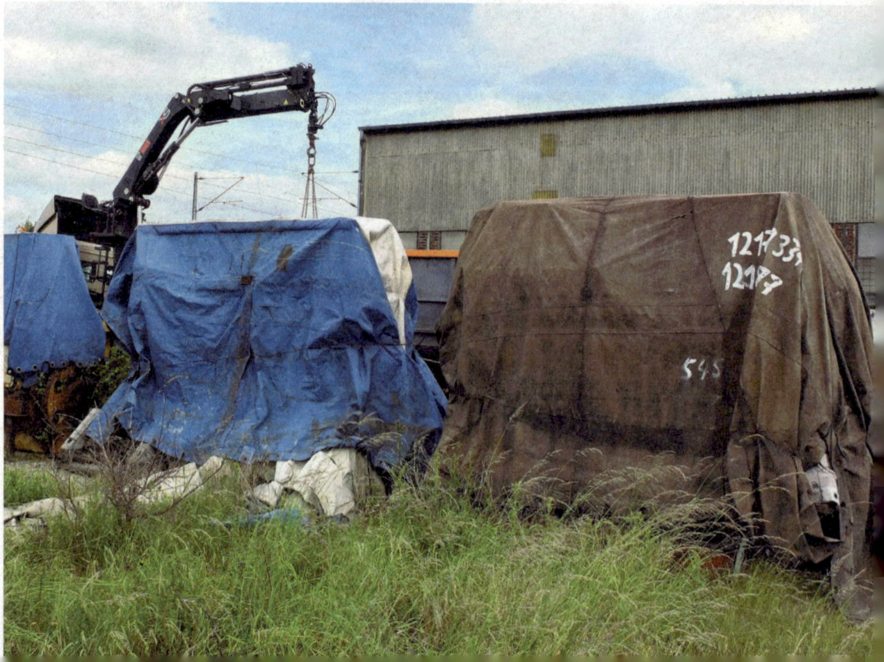

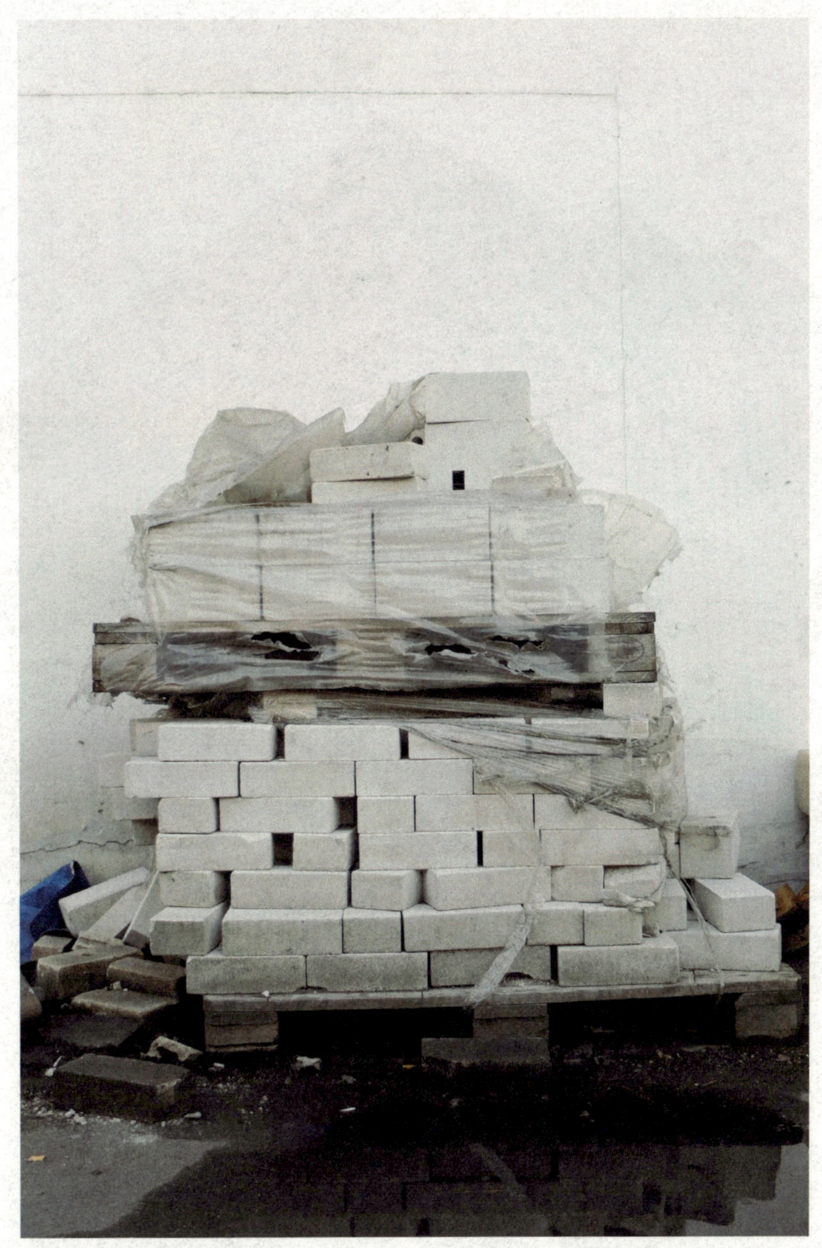

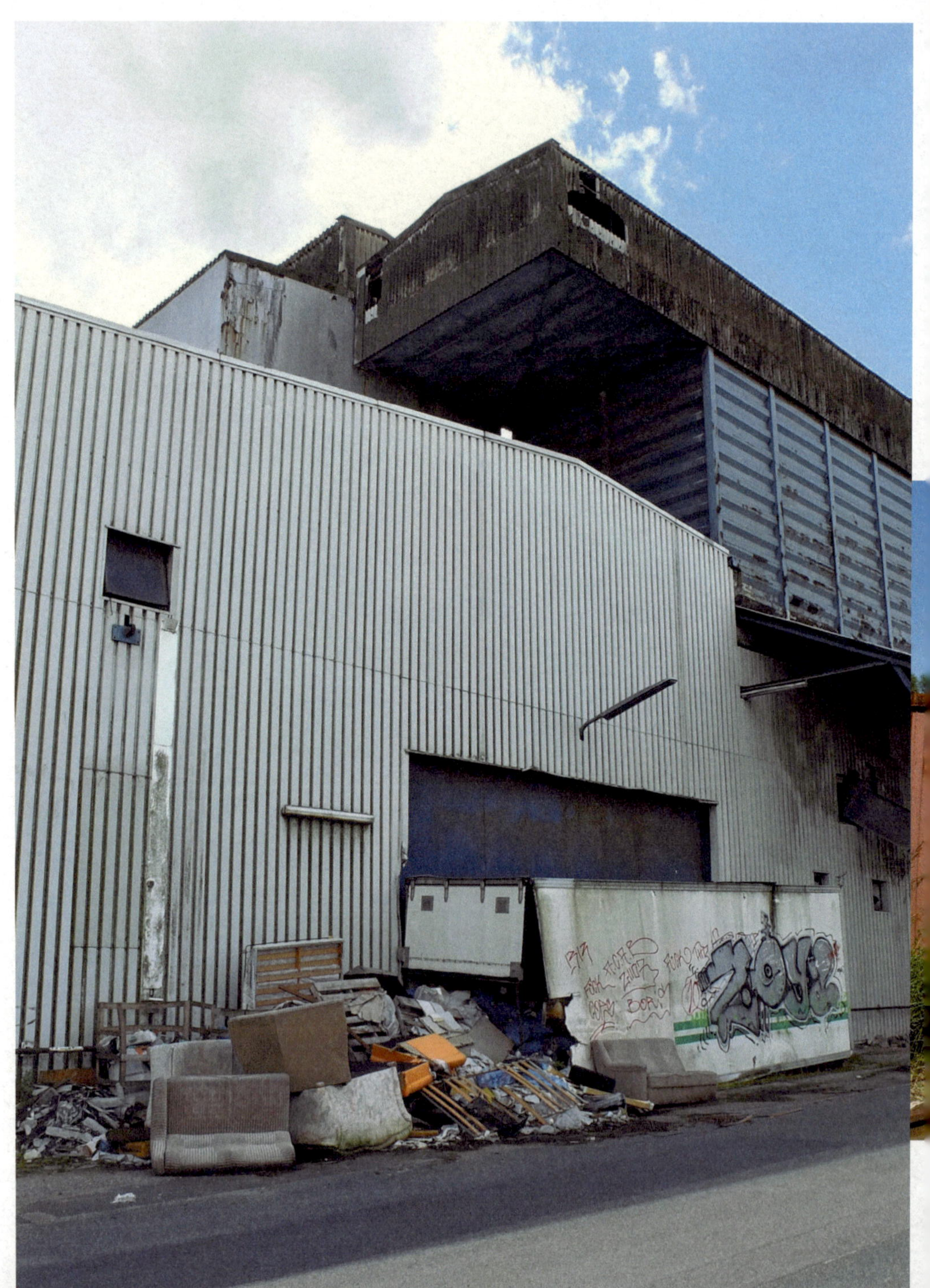

D

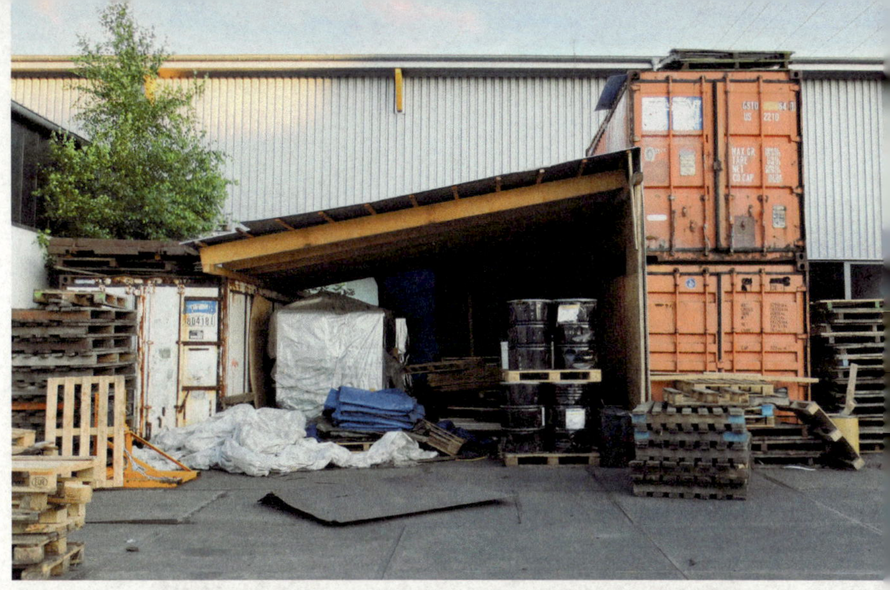

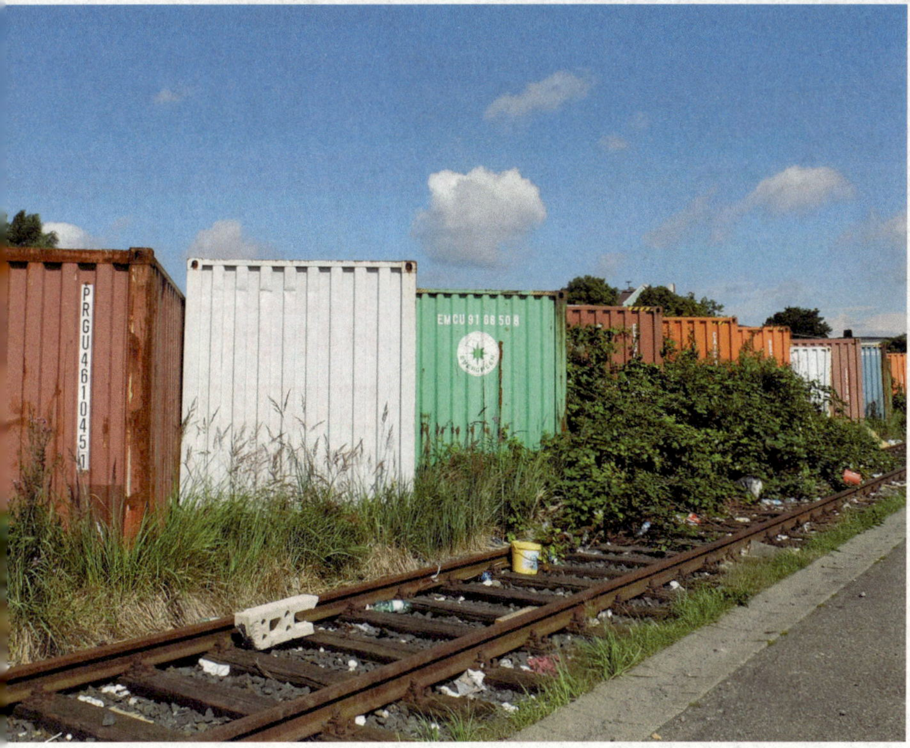

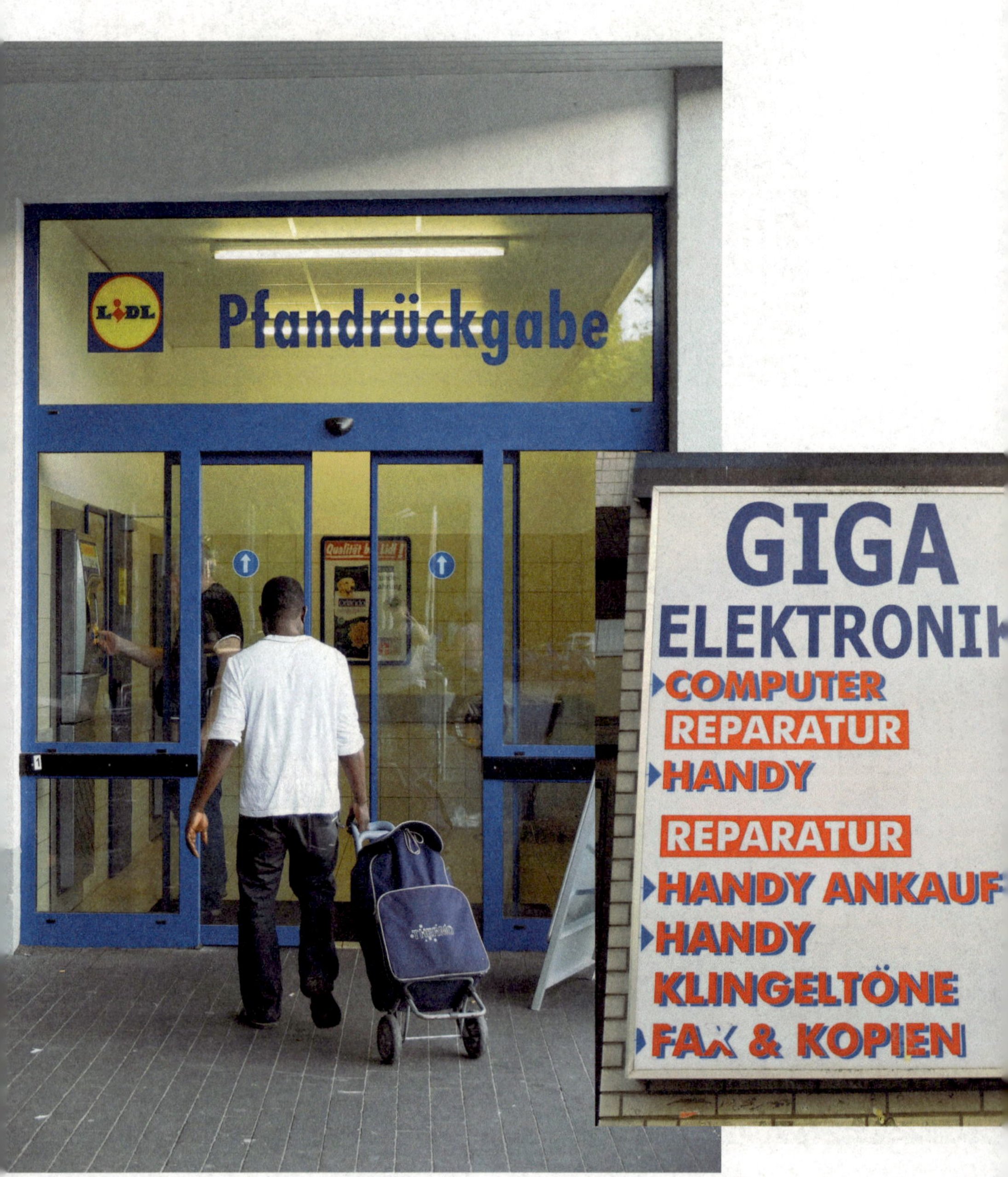
LIDL
Pfandrückgabe
Qualität bei Lidl
GIGA
ELEKTRONIK
COMPUTER
REPARATUR
HANDY
REPARATUR
HANDY ANKAUF
HANDY
KLINGELTÖNE
FAX & KOPIEN

In the meadow by the bunker or at Rotenhäuser Feld, pet owners tirelessly throw sticks. In this high summer season, they come very early in the morning before going to work, before the heat that will build up later. After work they again encounter the same dog owners. Apparently these regular meetings readily give rise to new friendships. These are repetitive routines of daily practices. This is too a recurring rhythm that apparently clearly structures the everyday life of pensioners. Several times a day they go out for a round or two with their aging, still faithful canine companions. Dogs and cats lie or sit by the window. Patiently waiting, eyes half-open, they are on the lookout for their masters and mistresses. The joy of reunion is pre-programmed. The ducks, gulls, and pigeons are fed by various animal friends. The gulls screech and gather around the former honey factory, fly down and fish out of the water the pieces of bread that a man throws into the Veringkanal. Slowly. The staged spectacle attracts passers-by who linger for a few minutes on the edge, watching the gulls close up. A grandmother with her grandson is feeding a large family of ducks. A welcome activity in the afternoon. A short break from everyday life.

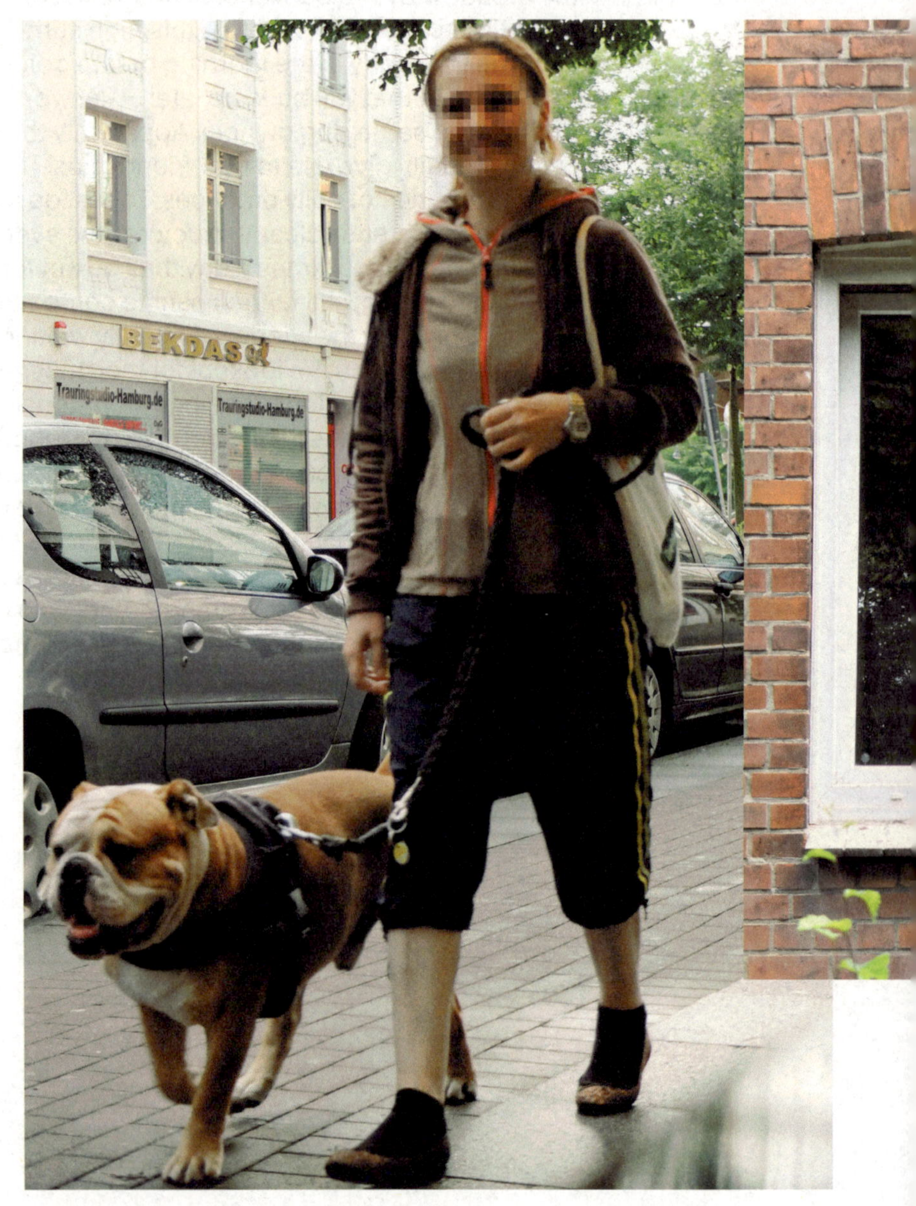

BEKDAS
Trauringstudio-Hamburg.de
Trauringstudio-Hamburg.de

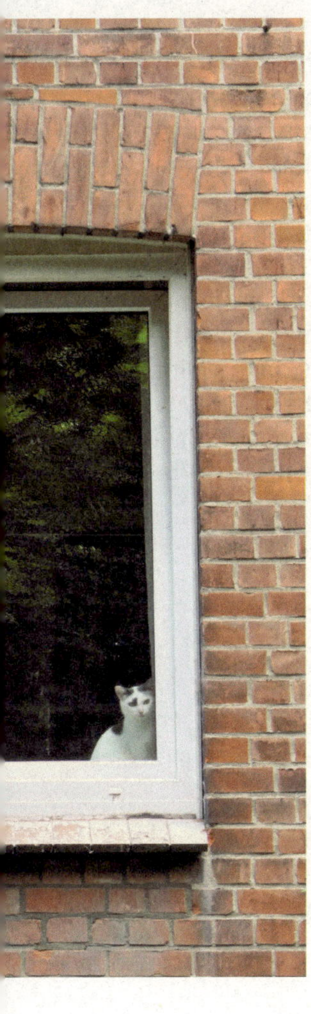

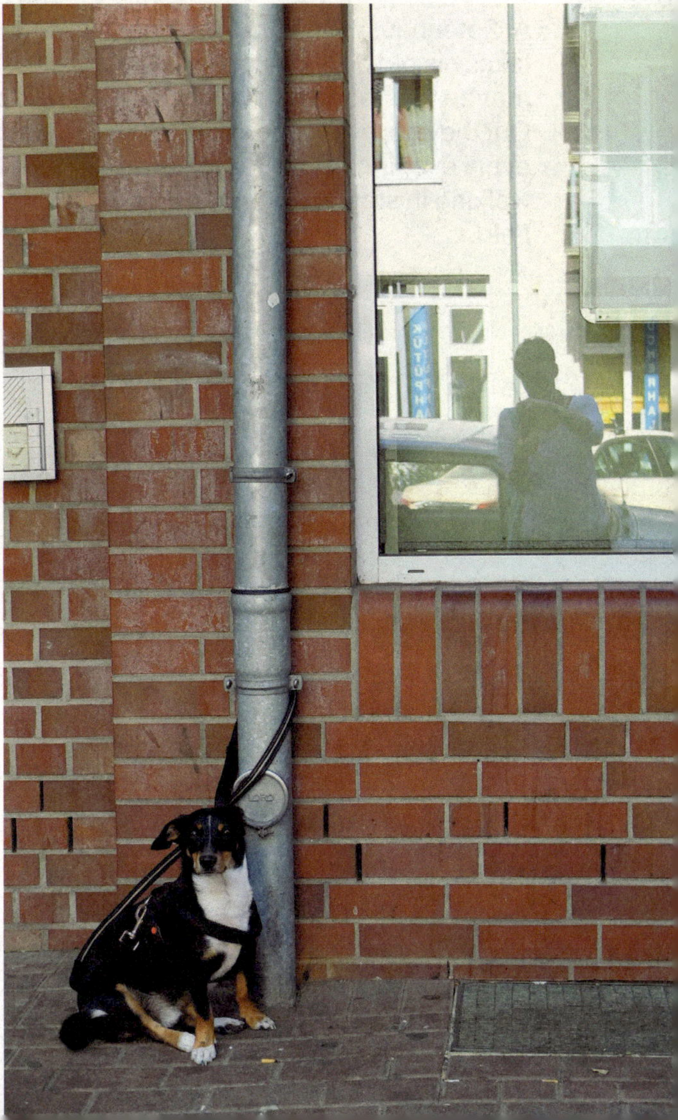

At Rotenhäuser Feld in the evening, the sun is still—just—shining.
Small, plump, and snorting, three
dogs pull their female owners
along behind them. On the big
meadow women tirelessly throw
stick after stick, watch as their
little ones run.

At Rotenhäuser Feld the neighbor
takes his old dog for a walk. One
maybe two rounds in the morning.
Out they go, every noon and
every evening. Together, leisurely
walking in step to Rotenhäuser
Feld.

The male orange cat from next
door slithers around the legs of the
man who owns the Corner Pub.
Peter, as the neighbor calls when
it's time to feed him, knows his
terrains with its hidey-holes well.

The kitchen window is closed.
The cat lady plays with the black
and white cats on the windowsill, stroking them. They wriggle
and stretch, unwavering stares
fixed on the front yard. Vis-à-vis
the UdN.

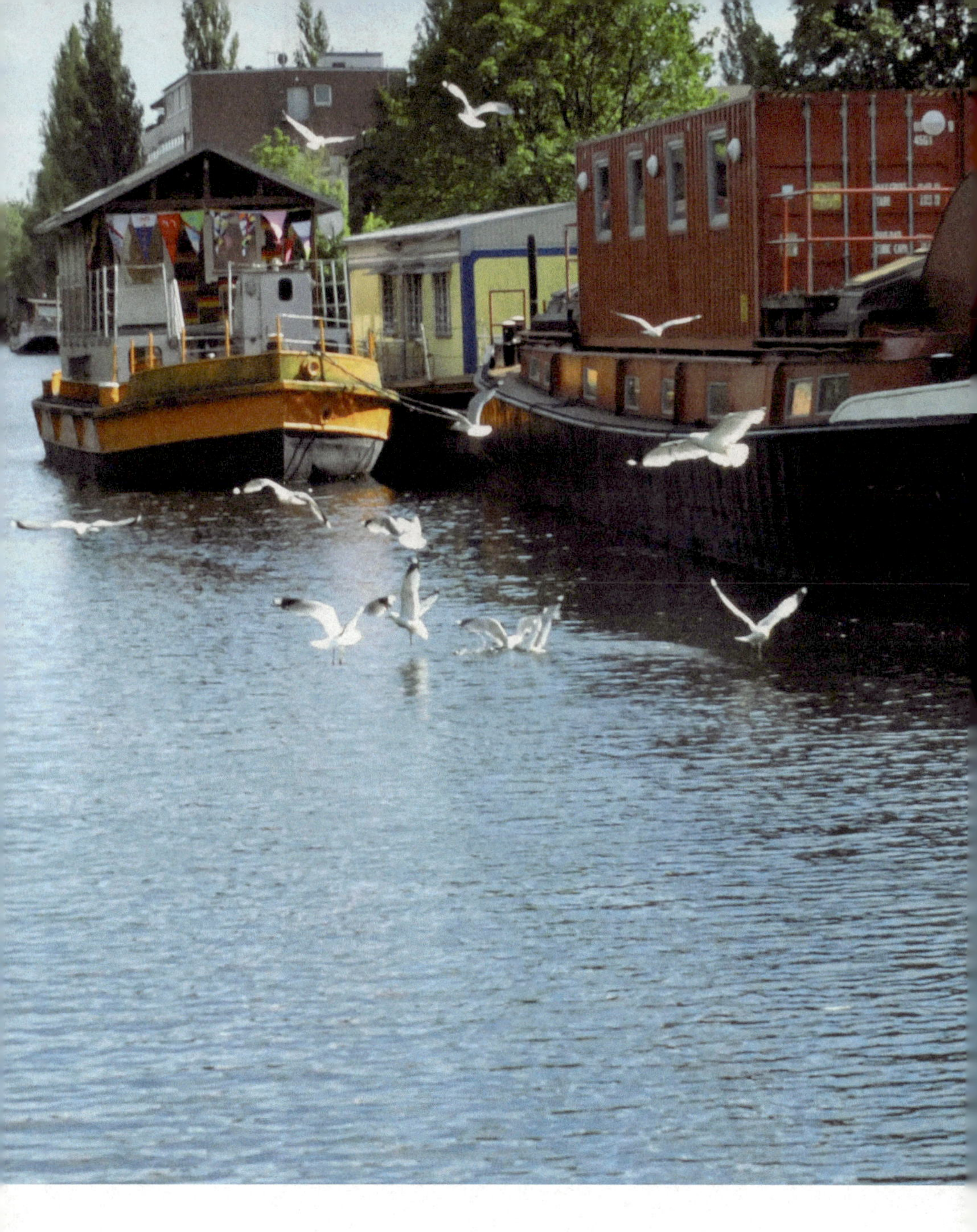

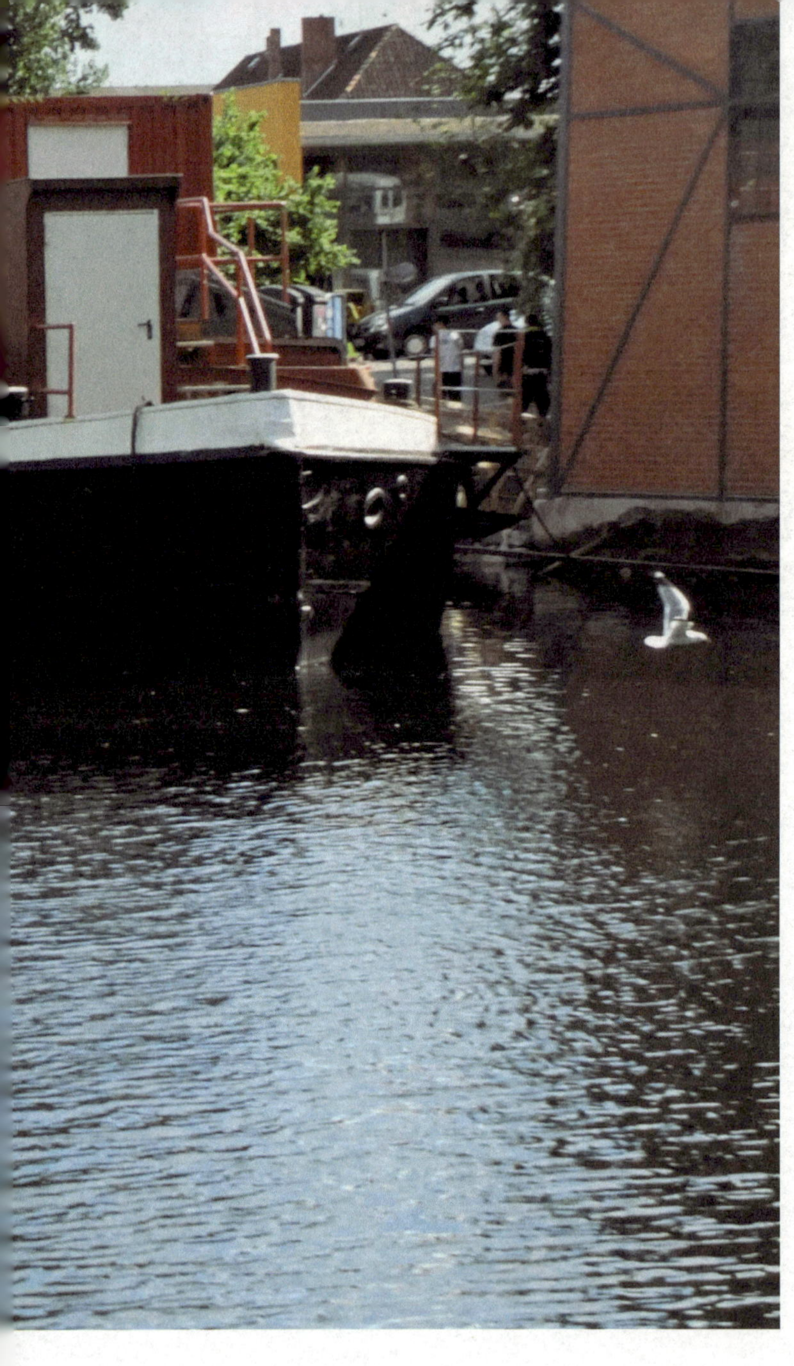

1

As a token of thanks for the work done in constructing dikes on the islands of Stillhorn und Moorwerder in the 14th and 15th centuries, the dike-builders were promised a plot of land. These settlers and their self-constructed farms were called "Höfner." The "Kötner," who moved to the islands later, bought or leased a small piece of land from the "Höfner." There they built their homes, thatch-covered cottages.

2

"Hökerei," der "Höker": Low German term for small traders.

There is a long tradition of growing vegetables on the Elbe Islands. In the 14th century, the fertile marshland was used by the first settlers[1]. The first inhabitants mainly engaged in subsistence farming and grew various cereals such as rye, wheat, barley, or oats for their own use. Cows were kept for milk and meat production. However, with the rapid population growth in Hamburg at the beginning of the 18th century, living conditions changed significantly on the Elbe Islands. Slow, laborious production of meat, milk, and cereals could no longer keep pace with increased demand, and it was crucial to switch to different agricultural methods. In the late 18th century, professionalized vegetable cultivation became established in northern Germany too. These smallholders, the "Höfner" and "Kötner," cultivated large areas, and grew very productive crops of potatoes, various legumes, and brassicas in their gardens and fields. They were known as "Greunhöker"[2]. They brought their green goods along the waterways to Hamburg's weekly market on small wooden sailing boats Connectors . Even if vegetable cultivation as an independent farmer was very difficult, and called for diligence, skill, and stamina, this sector nonetheless provided a livelihood for many people (cf. Geschichtswerkstatt Wilhelmsburg 2008: 13ff). To this day it is one of the most important economic sectors on the Elbe Islands. Meanwhile, the face of agriculture has changed. Greenhouses and polytunnels protect the delicate vegetables from the harsh marine climate. Larger, sometimes automated devices for harvesting or farming the fields facilitate work in most places. But manual labor is still in demand. Many businesses are supported by harvest workers from neighboring EU countries. Nowadays "Greunhöker" sell their wares at the Hamburg Wholesale Market, local farmers' markets, or in grocery stores. In addition to the most popular types of vegetables, such as spinach, lettuce, fennel, rhubarb, cabbage, or cucumber, they also produce cut flowers. The various structures and textures of leaves are woven together into a striped mosaic on the southern tip of the Elbe Islands. In addition to the large fields of vegetable crops, I notice small-scale "Greunhöker" activities scattered across the island. In the front garden of the houses, in the gardens of the mosques, in the

Wilhelmsburg intercultural garden, and on allotment plots, specific cultivation methods and individual variety compilations can be found as well as ornamental twists. Various varieties of runner beans, peppers, tomatoes, and Swiss chard are cultivated. Summer flowers like gladioli, zinnias, or bushy marigolds seem very familiar and at home in this place.

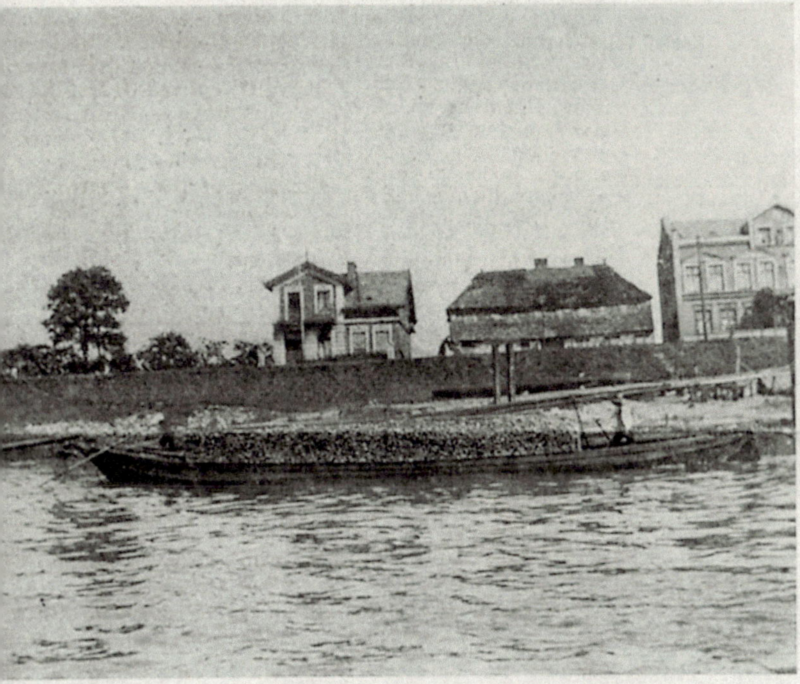

Ein Gemüseweer passiert den Reiherstieg. Links das Doktorhaus

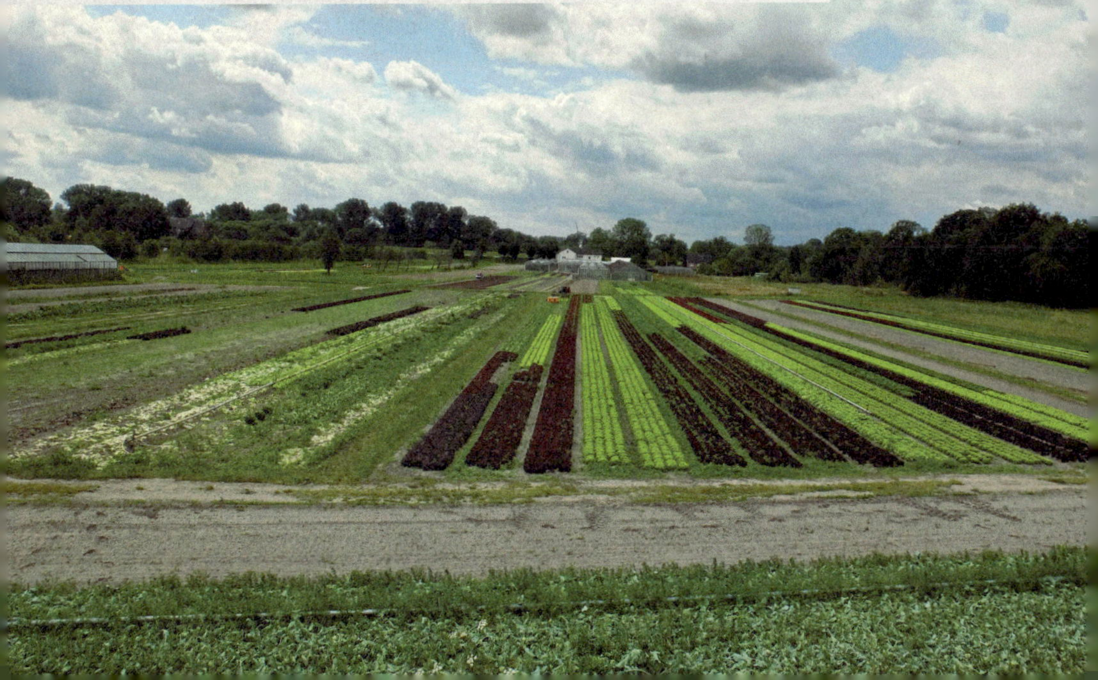

August Cohrs 80 Jahre alt

Seinen 80. Geburtstag feiert heute August Cohrs. Er stammt aus einer alten Wilhelmsburger „Grünhöker-Familie" (so nannte man früher die Gemüsebauern unserer Elbinsel) und erfreut sich bester Gesundheit. Seine Jugend verlebte er auf der Landwirtschaft der Familie am Buscherweg (früher Im Busch 66). Später übernahm August Cohrs den Betrieb von seinem Onkel Hein und stand nun ganz im beschwerlichen Leben der damaligen „Grünhöker". Denn um den Boden zu verbessern, schöpfte man Schlamm aus der Dove-Elbe und transportierte ihn mit einem großen Kahn zum Bestimmungsort. Auch August Cohrs arbeitete mit diesem Verfahren, mit dem sich schon Generationen von Gemüsebauern abplagten.

Trotz vieler Schicksalsschläge blieb August Cohrs immer ein hilfsbereiter Nachbar, der immer dann Hand anlegt, wenn Hilfe not tut; auch ist er jederzeit zu einem kleinen Klönschnack bereit. Im Rentenalter hat sich das nicht geändert. Besonders im Wilhelmsburger Heimatmuseum engagiert er sich und ist während der Öffnungszeiten stets da, um Aufsicht zu führen und für Ordnung zu sorgen.

So steht sein Leben noch immer im Zeichen stetiger Hilfsbereitschaft für die Nachbarn und die Allgemeinheit. Dafür sei ihm auch an dieser Stelle gedankt. Viele weitere frohe Lebensjahre, Gesundheit und Schaffenskraft wünschen wir ihm. Hol di fuchtig, August!　　　WZ

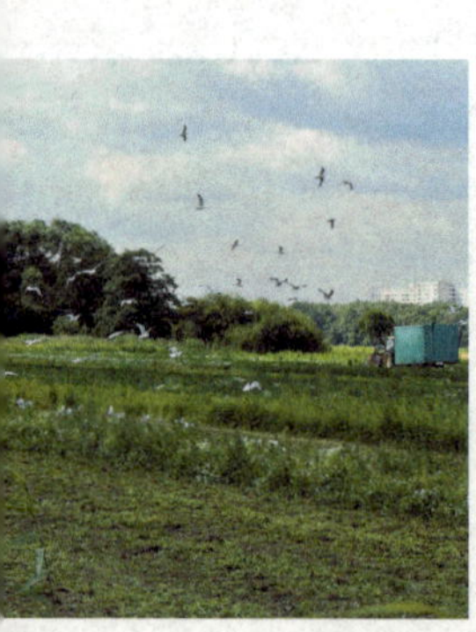

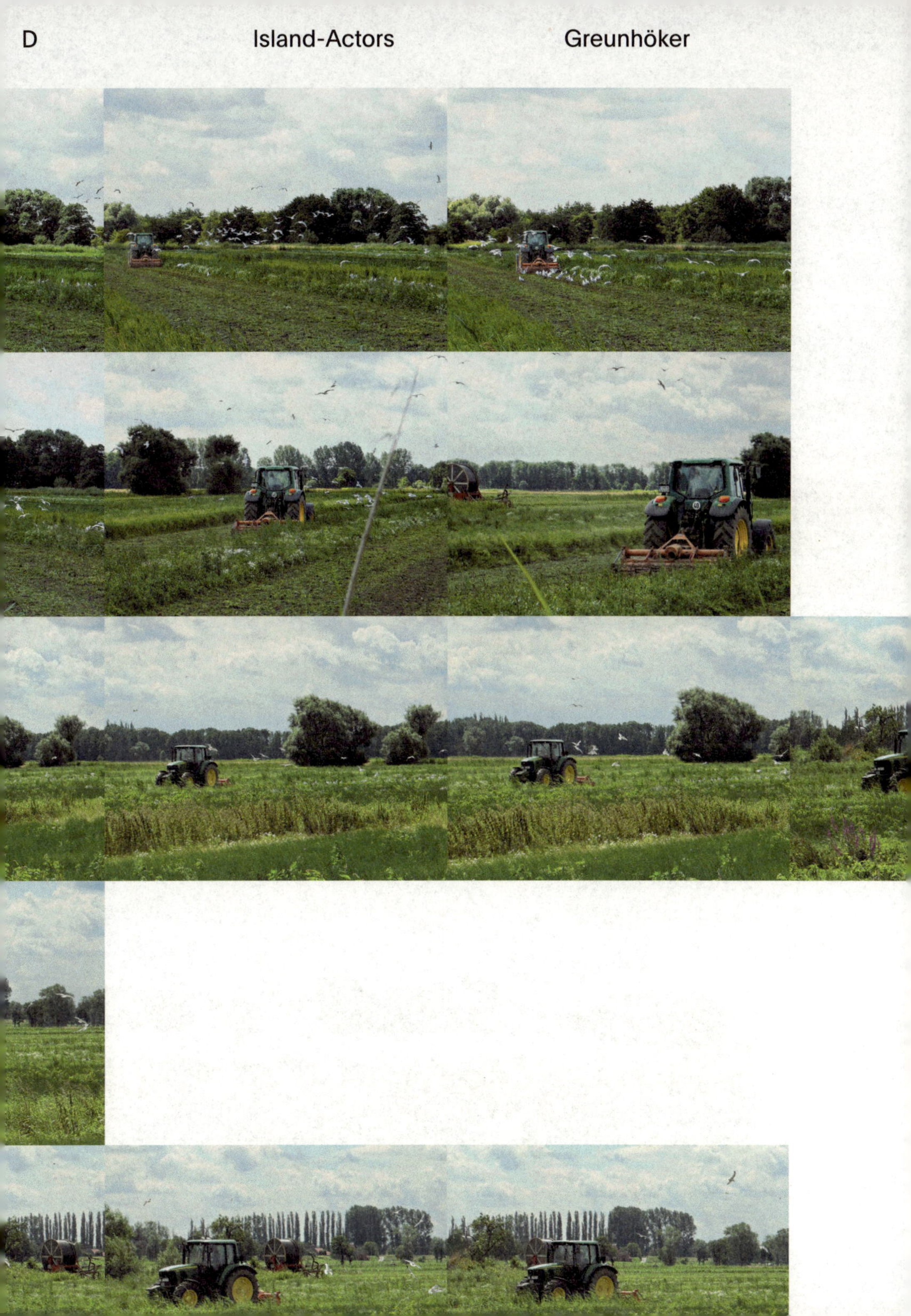

D
Island-Actors
Greunhöker

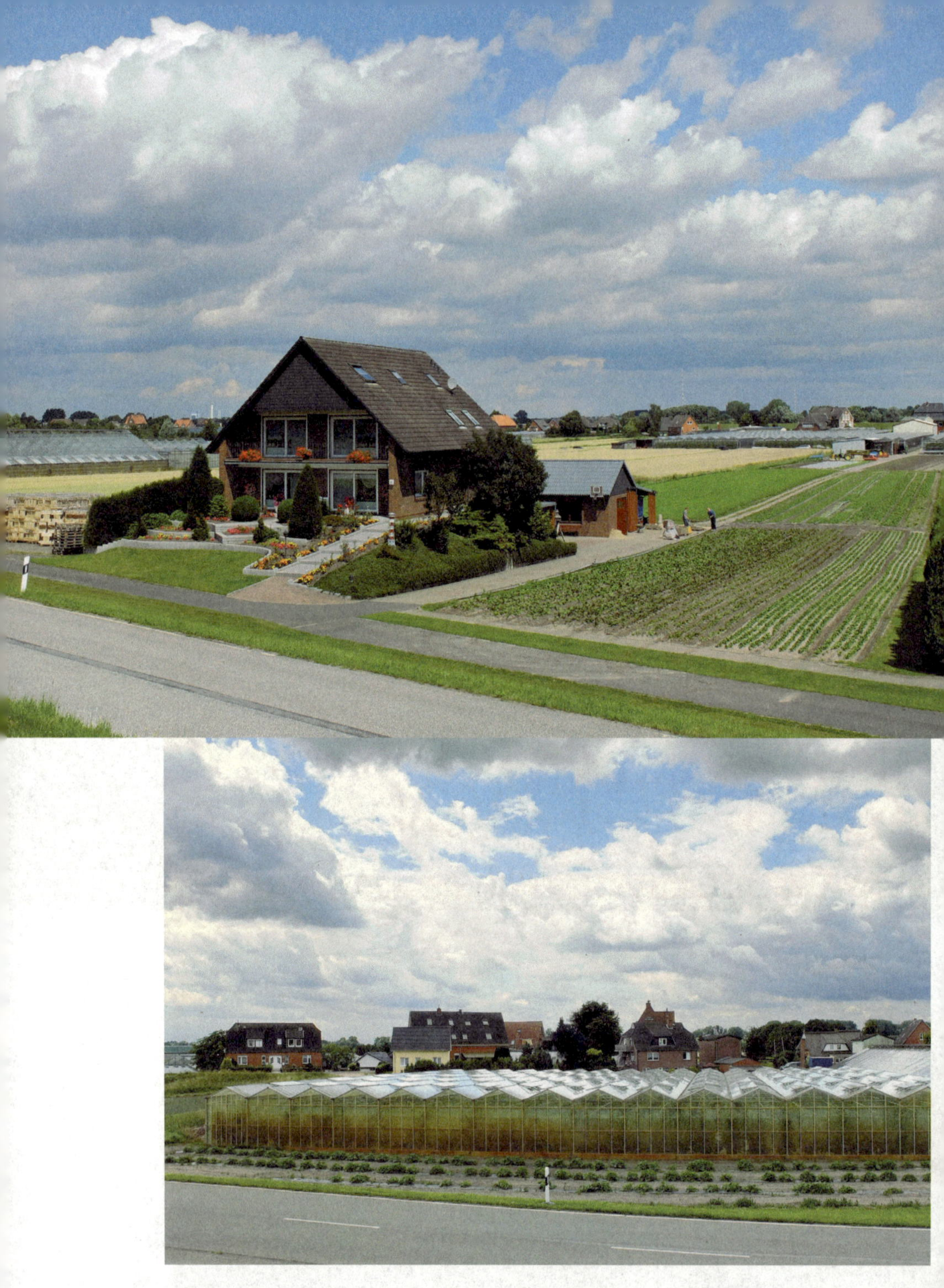

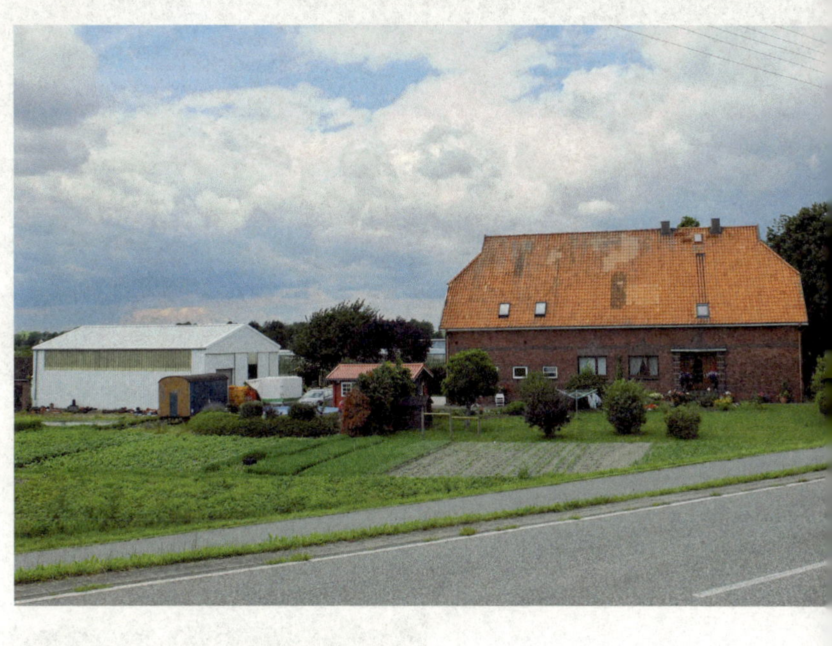

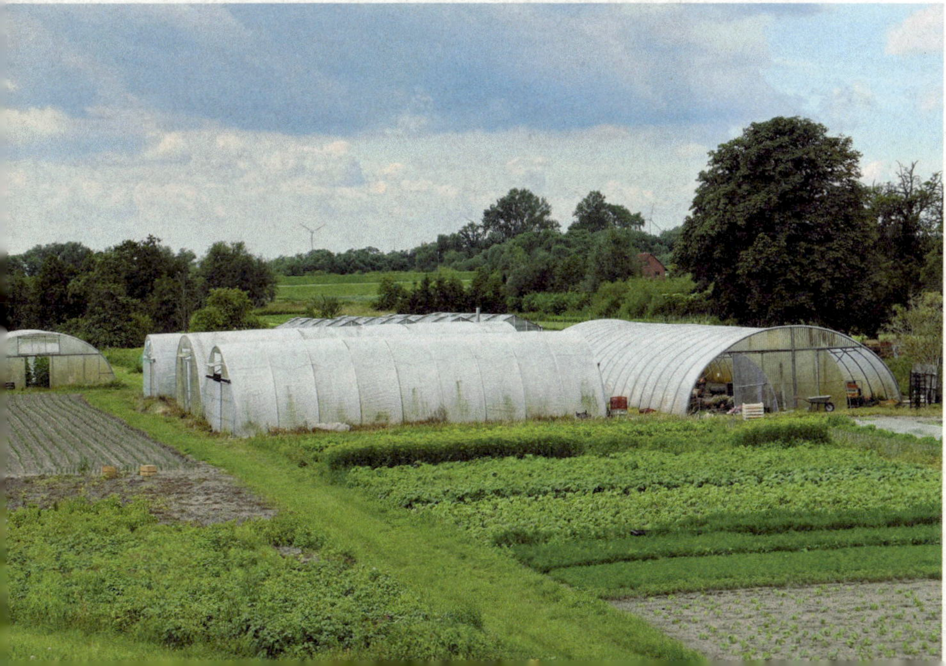

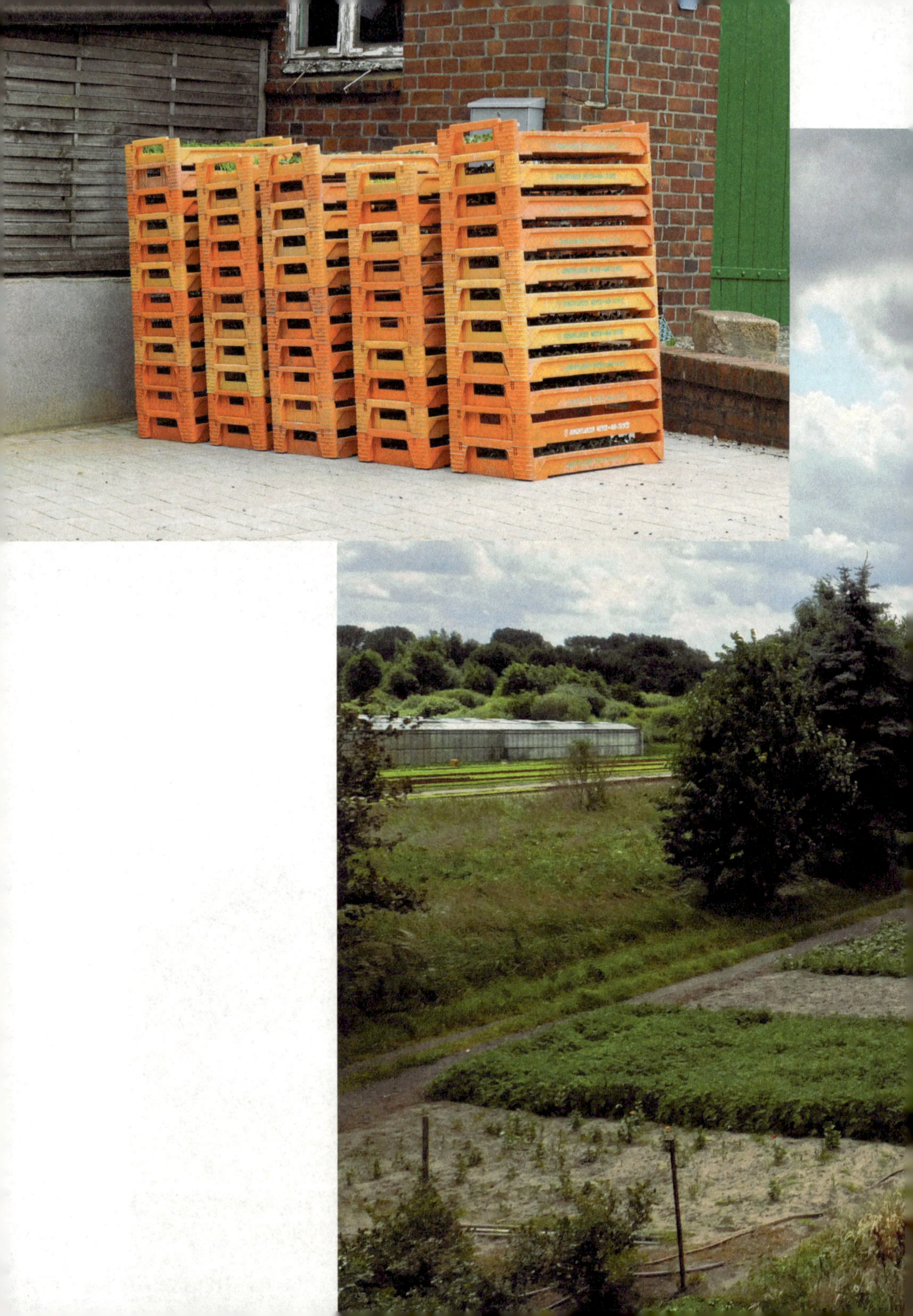

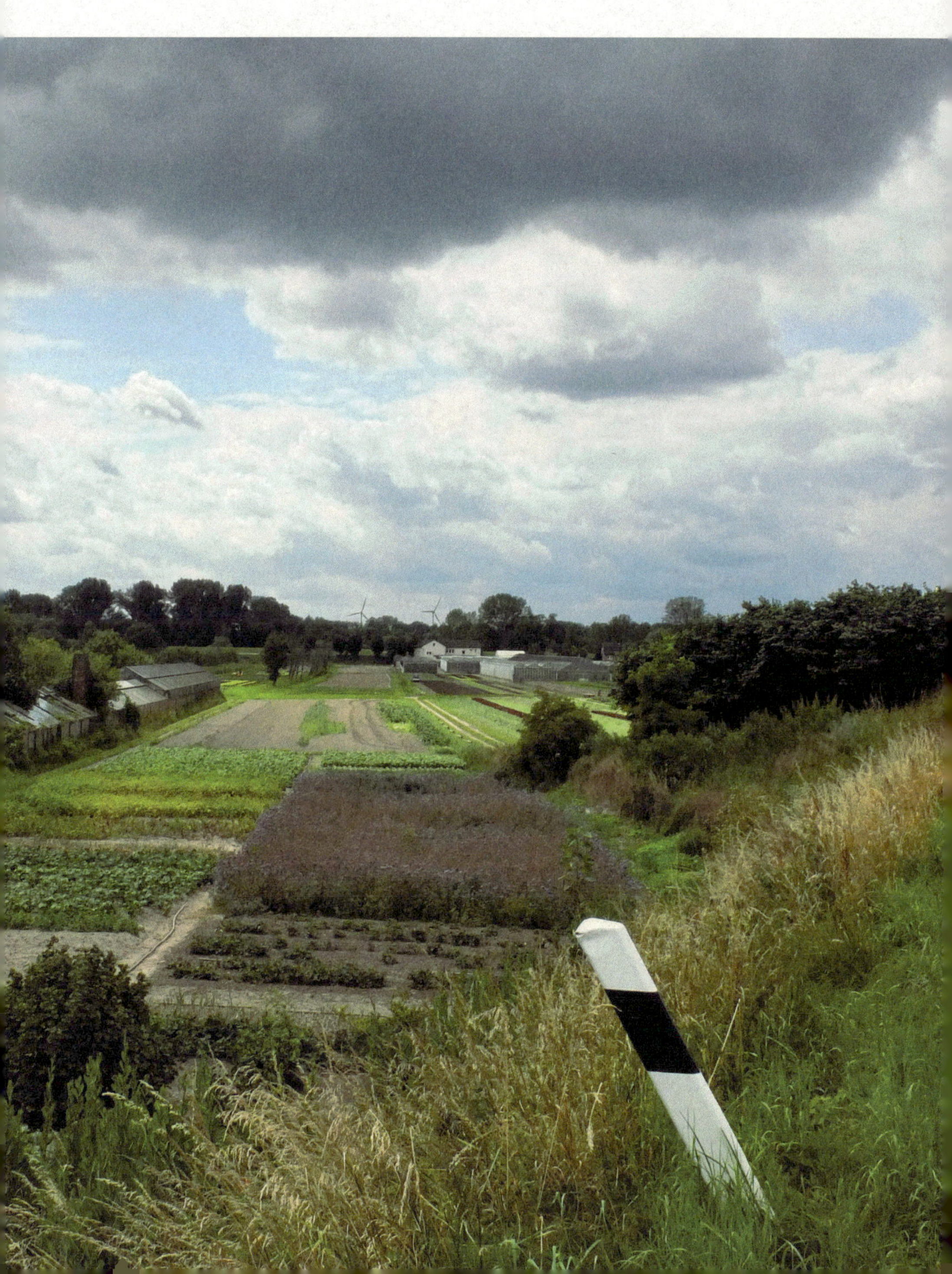

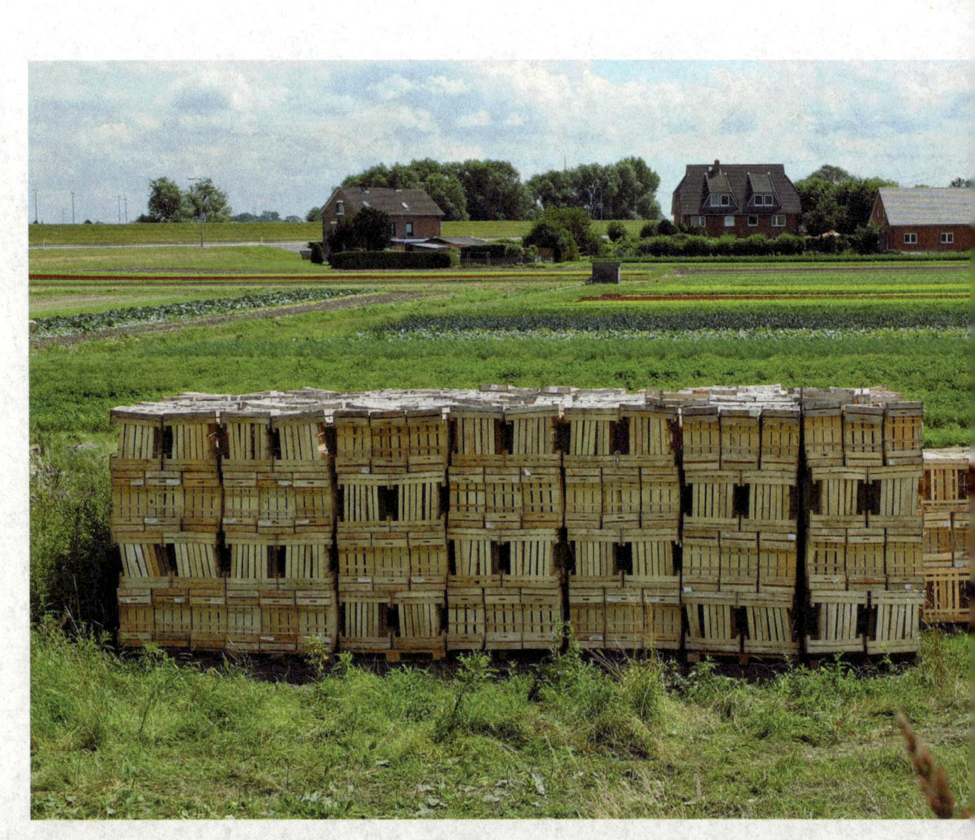

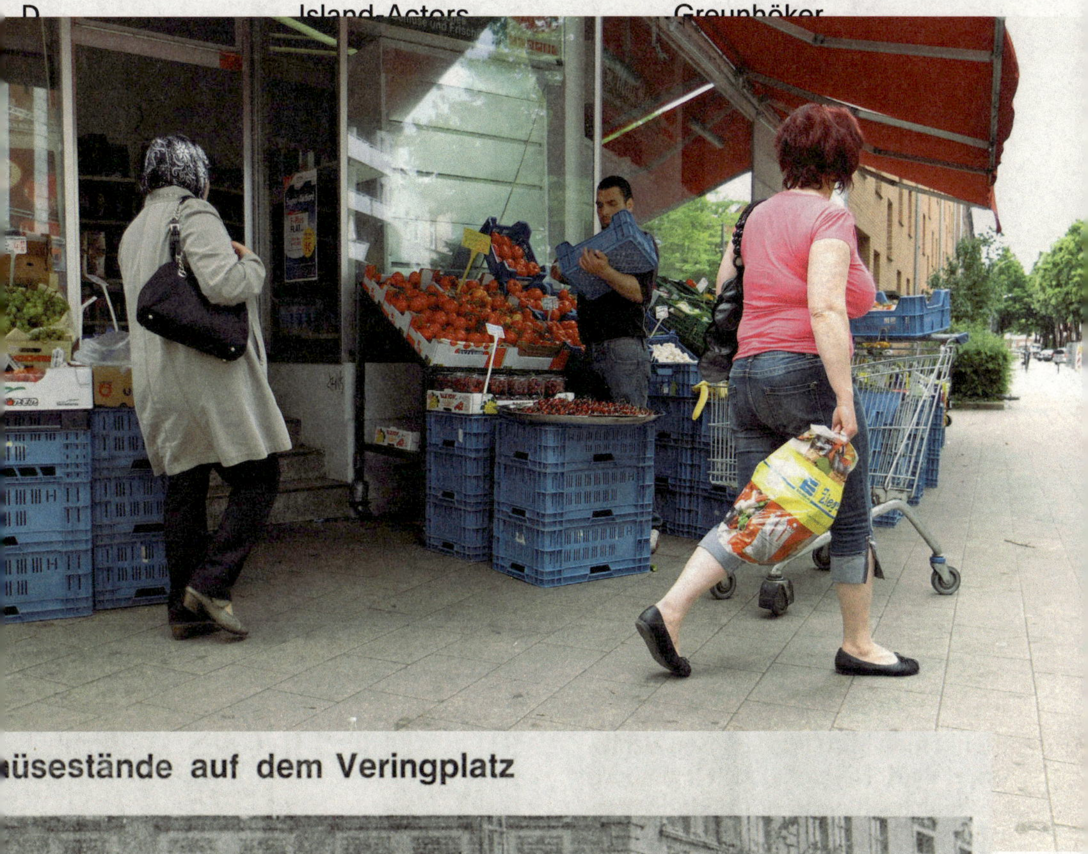

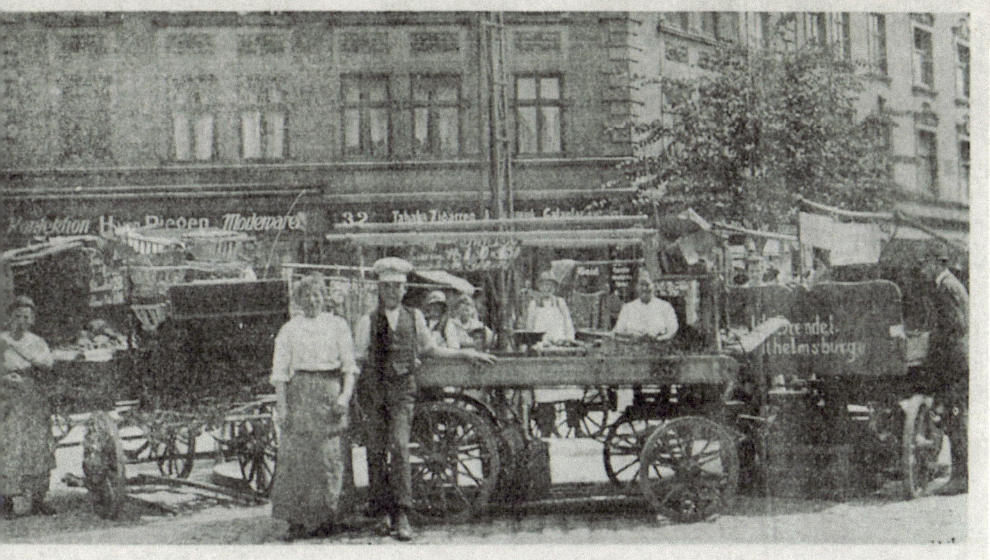

...üsestände auf dem Veringplatz

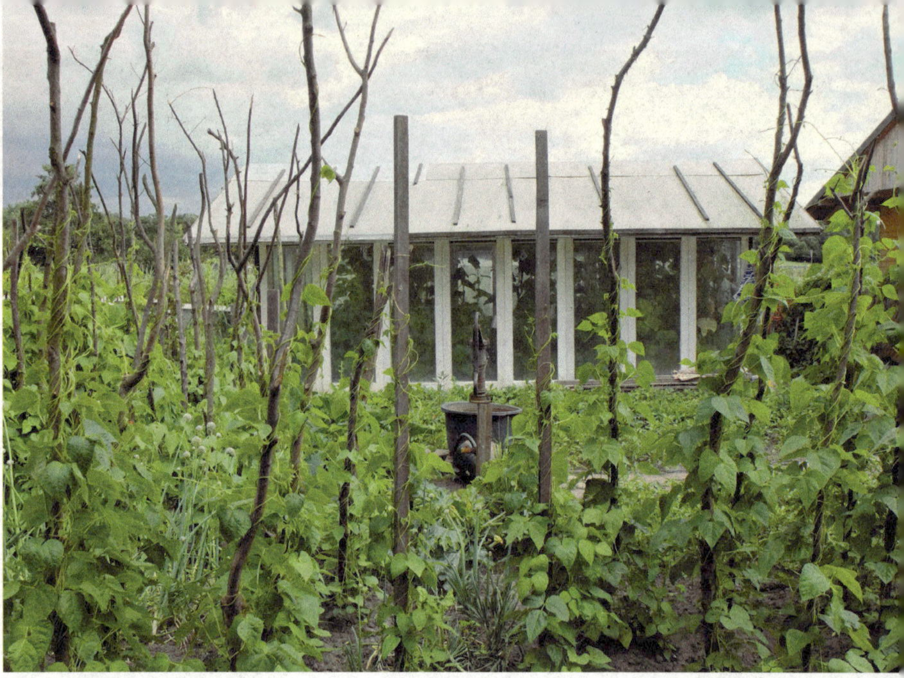

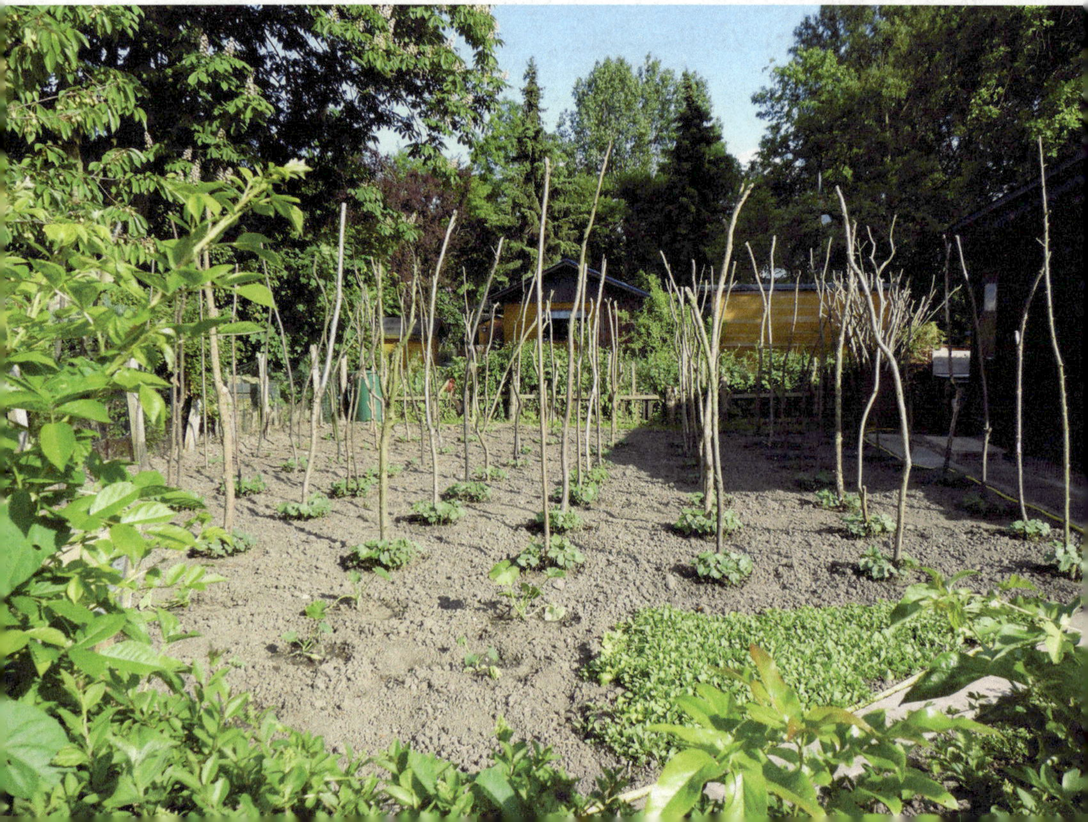

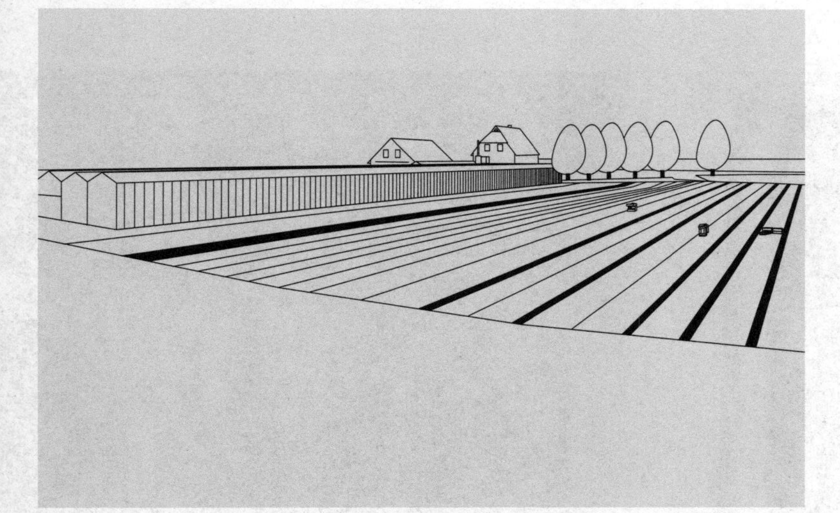

... Circular saws and the screech of gulls, tractors are making their way up and down the fields, brightly-colored lettuces are being harvested. Greenhouses and ornately decorated farmhouses dot the landscape. Südspitze is so very different from the other islands. The green in the color green around here glows bright. Here it is so incredibly lush, fertile, and wide-open ...

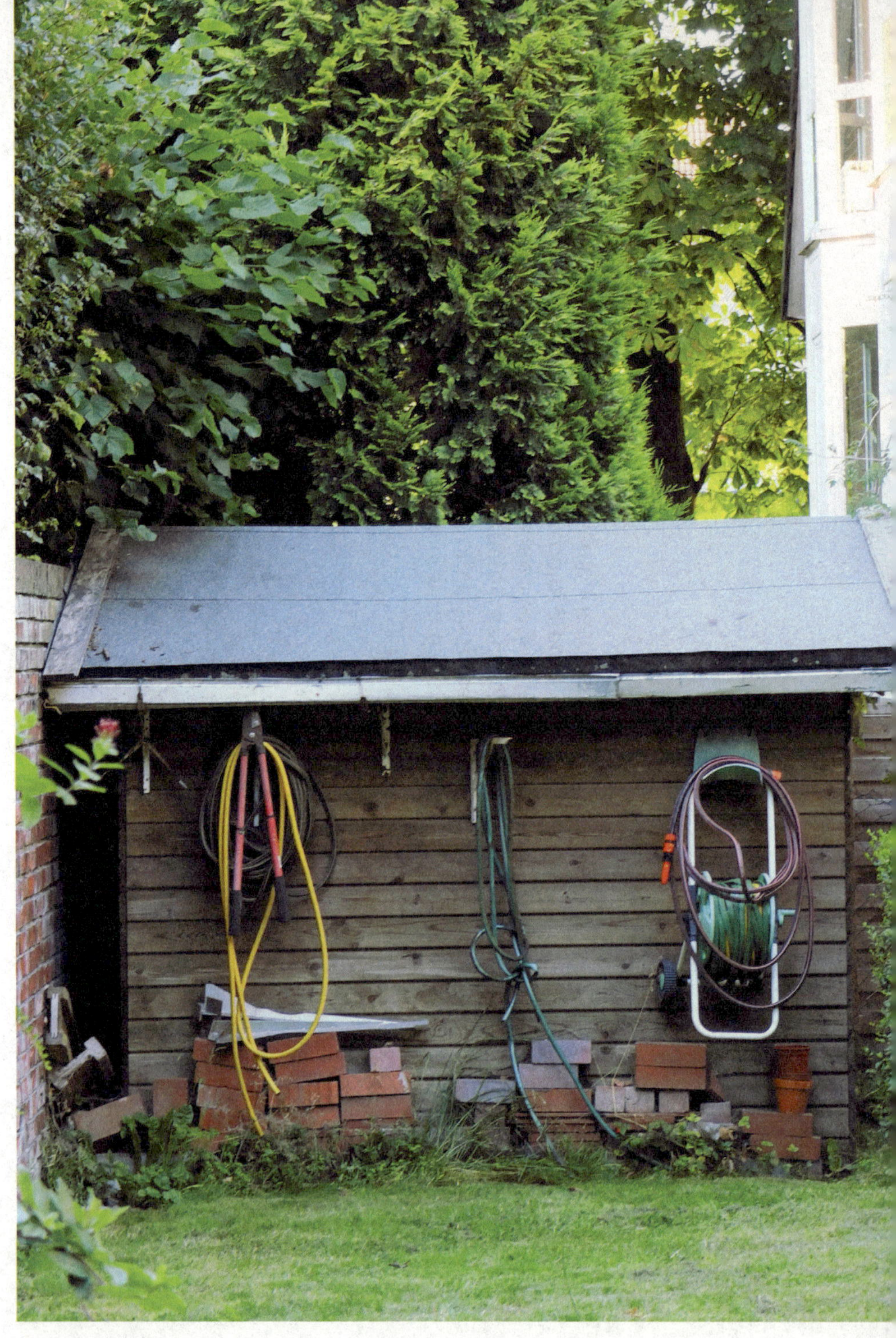

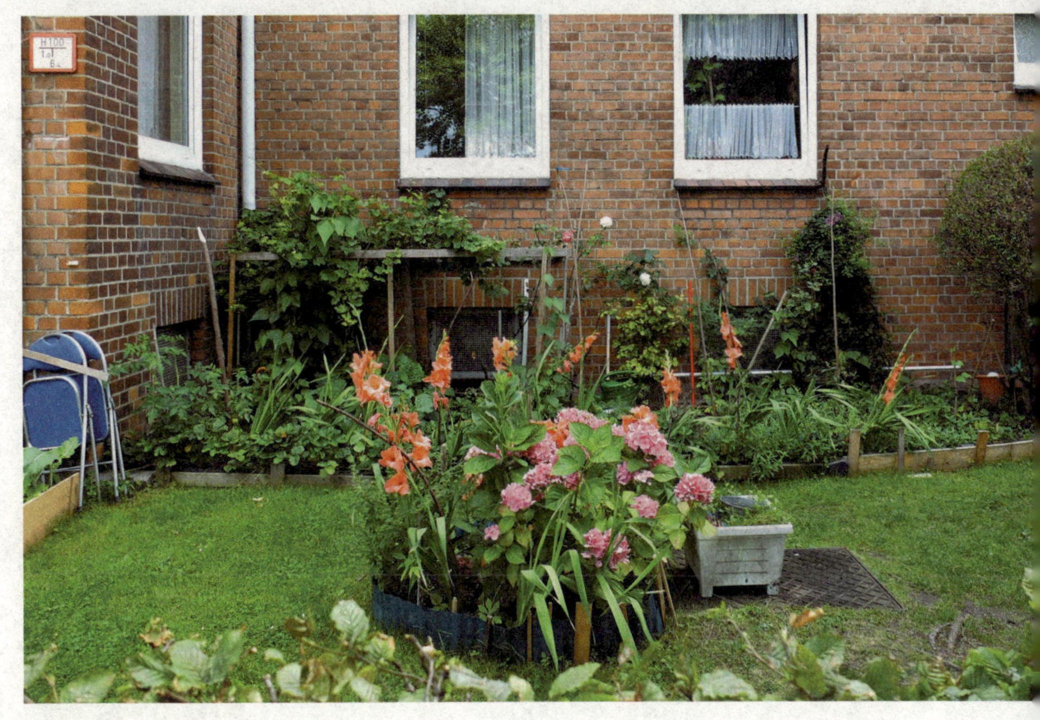

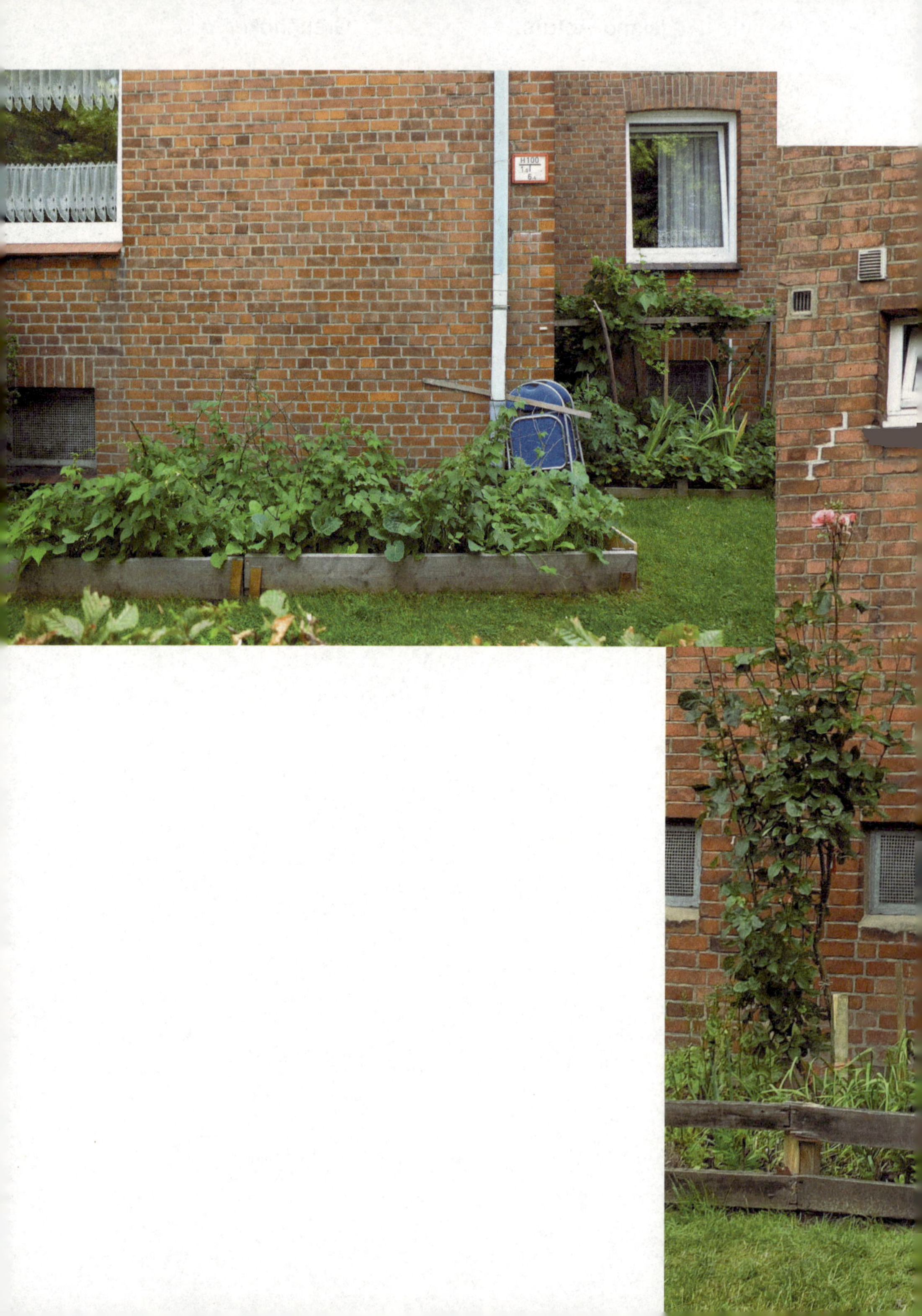

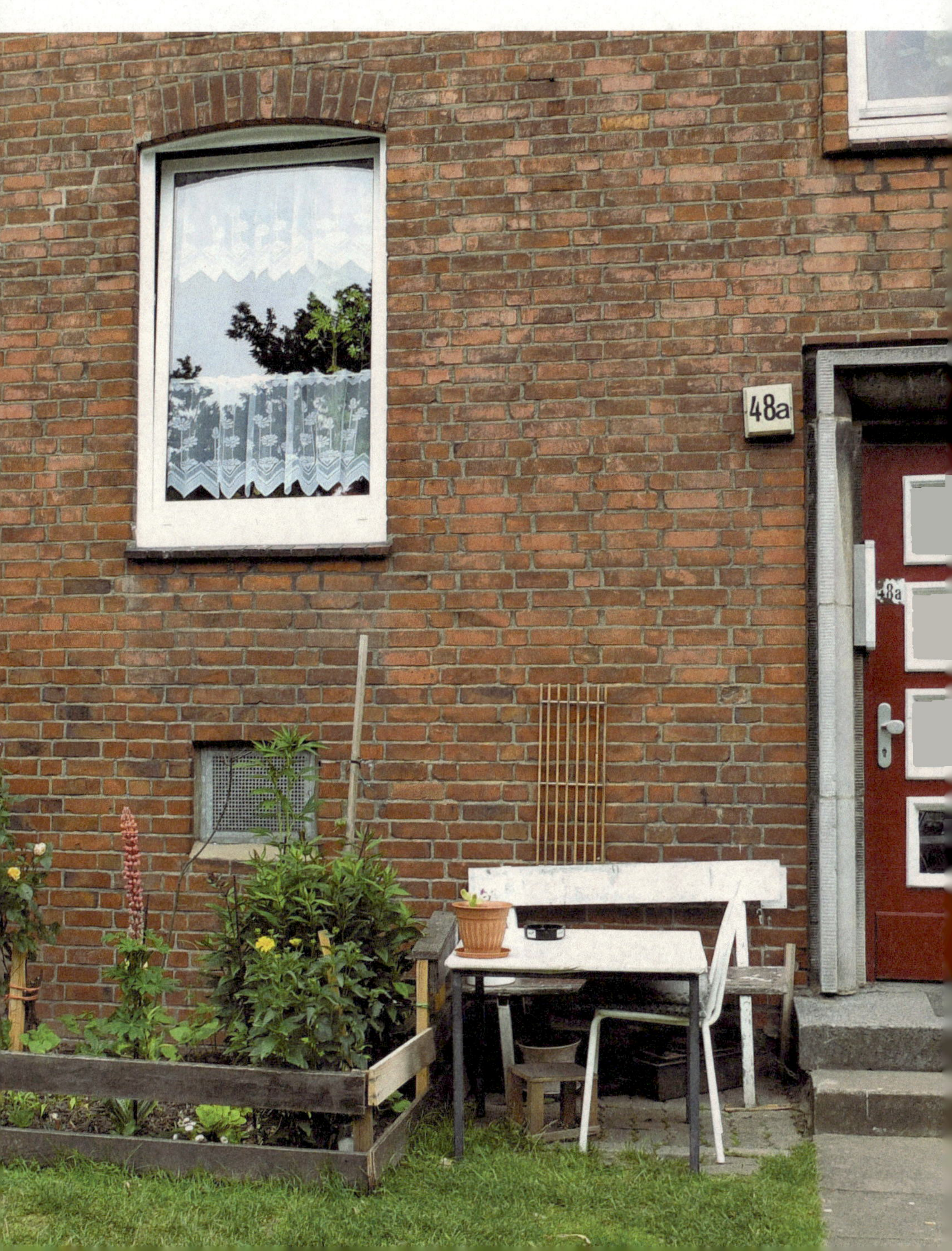
48a

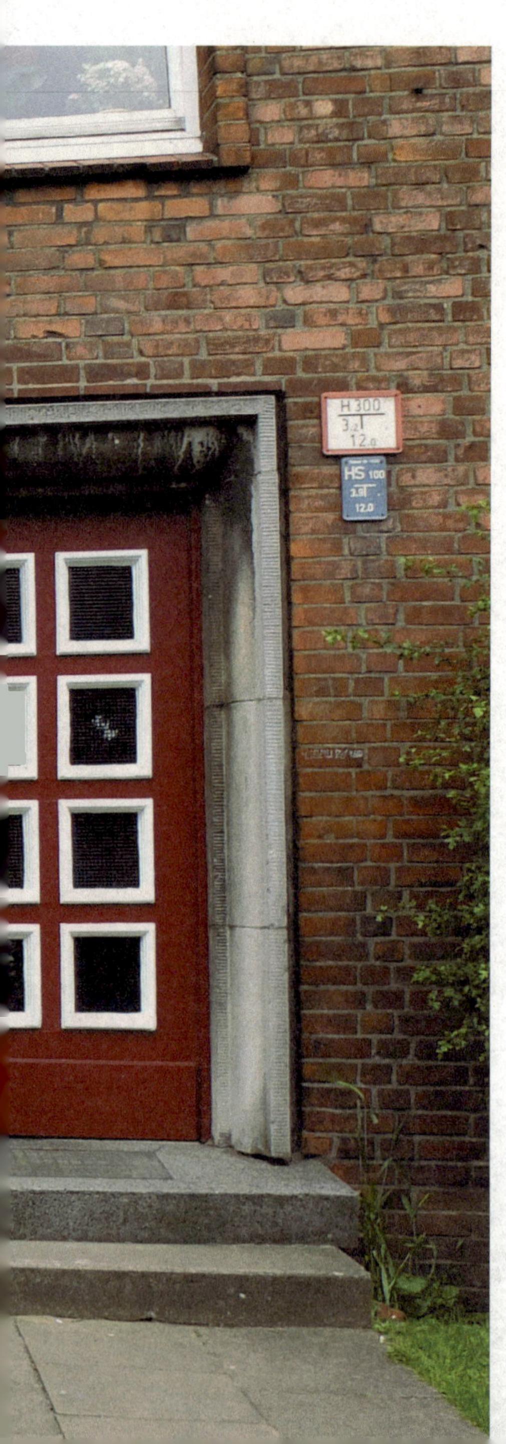

Full-time Mothers
—Free-time Fathers

Mothers take their toddlers to the nursery. Mothers take
their children to school, later they pick them up from there.
Mothers spend the afternoons in the park and playgrounds.
Watching the playing children from the benches. Food
and drinks are constantly available. They call their children
over from time to time, tell them to behave, the mothers
are strict, even loud. Mothers sit together with other mothers
in a circle of friends during the afternoons in various cafes,
rocking their children to sleep. It is a short break for everyone.
Mothers walk home with food-filled shopping bags, push-
ing all kinds of very well equipped baby strollers from various
manufacturers. Getting skillfully on and off the bus or the train
with them. Waiting silently until someone finally lets them
pass. Firmly holding the older sibling's hand all the while, or
with the child safely in sight. Carrying their children around
with various sling techniques. African women mostly
carry their infants on their backs. German mothers, however,
transport their children bound to their chests. Turkish women
opt exclusively for strollers, often models in muted colors.
At the traffic lights mothers distribute pacifiers, bottles, simit
rings, or rattling toys. The mothers can take off various items
of their children's clothing or put them back on again with
one hand. They are (im)patient, comforting their children and
talking on the phone at the same time. I see expectant
mothers too. Often. The fathers' faces beam and shine. After
work or on the weekends they proudly carry their youngest
offspring in their arms. The daughter is wearing a Sunday
dress, the father a suit. Small children, barefoot, take their first
steps in the grass holding their fathers' hands. They play
football with them, chase after the ball together. Happy about
every goal or each step. Fathers tease their sons. Playfully
testing their strength at times. They take breaks together,
drinking from a water bottle and cutting a melon into chunks.
The little son sits in his father's expensive car and plays with
the steering wheel, with the engine running. In the carport of
a newly built estate the colorful tricycle is parked next to the
father's motorcycle. The child's plastic green John Deere stands
next to the large, black, professional gas barbecue in a garden on the same estate. Toys for large and small. Grandfathers

have a man-to-man talk with their grandsons. Fathers take their boys to the mosque on Friday. And fathers go around the block in the evening with their children once again, buying them small plastic toys filled with colorful candies along the way.

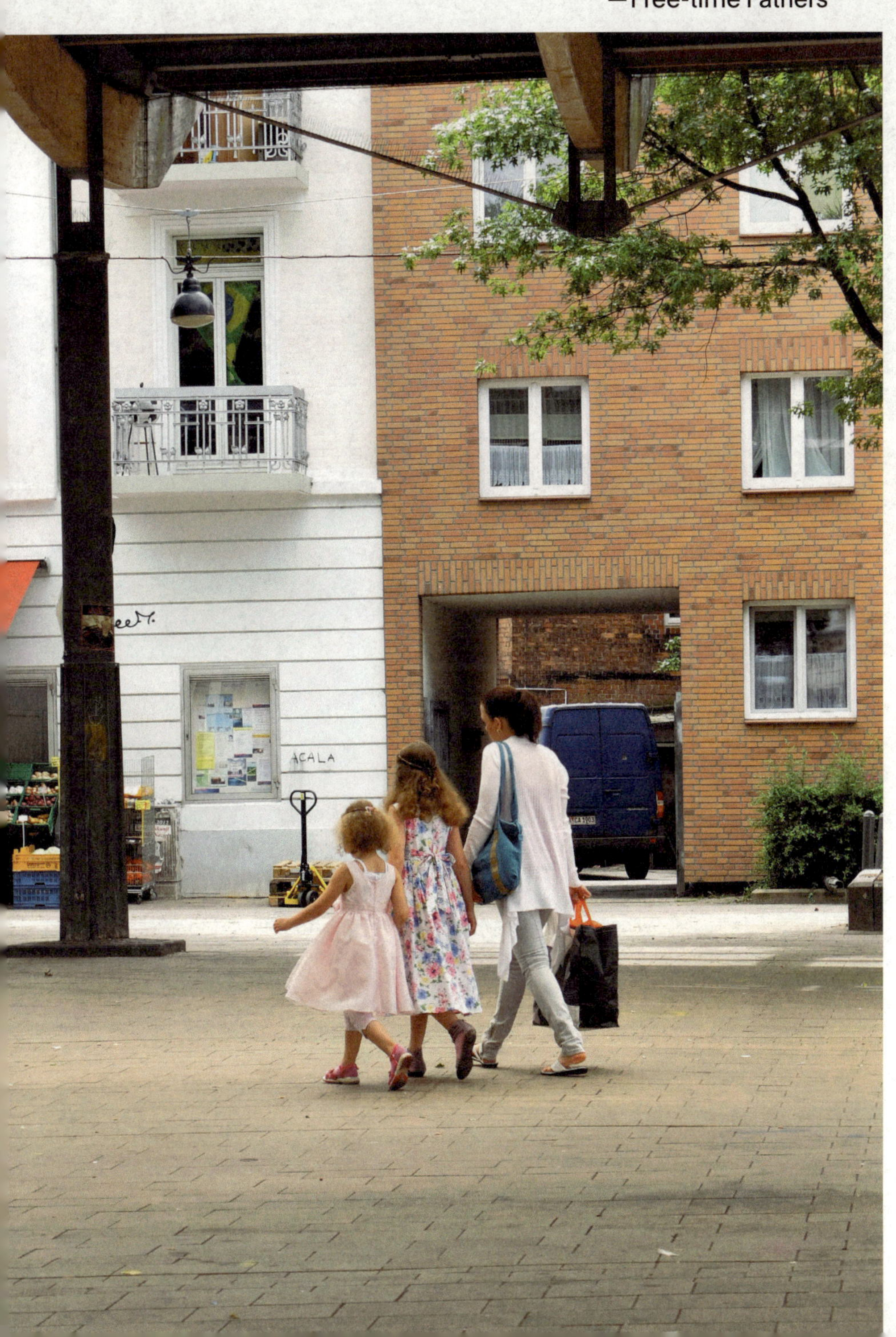

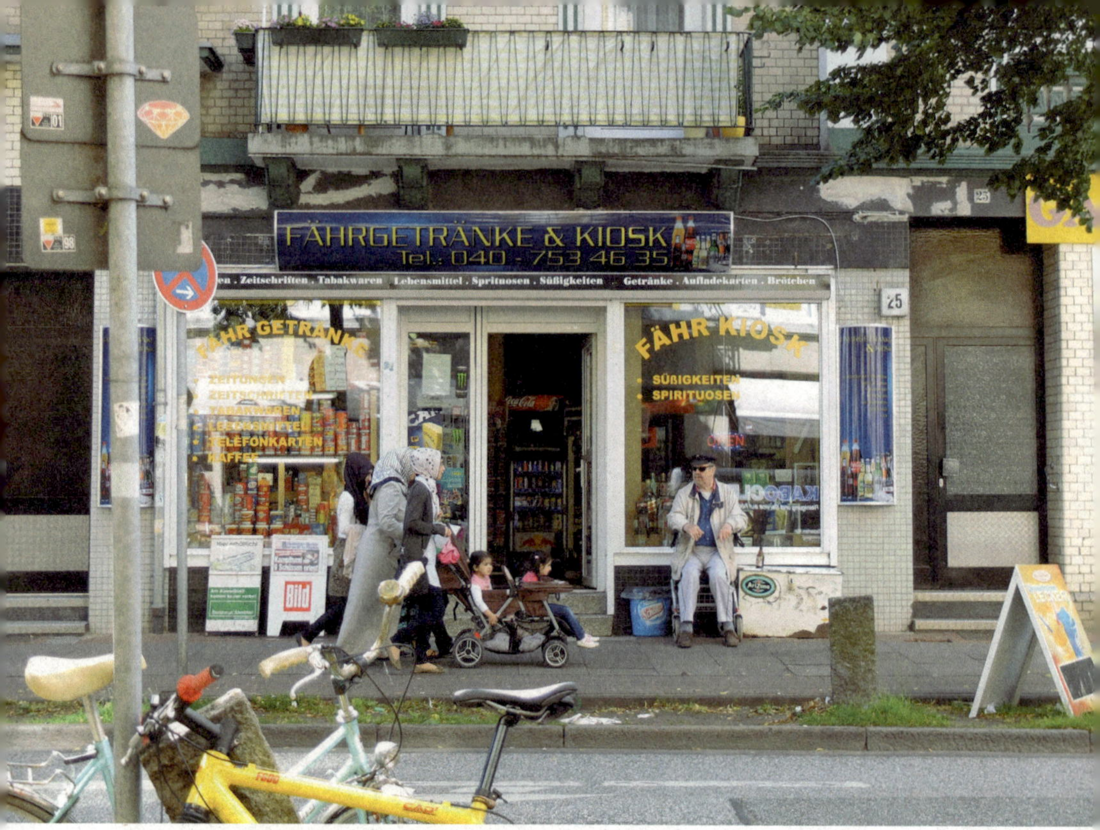

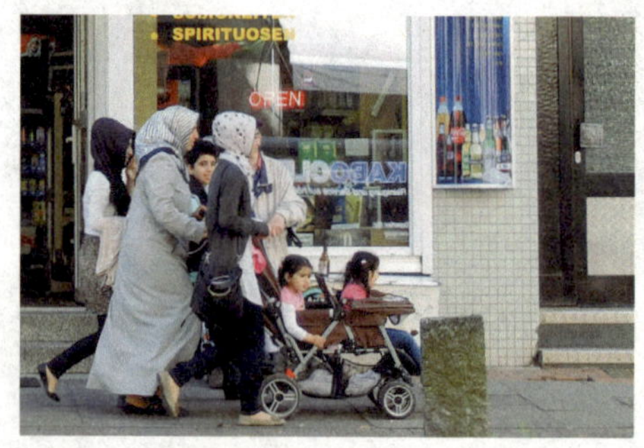

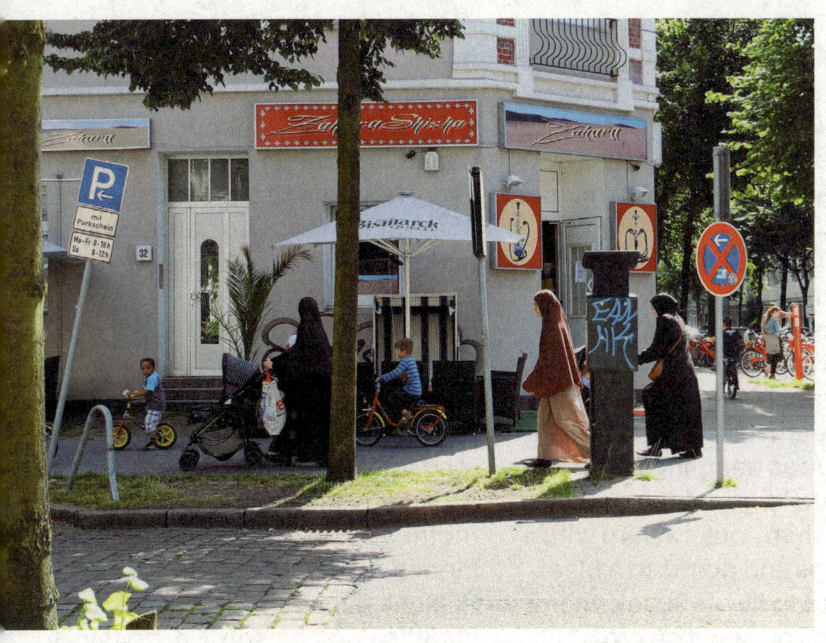

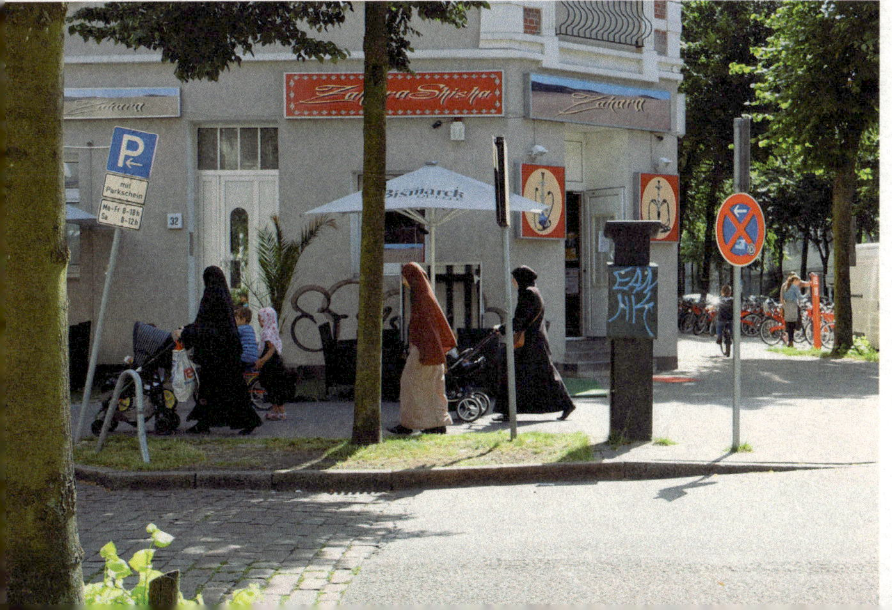

In the Portuguese Café Seu, young women with headscarves are chatting. Over-excited. Coca-Cola flows through their straws now and then. One or two strollers rock next to them. "It's none of her business anymore that I am married to an Arab now."

In the evening a father in a dark blue tracksuit with slightly gray peppered hair is strolling. Up and down in front of the condominium. On his forearm his little son, his arms and legs dangling in the air. His eyes are large, wide open. He talks to him, looks at him with a smile. Stops and points to a black crow about to fly off. "Look, there, a crow! Do you see it? A crow."

A Turkish father sits on a white plastic chair, holding in his right hand a garden hose. He sprays his squealing son with water; his wife meanwhile shampoos the carpet laid out on a tarp in the lawn. Every now and then, he aims again at the foaming carpet or at his laughing boy on Sunday, at the Rotehaus allotments.

In the evening the Porsche Cayenne sits outside Hans-Reimer Schumacher fish bar by the roadside. Next to it, a Mercedes is parked. Oscillating its pastel mother-of-pearl hues. A wiry, tanned man gets out. He joins the Porsche father. On the driver's seat his little Porsche son. He ignites the engine through the window. The power steering yields immediately. The small boy turns the steering wheel, pulls himself up on it. The men watch him, talking and smoking all the while. From time to time on the early Saturday evening the Porsche's horn is honked.

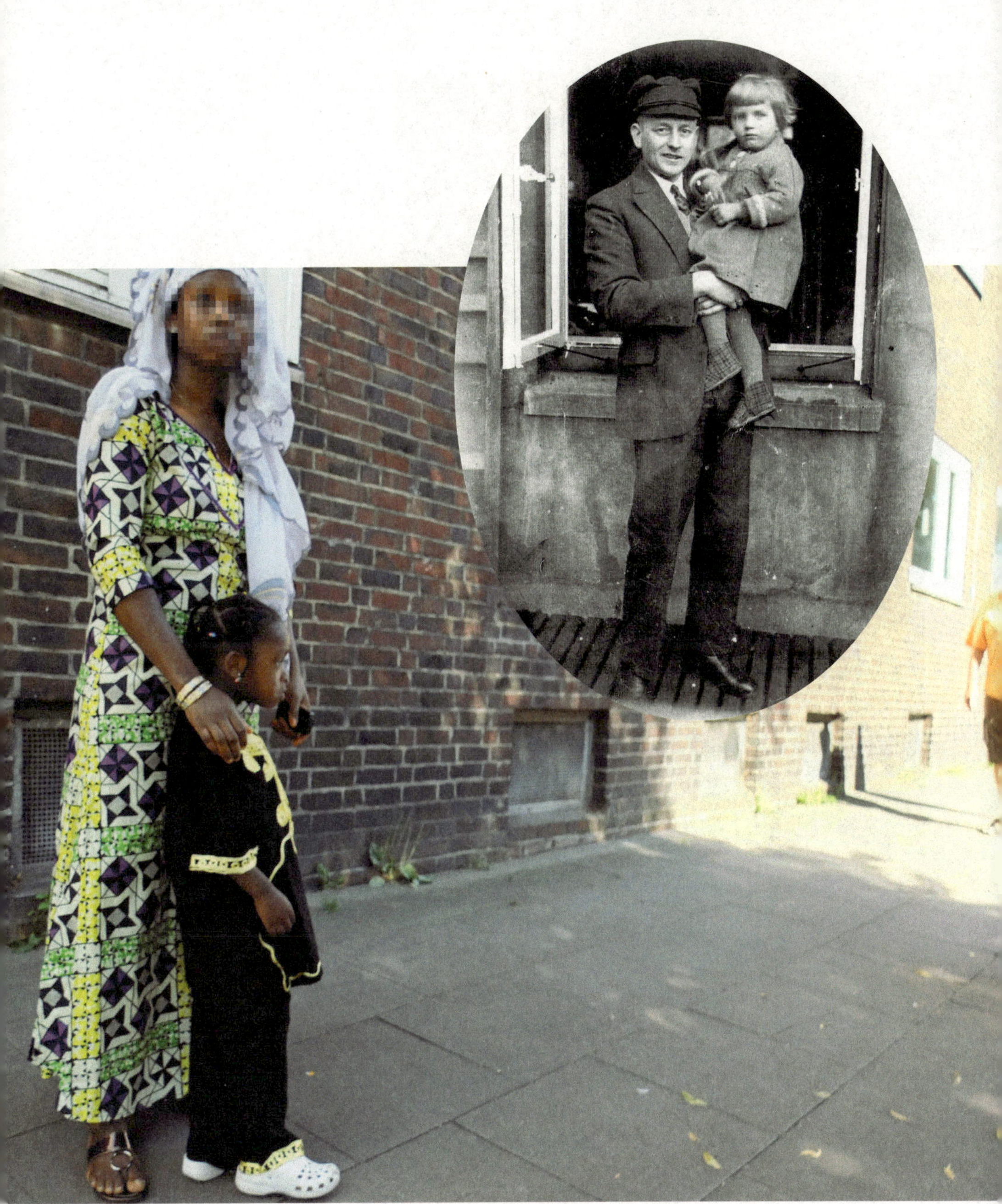

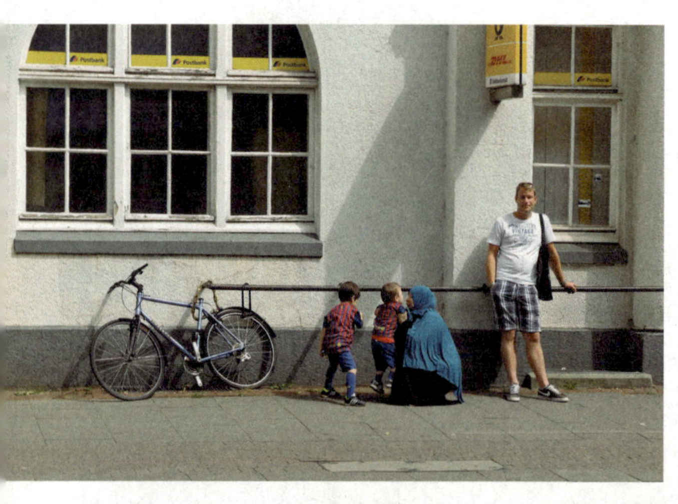

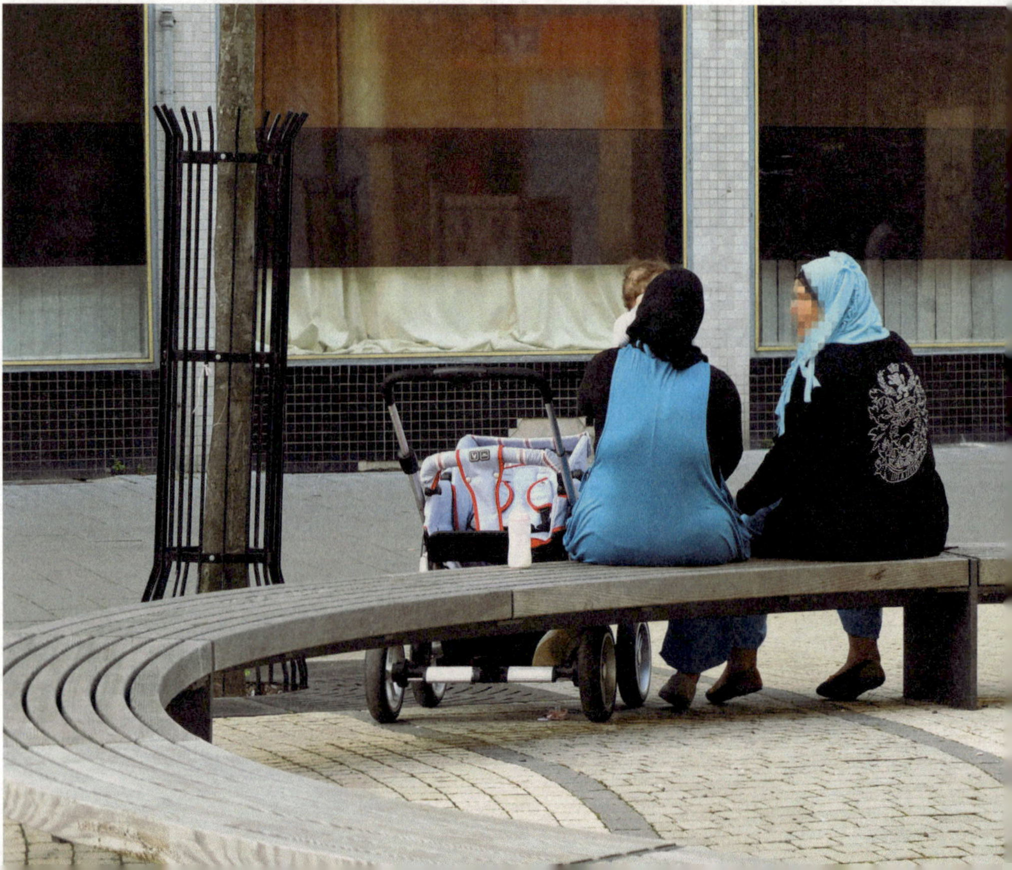

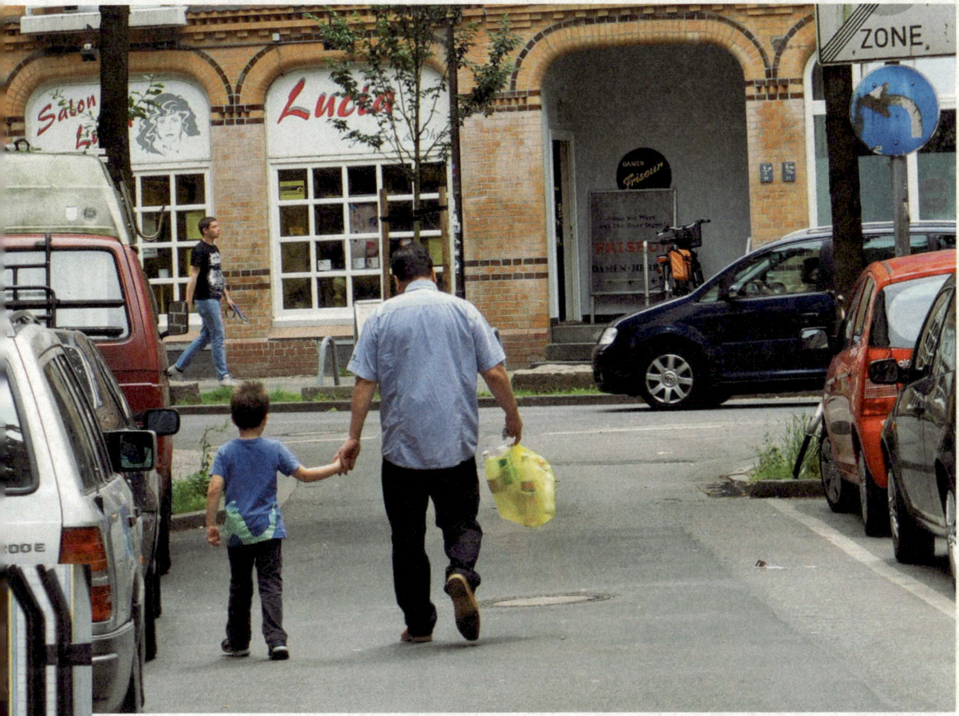

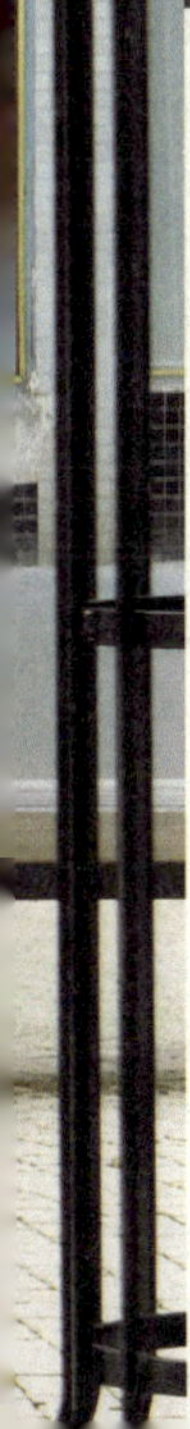

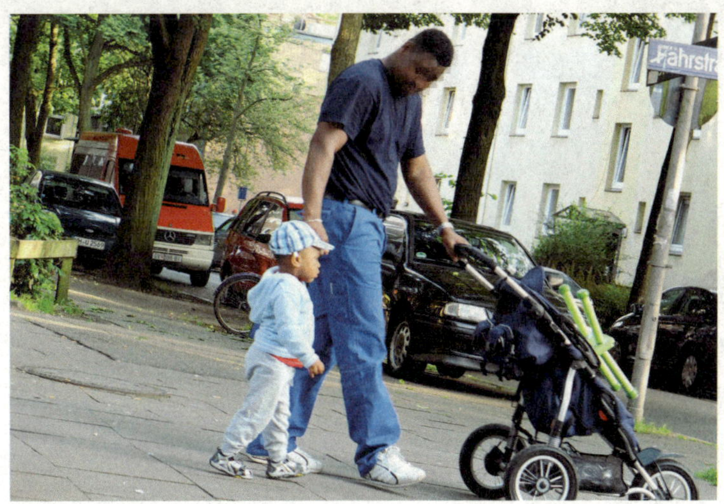

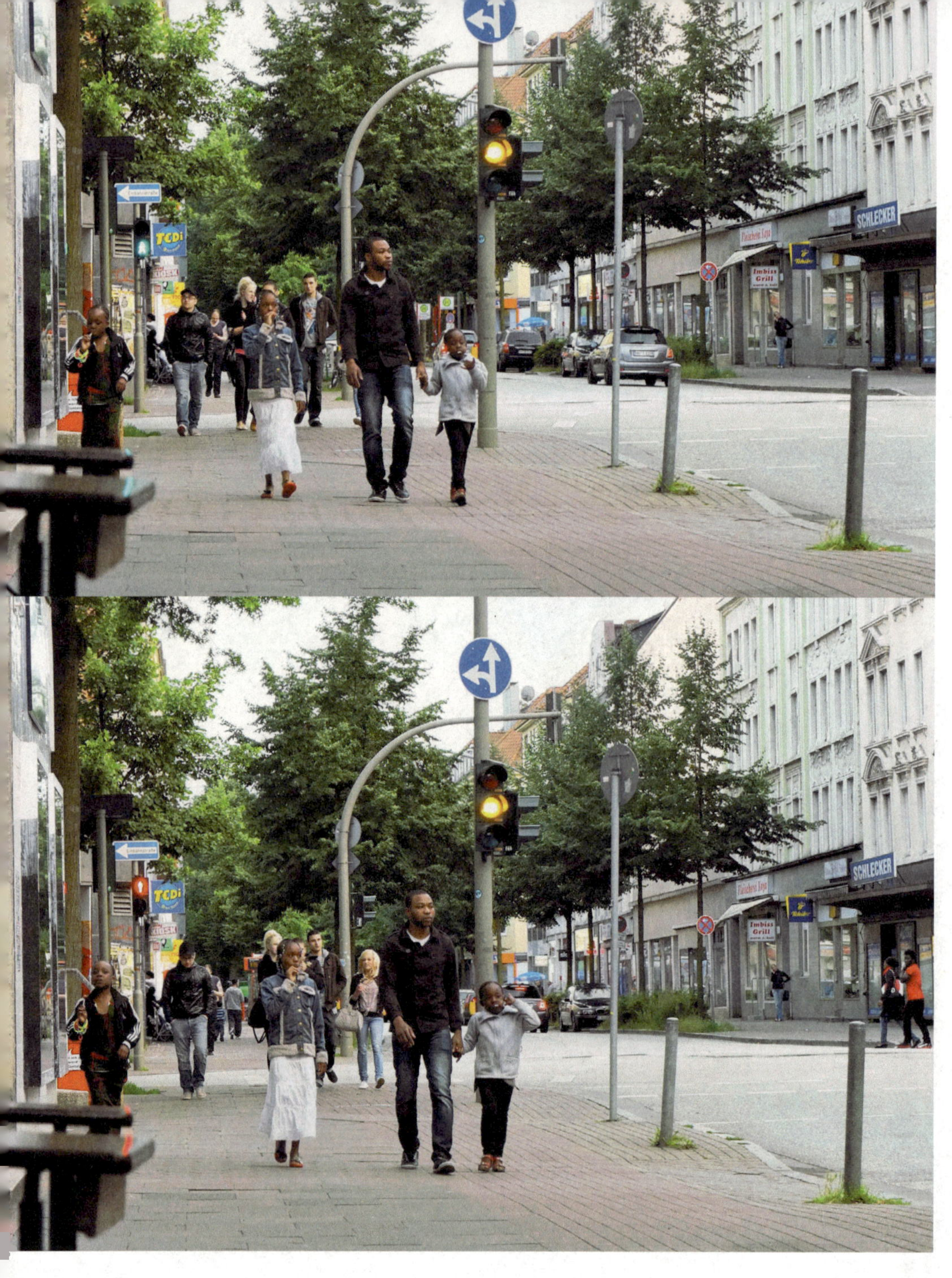

En-
TCDi
SCHLECKER
Imbiss
Grill
TCDi
SCHLECKER
Imbiss
Grill

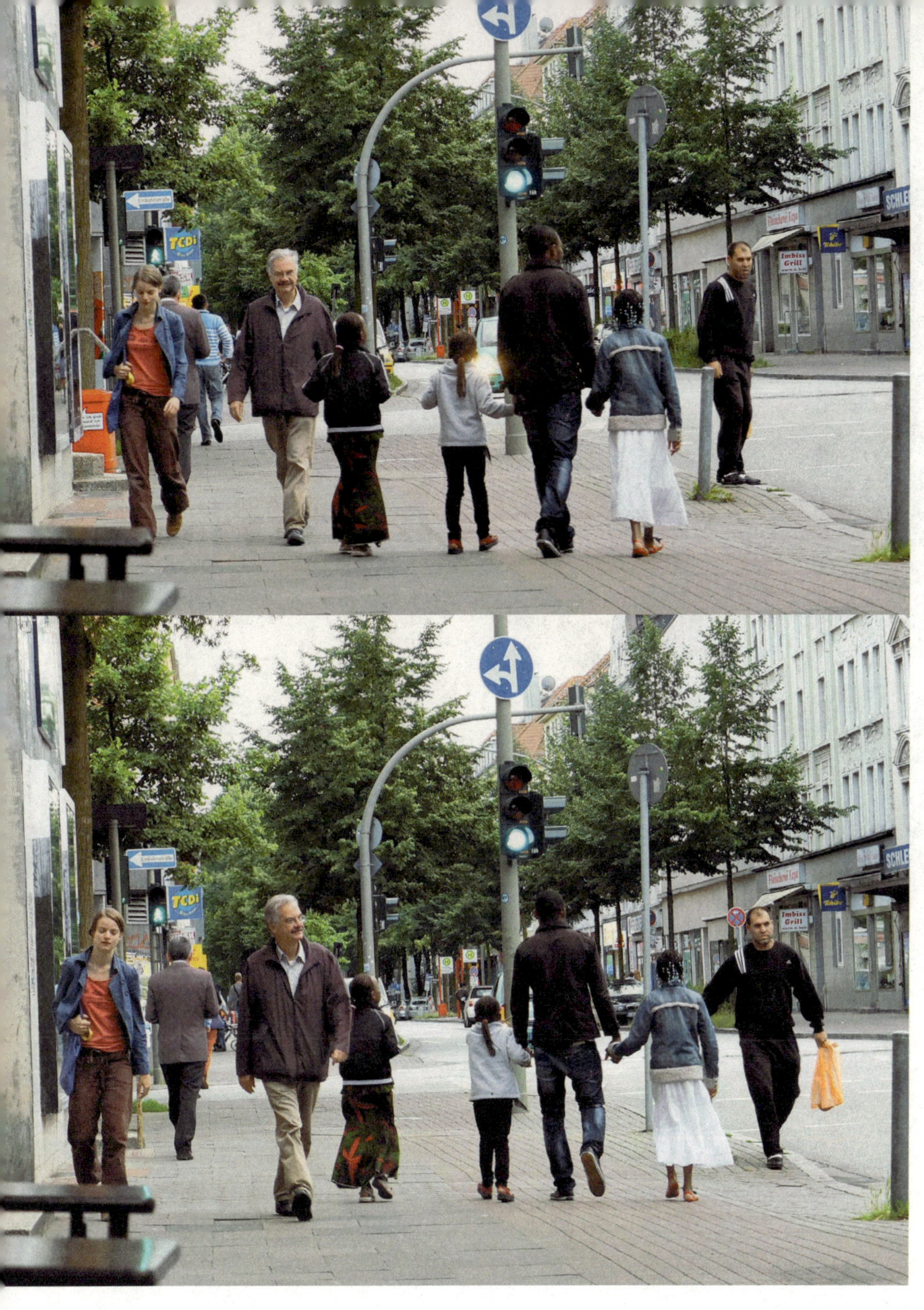

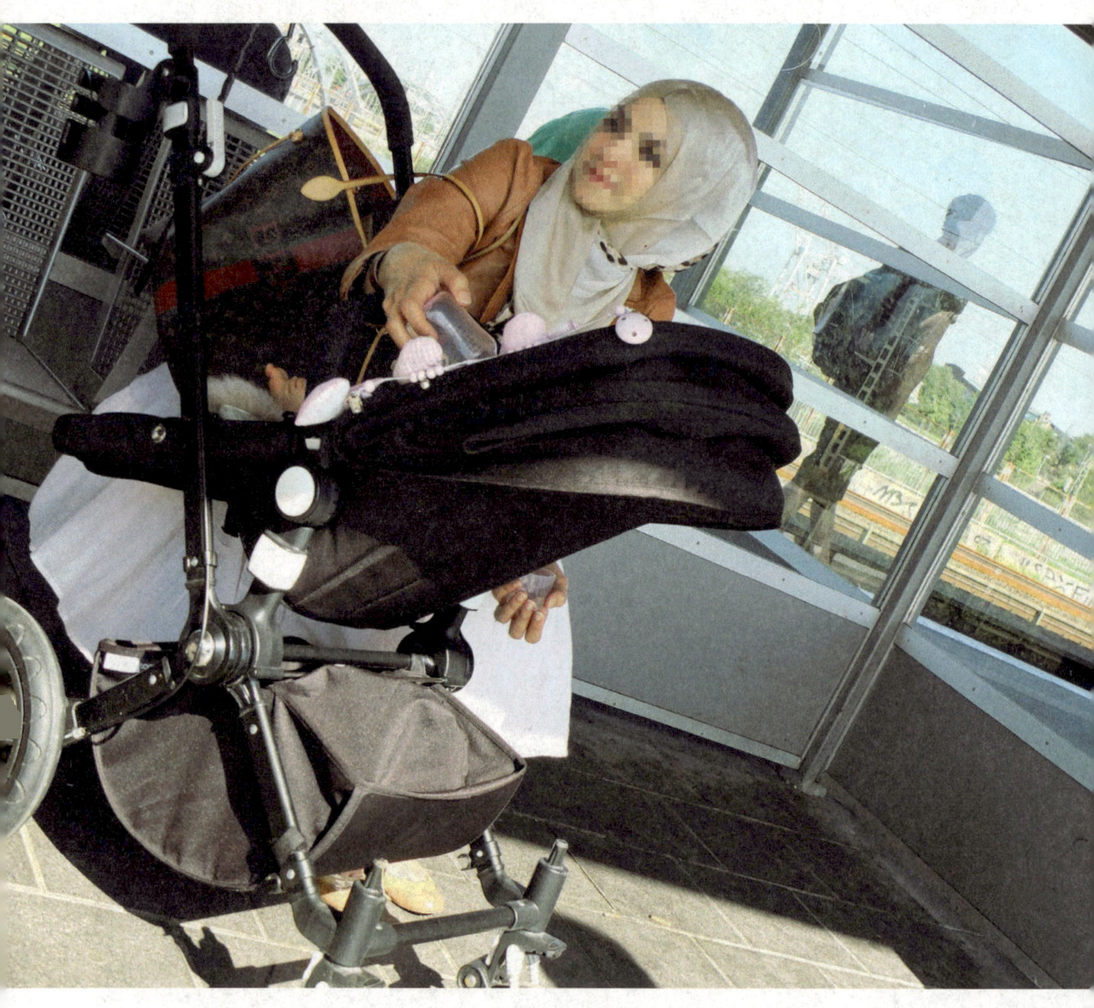

The only thing that actually recalls the wool-carding plant is the street name Bei der Wollkämmerei (At the Wool-carding Factory). Actually. The imposing brick building on Industriestraße (Industry Street, formerly known as Canal Street), was largely destroyed during World War II, the reconstructed building was demolished in the early 2000s. Now Punica Getränke GmbH bottles juices and sodas on the site. During my randonnée on the Elbe Islands I discover to my surprise and amazement a wool-carder in Wilhelmsburg. A wool-carder with a headscarf and long skirt, sitting in the evening on the doorstep with her carder-husband and sorting, tugging, and twisting a bag of soft white wool. Wool production in Wilhelmsburg!? Hamburger Wollkämmerei AG was founded in 1889 as a branch of Leipziger Wollkämmerei. As one of the largest factories, they fostered industrialization of the Elbe Islands. However, there were so few skilled workers available there when the factory was founded that carefully worded ads sought to attract workers from Saxony, Silesia, Poland, or Hungary: "We are hiring trained wool sorters. Report to: Hamburger Wollkämmerei" (Geschichtswerkstatt Wilhelmsburg 2008). Various apartments, a single women's hostel, a canteen, a bathhouse, and a company hospital (later known as Groß Sand Krankenhaus) were built for the two thousand predominantly Catholic employees (cf. Geschichte Alt-Wilhelmsburg). Despite the economic upturn, working and living conditions proved highly precarious. Twelve-hour shifts doing work that was both dangerous and unhealthy were par for the course. In addition, the Wollkämmerei AG paid the lowest wages on the Elbe Islands (ibid.). In 1906 there were strikes by employees, but their situation did not improve as a result. After the reconstruction of the infrastructure destroyed in the Second World War, guest workers from Spain and Italy arrived in Wilhelmsburg in the early 1960s. The young women quickly found work in the wool-carding factory, which was booming once again (ibid.). The trade of tailor or seamstress is frequently found on the Elbe Islands too. The tailors or seamstresses, originally from Turkey, Poland, Greece etc., are now older women or men. Through the windows I see them busy with the many different kinds of sewing jobs, with calm serenity and practiced dexterity.

On the doorstep in the front yard
next to the high gladioli, beans and
various kinds of peppers, a couple
are sitting at Georg-Wilhelm-
Straße. She is crouching, with
her flowered skirt, wool vest and
headscarf, on the edge of the
flowerbed. He sits on a plastic
chair. A white bag on the ground,
fibers of soft sheepskin swell
out of it. Some of it is lying on the
lawn too. Sorting hands, pluck,
pull, twist and twirl, piece by
piece. Cleverly and quickly, in the
front garden beneath the kitchen
window that sits ajar.

Kleider-Klinik

Änderungen • Reparaturen • Kunststopfen
Reinigungsannahme — Werbepreis spezialgereinigt:

Kleid 3,20   Mantel 5,50

Wilhelm Oelke • Schneidermeister
Wilhelmsburg, Veringstraße 167, Telefon 75 86 13

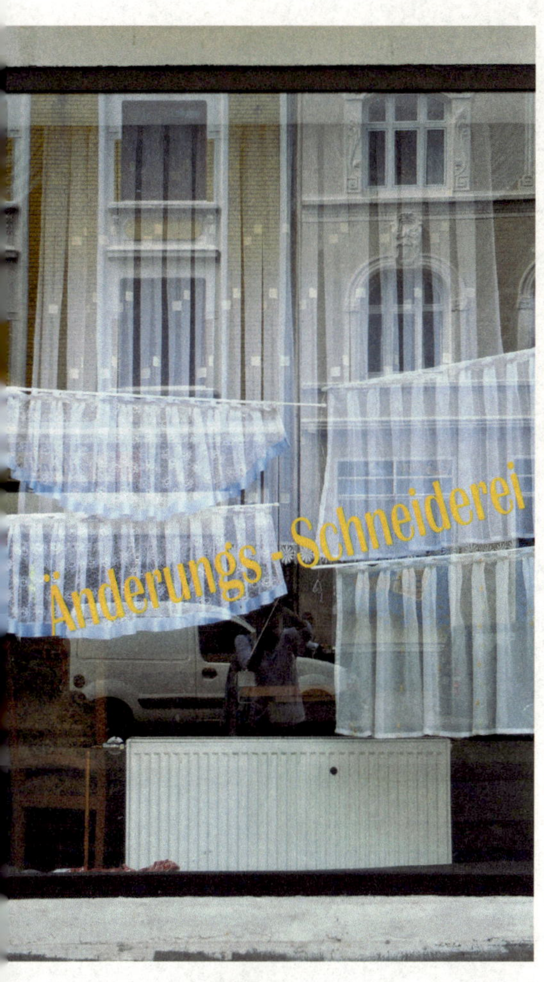

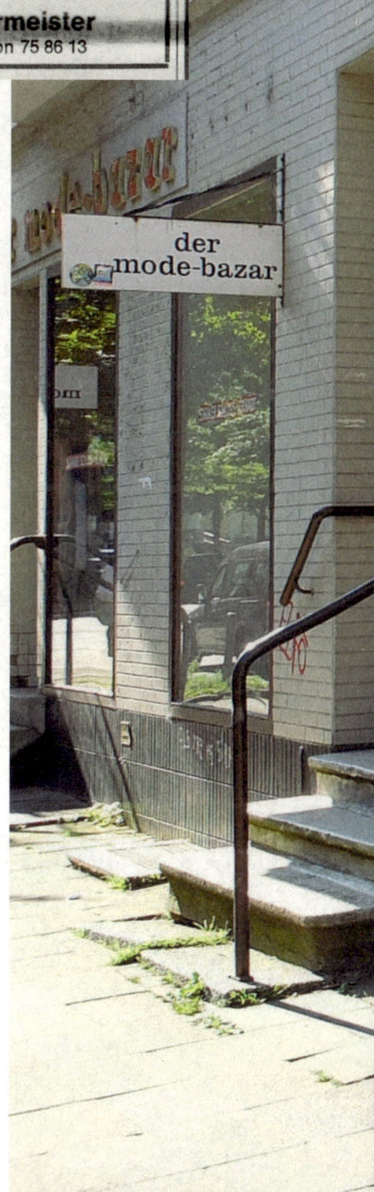

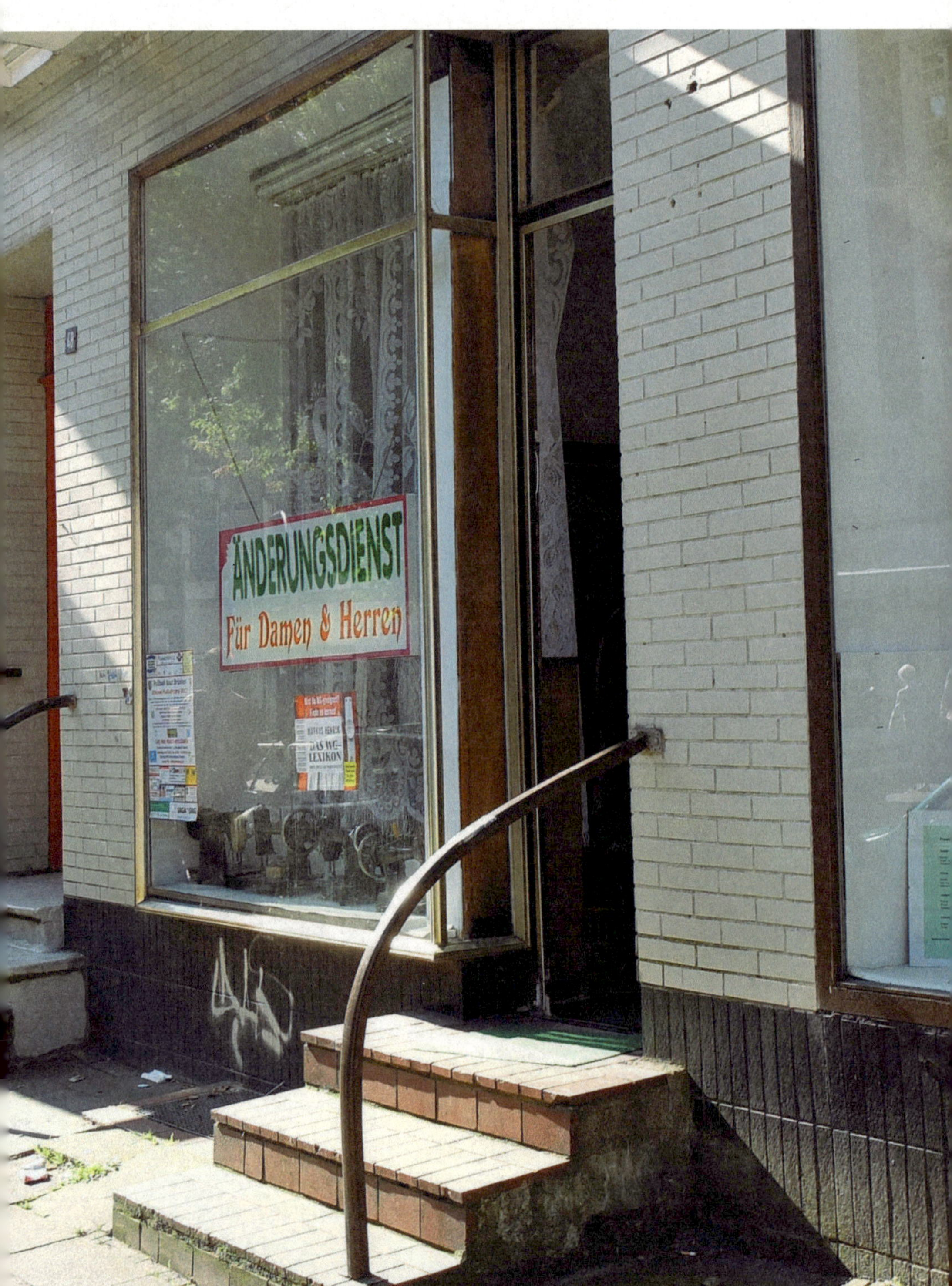

ÄNDERUNGSDIENST
Für Damen & Herren
DAS WG-
LEXIKON

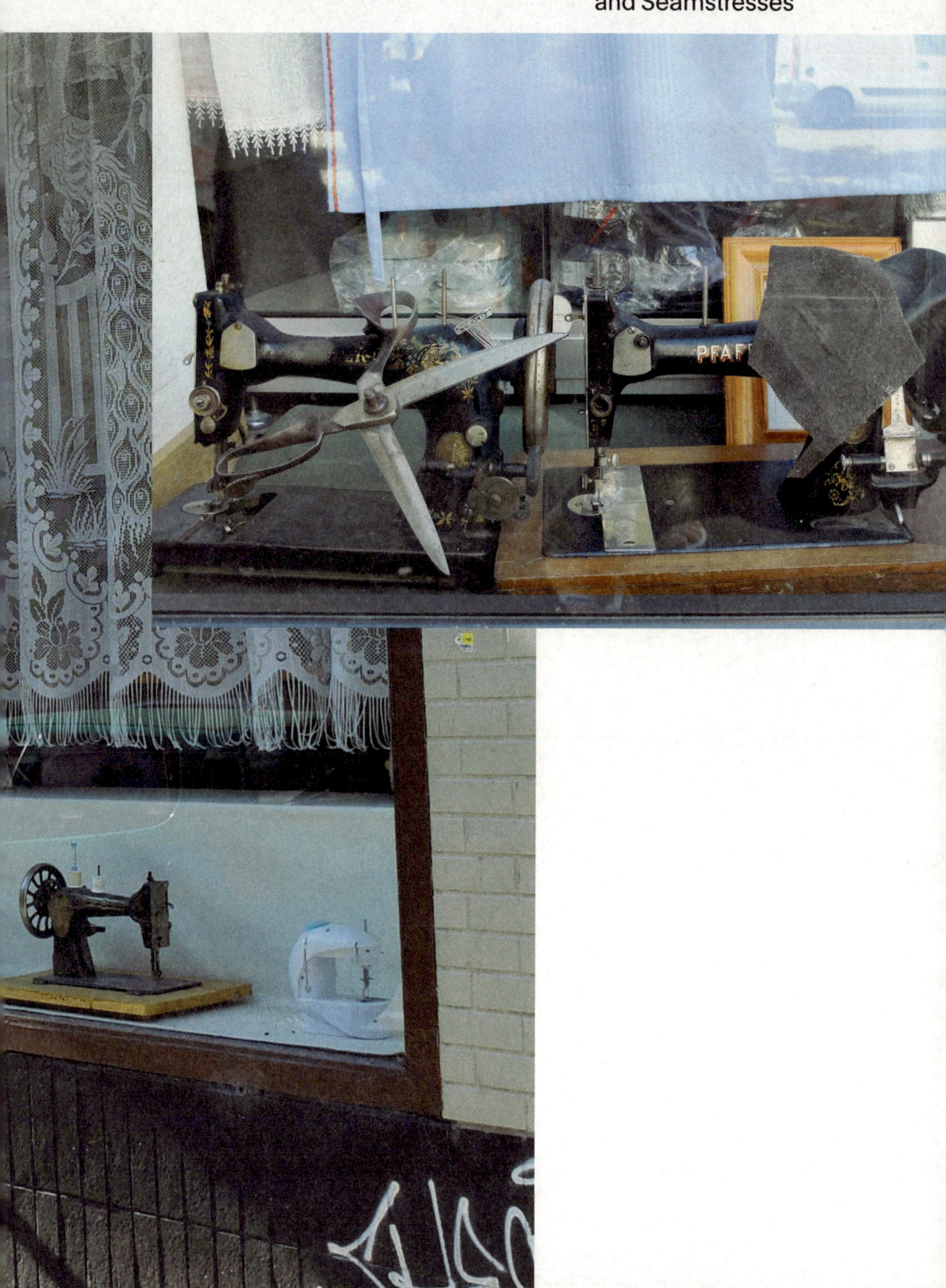

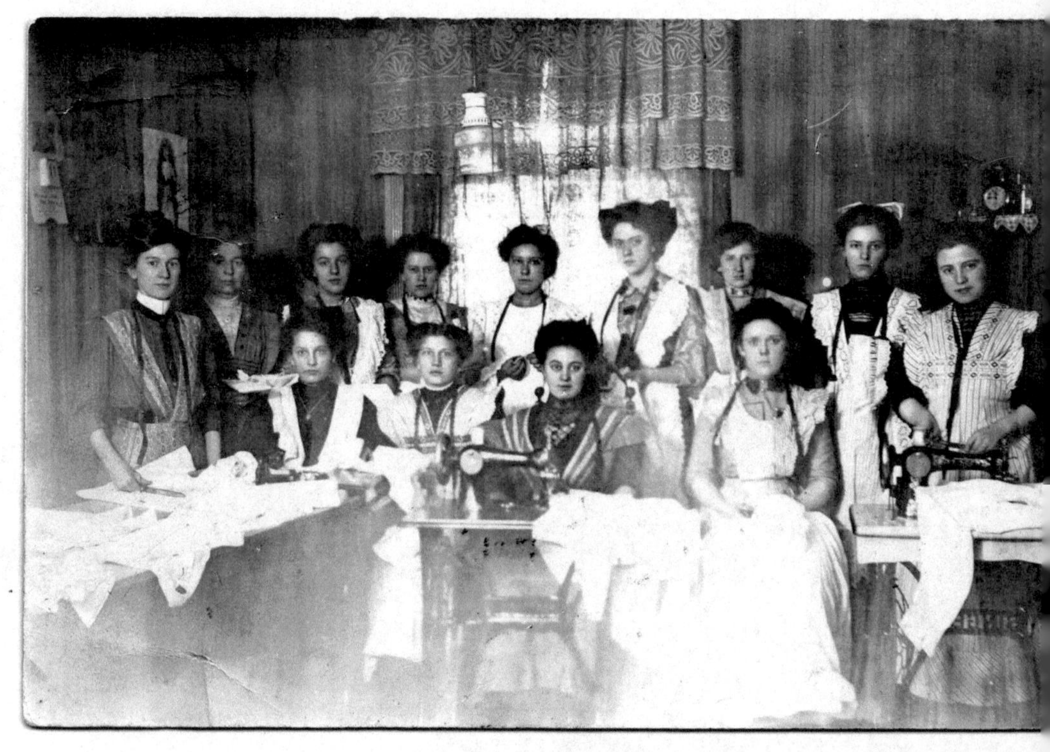

Textile codes and symbols develop their own language on the streets of the Elbe Islands. In various colored patterns and textures, the textile language communicates visibly clear yet at the same time flowing silently. Clothing like work overalls, men's suits, Ghanaian togas, or wrap dresses from traditional kente fabrics, breathable outdoor clothing, tracksuits, blouses, jackets, saris, jogging kit, burqas, jilbabs (abayas or djellabas), blue jeans, long shirts, flamenco skirts, ruffle skirts, ruffled skirts, tunics, qamis, women's suits, gowns ... and headgear such as chadors (hijabs or hidschabs), turbans, cowboy hats, straw hats, kippas, takke ... or accessories made of flowers, feathers, gold jewelry, bags, sunglasses ... are blended mixtures of customs, tradition, religion, leisure, work, trends, everyday life, originality ... The textile wearers refer via their appearance to their various countries of origin and / or circumstances. Their ethnic, religious, and cultural affiliations remain part of their identity. In this context, new and random references interweave. These are unstable connections, fleeting and ephemeral in their textile-based essence yet nonetheless experienced and perceived in this space. The practice of wearing textiles is festivity and everyday routine rolled into one. It is a cheerful, squealing, elegant, restrained, well-kept, individual, modest, confident, expressive, more brightly colored, more meaningful, symbolic, exotic, mythical, and legendary style of speech and expression at one and the same time. Lifestyle. The numerous clothing stores, the clothes racks at the weekly market, as well as the clothes lines in the backyards are also bearers of this language. They complement the linguistic picture and render its vocabulary denser and richer. Then. On the S-Bahn 31 / S-Bahn 3 platform at Hamburg Central Station, this site-specific language can be gradually guessed at until finally, at the Veddel S-Bahn Station if not before, it becomes an unmistakable reality worn upon the body.

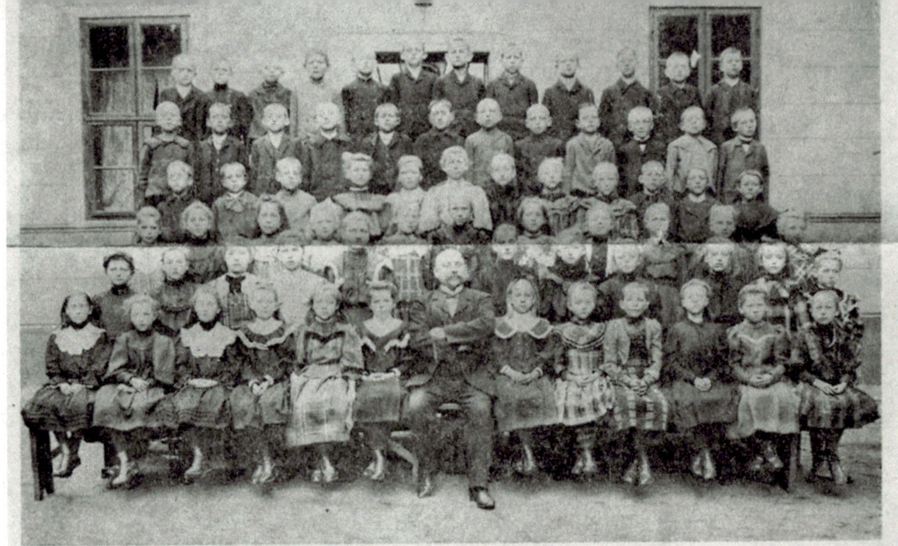

Lehrer Hennings mit seinen Schülern und Schülerinnen vor der Kirchdorfer Schule im Jahre 1908.

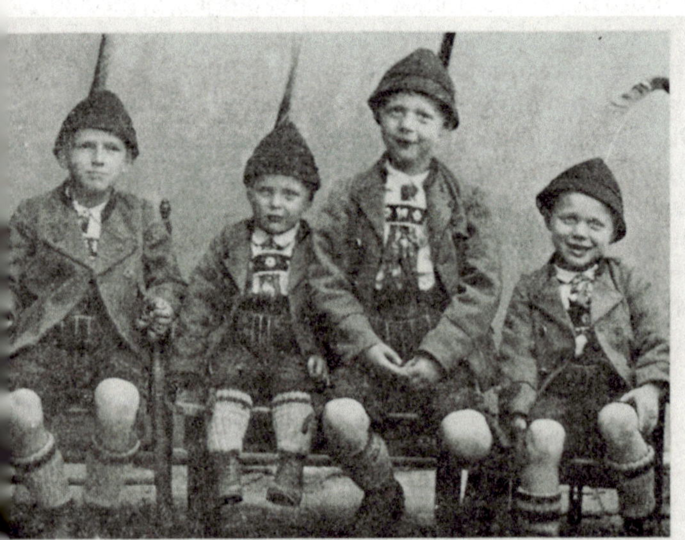

drei Jungen v. r. Alfred, Reinhold, Walter zusammen mit Max Nippold, dem Sohn des bekannten Grundstückmaklers

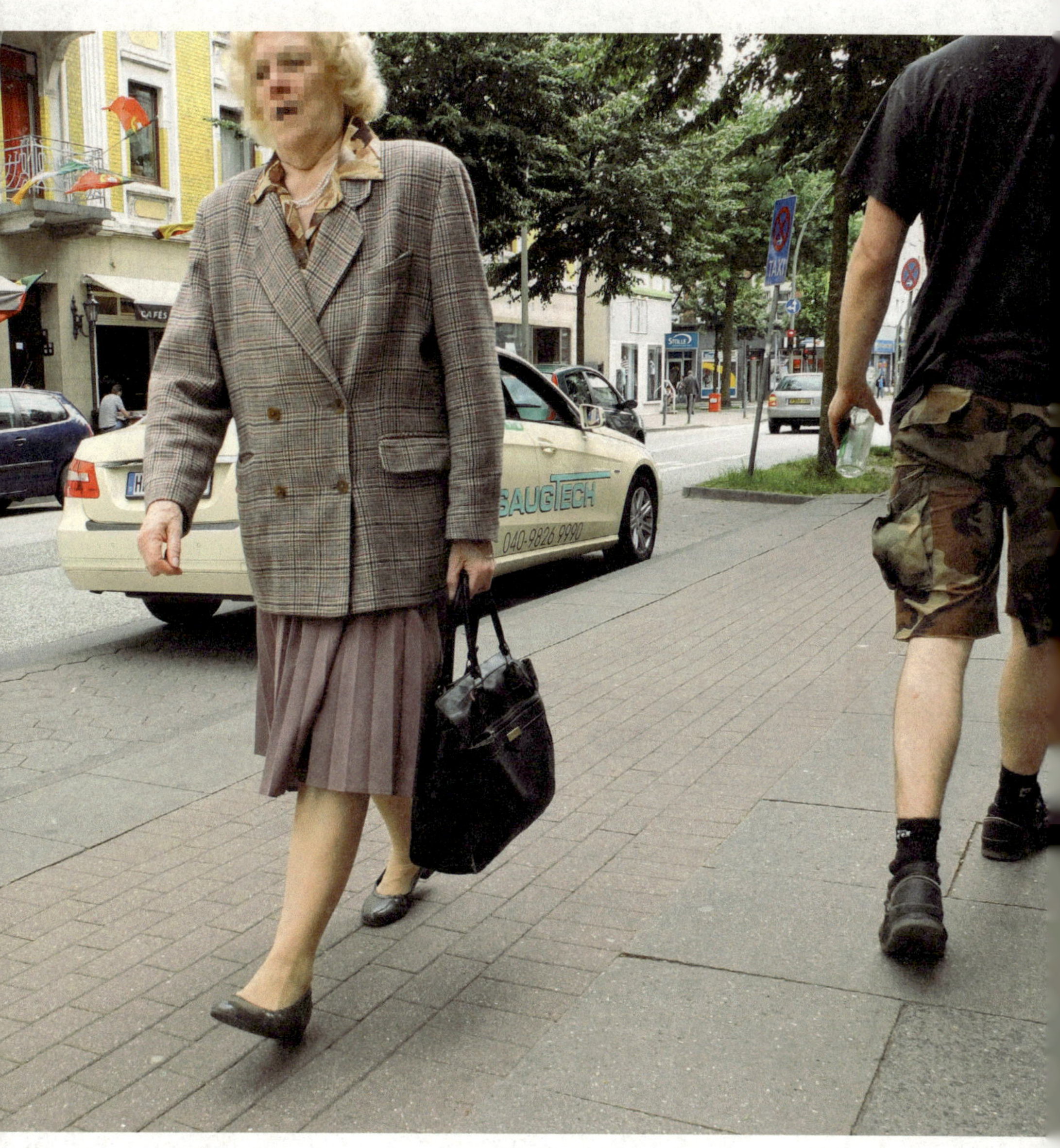
SAUGTECH
040-9826 9990
TAXI

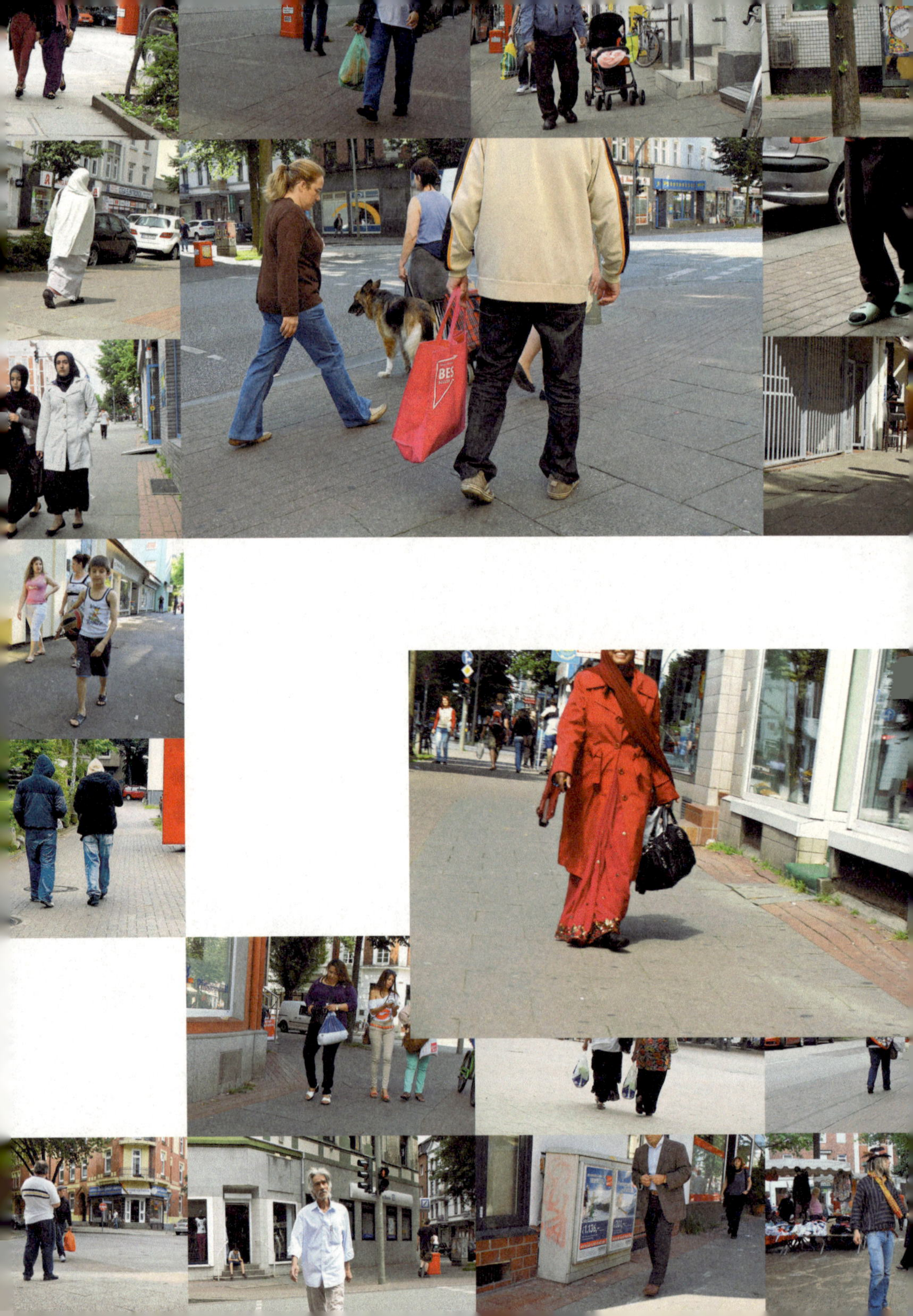

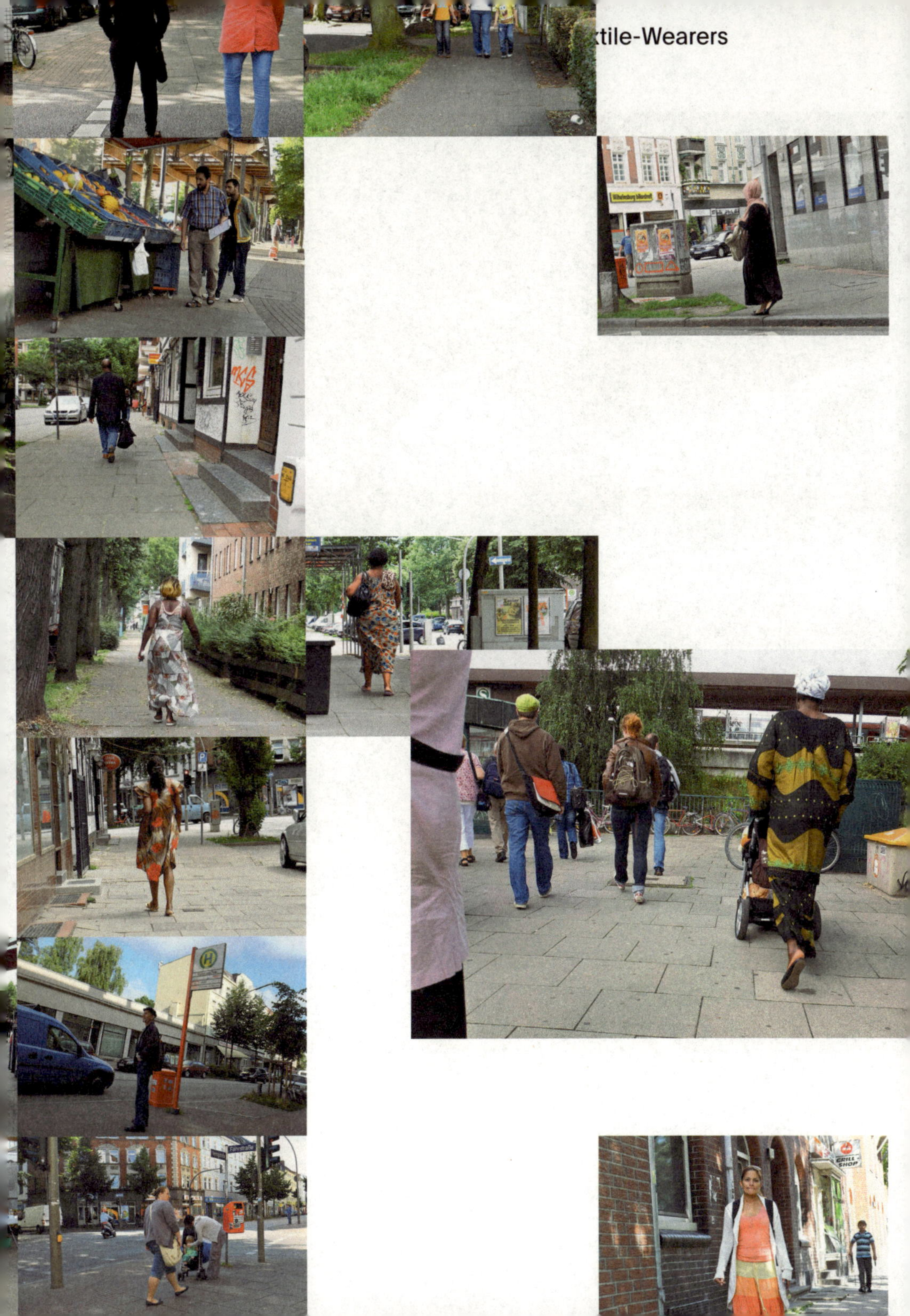

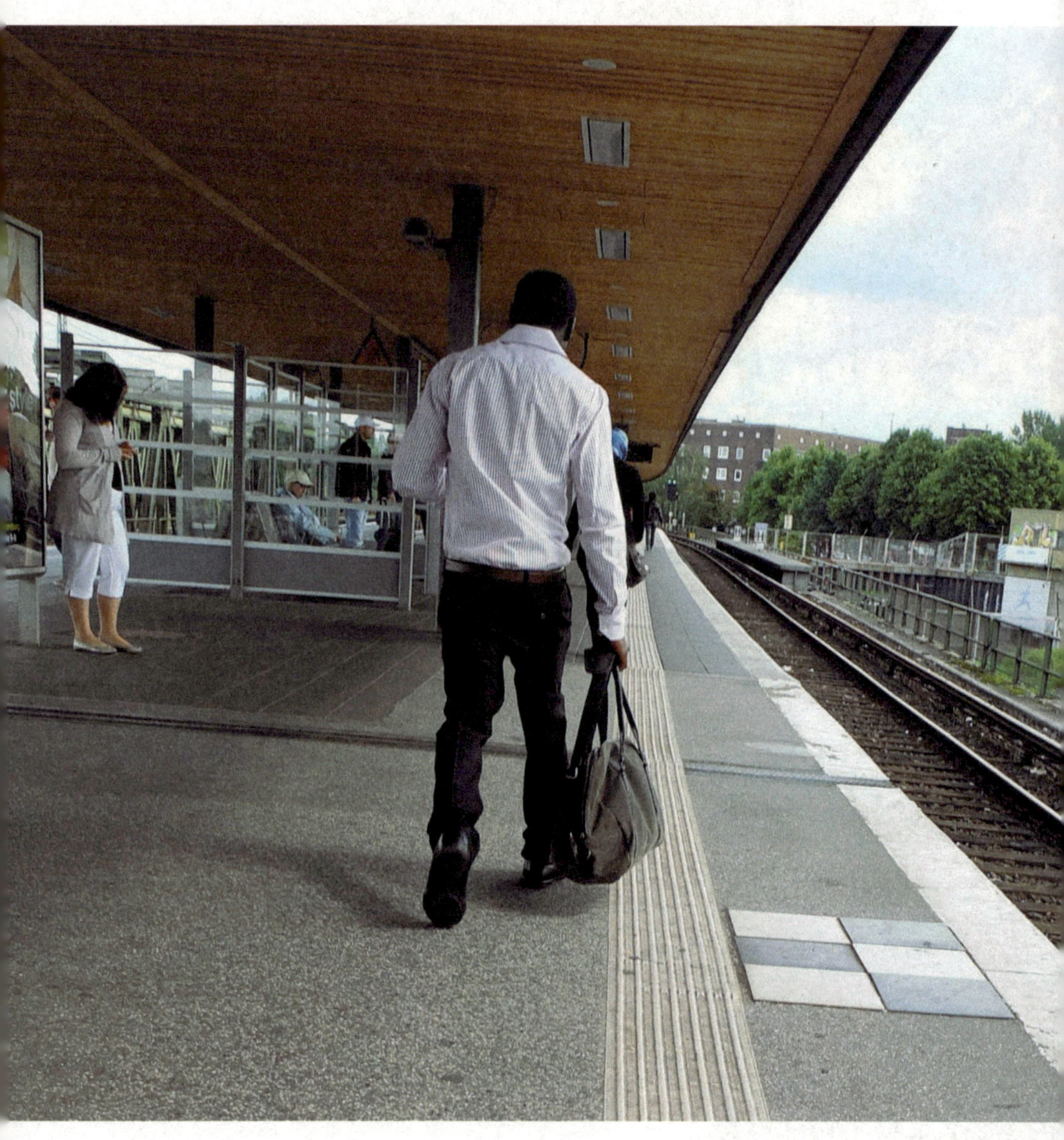

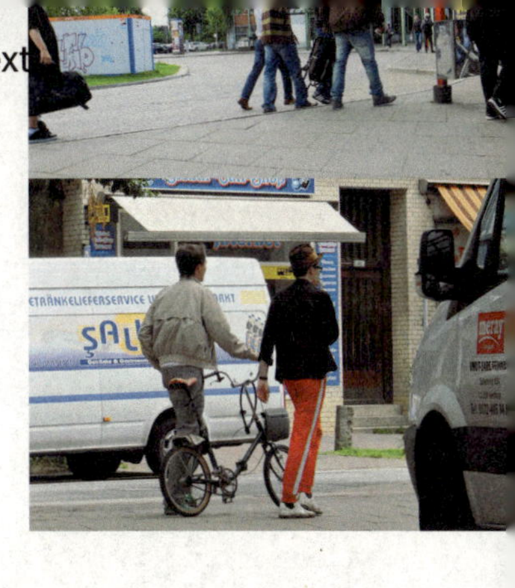

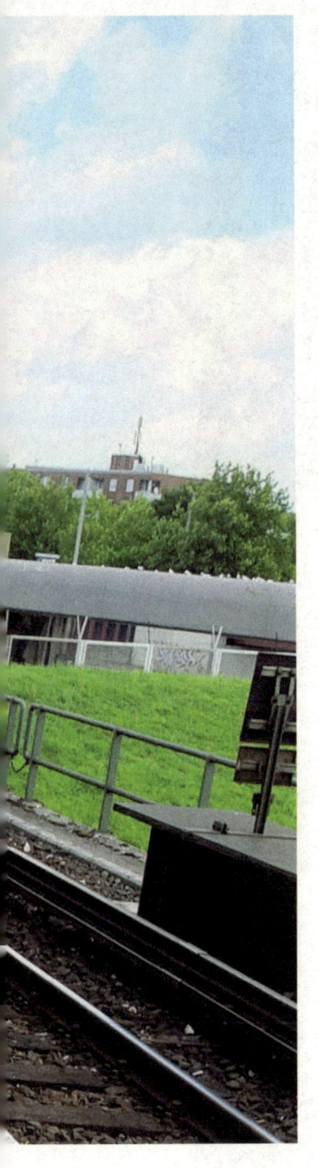

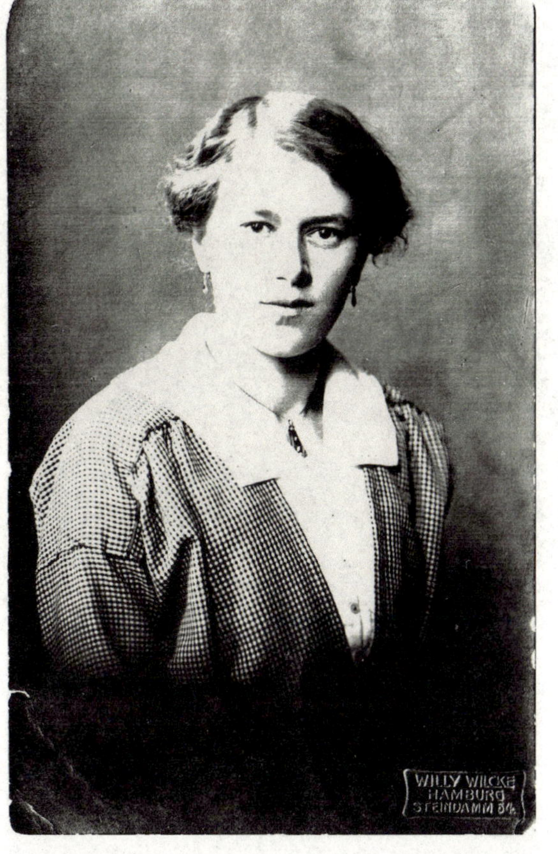

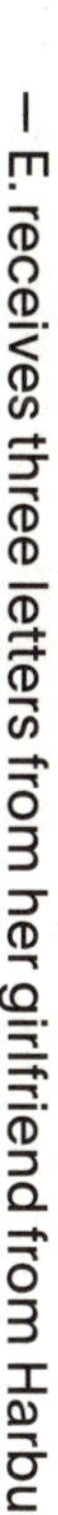
— E. receives three letters from her girlfriend from Harburg —

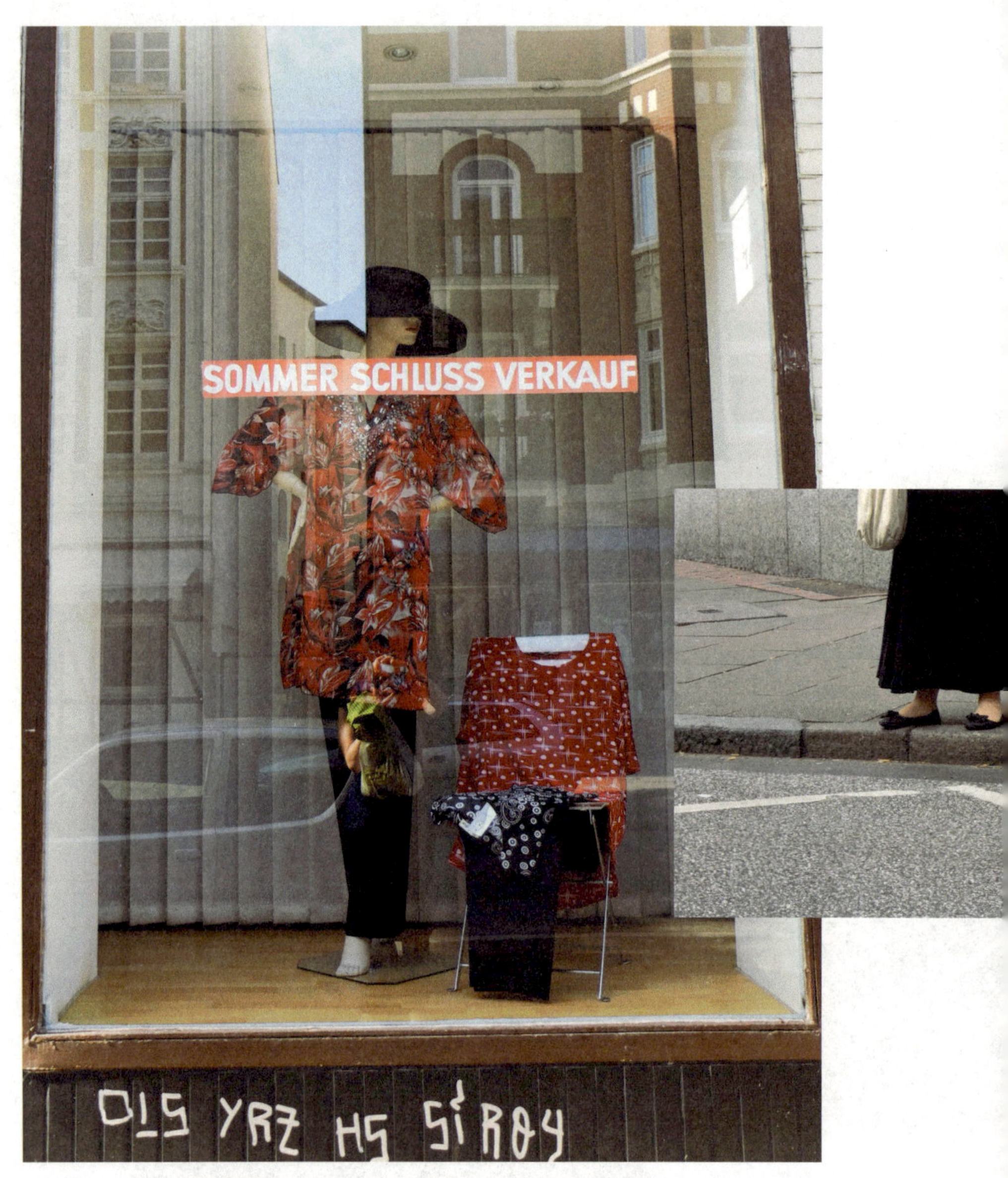

SOMMER SCHLUSS VERKAUF

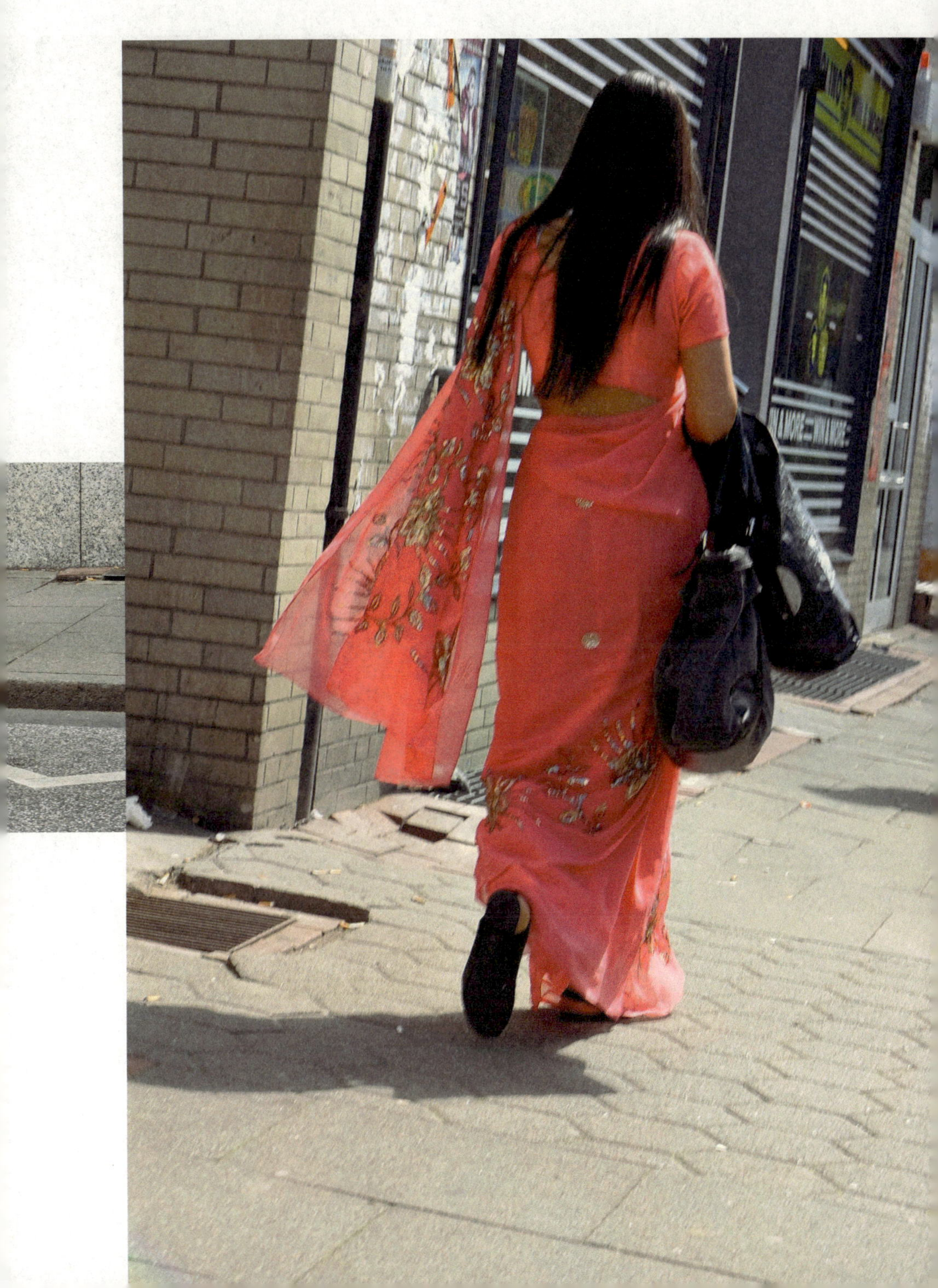

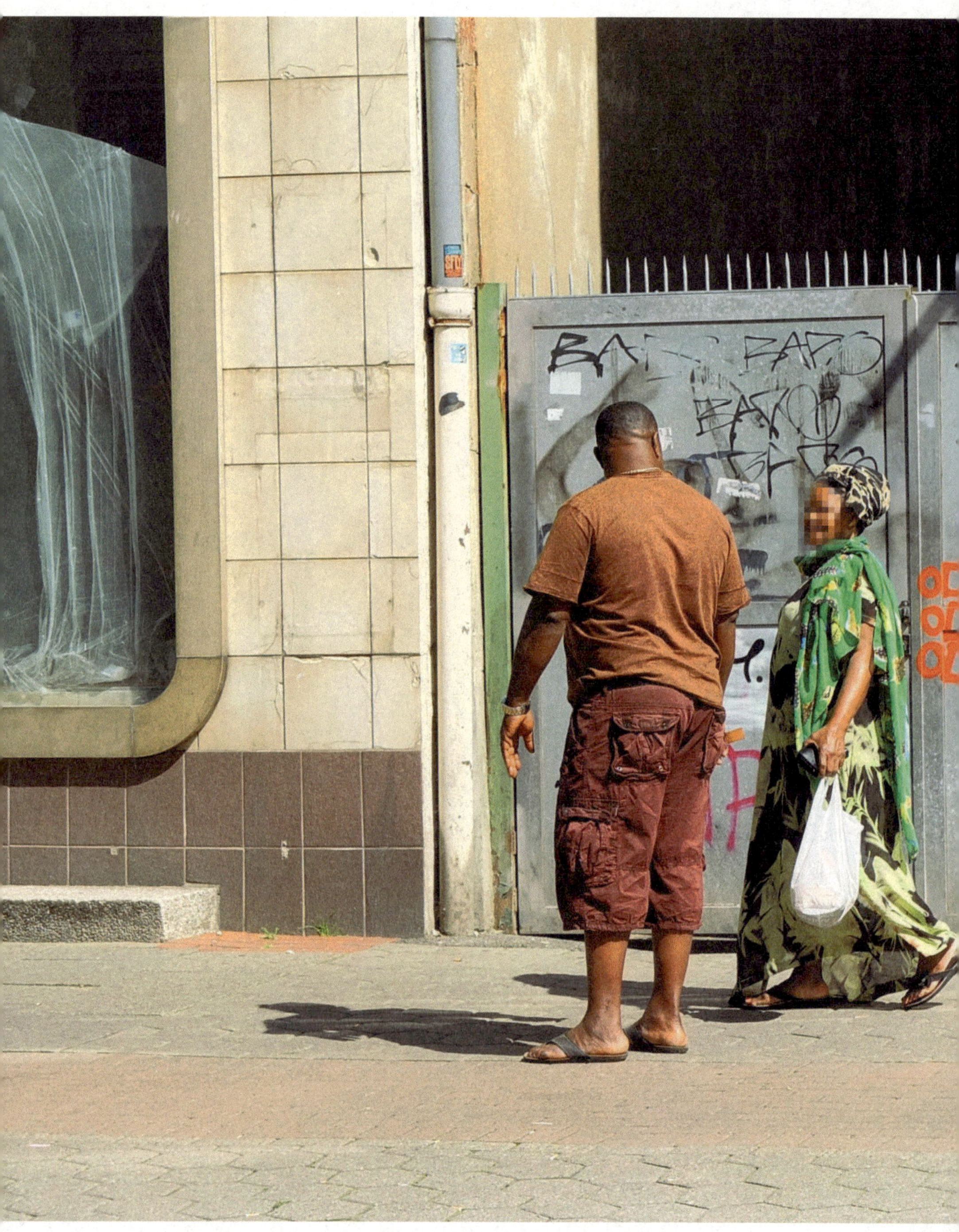

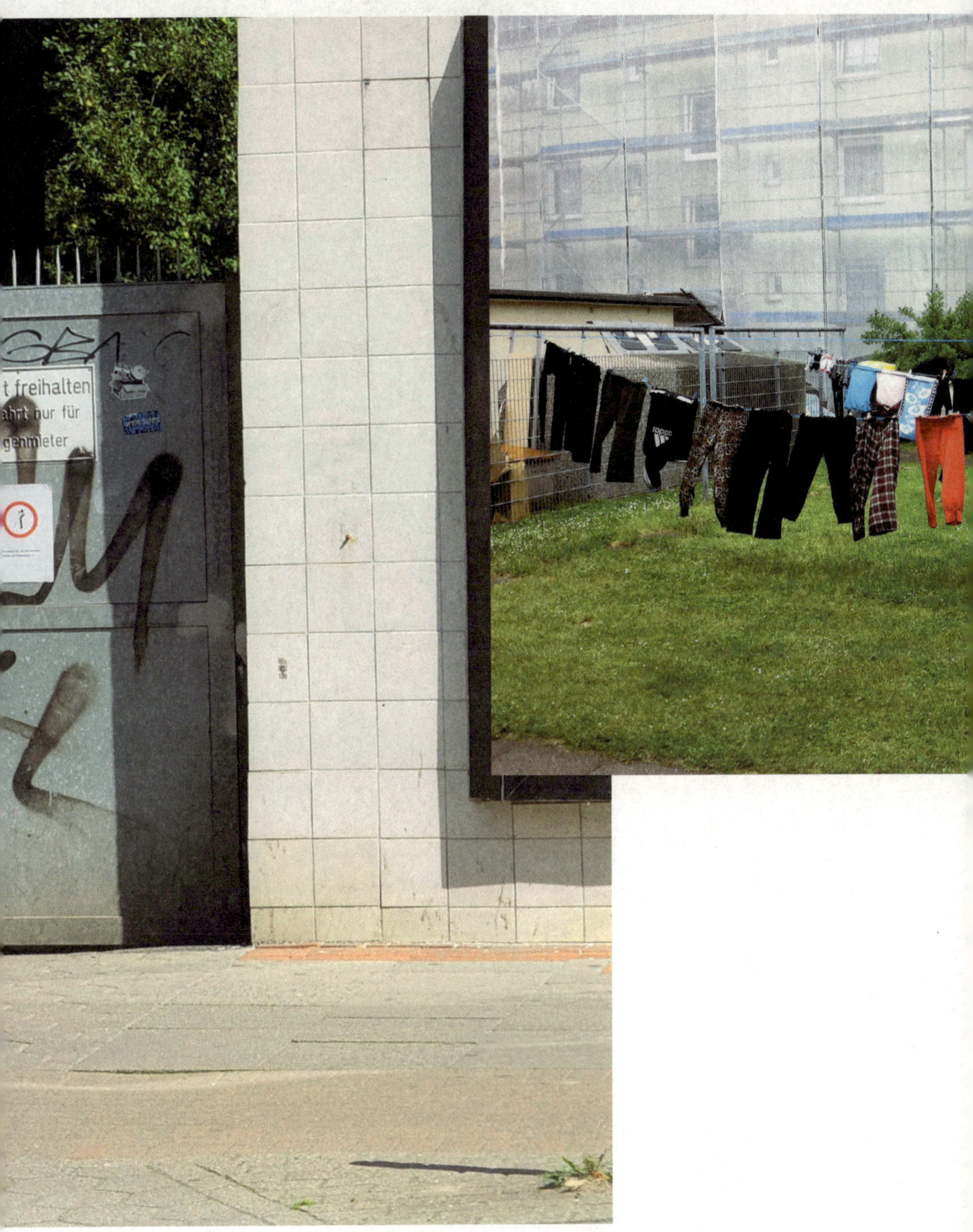
t freihalten
ahrt nur für
genmieter
adidas

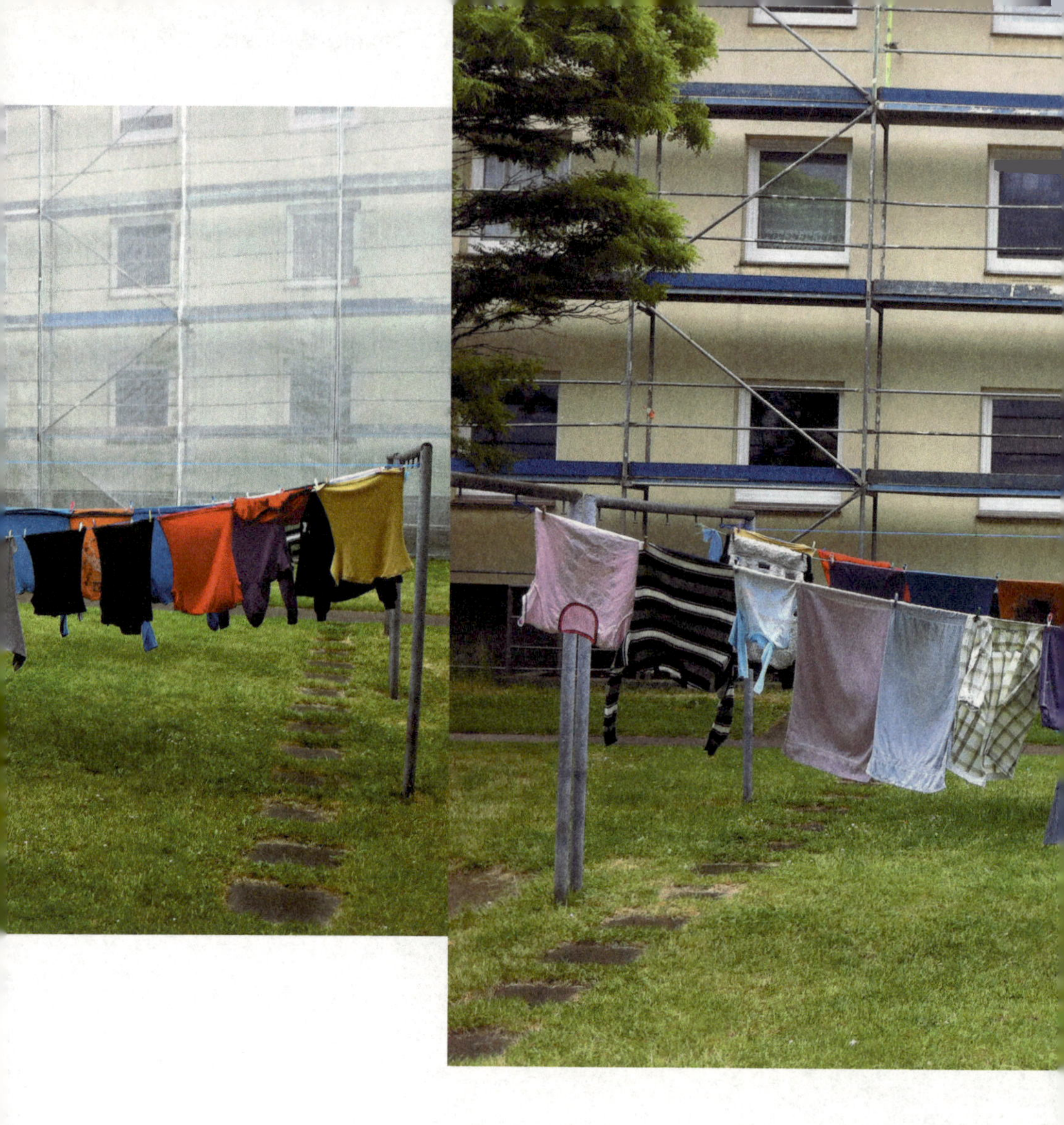

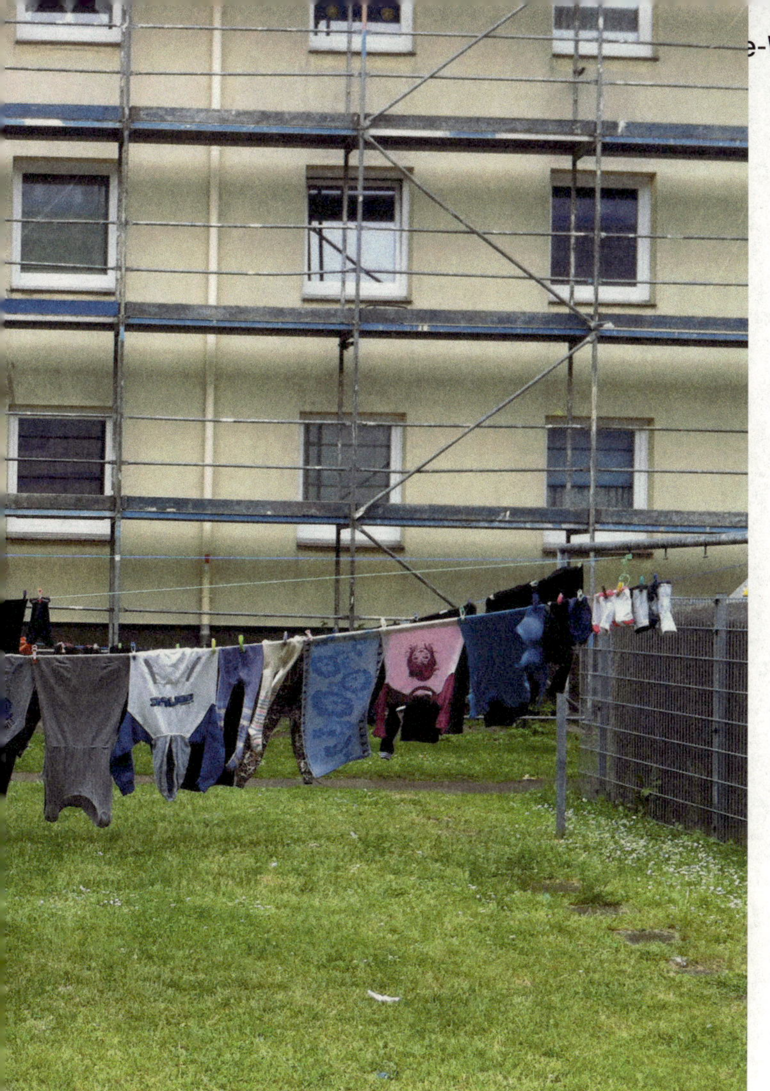

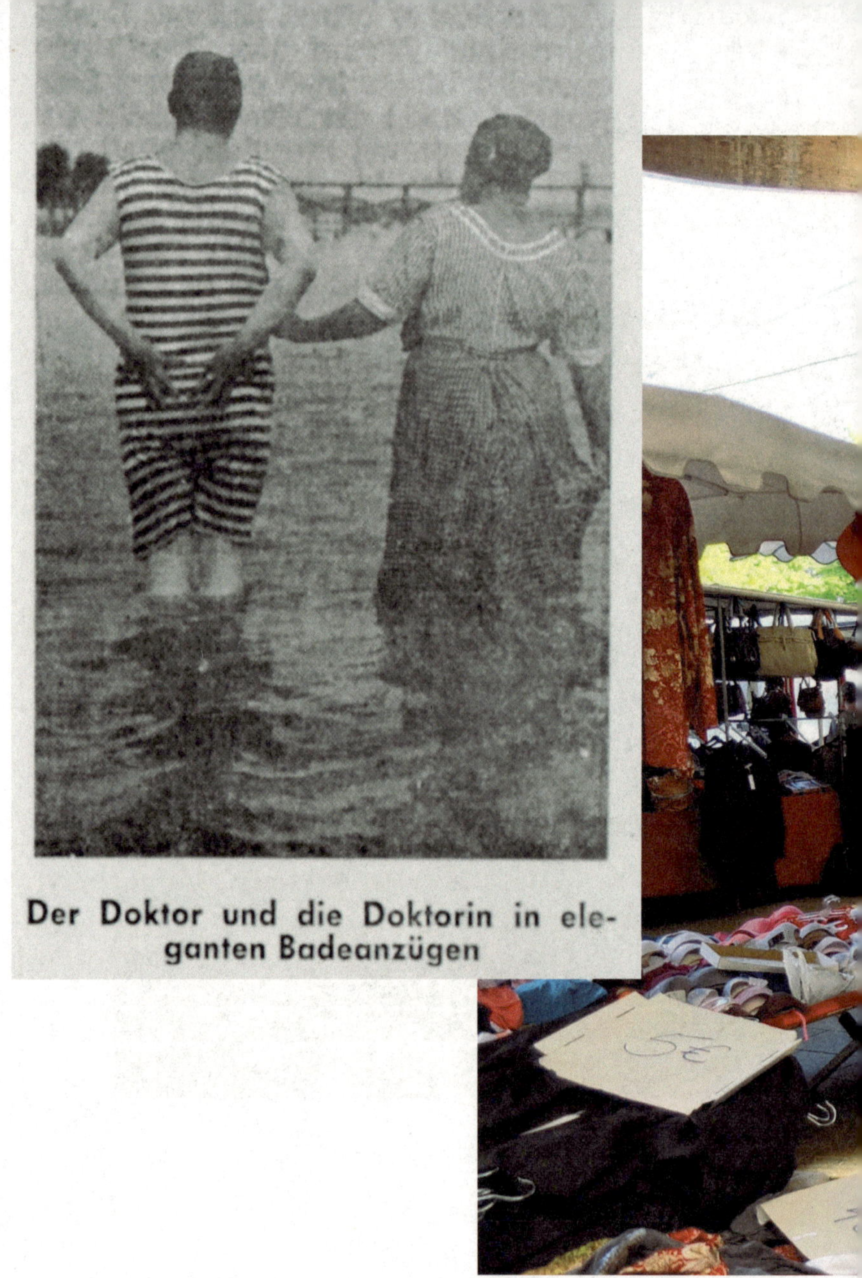

Der Doktor und die Doktorin in eleganten Badeanzügen

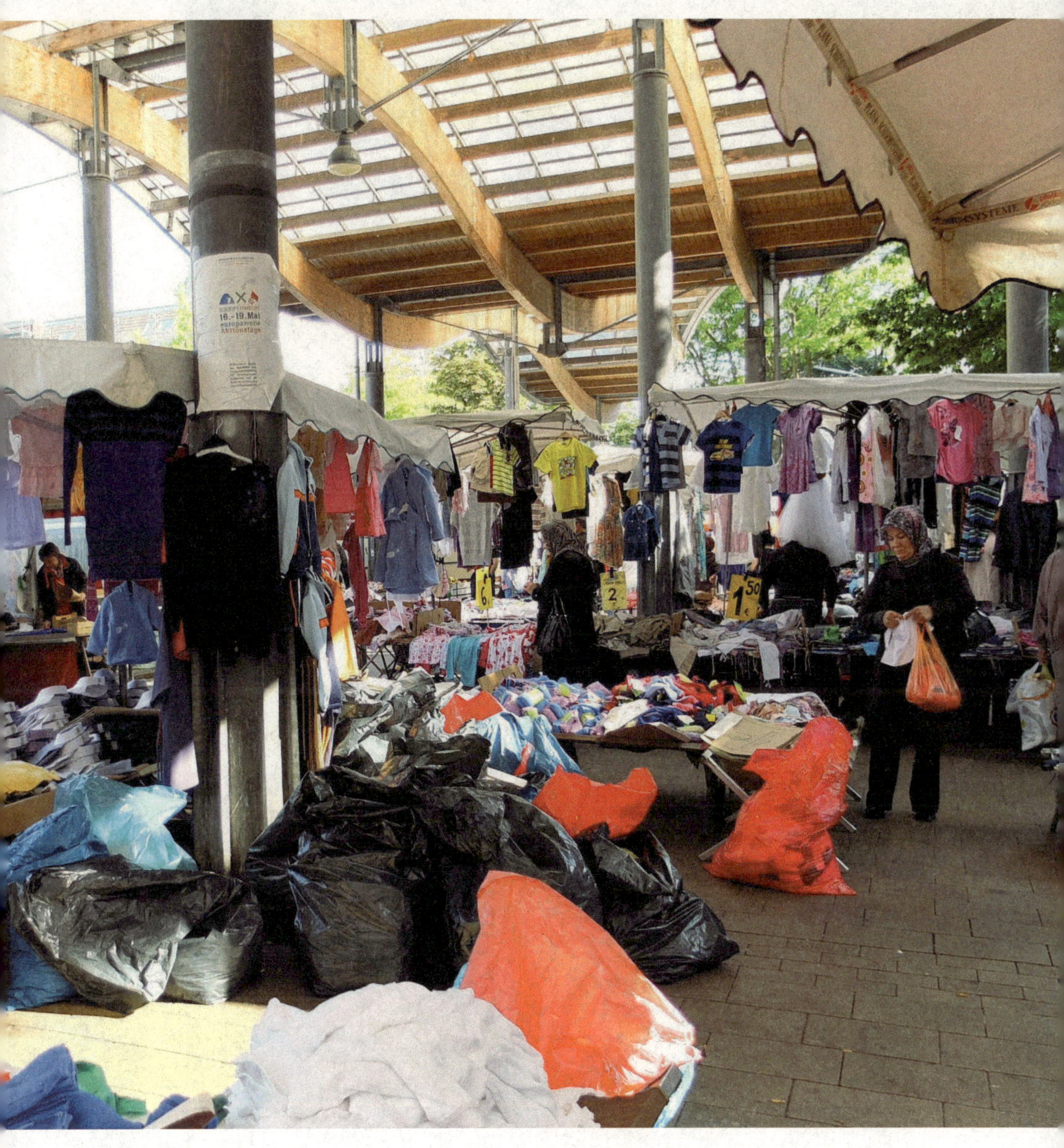

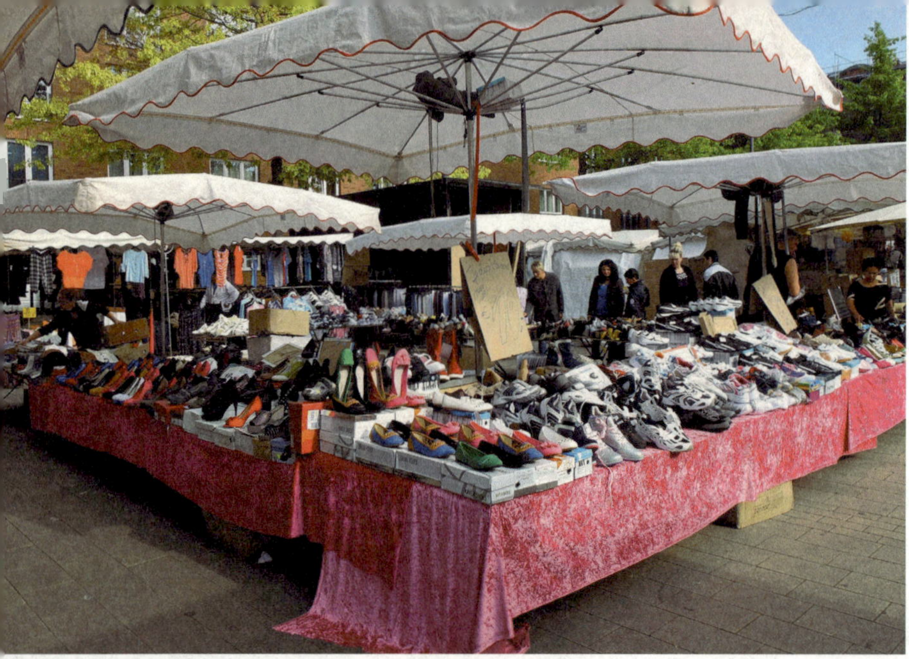

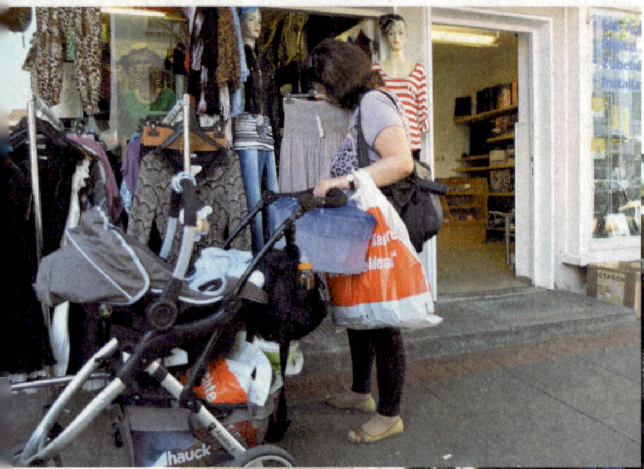

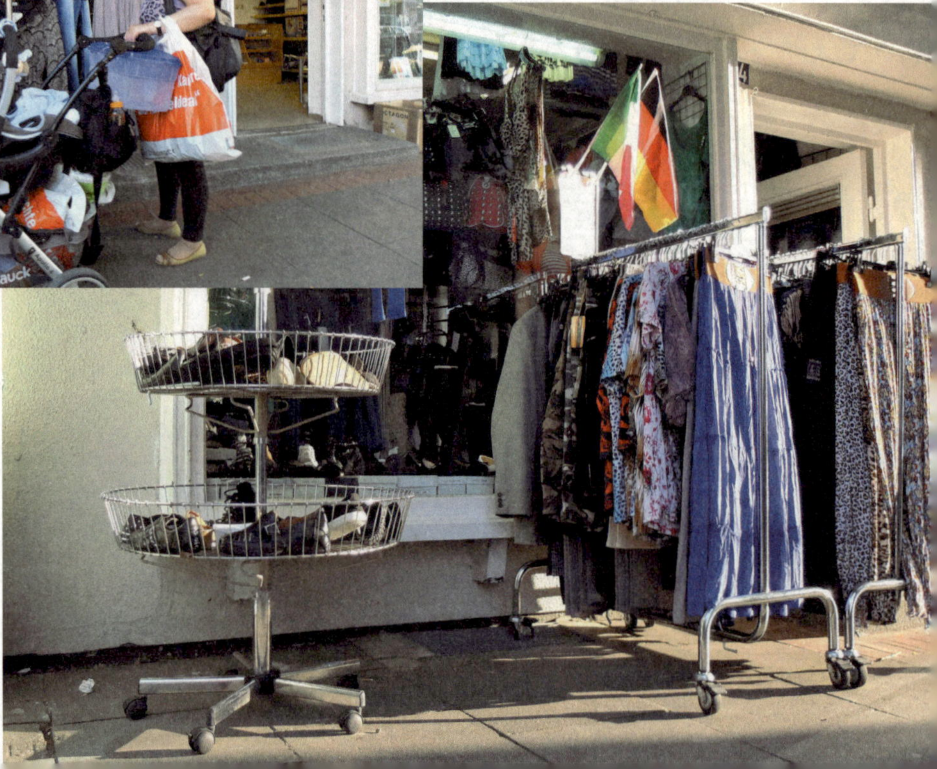

Fast sporty cars are important companions for many young men in Wilhelmsburg. The colored paint gleams, freshly polished. The relevant styling and care programs are available at the Superbox car wash or at the gas stations. The numerous car self-help workshops also offer an insight into relationships with these status symbols. The drivers of these tuned 'music boxes' also take great pride in their own appearance Show and Business . Turkish barbershops along Georg-Wilhelm- or Fährstraße are correspondingly well attended. Through the windows I watch as hair is shampooed, cut, and styled. The barbers skillfully cut the contours of bears, or shaving very nicely and neatly. From time to time I come across private nail studios and beauty parlors run by women amidst the detached and semi-detached houses. Informal and temporary beauty salons also numbered among my observations Temporary Outside Rooms .

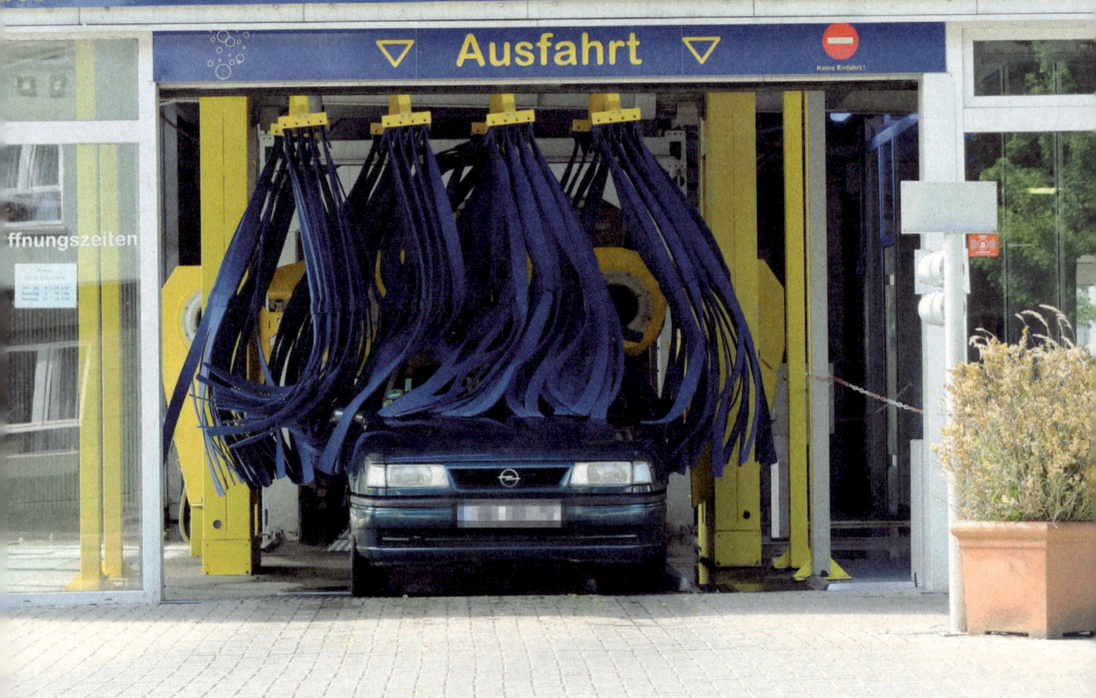

WASH
towäsche
Maximal sanft. Maximal rein.
Ausfahrt
Keine Einfahrt!
ffnungszeiten

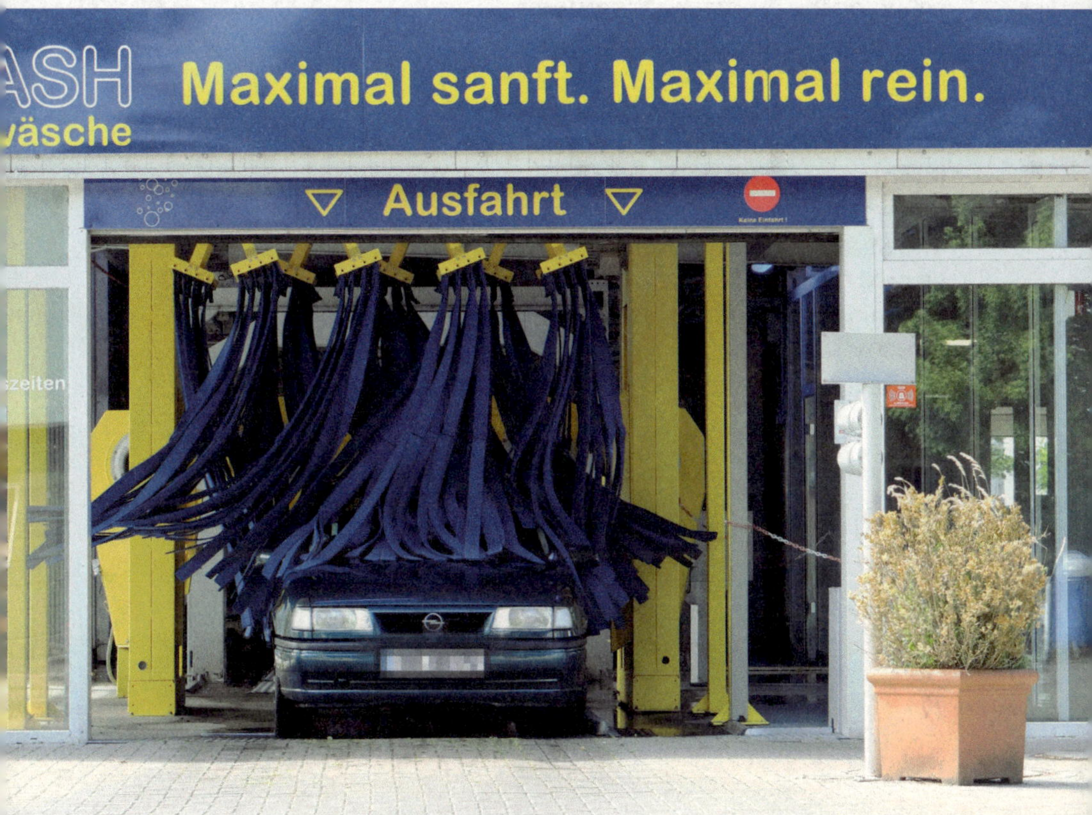
ASH
wäsche
Maximal sanft. Maximal rein.
▽ Ausfahrt ▽
Keine Einfahrt !
zeiten

Shortly after closing time on
the empty parking lot of the Turkish
supermarket, Sinti women are
sitting on the curbstone. Very beau-
tiful. They are lovely with their
long black shiny hair. One young
woman is lying across another's
lap on her brightly colored dress.
Bending over, she deftly plucks
the reclining woman's eyebrows
into shape. Little girls, little sisters
sit next to them with small dogs,
watching. They know this scene.
Already.

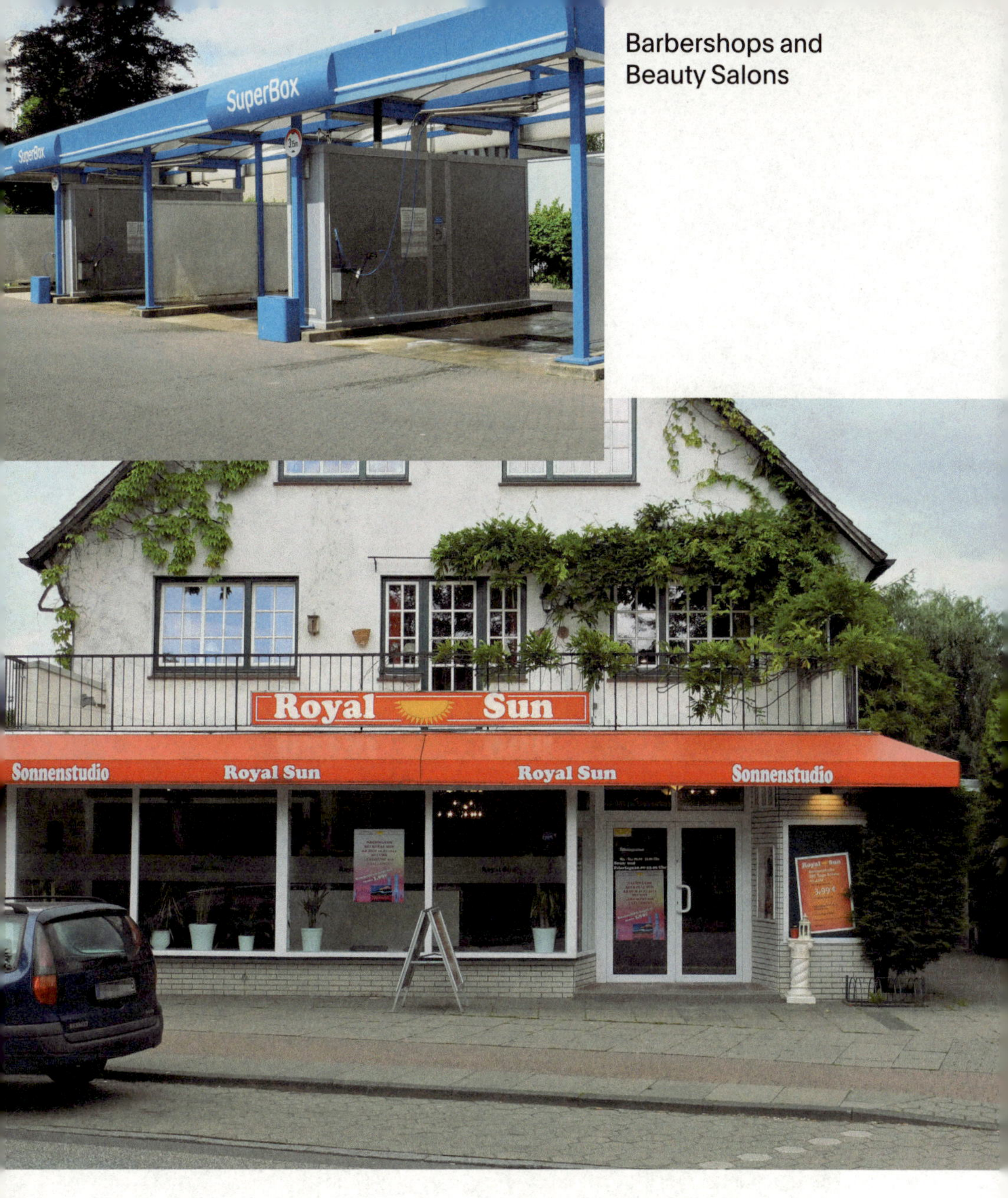

Barbershops and
Beauty Salons

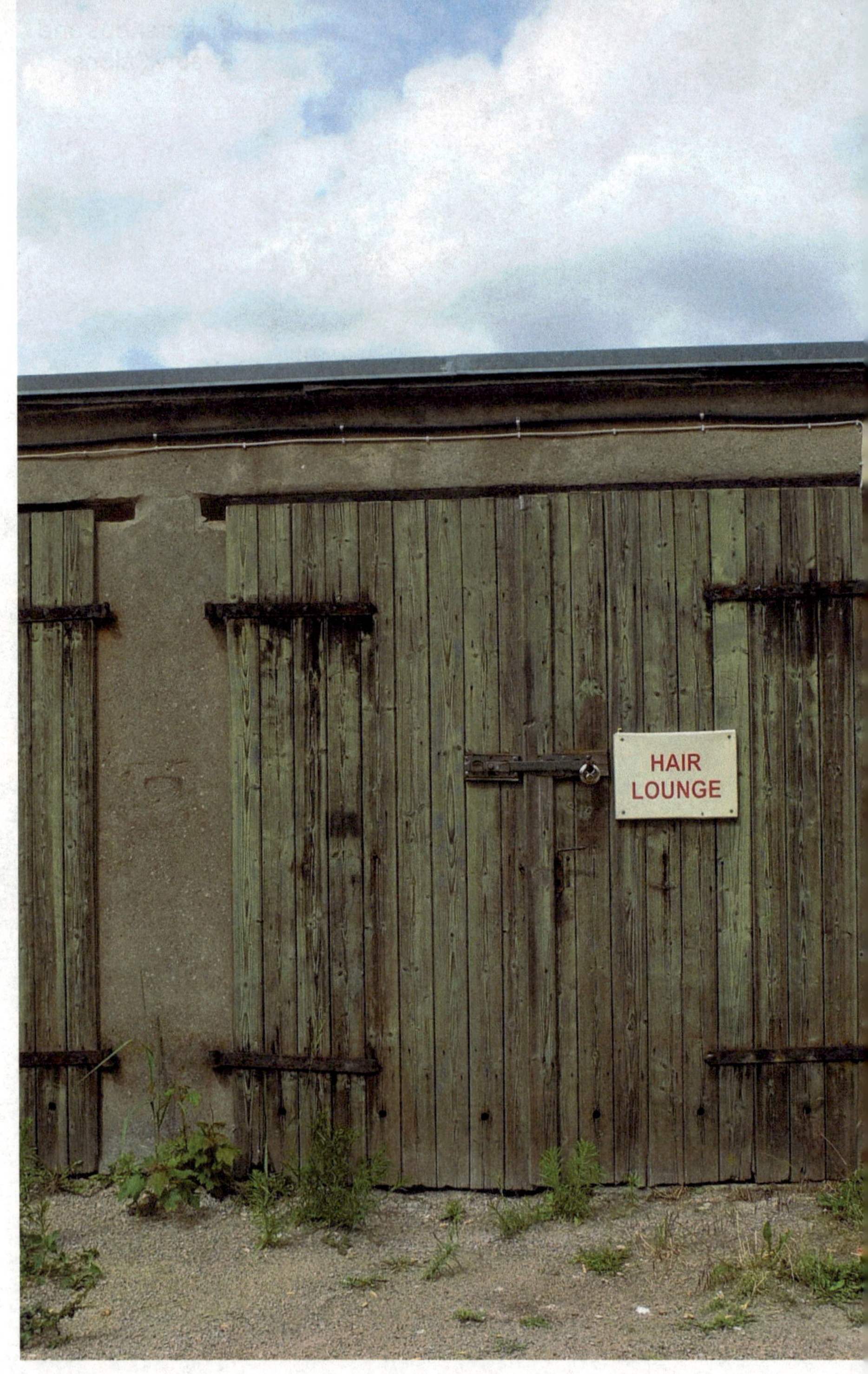

HAIR
LOUNGE

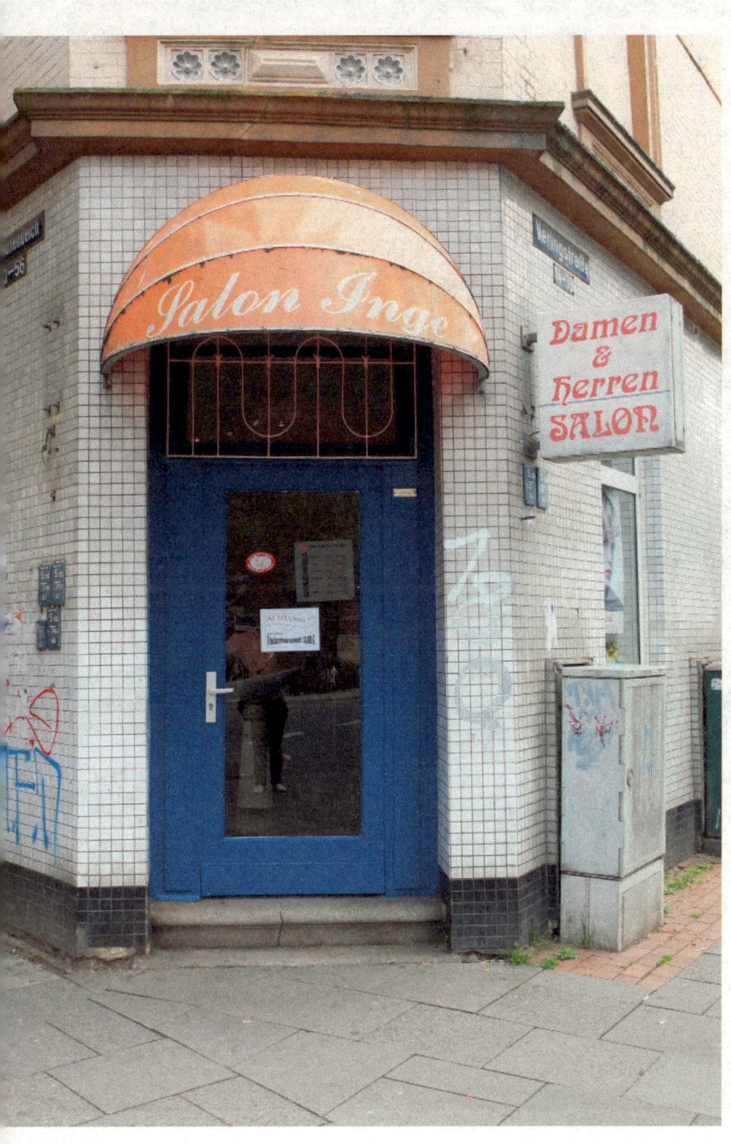
Salon Inge
Damen
&
Herren
SALON

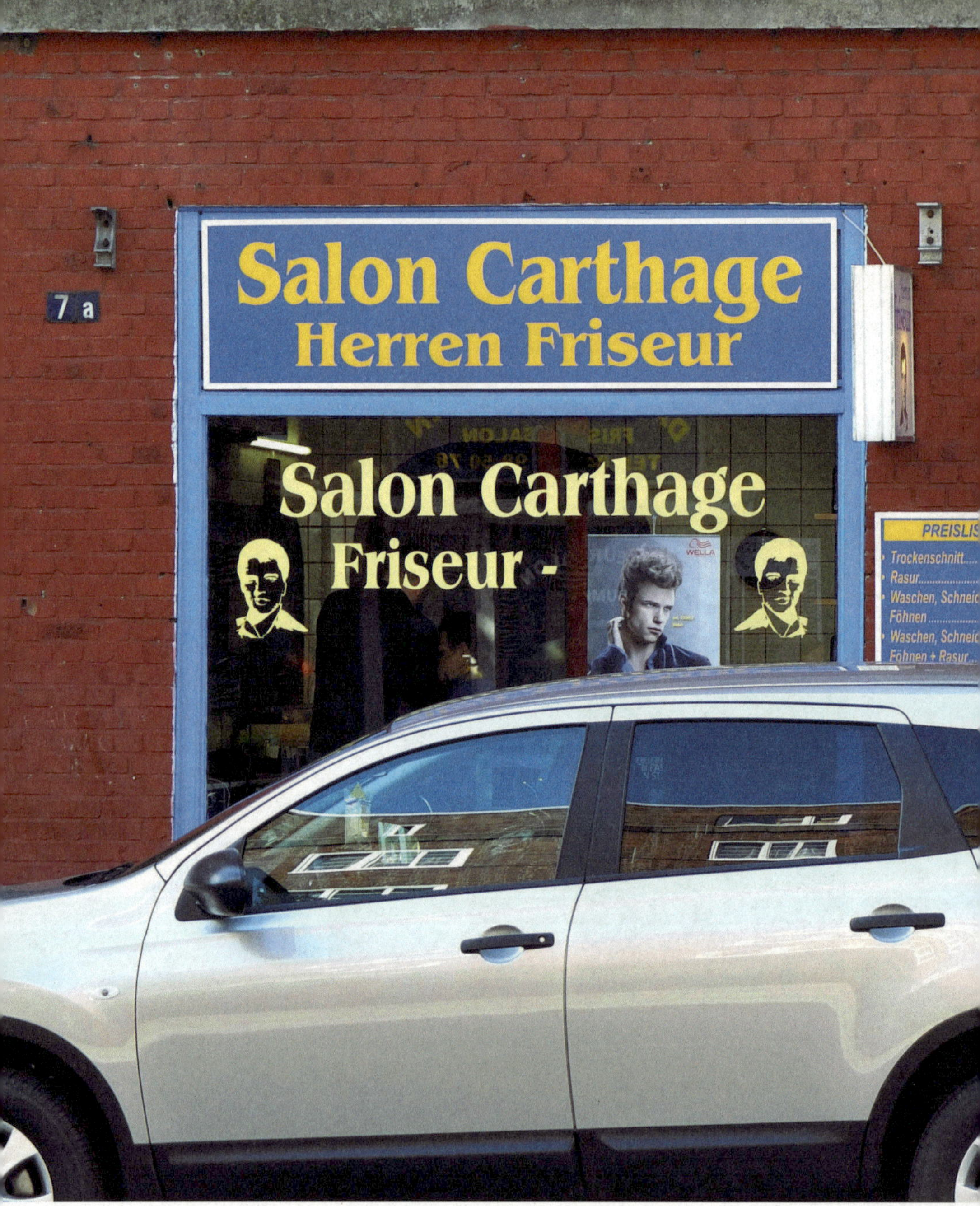
7 a
Salon Carthage
Herren Friseur
Salon Carthage
Friseur -
WELLA
PREISLIS
Trockenschnitt
Rasur
Waschen, Schneid
Föhnen
Waschen, Schneid
Föhnen + Rasur

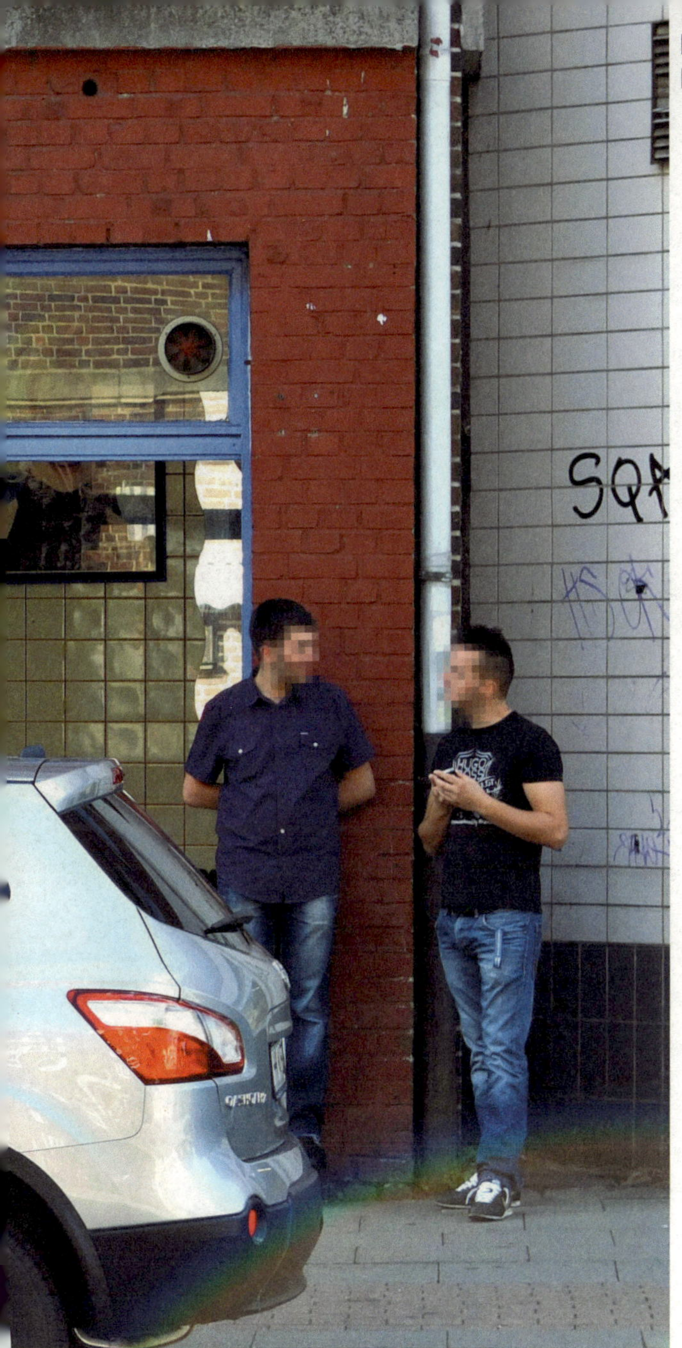

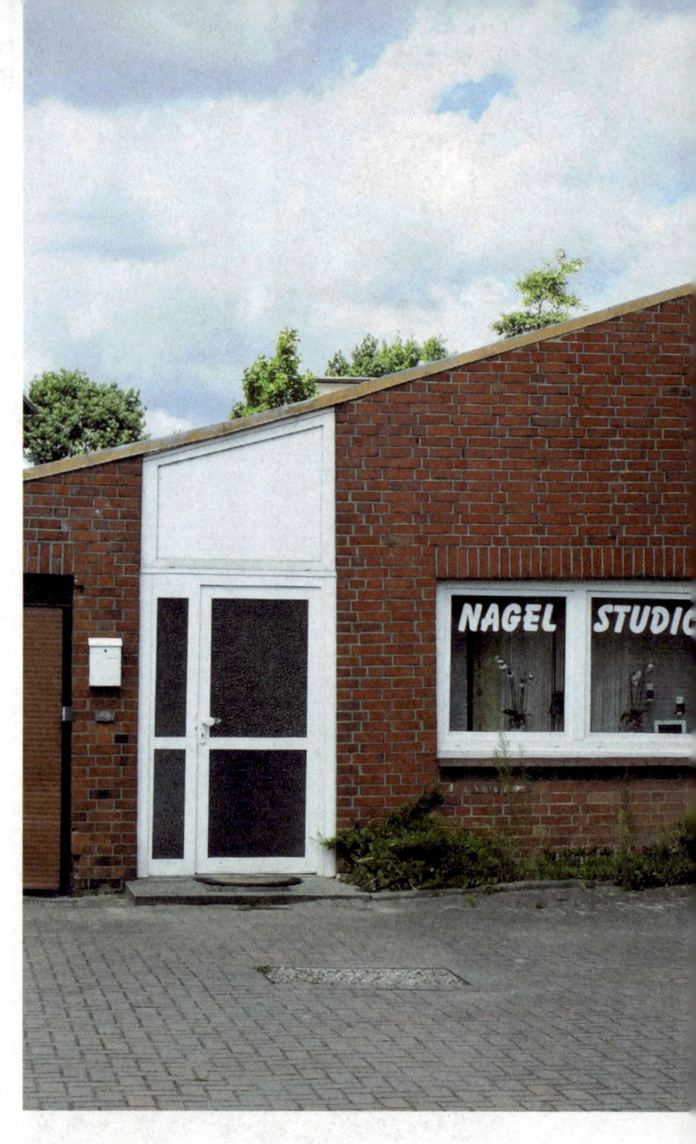
NAGEL STUDIO

...ıar 1995 erhoben wird, ...ınahme des Verkehrs ...ıfengebiet führen wür- ...ebenso wenig beant- ...Fragen nach großräu- ...ıngen. Dafür liege die ... nicht in Harburg, so

...ılhelmsburger wollen ...bißchen leben, oder ...am Leben bleiben", ... Herbert Wenzel ...ı von seiner Fraktion ...en interfraktionellen ...ıtsantrag.

...um die Flut vom ...die mit 6,02 Metern ...ıchste nach der Flut ...ar. „Das Wasser ist in ...uten um 2,63 Meter ...erläuterte Wenzel. ...ırg habe Glück ge- ...eine weiteren ungün- ...ren wie eine Springti-

eine Höhe von 7,20 Metern über Normal Null (NN). „Wir wären abgesoffen."

Der Dringlichkeitsantrag der SPD enthielt vier Forderungen, die auf Vorschlag der GAL um eine weitere ergänzt wurden. Danach fordert der Ortsausschuß einstimmig:

-die Deiche in kurzer Zeit auf eine Höhe von acht Metern zu bringen,

-die Deichrückverlegungsmaßnahmen bis auf weiteres einzustellen, da die Sicherheit absolut Vorrang habe,

-auf die Elbvertiefung auf 16,70 Meter zu verzichten,

-die Errichtung eines Sperrwerkes zu prüfen und

die Verwaltung aufzufordern zu prüfen, ob Überflutungsgebiete in anderen Bundesländern geschaffen werden können.

das Leben???" am Sonntag, 29. Januar, um 16.00 Uhr noch einmal im Bürgerhaus Wilhelmsburg, Mengestraße 20, aufführen.

Der Eintritt kostet zehn Mark. Personen, für die die Ermäßigung gilt, zahlen sieben Mark.

Vorbereitung auf die Geburt

kb - WILHELMSBURG. Eine „Vorbereitung auf die Geburt für Paare und Frauen" bietet die Elternschule Wilhelmsburg, Zeidlerstraße 75, an sieben Montagen zwischen dem 13. Februar und 27. März an.

Informationen und Anmeldungen bei Kursleiterin Diana Lührs, Telefon 04752-7534.

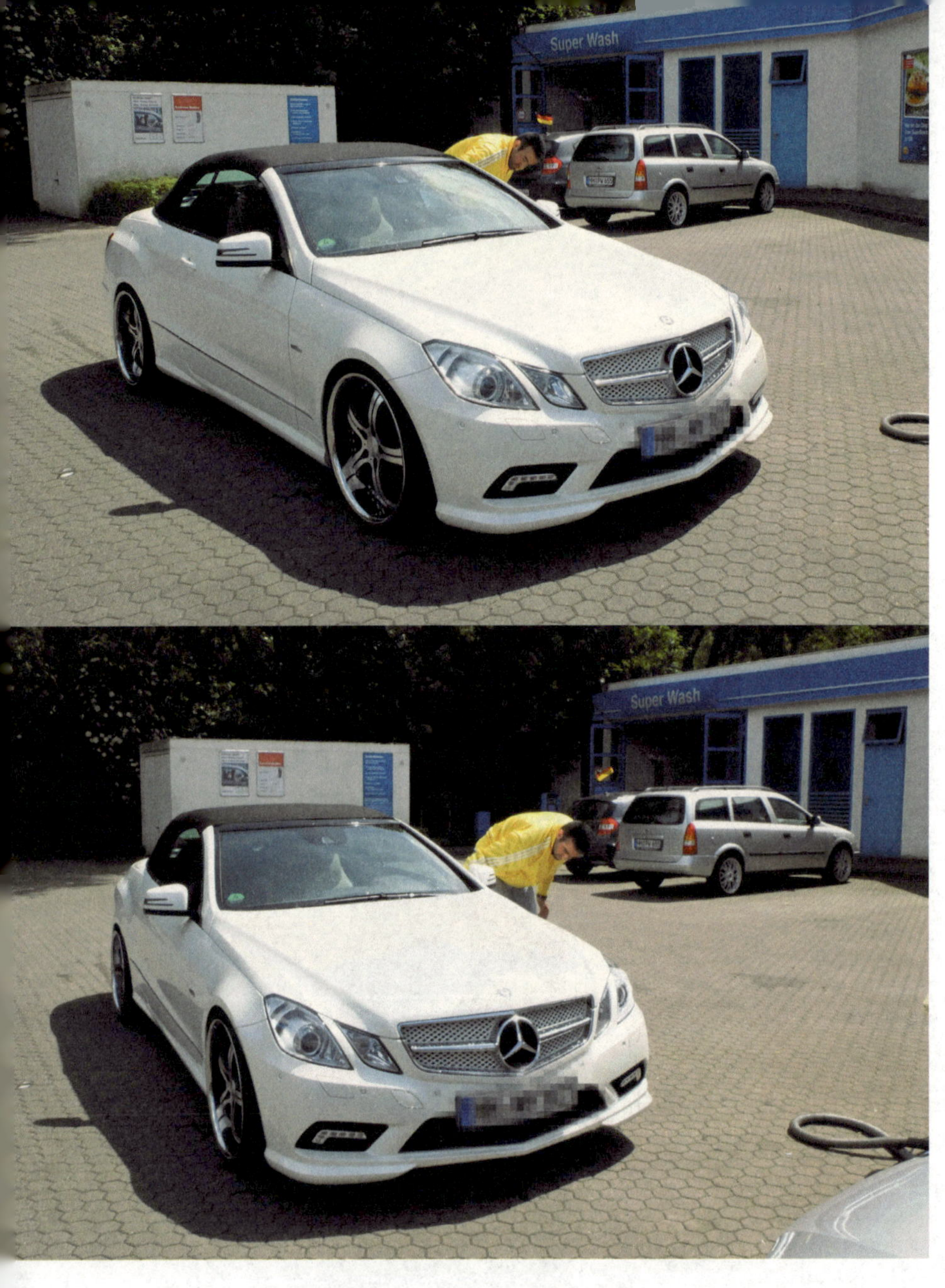

Super Wash

Augenbrauen
Zupfen !
5,-
Hier !!!
Heisswachs

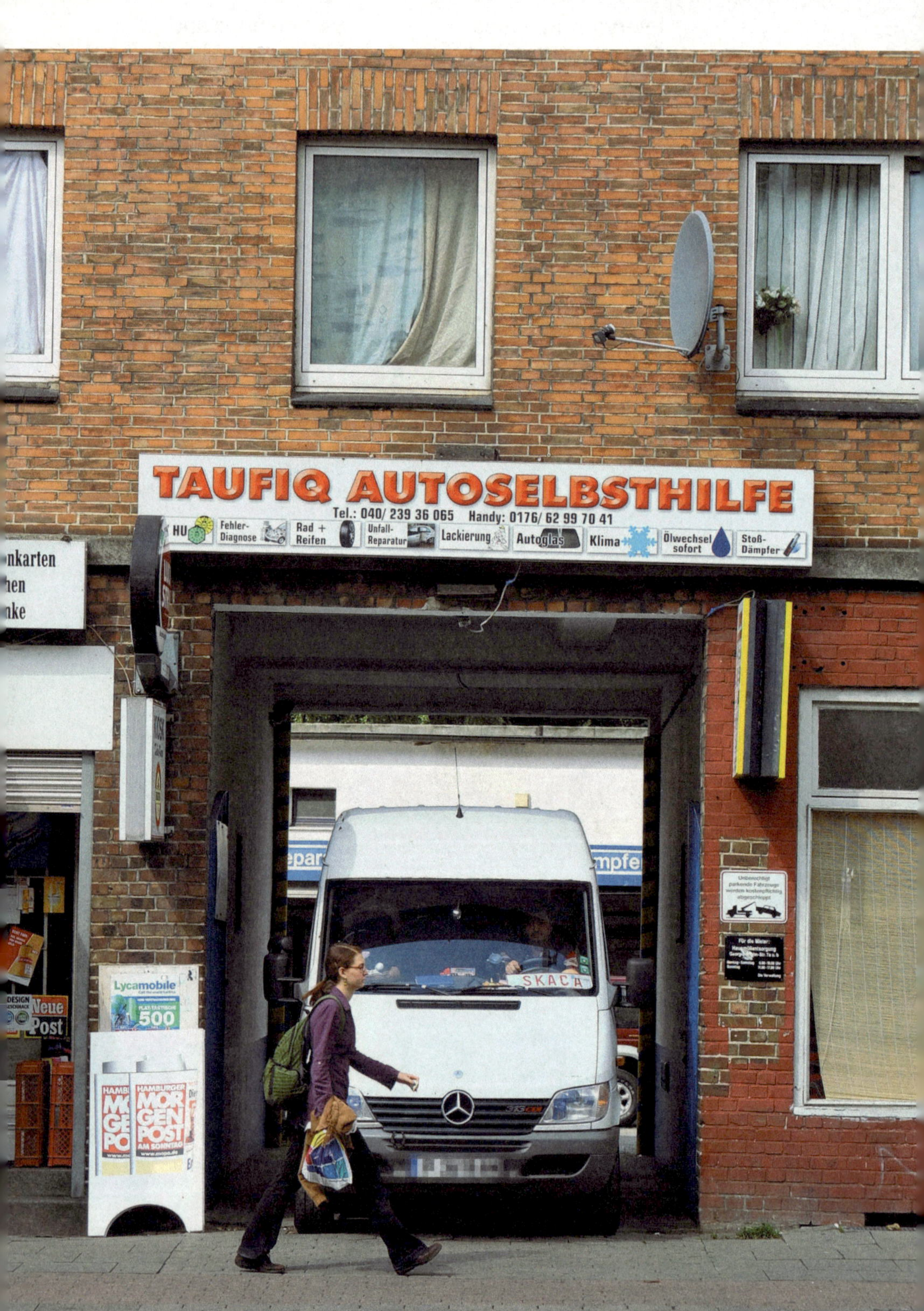
TAUFIQ AUTOSELBSTHILFE
Tel.: 040/ 239 36 065   Handy: 0176/ 62 99 70 41
HU
Fehler-
Diagnose
Rad +
Reifen
Unfall-
Reparatur
Lackierung
Autoglas
Klima
Ölwechsel
sofort
Stoß-
Dämpfer
Lycamobile
500
Neue
Post
HAMBURGER
MORGEN
POST
HAMBURGER
MORGEN
POST
AM SONNTAG
nkarten
ke

Breakfast and More
[In-vivo code]

The numerous fast food stands, kiosks, and small grocery
stores scattered around the port, or araound the commercial and industrial areas are already serving up the day's first
drinks and food to workers and truck drivers in the early
morning hours. Names like Uschi's Snack Bar, Rosi's Place,
The Coffee Bar, Snack and Sea, Breakfast and More, Food
for Everyone, or Selig Family Dekamarkt seem welcoming
and very promising in the rather dreary areas. One of the
owners told me "A lot of workers come to me for breakfast;
I get up at four clock and make fresh coffee and sandwiches
for them every morning." In his shop I could sense a trusting,
familiar atmosphere among the guests Territorial Stomping
Grounds . But it is not just workers who seek out these
family-like food sources during breaks and after work; school
pupils also appreciate the kiosks' wares on their way to
school. I often see children happily nibbling or slurping up
Chinese Yum-Yum noodle soups. A packet costs twenty-
five cents and, according to consumer reports they also taste
good when dry, as well as filling. Just pour hot water or even
sweet Coca Cola over the contents of the pack and wait until
the noodle soup and its aromatic additives soften. The colored
bags and small extra packets can be found in many places.
Close by you will find the remains of the neon-colored popsi-
cles packaged in plastic packets Stands for Lingering .

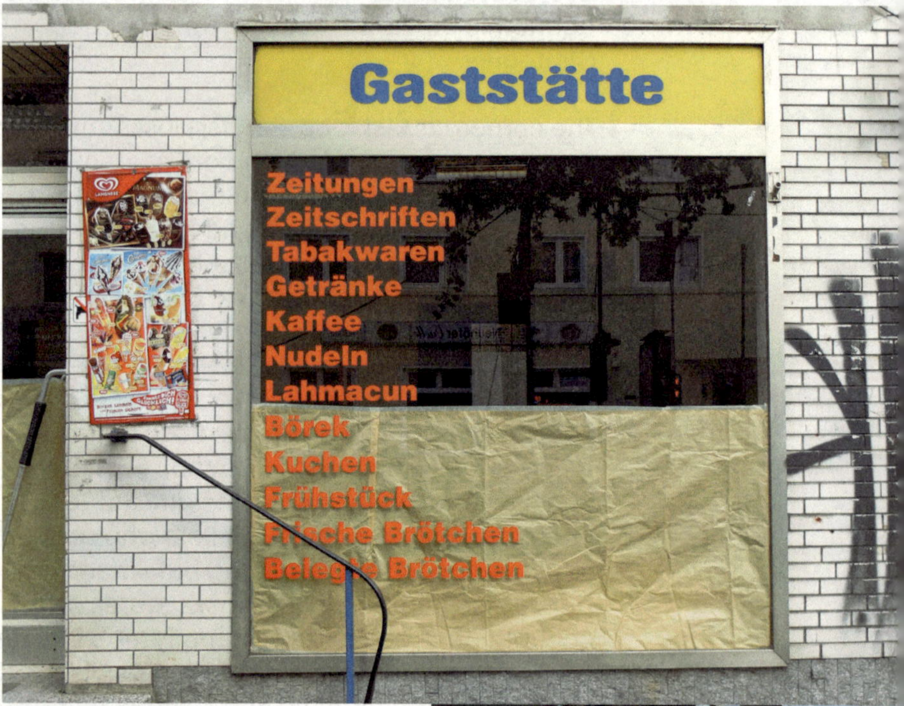

Gaststätte
Zeitungen
Zeitschriften
Tabakwaren
Getränke
Kaffee
Nudeln
Lahmacun
Börek
Kuchen
Frühstück
Frische Brötchen
Belegte Brötchen

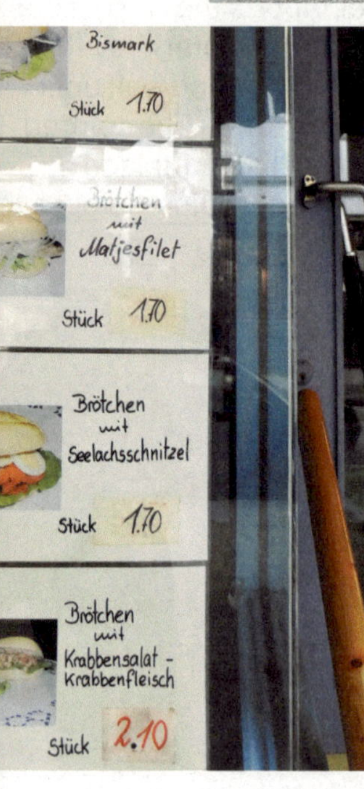

Bismark
Stück 1.70
Brötchen mit Matjesfilet
Stück 1.70
Brötchen mit Seelachsschnitzel
Stück 1.70
Brötchen mit Krabbensalat - Krabbenfleisch
Stück 2.10

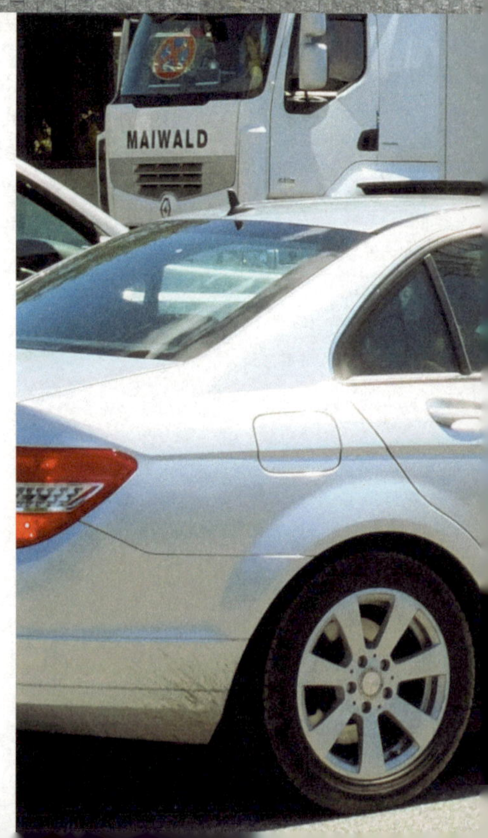

MAIWALD

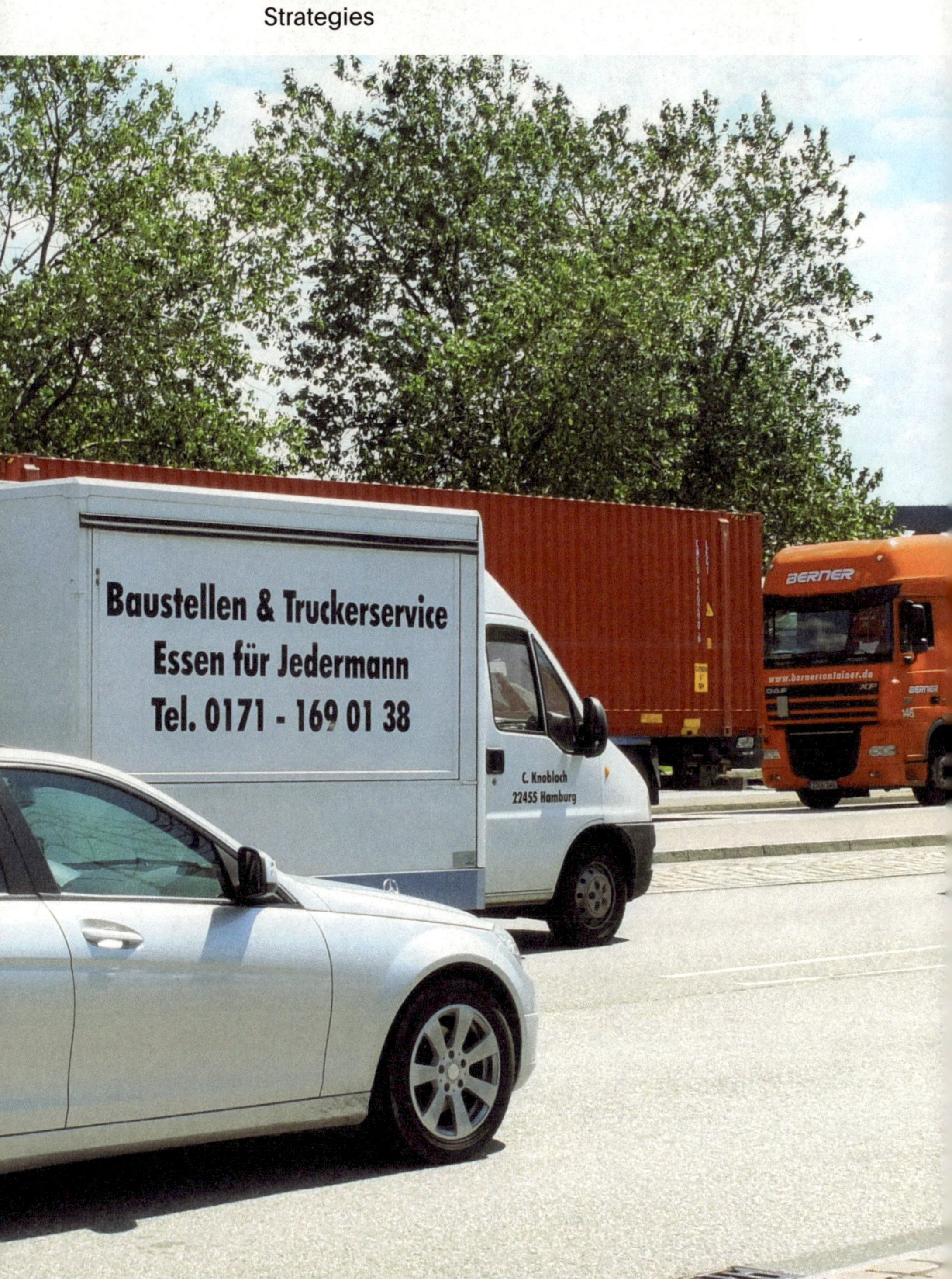
Baustellen & Truckerservice
Essen für Jedermann
Tel. 0171 - 169 01 38
C. Knobloch
22455 Hamburg
BERNER
www.bernercontainer.de

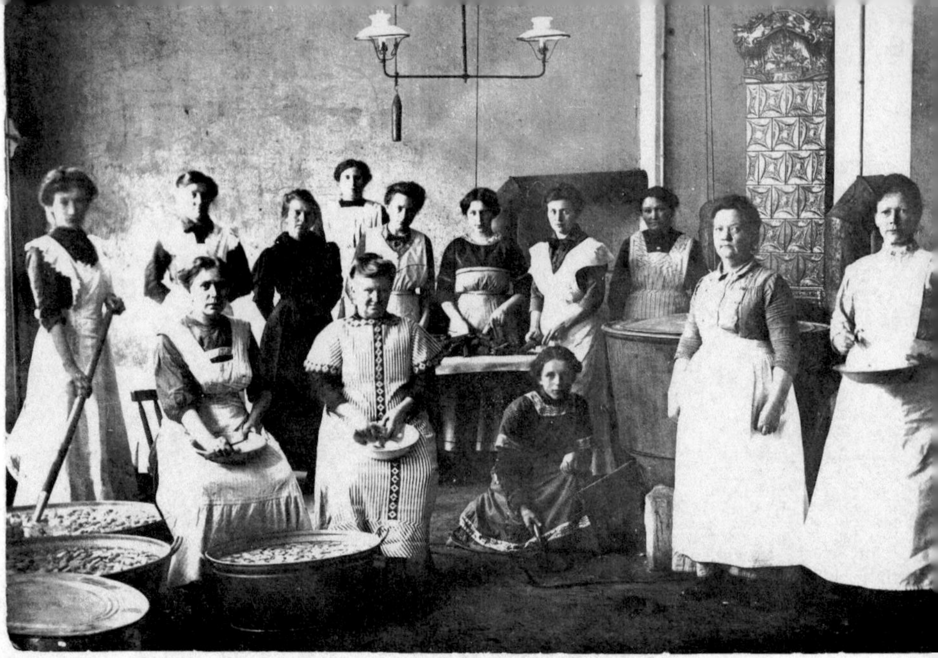

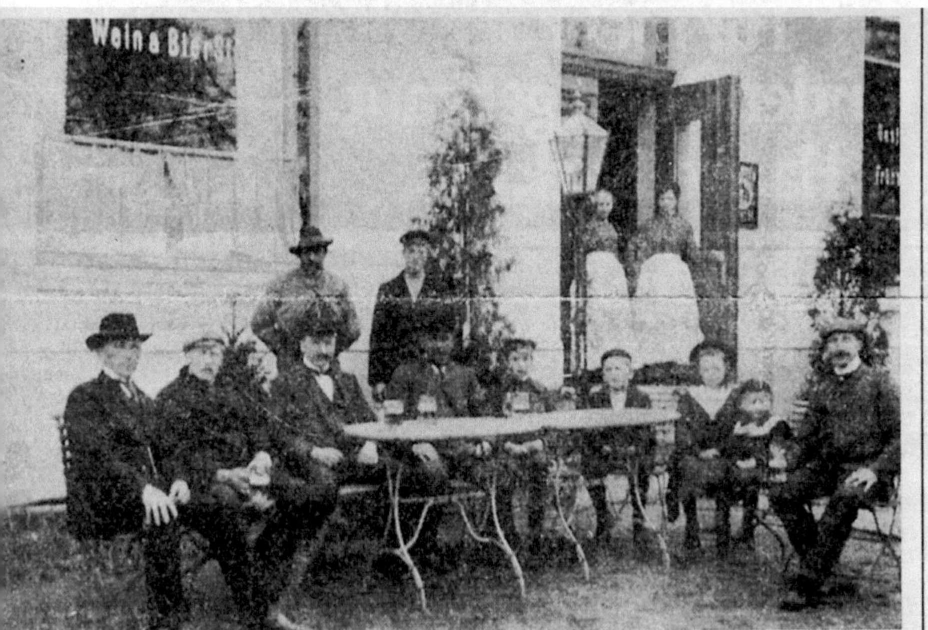

s war's — ein Foto von 1903. Beim Bier vor der Gaststätte traf der Fotograf auch Joh. Busch (4. von links), den
(5. v. links) sowie Camilla und Richard Busch (3. und 2. von rechts). Für die Kinder gab es natürlich kein
„kühles Blondes".

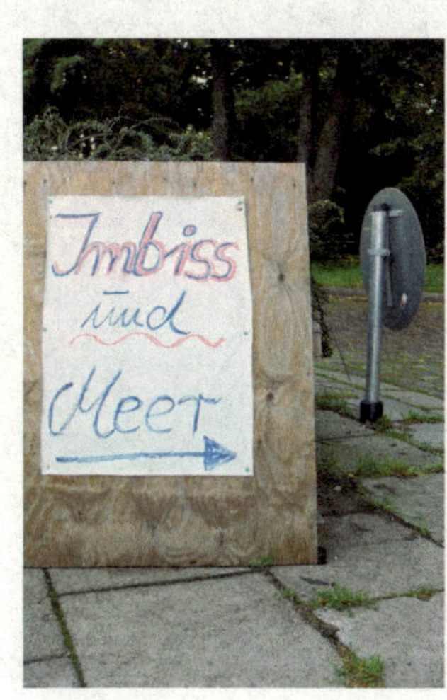
Imbiss
und
Meer

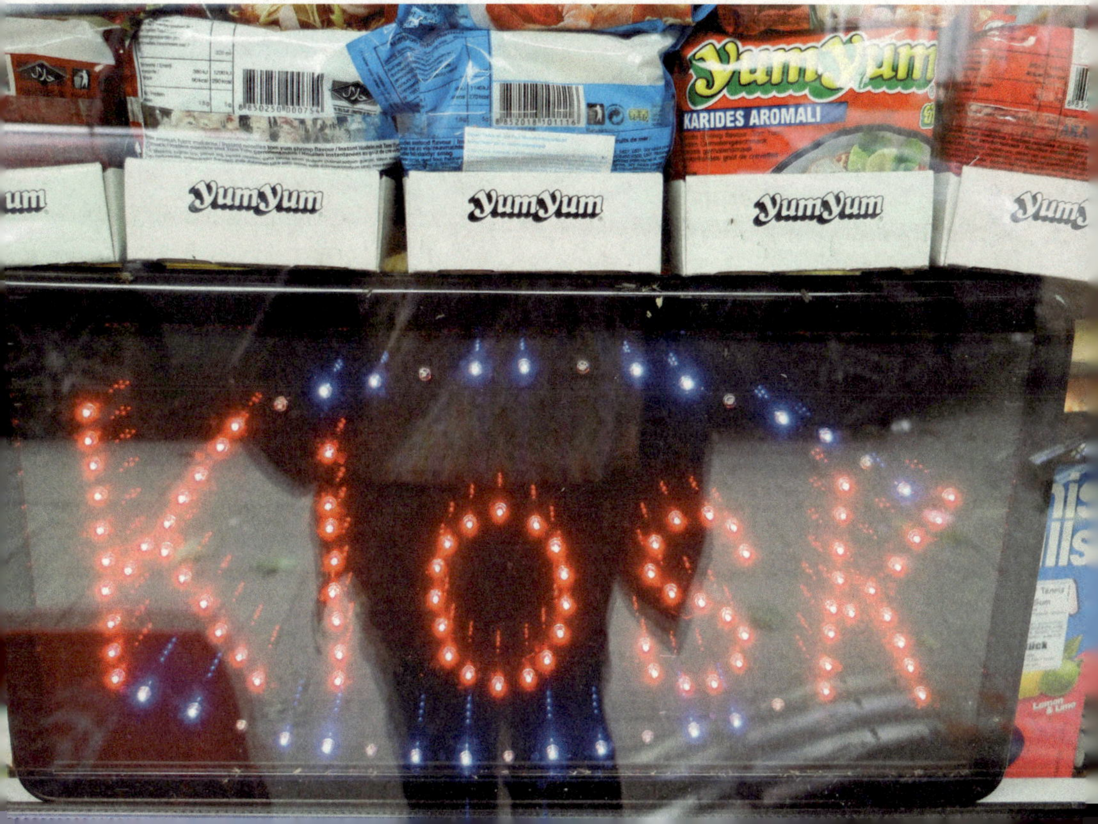

Currywurst
120g. Stück 190 Eu.
Frikadelle
Stück 15
Riesen-Currywurst
180g. Stück 250 Eu.
Schnitzel
ca. 250g. Stück 43
Krakauer Schinkenwurst
150g. Stück 210 Eu
Schaschlik
m. Zigeunersauce 260
Bockwurst
Stück 160 Eu
3 Kartoffelpuffer
m. Apfelmus 240
Feine Bratwurst
120g. Stück 170 Eu
Speck-Kartoffelsalat
Port. 170

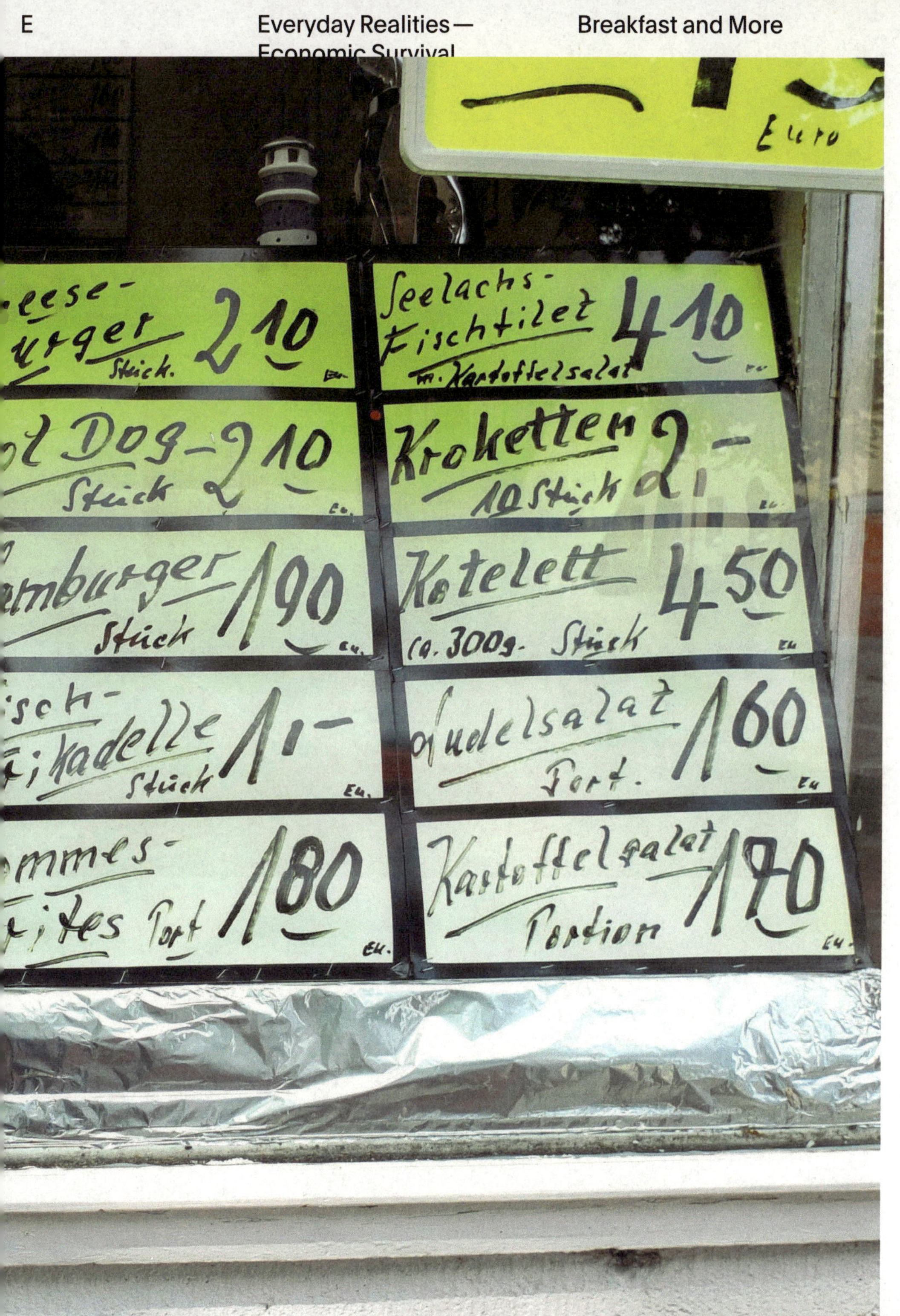
Euro
eese-
urger Stück 2 10
Seelachs-
Fischfilet 4 10
m. Kartoffelsalat EU
Dog 2 10
Stück EU
Kroketten
10 Stück 2 –
EU
amburger 1 90
Stück EU
Kotelett 4 50
ca. 300g. Stück EU
isch-
ikadelle 1 –
Stück EU
udelsalat 1 60
Port. EU
ommes-
ites Port 1 80
EU
Kartoffelsalat 1 70
Portion EU

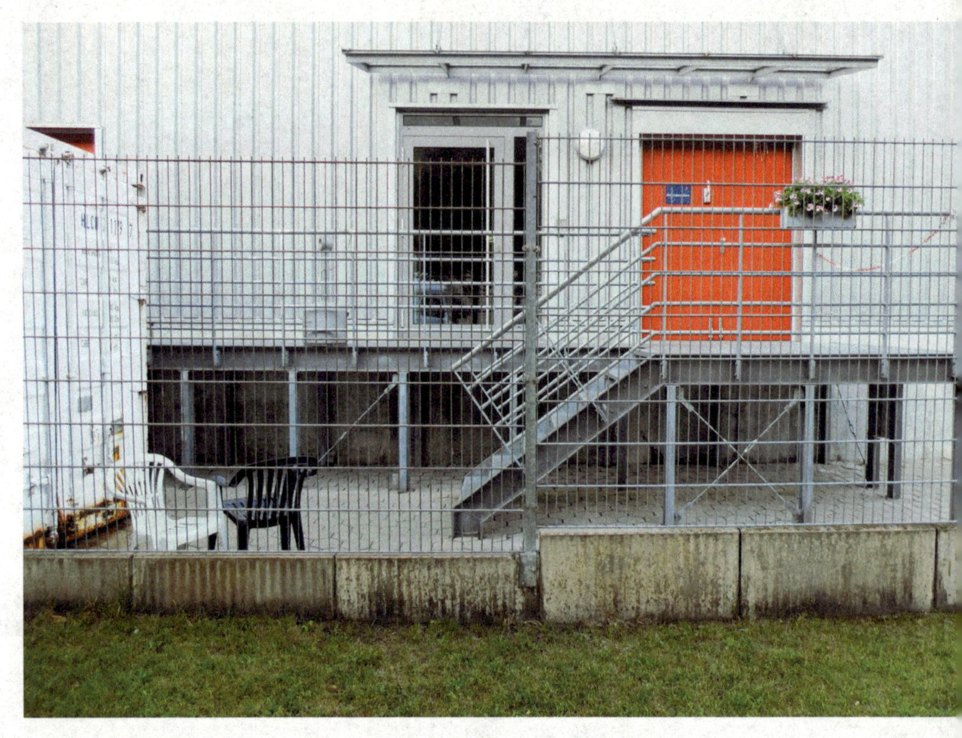

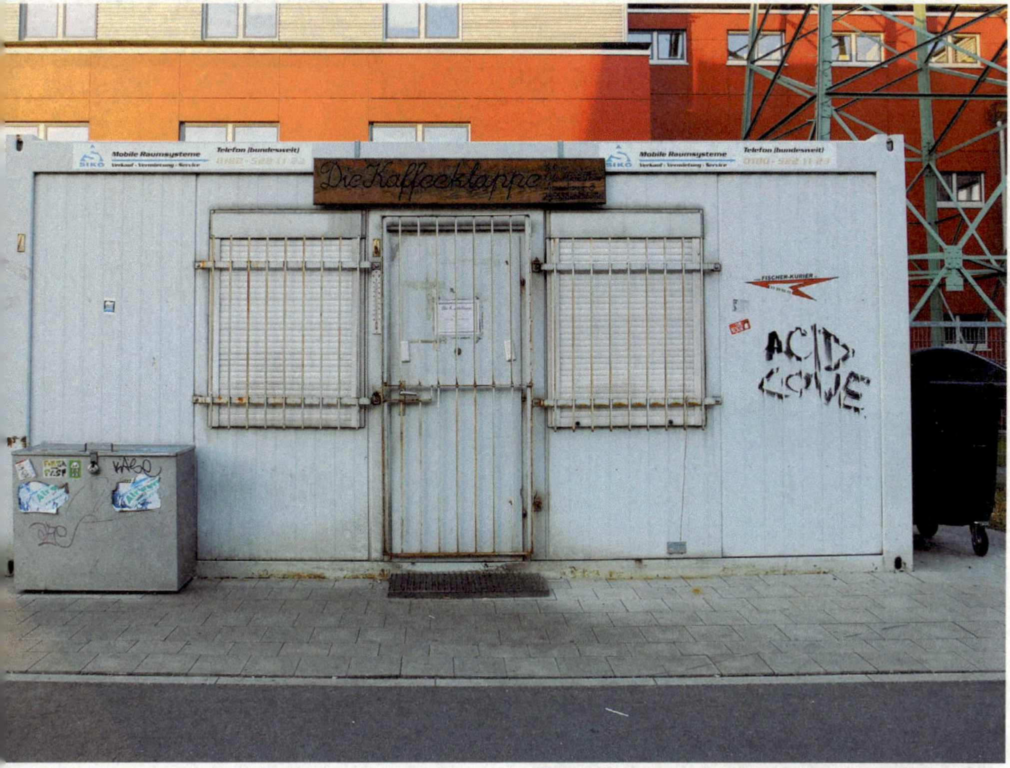

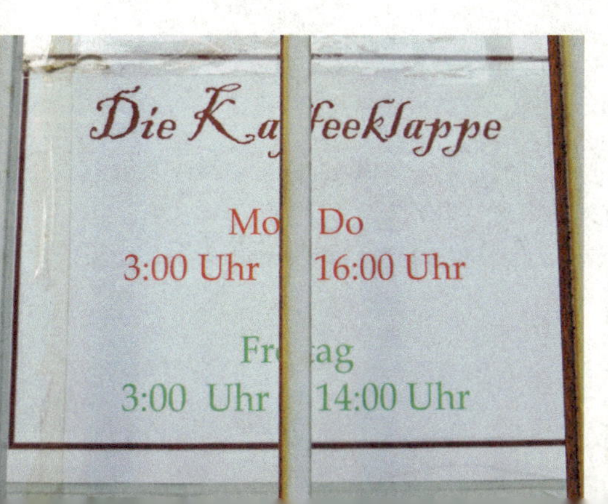
Die Kaffeeklappe

Mo   Do
3:00 Uhr   16:00 Uhr

Freitag
3:00 Uhr   14:00 Uhr

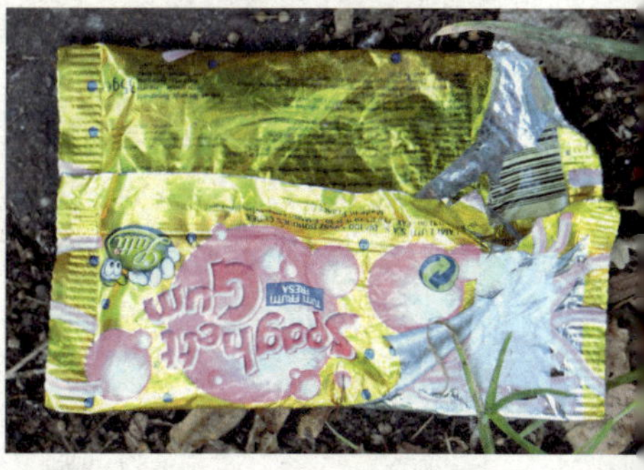

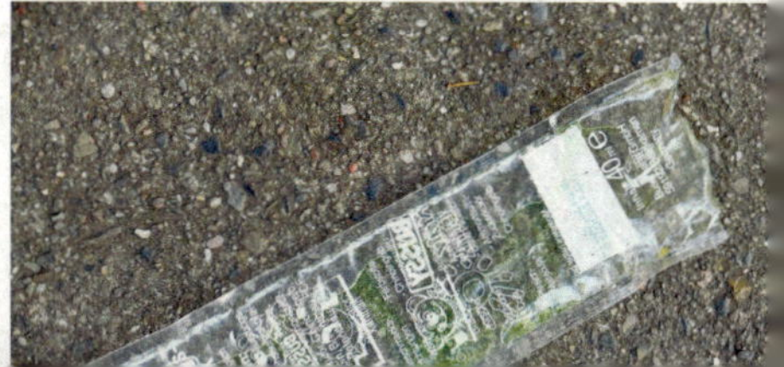

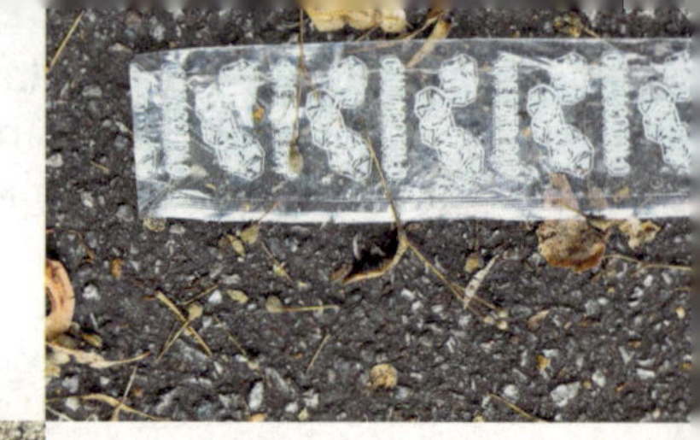

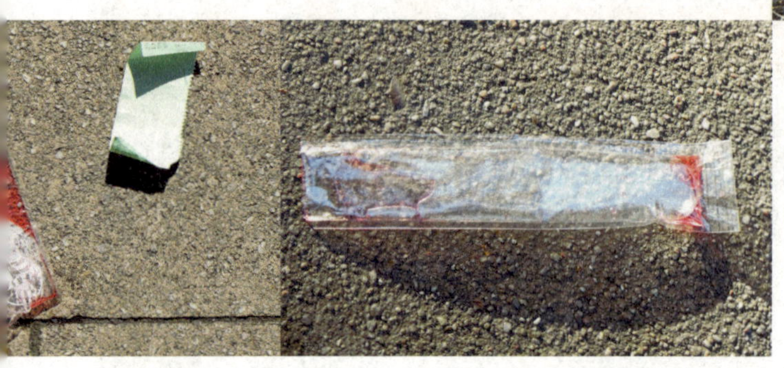

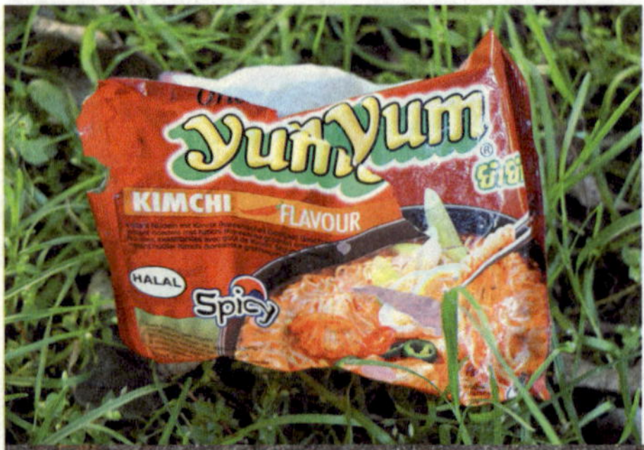

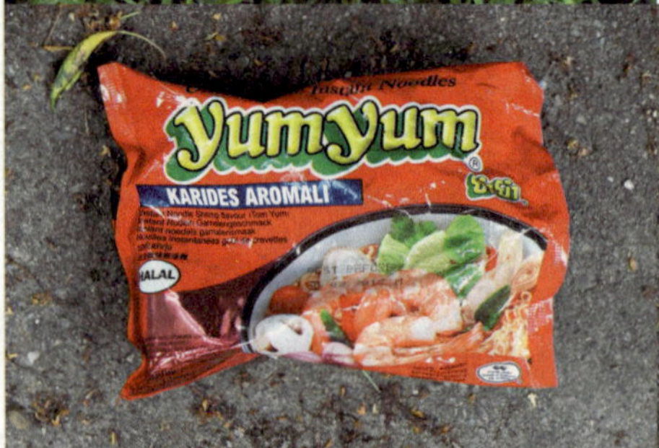

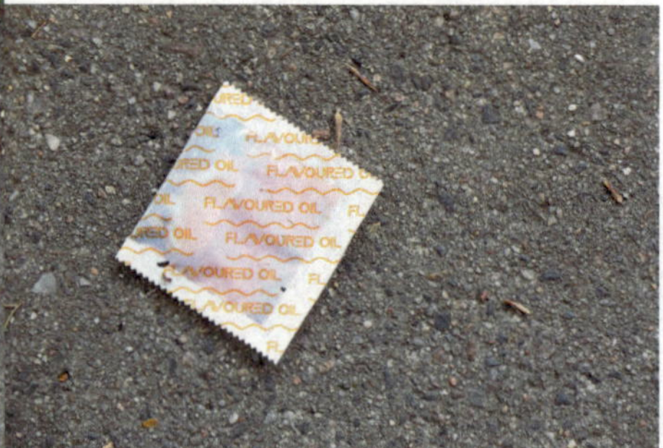

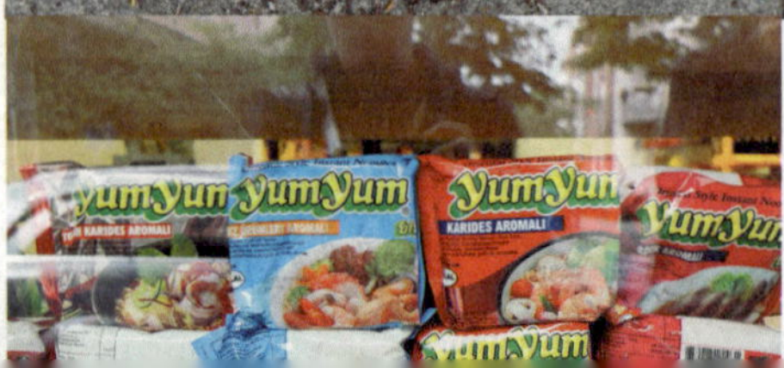

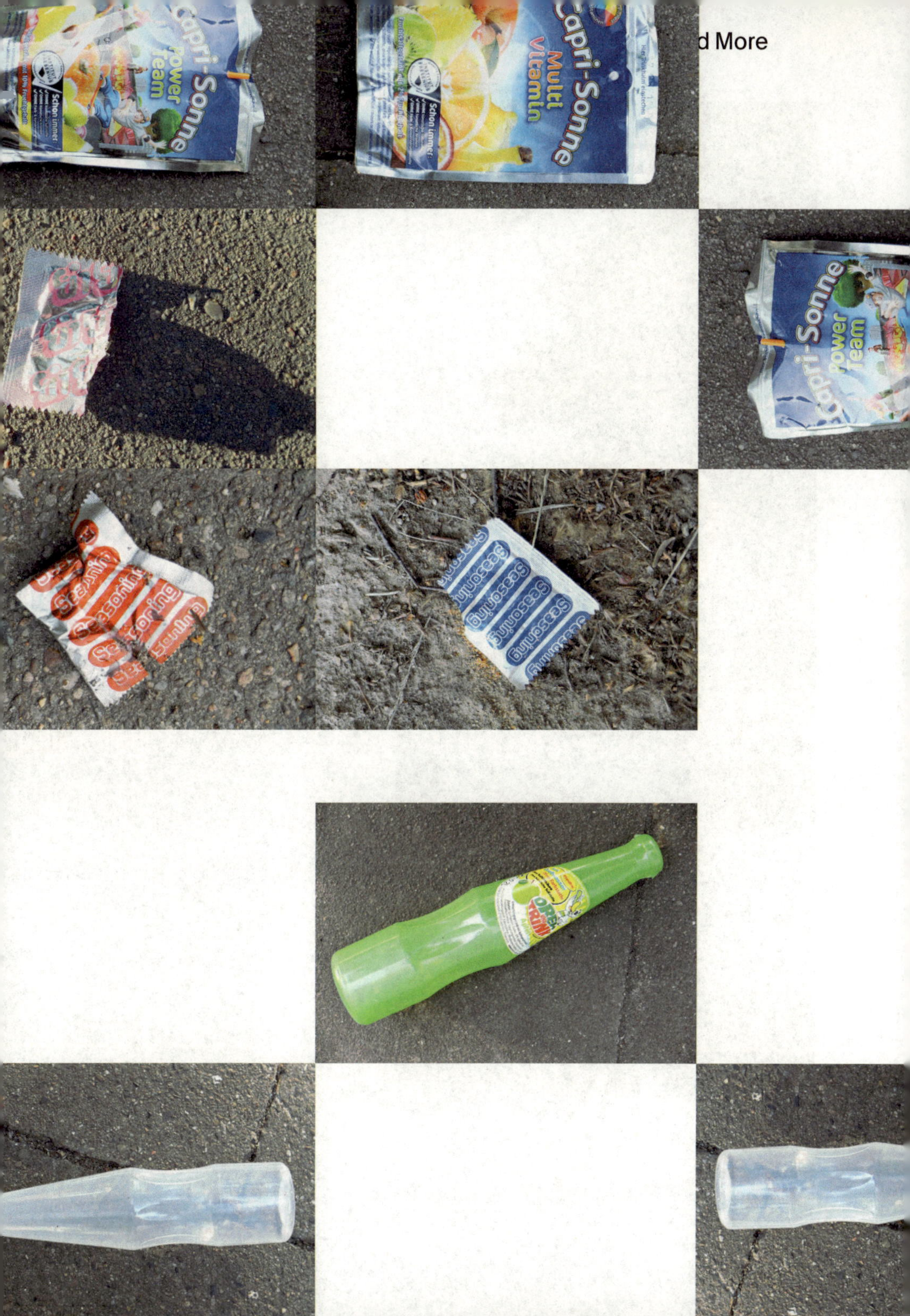
d More
Capri-Sonne
Power Team
Capri-Sonne
Multi Vitamin
Schon immer
Capri-Sonne
Power Team
Seasoning
Seasoning

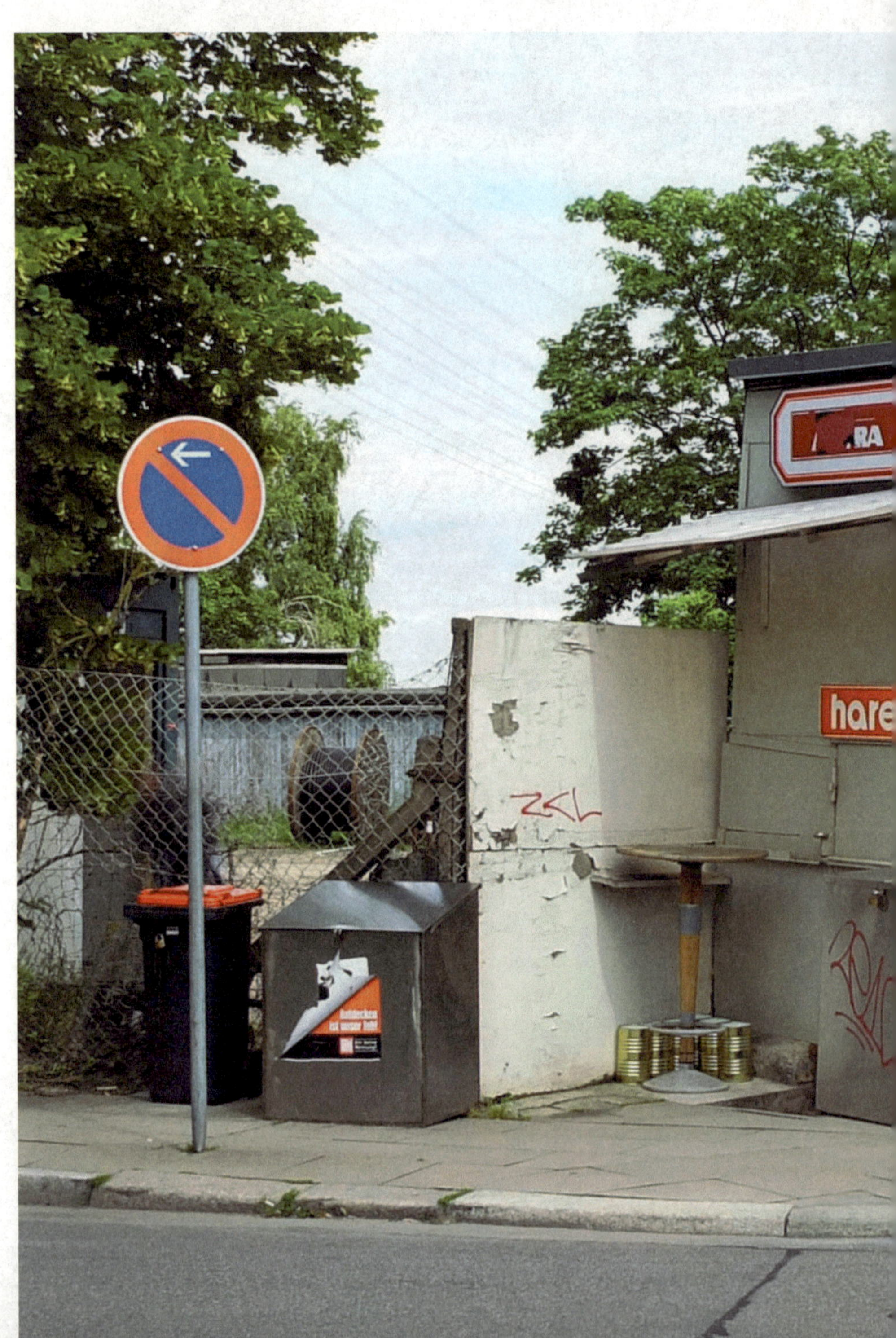
RA
hare
Bettdecken
ist besser jetzt

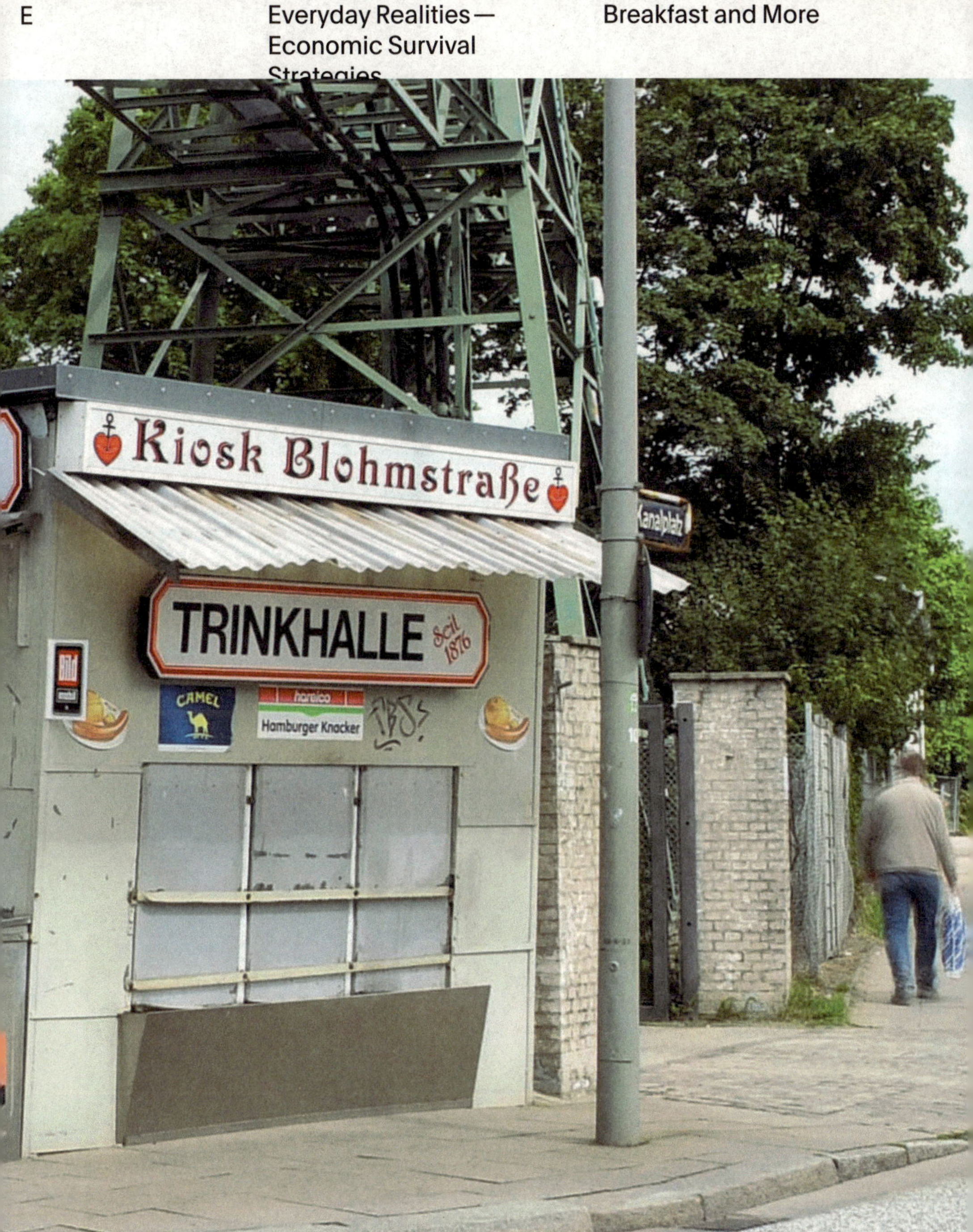
Kiosk Blohmstraße
TRINKHALLE Seit 1876
Bild mobil
CAMEL
hartico
Hamburger Knacker
Kanalplatz

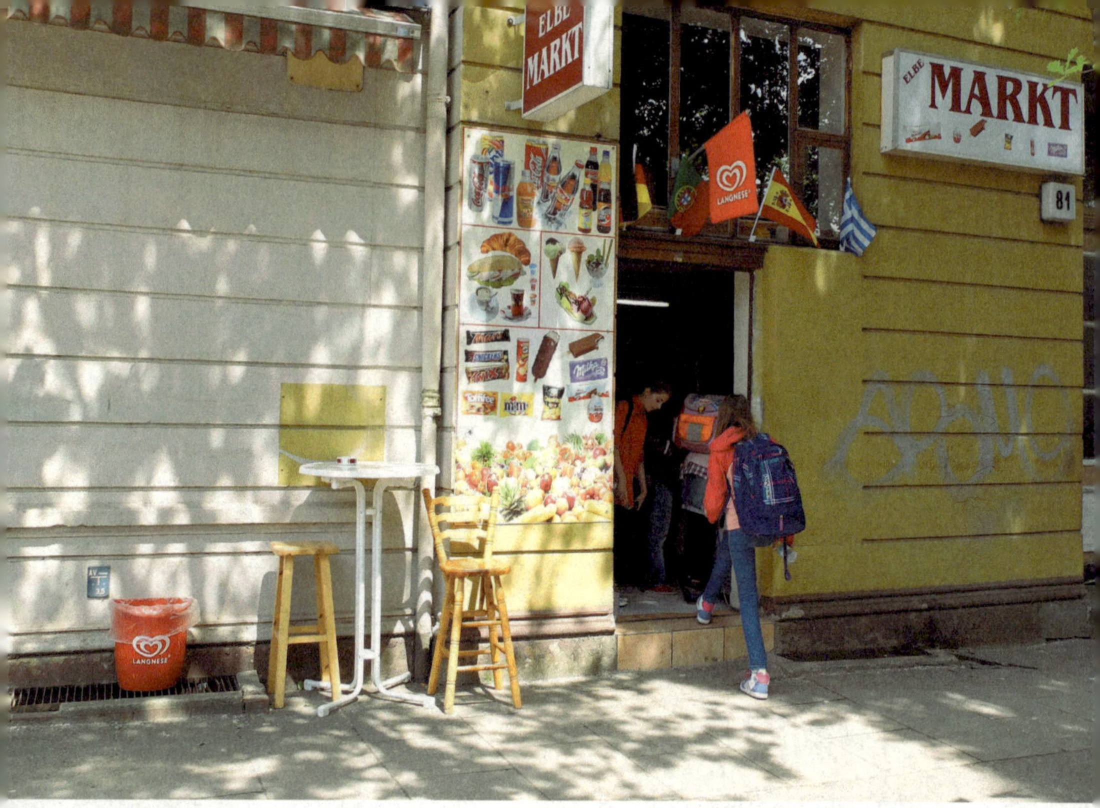

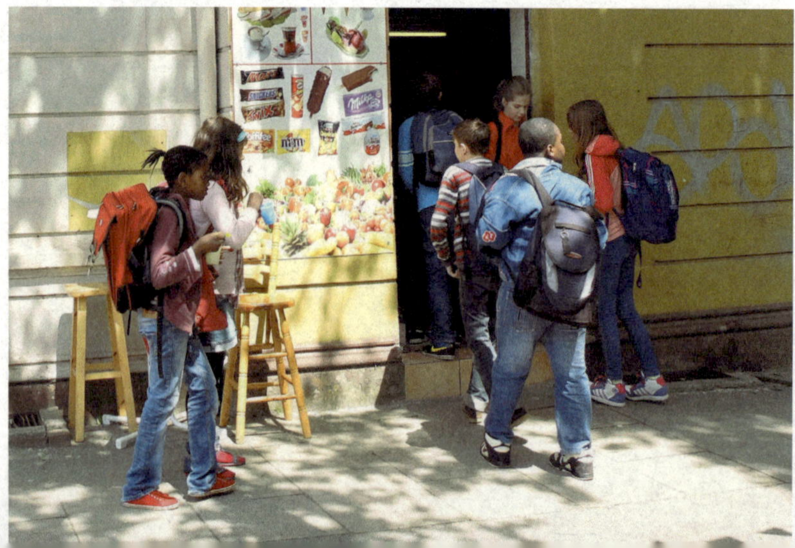

Everyday Realities —
Economic Survival
Strategies

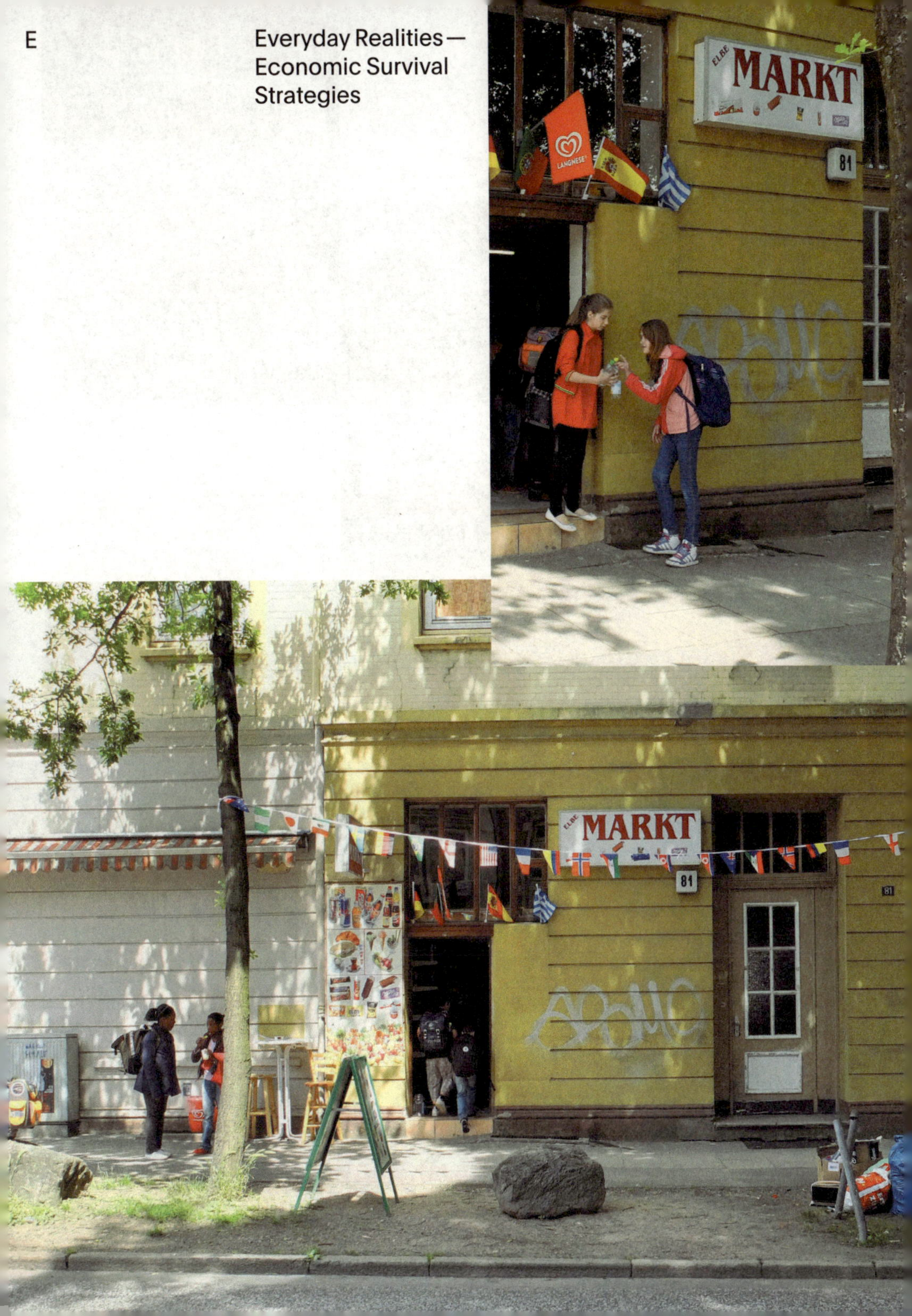

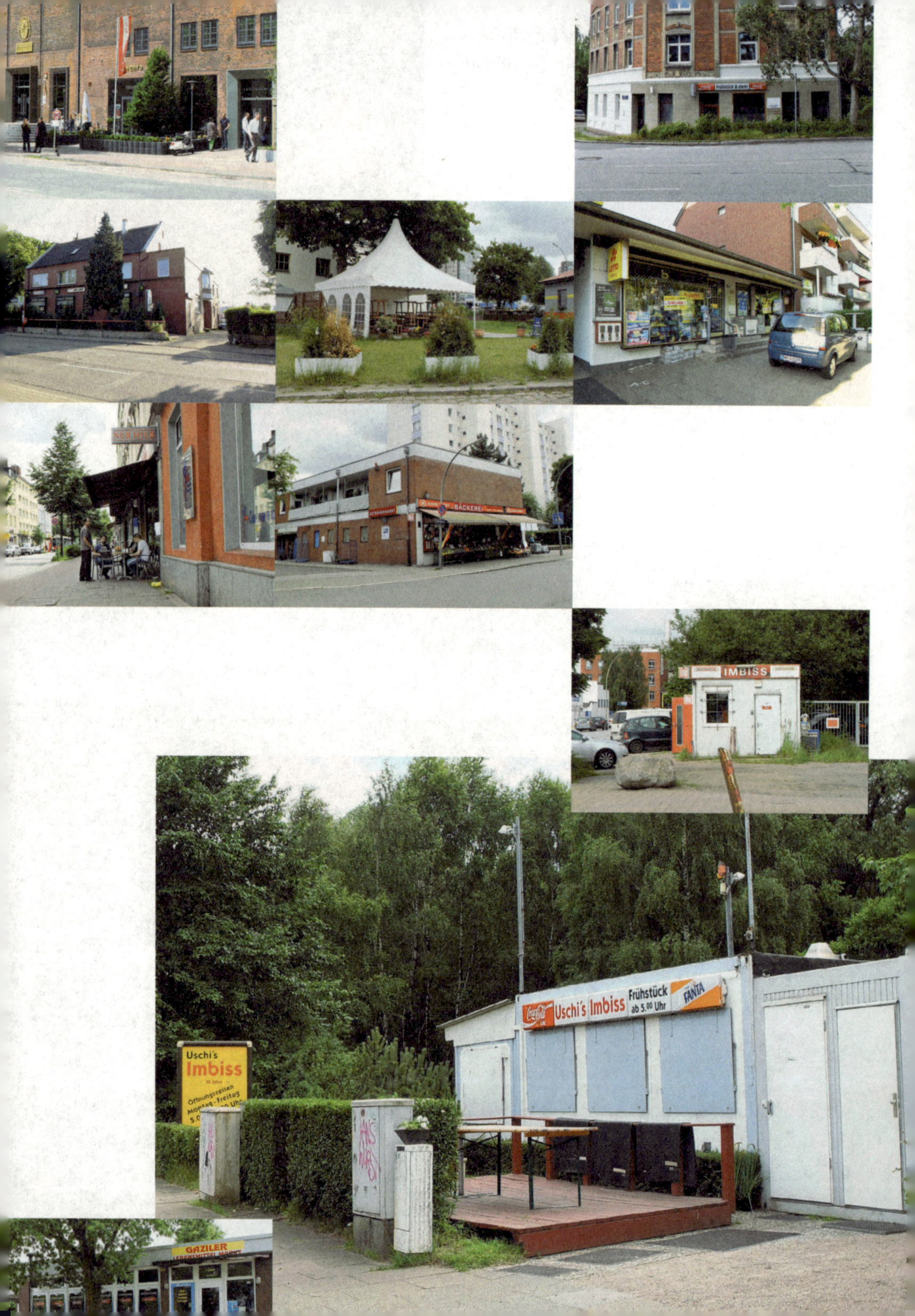

Uschi's Imbiss
Frühstück ab 5.00 Uhr
Coca-Cola
FANTA
IMBISS
GAZILER
LEBENSMITTEL MARKT
NUR DER
BÄCKEREI
LOTTO

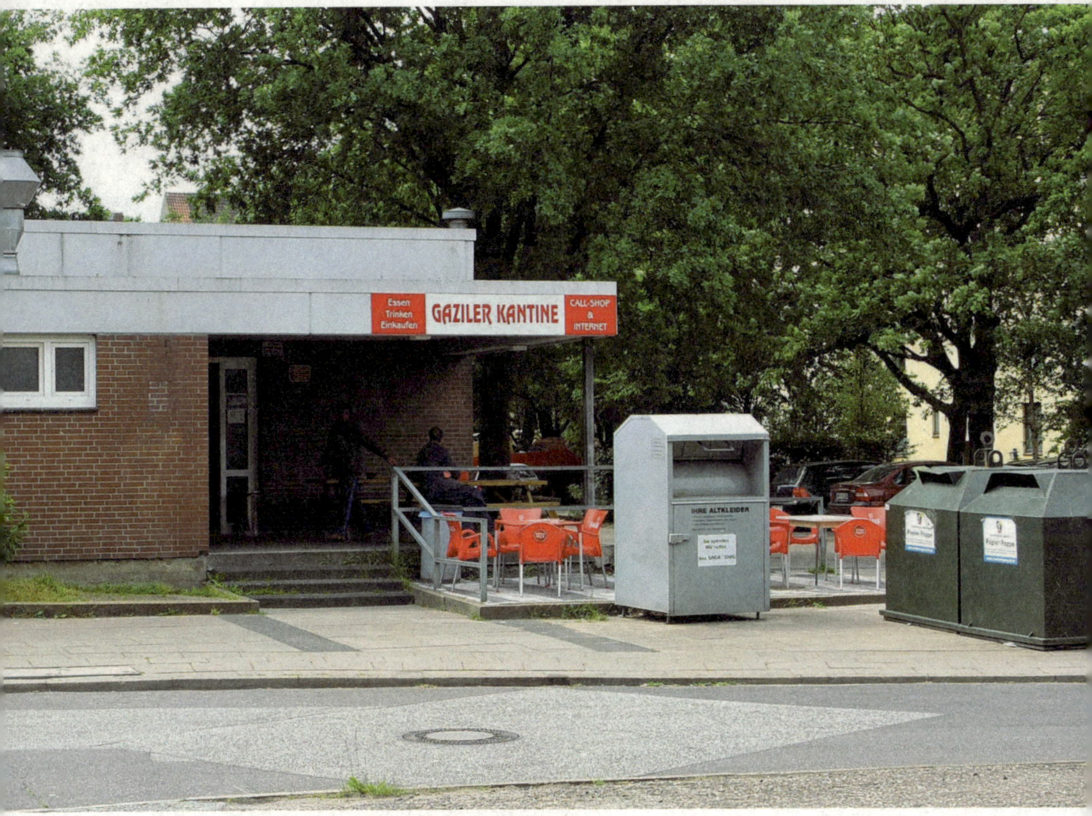

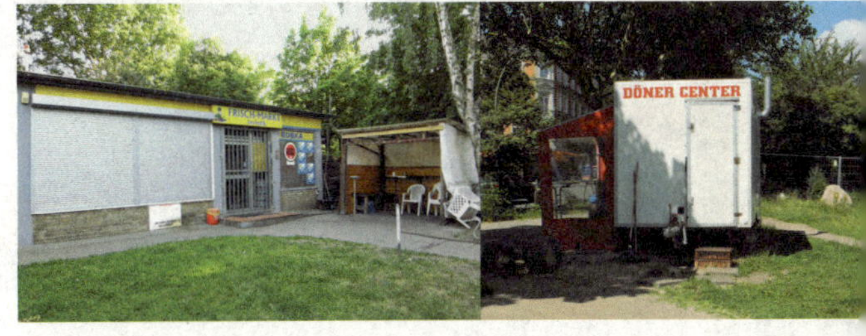

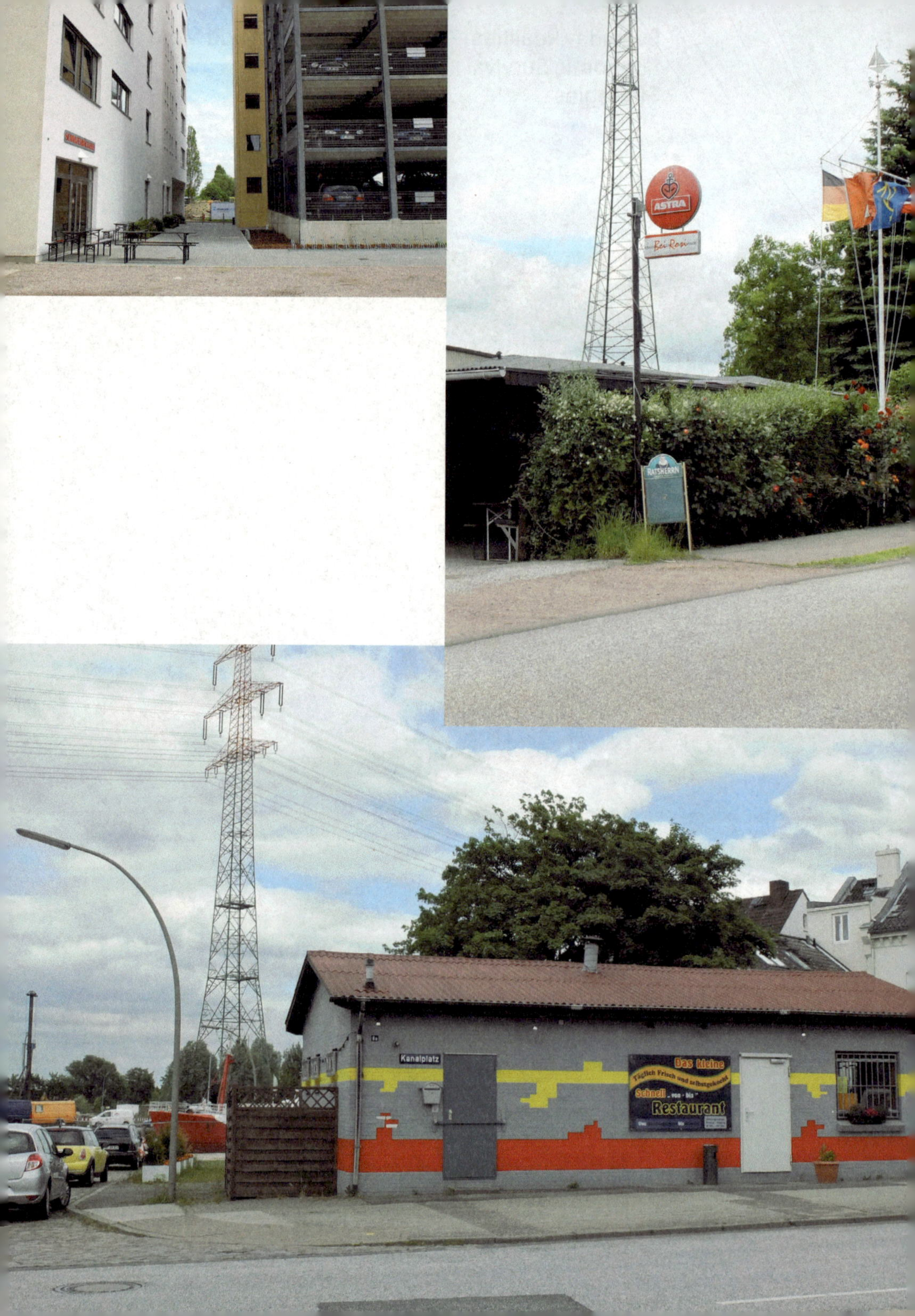

Everyday Realities —
Economic Survival
Strategies

**Win and More
[In-vivo code]**

Following some inner impulse, I head resolutely for Leihhaus Kurt at Mannesallee 27. For some time now, I have been
wondering what it looks like inside this mirrored building.
What I find are mute glass cabinets, filled with wedding rings,
gems, bracelets, gold chains, children's jewelry, old pocket
watches, and gilded alarm clocks. Well-worn family jewels,
handed down for generations. Countless tales. Next to them
laying indifferently, unused electrical appliances, DVDs,
computer games, and phones still in their plastic packaging.
Behind the bulletproof glass a man takes in the pawned
items, paying immediately in cash after a thorough exam-
ination. It is quiet, calm and anonymous. Families come and
go silently. The Bulgarians' wedding jewellery, as I read
later in the article entitled "Travelers of Hope" (Gezer 2011),
symbolizes the wife's honor. Often this will be pawned to
finance a fresh start in Germany. The brokerage and transport costs are not negligible; the wages paid are lower than
expected (ibid.). That is also probably how the family heir-
looms made their way into Leihaus Kurt. In the immediate
vicinity of the two pawnshops in Wilhelmsburg, the betting
parlors and gaming arcades clamor for attention with tempt-
ing promises such as "Win and More." Although the windows
are covered with advertising film, there is again and again
a chance to peep through an open door. Men of varying ages
and backgrounds sit in front of the flickering screens. The
atmosphere seems tensely euphoric. This is sports betting.
But the flashing machines in the darkened halls also promise
quick money around the clock. The pawnshops, gaming
arcades, and Western Union banks are often found in close
proximity to one another. The quest for happiness, hope, and
despair are often very close together. It is precisely these
moods that are often very palpable and tangible within the
space Life and Business .

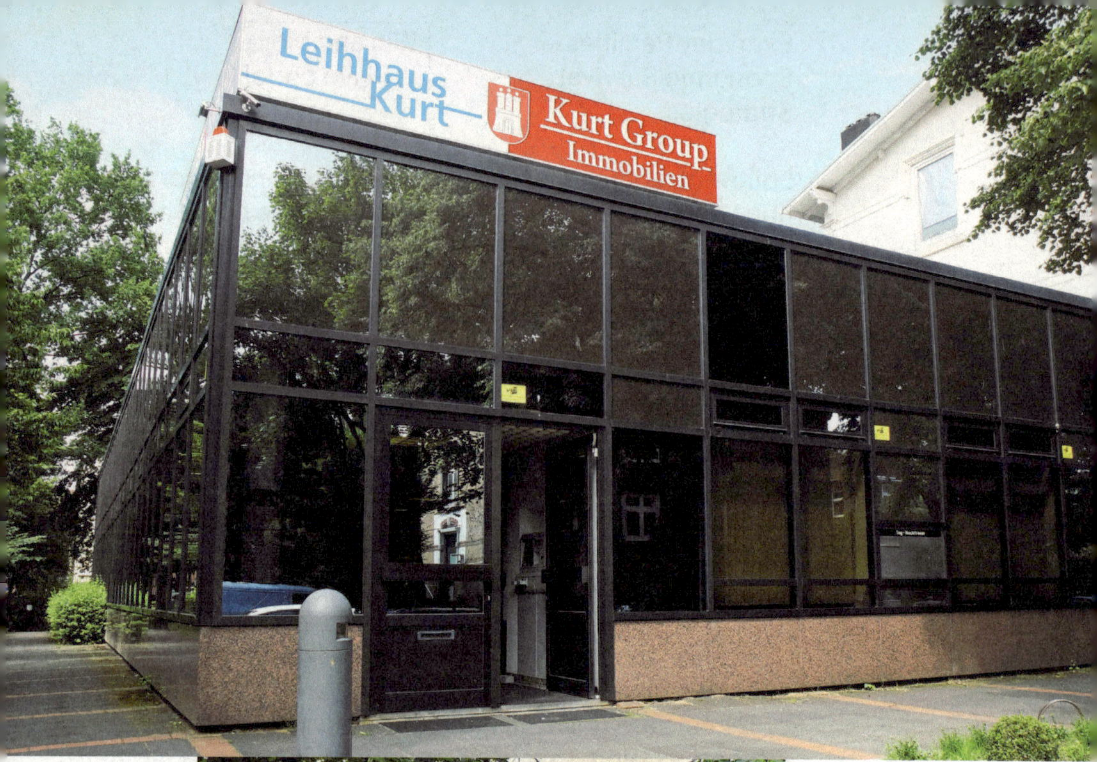

Leihhaus
Kurt
Kurt Group
Immobilien

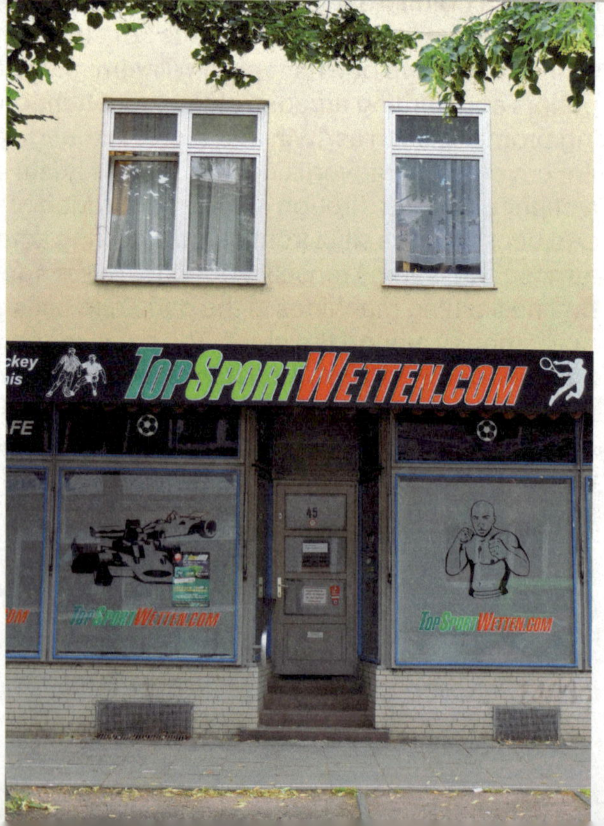

TopSportWetten.com
45

Everyday Realities—
Economic Survival
Strategies

Life and Business

For many people the Elbe Islands have been a "place of arrival and hope" (Saunders 2012) since they came into being. That all began back in the 14th century. In 1333 the aristocratic owner of Stillhorn concluded an agreement with the steward of neighboring Ochsenwerder Island to build the first embankments. The inhabitants of Ochsenwerder were to take charge of constructing the embankment on the southeast side of Stillhorn. By way of remuneration, they received a piece of land that they were allowed to cultivate and farm as the first settlers Greunhöker . Until 1660, according to data from the Wilhelmsburg History Workshop, the dike builders and settlers came from the neighboring, already reclaimed island of Billweder. In 1672 the lands of Stillhorn, Georgswerder, and Rothaus, which were already surrounded by embankments, passed to the Duke of Brunswick-Lüneburg, Georg Wilhelm. The new owner built more dikes to link up his possessions on Reiherstieg with the newly acquired land to form Wilhelmsburg Island No Dike, No Land . Many of his subjects from the Braunschweig-Lüneburg area subsequently moved to Wilhelmsburg (Wilhelmsburger Geschichtswerkstatt 2008: 7f). With increasing industrialization in the 19th century, large newly established companies like Wollkämmerei AG brought in skilled workers from neighboring Silesia, Poland, or Hungary Wool-carders, Tailors, and Seamstresses .
Around the year 1900, Hamburg was the second largest industrial city in the German Reich. Around half of all Hamburg's urban population had moved to the city by this time. People looking for work came there from Poland, and also from Austria, Russia, Scandinavia, Italy, Greece, Spain, Turkey, and even China (ibid.: 98). After the Second World War and the German Agreements on Migrant Workers, concluded with Italy, Greece, Spain, Turkey, Morocco, Portugal, Tunisia, and what was then still Yugoslavia, more guest workers arrived in Wilhelmsburg between 1955 and 1968. Many of them brought their family members to join them in due course, and have stayed in Hamburg to this day (ibid.: 99ff).[1] Initial conditions in their new homeland, were however often precarious and difficult. A persistent lack of housing

1
The Turkish community in Wilhelmsburg is the largest ethnic community in Hamburg. There are six mosques on the Elbe Islands. More than half of the ethnic Turks who live on the Elbe Islands have German nationality (Handelskammer Hamburg, 2004: 11).

means workers and their families are still living in overpriced and overcrowded dwellings even today (Gezer 2011). Anyone with a free room or bed rents it out, today just as they did back then, as an additional source of income (Geschichts-werkstatt Wilhelmsburg 2008: 89f). Signs indicating such offers often flap on building site fences. Since 1945, Sinti families from the large Weiss clan have lived on the Elbe Islands. In 1966 around five hundred members of the clan moved to the Georgswerder estate (ibid.: 105f). In the 1960s, the Elbe Islands experienced a population exodus due to the collapse of the economy, the increasing automation of the general cargo port and the enduring impact of storm tide flooding (1962). In the 1980s and 1990s accommodation was provided on the Elbe Islands for an influx of refugees, particularly from Third World countries and from Bosnia and Herzegovina (ibid.). Since the Schengen agreement in the early 2000s, the number of immigrants from Eastern European countries like Poland, Romania, and Bulgaria has grown significantly (Spiegel 2011/16). The main reason why people move from country areas or emigrate from other states is always similar. Coming from rural, rather impoverished regions, many seek their fortune in the German cities. But are districts like Hamburg-Wilhelmsburg prepared for these people "travelling in hope" (cf. Saunders 2012)? At present, the precarious situation of the most recent group of immigrants from Bulgaria, Poland, and Romania is very evident. Middlemen provide the local labor market with cheap, uninsured, but strong and willing workers. Despite underpayment and exploitation, the newcomers do not readily abandon the hope of a better life for themselves and their families. For many, the booming low-cost labor market is a worthwhile and simple business, for others it marks the end of their prospects for the future (Gezer 2011). In the course of my research I have observed the circumstances described in detail in this article over and over and again. The small vans with Polish or Bulgarian license plates parked along Rotenhäuser Damm or Rotenhäuser Wettern provide clues about the current human trafficking situation (ibid.). At first glance, they look like private travel companies: stickers of the Eiffel Tower, a setting sun, seagulls or the sea suggest tourist destinations. In fact, these vans transport people to construction sites, ports, and cleaning companies throughout Germany.

The windows are often blacked out with foil. If you look closely, you can identify the silhouettes of piles of blankets, plastic bags stuffed full, and work clothes. The agent's name and his contact details are clearly displayed on the vehicles. The middlemen sitting at the steering wheel take Europe-wide orders for laborers. On the seats in the back, the troops to be deployed are (already) sleeping their way toward their next assignment. The tearooms, the cafes on Stübenplatz, or the Veddel S-Bahn station are the informal employment agencies for those forces. The young men wait from the early morning hours for a job. Often times unsuccessfully. The wages are frequently three Euro an hour, with a working day of more than fifteen hours. Many barely speak German (ibid.). The wild campers on brownfield sites or informal caravans on company grounds are also striking ⟨Mobile Homes⟩. But there are also my repeated encounters with a Polish family man from the neighborhood, which reveal his hopeless situation.

Via the window of the research station University of the Neighborhoods (UdN) he tried (unsuccessfully) to steal my computer. Fear, terror, and despair were written all over his face, when he suddenly recognized me in my studio. He apologized to me repeatedly for the incident and then vanished without a sound through the dense greenery around the UdN. The only possible way to connect back with their foreign homes for these immigrants is provided by the global call shops and internet cafes. New openings of these connector sites can be identified in the neighborhood. In addition, the telephone boxes or parcel drop-off points offer further communication options ⟨Connectors⟩. In addition, the various Western Union banks in the Reiherstieg quarter or on the Veddel send hope back to home in monetary form, paid in cash. This goes on month after month, year after year.

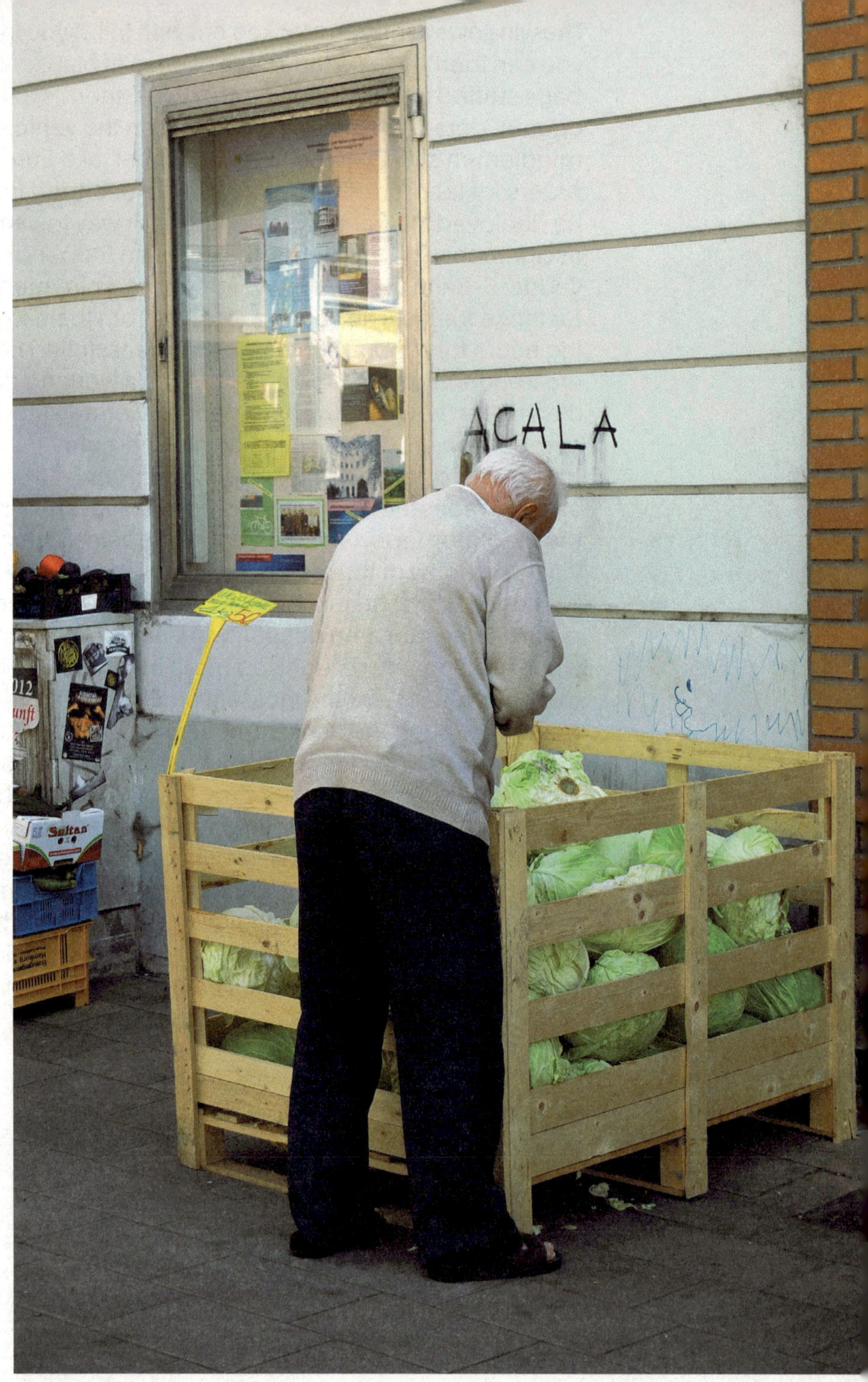
ACALA
Sultan

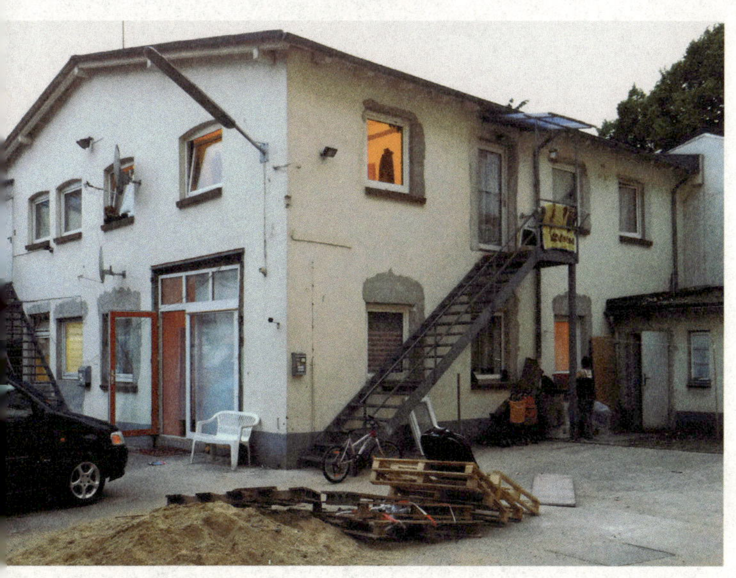

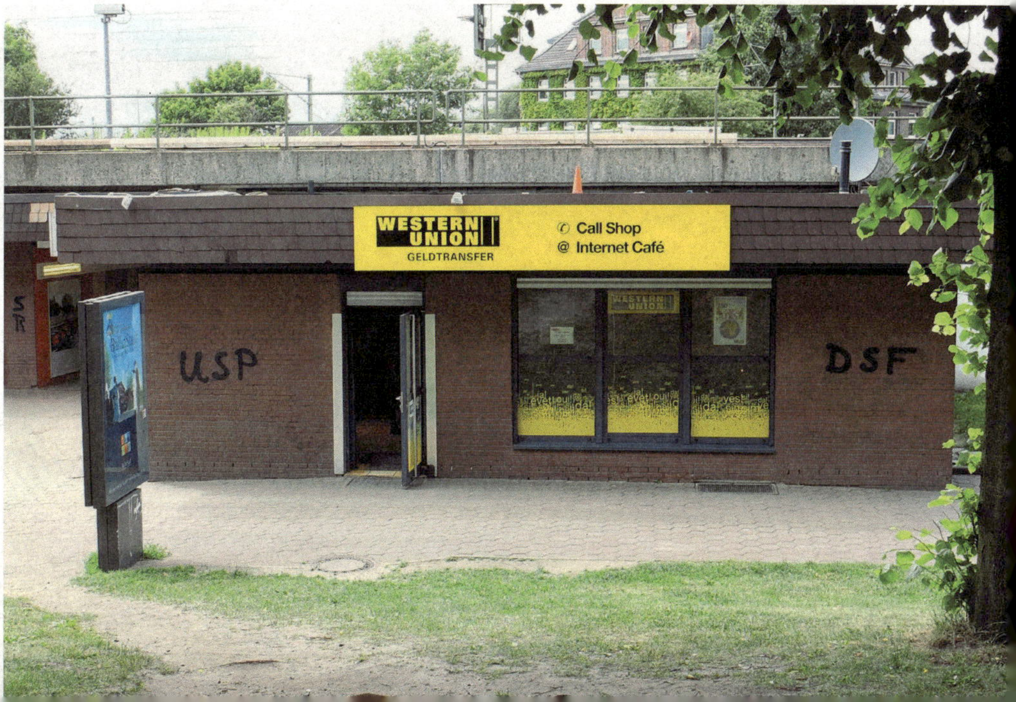

WESTERN
UNION
GELDTRANSFER
Call Shop
@ Internet Café
USP
DSF

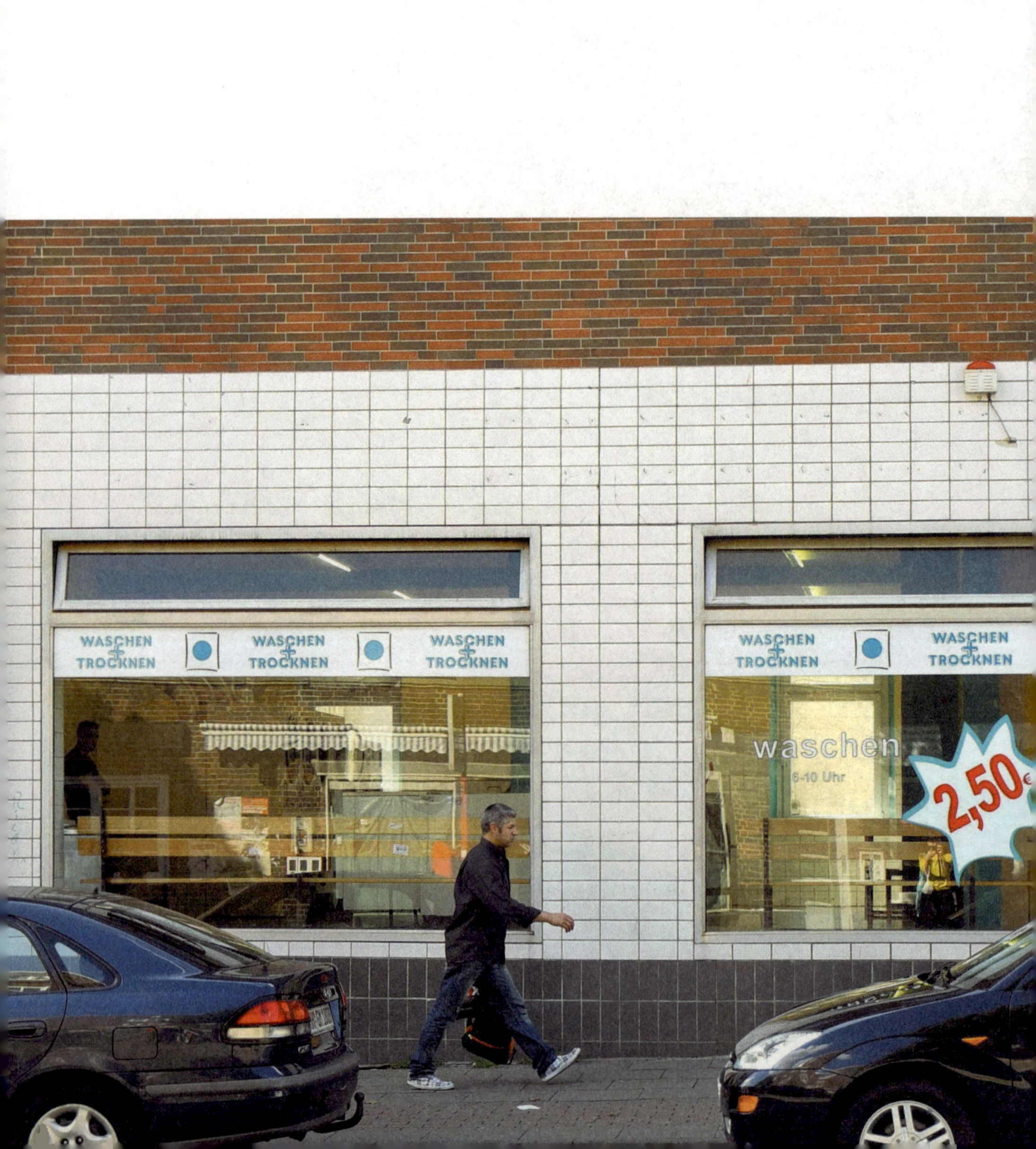

WASCHEN + TROCKNEN
WASCHEN + TROCKNEN
WASCHEN + TROCKNEN
WASCHEN + TROCKNEN
WASCHEN + TROCKNEN
waschen
6-10 Uhr
2,50 €

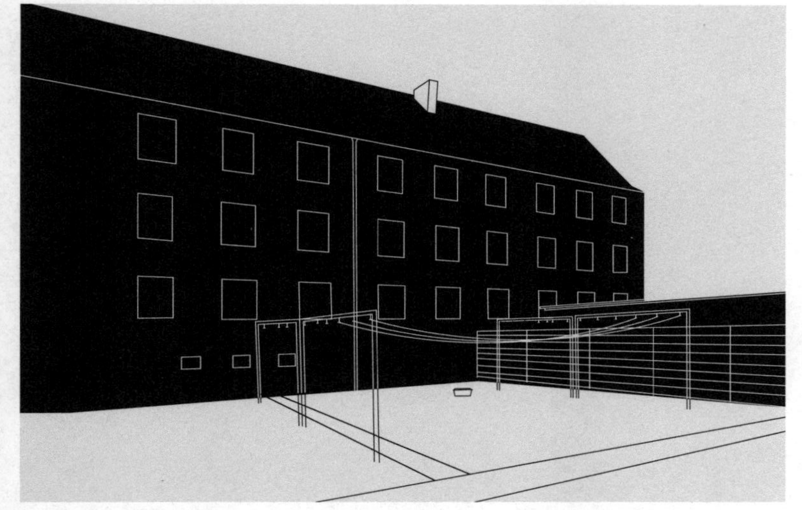

... a kiosk on the ground floor. Closed. History. Around the
corner, behind the house, is the courtyard. Four or five blue
overalls with a company logo sway gently in a row on the
clothesline. Next to them, awaiting for visitors, a small cluster
of plastic chairs. Blue and red and white. As everyone is
certainly busy, there is no-one there at the moment, it is
Monday afternoon ...

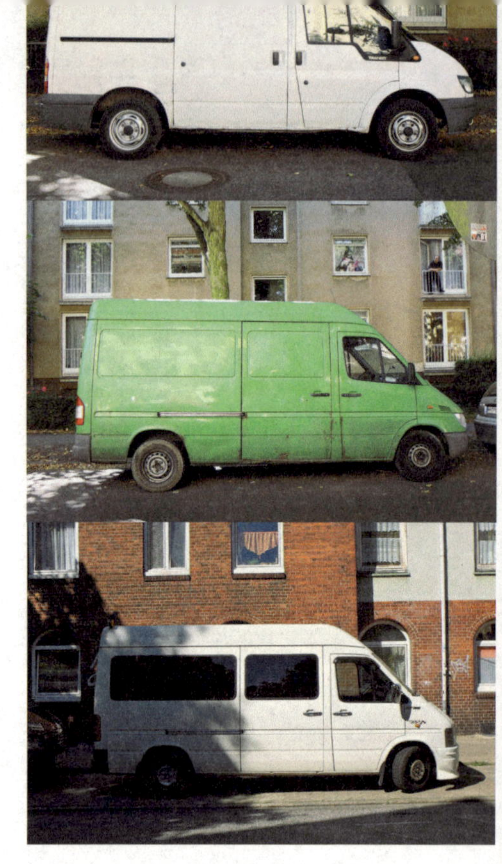

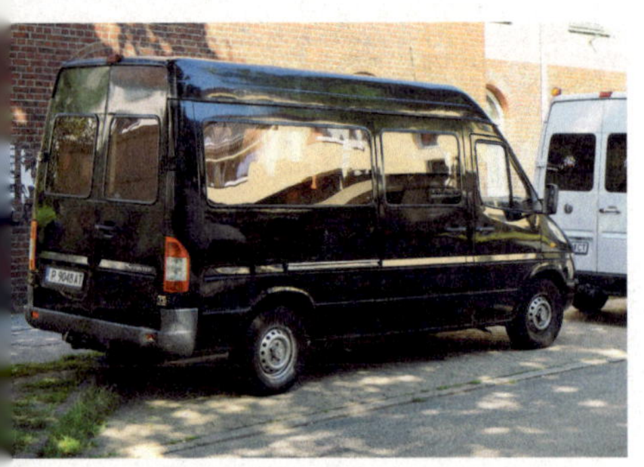

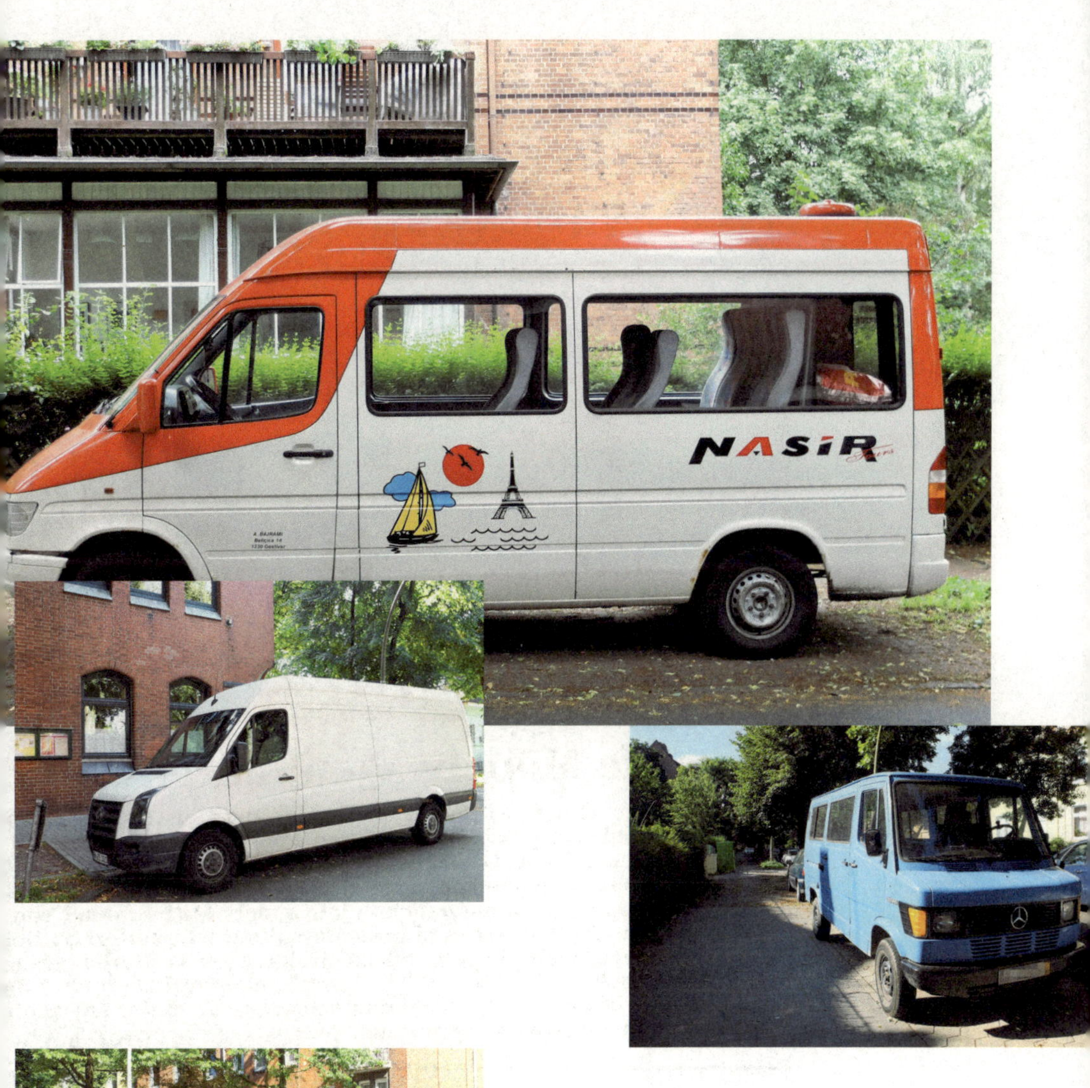

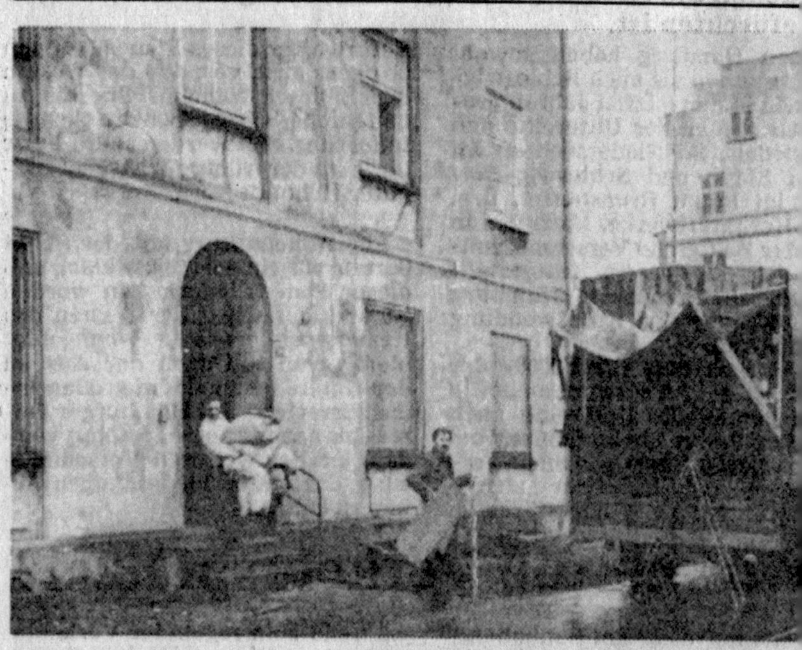

Die Möbelwagen fuhren vor

Seit dem Wochenende ist Neuhof noch mehr zur Geisterstadt gewo
Der 1. April bedeutete für Dutzende von Familien: Einzug in eine
Wohnung. Die türkische Gastarbeiterfamilie, die auf unserem Fot
gemieteten Möbelwagen belädt, wird künftig in Altona wohnen. So w
schleppten besonders am Sonnabend viele andere Mitbewohner von
hof Hausrat und Möbel. Während besonders die Gastarbeiterfamilie
Umzug bedauern, weil sie sehr billige Wohnungen verlieren, atme
wenigen Deutschen, die Neuhof am Wochenende verließen eher au
den letzten Wochen war der sterbende Stadtteil immer unansehnli
immer weniger lebenswert geworden.

OK (Foto: K.

Verlag »Wilhelmsburger Zeitung« Willy von Thaden.
Verlagsleitung Gertrud von Thaden, Redaktion Focko
Thomas (verantwortlich). Alle Hmb.-Wilhelmsburg,
Fährstraße 50, Tel. 75 82 80 und 75 89 08. Anzeigen-
preisliste Nr 11. Artikel, die mit dem Namen oder den
Initialen des Verfassers gekennzeichnet sind, geben
nicht immer auch die Meinung der Redaktion wieder.
Für unverlangt eingesandte Manuskripte keine Ge-
währ. Druck bei Bergedorfer Buchdruckerei von Ed.
Wagner, Hamburg 80.

Schlafzimmer
zu verschenken

Ein Schlafzimmer, sieben J
alt, weiß, Schleiflack, mit H
schrank und Matratzen, soll
schenkt werden. Interesse
melden sich bitte unter Te
75 75 66.

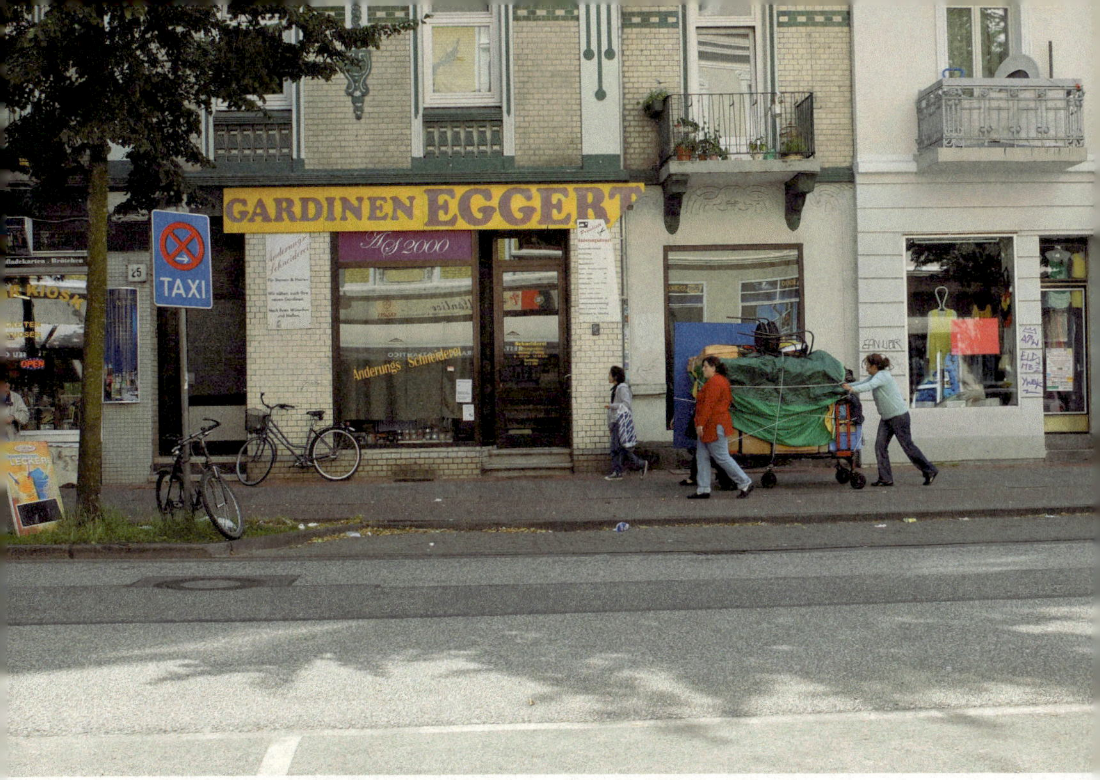

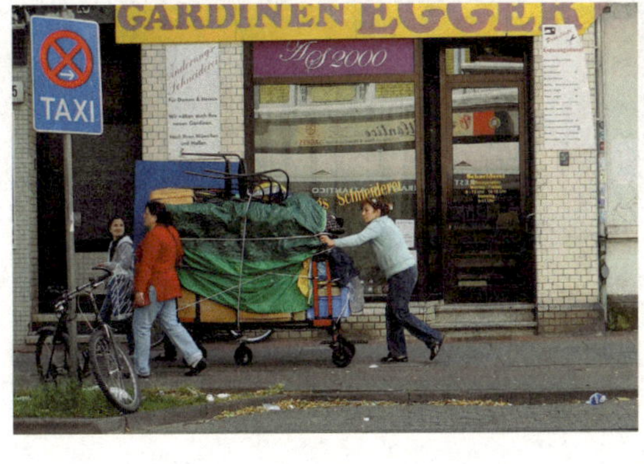

— Sitting, waiting, and observing for a long period —

249

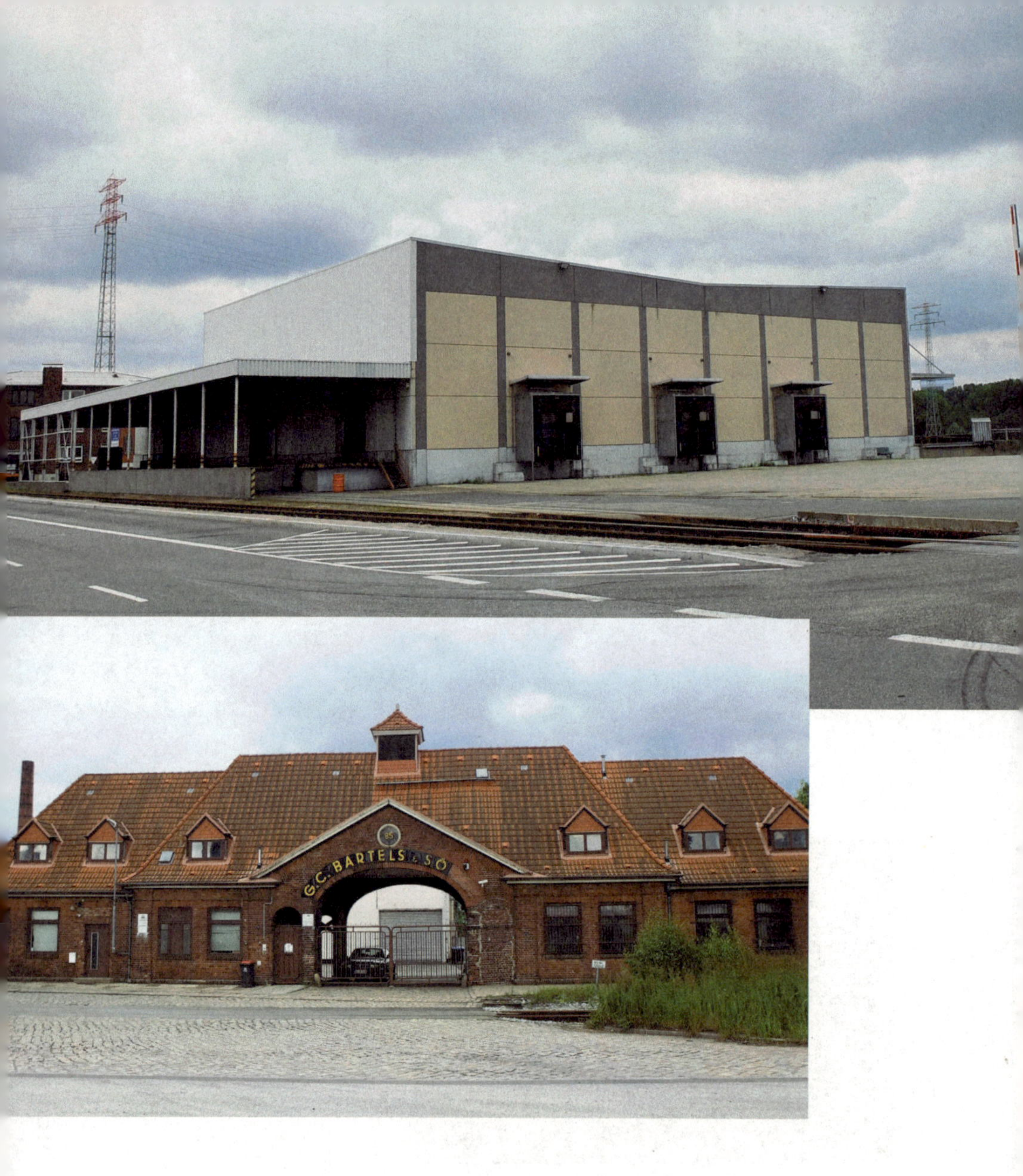

G. C. BARTELS & SØ

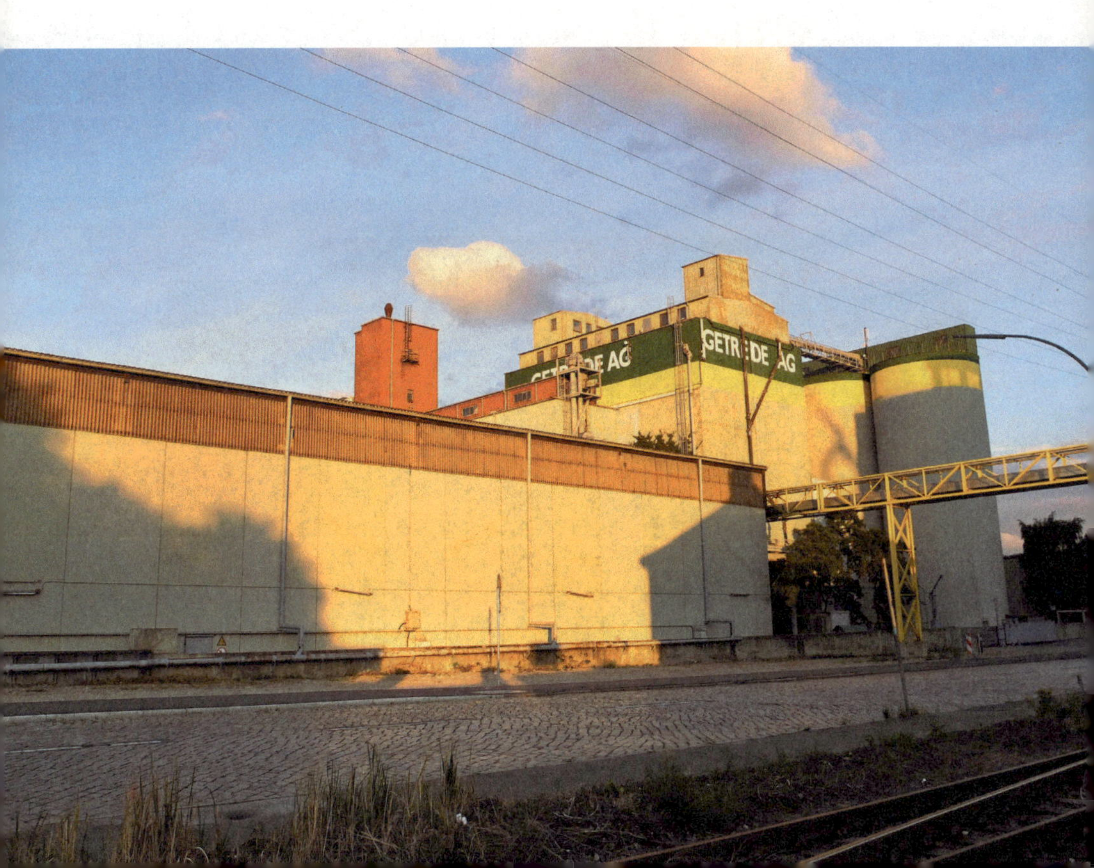

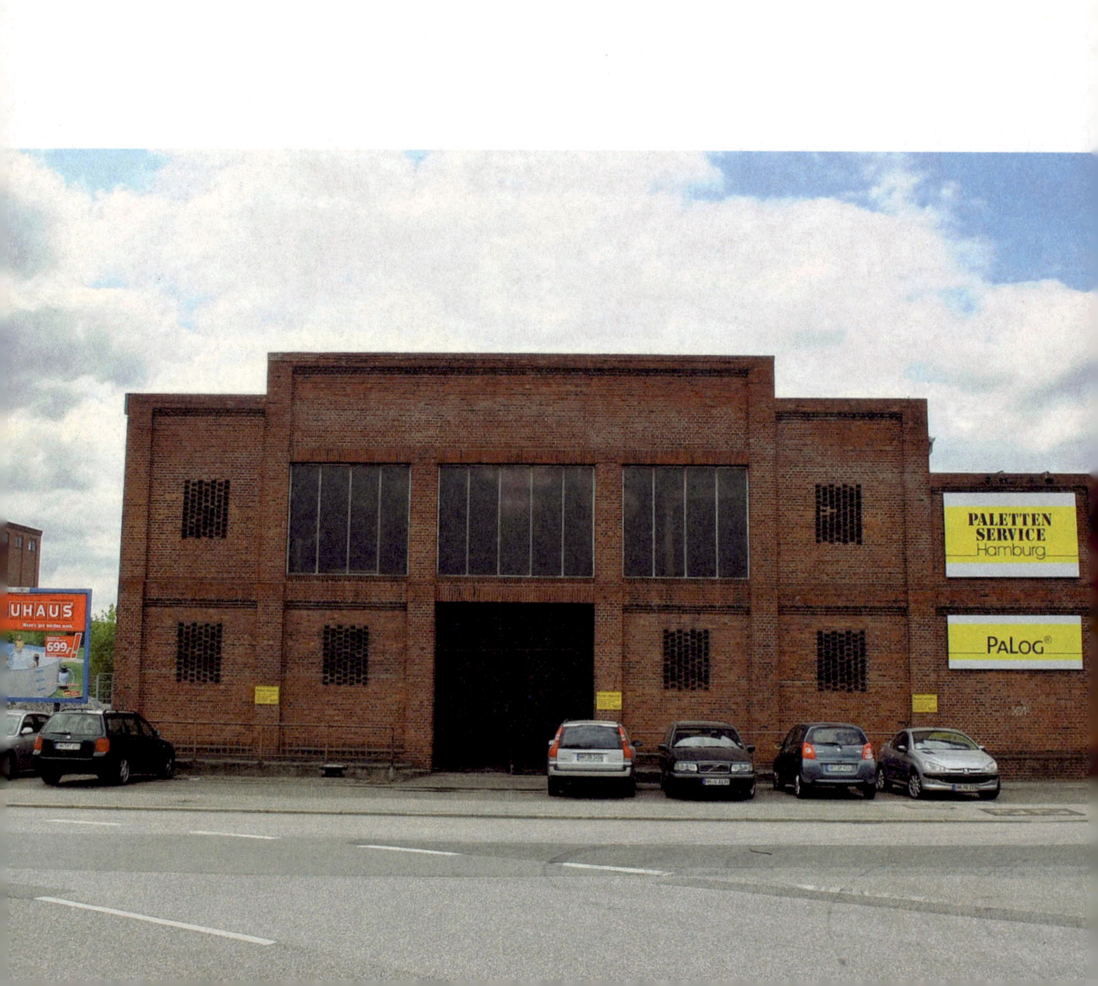
UHAUS
699,-
PALETTEN
SERVICE
Hamburg
PaLog®

ß!«), nur abstellen können sie
...Mißstände auch nicht sofort. Sie
...en am Dienstag, so Ewald Sier-
..., zur Versammlung, um die
...leme und Vorschläge der An-
...r aufzunehmen und dann mit
...e von Anträgen zu versuchen,
...lfe zu schaffen.
...e vier Initiatoren der Selbsthil-
...tion lassen jedenfalls nicht lok-
...Sie werden weitermachen und
...r sorgen, daß aus der Brack-
...e wieder – wie gehabt – eine
...e Siedlerstraße wird. Unter-
...ung bekamen sie auch. Am
...stag erklärten sich Elisabeth v.
..., Holger Elvers und Herbert
...ch bereit mitzuhelfen.

...s Wasser wird teurer

...e Hamburger Wasserwerke
...en den Preis für Trinkwasser
.. Juli erhöhen. Die Erhöhung
...0 Pfennig pro Kubikmeter be-
...en, so daß ein Kubikmeter
...kwasser in Hamburg künftig
...DM kosten wird. Dazu ist aller-
...s noch die Zustimmung des
...burger Senats erforderlich,
...sich in dieser Woche mit der
...sichtigten Erhöhung befassen

...s dem Klubraum ...

...einer Gaststätte am Veddeler
...n 2 entwendeten unbekannte
...r in der Nacht zum Sonntag ei-
...lektrogitarre und einen Ver-
...er.

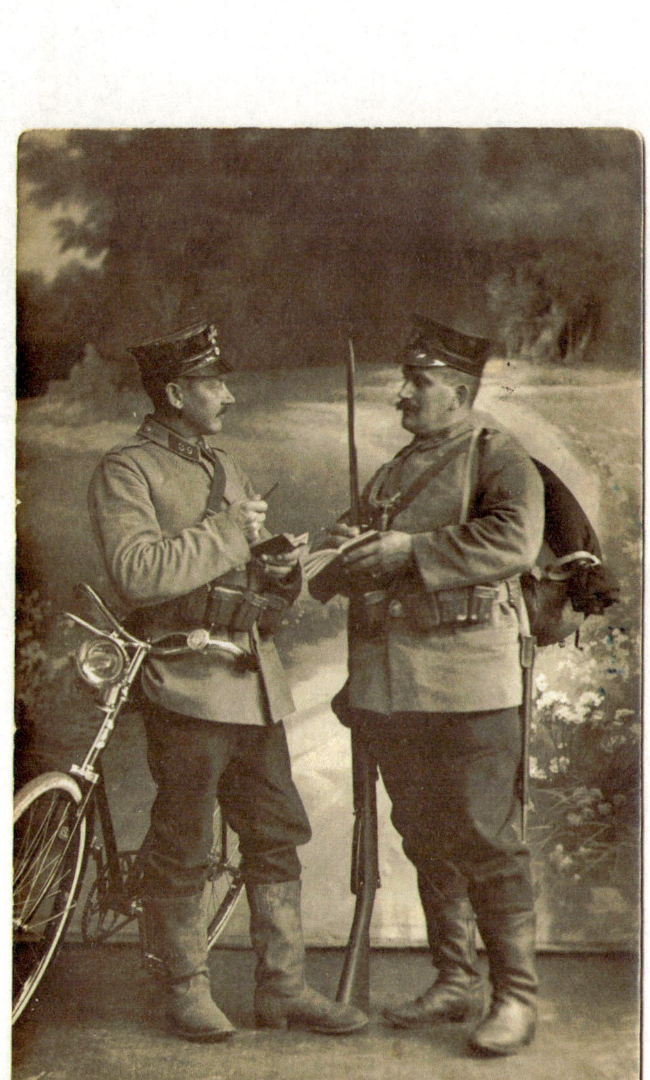

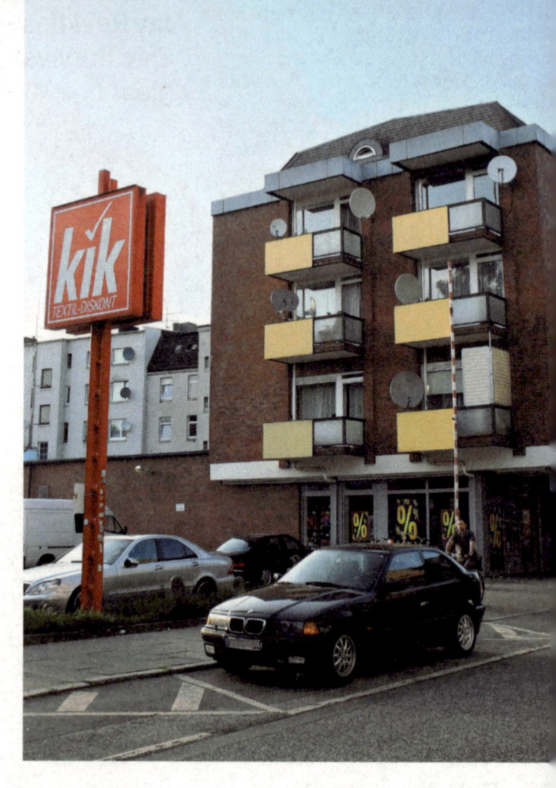
kik
TEXTIL-DISKONT

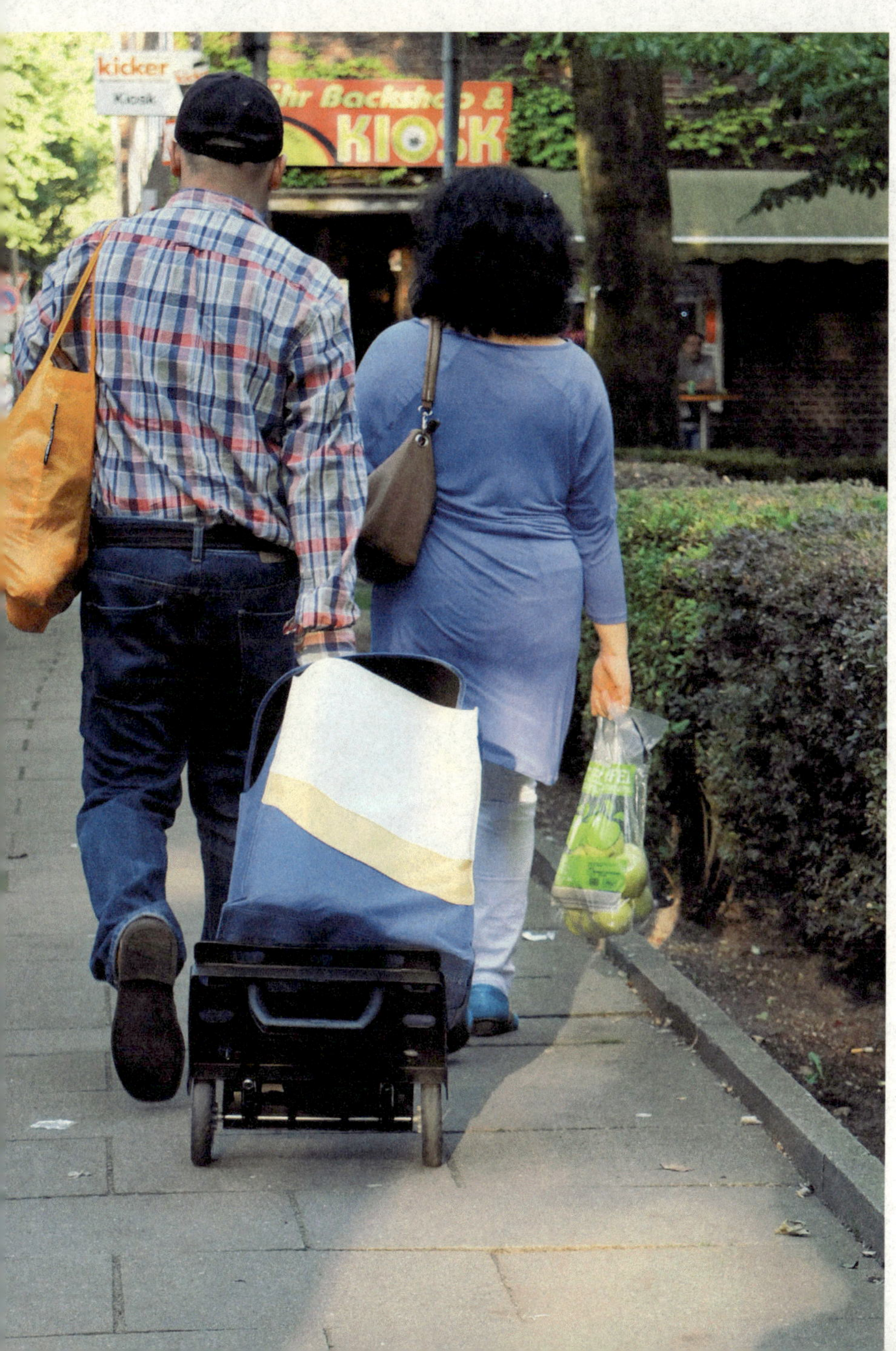
kicker
Kiosk
Ihr Backshop &
KIOSK

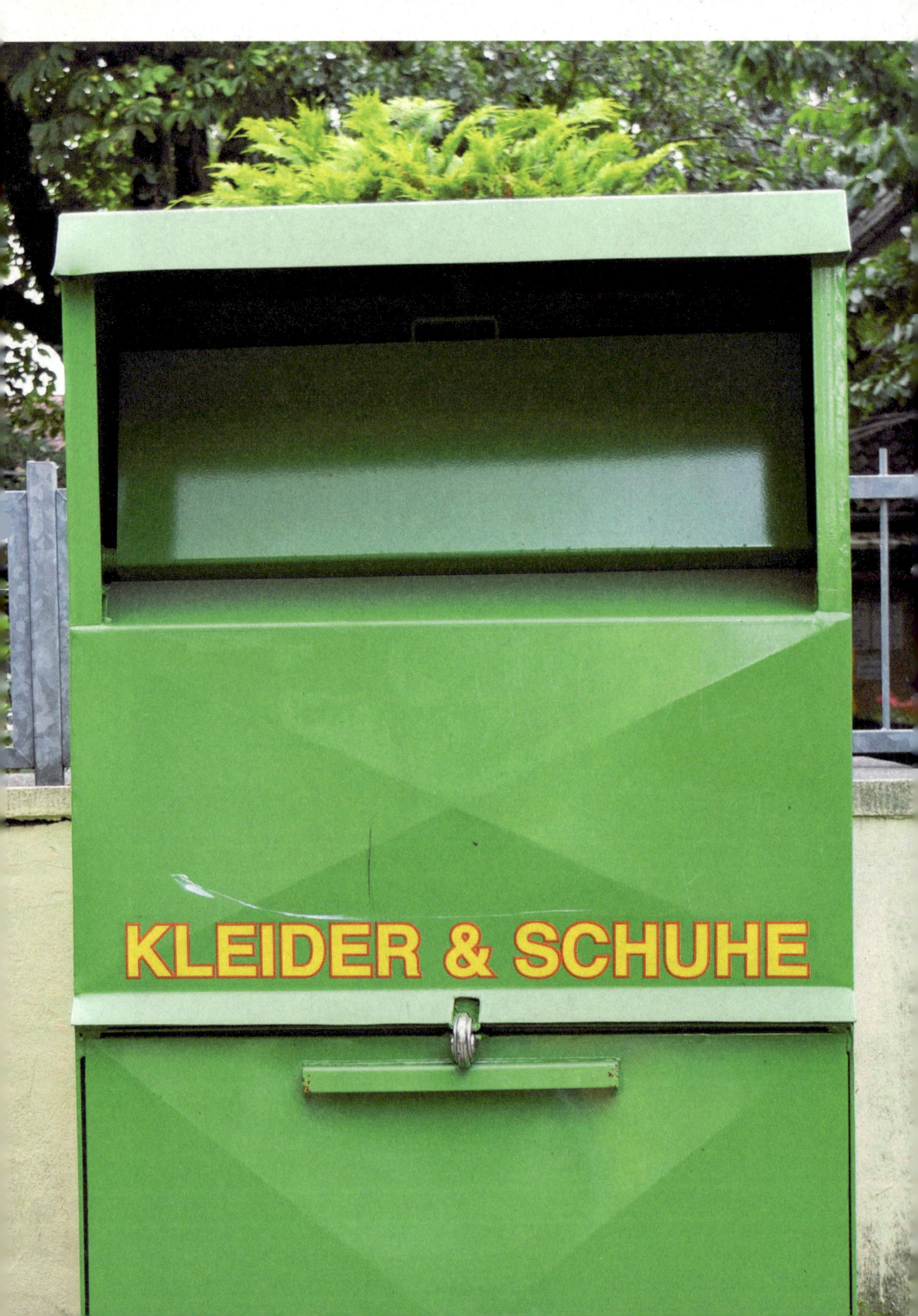
KLEIDER & SCHUHE

Ist ein Geschäftszentrum „drin"?

Genügen 450 Wohnungen, um ein Geschäftszentrum finanziell zu tragen?

Wir berichteten in der Weihnachtsausgabe über die erste Rammung einer 450 Wohnungen umfassenden neuen Wohnsiedlung in Kirchdorf. Dazu ereichten uns Anfragen, ob sich denn bei soviel oder sowenig Wohnungen die Errichtung eines modernen Geschäftsviertels lohne. Wir veröffentlichen eine der Zuschriften, die sich mit dieser Frage befaßt. Es heißt darin:

. . . ähnlich wie bei der geplanten Ladenstraße an der Mengestraße ist es heute bei den hohen Baupreisen äußerst schwierig, die erforderliche Wirtschaftlichkeit bei neuen Geschäftsvierteln zu erreichen. Ohne eine Verdichtung des Wohnungsbaues wird das kaum zu schaffen sein. So sollen sich die beiden zwölfgeschossigen Hochhäuser um einen Marktplatz gruppieren, der außerdem noch etwa 2000 Quadratmeter Geschäfts- und Gewerbeflächen erhalten soll. Alles liegt in unmittelbarer Nähe des geplanten S-Bahn-Haltepunktes Neuenfelder Straße-Nord. Außer den Wohnungen der DWG — es handelt sich um rund 350 Wohneinheiten — will die Bundesbahn-Baugesellschaft „Norden" in diesem Gebiet noch etwa 100 Wohnungen errichten.

Ob diese 450 Wohnungen ausreichen werden, um ein neues Geschäftszentrum zu tragen, wird von vielen Kennern der Verhältnisse bezweifelt. Zumal in den nächsten 10 Jahren kaum mit der neuen S-Bahn-Verbindung Hamburg—Harburg (und damit auch der geplanten Haltestelle an der Neuenfelder Straße) gerechnet werden kann.

Die WZ hat wiederholt darauf hingewiesen, daß an der Neuenfelder Straße (Nordseite) noch ausreichend Gelände für einen weiteren Wohnungsbau zur Verfügung stünde. Es

menhang mit der übrigen Wohnbebauung ist ein Torso, wenn nicht sogar eine Fehlplanung.

Deshalb meine ich, an der Neuenfelder Straße ist zunächst der Bau weiterer Wohnungen zwingend notwendig. Diese Auffassung deckt sich übrigens mit der der Unabhängigen Kommission zur Überprüfung des Hamburger Aufbauplanes, die ebenfalls eine Verdichtung an den S-Bahn- und U-Bahn-Haltestellen fordert.

A. A., Wbg.

Keine Überschwemmungen

Obwohl es in den letzten Tagen auch bei uns viel und häufig geregnet hat und reichlich Feuchtigkeit heruntergekommen ist, blieb die Elbinsel von größeren Überschwemmungen verschont. Auch das steigende Grundwasser blieb ohne sichtbare Wirkung. Pausenlos waren die Pumpen in den Schöpfwerken in Tätigkeit, um das Wasser aus der „Badewanne Wilhelmsburg" in die Außengewässer überzupumpen. So gab es an den Feiertagen keine Wassernot und keine Überschwemmungsgefahr für unsere tiefliegenden Gebiete. Nur südlich des Bahnhofsviertels standen einige Schrebergärten unter Wasser. Dort war die Entwässerung durch ein großes Bauvorhaben gestört, und die Bracks waren randvoll Wasser.

Ausgerechnet das Standesamt

Während der Weihnachtsfeiertage hat ein unbekannter Täter offenbar mit einem Luftgewehr eine Fensterscheibe im ersten Stockwerk unseres Rathauses zerschossen. Mit etwa fünfzehn Schuß wurde die Doppelglasscheibe total zertrümmert. Warum sich der Täter ausgerechnet das Trau-

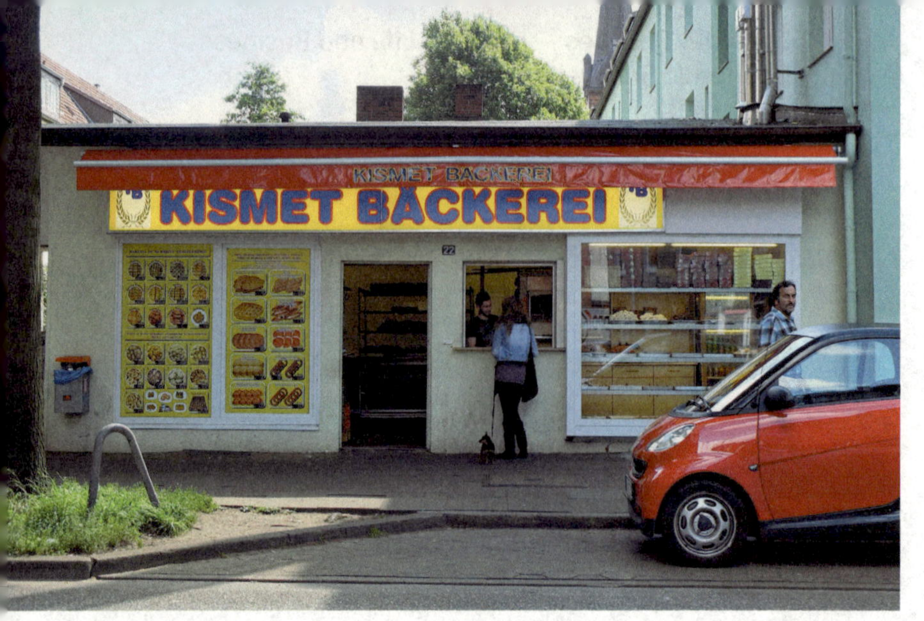

KISMET BÄCKEREI
KISMET BÄCKEREI
Fleischerei Kaya

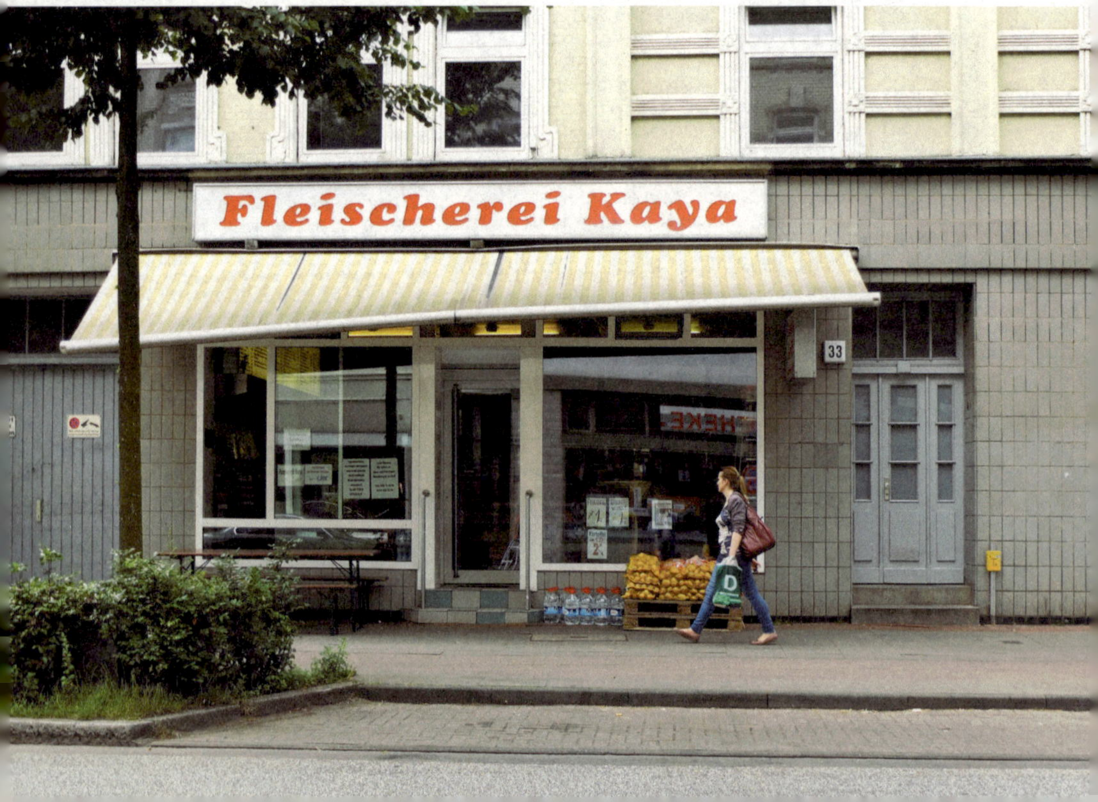

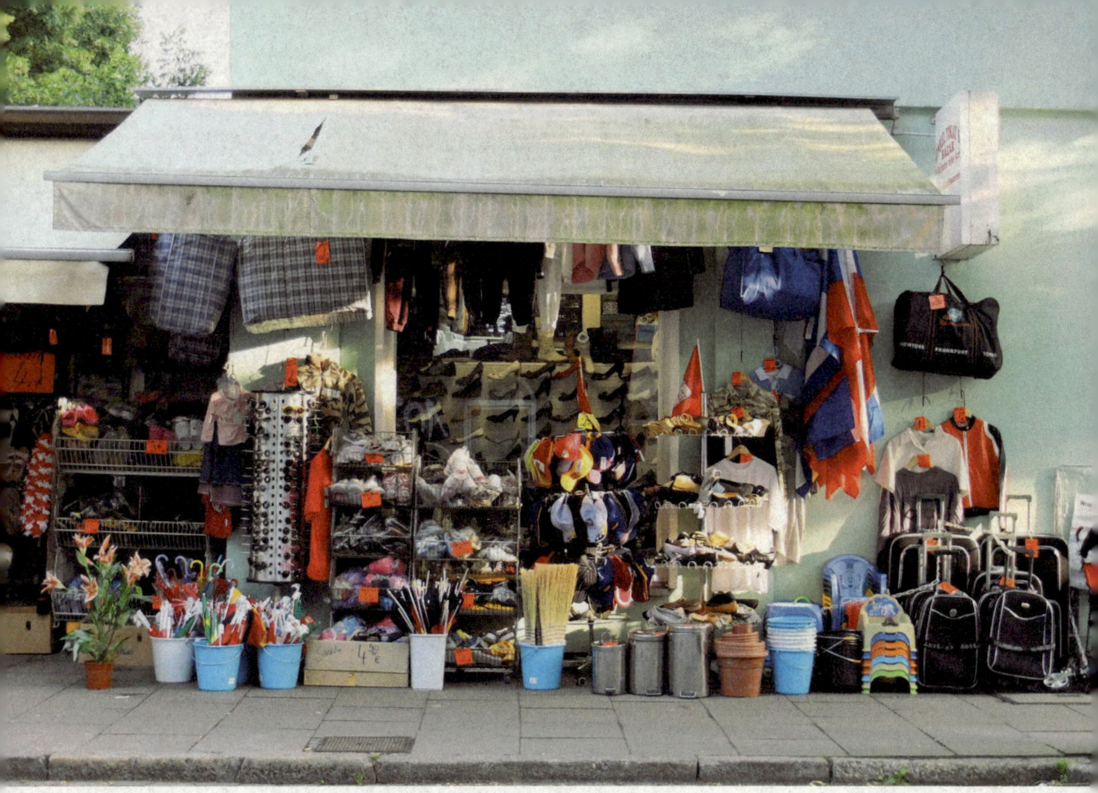

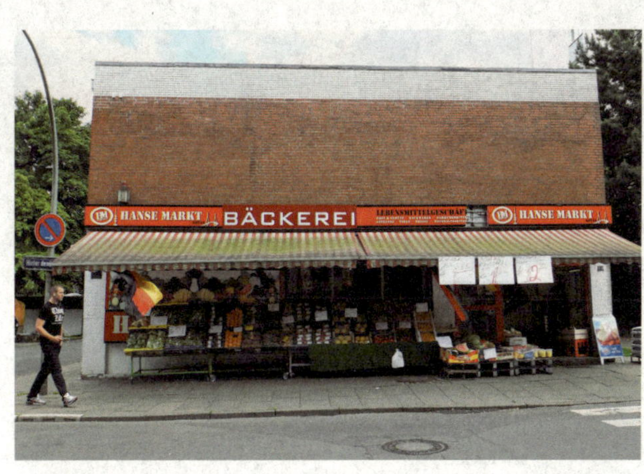

HANSE MARKT BÄCKEREI LEBENSMITTELGESCHÄFT HANSE MARKT

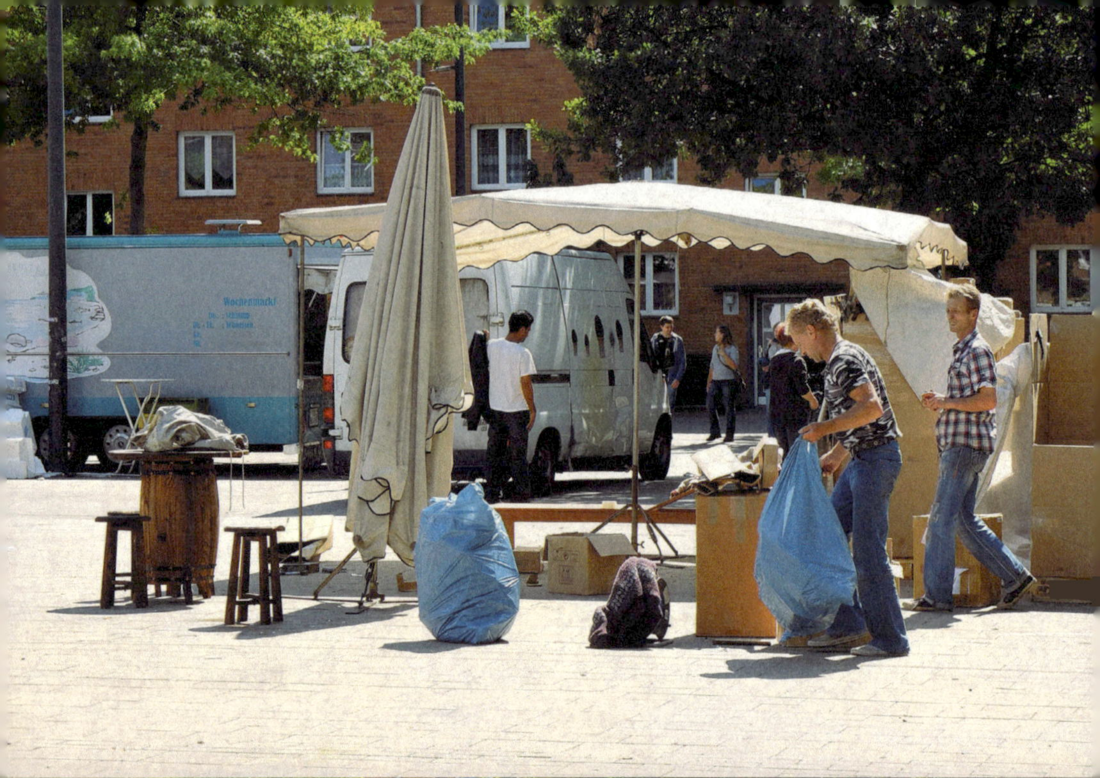
Wochenmarkt

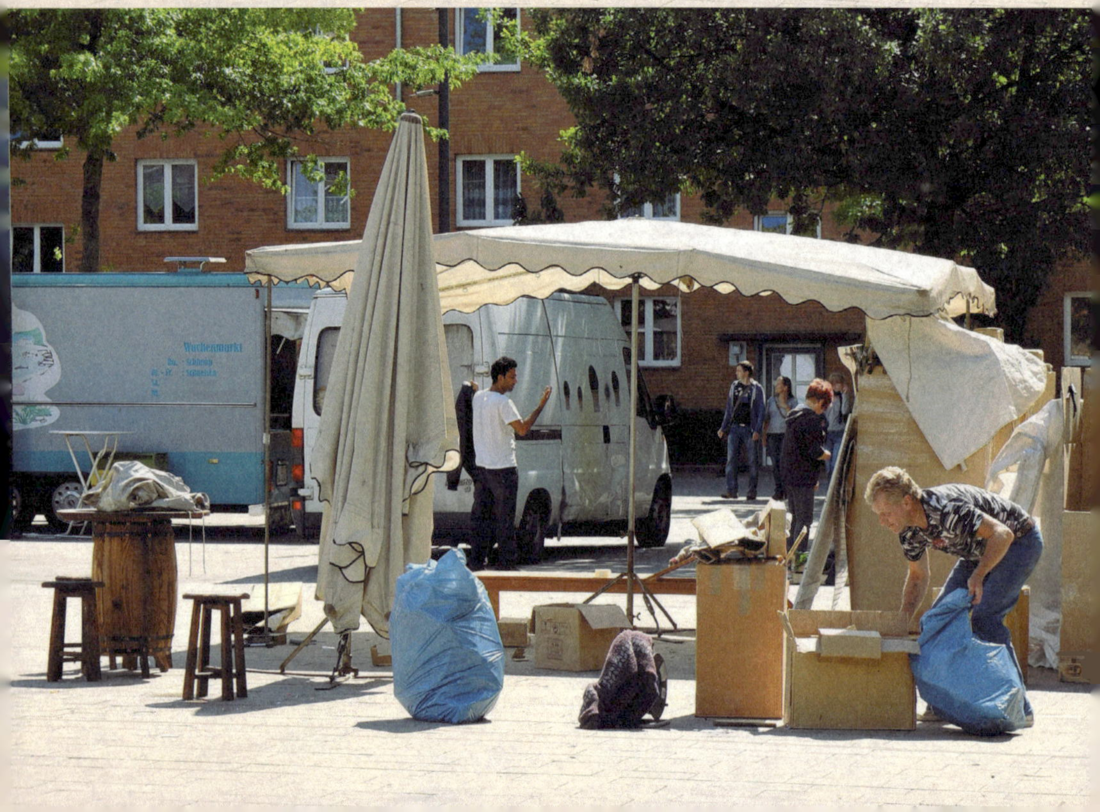
Wochenmarkt

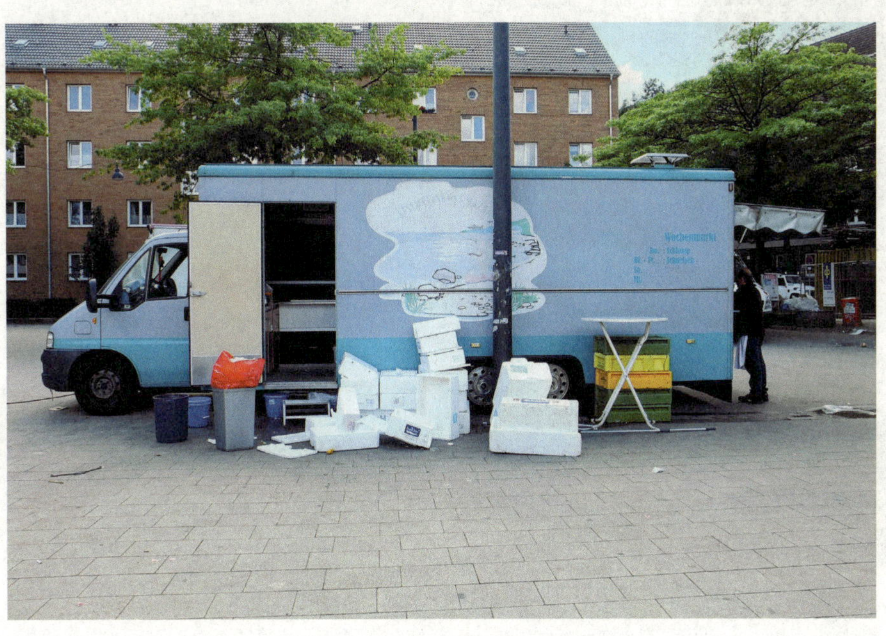

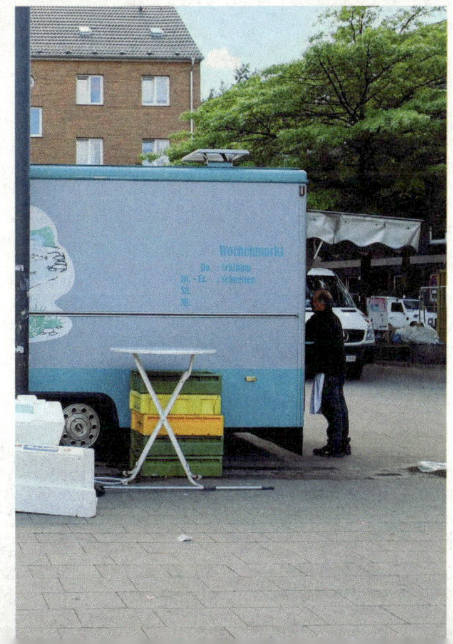

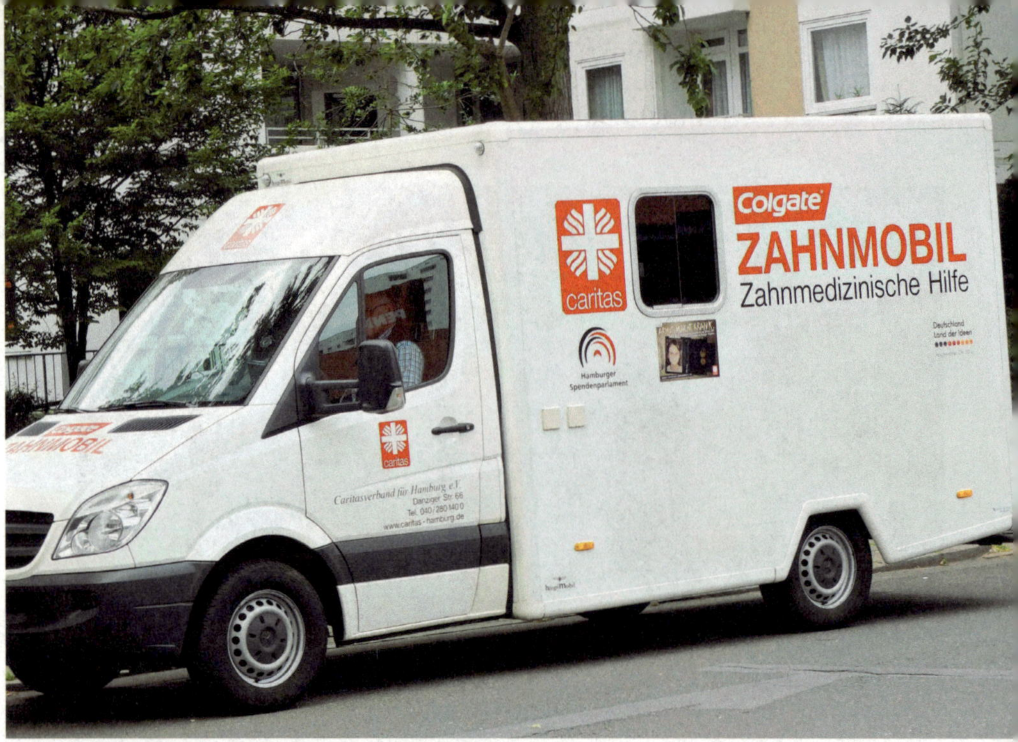

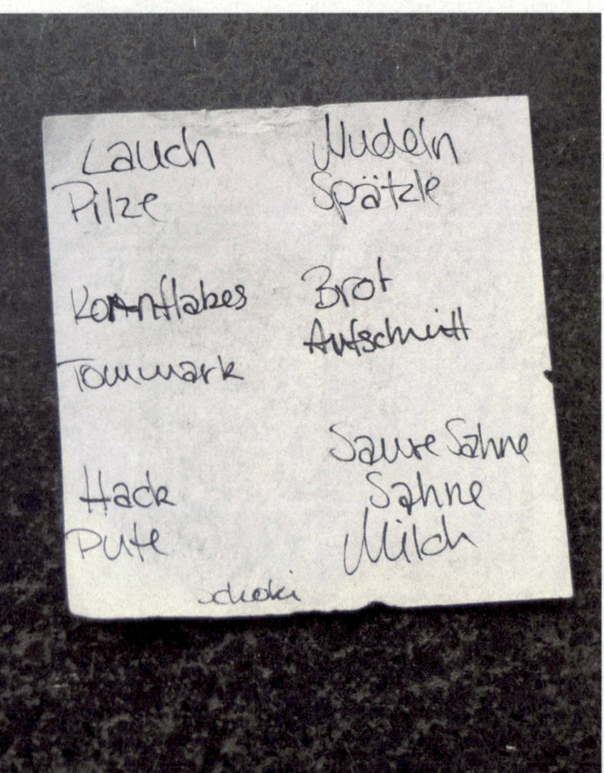

Lauch
Pilze

Kornflakes
Tommark

Hack
Pute

Nudeln
Spätzle

Brot
Aufschnitt

Saure Sahne
Sahne
Milch

Different practices of moving or transportation can be found. It is above all the bright colored containers that shape the look of the Elbe Islands. Since the 1960s, the former general cargo and freight port has been increasingly automated due to conversion of the port into a container terminal Rural Opulence . Since then it is impossible to imagine the waterways, tracks, or roads without containers, mobile and stacked high. Incessant flows of goods heading for markets at home and abroad. With the gantry cranes at work it is impossible to ignore the sound. Public transport like the suburban train lines S 31 / S 3, the number 13 bus, or the passenger ferries of HADAG Gesellschaft link the islands to the neighboring centers of Hamburg and Harburg. For the residents and / or workers these are important connectors in everyday life Connectors . Until the 1970s there was a direct tram line between Wilhelmsburg and Hamburg Central Station. Today the number 13 bus connects the various residential areas between Veddel and southerly Kirchdorf in a 10–20 minute cycle. In addition, a second City Bike station supplements public transport. Walking aids such as walkers and canes are among the commonly observed modes of locomotion in everyday life. Along the way, people keep their eyes peeled for a place to sit and have a rest Stands for Lingering . The so-called Porsche at your heels[1], strollers or fairly often even shopping carts have gained the upper hand among various population groups as movers and transporters for goods to move right to the front door. You can often see the empty carts parked out in the street. If need be they are (re)activated. Even collectors and sorters use these repurposed transporters for their returnable bottles or other goods they have collected Collectors and Sorters . The general prevalence of the classic plastic bag is striking. People carry the semi-transparent bags from the Turkish markets or kiosks and the more stable versions from the competition, Lidl and Co, at all hours of the day and night. Young people with blue IKEA bags or custom-printed tote bags are (still) rarely encountered on the Elbe Islands. Since the free port has become freely accessible in the last few years, recreational forms of locomotion on skateboards or inline skates are nothing unusual. The smooth blacktop is an outright invitation to the

1
These are wheeled shopping trolleys that people pull along behind them.

skaters. On the weekends at the various canals, or on the Dove-Elbe, you can spot the occasional motorboat, paddle boat, or majestic looking swan pedalo for rent from particular mooring places or docked in small private ports Playfully .

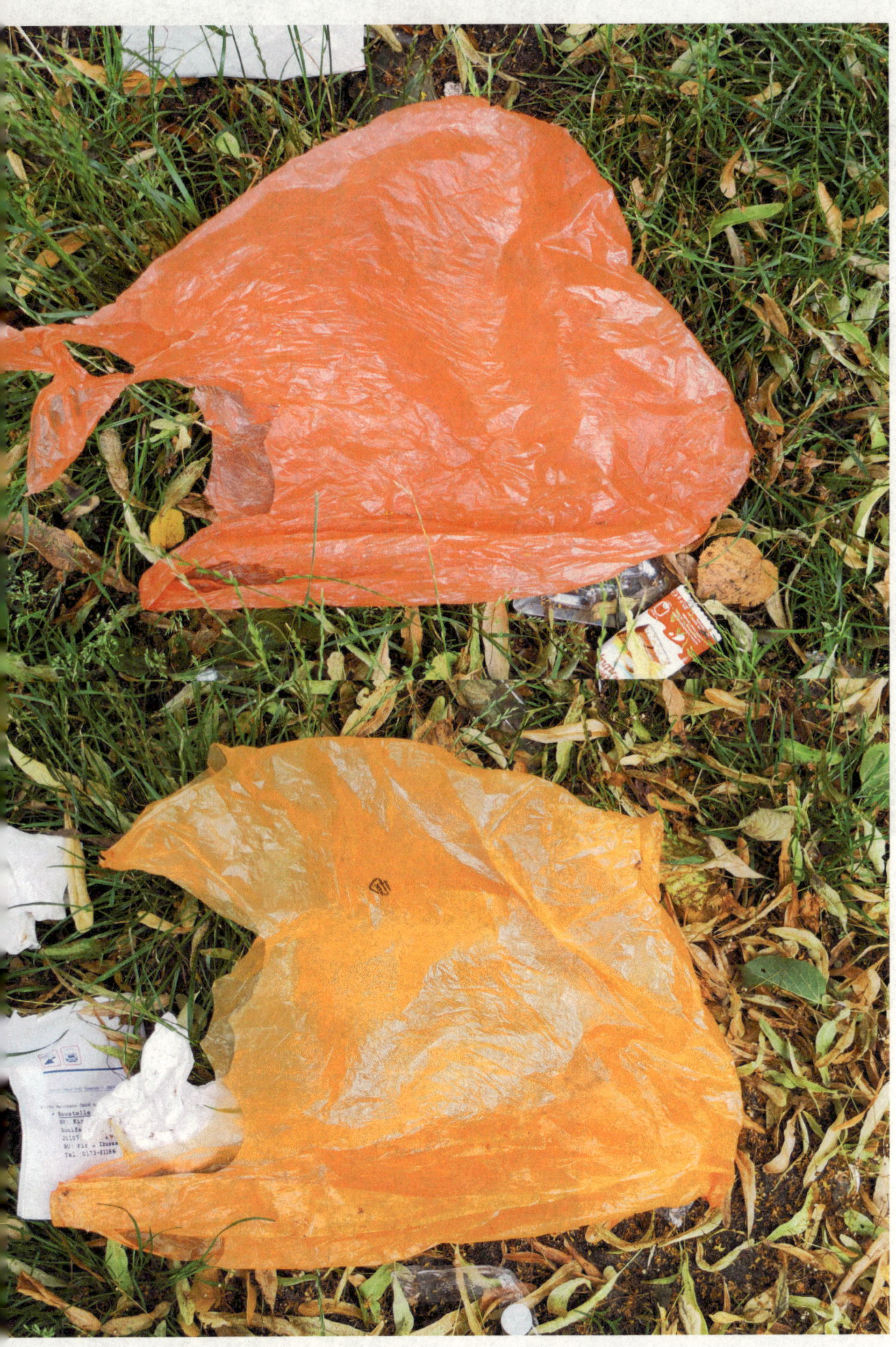

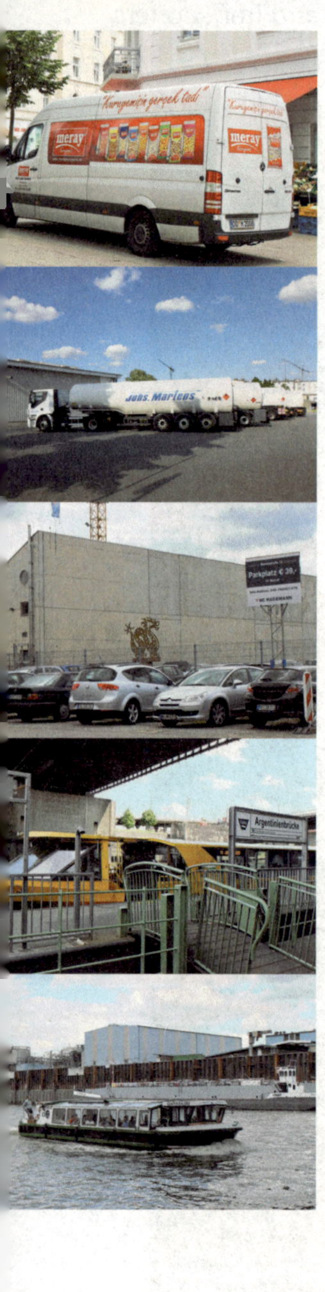
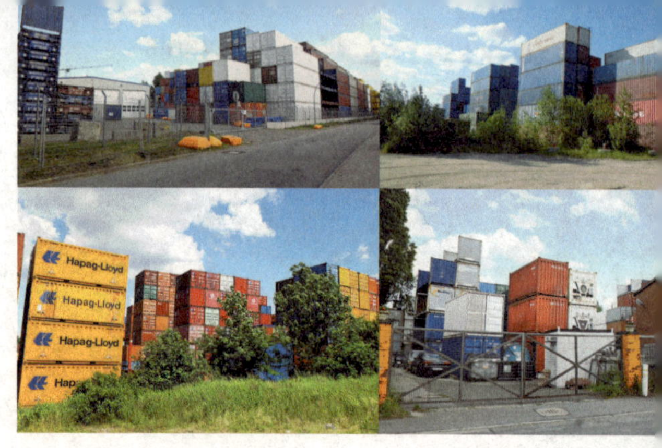
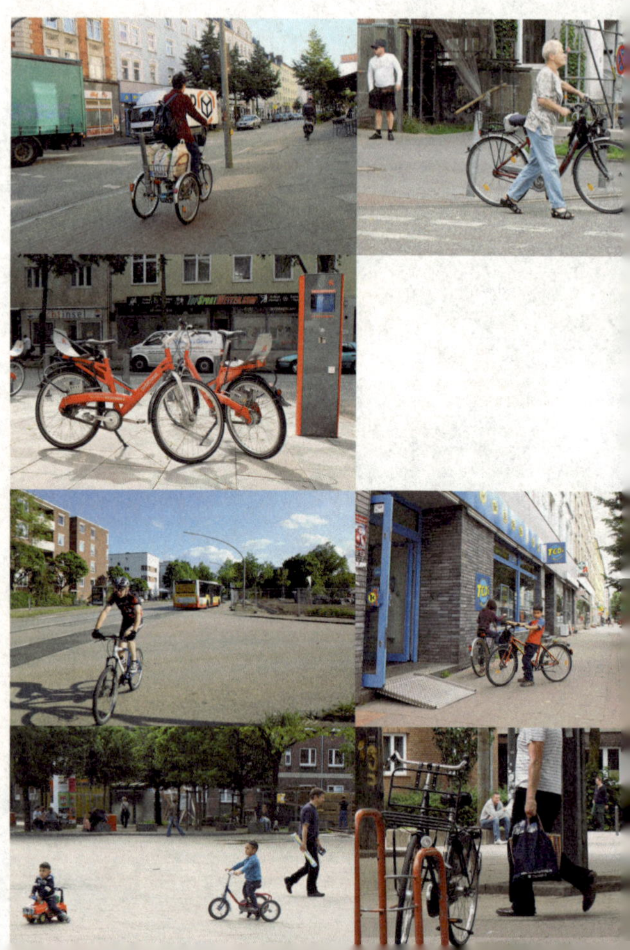

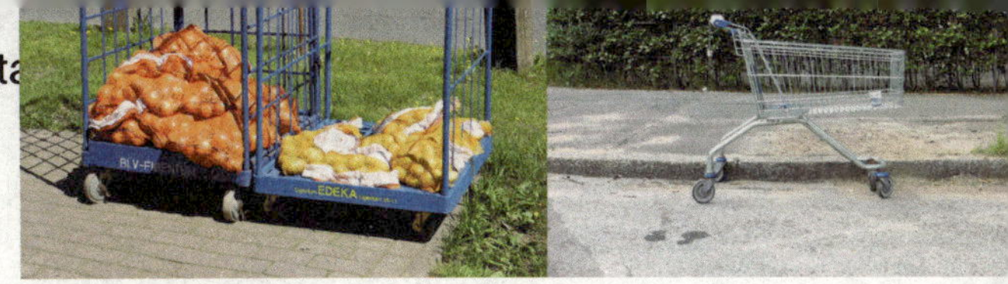

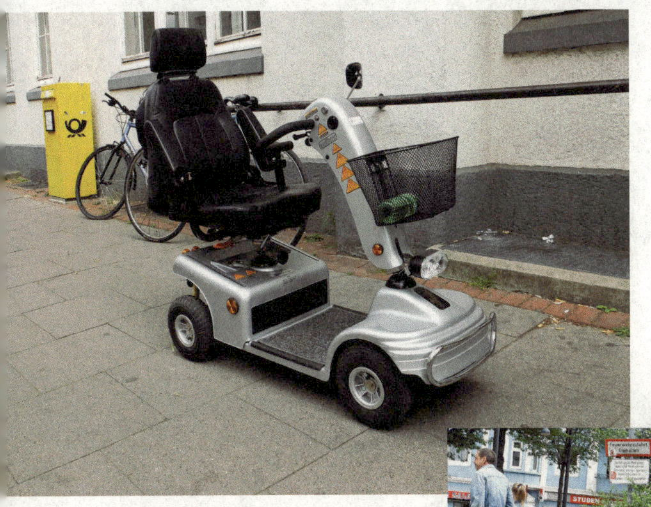

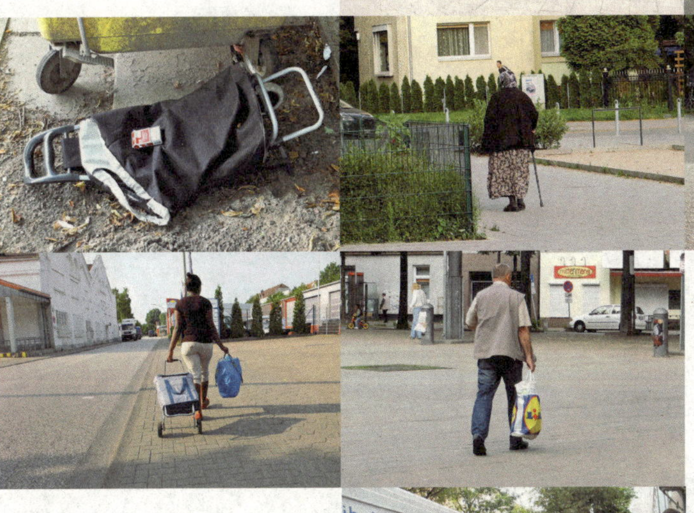

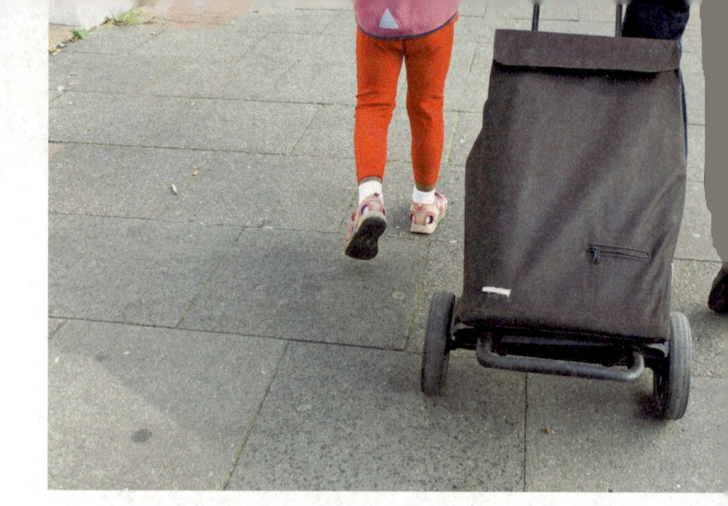

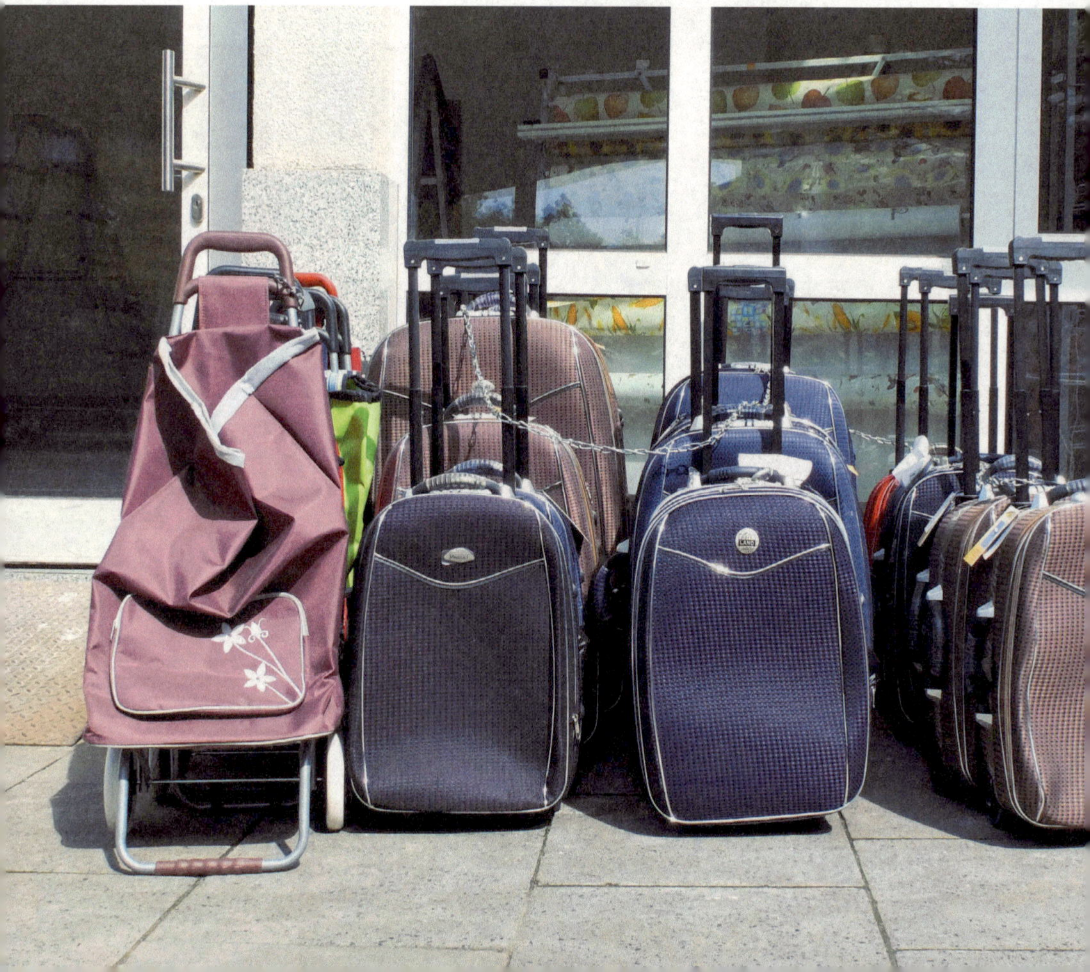

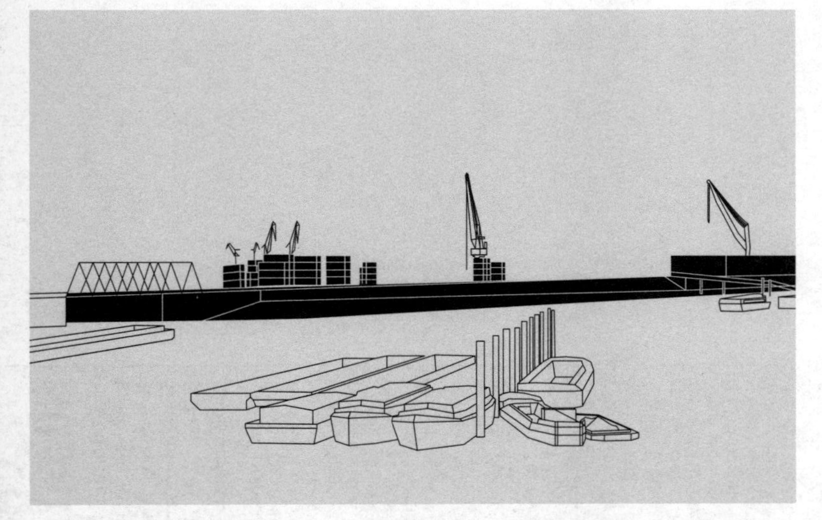

... the path suddenly stops which causes me to suddenly feel deeply surprised. Then finally comes the Oderhöft shipping pier. There are already tourists on board. Two, three, workers come down the bridge at a leisurely pace. Pirate types. The end of their shift. They do not talk and do not smoke, they only nod to the captain ...

Containerverkehr nach Südafrika wird aufgenomme[n]

Container bestimmen zunehmend den internationalen Güterv[er]kehr. So wird beispielsweise Hapag-Lloyd, die größte deuts[che] Reederei, bis 1979/80 den überwiegenden Teil ihrer gesam[ten] Liniendienste auf die Fahrt mit der genormten Kiste umgest[ellt] haben. Auf dem Programm steht als nächste Container-Relati[on] die Karibik.

Noch zuvor, Mitte 1977, erschließen die Deutschen Afrika-Linien gemeinsam mit acht Schiffahrtsunternehmen dem Container ein weiteres Fahrtgebiet: Südafrika. Hamburg zählt zu jenen europäischen Haupthäfen, die von dieser als „Container Club" apostrophierten Südafrika-Konferenzreedergruppe bedient werden.

Trotz der aktuellen Entwicklung in Südafrika erwartet Hamburg in diesem Zusammenhang einen starken Zuwachs seines Containerumschlags. In dieser Haltung sieht sich der Elbehafen aufgrund der Prognosen deutscher Schiffahrtskaufleute und Spediteure, aber auch südafrikanischer Wirtschaftskreise durchaus bestätigt.

Welche Bedeutung diesem Markt aus deutscher Sicht zukommt, zeigt die Entwicklung des Warenaustausches mit der Republik Südafrika. Im vergangenen Jahr exportierte die bundesdeutsche Wirtschaft Güter im Werte von 3,4 Mrd. DM; die Importe aus der Republik beliefen sich auf 2,2 Mrd. DM. Über 90 Prozent der Ausfuhren entfielen auf gewerbliche Fertigwaren, die bekanntlich die Basis für den Containerverkehr bilden. Über Hamburg, das aus Tradition eine starke Stellung im Südafrika-[...] im Jahre [...] [...]ut 540 000 t [...]5 waren es [...]dings rund

Die Anstrengungen der Südafri[ka-]Konferenzlinien zeigen, welches [Ge]wicht sie dem Container in die[ser] Relation beimessen. Sie werden ze[hn] große Containerschiffe zwisch[en] Nordeuropa und der Republik [im] Süden Afrikas einsetzen, die jew[eils] rund 2400 bis 2500 Großbehälter [be]fördern können. Im Jahre 1980 [wird] dieser Dienst dann seine volle L[ei]stungsstärke erreichen. Die Inve[sti]tionen für diesen Verkehr werd[en] einschließlich der Umschlagsanla[gen] in Südafrika und der dort notwen[di]gen Infrastrukturmaßnahmen umge[ge]rechnet mehr als drei Milliarden [DM] kosten.

Kredite für dürregeschädigte Bauer[n]

Finanzierungshilfen von 85 000 [DM] hat der Bürgerausschuß auf Ant[rag] des Senats am Mittwoch für lan[d-] und forstwirtschaftliche Betri[ebe] bewilligt, denen die Trockenheit [des] letzten Sommers existenzbedrohe[nde] Schäden zugefügt hat. Weitere 85 [000] DM stehen der hamburgisch[en] Landwirtschaft aus Bundesmitt[eln] für diesen Zweck zur Verfüg[ung]. Damit können insgesamt 1,2 Mill[io]nen DM Kredite verbilligt werden.

Weitere Voraussetzungen für [die] Vergabe der Mittel und die näher[en] Einzelheiten über die Durchführu[ng] des Antragsverfahrens werd[en] durch Richtlinien der Behörde [für] Wirtschaft, Verkehr und Landwi[rt]schaft geregelt.

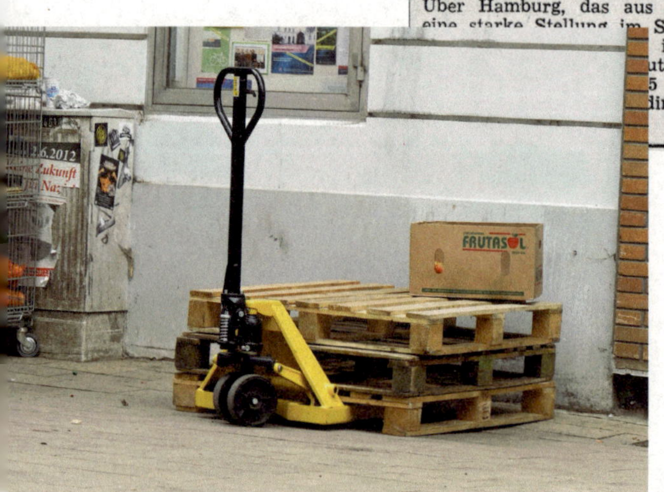

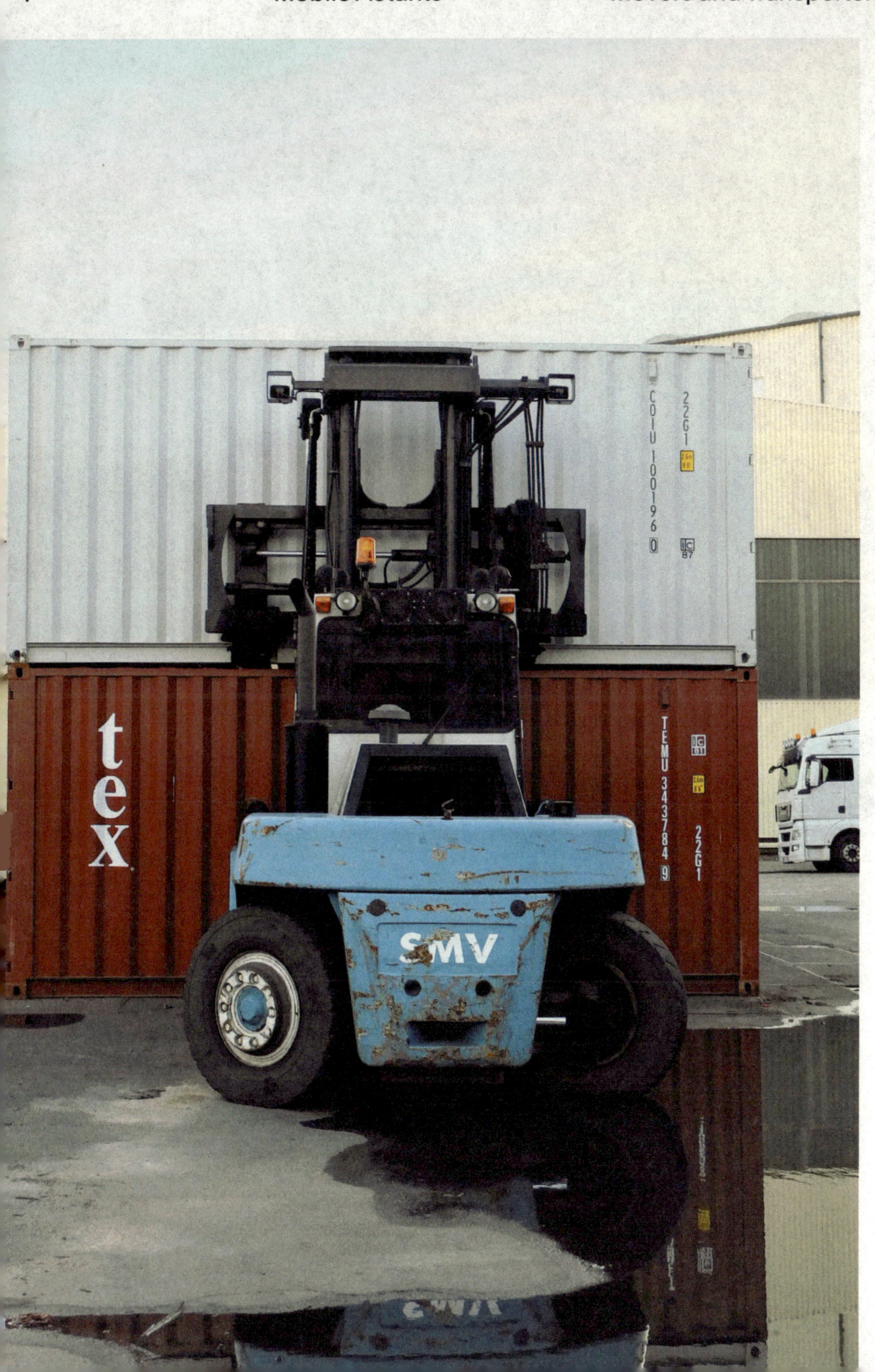
COIU 1001960
22G1
tex
TEMU 343784 9
22G1
SMV

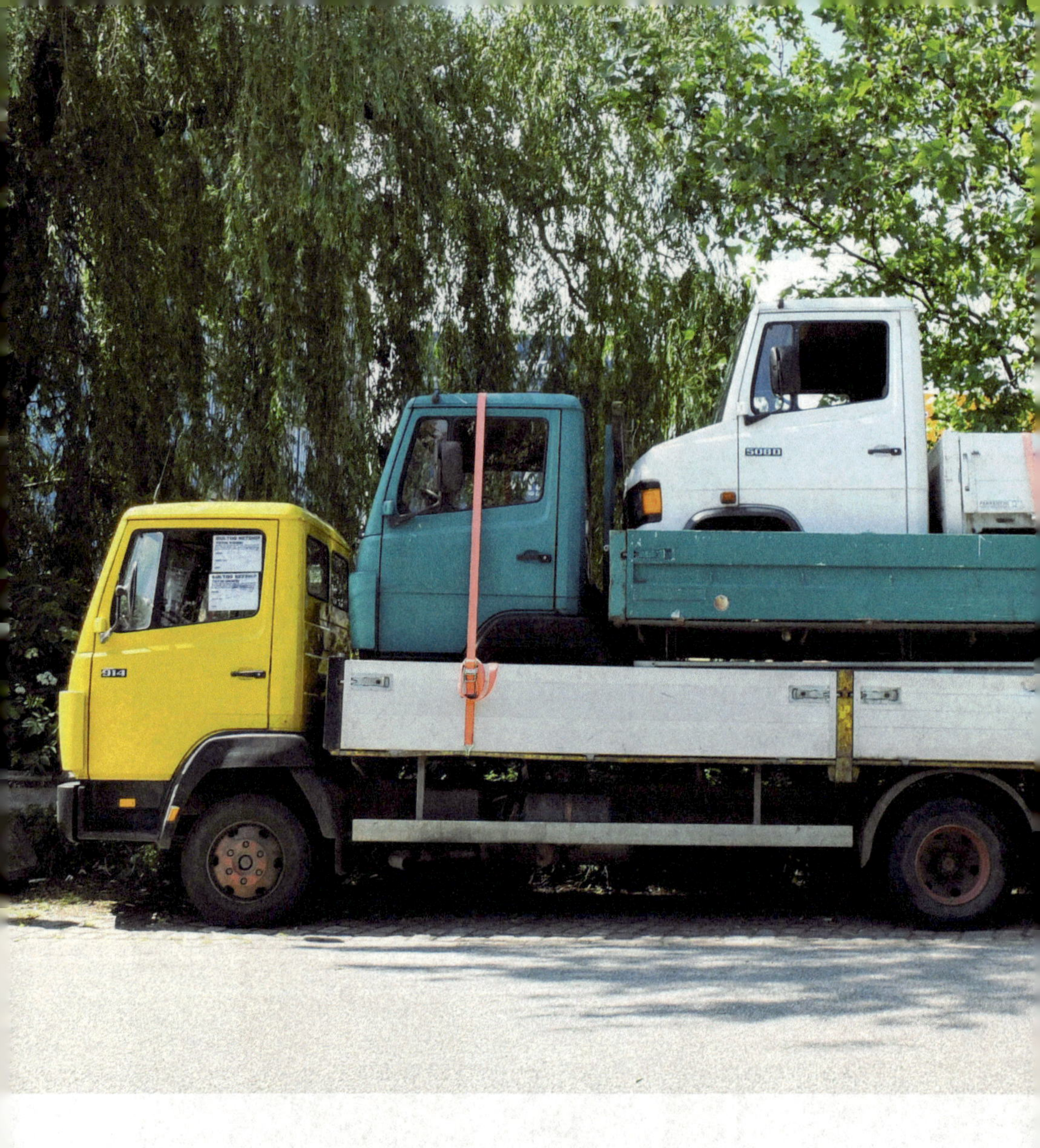

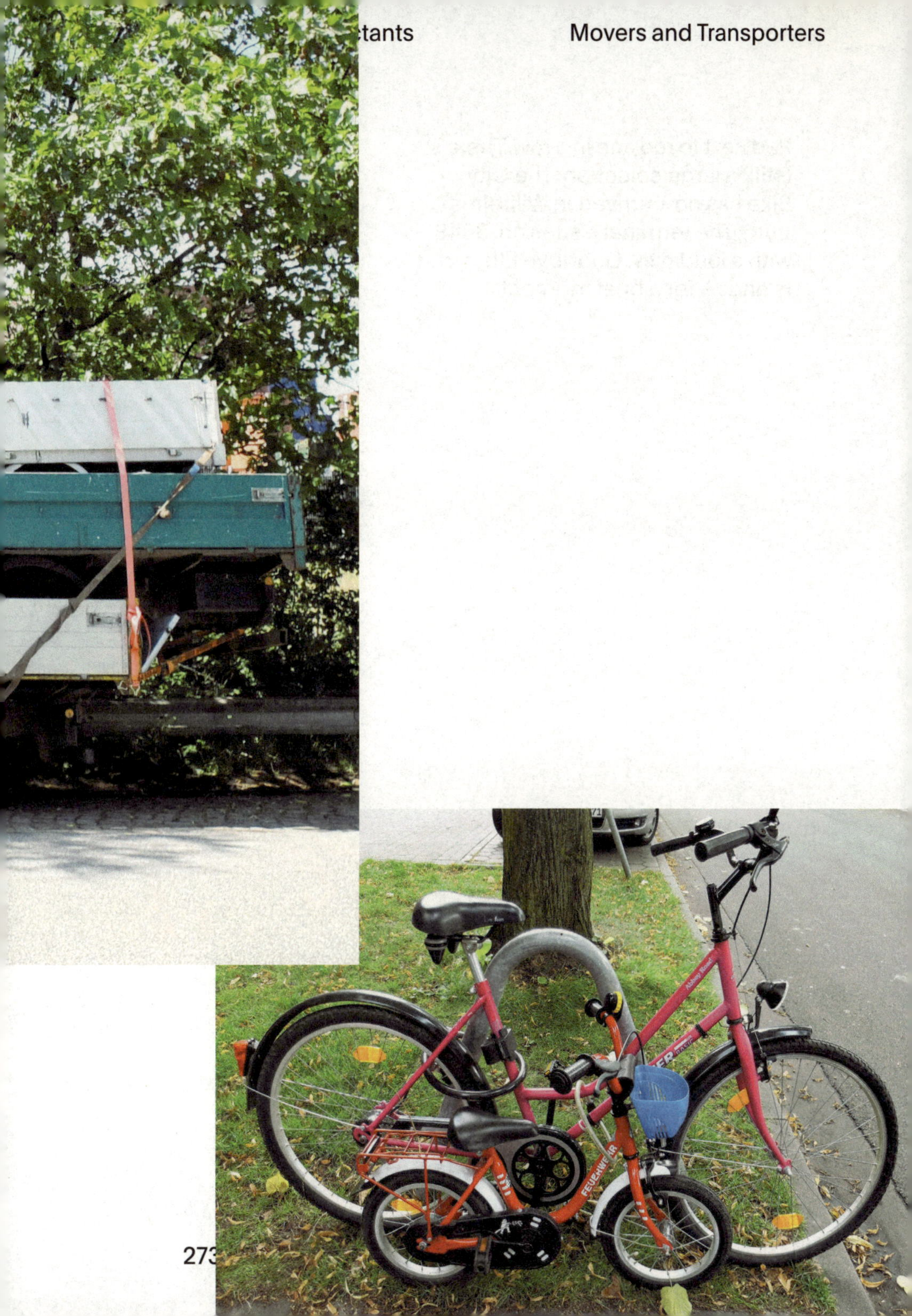

Red next to red and in a row. There's
(still) a large selection. The City
Bike has now arrived in Wilhelmsburg. The terminal issues no. 8049
with a loud hiss. Goodbye Elbe
Islands—for a brief moment.

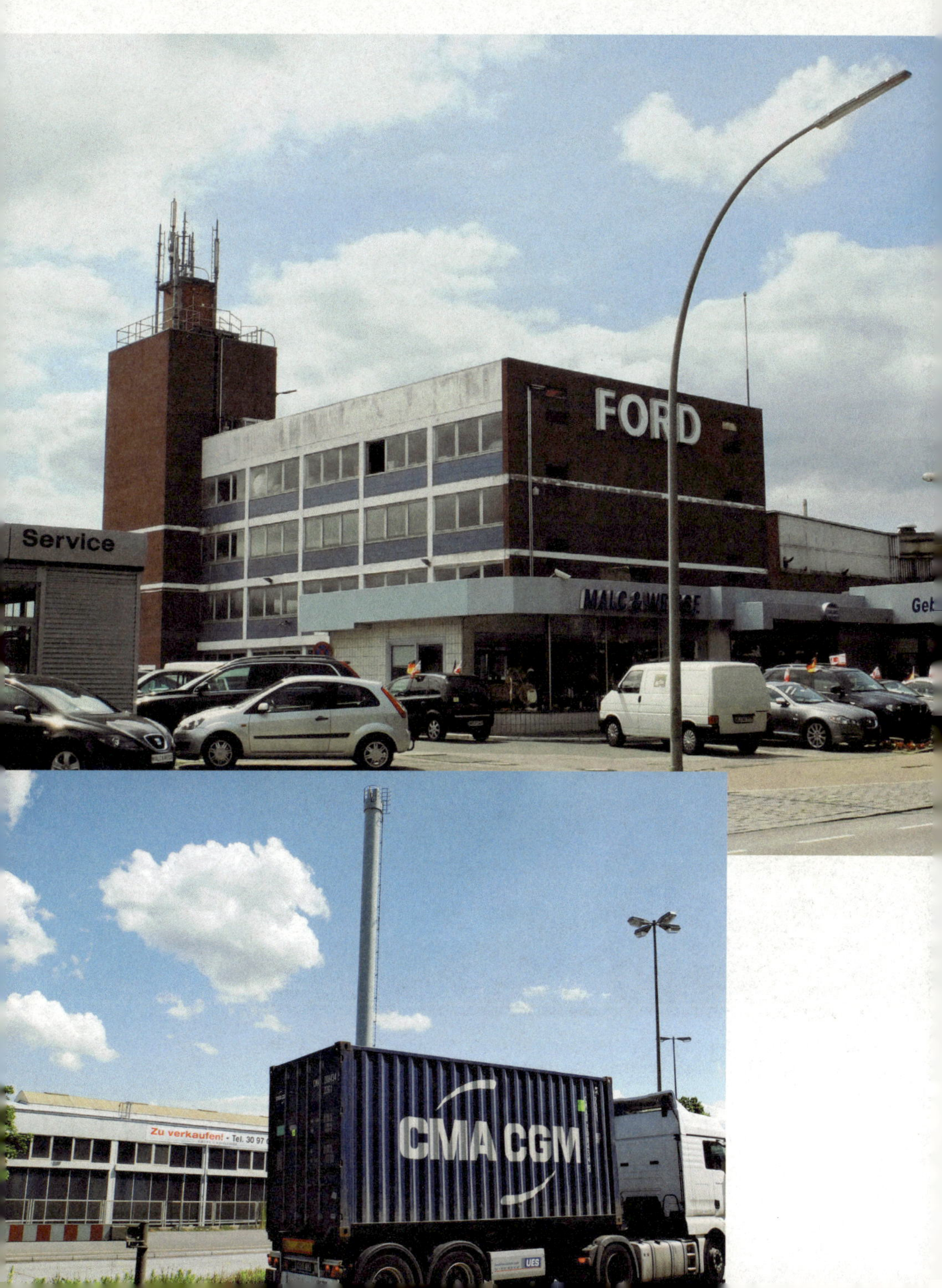
Service
FORD
MALC & WEISE
Geb
Zu verkaufen! - Tel. 30 97
CMA CGM

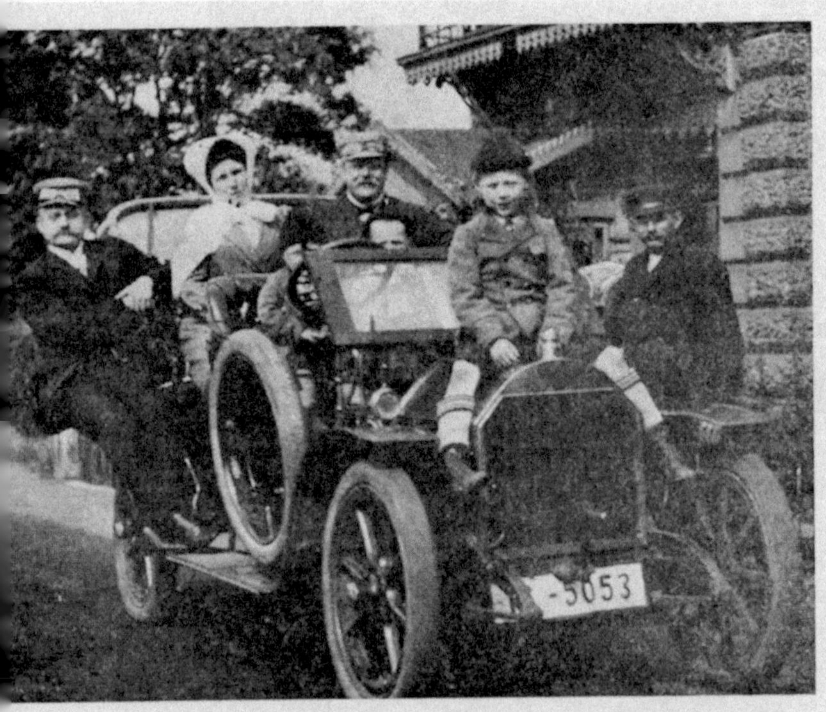

berühmte alte Opel. Im Fond der Doktor mit Frau. Reinhold jr. als Kühler-
figur, am Steuer Alfred und Walter. Vor dem Haus am Reiherstiegdeich

Important connectors in and between areas on the Elbe Islands still include the expressway A1, the crossing-free Reichsstraße, the Elbe Bridges, the Elbe, the rail tracks and the non-tidal waterway network. These are the central axial north-south links. These built structures, which are massive in places, reveal the technical development and economic importance of Wilhelmsburg as a hub and industrial site in the late 19th to mid-20th century Change-Comma-Pause . The trigger for its accelerated development was the increasing level of port operations and traffic at the port facilities, opened in 1888 in Hamburg. Areas with water links were in great demand, so the construction was fostered by side-reinforced channels. These followed the topography of the pre-existing agricultural drainage network No Dike, No Land . As time passed, an intermeshing system of connectors and links developed, made up of navigable locks, canals or folding bridges that were often named after the entrepreneurs and investors associated with them (Veringkanal, Ernst-August-Kanal, Jaffé-Davids-Kanal, Neuhöfer-Kanal). The last canal was finally built in 1924. For many people it was not just the economic outlook on the Elbe Islands that changed after the collapse of industry, the conversion and automation of the cargo port into a container port, and the catastrophic flooding in the 1960s. A huge wave of emigration caused population shrinkage. Today the Elbe Islands are primarily a residential area for 50,731 inhabitants.[1] Various forms of public transport such as buses, suburban trains, or ferries continue to play an important role for mobility in everyday life Movers and Transporters . However the unlimited connectivity provided by various information and communication technologies forms part of the islands' everyday life. Numerous satellites or cell towers receive the local stations. Internet cafés, global call shops, and private travel agencies draw attention to themselves with their various services and limitless connectivity. Cheap international rates or European bus and plane trips point to the far-flung, enduring family ties of the various ethnic groups.

1
Of these, 32.7%
come from abroad
and 56.8% have
a migration back-
ground. A total of
158 different
nationalities live on
the Elbe Islands.
(Statistisches Amt
für Hamburg und
Schleswig-Holstein,
figures in
December 2011)

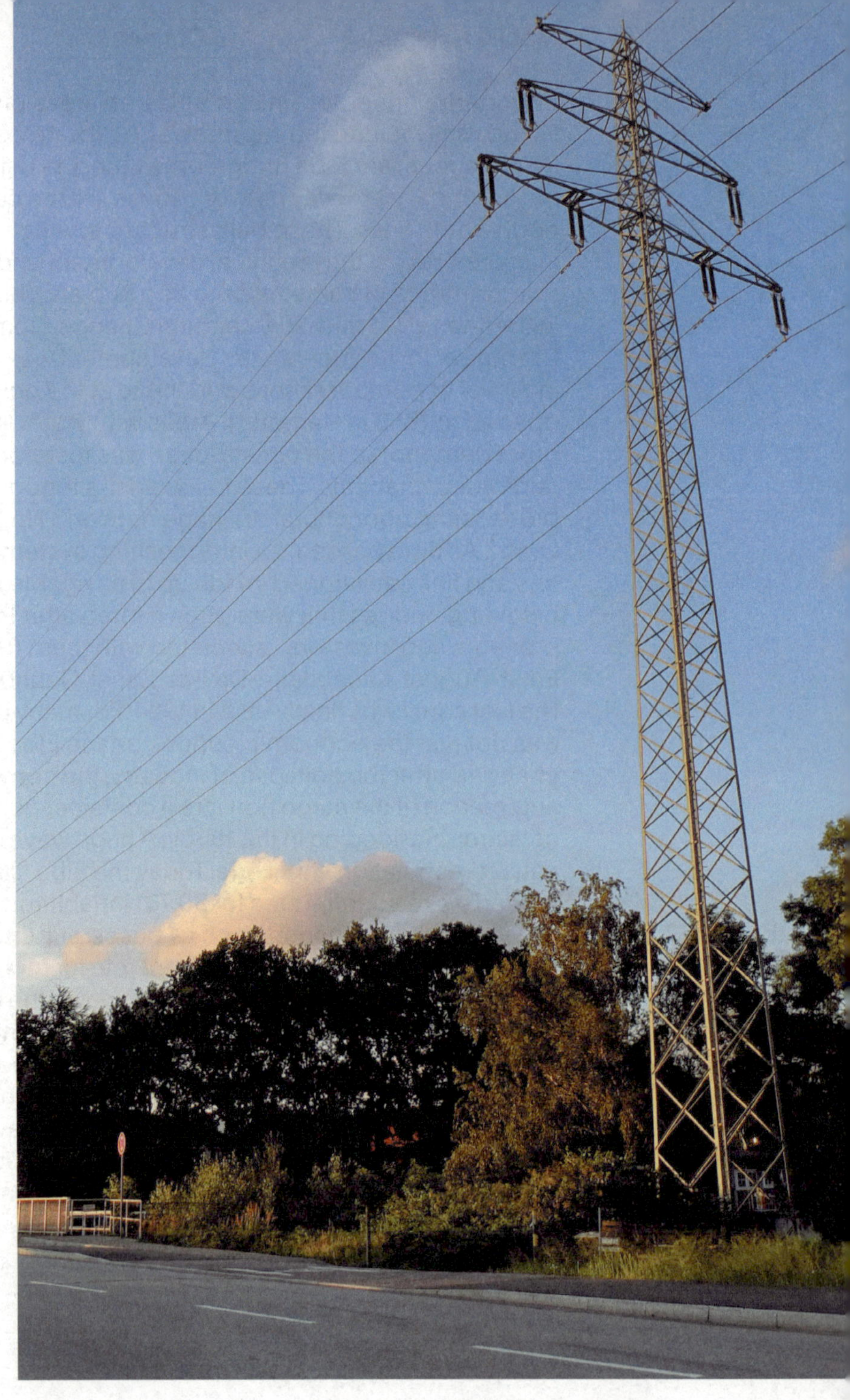

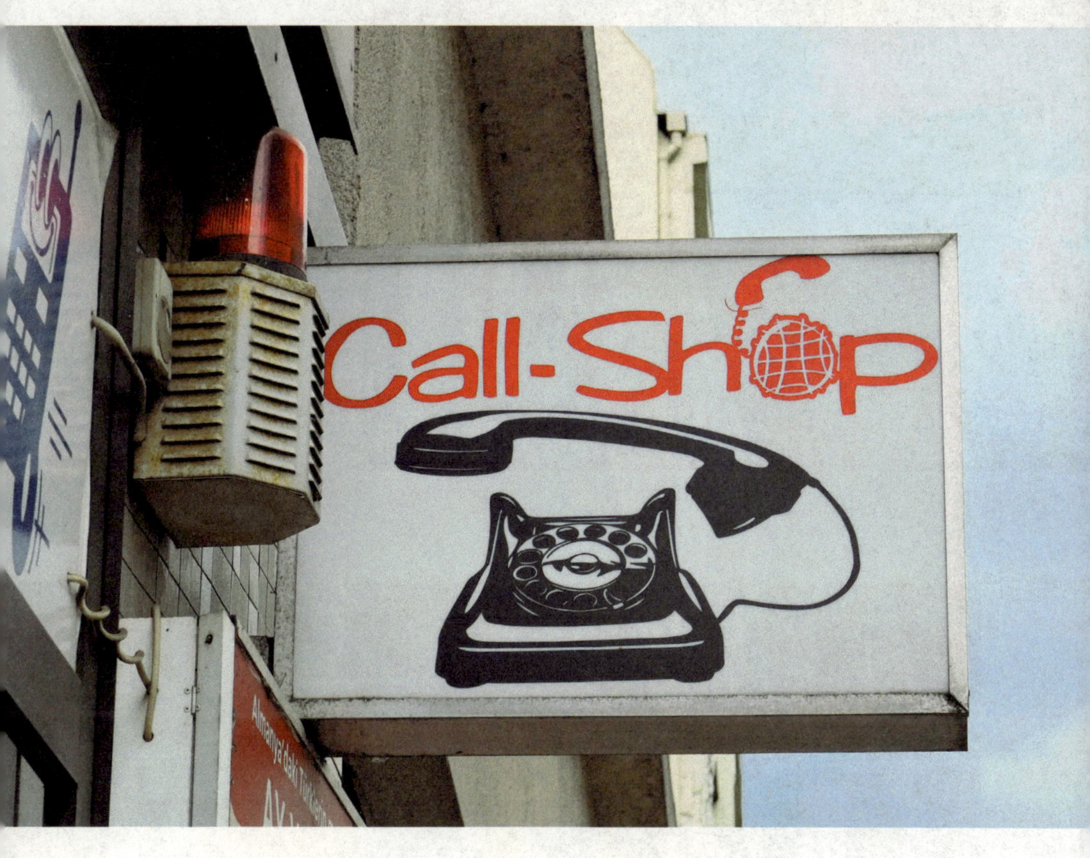
Call-Shop

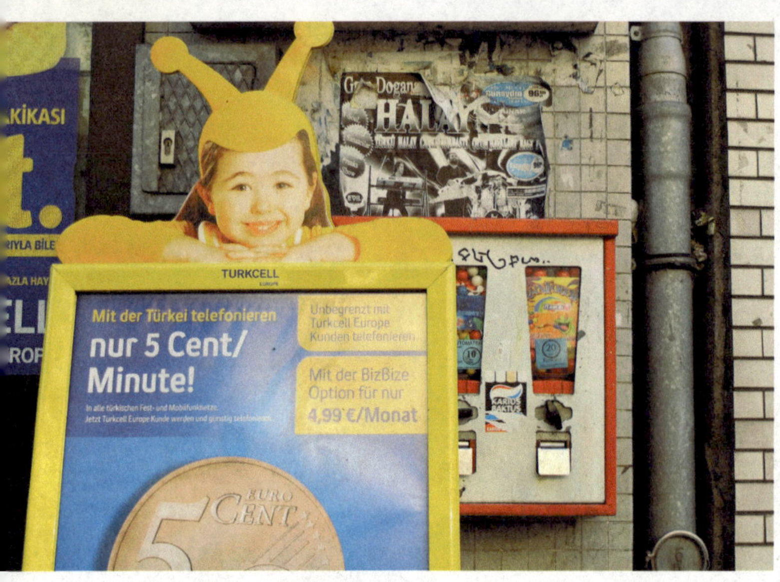

KİKASI
t.
RIYLA BİLE
AZLA HAY
ELL
ROF
TURKCELL
EUROPE
Mit der Türkei telefonieren
nur 5 Cent/
Minute!
In alle türkischen Fest- und Mobilfunknetze.
Jetzt Turkcell Europe Kunde werden und günstig telefonieren.
Unbegrenzt mit
Turkcell Europe
Kunden telefonieren
Mit der BizBize
Option für nur
4,99 €/Monat
EURO
CENT
5
Dogan
HALAY

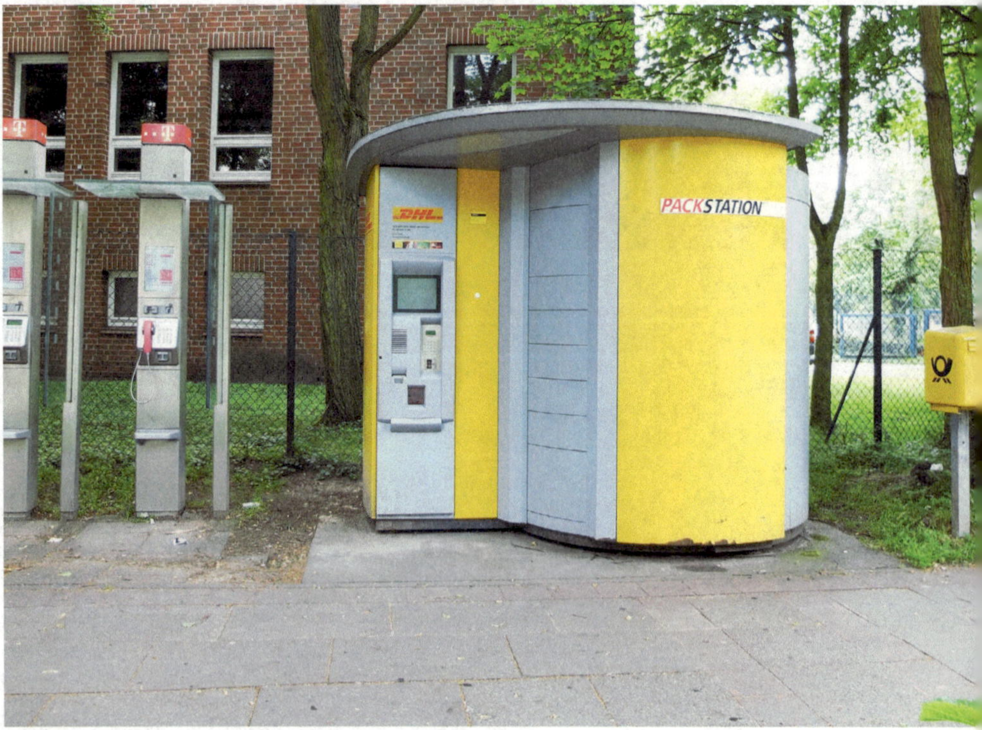

DHL
PACKSTATION

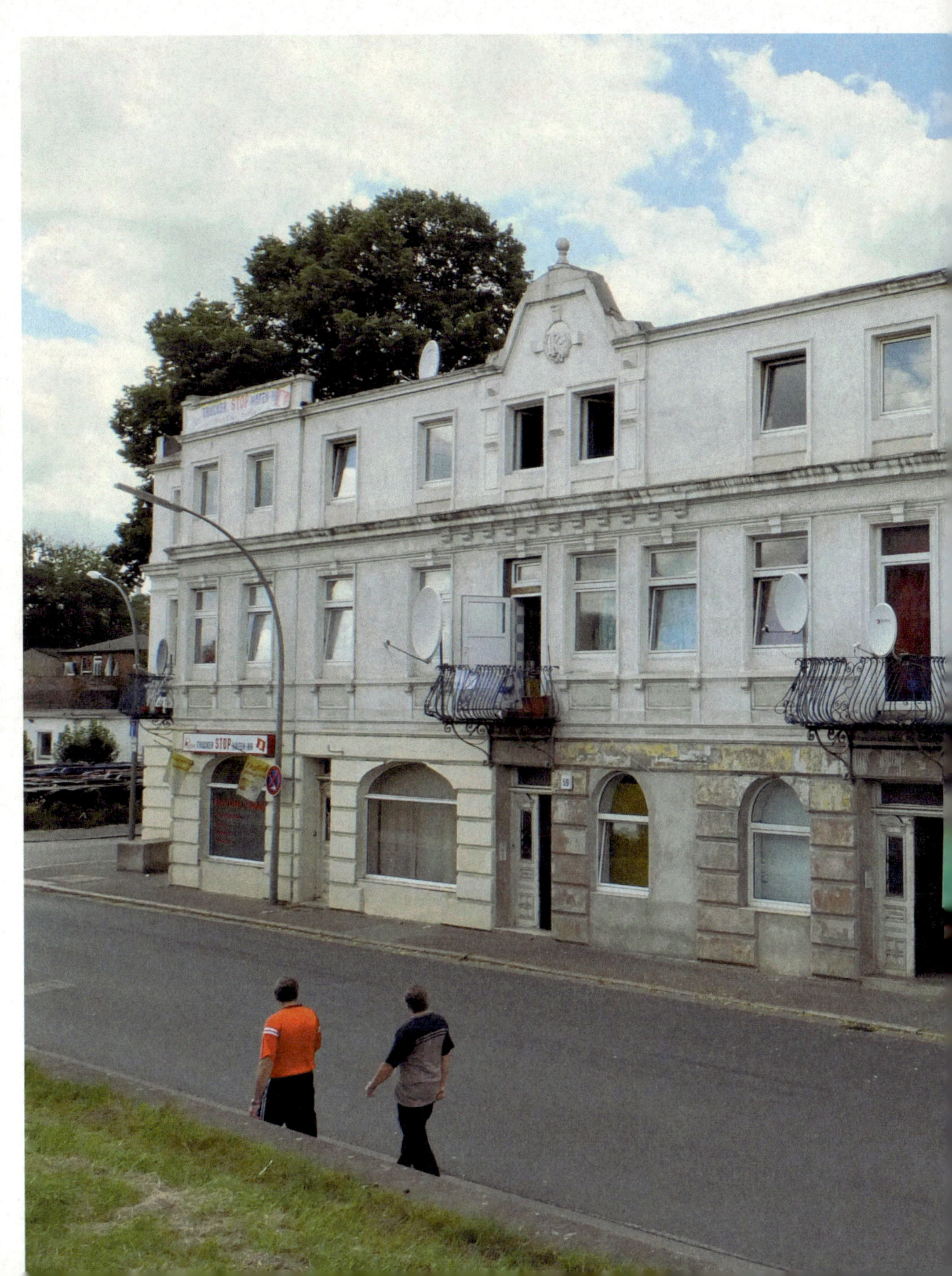

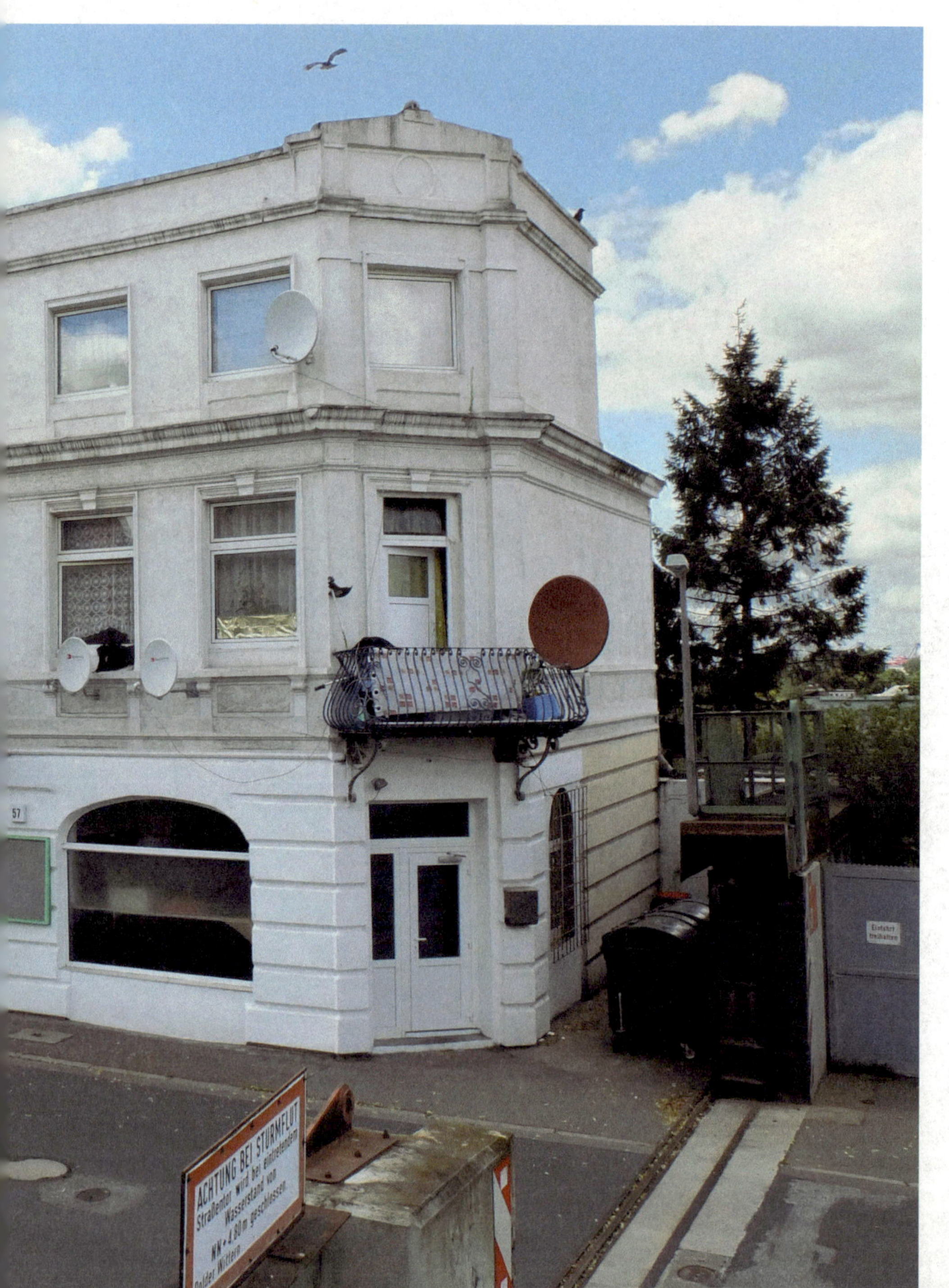
ACHTUNG BEI STURMFLUT
Straßentor wird bei eintretendem
Wasserstand von
NN + 4,80 m geschlossen

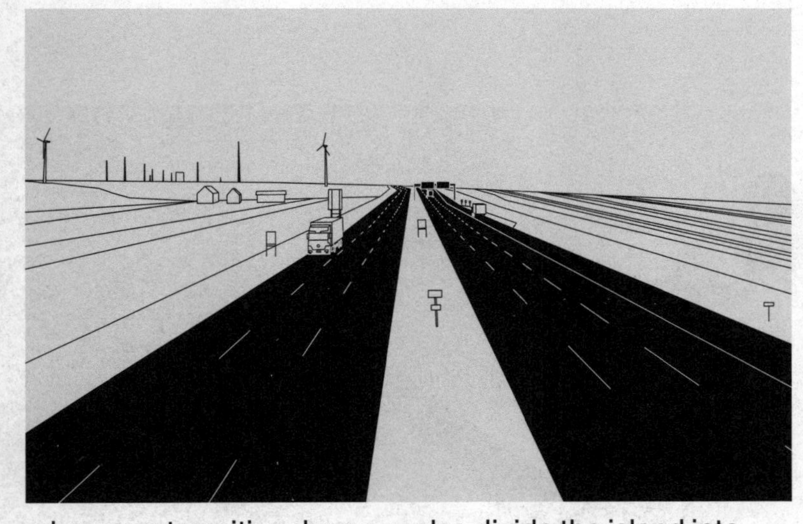

... however transitional spaces also divide the island into other islands. Islands are set between one another, detached or separated from each other. Various everyday realities ...

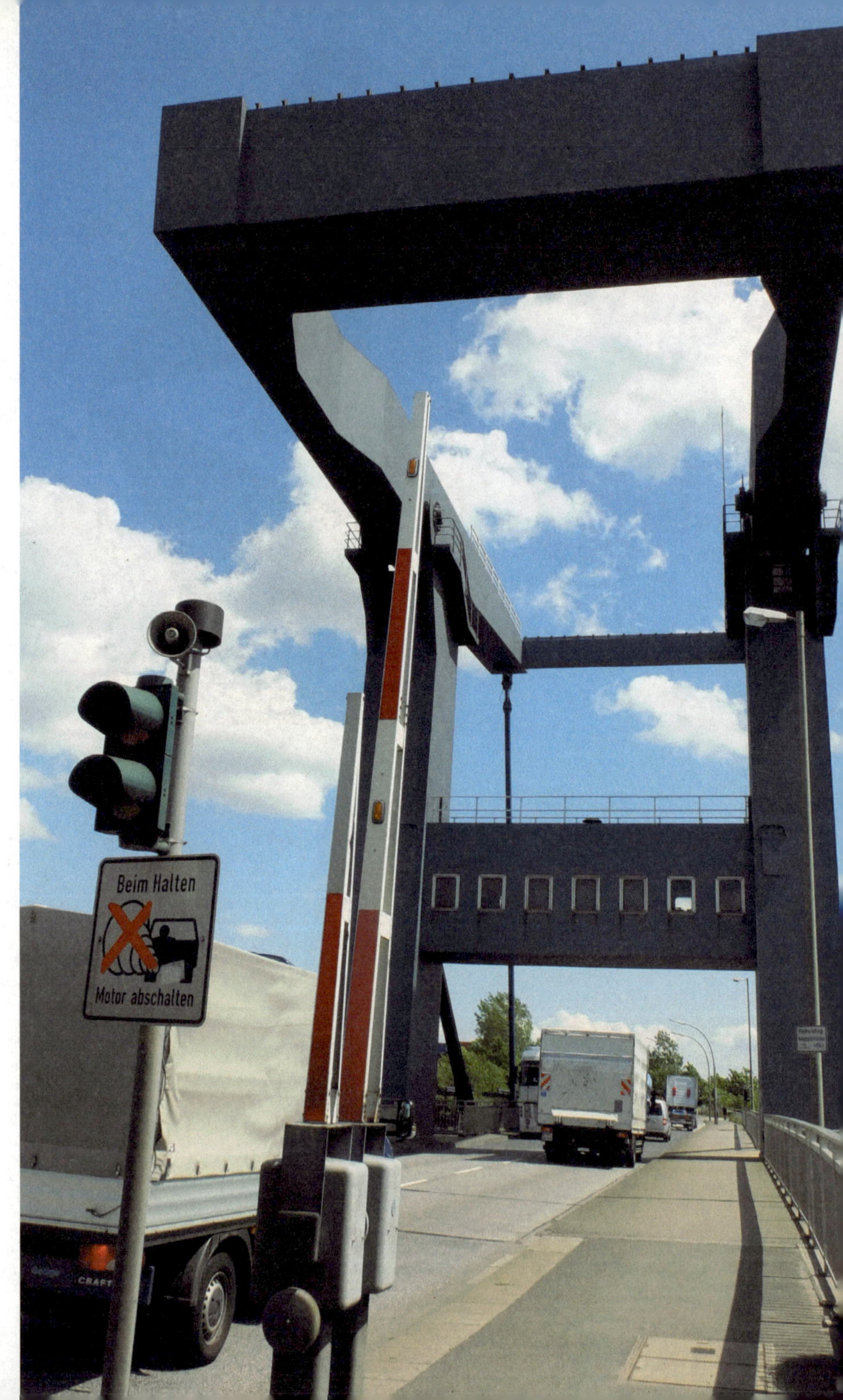
Beim Halten
Motor abschalten

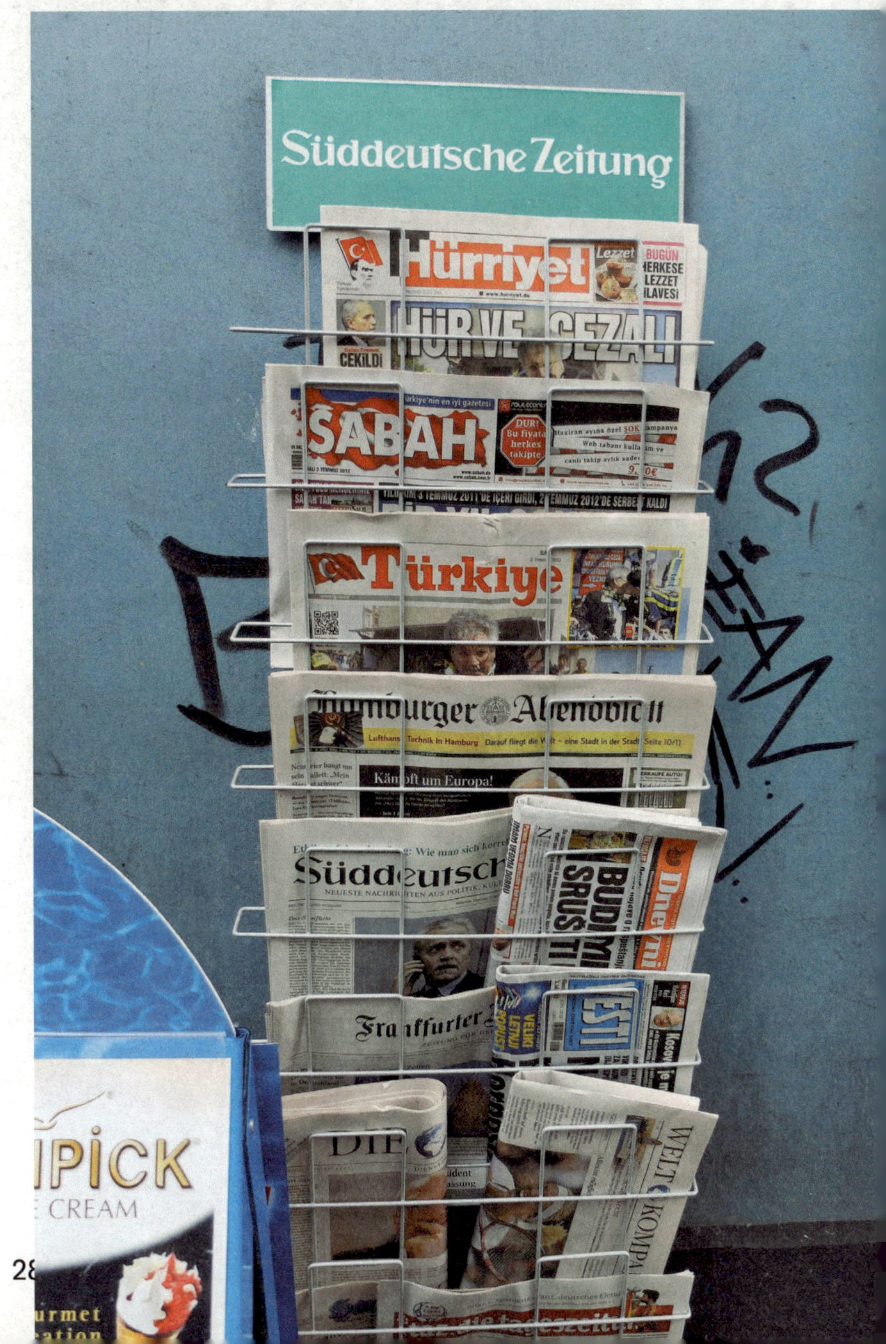
Süddeutsche Zeitung
Hürriyet
HÜR VE GEZALI
SABAH
Türkiye
Hamburger Abendblatt
Süddeutsche
Frankfurter

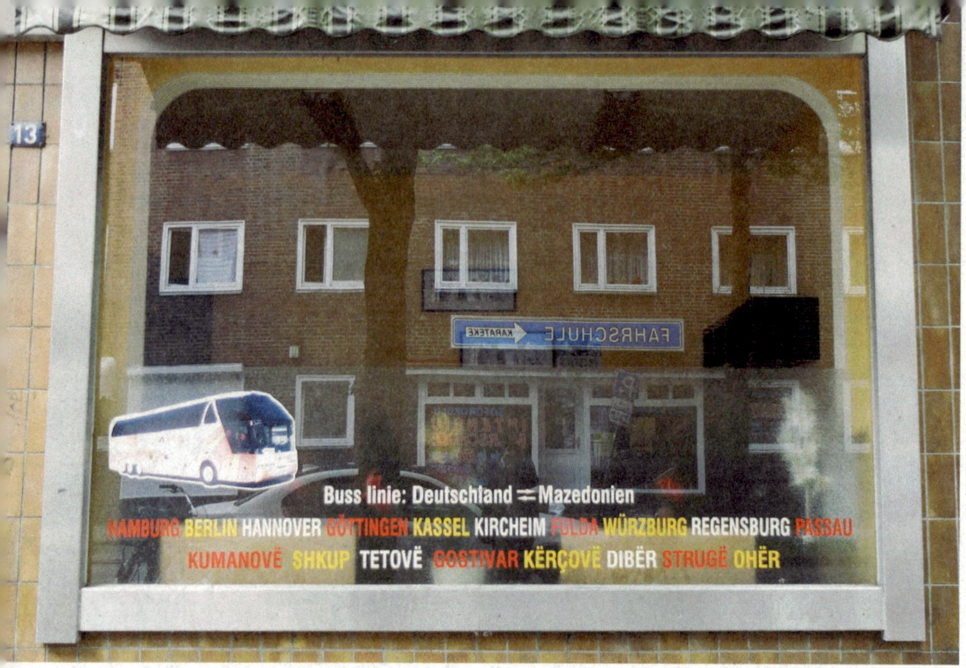

FAHRSCHULE
KARATEKA
Buss linie: Deutschland ⇌ Mazedonien
HAMBURG BERLIN HANNOVER GÖTTINGEN KASSEL KIRCHEIM FULDA WÜRZBURG REGENSBURG PASSAU
KUMANOVË SHKUP TETOVË GOSTIVAR KËRÇOVË DIBËR STRUGË OHËR

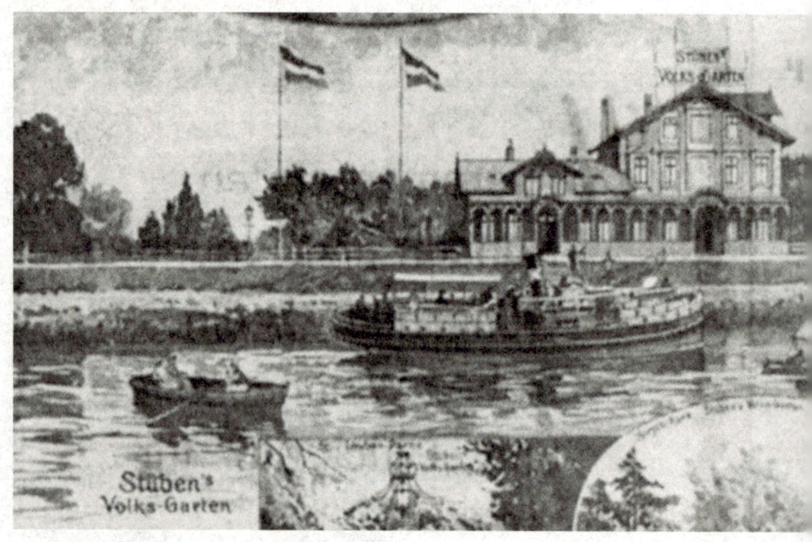

Stuben's
Volks-Garten

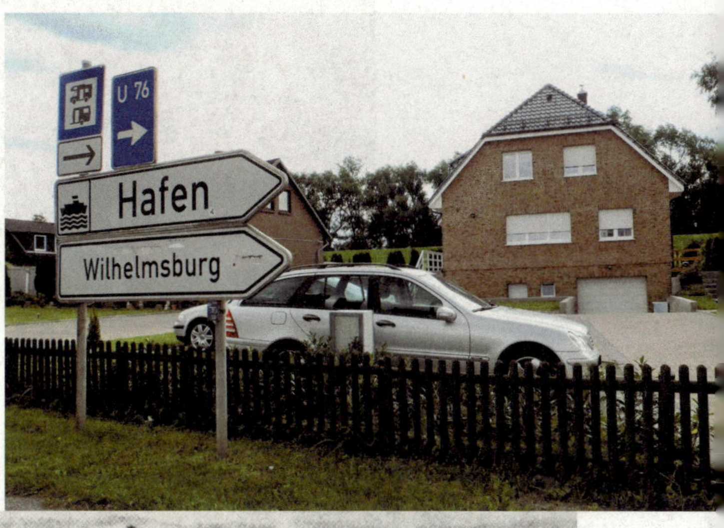
U 76
Hafen
Wilhelmsburg

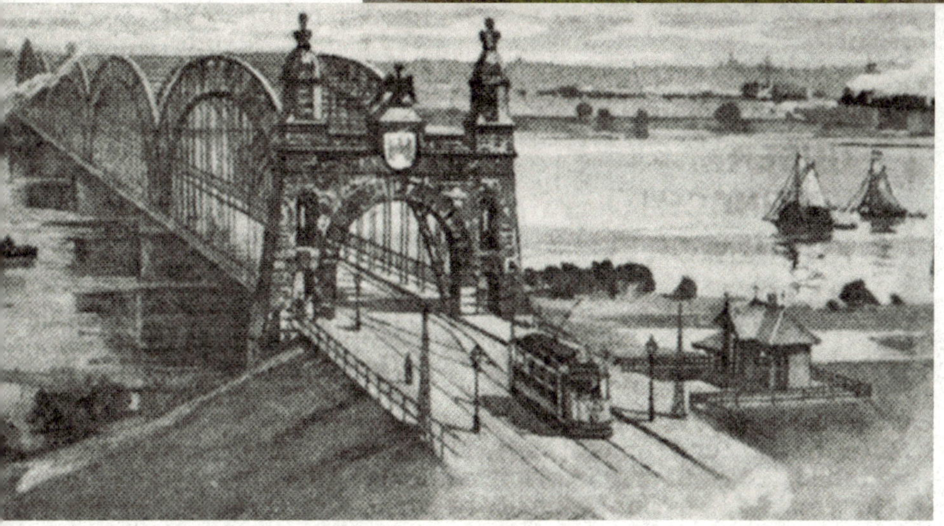

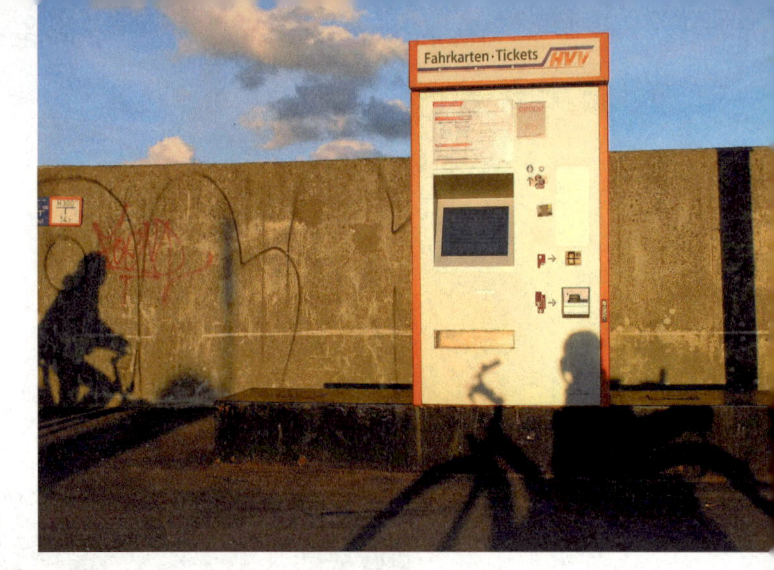
Fahrkarten·Tickets HVV

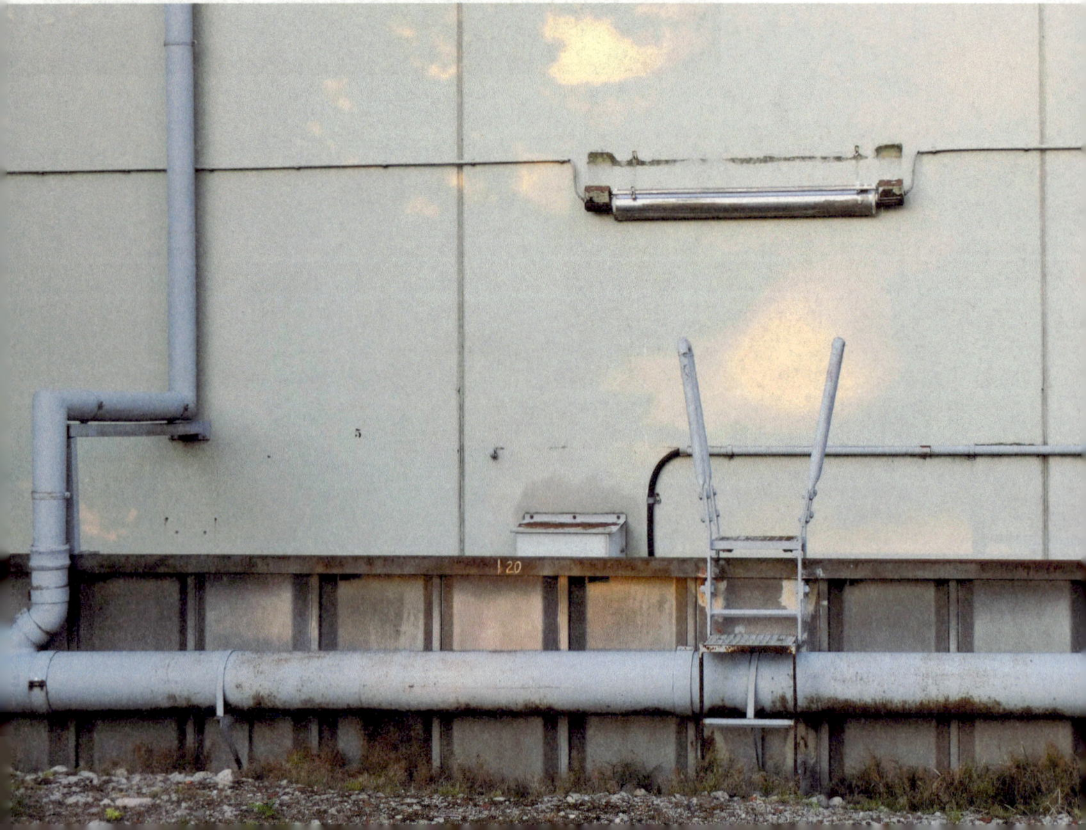

Highly contrasting states of consciousness are expressed in this site-specific practice, involving various actors. Indecision and boredom or determination and representation. The circling around is repeated several times weekly, daily, or even hourly in uniform movements. It is sometimes akin to strolling or aimless rambling, but also resembles very focused, concentrated, or thoughtful circulating. I observed the preferred times of day for this practice. For example, young women from the Sinti-Roma families mostly stroll on weekends and late at night. The jogging couples regularly run their rounds in the early evening. The ice cream van, in contrast, loops around all day long. The selected actants —a bright bell or formal clothing—draw attention to themselves in their own subtle way. The area encircled is emphasized by the practice, written into space. The production of space is made through repetition.

Proudly young women on the sidewalks stroll side by side. They look
straight ahead, talking quietly.
Hold hands or push strollers ahead
of them. Mothers, daughters,
sisters. They wear long, slightly
trailing frilly skirts, colorful scarves
around their shoulders, gold
jewelry in their ears, floral deco-
ration in their hair. Long black
braids down to their hips. They
look confident with their upright
posture, seeming in a certain
sense inviolable, concentrated.
They walk slowly, round by round.
Naturally proud.

At Rotenhäuser Feld in the evening, the sun is—just—still shining.
A couple is jogging. Lap after
lap. She wears a white headscarf
and a beige tunic dress over
trousers. Her husband in blue
jeans and T-shirt runs just slightly
behind her. On his wrist a
heavy watch. Several times in
the park during the evening,
just before the sun sets behind
the trees.

In the late afternoon out and about
with a semi-translucent plastic bag
on the road, our paths cross.
Several times today. The turquoise
shorts with white patterns recall
Hawaii, the beach, the sun, and the
sea. Black hair curled. Music seeps
out of white ear plugs. He does
his rounds several times. Aimless
today?

19:02, 19:07, 19:08, 19:22 it rings
a few times. Every day light and
welcoming, even when it rains.
The ice cream van does its rounds
as usual in the late afternoon.
Hello summer, when do you
actually start?

It is still early in the morning, the
windows are wide open. The rain
has subsided. The air is wet
and cool. Heavy drops fall from the
trees. Again and again. The sweeper
on Rotenhäuser Damm is audible. Moves up and down, turns in
circles. Then the bells ring seven.

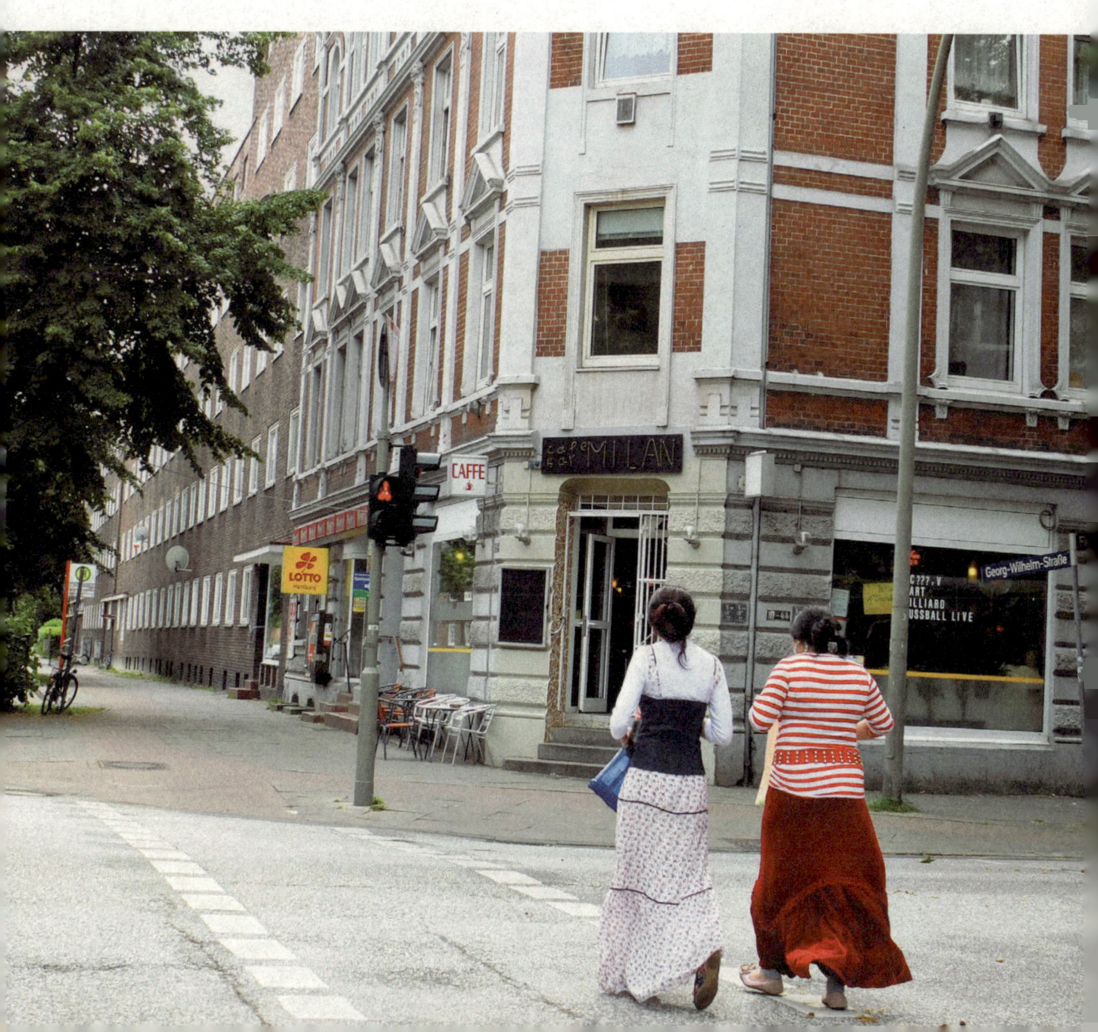
cafe
bar MILAN
CAFFE
LOTTO
Georg-Wilhelm-Straße

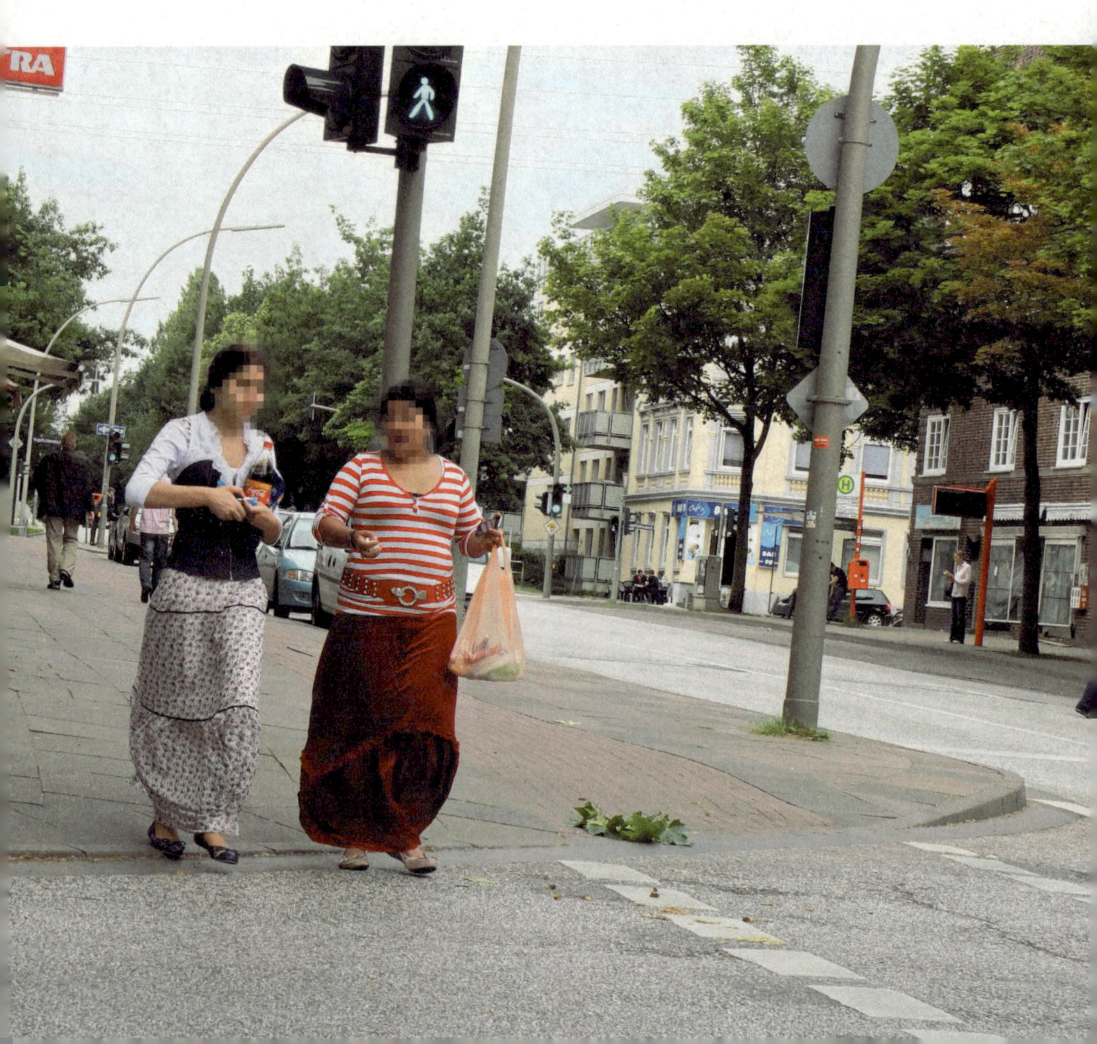

Mainly in the evening, especially on weekends, driving for show is on the program in Wilhelmsburg. Fast, sporty cars race along the main roads, such as Vering- or Georg-Wilhelm Straße. Preferably anywhere that the small restaurants, cafes, tearooms, and fast food stands are bustling. The cars brake abruptly at traffic lights, then drive off shortly afterwards with a loud kick start. This is not only a tried-and-tested attention-seeking strategy of young men, but is also a (playful, non-hazardous) trial of strength between friends. During these brief excursions, in addition to the fresh hot rod model, the girlfriend in the passenger seat is presented proudly to the audience | Barbershops and Beauty Salons |. Rhythmic music pours out of the wide-open windows. Good luck charms on rear-view mirrors vibrate to the basses. Phone conversations are conducted when driving or stopped. Long hours and non-stop business. Stop and go.

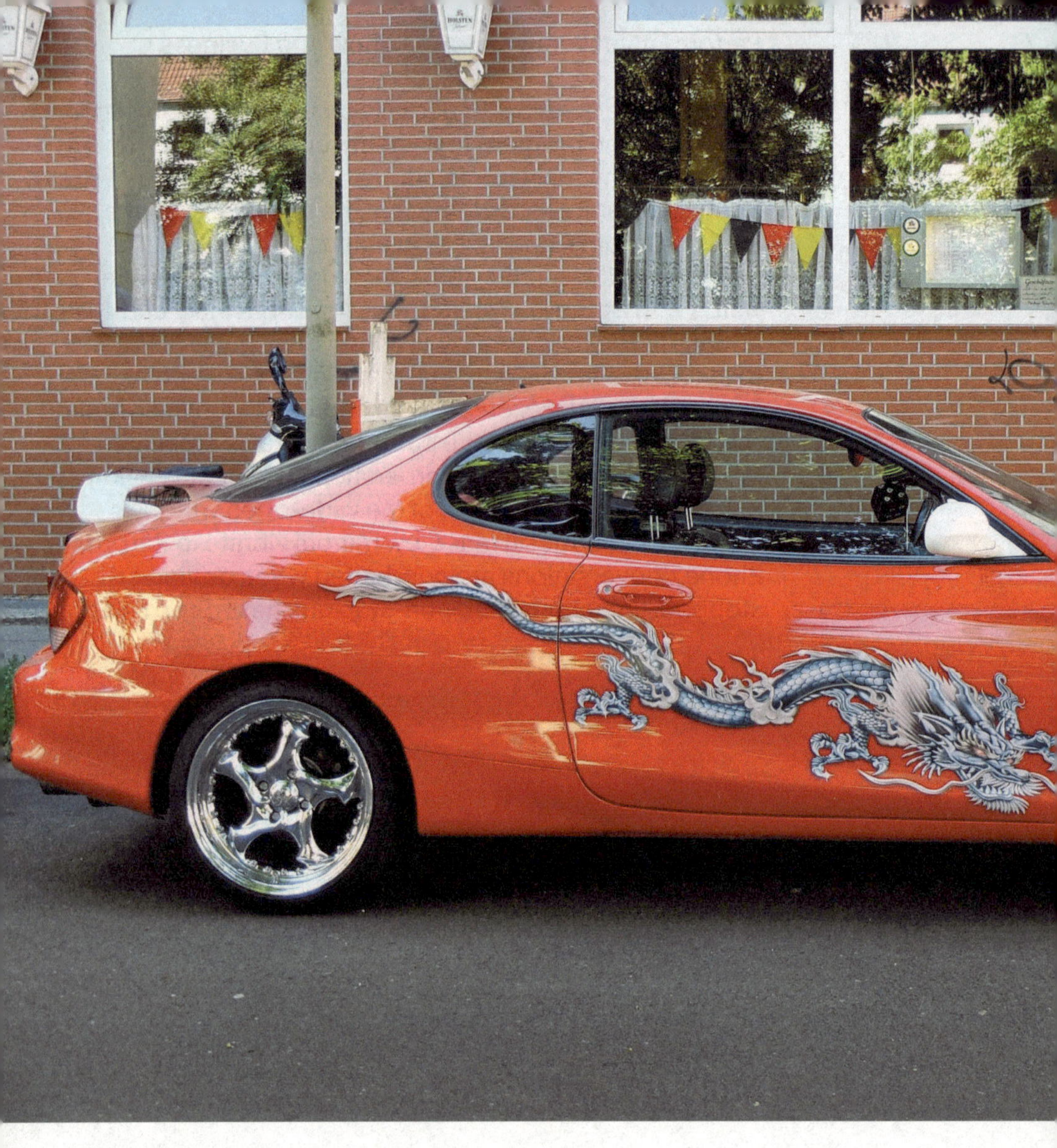

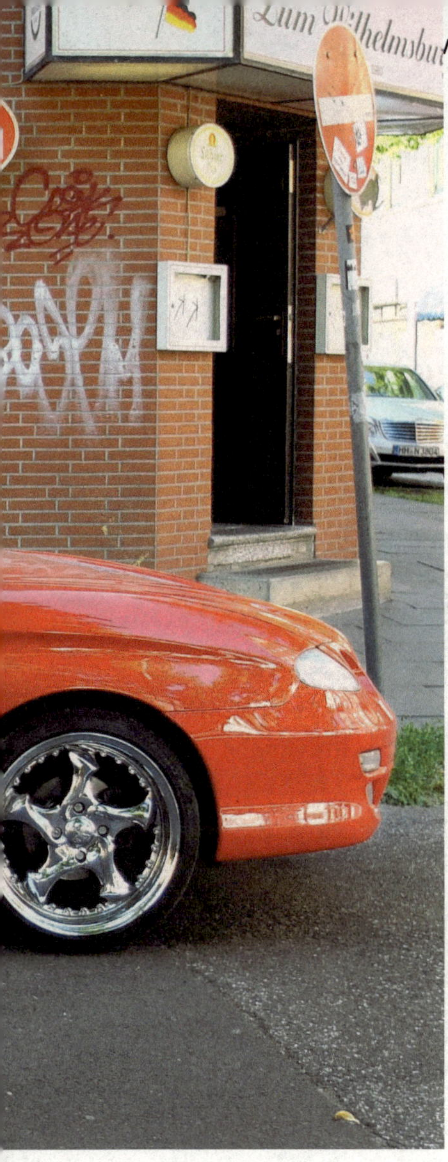

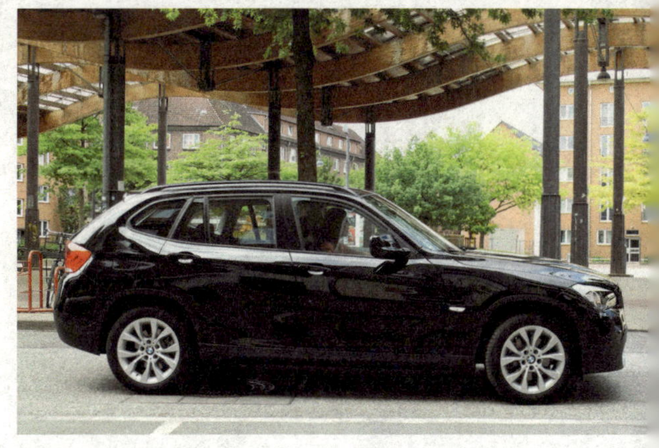

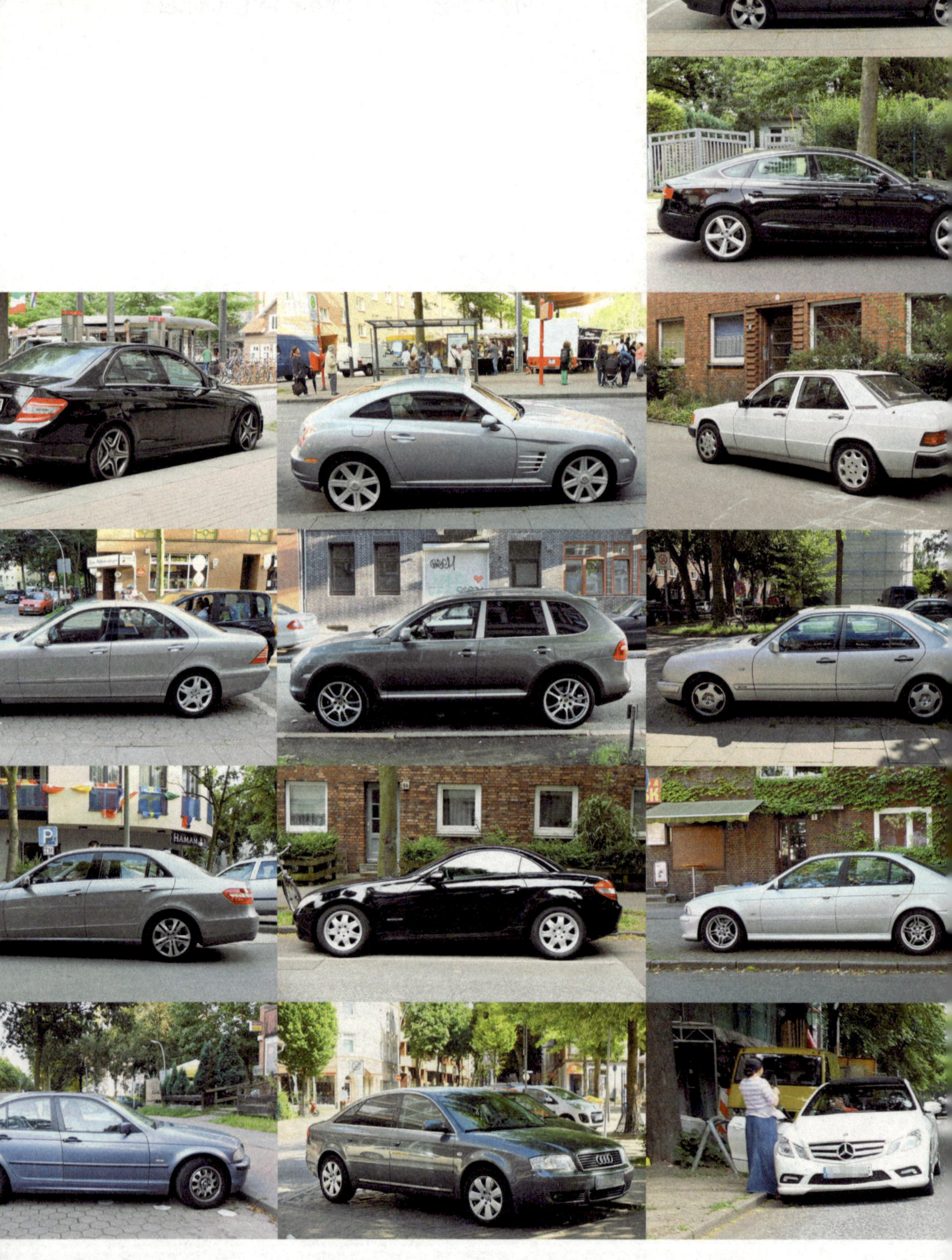

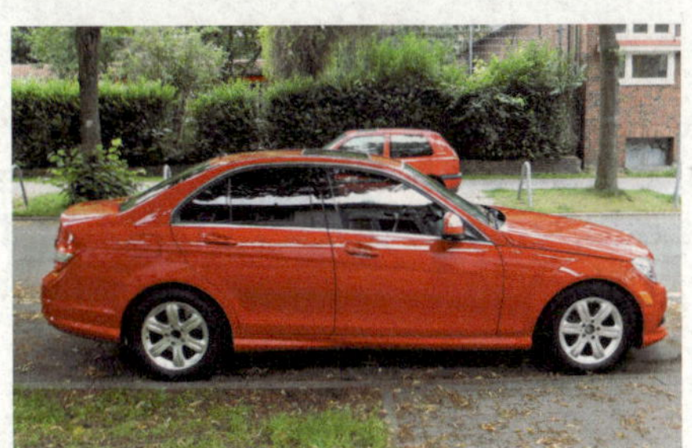

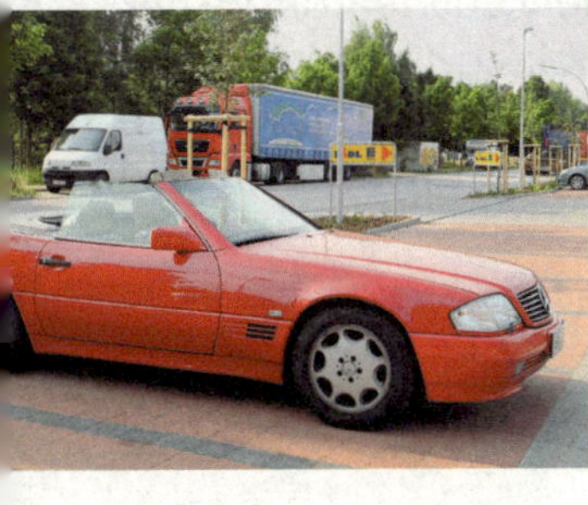

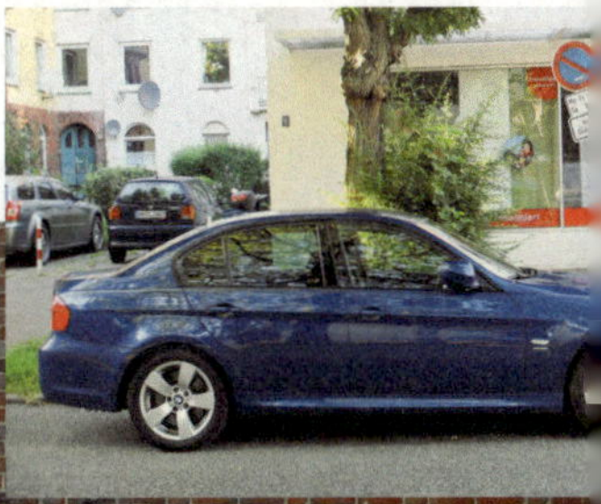

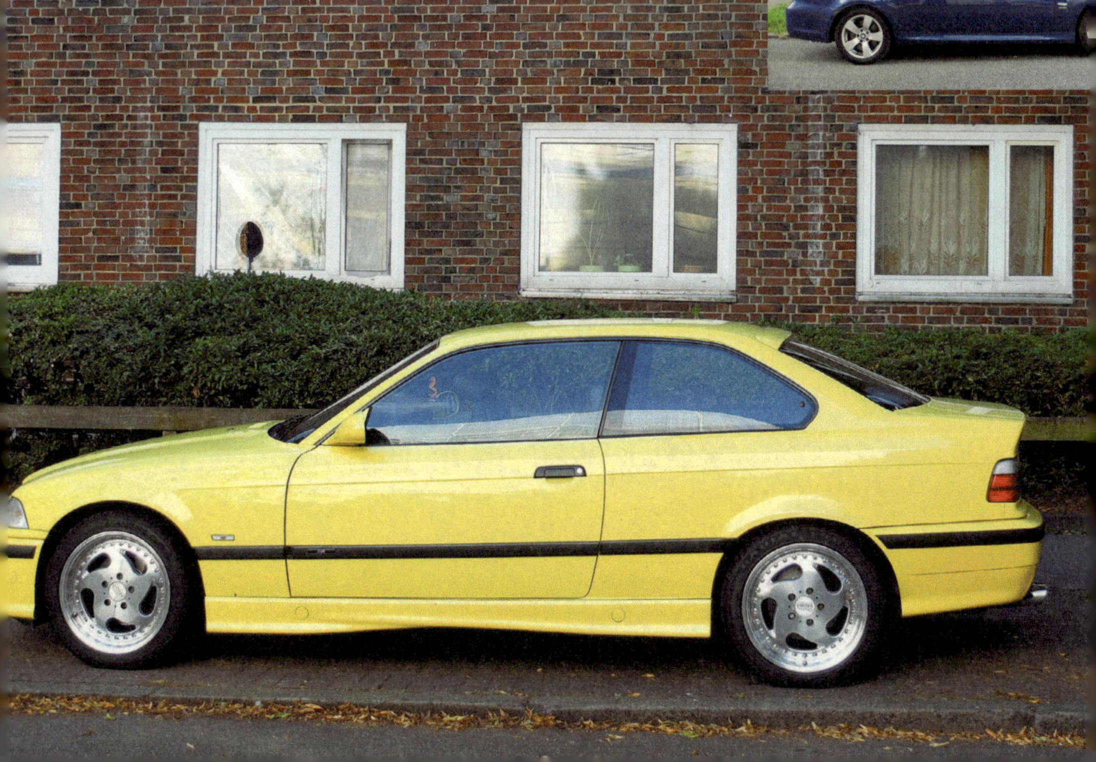

Something hangs in the air,
in the evening, at dusk, the mood
high-spirited. Loud, squealing,
and screeching. Showtime
Wilhelmsburg.

The loudspeakers inside are turned
up high, the bass clearly noticeably.
The car is almost standing still
on the street. Put to one side for
a moment. The engine is running
too. Men in jeans and sneakers
with precisely cut beards are talking and smoking, listening to
their music. The cans stay on the
roof until the car drives off again.

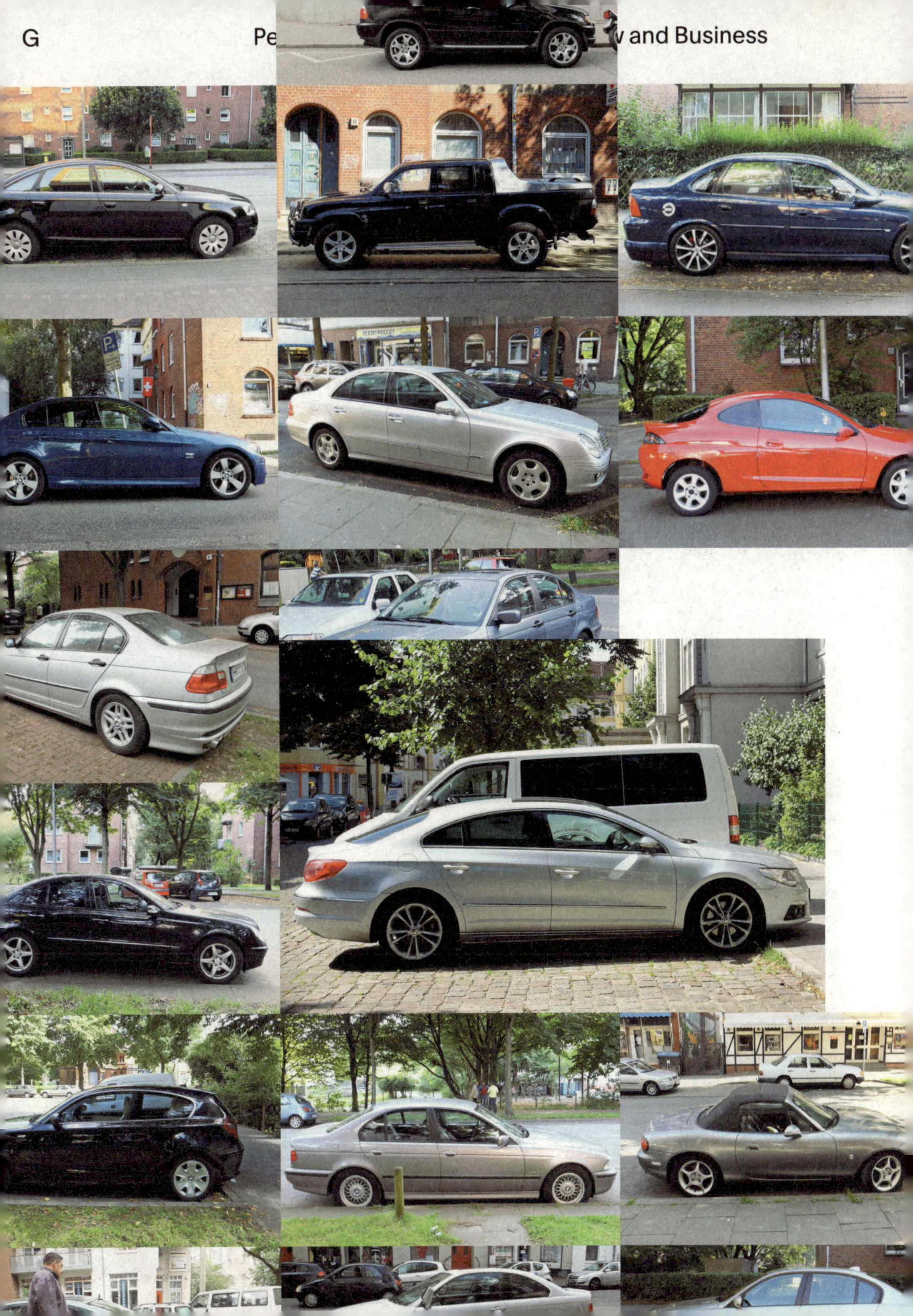

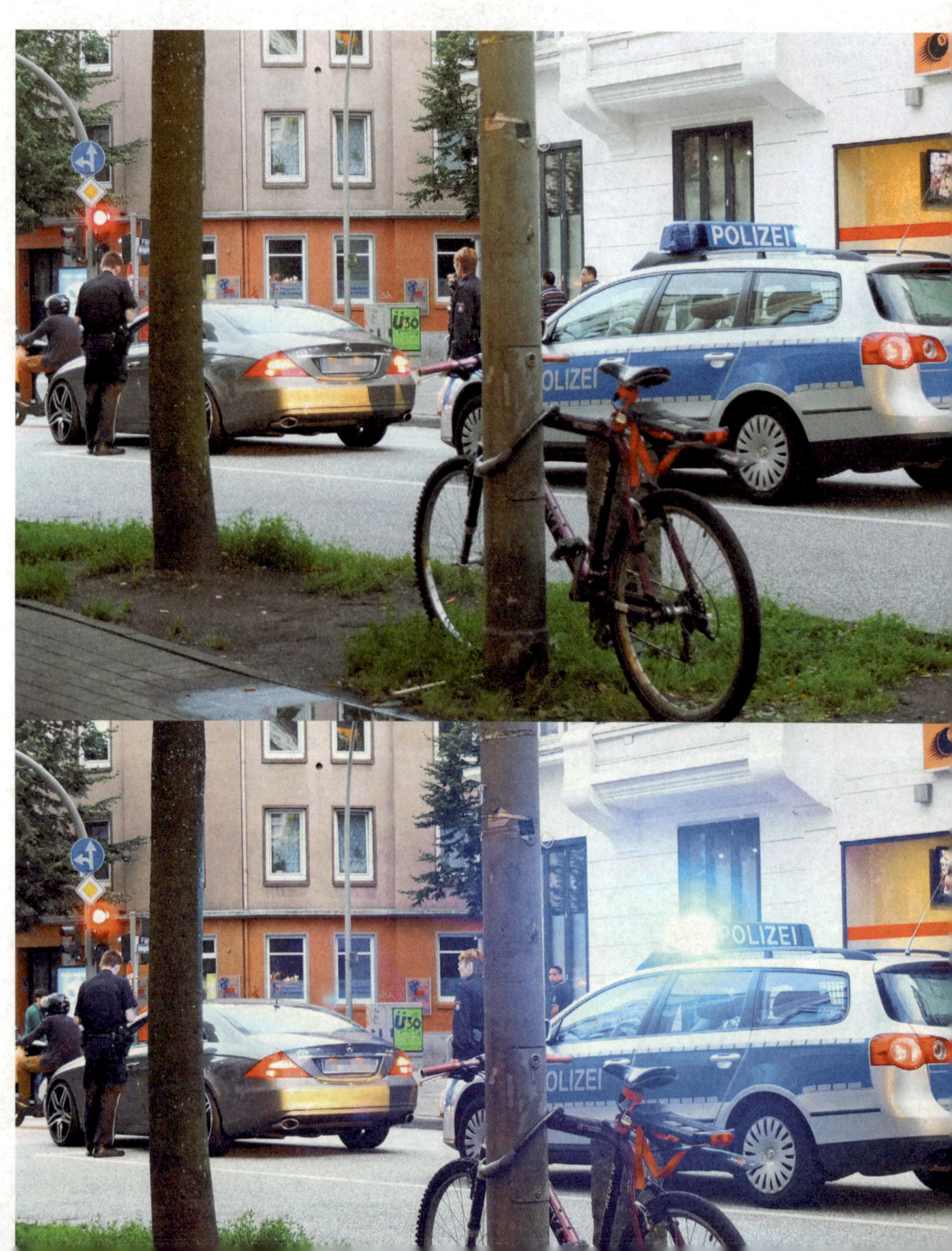

Communication with
[In-vivo code]

Windows communicate with me. They ... ask wave warn irritate offer sell exhibit show laugh open insert small ads conceal hide bore overload chat gift wish forget decorate linger close betray take on age fade break adorn give away secrets position provoke harmonize blink shine dance bend look forward ventilate change activate rust break out link speak integrate relate invite leave out open up close hang out sing squeak rattle clatter tilt click steam up look take a look out wait for ...

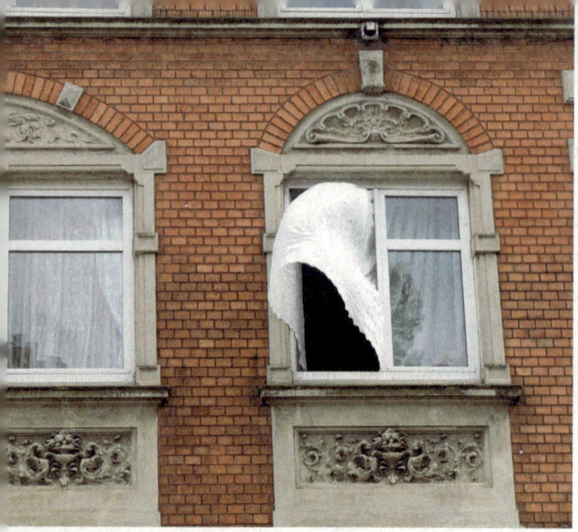

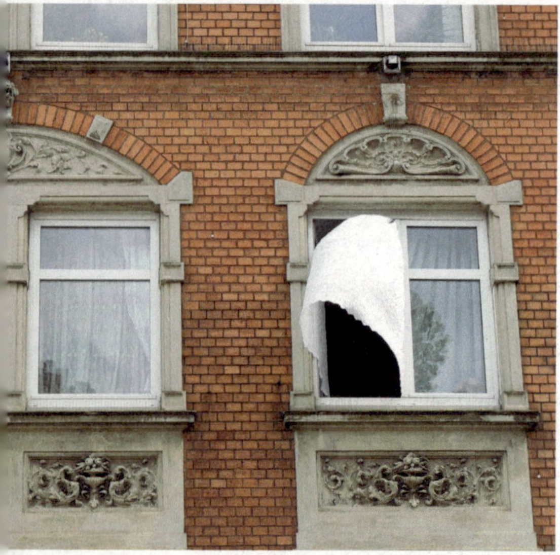

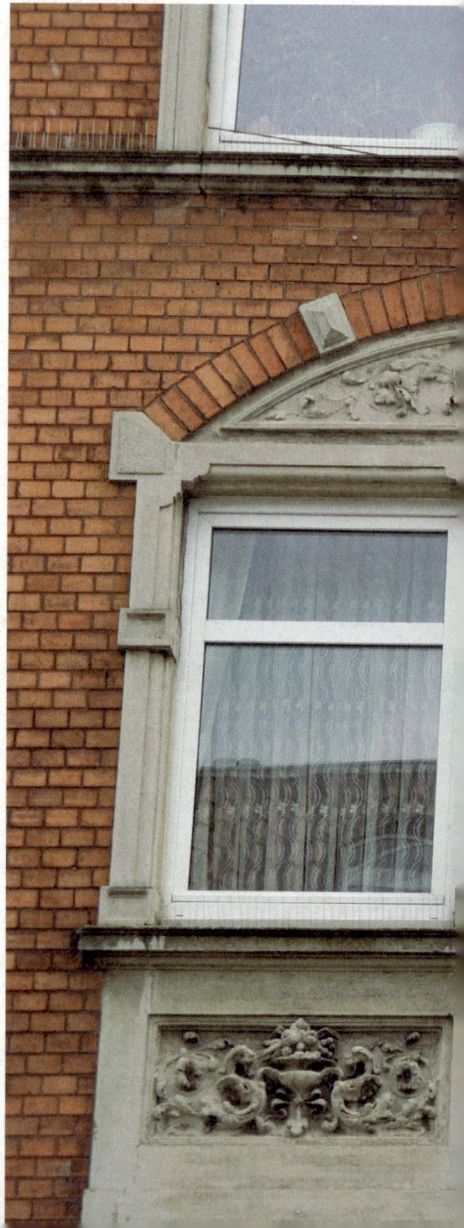

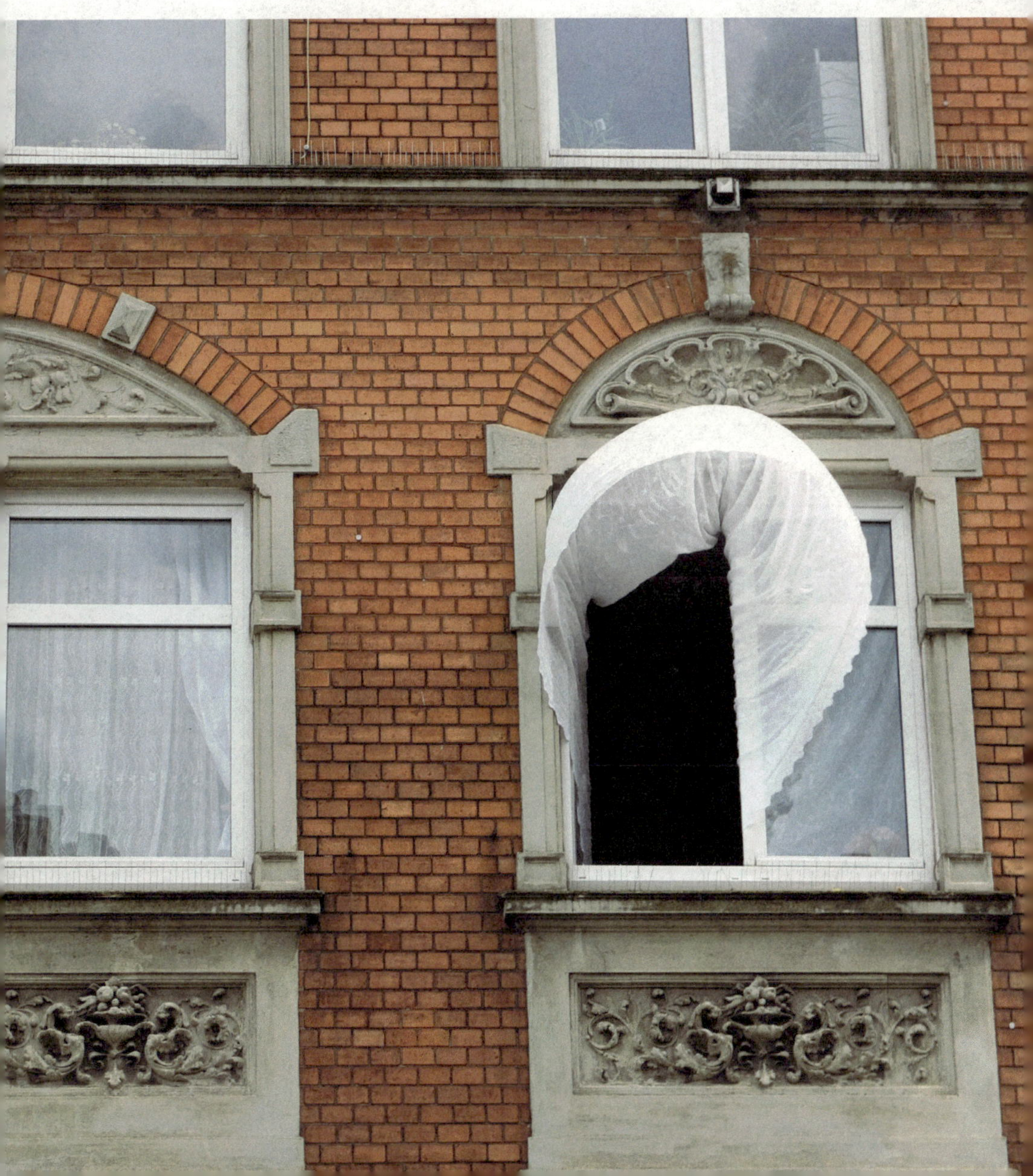

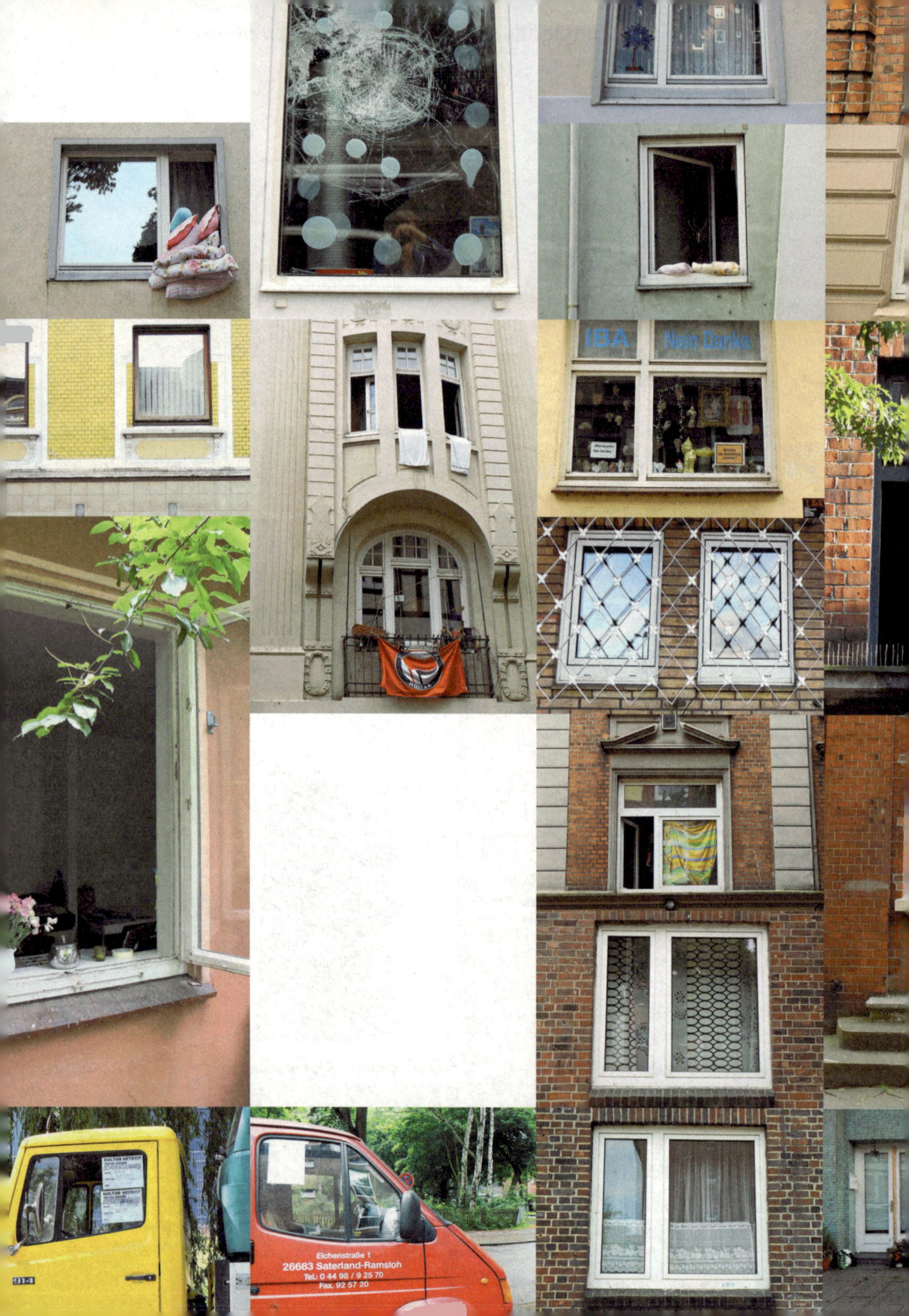
IBA
Nein Danke
Eichenstraße 1
26683 Saterland-Ramsloh
Tel: 0 44 98 / 9 25 70
Fax. 92 57 20

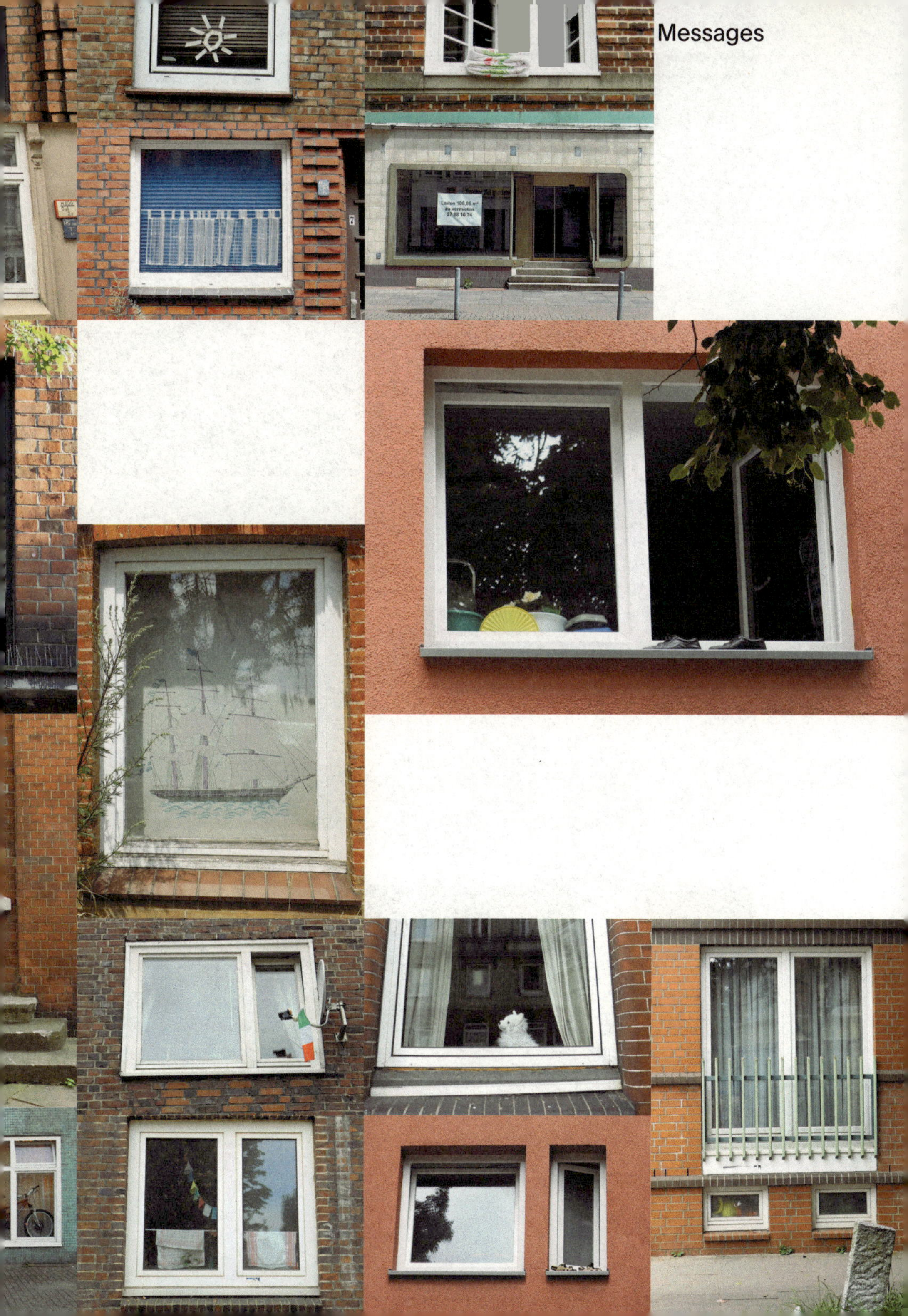

Messages

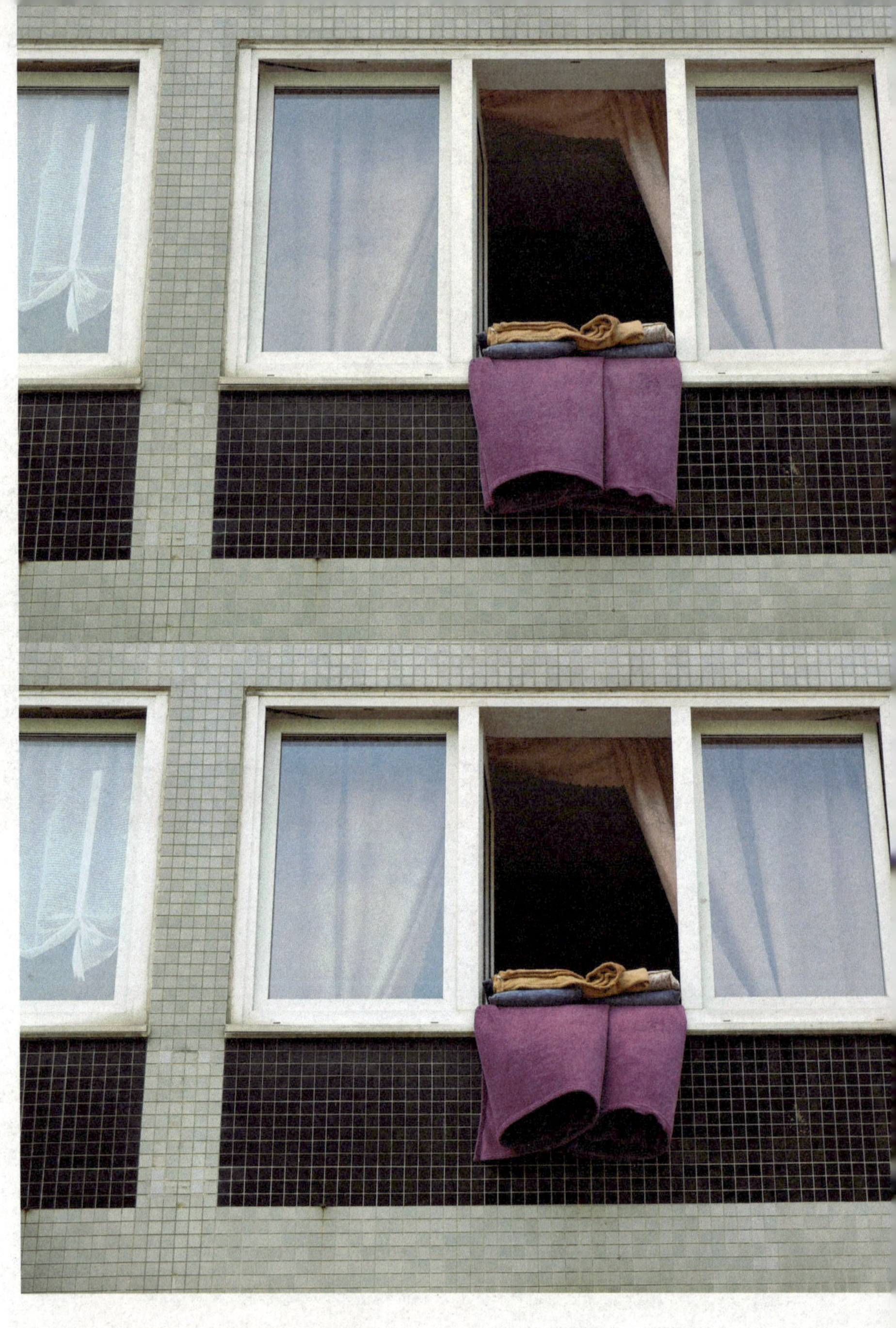

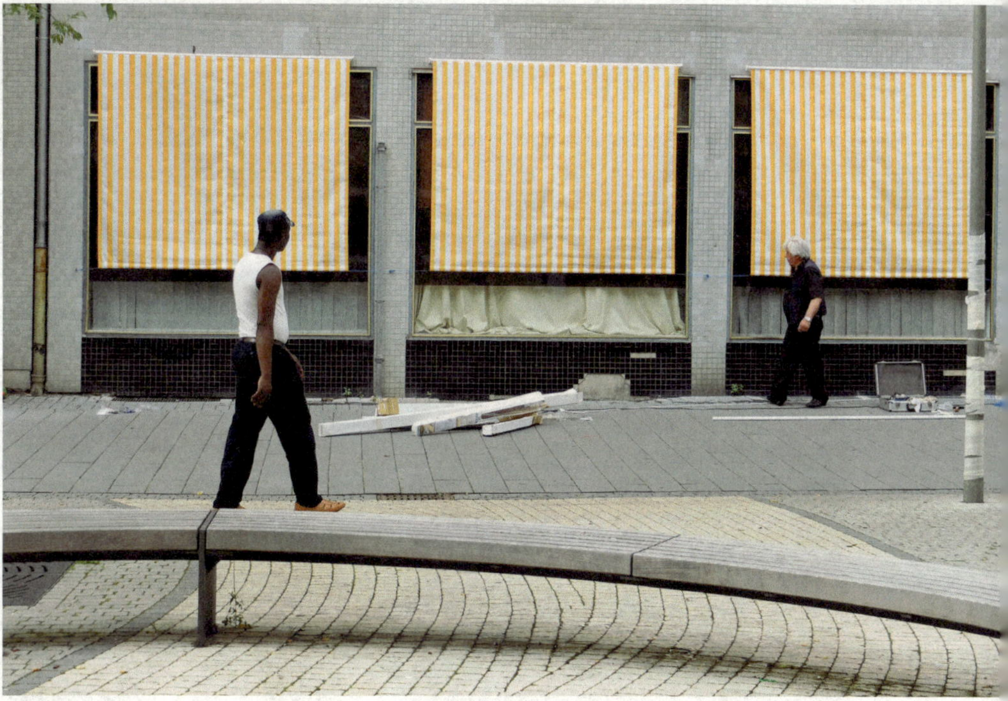

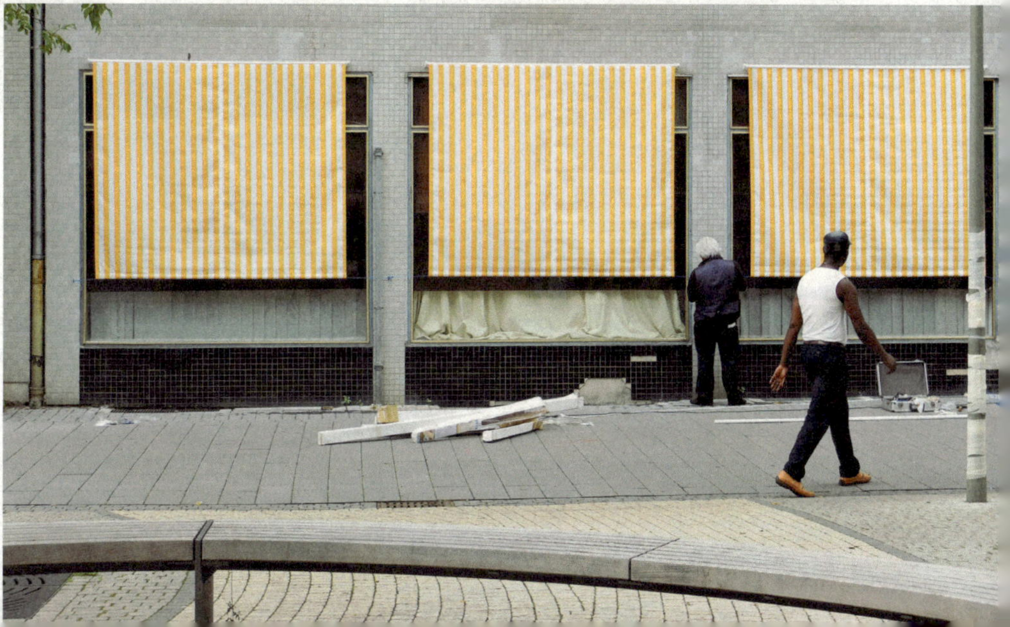

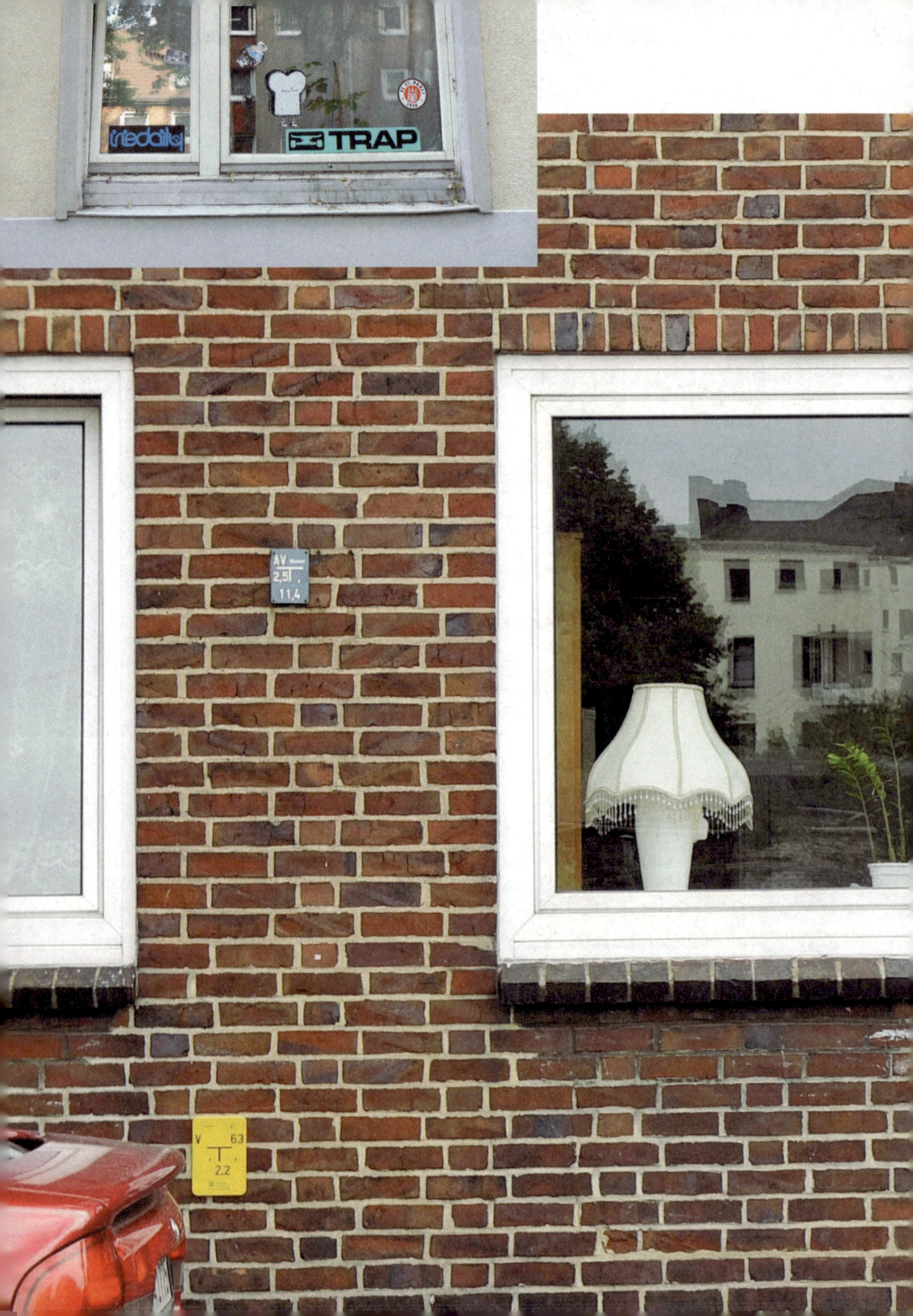

iriedaily
TRAP
AV Wasser
2,5 ⌐
11,4
V   63
T
2.2

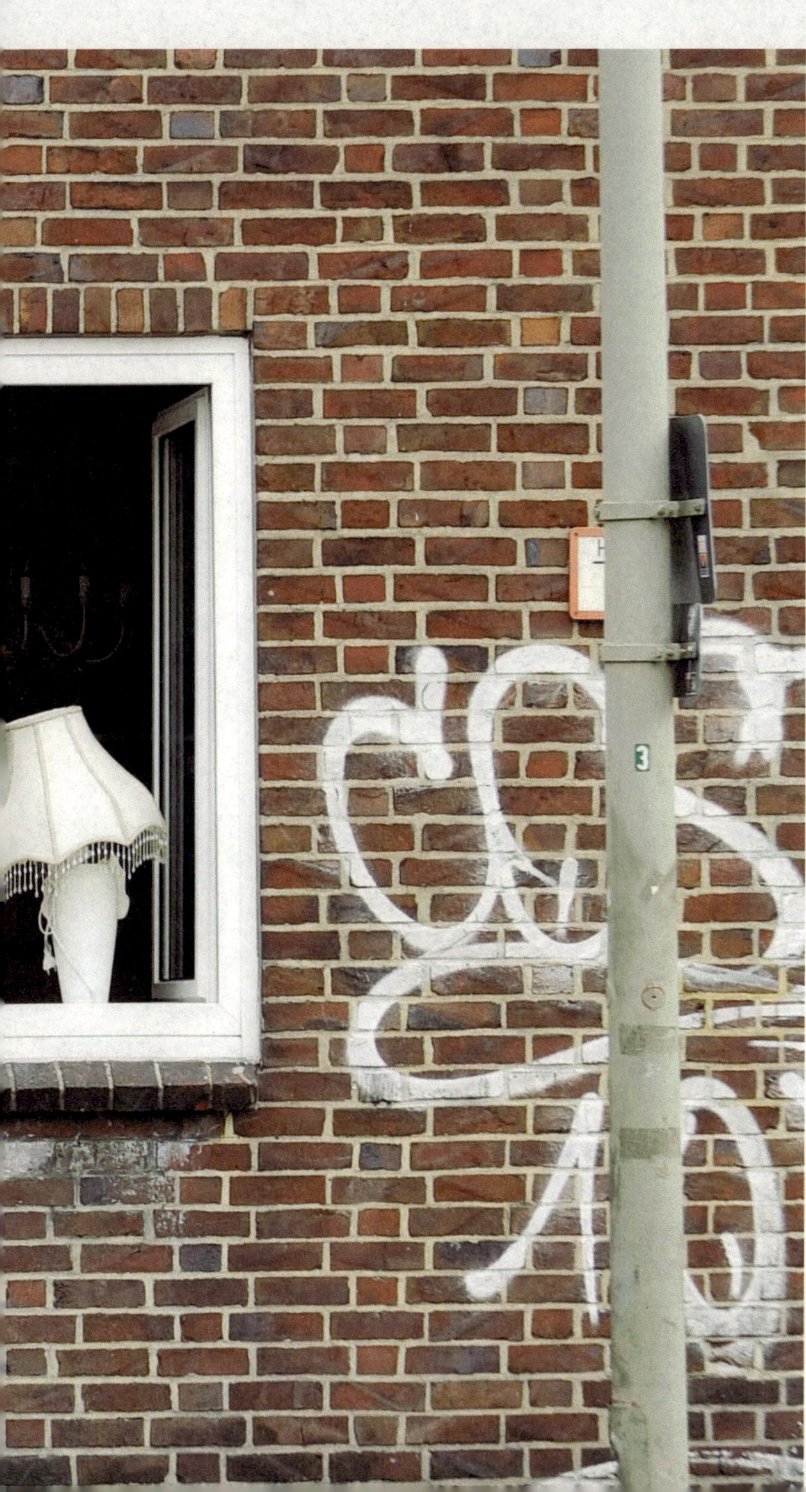

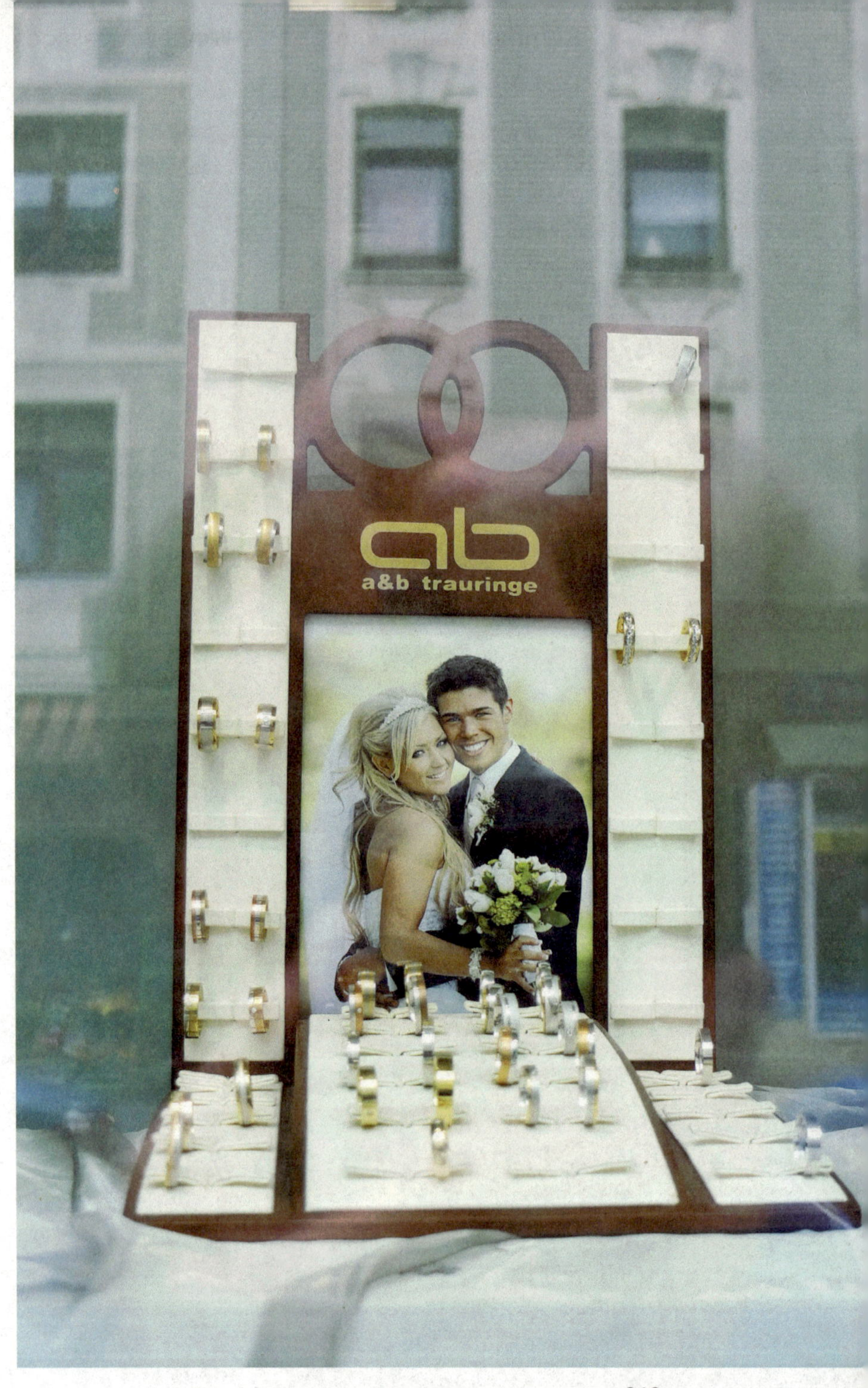

ab
a&b trauringe

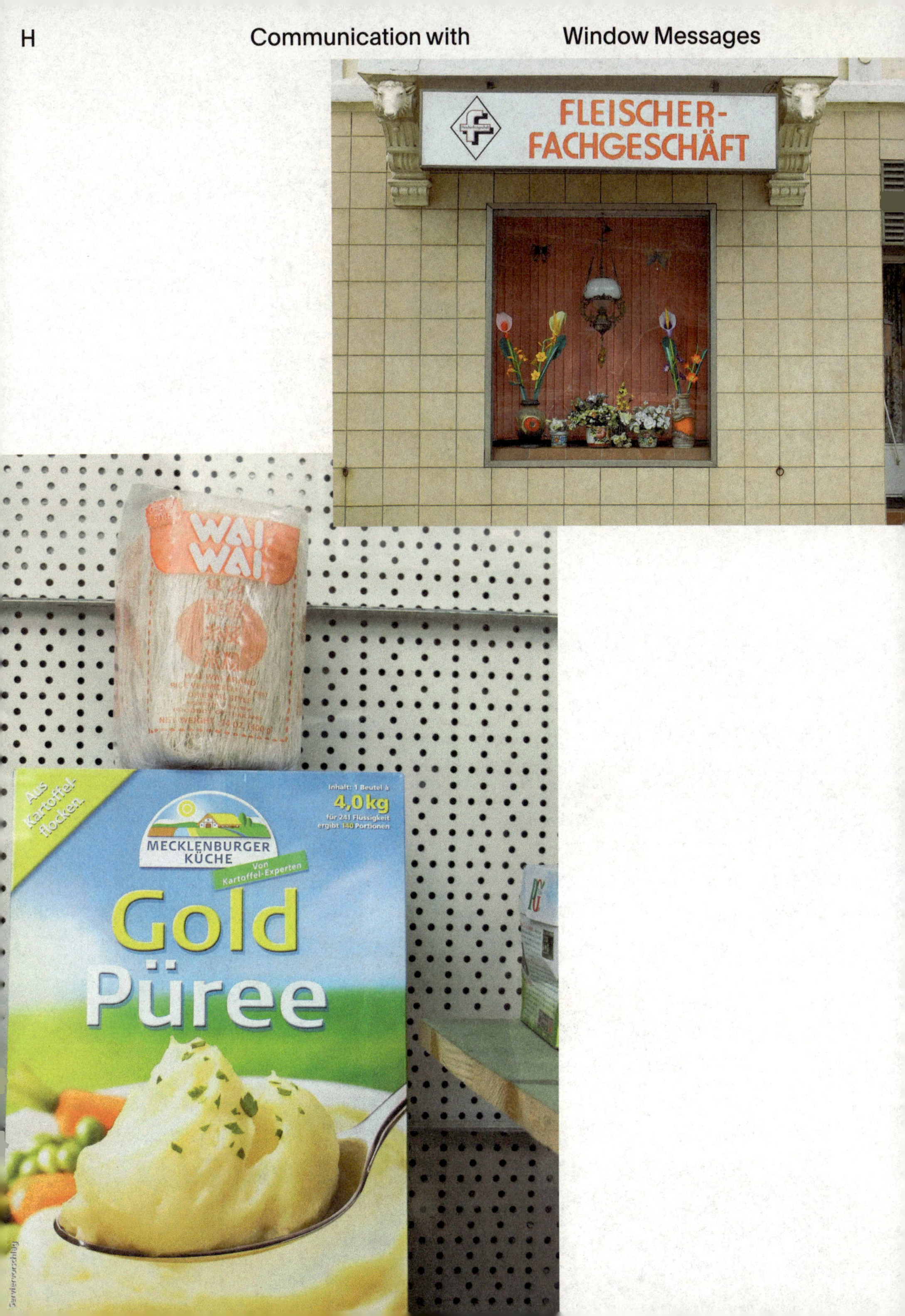
FLEISCHER-
FACHGESCHÄFT
WAI
WAI
Aus
Kartoffel-
flocken.
MECKLENBURGER
KÜCHE
Von
Kartoffel-Experten
Inhalt: 1 Beutel à
4,0 kg
für 24l Flüssigkeit
ergibt 140 Portionen
Gold
Püree
Serviervorschlag

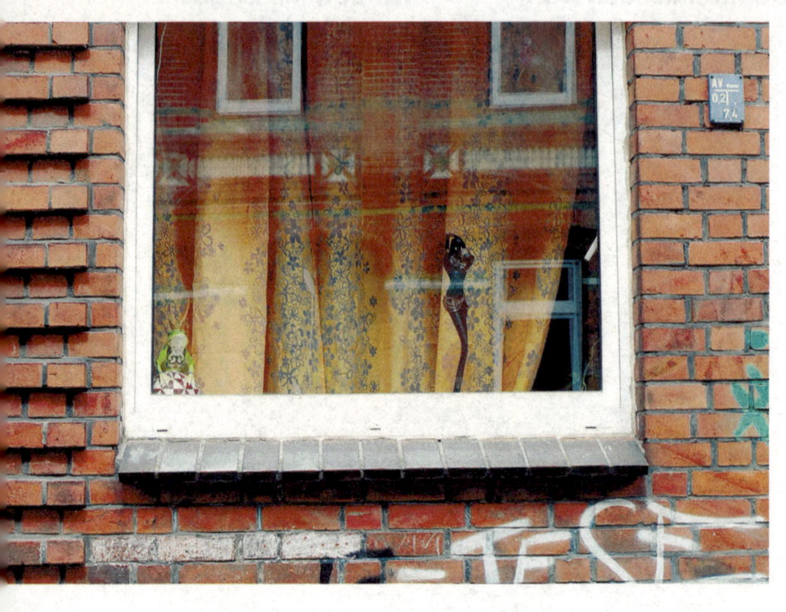

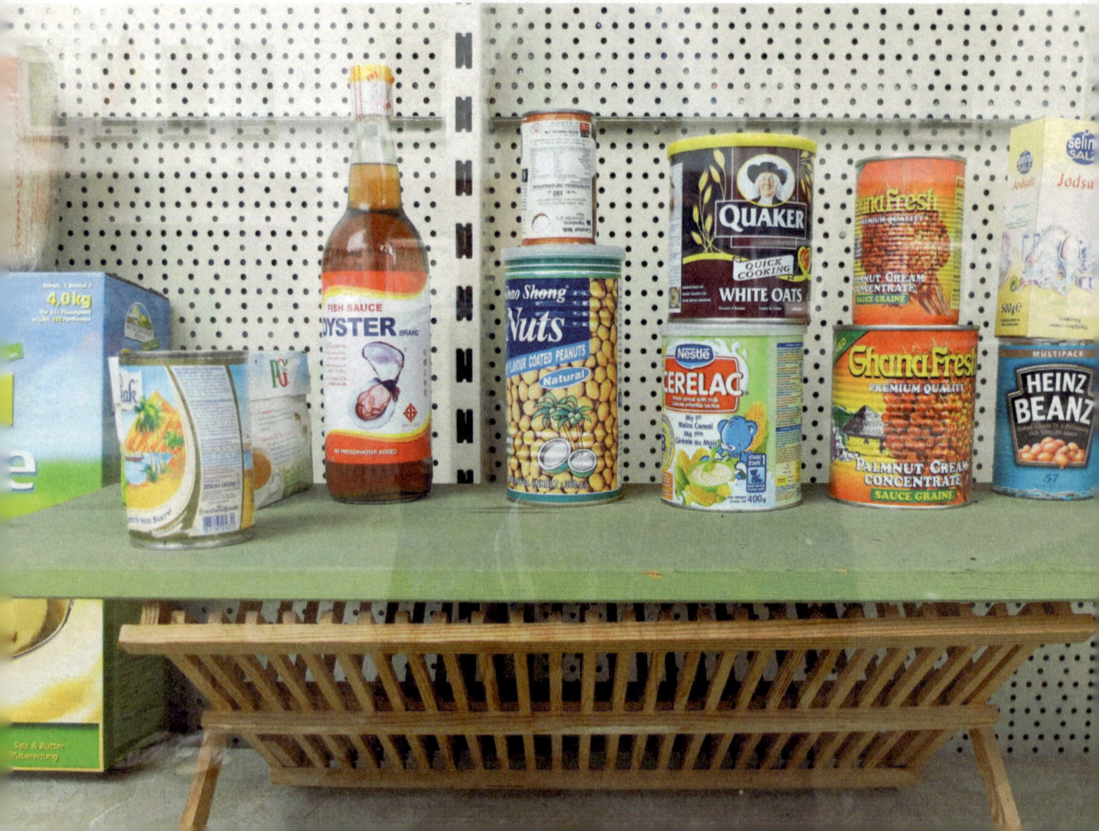

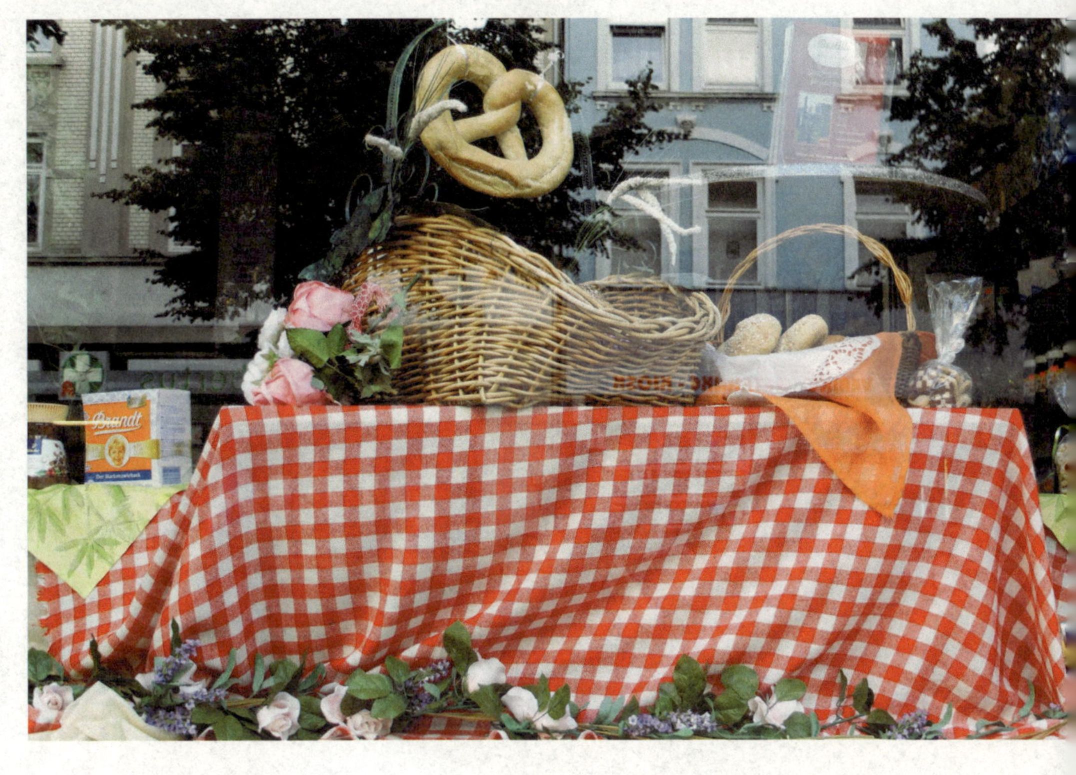

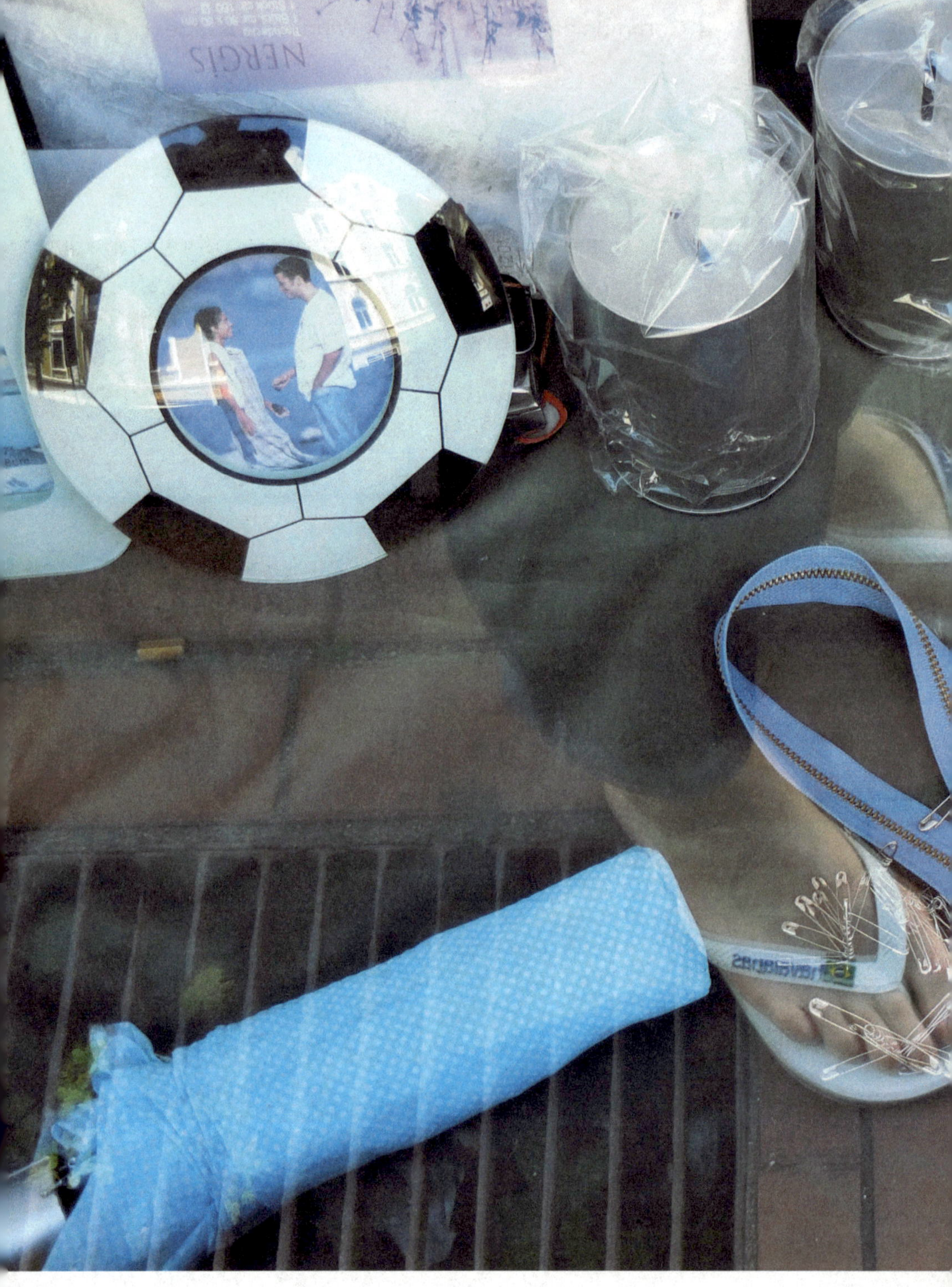

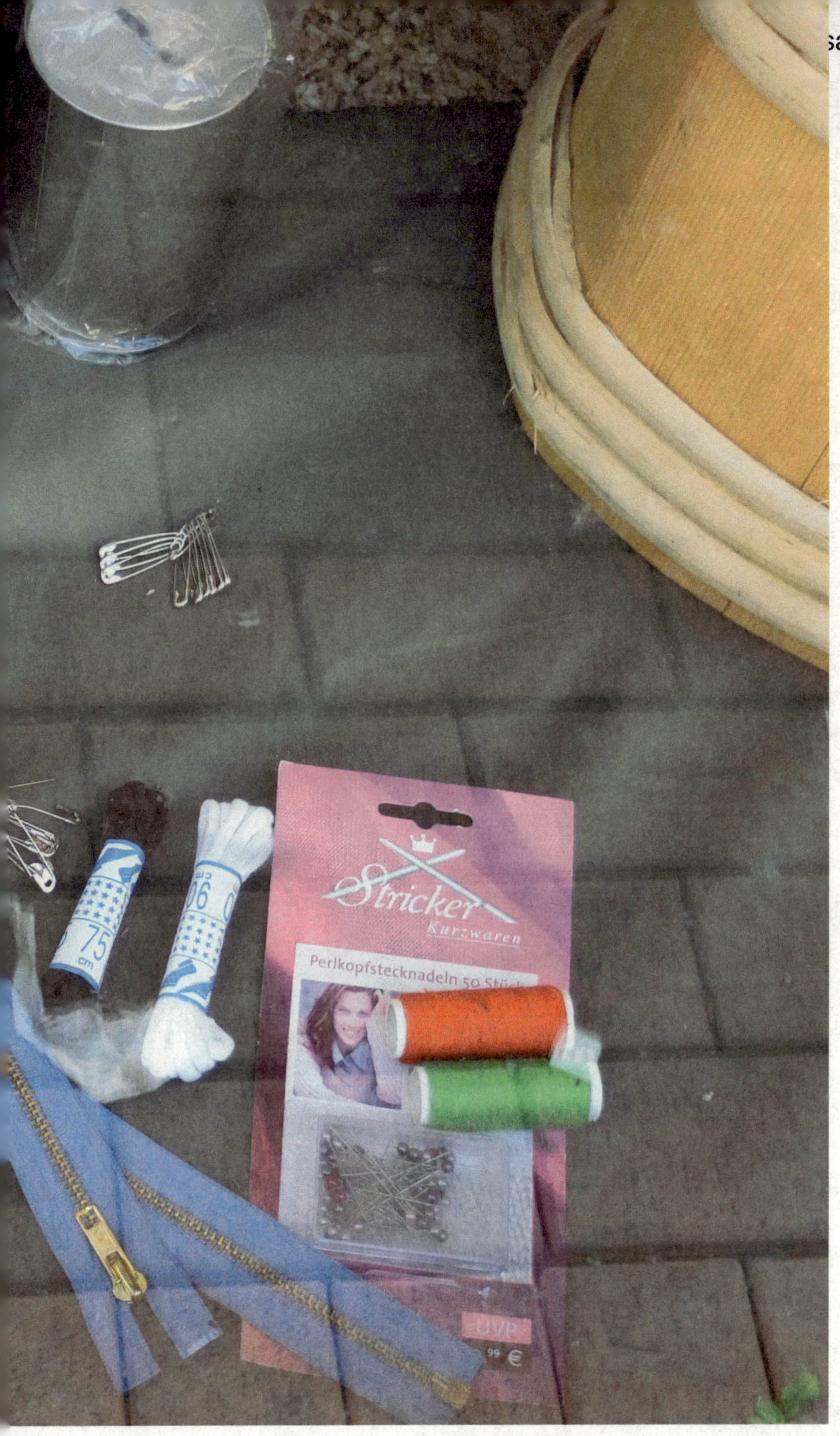
Stricker
Kurzwaren
Perlkopfstecknadeln 50 Stück
75 cm
90 cm
UVP
99 €

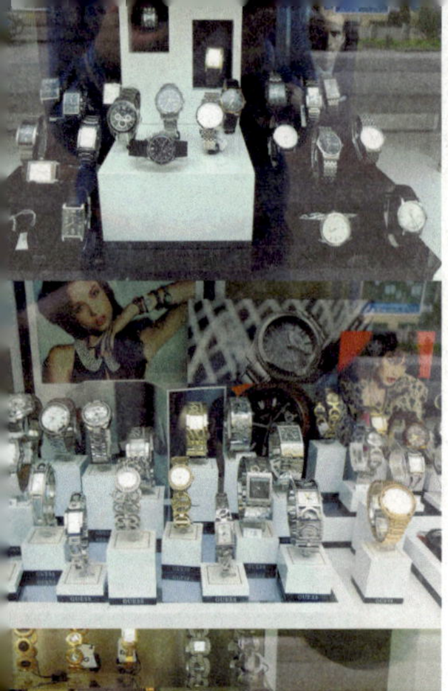
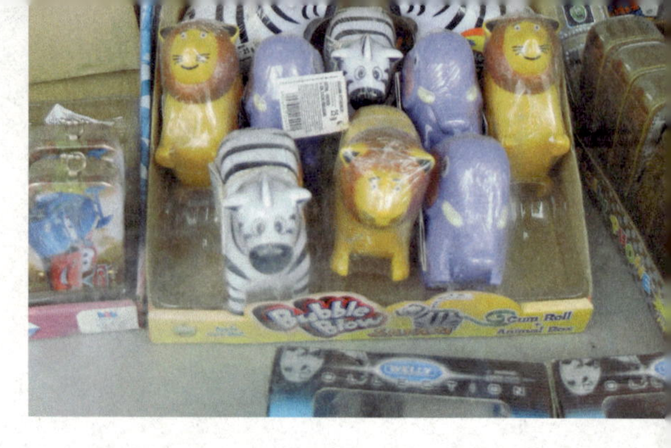
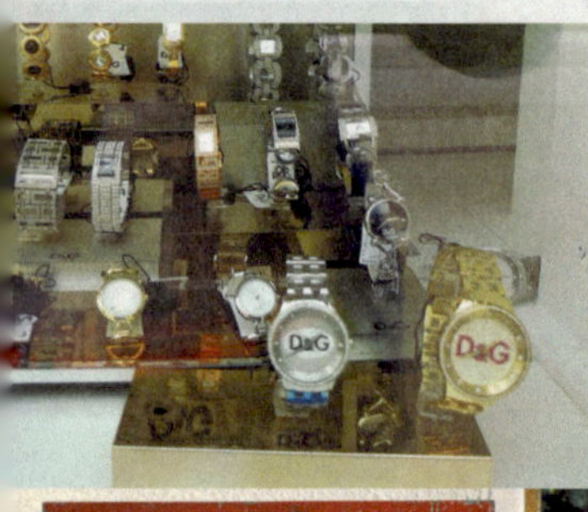
Bubble Blow
Gum Roll
Animal Box 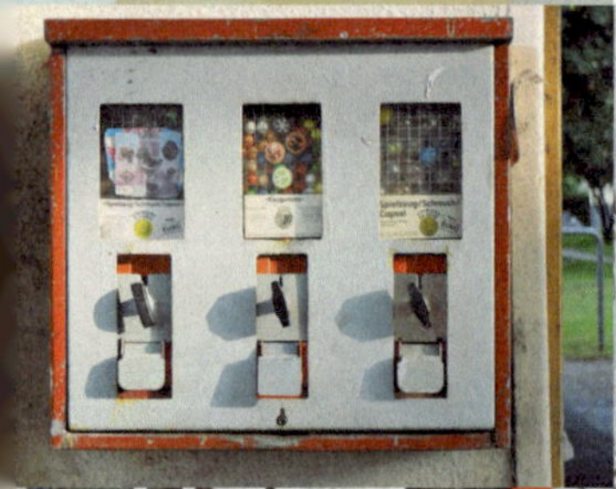 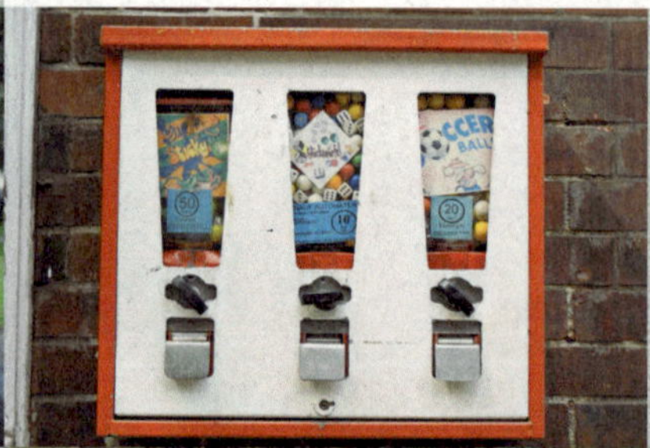 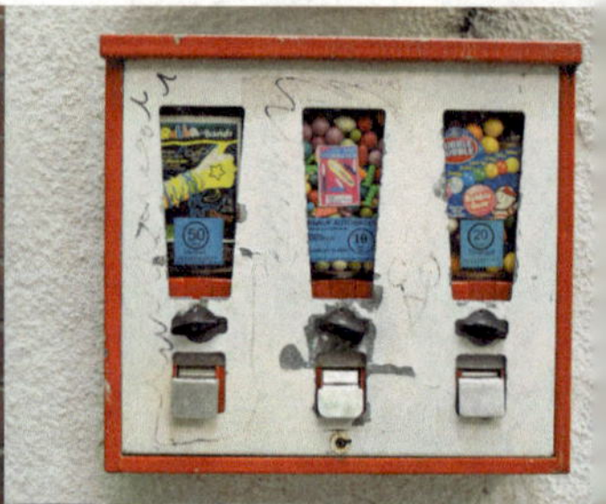 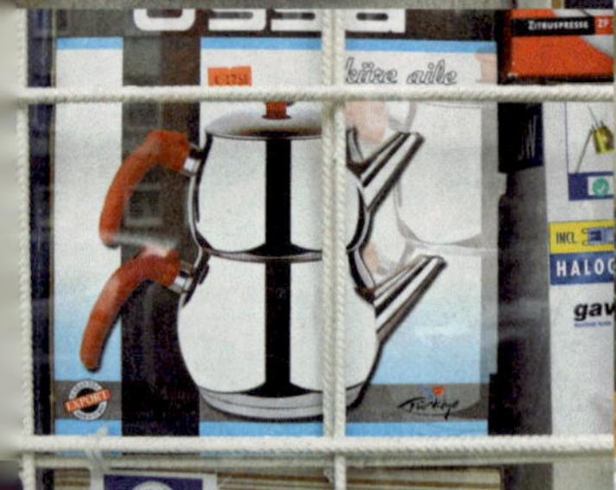 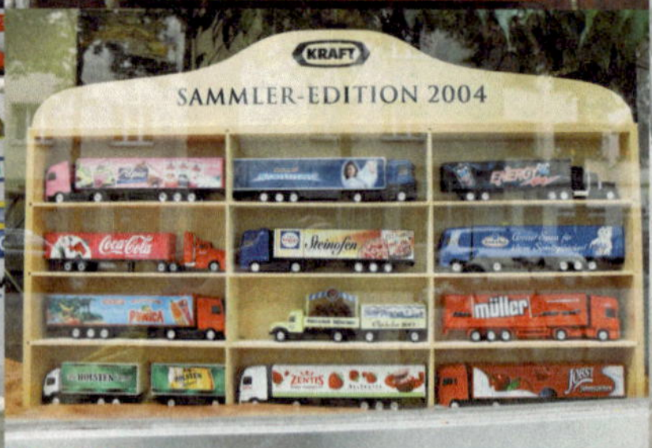
D&G
D&G
SOCCER BALL
50
10
20
KRAFT
SAMMLER-EDITION 2004
Coca-Cola
Steinofen
müller 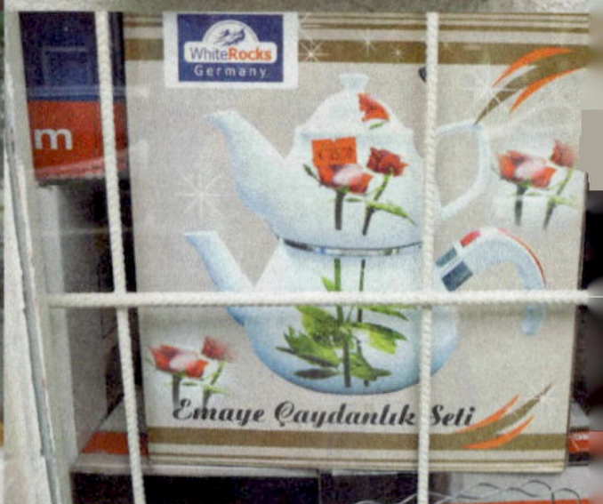
HOLSTEN
ZENTIS
WhiteRocks
Germany
Emaye Çaydanlık Seti
A.I.D.
Fu Fu Flakes
FUFU
LA MIRAN

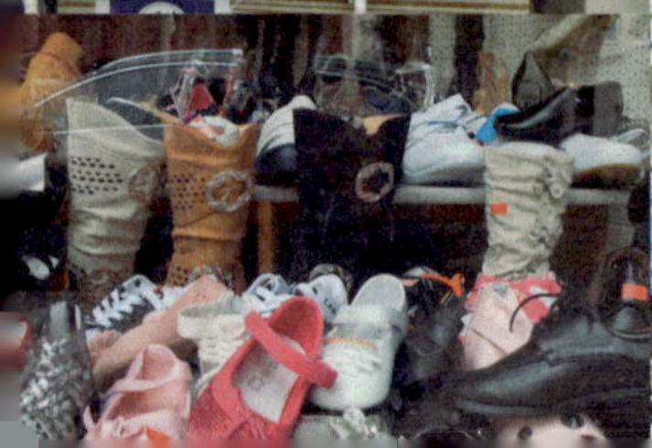

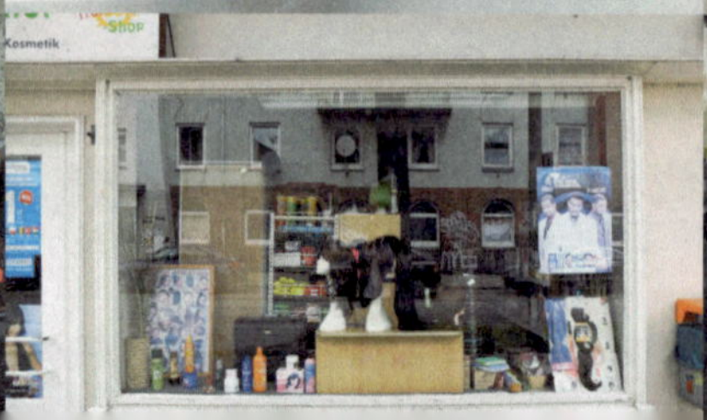

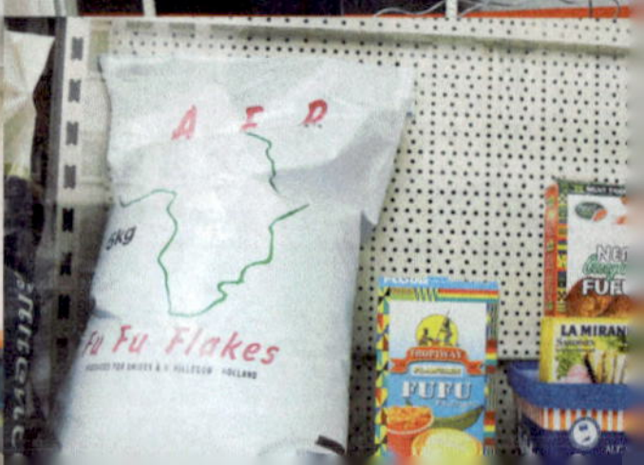

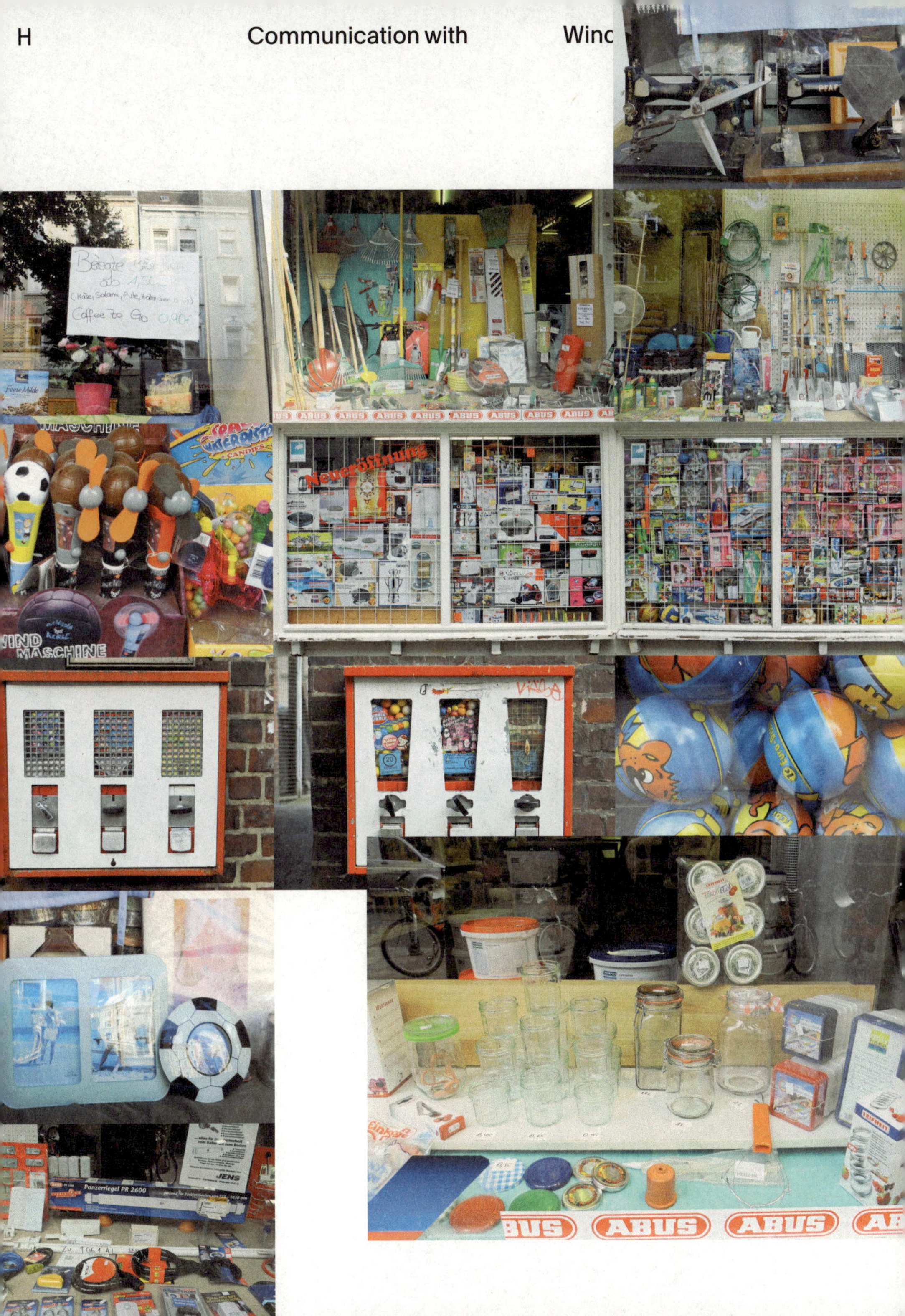

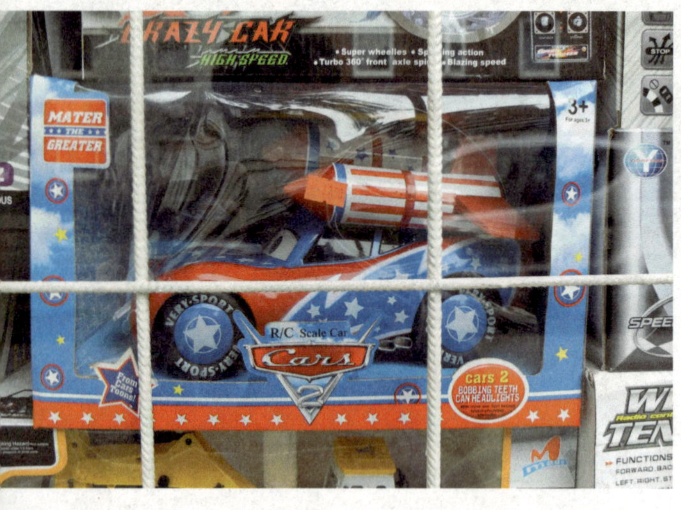
CRAZY CAR
HIGH SPEED
• Super wheelies • Spinning action
• Turbo 360° front axle spin • Blazing speed
MATER
THE
GREATER
3+
For ages 3+
R/C Scale Car
Cars
2
Cars 2
BOBBING TEETH
CAN HEADLIGHTS
From
Cars
Toons!
STOP
SPEED
WI
TE
FUNCTIONS
FORWARD, BAC
LEFT, RIGHT, ST

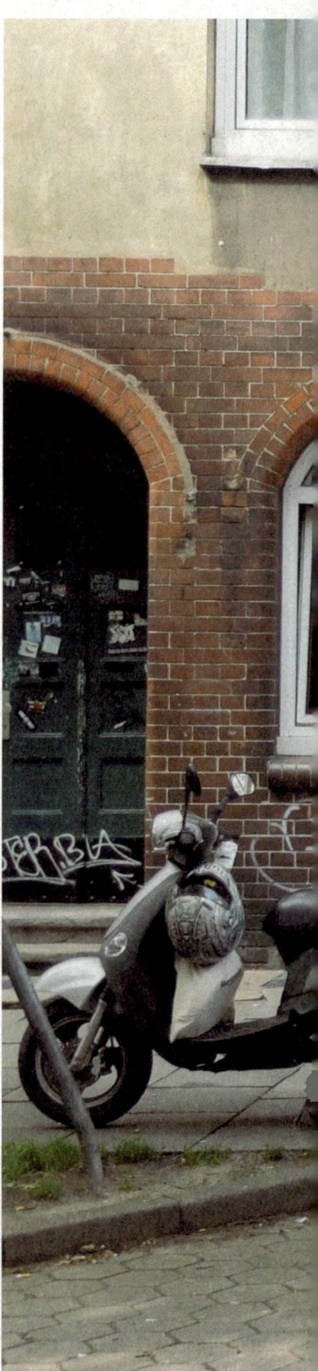
SERBIA

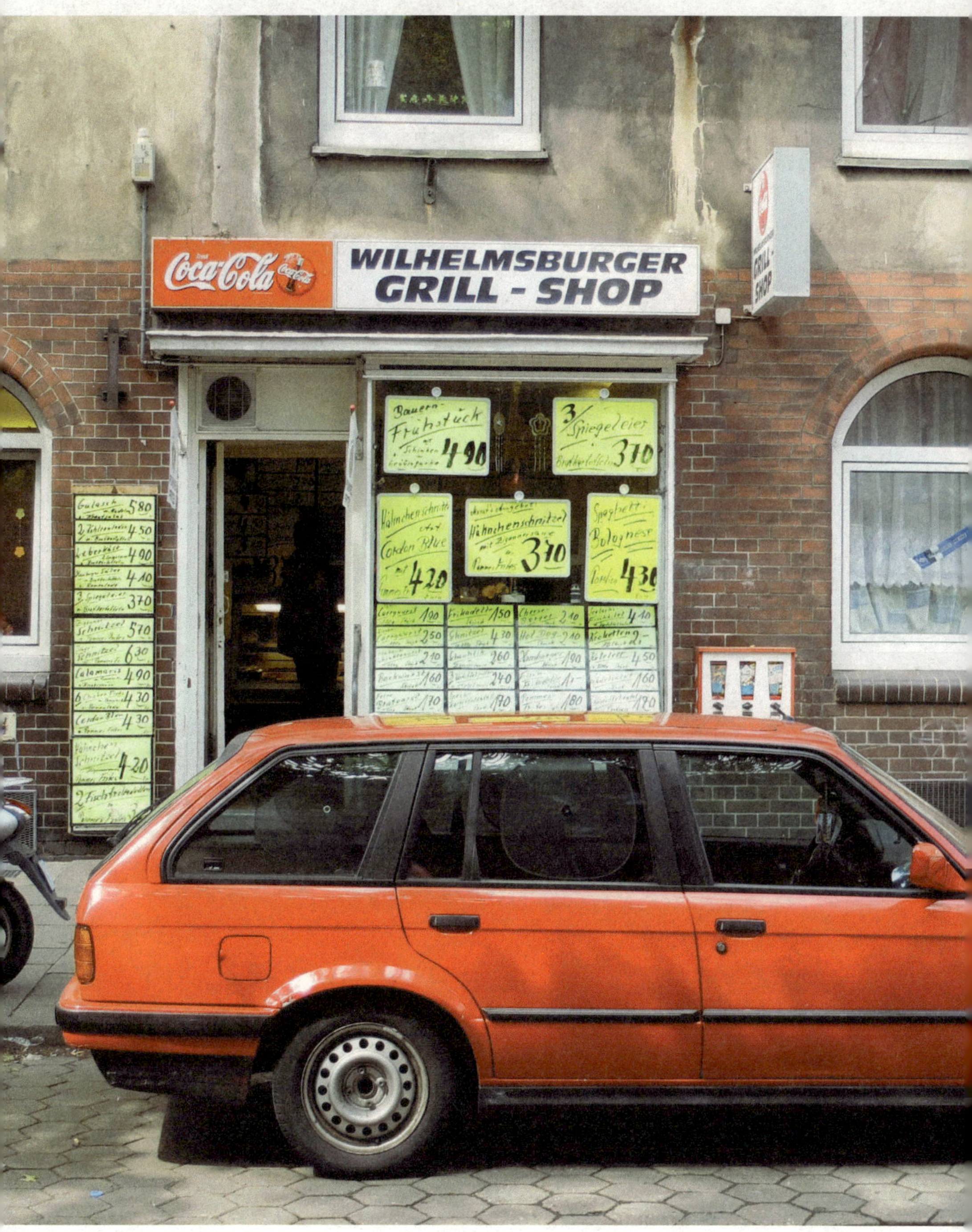
Coca-Cola
WILHELMSBURGER
GRILL - SHOP
GRILL-SHOP

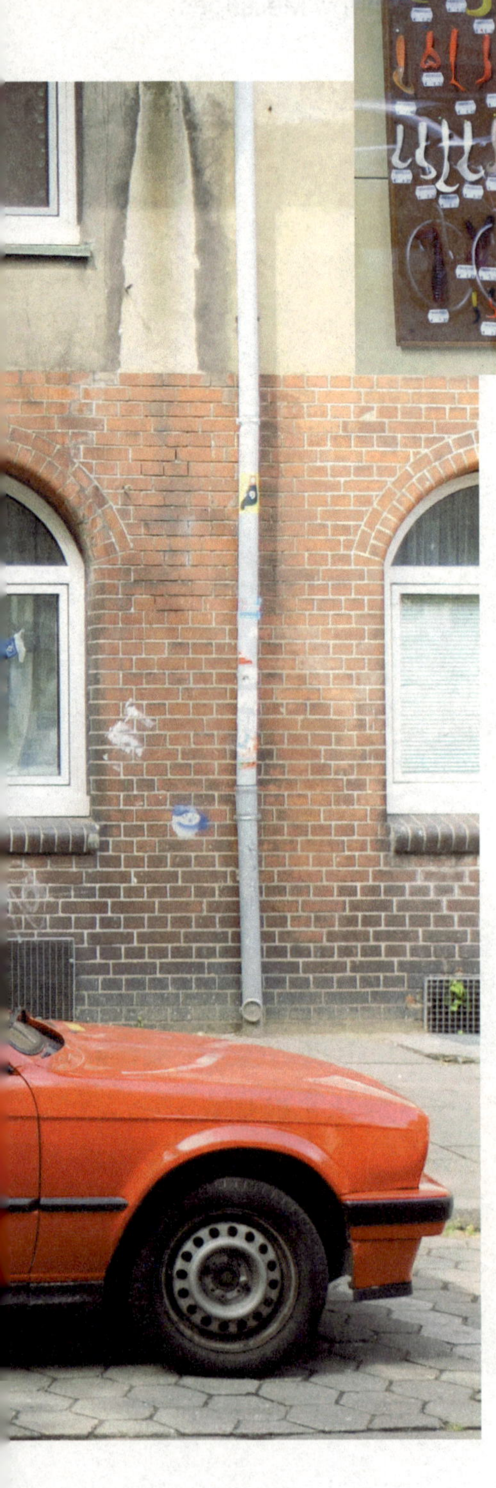

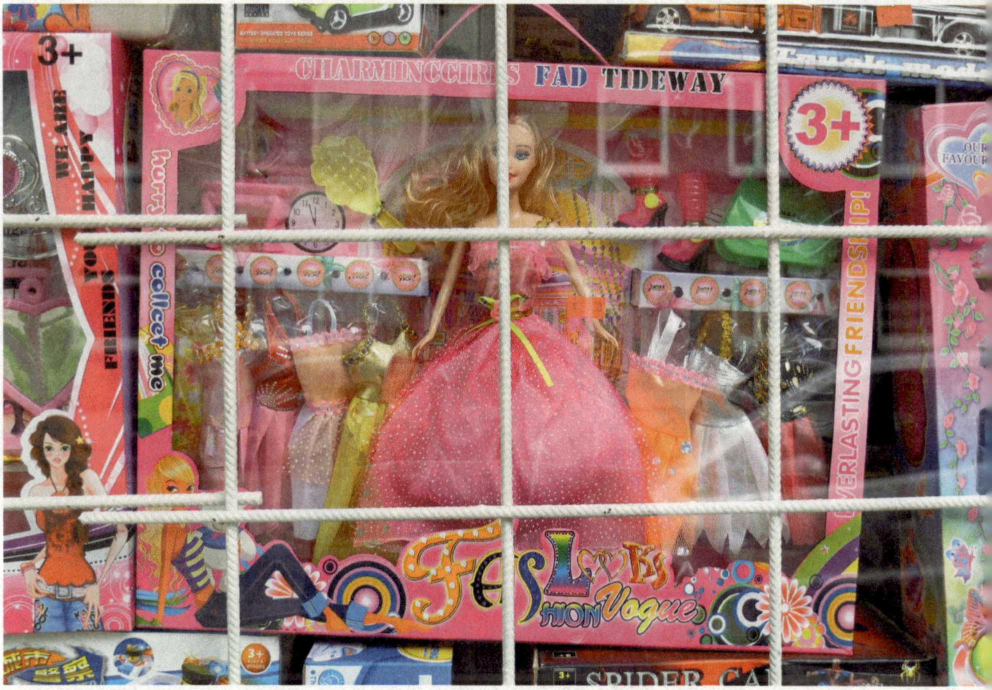

3+
CHARMINCGIRLS FAD TIDEWAY
3+
WE ARE HAPPY
FRIENDS YOU
collect me
horry
EVERLASTING FRIENDSHIP!
OUR FAVOUR
FASHION Vogue
3+
SPIDER CA

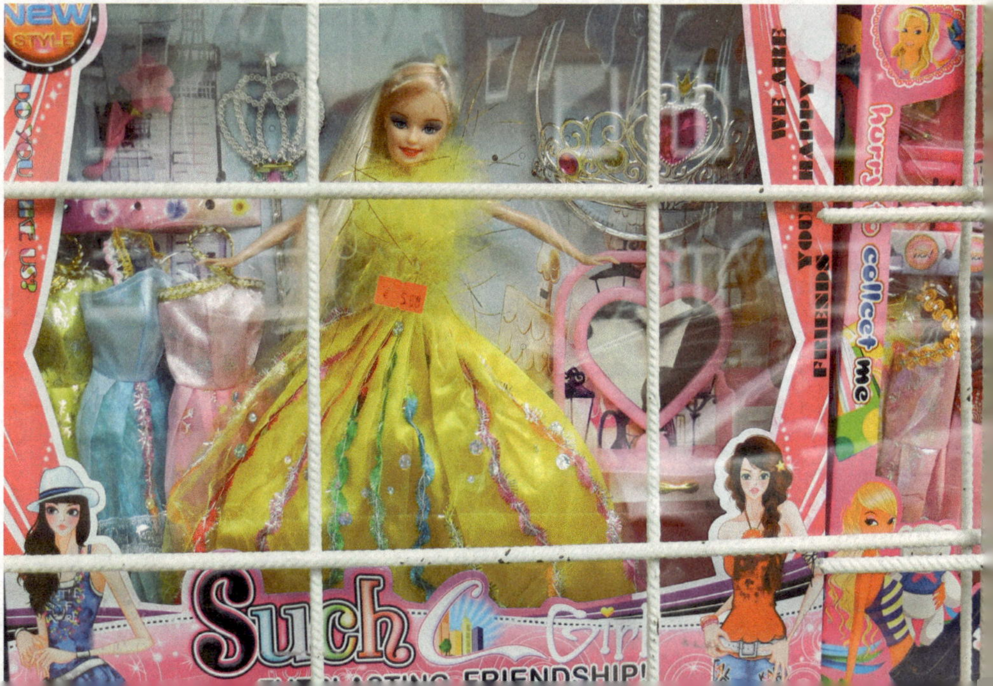

NEW STYLE
DO YOU LIKE US?
WE ARE HAPPY
YOUR FRIENDS
collect me
horry
Such Girl
EVERLASTING FRIENDSHIP!

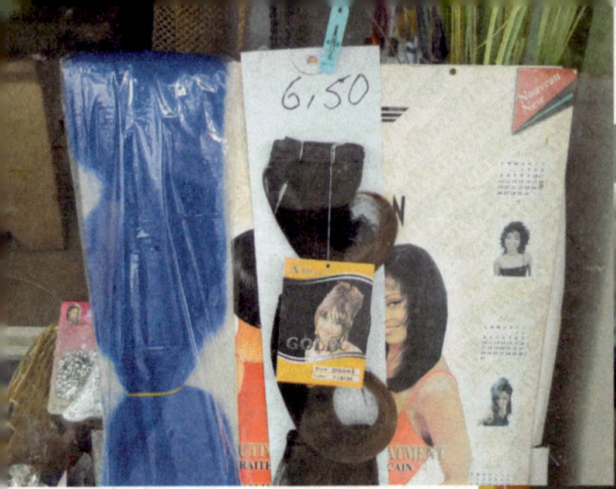

6.50
Nouveau
New 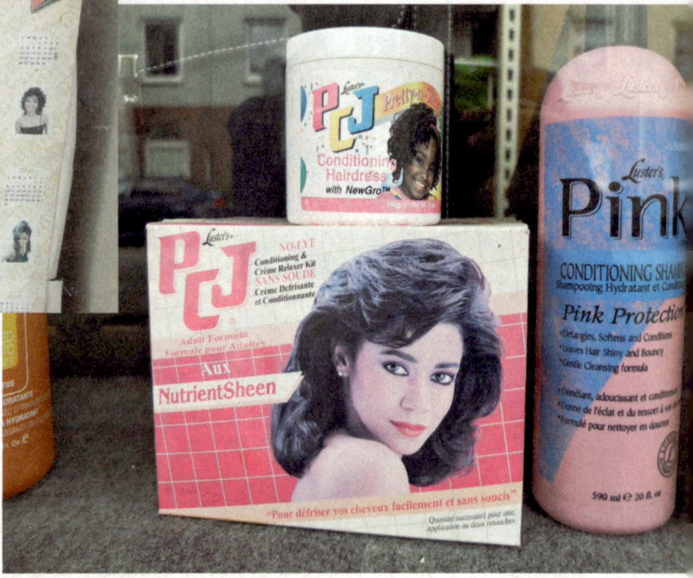
GOLD
PCJ
Pretty-n
Luster's
Conditioning
Hairdress
with NewGro™
Luster's
PCJ
NO-LYE
Conditioning &
Crème Relaxer Kit
SANS SOUDE
Crème Defrisante
et Conditionnante
Adult Formula
Formule pour Adultes
Aux
NutrientSheen
"Pour défriser vos cheveux facilement et sans soucis"
Quantité nécessaire pour une
application ou deux retouches
Luster's
Pink
CONDITIONING SHAMPOO
Shampooing Hydratant et Conditionnant
Pink Protection
• Detangles, Softens and Conditions
• Leaves Hair Shiny and Bouncy
• Gentle Cleansing formula
• Démêlant, adoucissant et conditionnant
• Donne de l'éclat et du ressort à vos cheveux
• Formulé pour nettoyer en douceur
590 ml ℮ 20 fl. oz

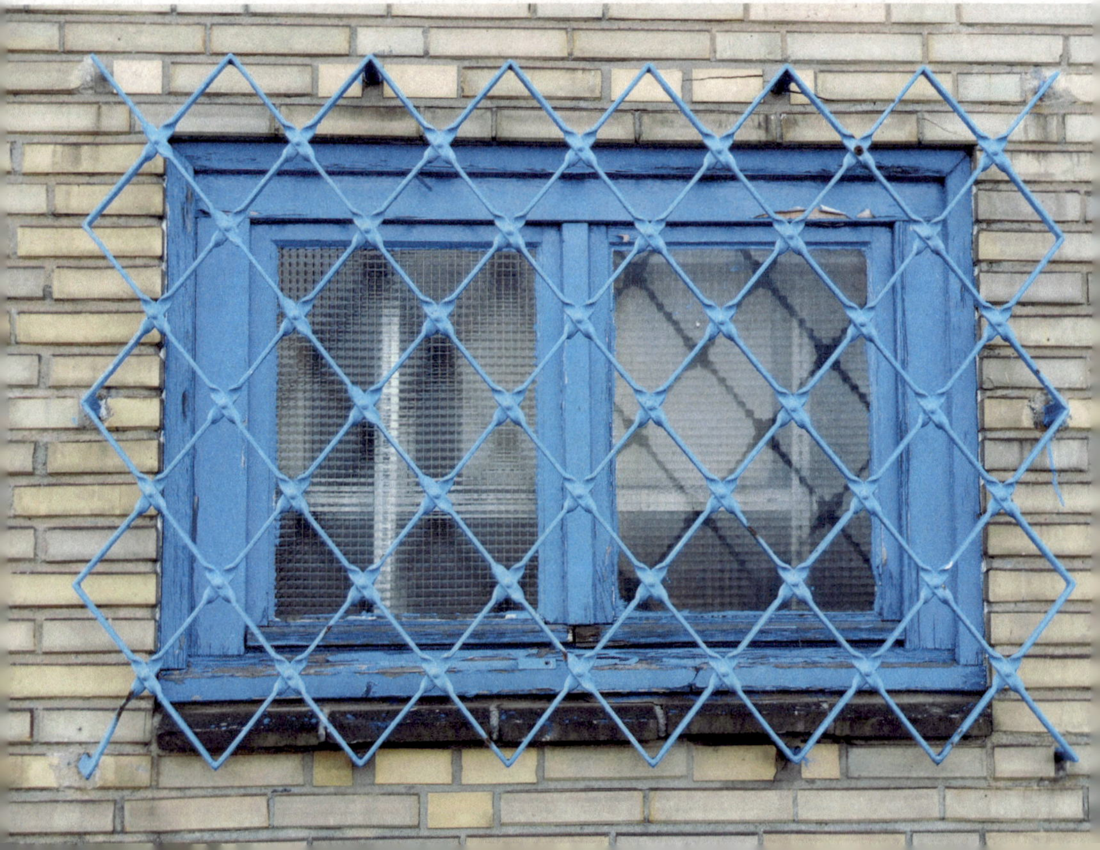

<table>
<tr><td>Communication with
[In-vivo code]</td><td>Stage Directions
from the Field</td></tr>
</table>

Excuse me, you need an appointment to enter. Drivers on company premises do so at their own risk. Keep entrance free. Pay attention when traffic lights change. Video surveillance. No pictures. Keep the courtyard gate closed at all times. That's no good, get out of here, scamper! [In the background a car horn honks several times, loud and clear] Private property; no trespassing! Alight only at Kirchdorf Süd. Is that forbidden? [He asks in broken German, worried] No, of course not! No picture, sie ist meine Schwester! [She immediately deletes the photo on the camera] Give way. And. Beware: ordnance salvaging. Drive to the end of the road, that is where the cycle path starts. [An invisible voice over the loudspeaker] Once again—reverse and drive to the end of the road, the bike path begins there. Hello?! [Short break] Hello!? [Unfriendly male voice from off-screen] So you don't want to cooperate with me? [Security person No. 2 behind the curtain; it is still dark, the first timid chirping of birds is audible] They have refused to cooperate. Disturbance Sensor 1 [The sensor sounds incessantly, at regular intervals] No. 2 alerts the police. [Three uniformed officers search the room, take the personal details of those present] The bombs detonate properly. [The actants are out of control, she wakes up from the actant party] Inform your foreign neighbors! [The megaphone distorts the announcement] Assembly point in case of storm surge. Stop. Evacuation route ahead. [But I—will stay]

This is Hamburg Mitte District
Office. Attention please attention
please. An unexploded bomb was
found in Rotenhäuser Straße at
the fire department. The bomb will
be defused today by 3 p.m. That
means that from 2 p.m. to 6 p.m.
you should not go outside. Please
stay at home and keep windows
and doors closed and keep away
from them. Watch out for more
announcements and inform your
foreign neighbors. Attention please
attention please. This is ...

It is eleven clock in the morning. It is still relatively quiet on Rotenhäuser Feld. It's a Sunday and it's windy. The sun is out. I head decisively for the first bench. The one where people like to barbecue aka the kitchen-bench Temporary Outside Rooms . A used, blackened wire grid lies on the seat surface. A lot of papers and packaging are scattered on the ground, the empty shells of sunflower seeds — conversations I read. I sit sideways on the bench. Now I start to stick the Post-its to the backrest. I notice at once that they do not stick well, even worse than I had originally thought. Presumably, the backrest is greasy with the meat grilled there before. In addition the surface is mossy. In short, it is difficult to keep the fluttering pieces of paper in their ephemeral nature. I must (unfortunately) put a stop to that with additional tape. The aesthetics do not convince me. But this list is meant to remain on the backrest. Even in the midst of the process, I realize that this intervention is a prototype again. It is the simplicity of this intervention that makes it difficult. Each actant brings its own distinct qualities, its dispositions along with it. Where to attach the pen, how to capture the paper again after the next gust of wind? Which language first, in what order and with what rhythm should I repeat the sentences HERE+I / HIER+ICH / ICI+MOI / BARAYA+BEN / BURAYA+BEN / HERE+I / TYK+A3 / TUTAJ+I / ZDE+I / AQUI+EU / AQUI+IO / HER+JEG / AQUI+YO / UNE+KETU / ЗДЕСЬ+Я /...? This bench is ready. I go to the next one, where the gang of youths usually sits. As I do so, I can see the first visitors to the park approaching the kitchen-bench intervention approach and stopping there. A man picks up the pen. The game commences. I attempt to improve the sticking technique and arrangement for the next bench. The wind doesn't make things easier though. A significant participant in my intervention. The next bench is regularly visited by the old ladies with their walkers. This walker-bench is already getting the sun. Then I go on to the playground, where I have often seen Turkish mothers with their children. Here two women look at me. They both look tense. Call out their children's names, admonishing them to be good. Laboriously I pick up some of the Post-it notes, blown away by the wind. I go onto the sports field, here something is always happening all day long. By the pitch I consider whether I should continue my intervention on the seated grandstands. I opt for the classic bench model. My chosen bench is in the passage to the avenue of lime trees. A girl talks to me, asks me what I'm doing. Finally, I attach my magenta notes opposite the senior citizens' day center. There I bump into our UdN neighbor with his old dog Animal Lovers . He tells me in detail about his numerous leg surgeries over the last seven years. He was in the Groß Sand Krankenhaus in Wilhelmsburg every time Wool-carders, Tailors, and Seamstresses . I stick my notes on the last two benches near the children's home. I even highlight a hidden bench with Post-its. It is a kind of mini cooking place outside. The last bench is especially good for sticking notes on thanks to its smooth surface. I leave visible the messages cut into the wood. "He didn't shoot me dead," "Tunis," and next to this beats a heart with an arrow. Overall, I picked out nine benches, there are certainly as many again in the park. After setting up the intervention I walk to the nearest Turkish takeaway coffee shop and buy myself a coffee. When I come back there are several people in the park. It's nearly one o'clock in the afternoon. One of the older ladies, meanwhile, has now sat down on 'her' bench and is quite obviously waiting for her walker girlfriends. She had torn the Post-it note (as a neighboring observer told me, she must have recognized me) off the back of the bench, clearly very upset, before finally sitting down on her pink cushions Territorial Stomping Grounds . However, four notes remained hanging. Why? Various people head straight for the benches, stop abruptly, read, discuss. Apart from the first visitors, I rarely see someone who actually writes something. They have added more languages to my current language set: Greek, Arabic, and other languages that I do not recognize despite their comments. Now the gang of youths come from around the corner. However the boys do not sit on their gang-bench, but next to it. They make phone calls, listen to music from their mobiles. Just like they always do, but this time on another bench. The benches are occupied by the Post-its, the visitors back off. Here and I. The effective power of the small notes is clear. On one hand, they are attractive and at the same time they are confusing. Many park visitors keep their distance, seeing or listening to what others are saying, reading, or writing. Later I see W. on his usual collection round by bike. Although he is in his bottle-search mode, he does actually stop Collectors and Sorters . He takes the pen, takes off the lid. He crumples up the paper on which he wrote something, and throws it away, clearly angry. On the neighboring bench, a colleague asks what it says, actually, and what it is all about. They talk about it, from bench to bench. "These idiots" I hear them say as they wind up. On my first tour I found that sporadic messages had been left. Some notes have drawings or signatures by children. Cryptic answers. Yes, it's about the process. It's about a playful dialogue with the actors and actants. The bench as a territorial stomping ground and a stand for lingering too Appropriations . On it people recline, cook, barbecue, eat, sleep, kiss, wait, cry, dream, rest, read, think, and relax ... It is shrouded in count-less open-ended stories. They can be found everywhere. The colored pieces of paper intervene in their ephemeral and garish way in the park program. Unexpected interruptions, assertions of ownership are made clear, unusual distances, new proximities, question marks, and changes of perspec-tives have emerged. With the intervention 'Here and I,' I was able to read and recognize the park program in a whole host of different ways. Overall I have hung up 200 Post-its. Many of them have vanished quietly in their ephemeral way. Others stay in place for longer, hanging in their tempo-rary destinations. Finally, I go one last lap around Roten-häuser Feld. Look at the last Post-its. On the ground a few loose sheets greet me here and there; I leave them to time and space.

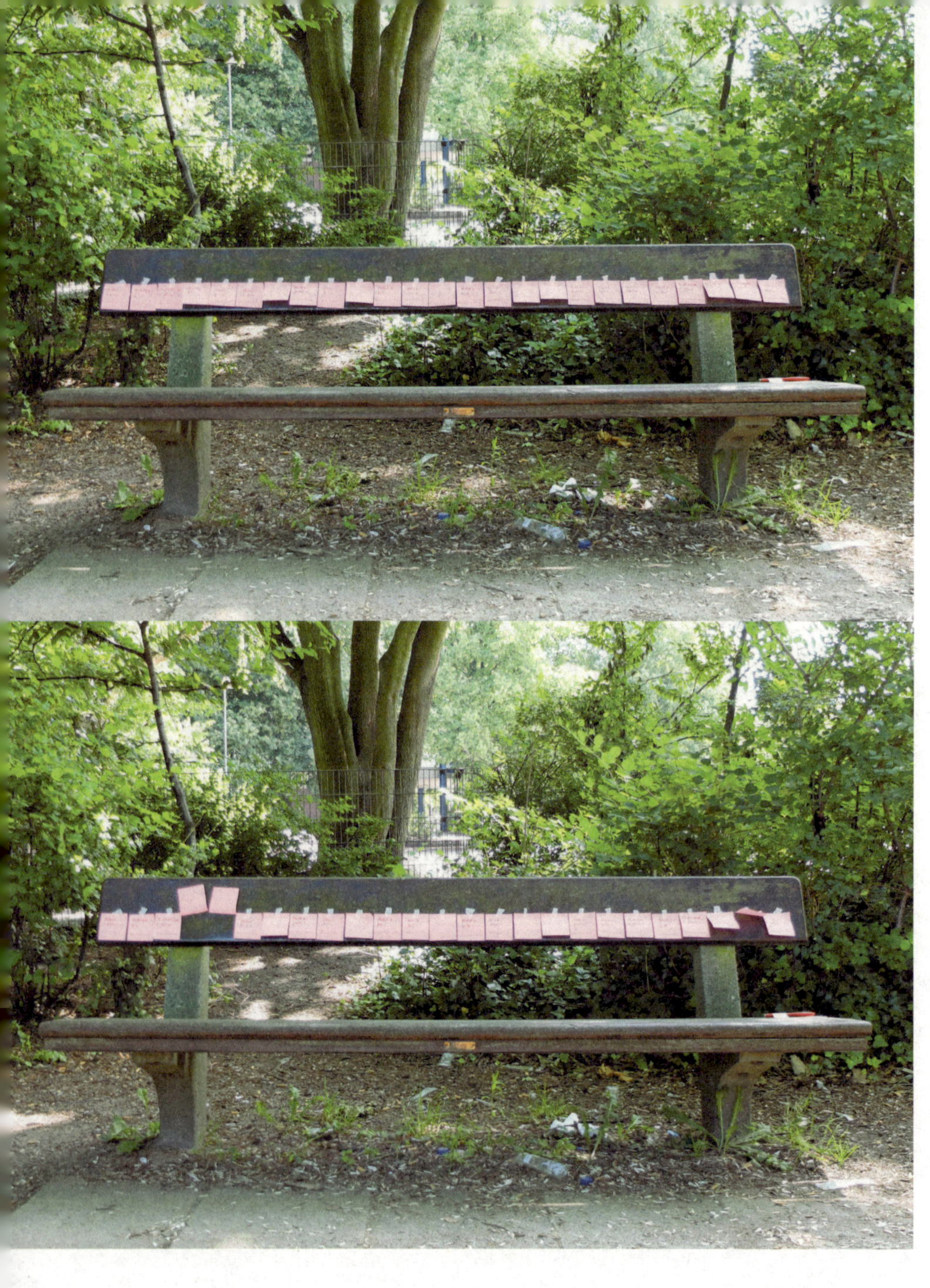

Communication with [Links]
[In-vivo code]

Link 1: The Peute industrial zone smells of chocolate. The
Kleiner Grasbrook port area exists as a Rosa canina-cutlet-
cocoa fragrance blend. And to boot, the limes are blossom-
ing again. Everywhere the scent of flowers mingles with
the dust of the dry port. It makes a noise in the ears. The privet
in the port area Neuhof transports me instantly to St. Prex,
near Lausanne. It is summer 1979. I can still see deep blue,
glowing Lac Léman through the fragrant hedge. The children
speak unfamiliar French.
Link 2: Back to Neuhofer Damm, on a path to the side a
vista to the west opens up briefly: containers, harbor, canals,
railway tracks. I pass Nippoldstraße. "Nippoldstraße is the
main street on Neuhof Peninsula. It links Köhlbrandbrücke
to Reiherstieg. It is named after Berlin merchant Ferdinand
Nippold, who was born in 1871 in Berlin and died in Wilhelmsburg in 1929. In the mid-17th century, the first farmers settled
on Neuhof. They ran dairy farms and grew vegetables
[Greunhöker]. In 1672 Grote Otto the 11th acquired the island,
which until then had been called Karkhoff. In 1813 during
the siege of Hamburg by the Napoleonic troops all Neuhof's
inhabitants were expelled. Twelve years later a good 400
people were living on the island again: there were fishermen,
dairy farmers, ship carpenters, craftsmen, and day laborers.
In 1818 the first steam ship sailed, the "steam ferry for the
privileged," from Hamburg to Harburg with a stop on Neuhof.
In 1845 commercial lines sailed to Reiherstieg [Connector].
In 1888 the free port of Hamburg and the shipyard Oelkers
came into being [Lost—Abandoned—Wait]. In 1896 Baron Otto
von Grote sold the island. (...) At that time there were mainly
pastures and farms on Neuhof. About 700 people lived there.
The buyer was a Berlin Handelsgesellschaft, which con-
sisted of various banking houses. The banker Friedburg had
smelled a good business opportunity as the site was so close
to the port: "With a glance I convinced myself that Neuhof,
bordering directly on these facilities, would sooner or later
be of very considerable value for industrial or other enterprises
(...)." Neuhof was a Prussian fief, so neither taxes nor duties
for Neuhof had to be paid to the lords. (...) The Prussian king
approved the conversion into a free estate and the estate

changed hands for 2.25 million marks. (...) Given its location
and the prospects for its future development, the amount
seemed reasonable. It cost about one mark per square meter.
The Berliner Handelsgesellschaft (...) and various other
cash-rich investors founded the Neuhof Corporation and
appointed Berlin merchant Ferdinand Nippold as manag-
ing director. (...) Nippold put a lot of energy into developing
the Elbe Island and establishing industrial enterprises
there. (...) Among the people of Neuhof, his authoritarian
style quickly earned him the nickname 'King Ferdinand'"
(Elbe Wochenblatt: 1995).
Link 3: With the American Line I finally end up in China Town.
There, on top of a lonely pillar at Argentienbrücke, stands the
Golden Calf (artist Elisabeth Richnow; see action "No man
is an island") on a red box. Lost in Translation. I can hardly ever
decipher the labels on the containers. But to make up for that
there is American Pizza and Chinese food free delivery.
Link 4: The residential area by the old Elbe Bridge manifests
as rather discreetly British. Perhaps it is going to rain again?
The clouds hang low, very low over the Elbe Islands. Is the
new, converted, and extended port of Harburg like HafenCity
or is it more like Rotterdam? I'm not sure.
Link 5: The Reiherstieg quarter is enveloped in a hint of
freshly baked waffles. Actually, all the time from Monday to
Sunday it is like this. Depending on the direction of the
wind, the cloud from Palm Oil Refining reaches us sometimes more, sometimes less clearly.
Link 6: The school bus to Osterøy waits not far away. For me?
Who would ever have thought that? With a surface area of
328 square kilometers, this is the largest island in Norway not
directly located in the open sea. 1,533 kilometers from
Wilhelmsburg. I choose the route via Sweden. Over land and
without taking the "expressways"(!) (Serres 2009/1998: 271).
Right at that moment the school bus to Osterøy is being
resprayed Barbershops and Beauty Salons . Terminal stop
Vogelhüttendeich?
Link 7: Bits of language accompany me everywhere. Turkish-
German, Bulgarian, Russian-German, Arabic, Russian,
English or American English, Portuguese-German, Turkish,
Bulgarian, German-Turkish, Low German, Swiss German,
Russian, French, German, Italian ... even if I do (not) always
understand, I dream up situational translations for everyday

life. Then I actually leave Wilhelmsburg for several hours.
Link 8: Two days at Documenta. An exhibition in Kassel.
"I document your existence. (...) You choose the location."
Yes, I chose my research field.
Link 9: After the visit in Harburg my mood slithers out of tune.
The (imaginary) Castle of Harburg is nowhere to be seen.
Instead, a red strawberry stand selling raspberries glows all
the more intensely and strikingly. Learning from Las Vegas—
in Wilhelmsburg too!

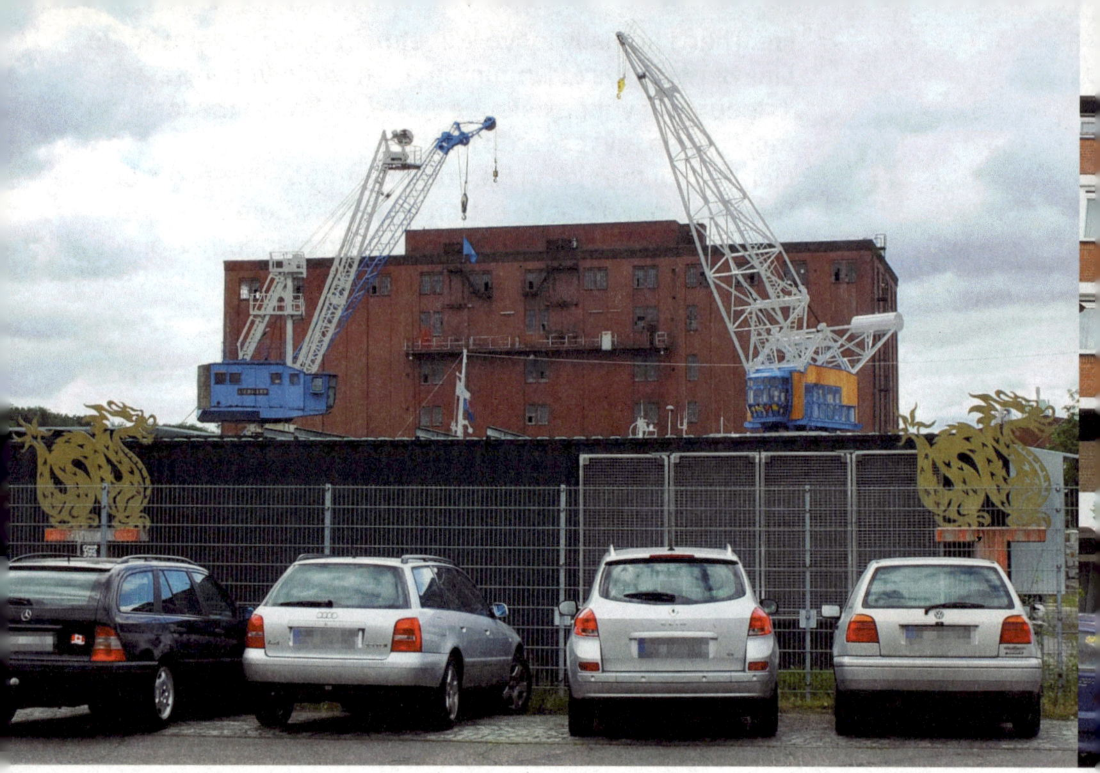

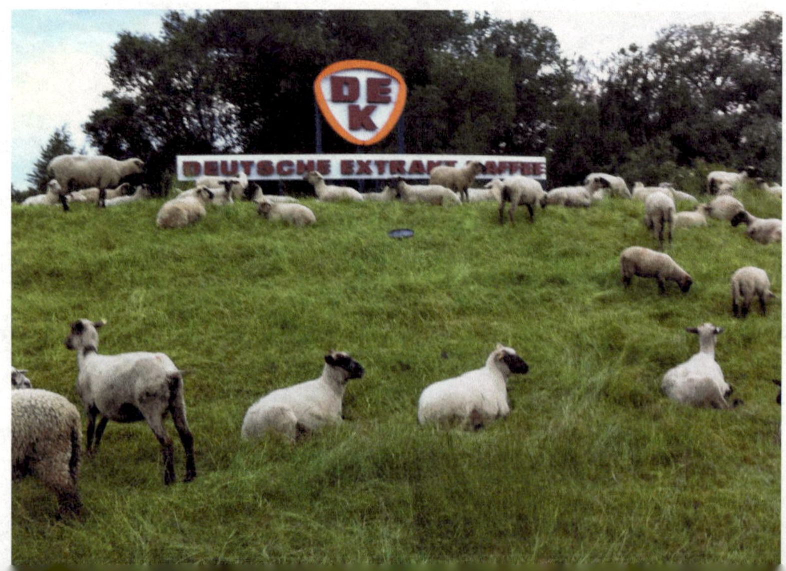
DE
K
DEUTSCHE EXTRAKT KAFFEE

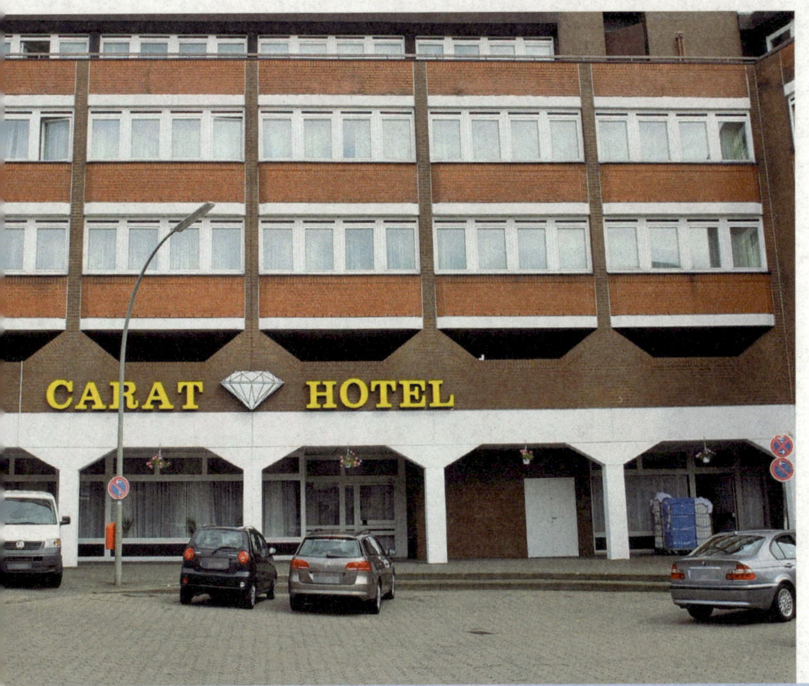
CARAT HOTEL
PRINCE

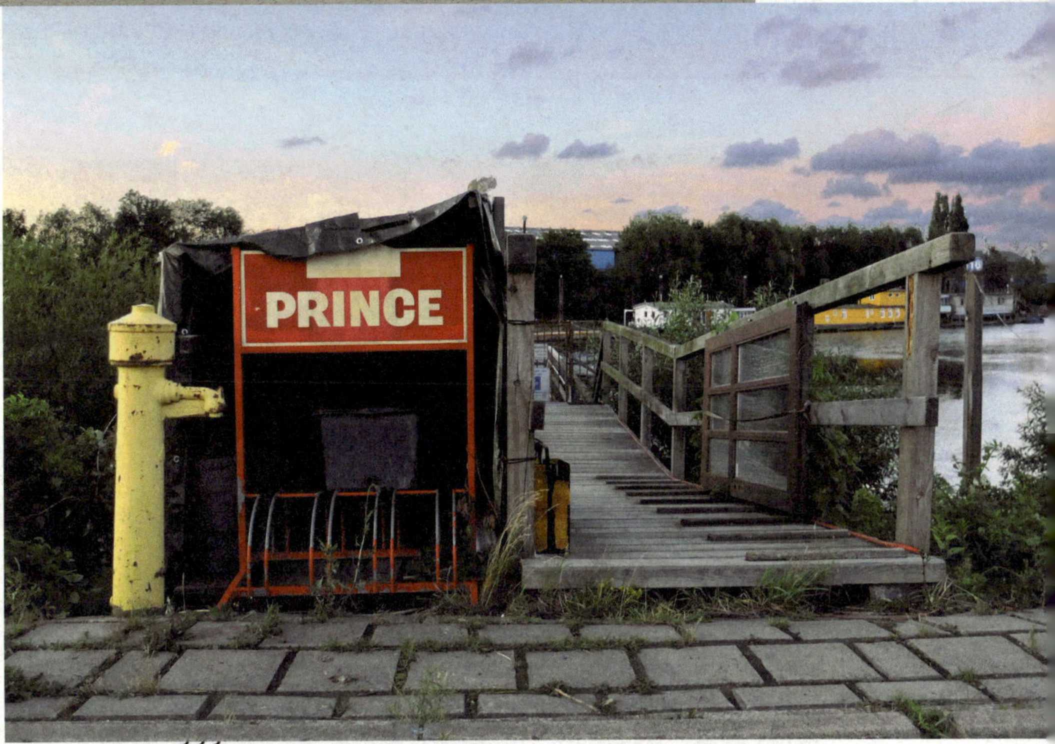

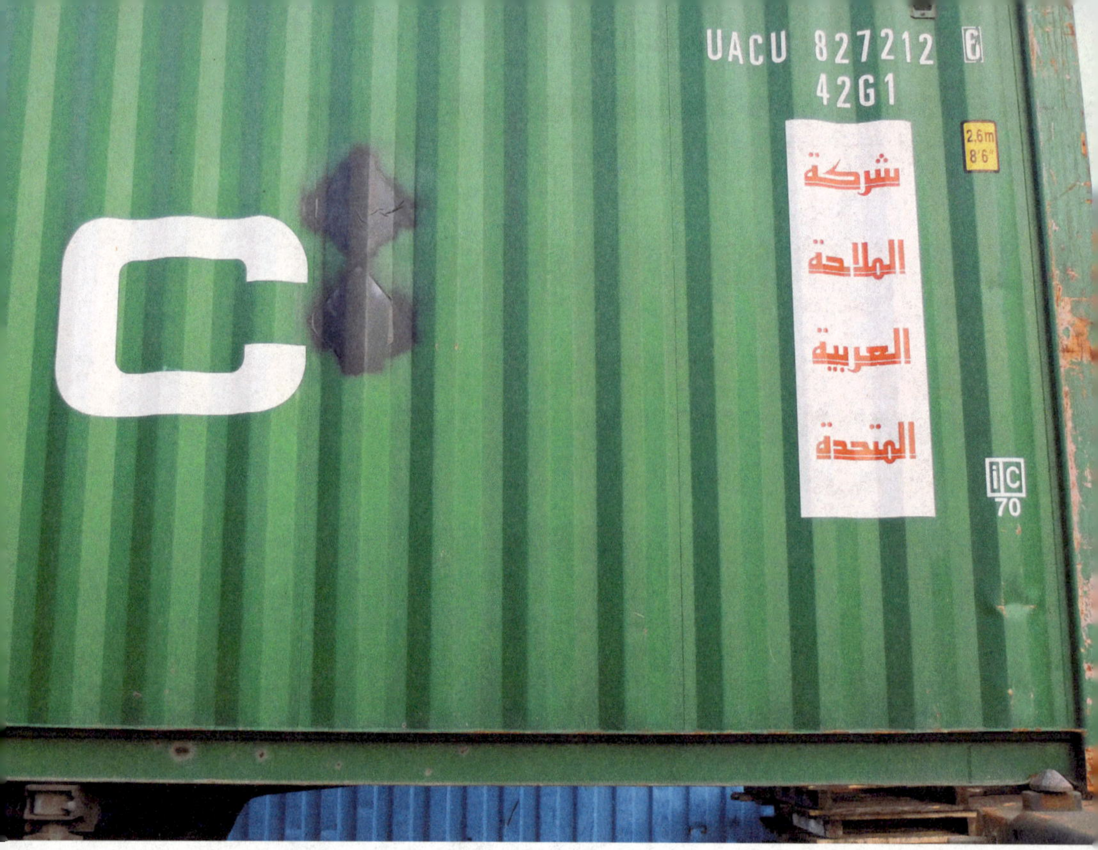

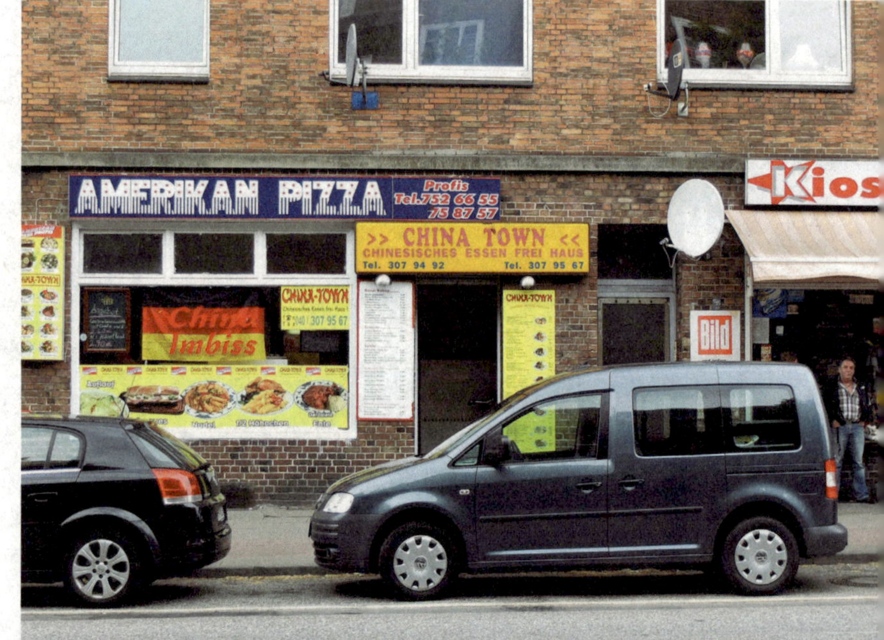
UACU 827212
42G1
2,6 m
8'6"
شركة
الملاحة
العربية
المتحدة
C
70
AMERIKAN PIZZA
Profis
Tel.752 66 55
75 87 57
>> CHINA TOWN <<
CHINESISCHES ESSEN FREI HAUS
Tel. 307 94 92
Tel. 307 95 67
China
Imbiss
Kios
Bild

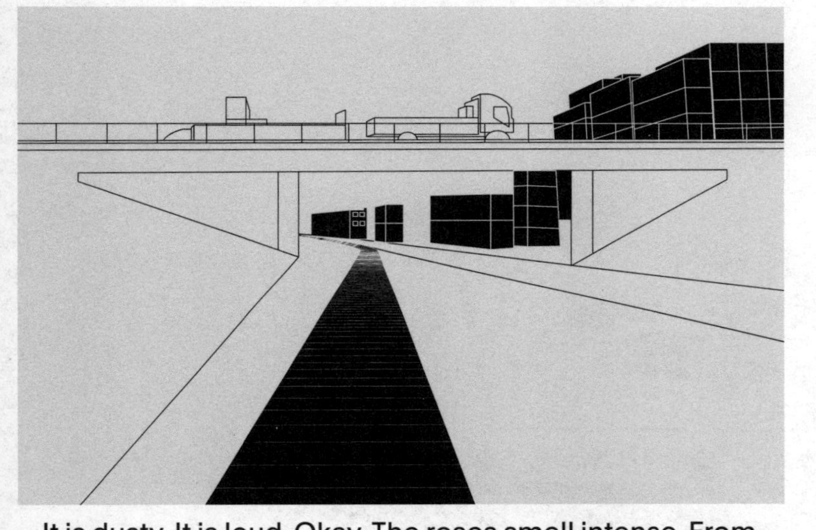

... It is dusty. It is loud. Okay. The roses smell intense. From somewhere in one of the halls the smell of fried chops float over to me ...

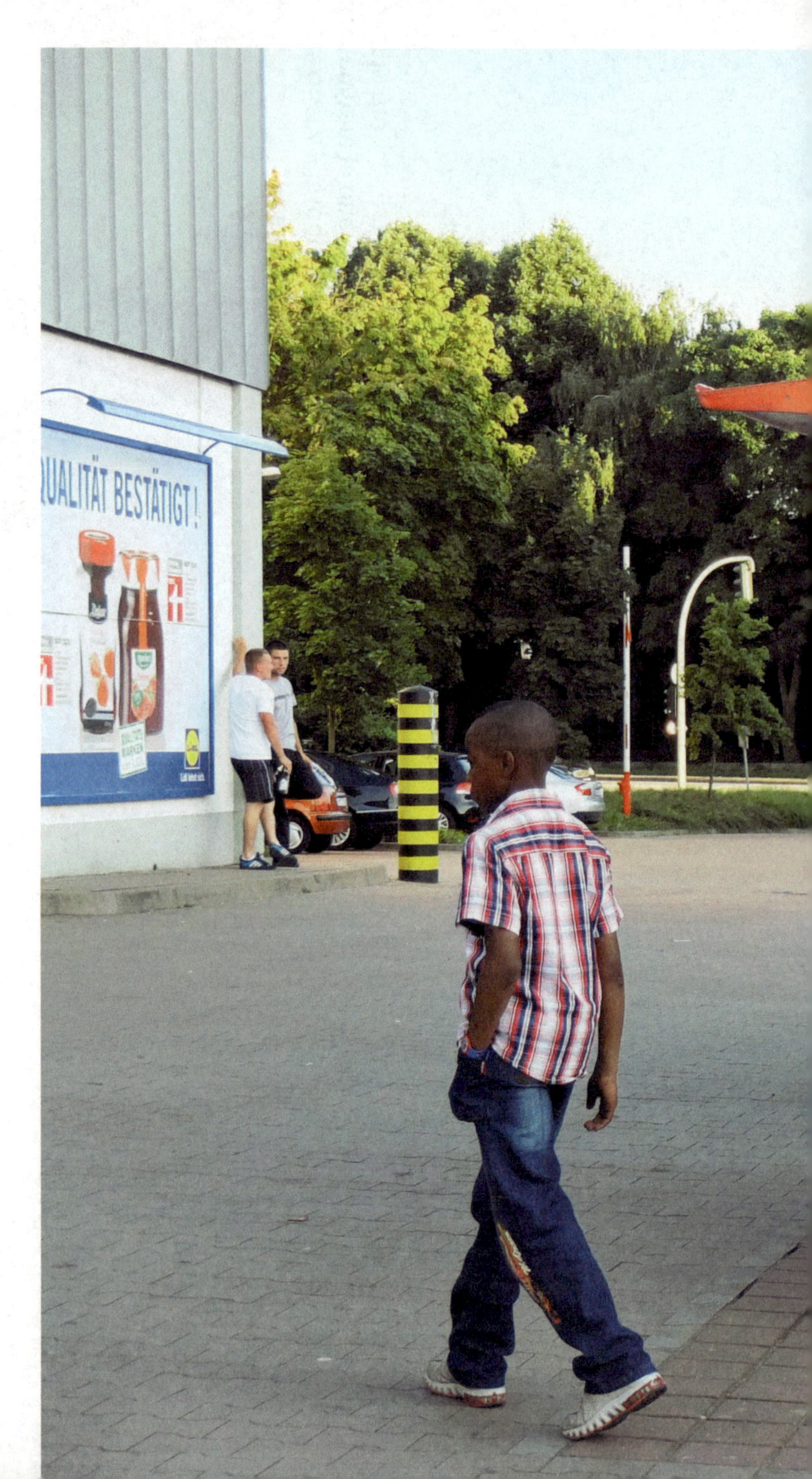
QUALITÄT BESTÄTIGT !
Lidl

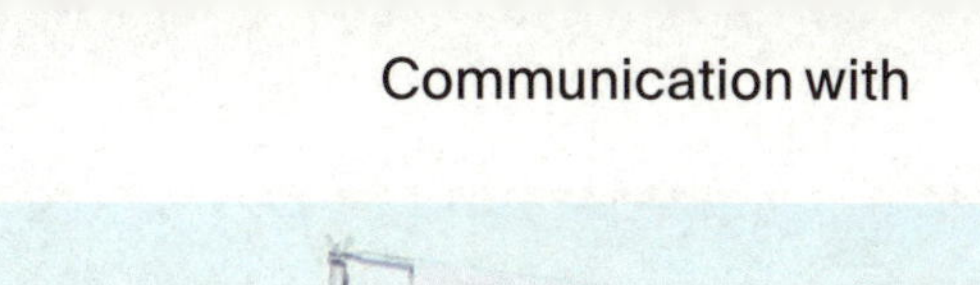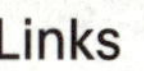
Himbeeren

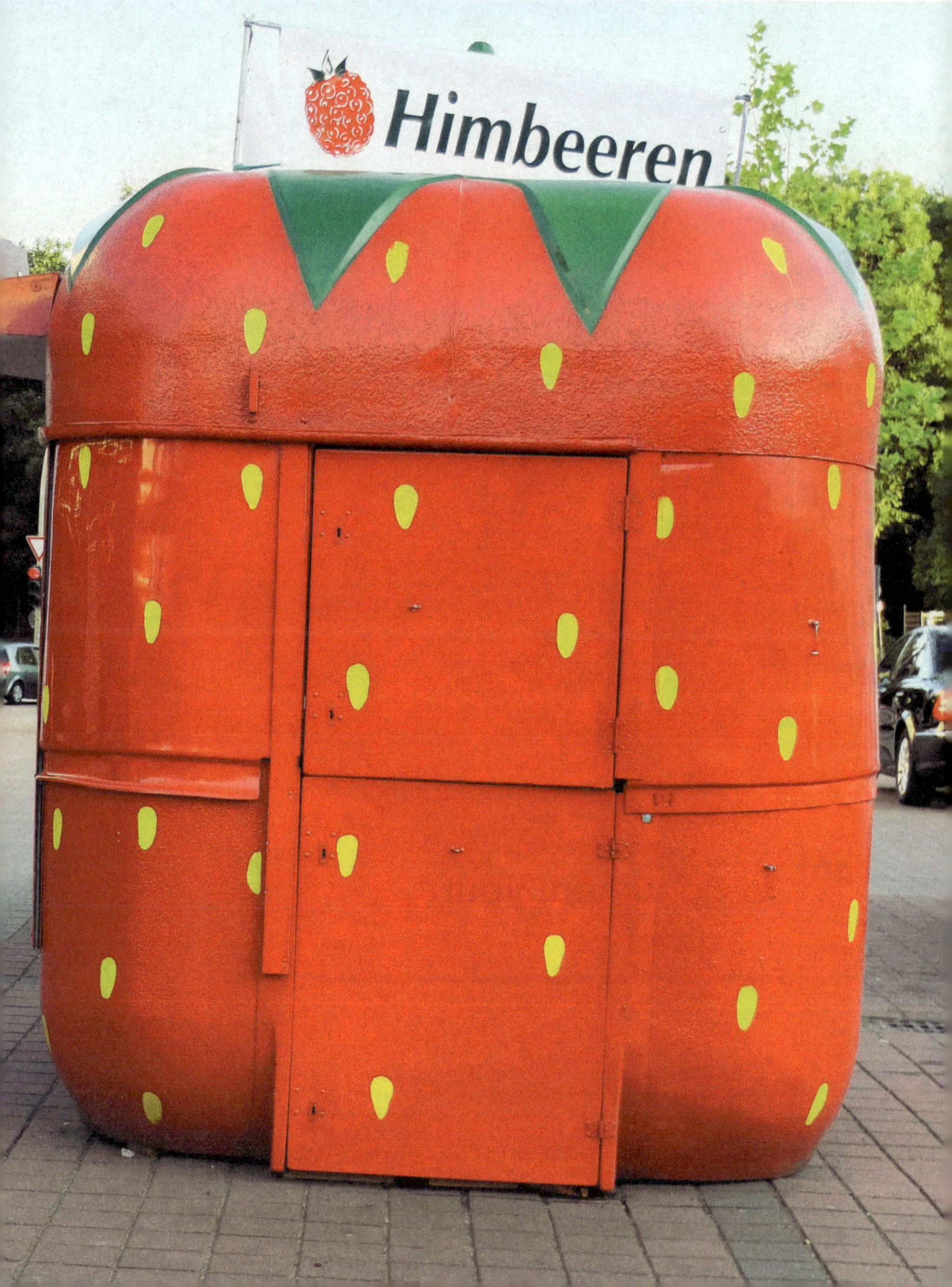

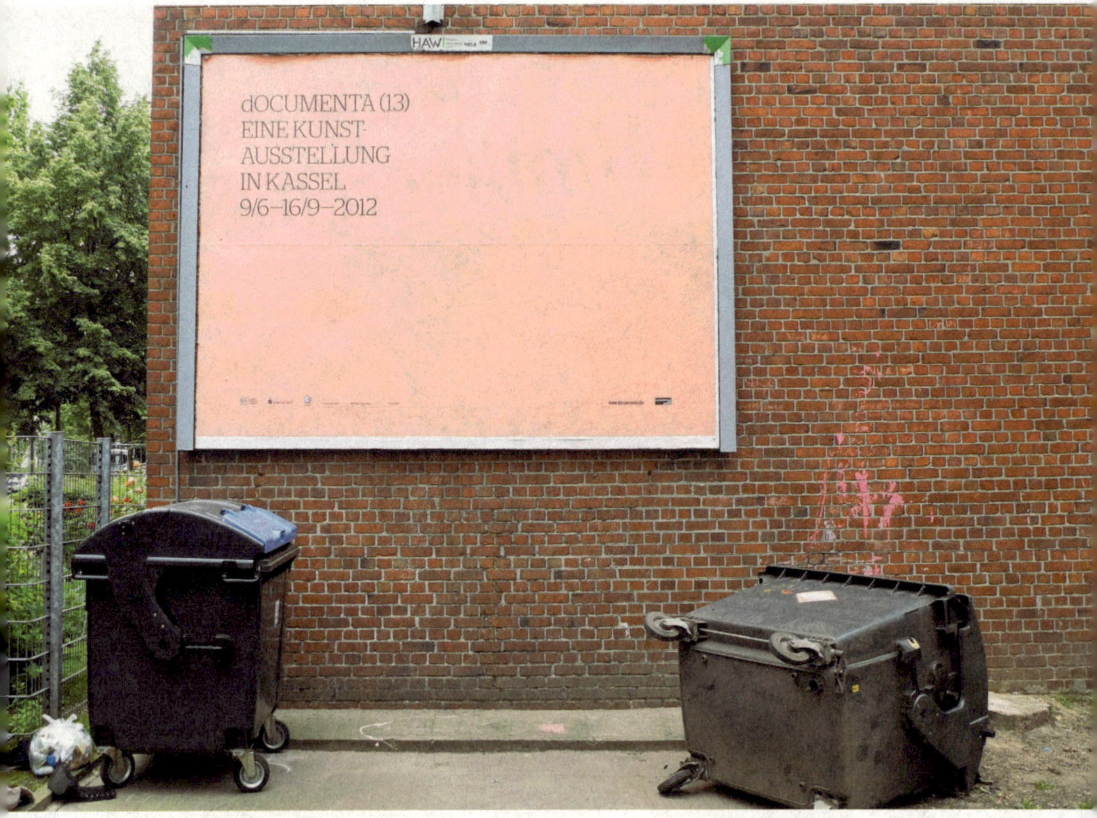

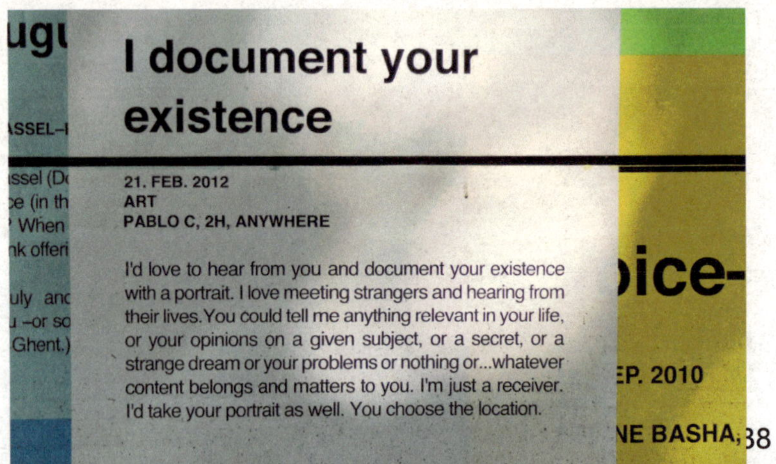
dOCUMENTA (13)
EINE KUNST-
AUSSTELLUNG
IN KASSEL
9/6–16/9–2012

ugu
ASSEL–
ssel (D
ce (in th
When
nk offeri
uly and
u –or so
Ghent.)
I document your
existence
21. FEB. 2012
ART
PABLO C, 2H, ANYWHERE
I'd love to hear from you and document your existence
with a portrait. I love meeting strangers and hearing from
their lives. You could tell me anything relevant in your life,
or your opinions on a given subject, or a secret, or a
strange dream or your problems or nothing or...whatever
content belongs and matters to you. I'm just a receiver.
I'd take your portrait as well. You choose the location.
pice-
EP. 2010
NE BASHA, 38

Yes, they are here too. These sad houses, buildings, and halls. They look timeless and are located in this "no longer or not yet," waiting loop (Schneider; Baumgärtner 2000: 12f). Nor do they know where to go, or how long this state lasts. An awakening or a transformation? Is it forward or backward? Have they given up or do they lead silent lives of their own as living blind spots (cf. Lefebvre 1991/1974) of these islands? Namely as meeting points of (in)visible figures and a green wilderness that move in without a word and appropriate the emptiness? Many ownerless windows and doors are locked or broken. Between the glass splinters blow prematurely graying curtains. In the courtyard plastic bags lie around aimlessly. An apocalyptic mood or "Lost Places" (cf. Hamburg Kunsthalle)? In numerous locations it is precisely this feeling that creeps over me. Countless thousands of square meters of land are for sale or temporarily free Plus . But what to do about it? I dial the number of the company OTTO DÖRNER GmbH & Co. At Neuhöfer Damm 98, 25,000 square meters have been for sale for some time now. This was previously the premises of the Johann Oelkers Shipyard for repairs, conversions, and new-build vessels Links . They cannot give me a price for the site on the phone. They are expecting offers from interested parties. The geographic location and transport links are very good, any legacy pollution properly has been removed since 2004. Elbe Islands speculation for container storage space? What happens until the site is sold, and what about the other buildings or halls? Are they also projection surfaces for logistics companies? Wait! Or are they waiting for a new interpretation, reinterpretation, reprogramming of their inherent potentials? The sense of being lost also creeps over me at the sight of some houses. These are the real flipside of the Elbe Islands. Sad tristesse. It is emergency housing, just like the busy Harburger Chaussee. The football pitch in the yard appears deserted. The people who live here store their food on the windowsills (probably) due to lack of refrigerators, electricity, or lack of space. The laundry center is open twenty hours, with washing particularly inexpensive between six and ten clock in the morning. Many men try their luck as day laborers at the Veddel S-Bahn Station or on Stübenplatz. These are the two central, informal employment services ┌ Life and Business ┐. A very mysterious tension develops in some port, commercial or industrial area at times. Especially when the fences are high, the streets are empty, and the windowless buildings look emotionless. What is happening? Especially if I want to follow a trail, the watchful guards and security staff make it clear to me that I had better leave ┌ Stage Directions from the Field ┐. These reactions are certainly reinforced by my not entirely conventional appearance, my interested gaze and my companion, the camera. In addition, I rarely meet any women. There are male-dominated worlds. Neither they nor I know how to deal with that. Opaque transactions. Loud horns. Barking dogs. I leave.

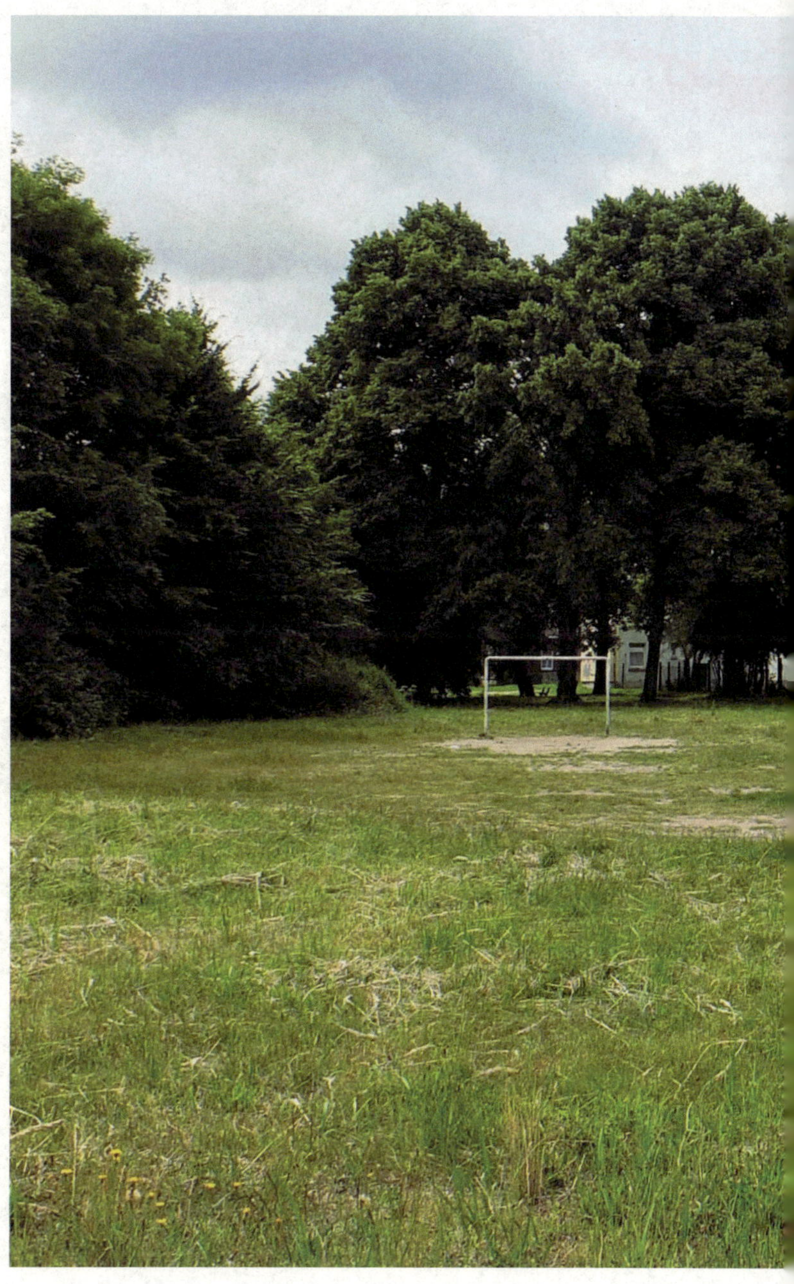

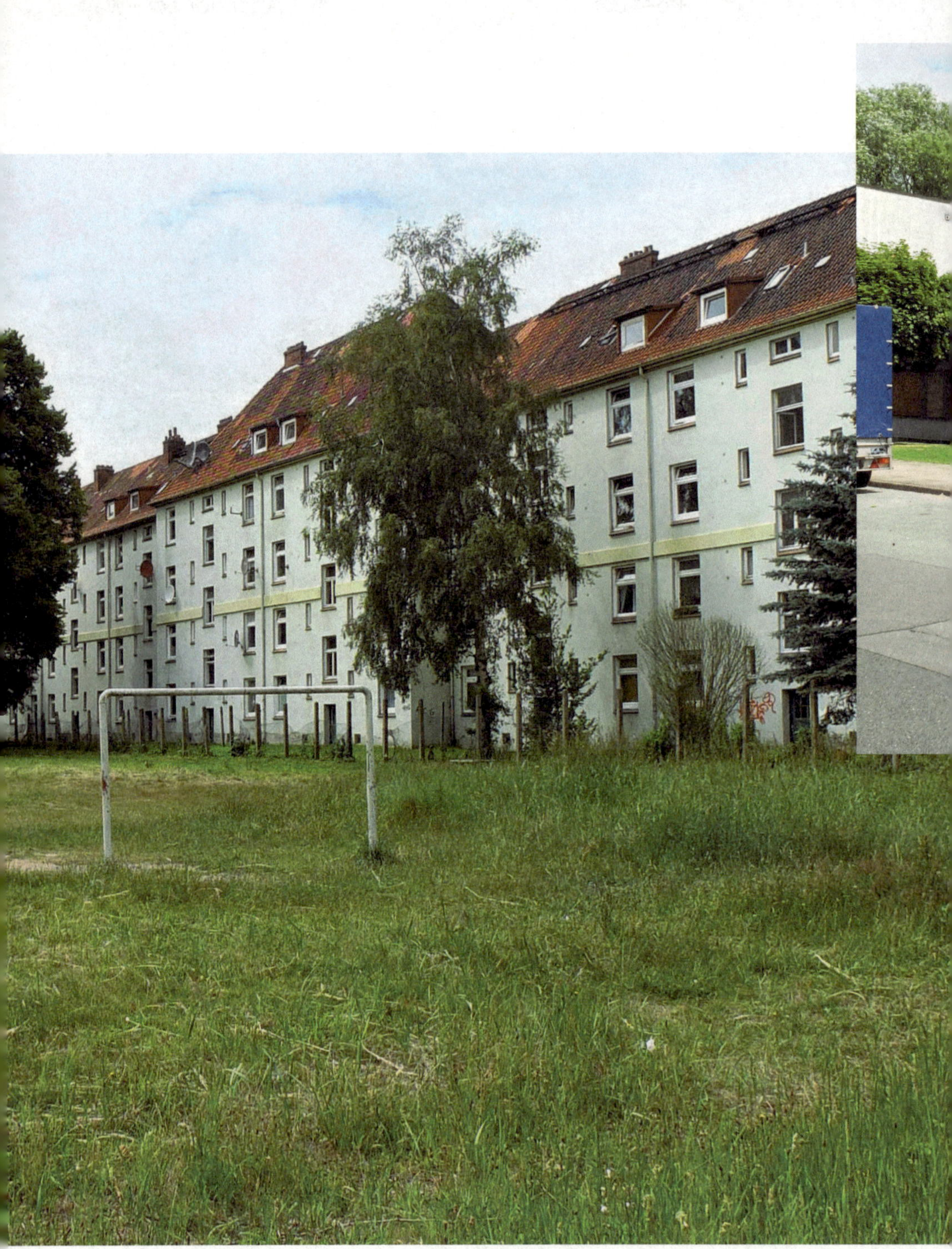

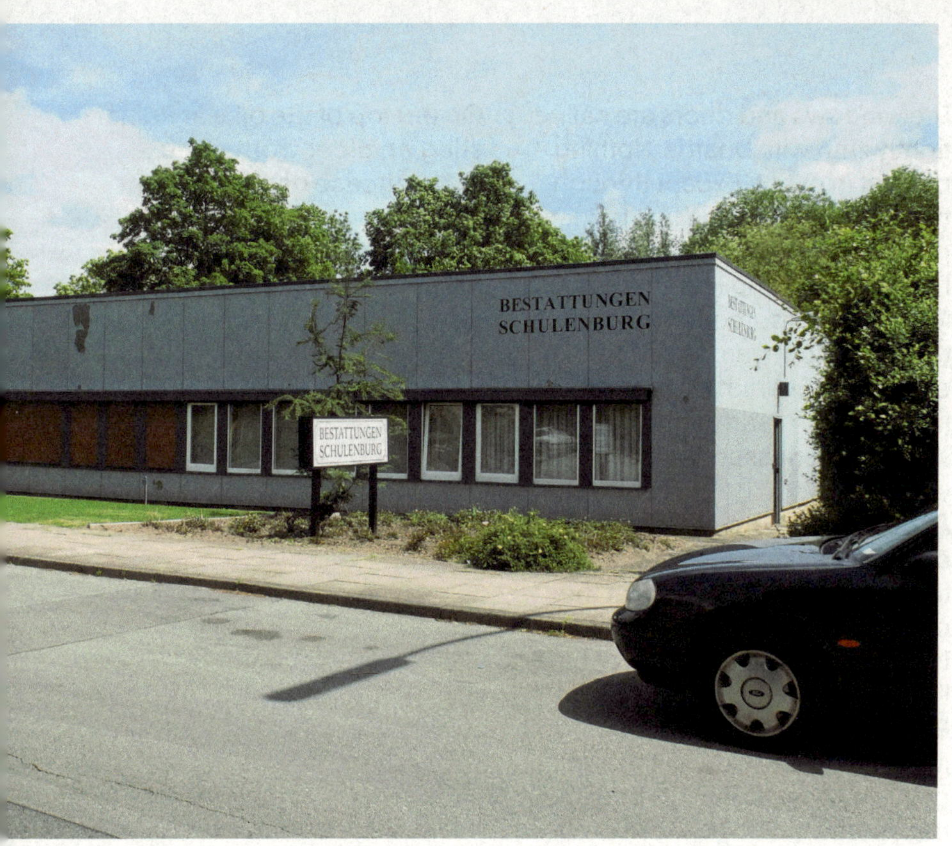
BESTATTUNGEN
SCHULENBURG
BESTATTUNGEN
SCHULENBURG

The windows and doors are nailed
tightly shut with boards. Nothing
can get in or out. Except through
the cracks, where the first pioneer
plants are squeezing their way in.
The brick building lets it happen.
Mute. Parts of something fly through
the dusty courtyard. A desert
of asphalt. Everything seems
motionless, clearly vanquished.
Verloren. Verlassen. Wait!

At dusk cats roam around on the
disused tracks in the garbage that
fills the air. Dark cars park at the
old slaughterhouse. Looking in
is unwelcome. Dogs bark behind
high walls and barbed wire.
Shadowy outlines of young people
jumping up and down at the end
of this byway. Night falls over the
tracks too.

On the top of the dike at Reiherstieg an older woman sits.
The staircase divides in front
of her, toward Fährstraße
or Fährstieg. She greets the few
passers-by who switch to one
side or the other, quietly nodding
—in the twilight.

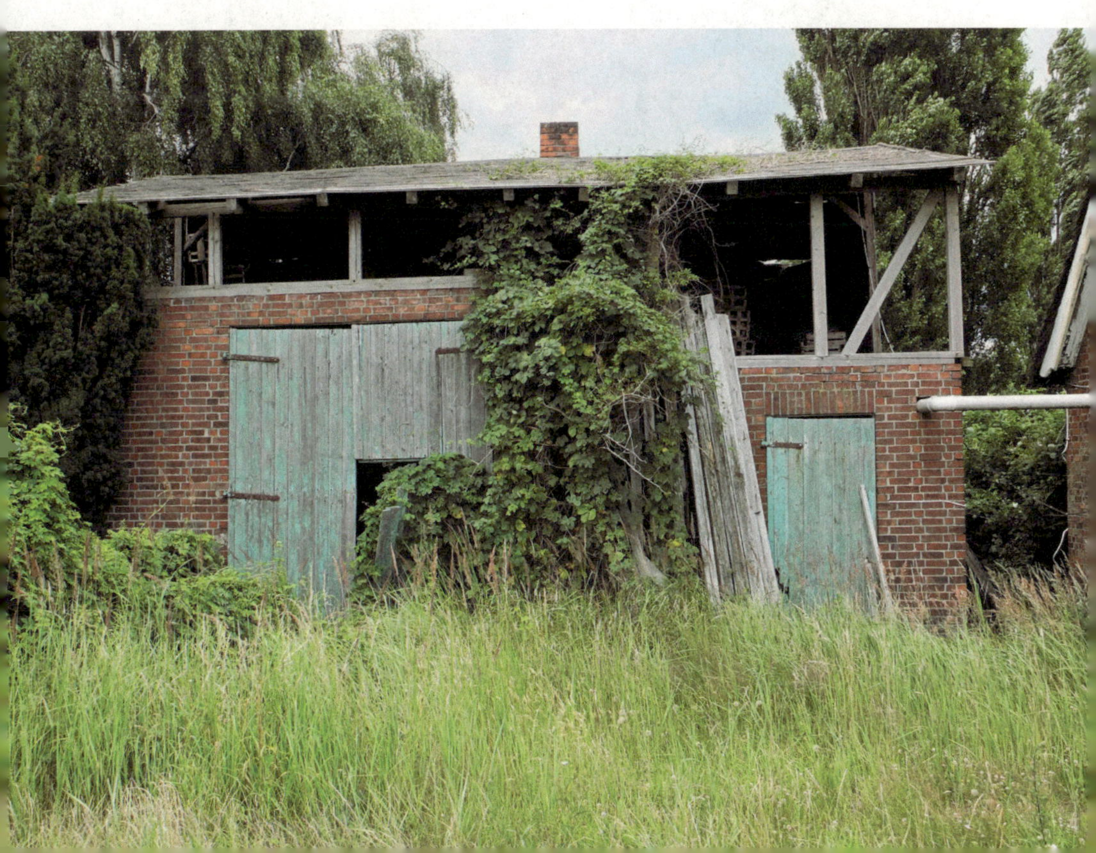

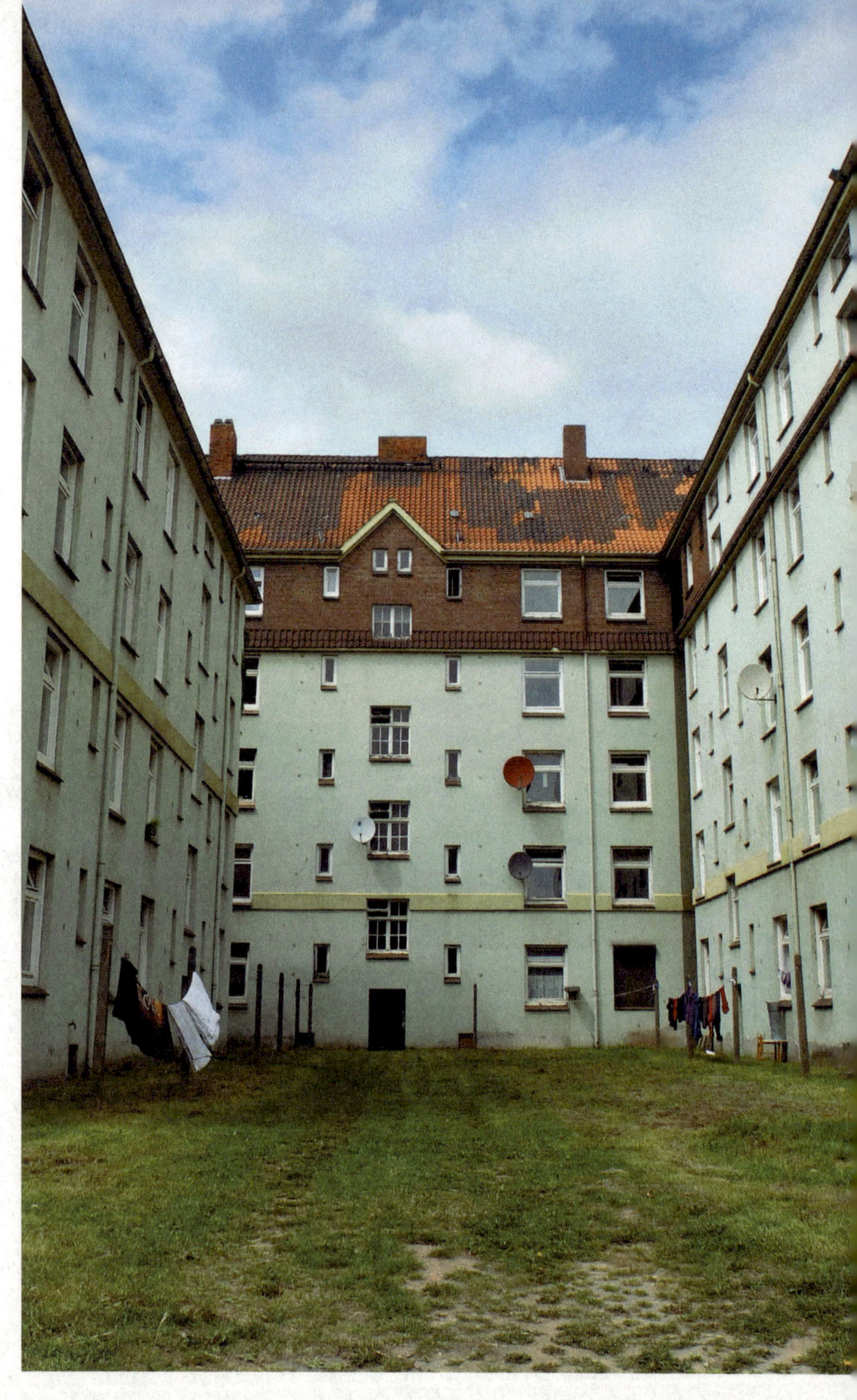

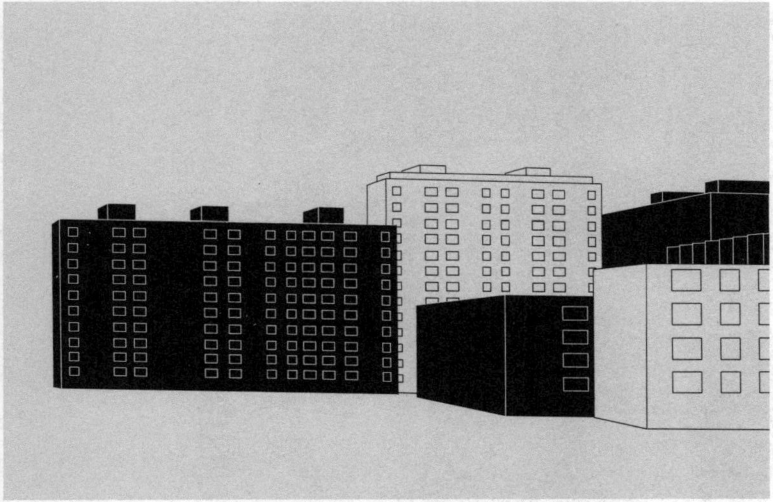

... reach the back of the apartment block. Satellite dishes
at the windows. It somehow reminds me of rural parts of East
Germany. Rather desolate, even as I read some signs that
there must be young tenants living here. Ikea fabrics or lamps
from the current catalog can be spotted here and there in
the windows — probably student flat-shares or young couples'
flats ...

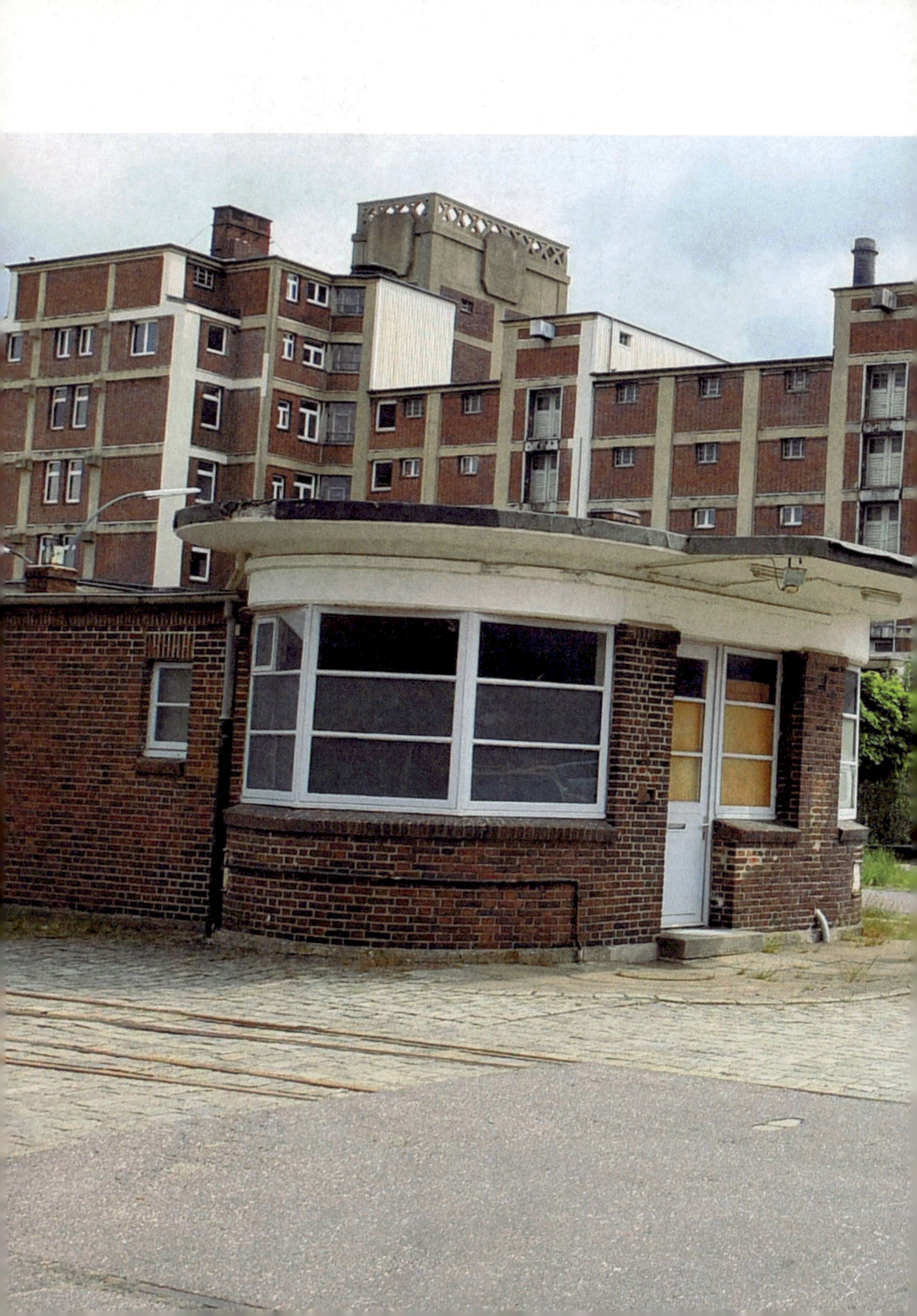

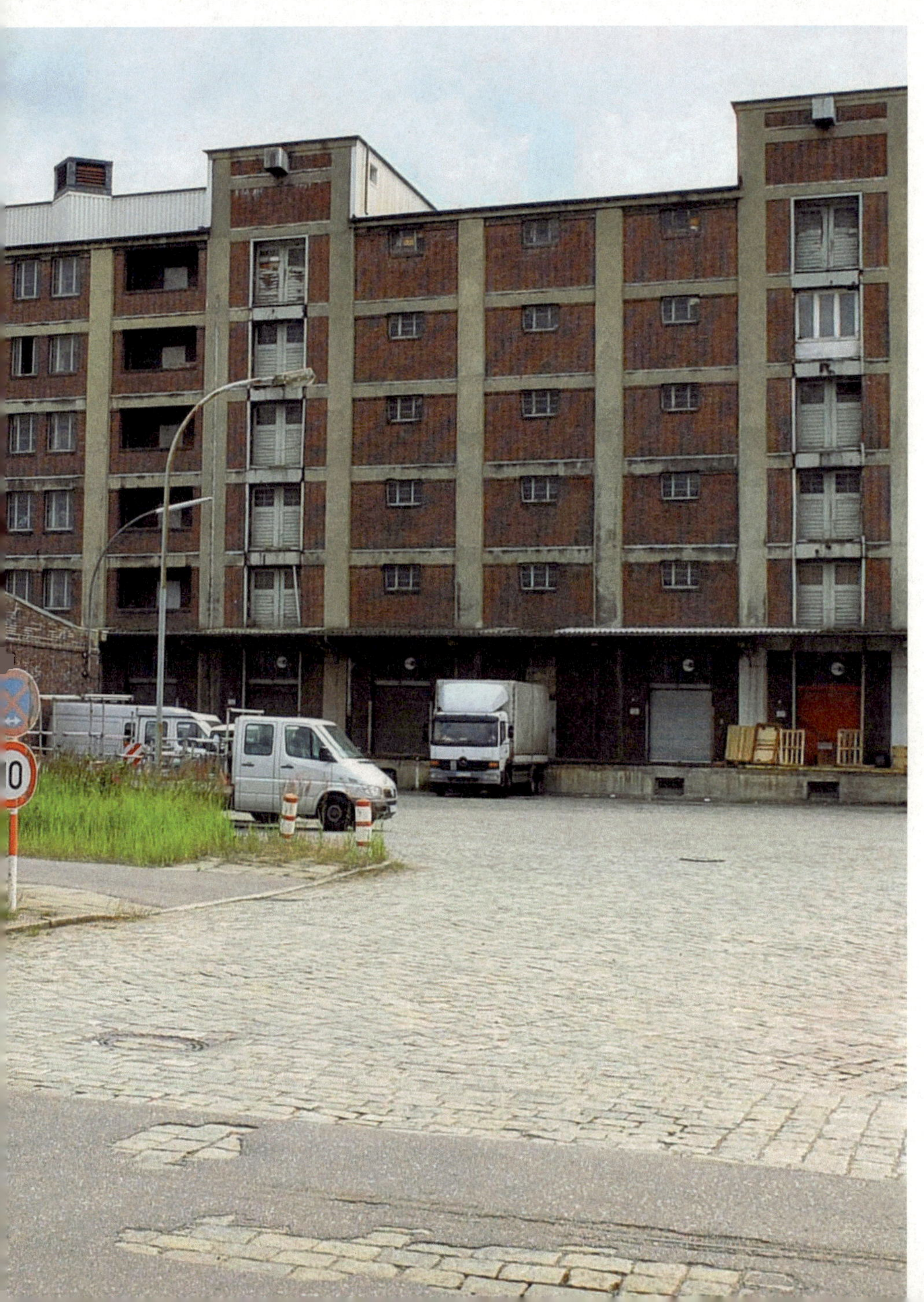

— The ice cream vendor honks loudly —

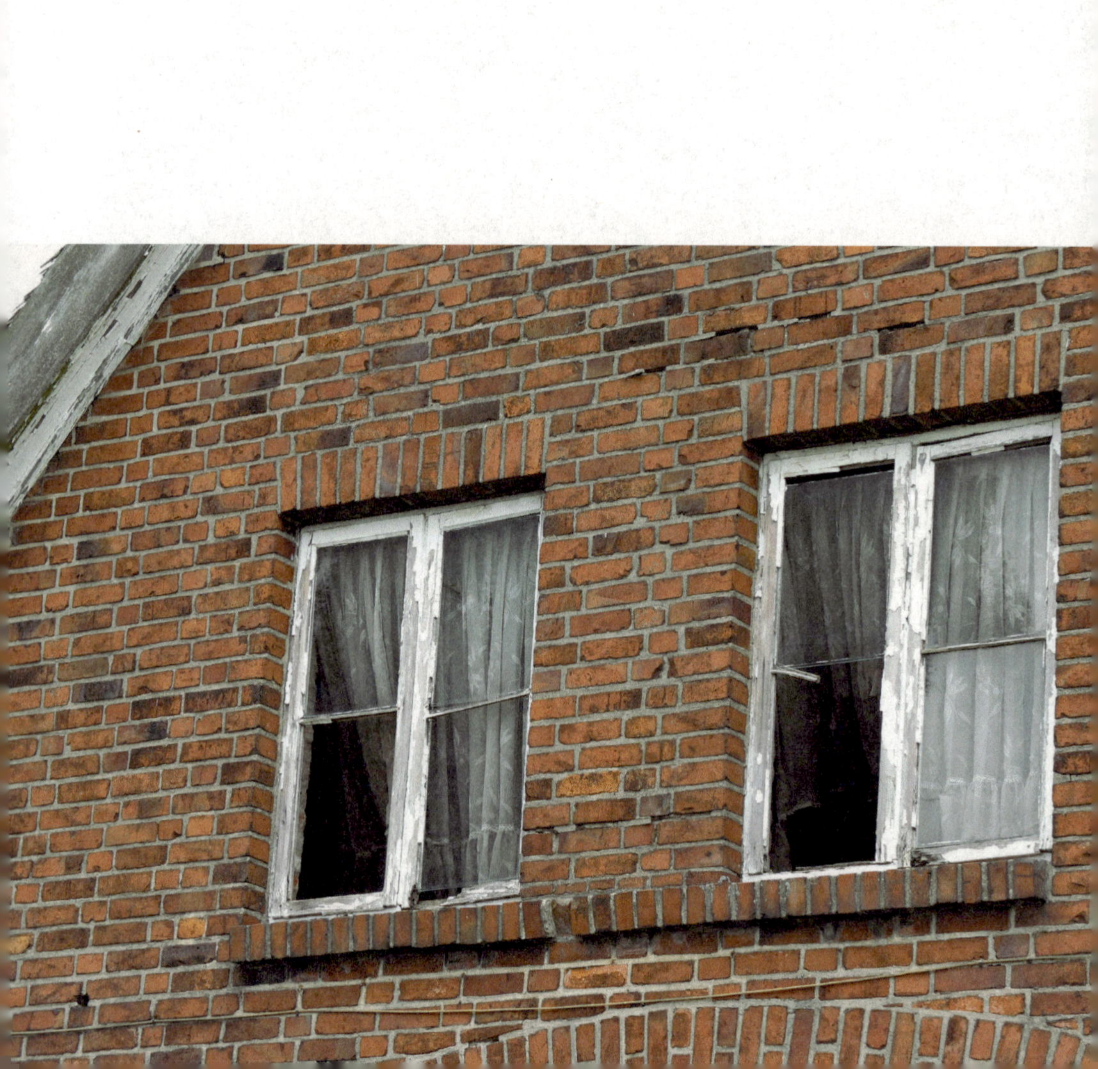

The soap bubbles shine as they float, bursting the next moment. A girl with an automatic (!) bubble machine makes hundreds of these airy and fascinatingly elusive bubbles on Stübenplatz (place purchased, as she informed me: Phoenix Center Harburg). Again and again I experience many such entertaining instances, along with other very offbeat, creative, and playfully improvised moments. They are independent of age and culture, time, and place.

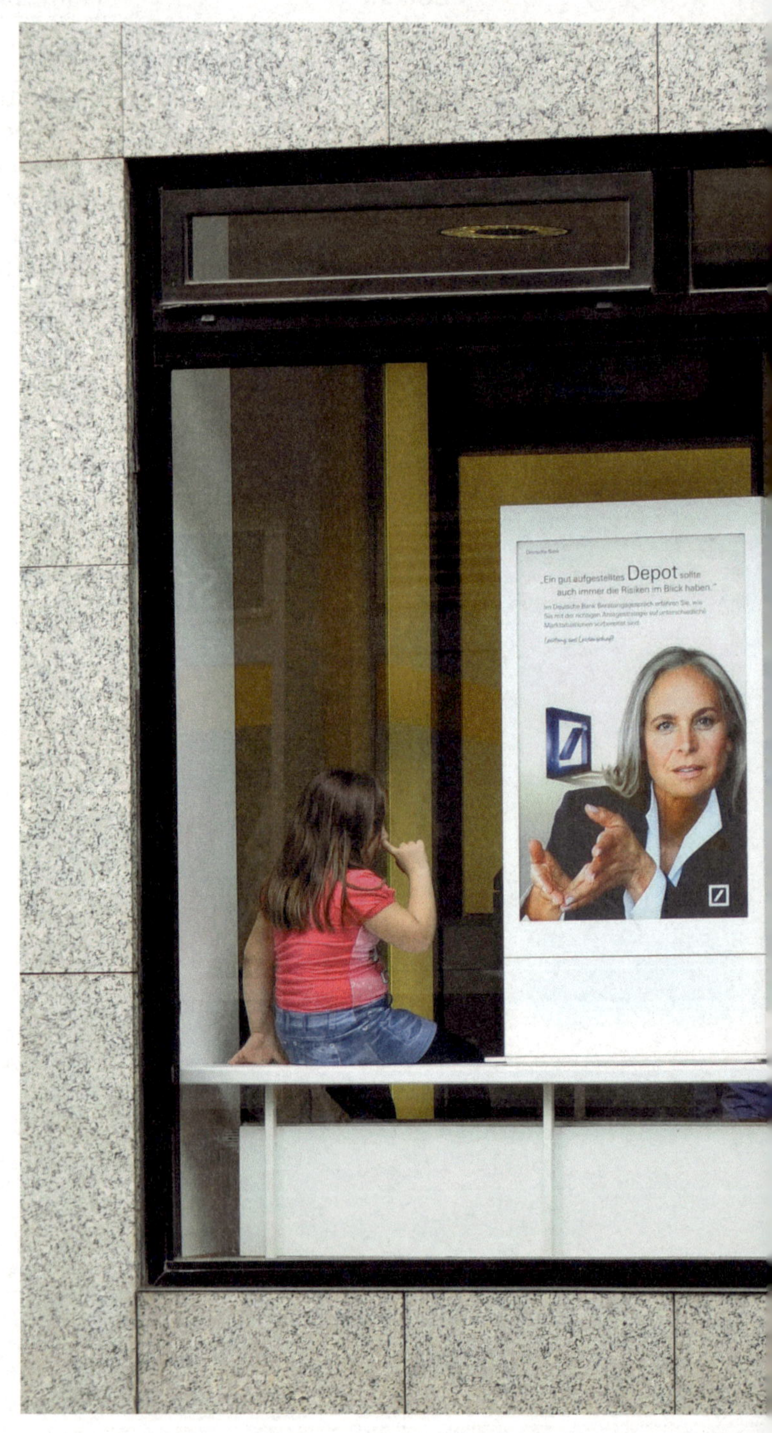

Deutsche Bank
„Ein gut aufgestelltes Depot sollte auch immer die Risiken im Blick haben."
Im Deutsche Bank Beratungsgespräch erfahren Sie, wie Sie mit der richtigen Anlagestrategie auf unterschiedliche Marktsituationen vorbereitet sind.
Leistung aus Leidenschaft?

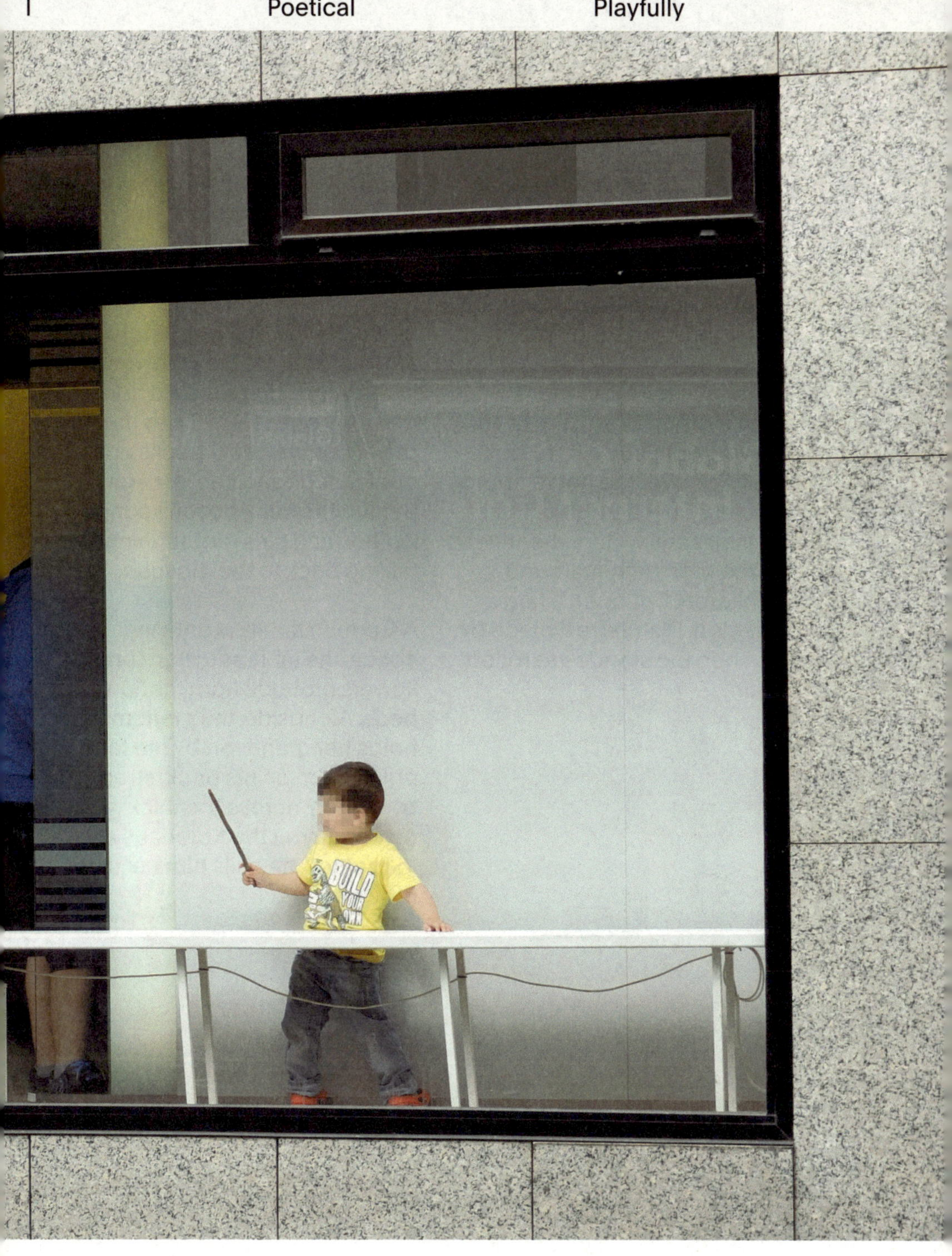
BUILD
YOUR
OWN

At the Zollhafen a young man
with a brown jacket is sitting in the
high, wiry grass. The loud street
noises intrude right up to the dike.
A mild evening wind blows from
the west. He is singing. Plays a
tune with his guitar to accompany
it. At twilight. Apparently silent.

At Rotenhäuser Feld in the
evening a group of Muslim men
are playing volleyball. Barefoot.
The ball flies over the net to improvised rules. On the edge of the
game their sons watch attentively.
Later. The men gather around
their children. Cut open a large
watermelon. Distribute it piece by
piece. Then the stands are rolled
up again.

It is Sunday, a silver Mercedes
drives slowly on the tree-lined
footpath. Behind the car run
a dozen young women and girls
laughing, talking on Rotenhäuser
Feld. In the meadow they play
football in their long dresses and
headscarves. The ball flies high
and far. Their clothes blowing
in the wind. There are no goals
and only one team? Then the
driver comes back; packs up the
cooler bags and carpets again.
Behind the car a dozen young
women and girls run laughing and
talking back to the mosque.

A German family is drinking
coffee, the table set. High summer
flowers protrude from the flower
beds. Alongside, the grandmother
holds her grandson by the feet,
pulling him on his back, stretch
by stretch, across the thick grass,
on Sunday, at the Rotehaus allotments. She calls him her lawn-
mower.

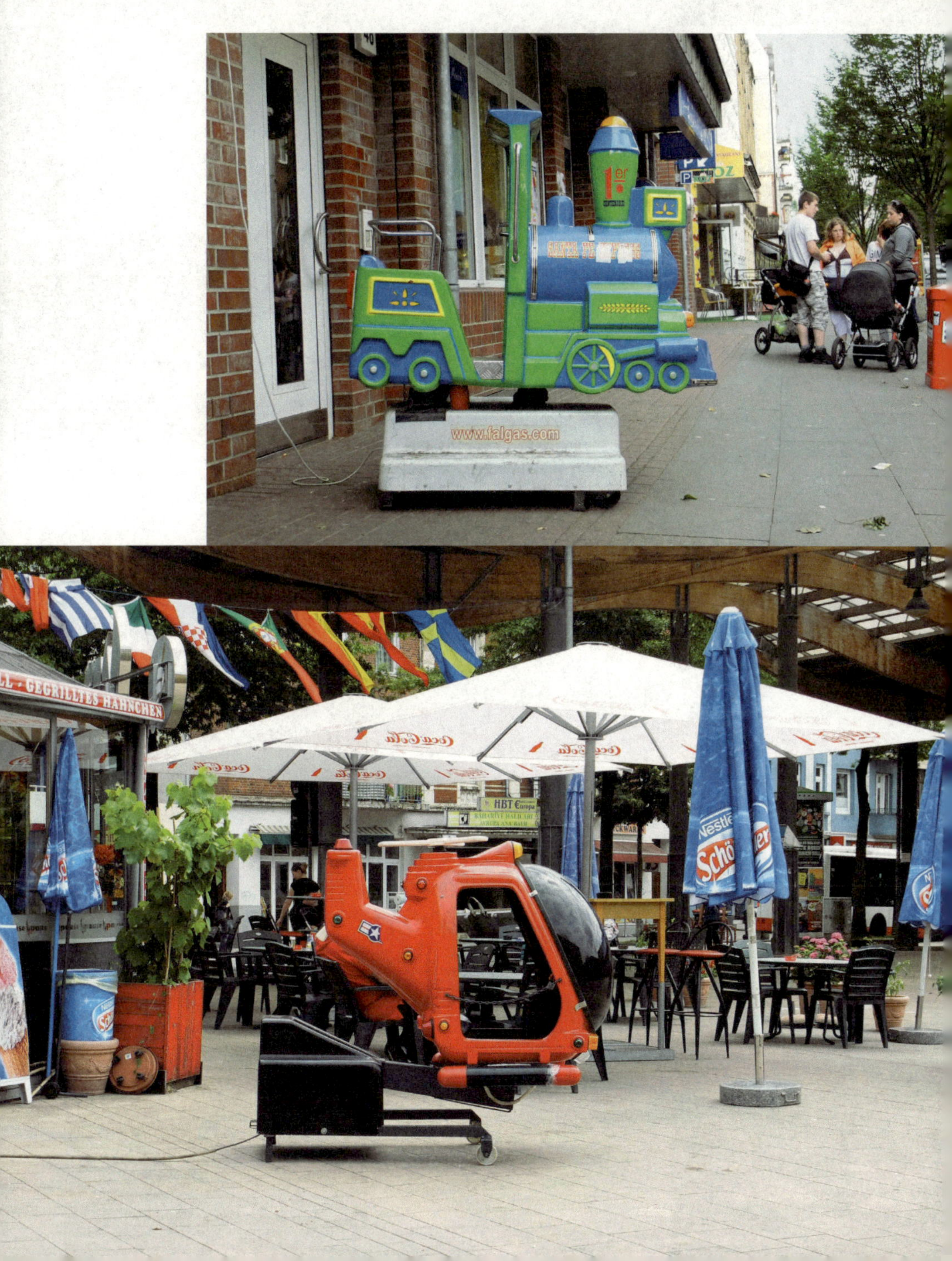

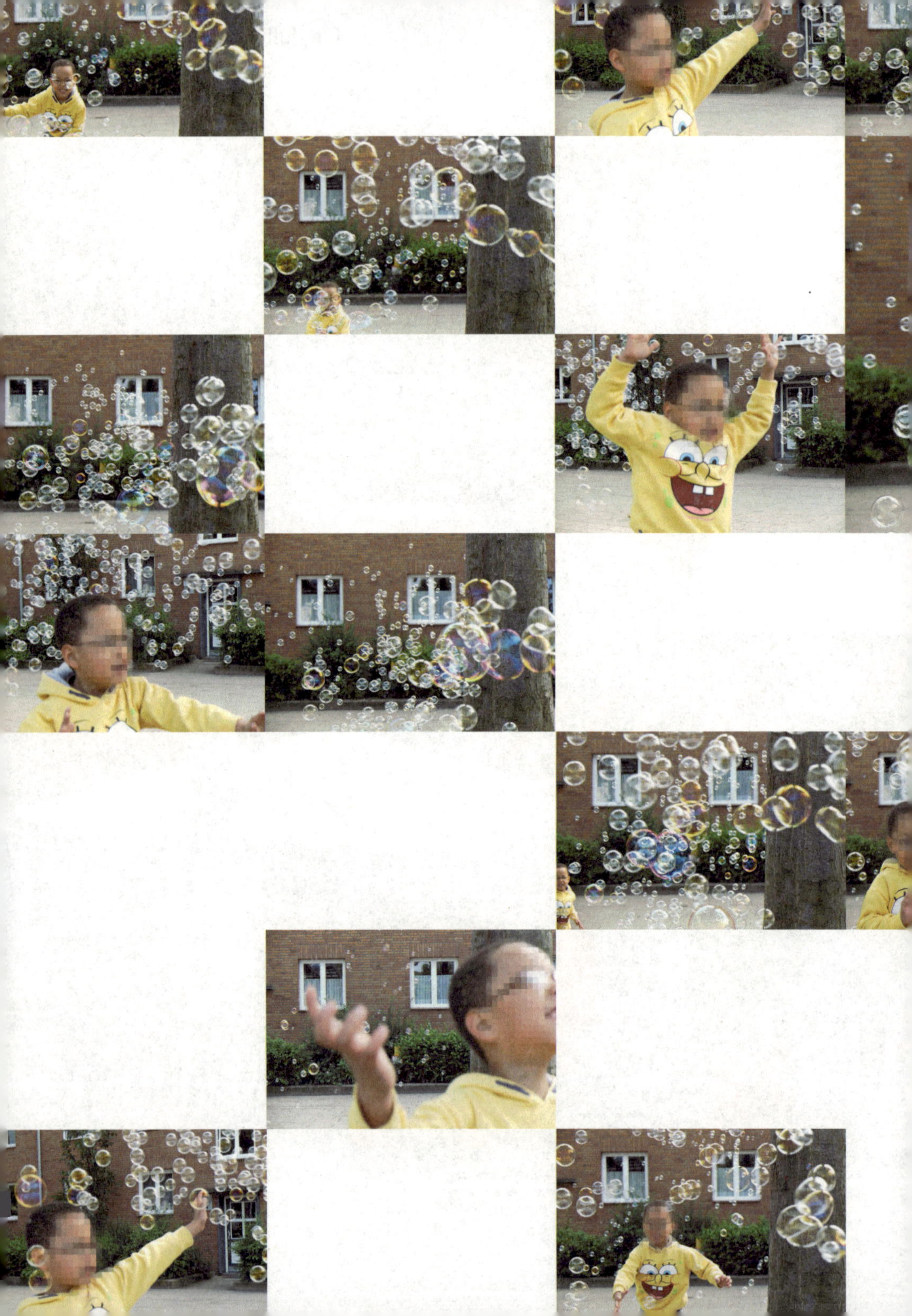

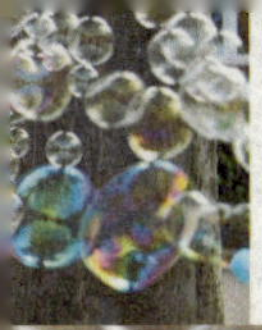

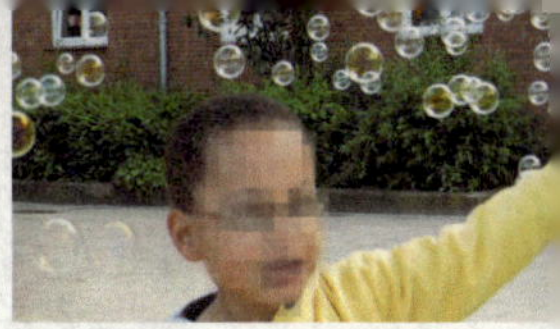

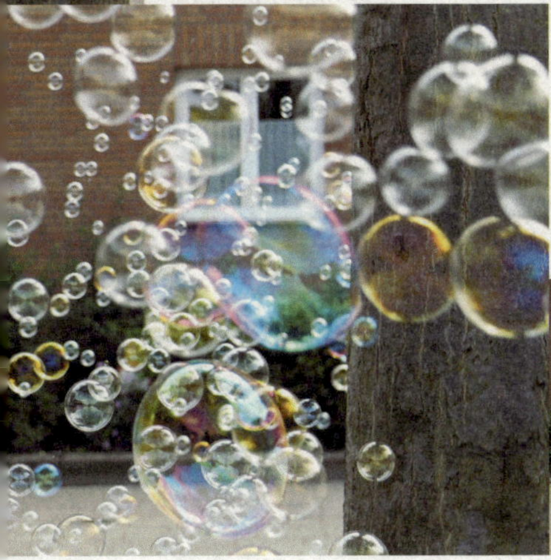

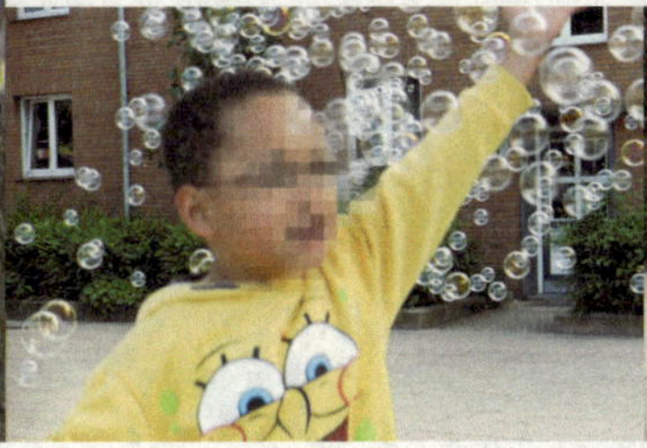

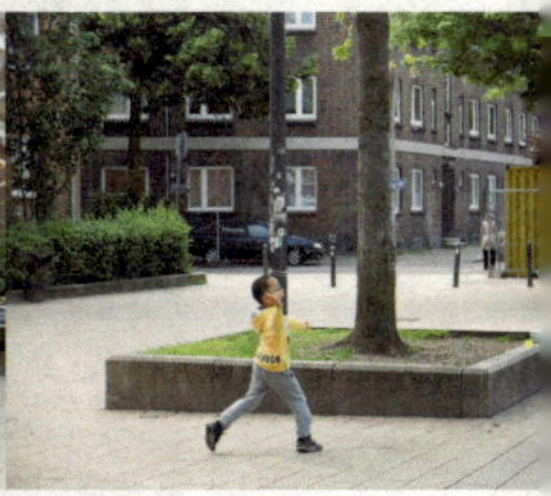

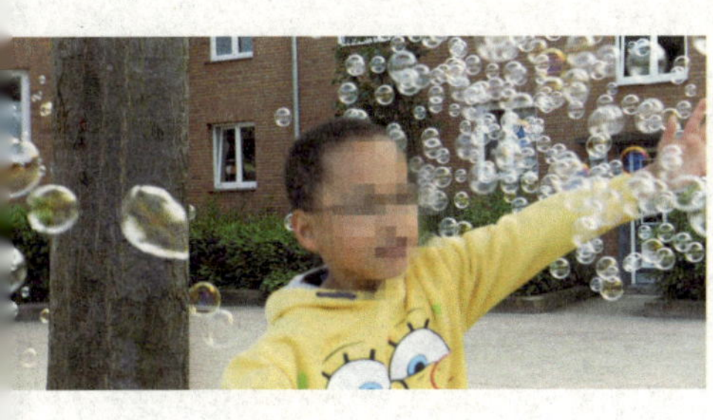

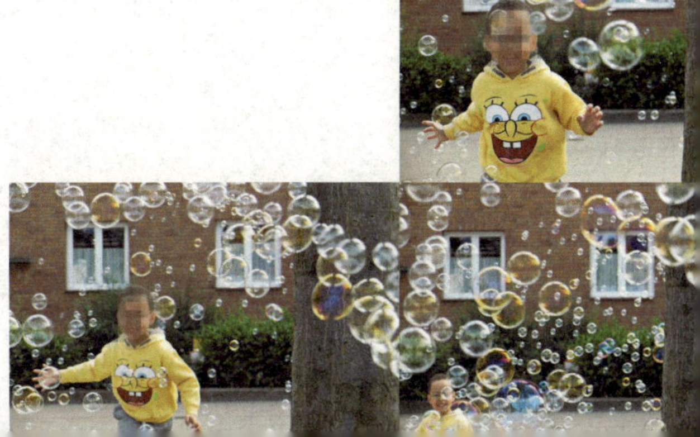

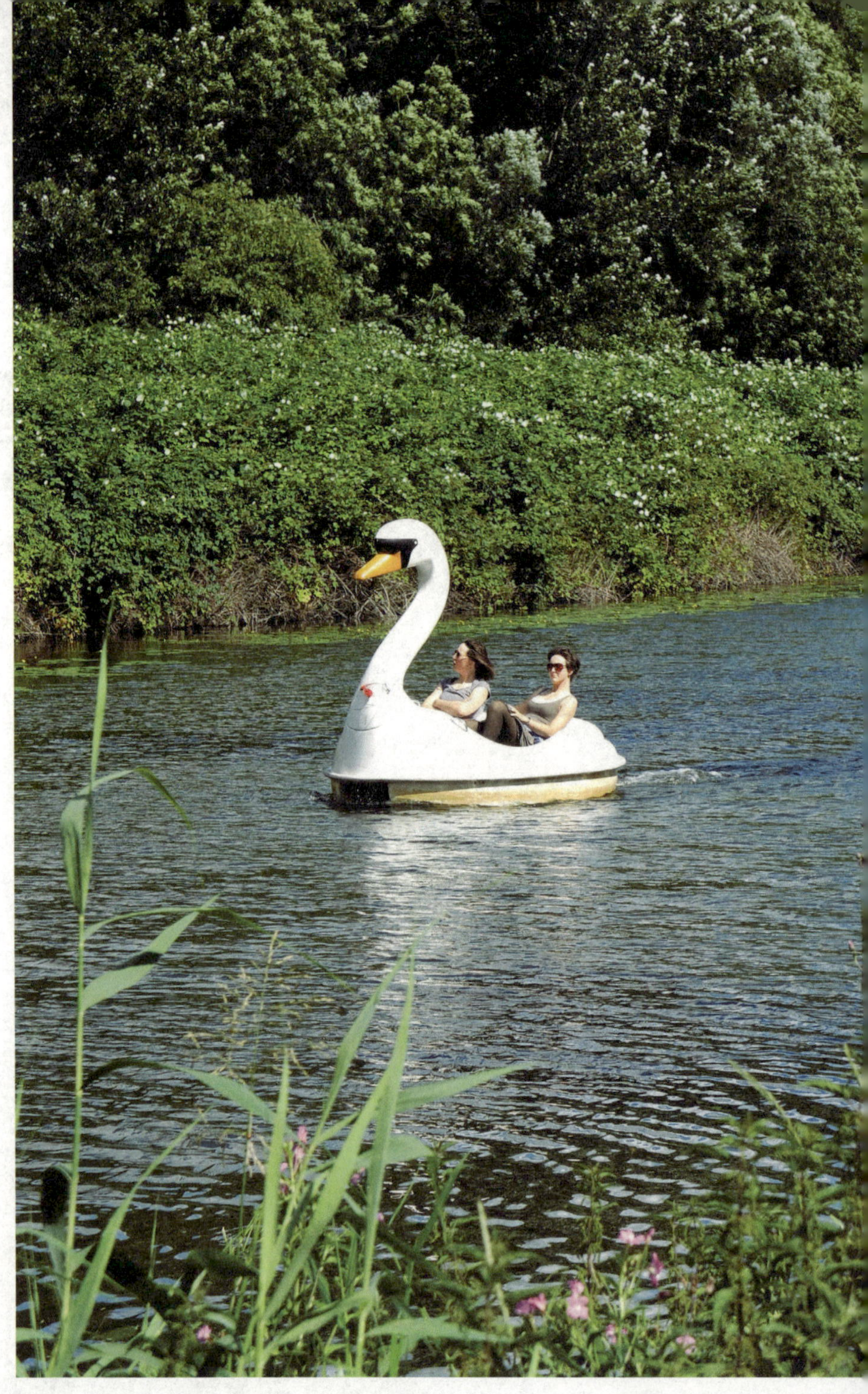

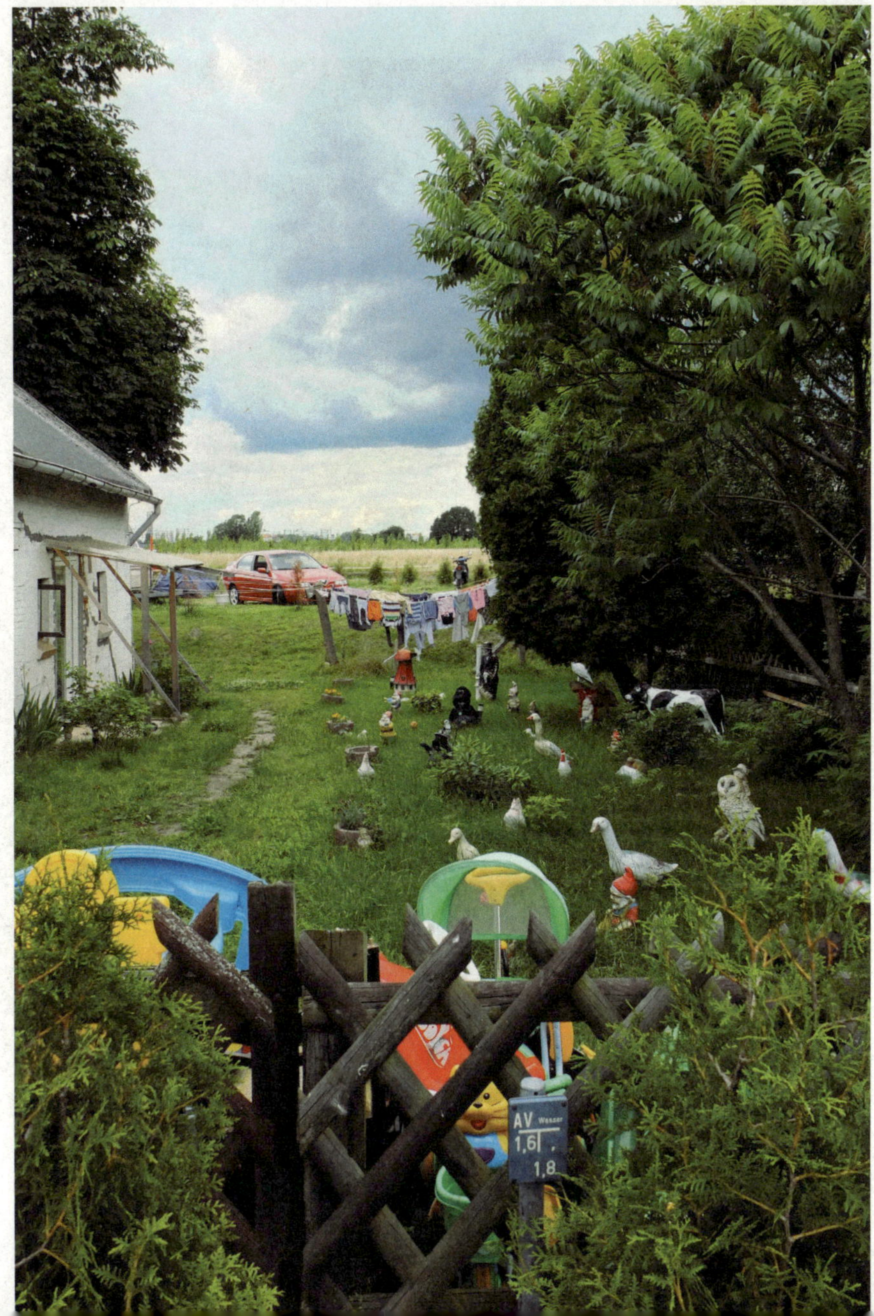

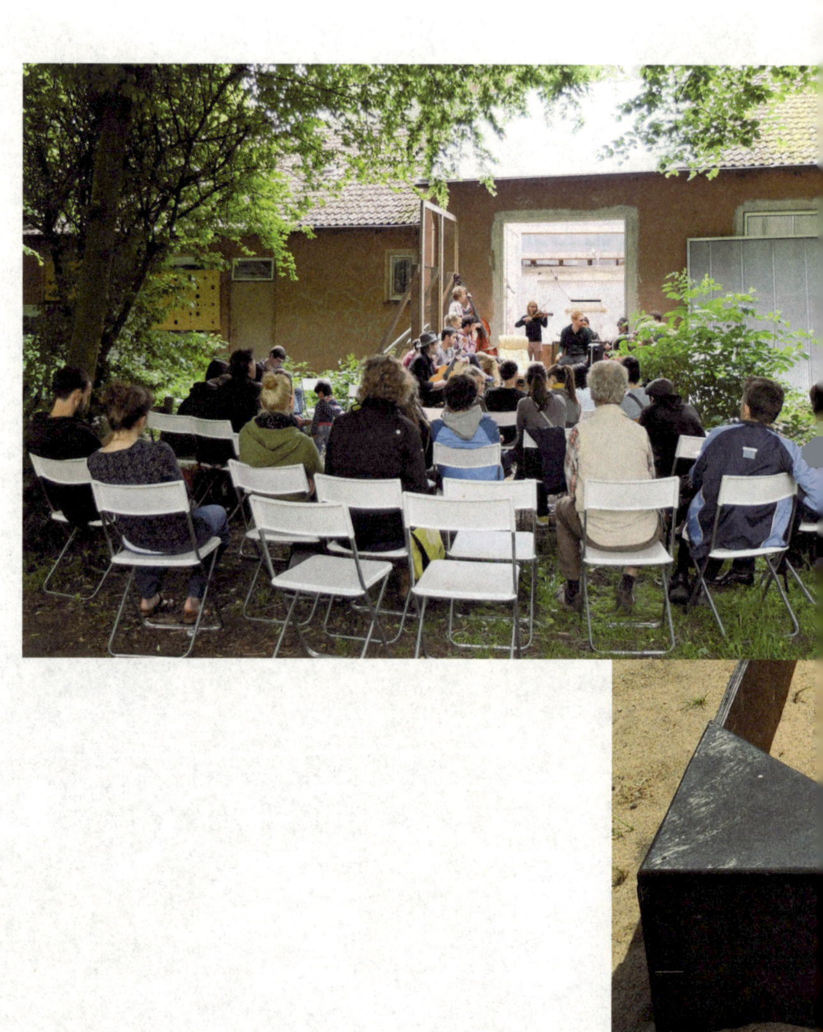

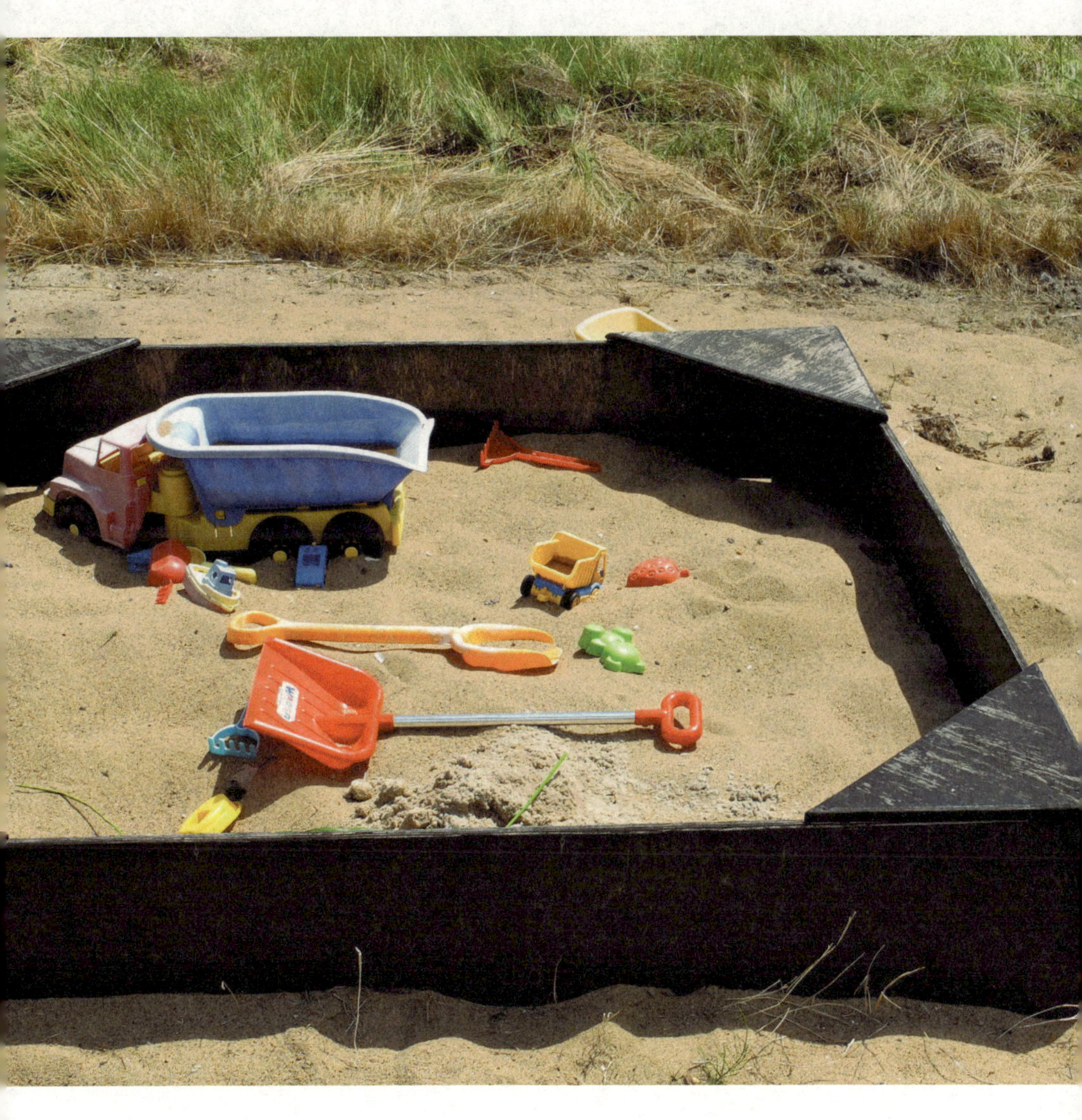

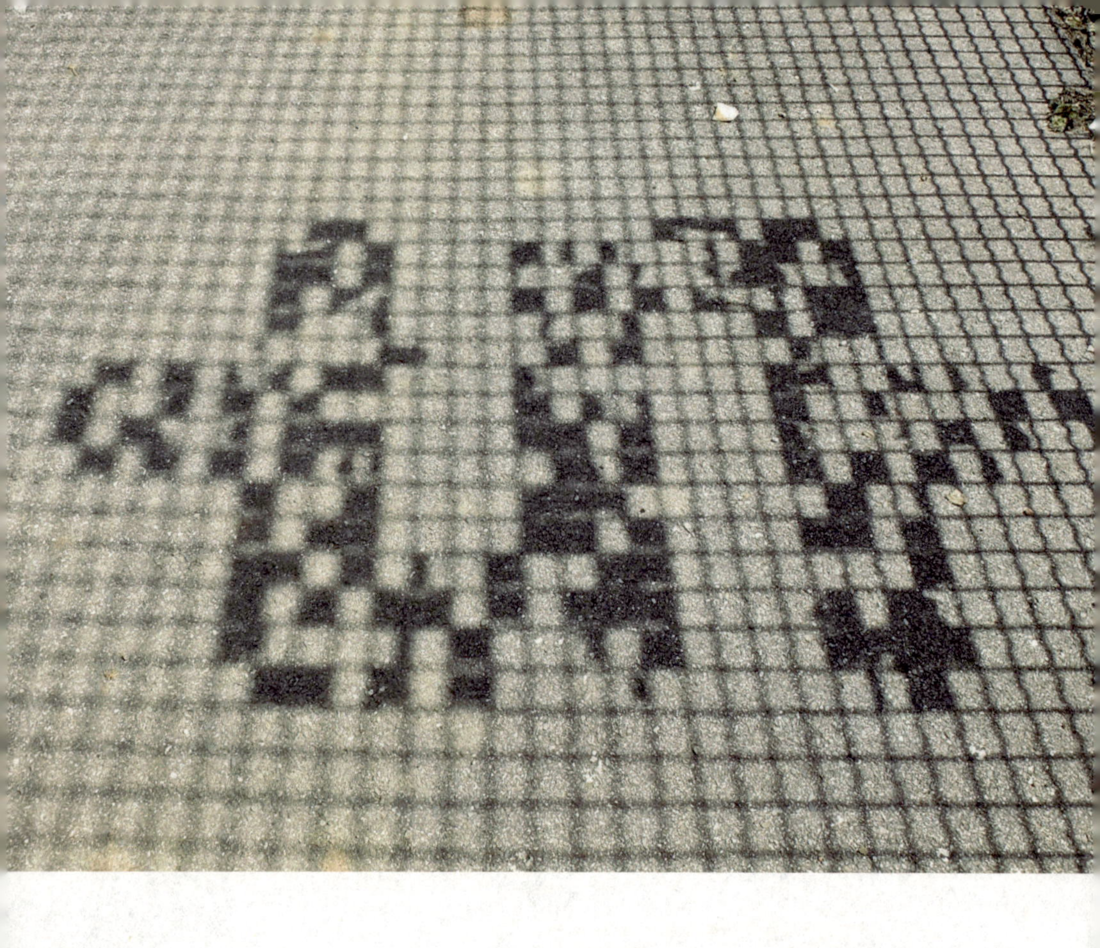

No Dike, No Land
[In-vivo code]

The Brock landscape (Brock, Low German: marsh, swamp) evolved over several centuries from an archipelago of islands to today's urban Elbe Islands │Change-Comma-Pause│. Through human intervention, the form of the Elbe Islands was continuously shaped transformed. Without the dykes and their sophisticated drainage and irrigation system, this cultural landscape would not exist. It is thanks to these land engineering measures that living space and housing could be created, livelihoods secured (initially through fertile arable land). At the same time the dikes have determined social and political coexistence, as well as economic growth, from the beginning. The probably fifteen or sixteen individually reclaimed areas were developed due to the territorial and profit interests of the islands' rulers (cf. Geschichte Alt-Wilhelmsburg). In 1333 in Stillhorn, the first dikes were created by conscripted peasants from neighboring islands │Life and Business│. As a reward they were given a piece of land and established, as so-called "Höfner," their farms along the dikes │Greunhöker│. As "dike oath-givers" they had to carry out "dike duty." At regular intervals they had to check and repair the dike sections (cables) assigned to them (Wilhelmsburger Geschichtswerkstatt, 2008: 17ff). The "dike load" (maintenance costs) had to be paid by the "Höfner." Only extraordinary dike loads after large storm surges could be shared with the populace in general, since many livelihoods were dependent on the stability of dikes. Maintenance was however very time-consuming and costly, particularly parallel to farming the fields and arable land. In order to avoid this responsibility, the "Höfner" leased areas by the dikes to later arrivals, the "Kötner" (lessees) or "Häuslinge" (day laborers). For the settlers from lower social classes, these contracts often meant financial ruin (ibid.: 18ff). Later, "dike associations" of elected "dike oath-givers" and the presiding "dike steward" regulated the maintenance of the embankments (cf. "Die Ratten hatten den Deich unterwühlt," in Wilhelmsburger Zeitung 1954). Today it is mainly grazing flocks of sheep that carefully and tirelessly maintain this collective good.

„Wir ziehen da nicht wieder ein!"

Flutgeschädigte Mieter organisierten sich

m Montag trafen sich etwa dreißig Mieter aus den Häusern
Ernst-August-Deich im Wilhelmsburger Ortsamt. Es handelte
um Personen, die in den Erdgeschoß-Wohnungen des Häuser-
ks am Ernst-August-Deich leben und denen die diesjährige
am übelsten mitspielte: Sie können ihre Wohnungen derzeit
t benutzen.

e meisten von ihnen kamen bei
andten und Freunden unter, so
nur wenige Personen im Not-
tier in der Schule Fährstraße
cht suchen mußten. Doch wie
es weiter?

n eine Antwort auf diese Frage
ekommen, suchte man geschlos-
in Gespräch mit Ortsamtsleiter
ann Westphal, der sich bereits
end der Flut ein Bild von den
hungen am Ernst-August-Deich
cht hatte.

rnächtigt und sehr erregt, rede-
ie Betroffenen zunächst wahl-
urcheinander. Erst als sich die
üter etwas beruhigt hatten,
te Westphal mit einigen Infor-
onen dienen. Westphal: „Ich
Ihnen kein Geld geben, ich
auch nichts anordnen — ich
die Weisungen des Senats ab-
en. Seien Sie aber versichert,
alle zuständigen Stellen über
Lage in Kenntnis gesetzt wor-
sind." Verständlich der Unmut
Mieter, denen bei jedem Hoch-
er der Keller vollläuft (im Jahre
fünfmal) und bei denen das
er diesm
in der
liegt vor
weder E
in der v
alten, noc
Nach läng
Westph
Essen in
serviere
geeigne
der Jug

stätte) Sorge zu tragen. Ebenso be-
stehe die Möglichkeit, die Betroffenen für „obdachlos" zu erklären und
dann für eine zumutbare Übernach-
tungsmöglichkeit zu sorgen (Hotel).

Die Mieter vom Ernst-August-
Deich wissen, daß dies nur eine vor-
übergehende Lösung für die nächsten Tage darstellt. Ihr Anliegen ist
daher auch „längerfristig": Die Interessengemeinschaft der Betroffenen erklärt die Wohnungen zu Recht
für „unbewohnbar" und erhebt die
Forderung nach **neuen** Wohnungen.
Hier verwies Westphal wieder auf
den Senat, der sich zunächst mit dem
Hausbesitzer (der Häuserblock am
Ernst-August-Deich gehört einem
Privatmann) in Verbindung setzen
müsse, um Rechtsfragen abzuklären.

Den Betroffenen wurde zugesagt,
der Senat werde noch im Laufe des
Tages Antwort geben auf die Forderungen der Interessengemeinschaft,
(„Wo sollen wir hin? Für wie lange?
Wer entschädigt uns?") Man will gemeinsam darauf warten, denn nur
der Senat kann entscheiden.

Bleibt zu hoffen, daß der Bescheid

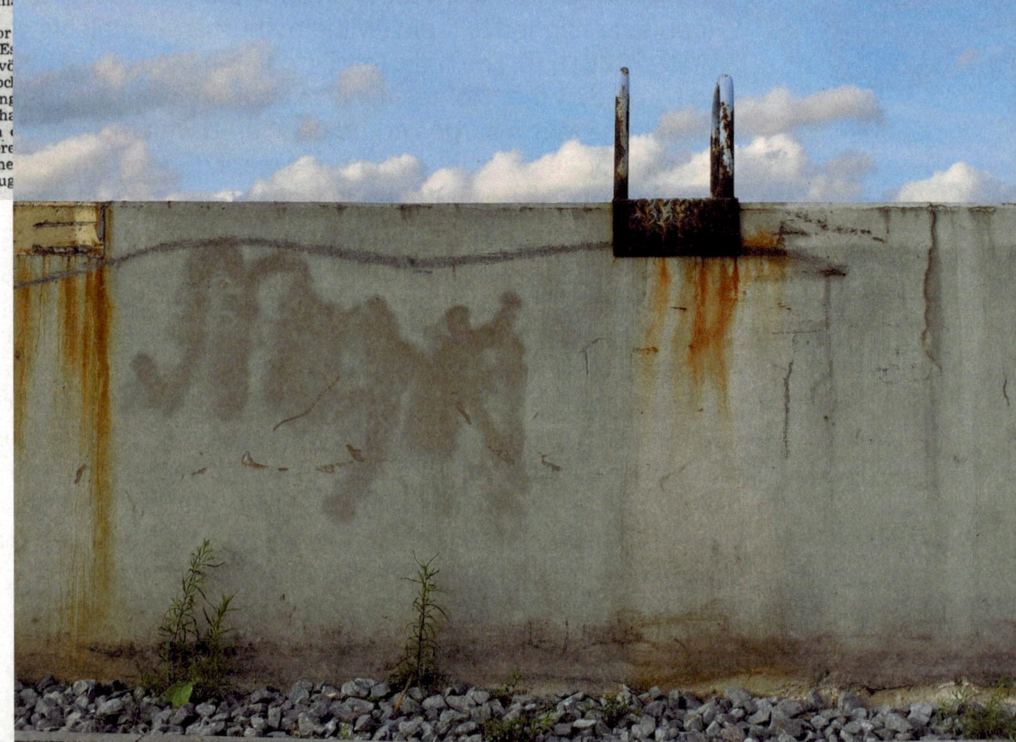

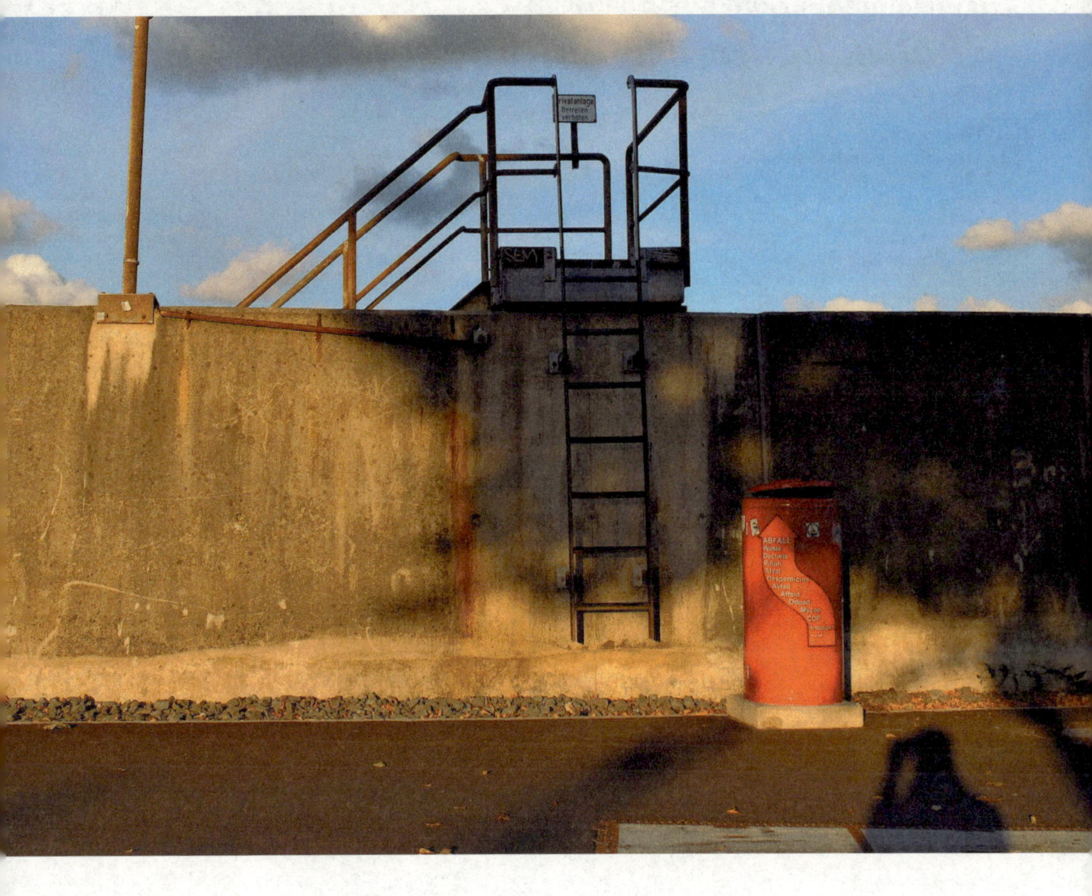

Ratten hatten den Deich unterwühlt

Deichvogt, Deichgeschworene, Anlieger und nicht zuletzt die freiwilligen Feuerwehren aus Kirchdorf und Moorwerder befanden sich Sonnabend und Sonntag in höchster Alarmbereitschaft. Am Finkenriek waren es offenbar Ratten gewesen, die sich im Deich Gänge gegraben hatten und dadurch den hochgehenden Wassern Angriffsflächen boten, die sehr leicht zu einer Katastrophe für die gesamte Elbinsel hätten ausarten können. Dem Deichvogt Adolf C o r d e s wurde von den Anliegern in Finkenriek rechtzeitig bei seiner Kontrollfahrt durchsickerndes Wasser gemeldet. Die sofort in die Wege geleiteten Maßnahmen in Zusammenarbeit mit Deichverband, Polizei und Feuerwehr bewahrten die Elbinsel vor dem Schlimmsten.

Als in den Mittagsstunden des Sonnabends die Autobusse der HHA-Linie 54 kurz vor der Veddel bereits durch Wasser fahren mußten und vorübergehend die Fahrgäste der Bundes-bahn vor dem Bahnhof Veddel die Feuerwehr bemühen mußten, um trockenen Fußes die Züge zu erreichen, da sah mancher Bürger auch einmal auf den außerordentlich hohen Wasserstand der Elbe und des Zoll-Kanals. Hochwasser-Böller-Schüsse wiesen schließlich auch die restliche Bevölkerung bei dem orkanartigen Sturm darauf hin, daß in Hamburg außerordentliches Hochwasser hatte. Unheimlich heulten im Wilhelmsburger Osten dann noch die Sirenen zum Einsatz der freiwilligen Feuerwehren dazu.

Fast auf den Tag ist es 98 Jahre her, daß Wilhelmsburg seine letzten großen Deichbruch-Katastrophen erlebte. 1855 brachen die Deiche an mehreren Stellen und die Fluten überspülten die gesamte Elbinsel. Das Brack am Sperlsdeich ist Zeuge dieser Unglücksnacht. Als danach scharfer

(Fortsetzung siehe nächste Seite)

Frost einsetzte, war ganz W[...]burg wochenlang eine einzige [...]de Eisfläche. Erst nach und n[...] lief sich nach Einsetzen von [...]ter das Wasser wieder.

Nur die alteingesessenen W[...]burger, die ihre Häuser unr[...] hinter dem Deich haben, wiss[...] von ihren Vorfahren von der [...]ren, die Sturmfluten und Dei[...] heraufbeschworen haben. N[...] eingangs erwähnten letzten U[...] nacht im Jahre 1855 brachte [...] Deiche auf ihre heutige Höhe [...] stärkte sie. Seitdem ist die Ins[...] von größeren Unglücken versc[...] blieben.

Während seiner Kontrollfah[...] mierten Anlieger in Finkenr[...] Deichvogt Adolf C o r d e s [...] daß dort der Deich Wasser du[...] An Ort und Stelle überzeug[...] die Herren des Deichverban[...] Feuerwehr und Polizei davo[...] hier offenbar Ratten den Deic[...] höhlt hatten. Dadurch wurd[...] Fluten Angriffsflächen preisg[...] Sie hätten bei Nichtbeachtu[...] Schutzdamm zerstört und die [...] hätten ungehindert ins Hinterl[...] fließen können. Sofort traf ma[...] forderlichen Maßnahmen. Zum [...] mal heulten die Sirenen ihr [...] liches Lied und die Männer a[...] machten sich daran, das gese[...] Loch zu stopfen. Das mißlang i[...] als das zur gefährdeten Ste[...] förderte Material fortwährend [...] von den Wassern fortgesc[...] wurde. In Zusammenarbeit [...] Stackmeisterei Moorwerder [...] man bis Sonntag insgesamt [...] füllte Sandsäcke bereit und ha[...] die erste Gefahr beseitigen kö[...]

In Götjensort wurden am [...] abend die Bewohner leicht g[...] Wohnlauben aussendeichs v[...] Feuerwehr aus ihren über[...] Heimen geholt. Höher und [...] stieg die Flut und fortwähren[...] die Hochwasser-Böllerschüss[...] Hamburg herüber zu hören. U[...] lich heulte der Orkan über d[...] gelegene Eiland dahin. Dar[...] wann riefen die Sirenen ern[...] Männer der freiwilligen Feue[...] zu gefährdeten Stellen. Tag un[...] waren die Männer auf den Bei[...] sie haben mit ihrem Einsatz [...] insel vor Verheerungen unv[...] baren Ausmaßes bewahrt.

Auch die Vertreter der Be[...] der Polizei, unter ihnen Ortsan[...] S t r a u s s begaben sich na[...] Finkenriek. Mit vereinten Krä[...] es gelungen, das Schlimmste ab[...] den, ohne das die Überzahl d[...] insel-Bewohner sich überhaup[...] unmittelbaren Gefahr bewußt [...] Das Hochwasser erreichte 2,60 [...] normal und stand bis etwa [...] den Deichkronen heran. Die fre[...] Feuerwehr Moorwerder überna[...] Nachtwache zum Sonntag. Du[...] Stackmeisterei Moorwerder wa[...] Hilfstrupps jeweils von den zu[...] tenden Fluten aus Cuxhaven [...] richtet.

Durch den anerkennenswert[...] satz aller Beteiligten ist eine [...] bruchkatastrophe unüberse[...] Ausmaßes verhindert worde[...] unmittelbare Gefahr aber hat [...]

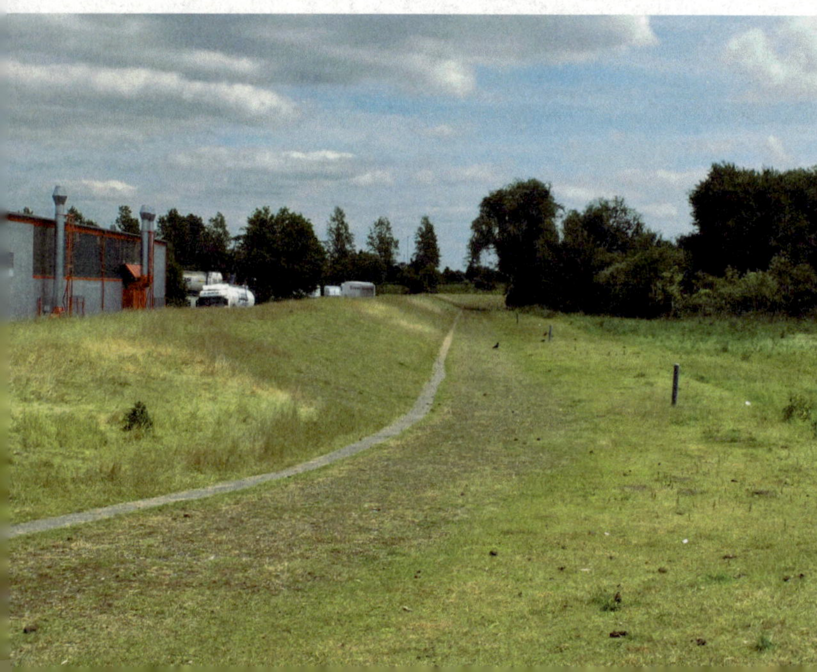

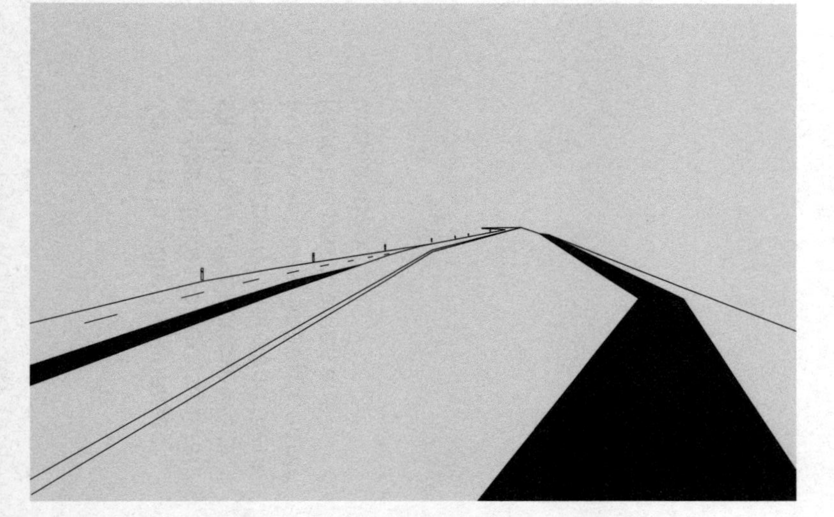

... Immediately this time I find the right path to the dike.
Two Albanian men walk toward me, a young man with a guitar
is sitting on the grass. With a strong wind blowing, it is noisy
up here on top of the dike. At the edge of the embankment, on
the smooth strip of asphalt, a very small girl is learning to
walk. Her mother is only supporting her with one hand. People
are out strolling, flâneurs come toward me. I have almost
reached the lock ...

Several hundred kilometers
of dikes. Dike walkers sauntering,
strolling on the narrow, well-
trodden path — here and there
and over there. Sheep, people.
Here the panoramas are
unbounded.

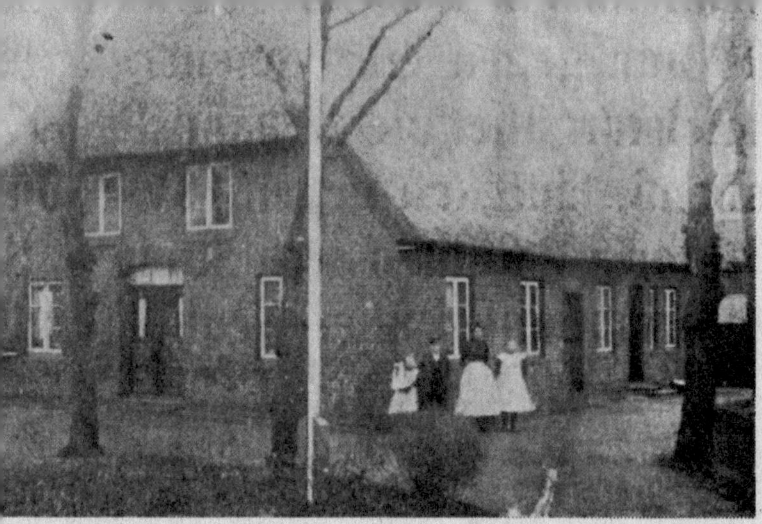

das größere weiße Haus am Hauland an der Reichsstraße steht, stand
s schöne Sieversche Bauernhaus. Vor dem Haus stehen Tante Line und
nseres Erzählers. Damals dachte noch niemand an die Reichsstraße. Die
r dieses Artikels sind so undeutlich, weil sie bei der Flut im Wasser ge-

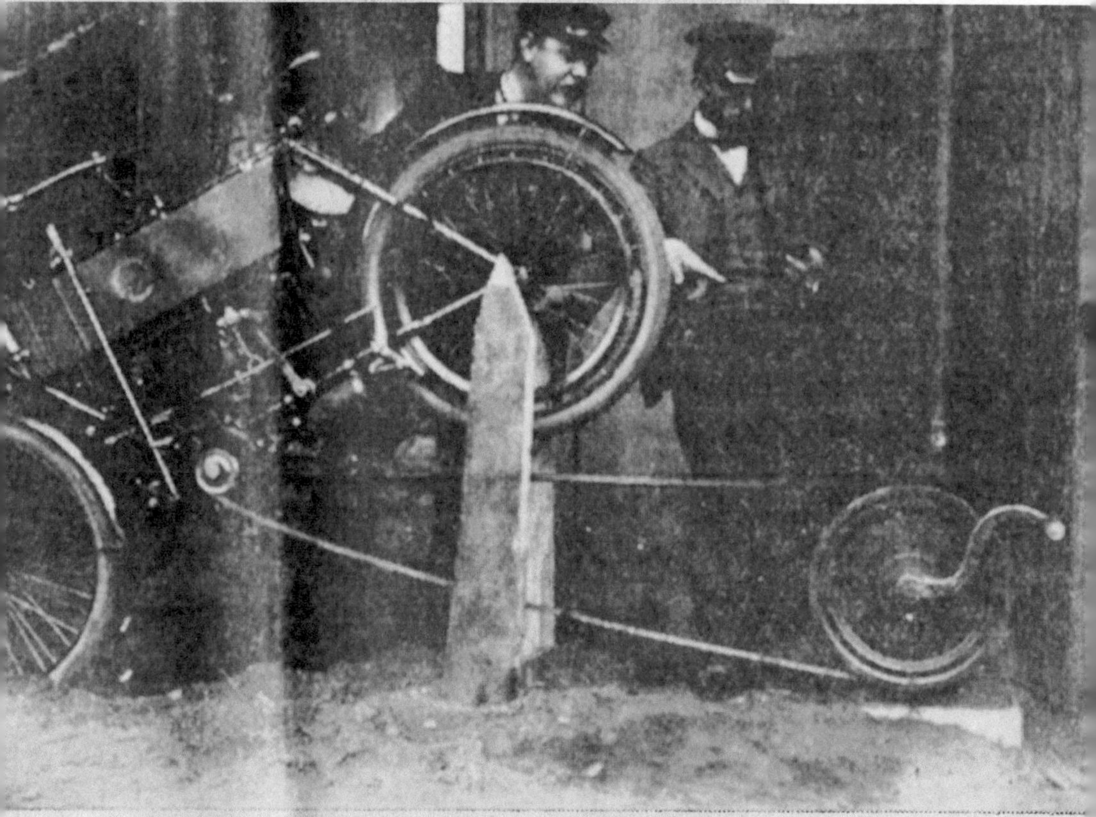

Das Motorrad „zweckentfremdet" als Antrieb für die Wasserpumpe

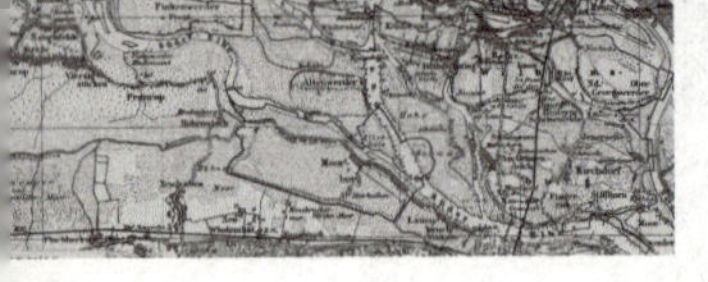

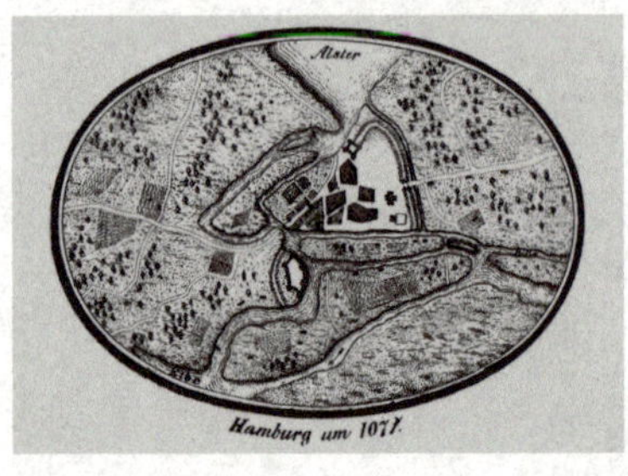

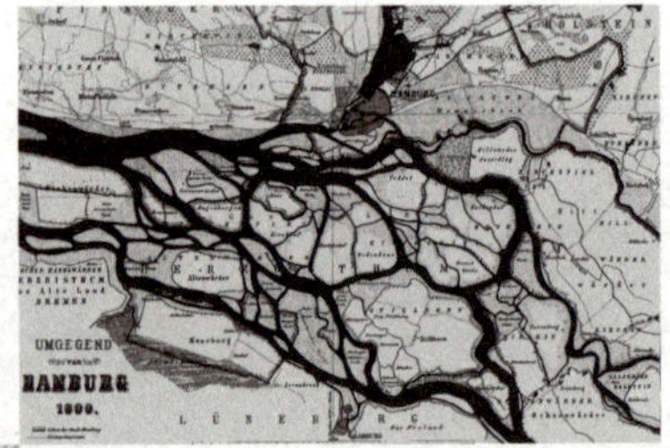

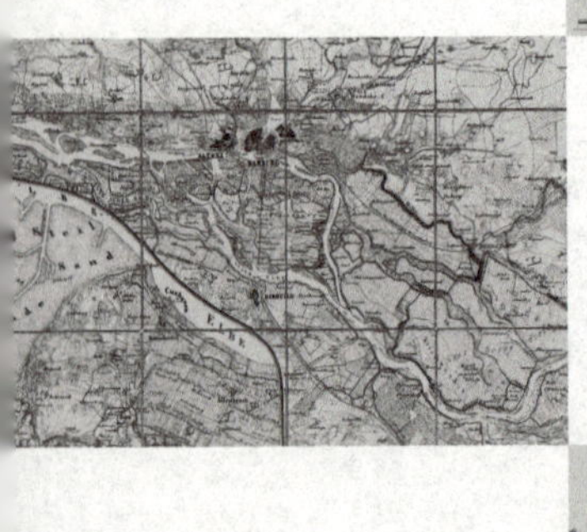

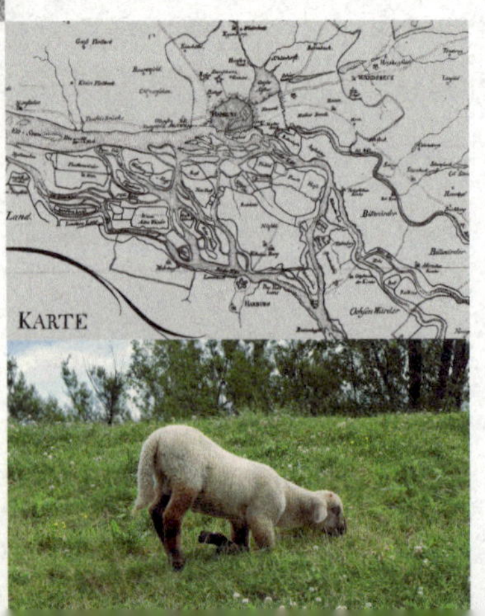

370

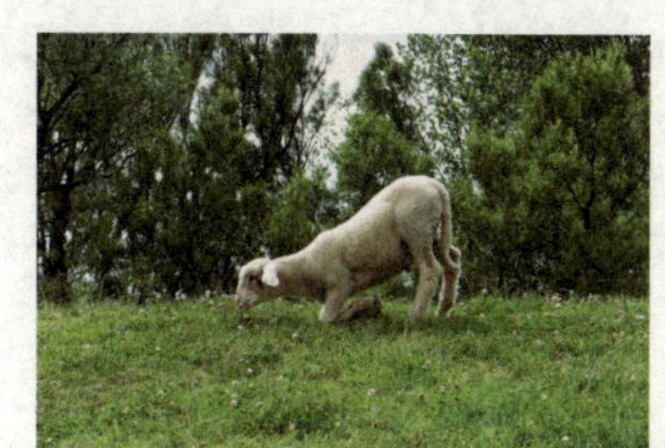

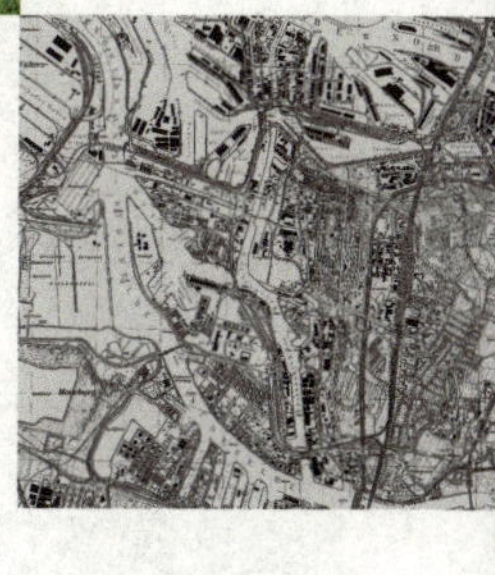

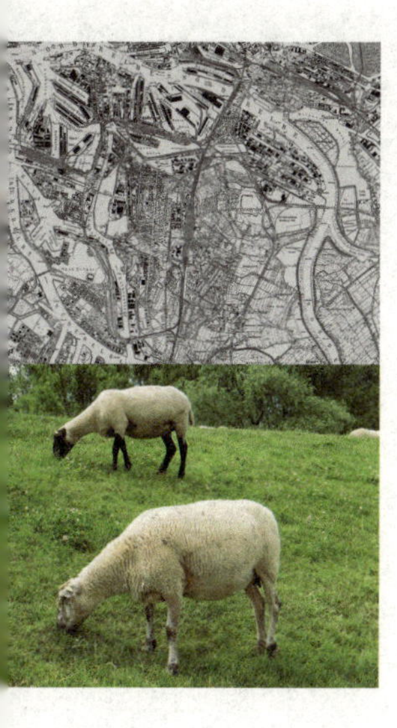

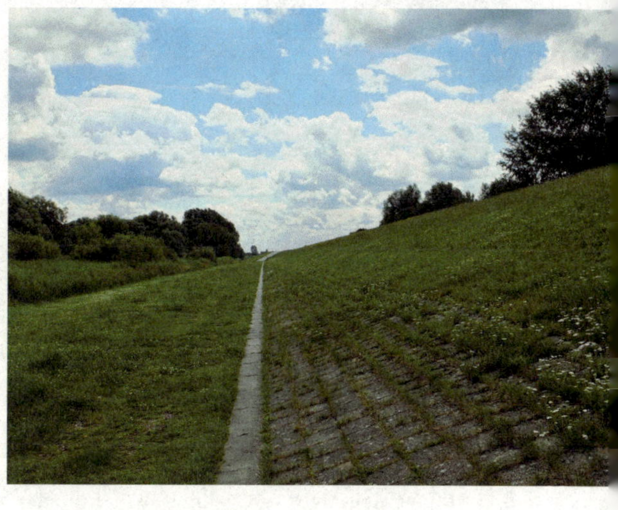

Die schwerste Sturmflut seit Menschengedenken

Wasser war höher als 1962 — Die neuen Deiche bestanden i[hre] Bewährungsprobe — Ungewöhnlich große Schäden im ungesch[ütz]ten Deichvorland — Keine Todesopfer in Wilhelmsburg — Vi[ele] Schaulustige in der Flutnacht — Dank gebührt allen Helfern

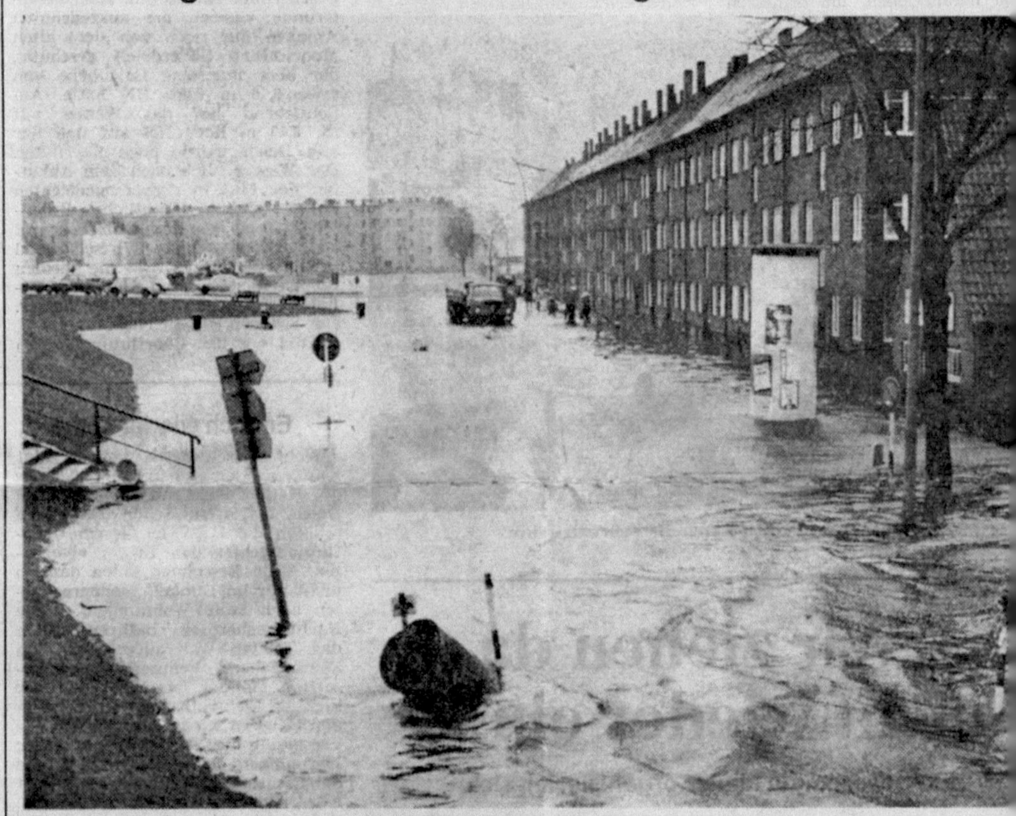

Ernst-August-Deich: Das Wasser stieg und stieg

Wilhelmsburg ist noch einmal davongekommen. Die schwerste Flutkatstrophe seit Menschengedenken mit Wasserständen von 6,40 Metern über NN — das sind 62 Zentimeter mehr als bei der Flutkatastrophe von 1962 — forderte keine Menschenleben. Die von den neuen Hochwasseranlagen geschützten Teile unserer Elbinsel blieben unversehrt. Sehr schwer mitgenommen wurden dagegen die übrigen nicht eingedeichten Gebiete Wilhelmsburgs. Viele Straßen mußten wegen Überflutung gesperrt werden. Auch Neuhof und die gesamte Hohe Schaar sowie Kattwyk standen zeitweilig etwa 1 Meter unter Wasser. An den Hochwasserdeichen und an anderen hochgelegenen Stellen waren viele hundert Pkws und Lkws abgestellt. Viele Schaulustige standen auf den Deichen.

satzfahrzeuge. Es gab mehrere [Un]fälle bei dieser Gelegenheit. [Viele] Wilhelmsburger aus den Üb[erflu]tungsgebieten verließen recht[zeitig] ihre Wohnungen und hielten si[ch bei] Verwandten am sicheren Ort au[f.]

Kirchen waren gut bes[ucht]

Die Gotteshäuser beider Ko[nfes]sionen sowie der Religionsge[mein]schaften wiesen am Sonntagm[orgen] einen außergewöhnlich guten B[esuch] auf. Die Frühmesse in der St. [Bo]fatius-Kirche war überfüllt. Au[ch]

1
As it was envisaged that the port industry would continue to spread across the entire north-west section of the Elbe Islands, the original plan from the 1960s envisaged construction of a further 30,000 homes. However the general cargo port soon changed into a container port. Further housing construction was therefore suspended. The housing estate in Kirchdorf-Süd ultimately comprised 2,200 homes with buildings up to fourteen stories high.

And then the endless pastures, fields, and paddocks begin. The sky and the country are spread out wide, opening to the south. Elbe Islands' panoramas are as far as the eye can see. Intertwined and flowing are greens and blues. Magnificently decorated, thatch-covered farmhouses or horse farms with opulent flower gardens. Greenhouses, vegetable fields, and orchards are arranged in between long ribbons Greunhöker . Sheep, horses, and goats complete the picture of a carefully cherished cultural landscape. Then in contrast, the towering scenery of the large housing estate Kirchdorf Süd on the horizon. It was built as a dormitory and recreation center for port industry workers and their families in the early 1970s. The islanders in particular were reliant on this modern new-build as many houses were destroyed during the 1962 storm surge flooding.[1] This mono-functional architectural style, typical of that time, does not refer in any way at all to its setting. Built on former agricultural land, the estate is withdrawn and introverted vis-à-vis the adjacent residential neighborhood. Ten years after completion, 140 flats were already standing empty. To counteract further vacancies, structural rehabilitation work was carried out for the first time in the mid-1980s. The contrasts, in fairly close proximity, could not be greater. The highway cuts through both realities. I continue to choose the countryside. The rural guesthouse at Moorweder Norderdeich is taking a day off. It is anyway very quiet, very still between the dikes. No wind at all. Few other movers and transporters are out and about Movers and Transporters . My step, my pace slows accordingly. I explore in depth, looking from the top of the dike or up close, the picturesque Elbe Islands of Stillhorn and Moorwerder, both of which came into being as a result of the dike construction in 1333 No Dike, No Land .

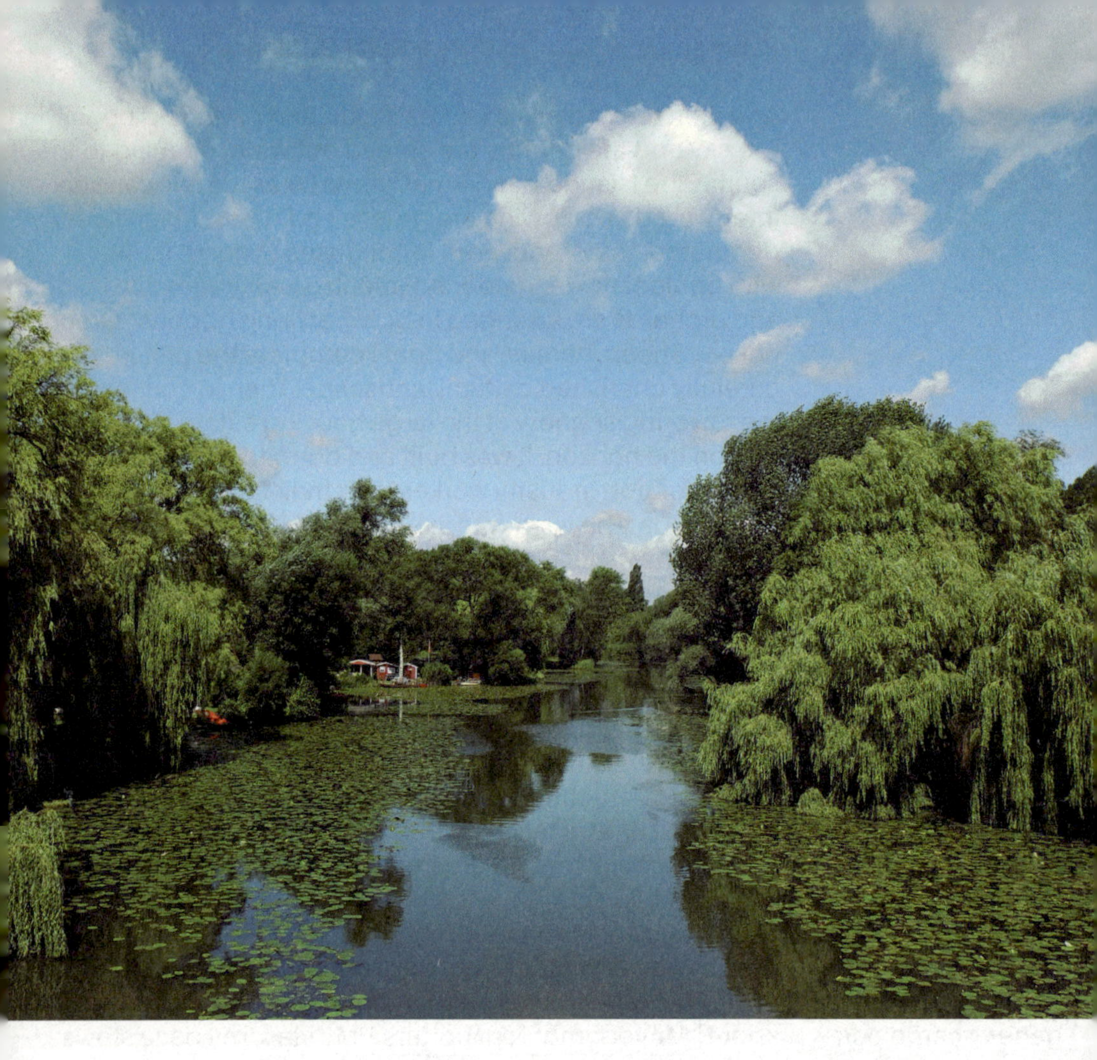

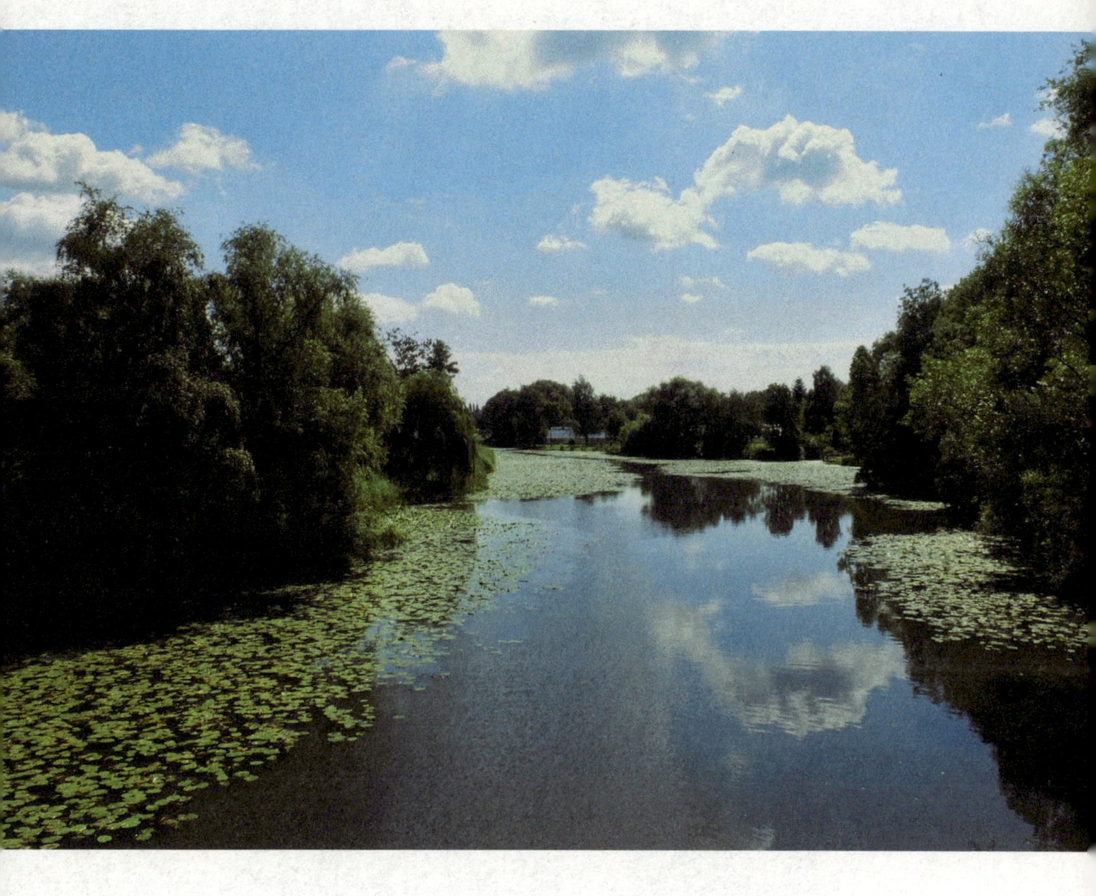

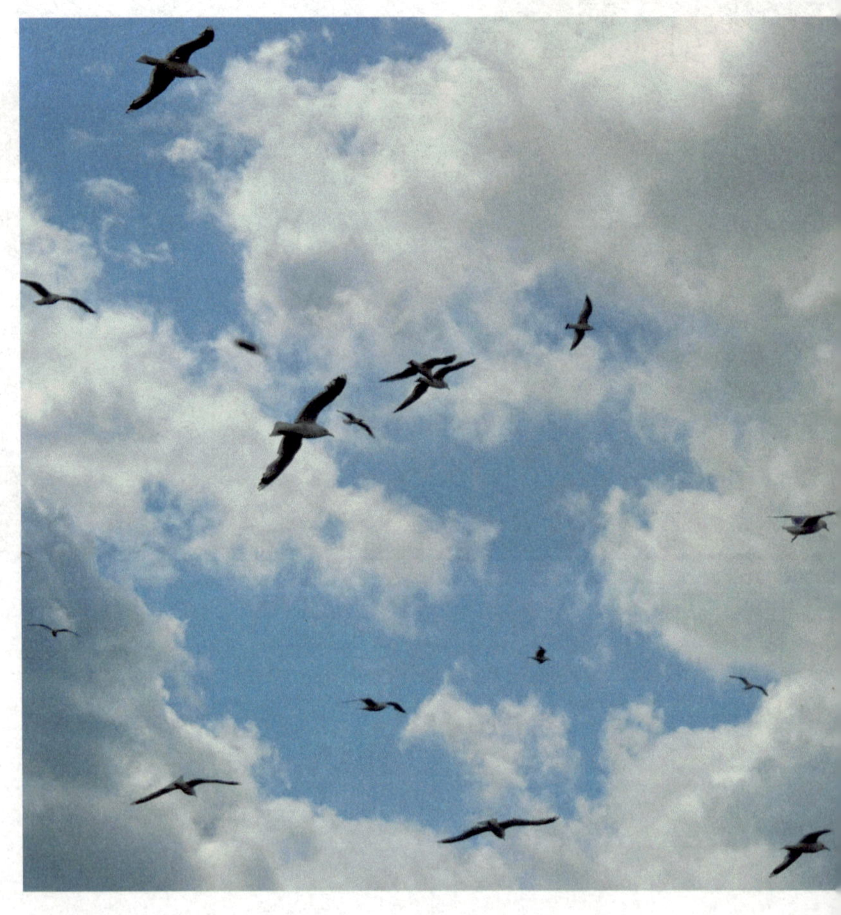

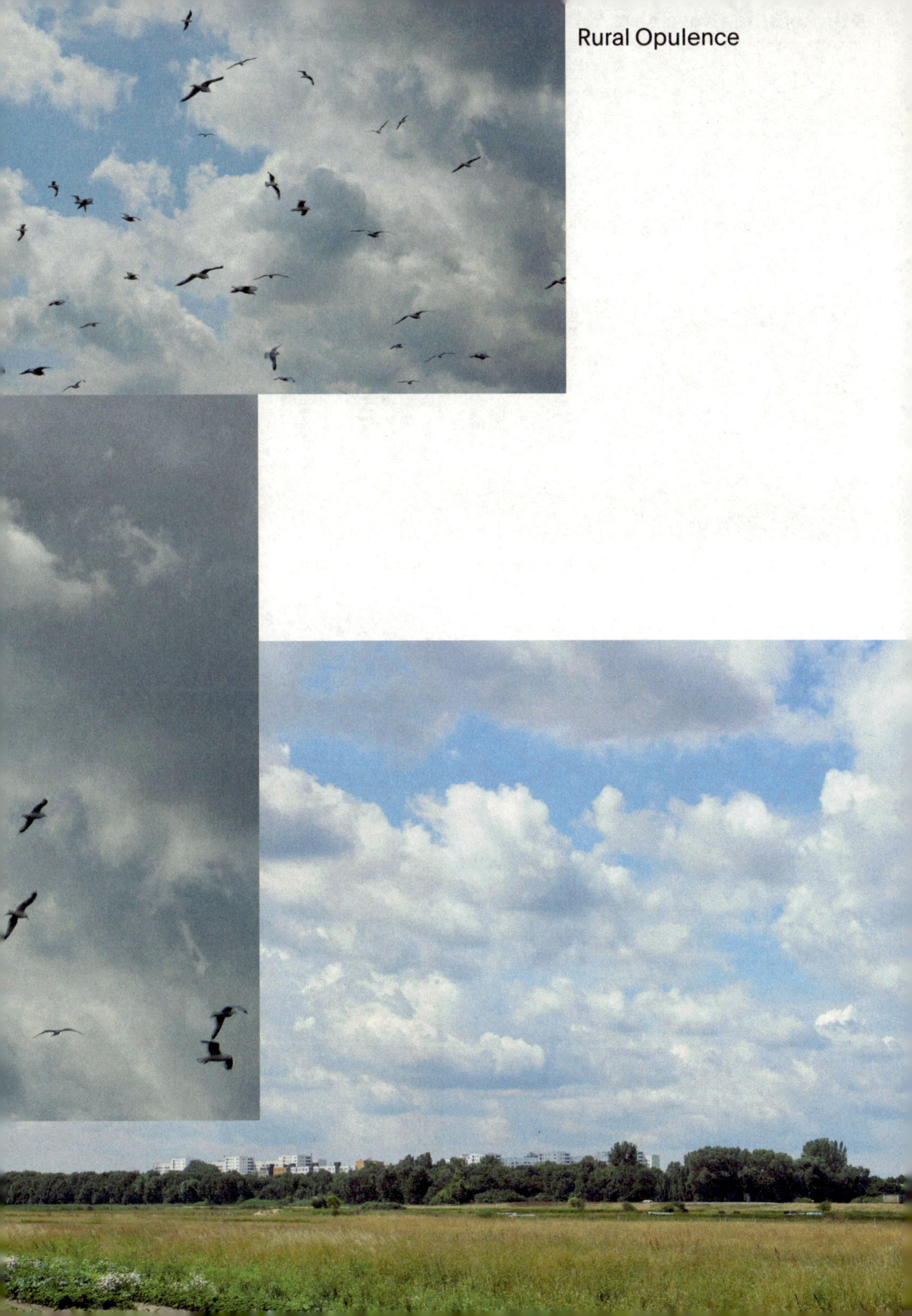
Rural Opulence

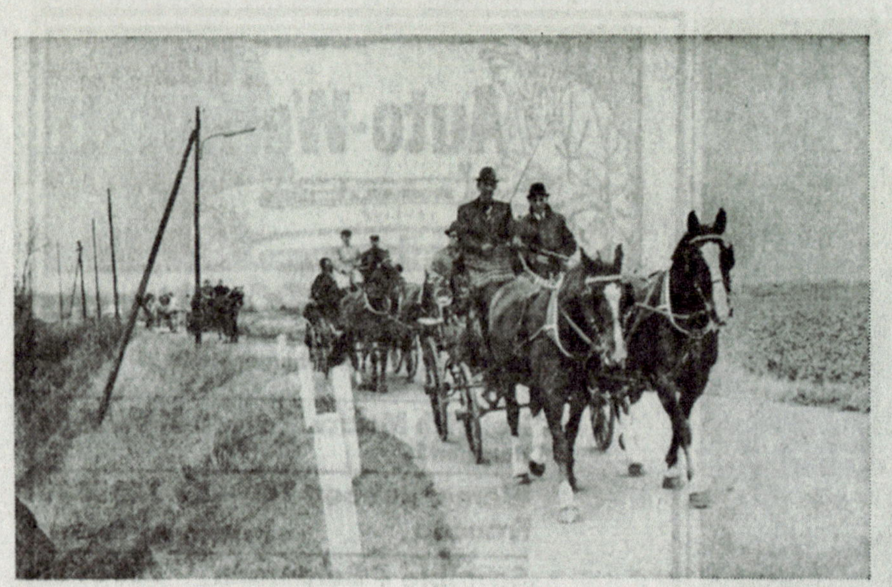

Vielbestaunter Ausflug: Kutschen bei der Fahrt durch Wilhelmsburg   Foto: NISS

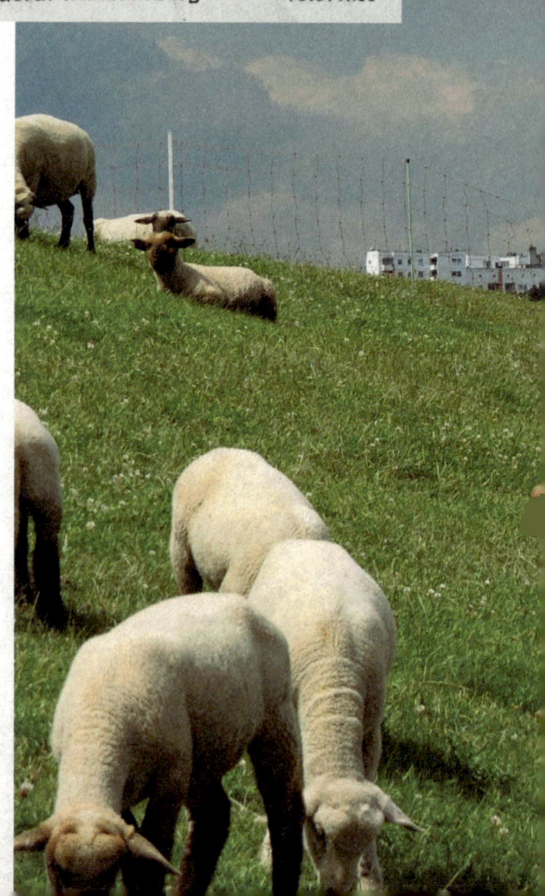

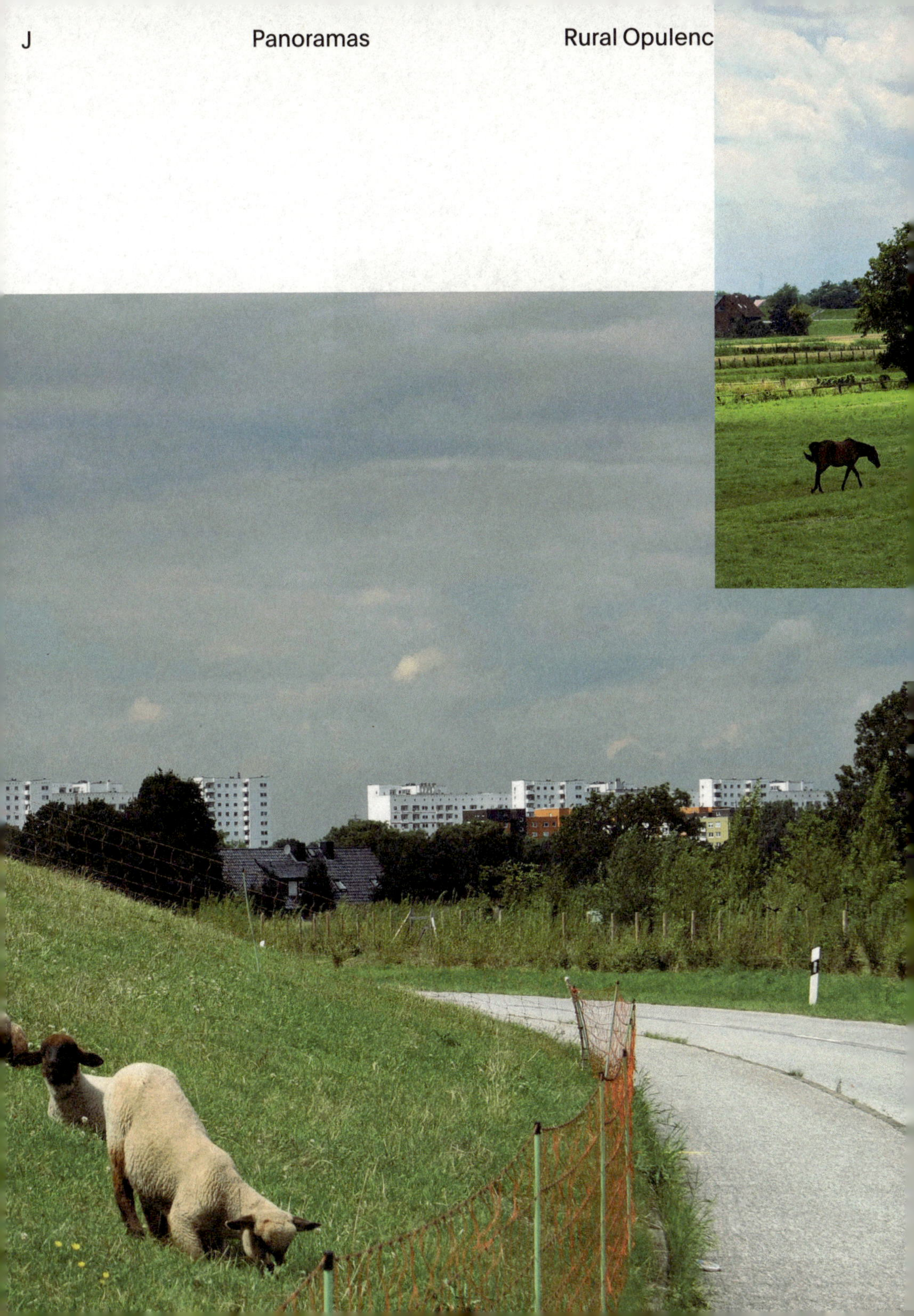

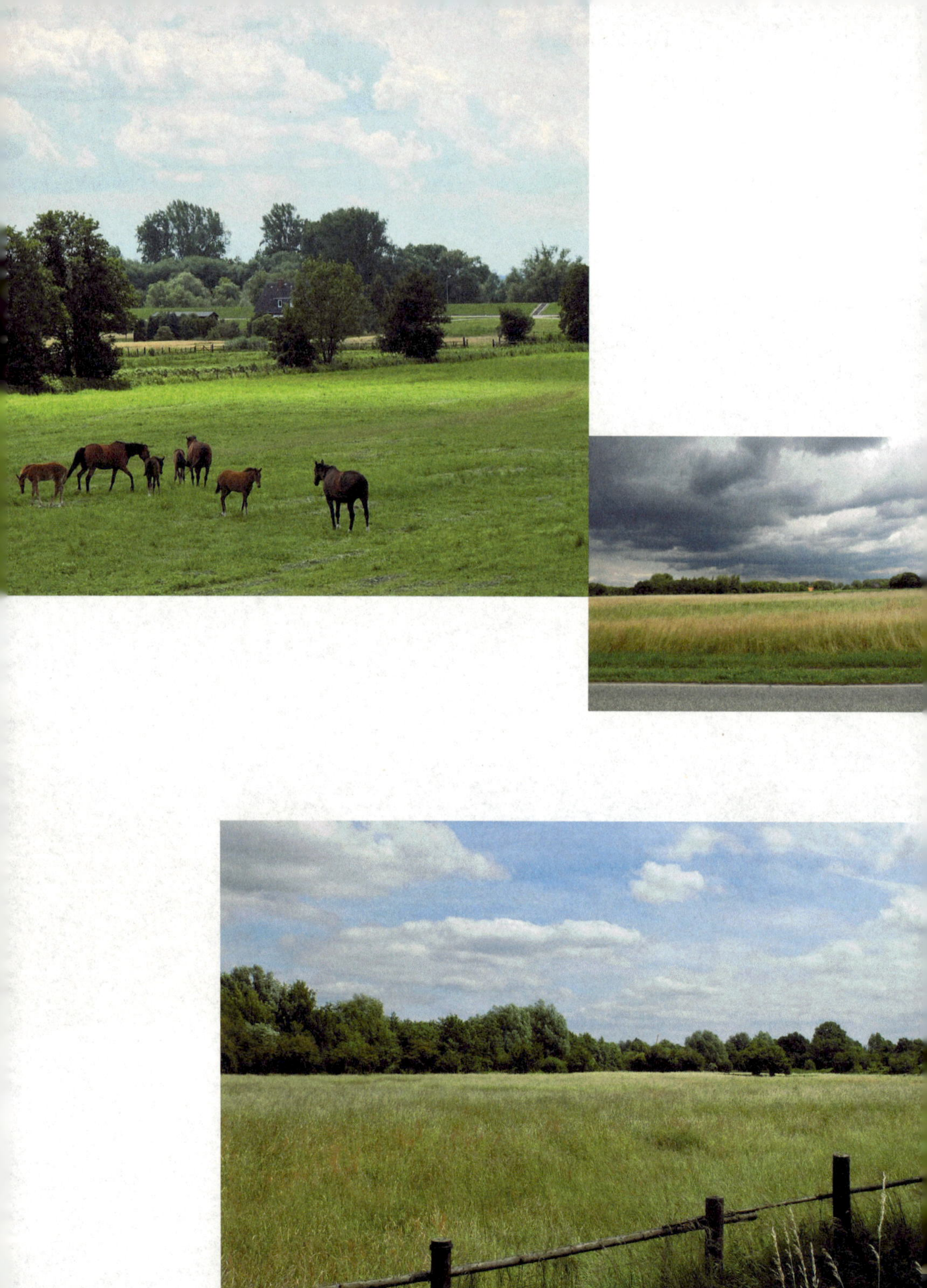

Wide vistas, light, air, and space. Emptiness. Building density. Minimum and maximum dimensions and volumes: container-detached houses, large housing estate. In the midst of this, hidden corners and niches are produced. Panoramas of contrasts and contradictions. Multiplicity. (Un)known realities in the immediate vicinity. Diverse inequalities, idiosyncrasies, and similarities. Warehouses, store rooms, transshipment points for goods, knowledge, and everyday practices. Seclusion or proximity? Being forgotten or waiting for? Gray-bright, hot-cold, gruff-charming, dismissive-inviting. Rejecting. Very loud, very international. Traces of overwritten text: an island-palimpsest. Solid, stable. Fragile. Connections, openings and territorial explorations. Appropriations. Invitation and farewell at one and the same time.

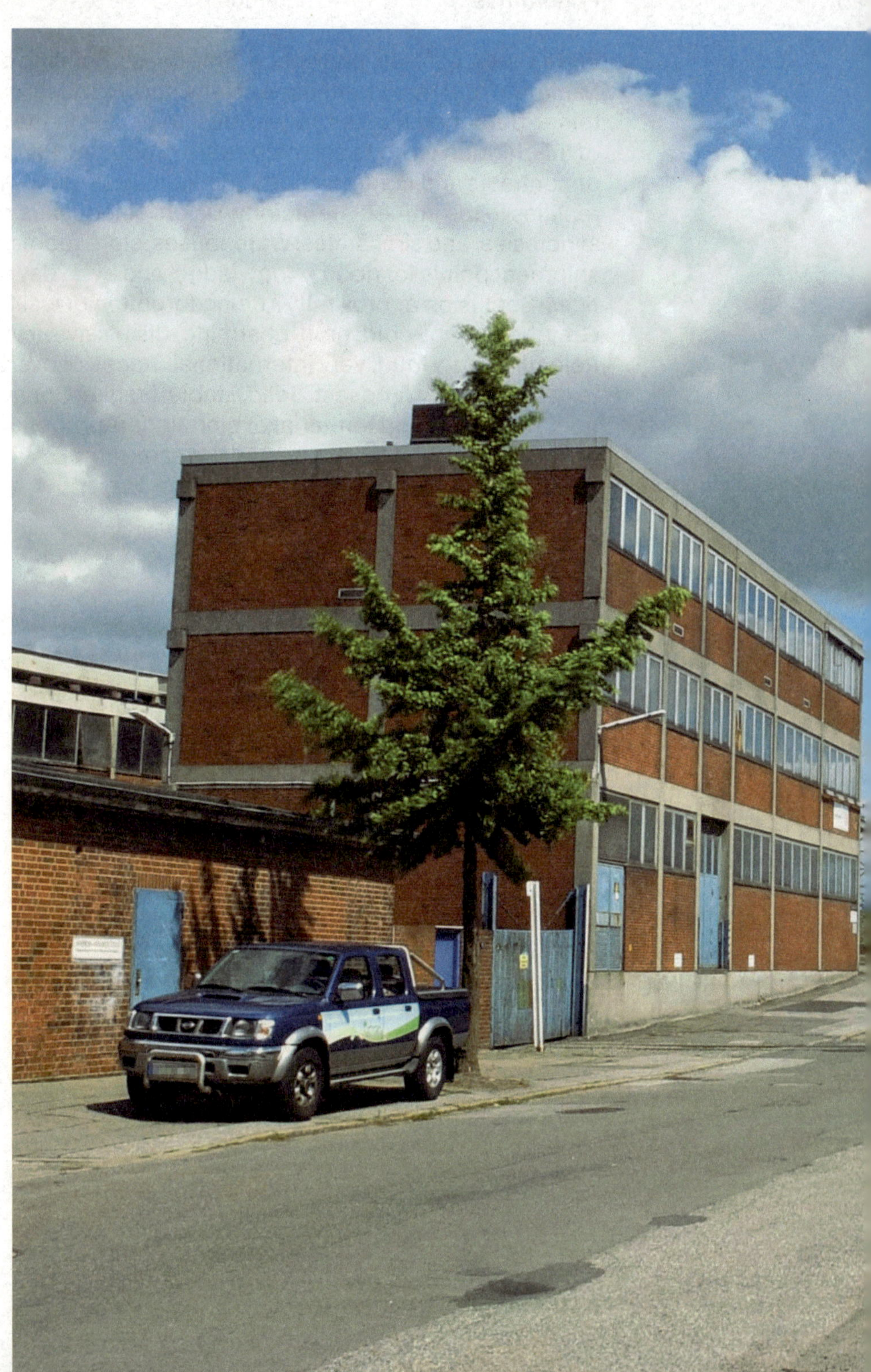

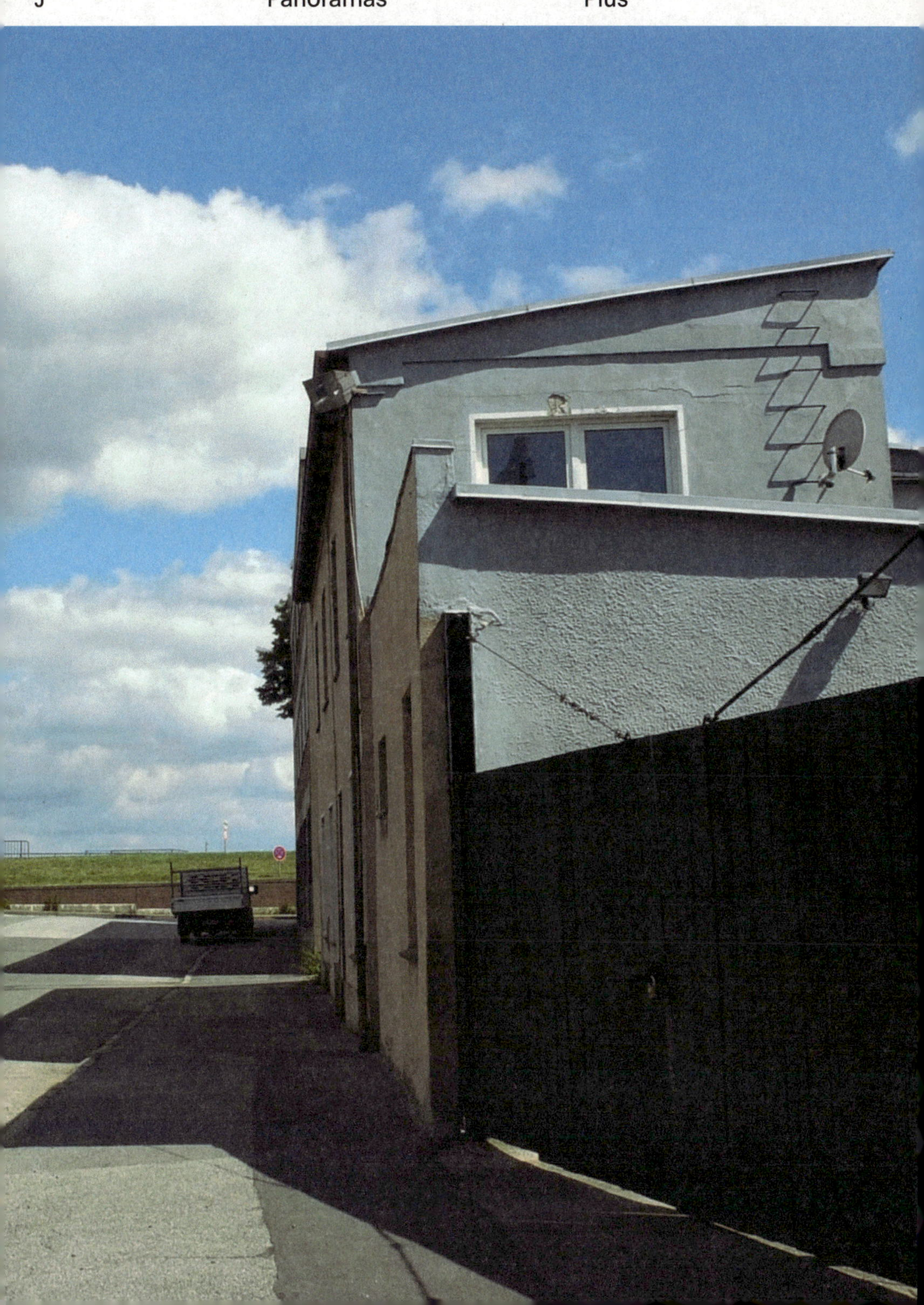

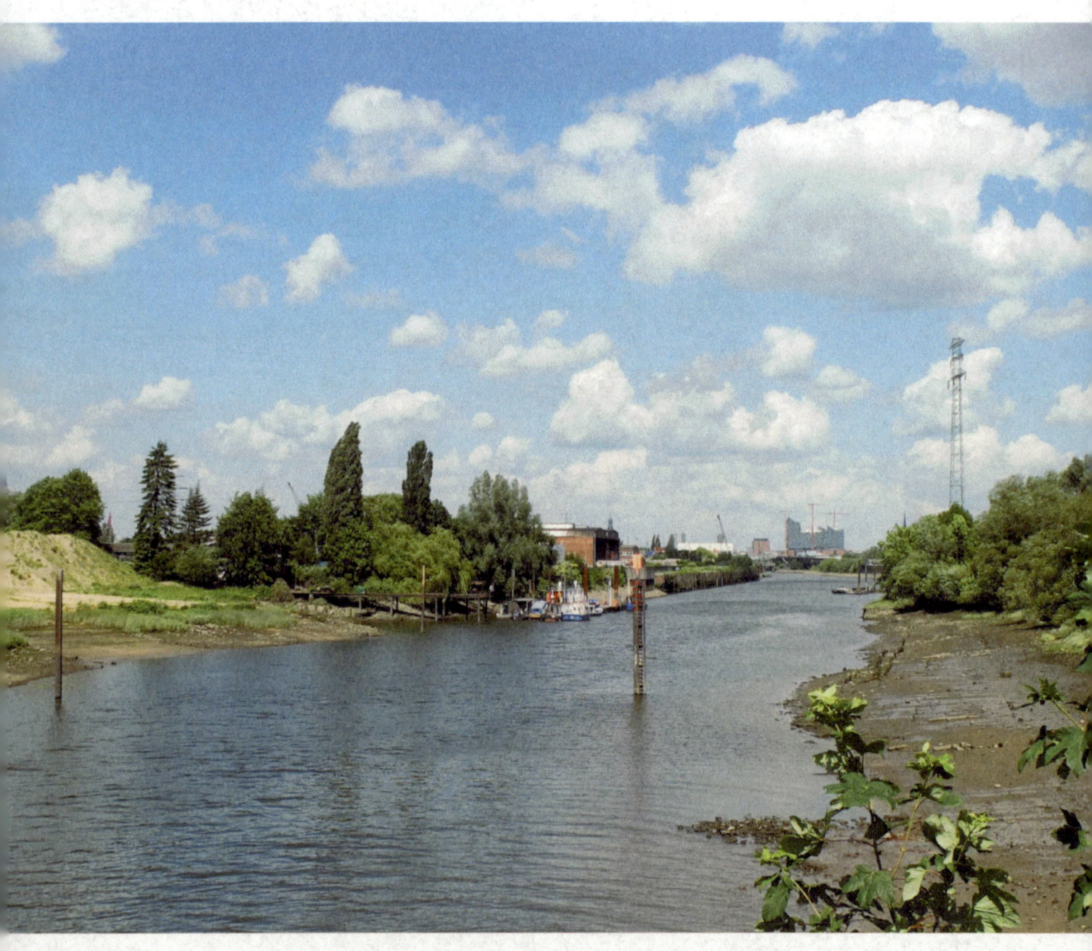

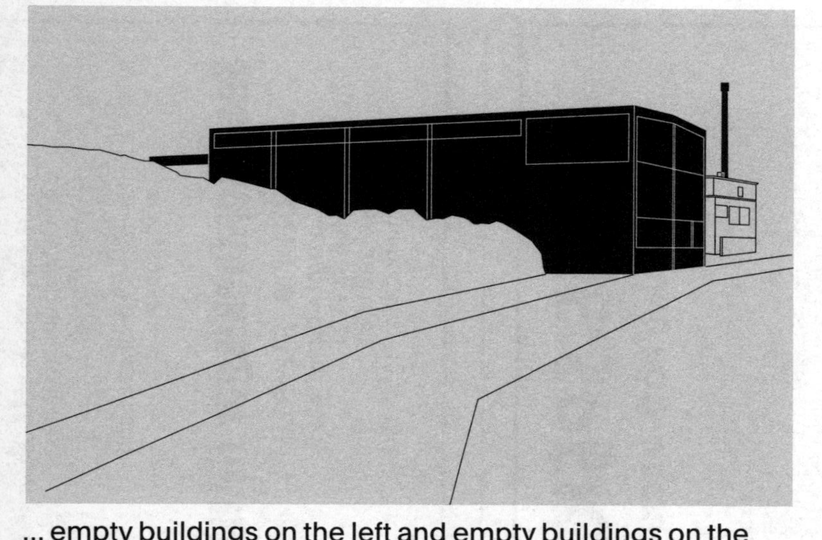

... empty buildings on the left and empty buildings on the right. There are 25,000 squared meters for sale. Plus there are heaps of sand. A boat parked for a while. Empty spray cans are on the ground. From the outside the wilderness is creeping in. The hall is like a cathedral, gigantic and high. Air. Emptiness. Walls ...

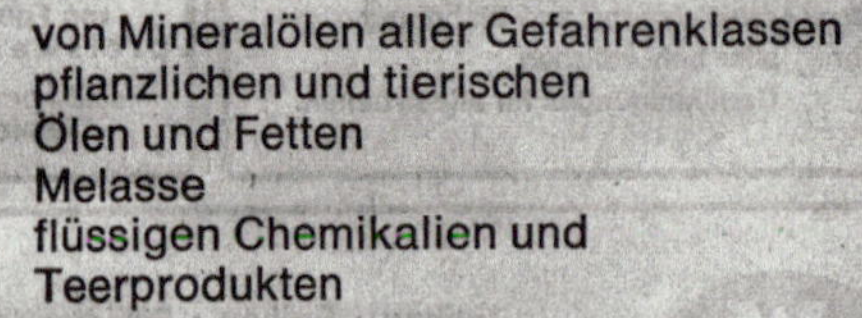

von Mineralölen aller Gefahrenklassen
pflanzlichen und tierischen
Ölen und Fetten
Melasse
flüssigen Chemikalien und
Teerprodukten

Seehafentanklager HANSAMATEX

KÖHN & KUYPER
Hamburg 1 • Domstraße 9
Telefon 33 11 71
Telex 2 161 960
Drahtanschrift: HANSAMATEX

RETHE-SPEICHER

ERICH UND ROLF MACKPRANG

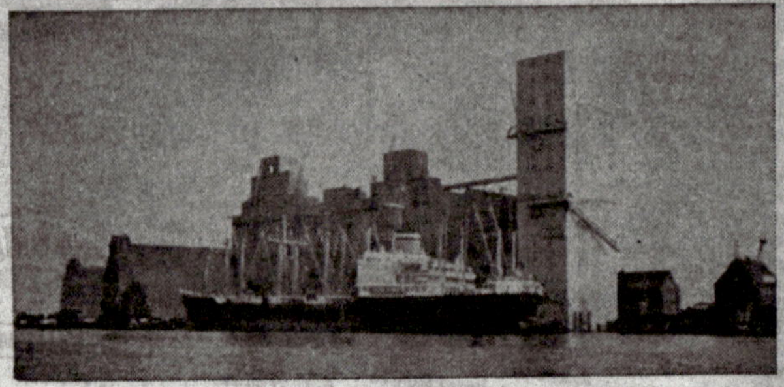

Seit 1938 in Wilhelmsburg an der Rethe

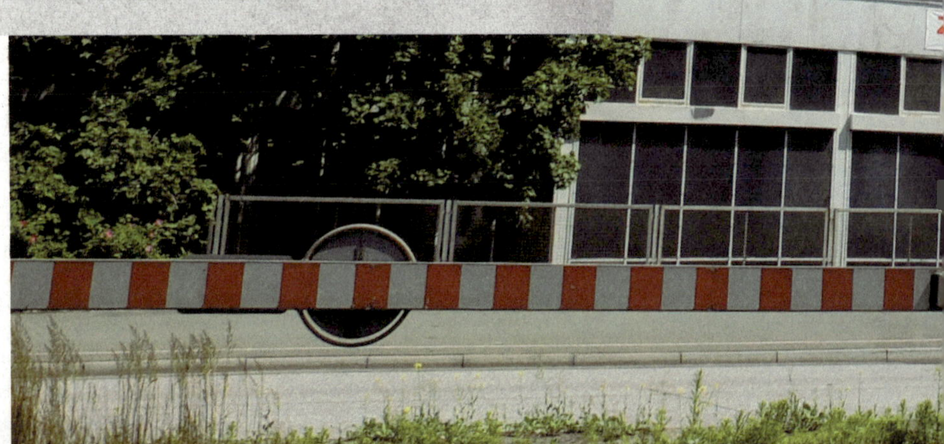

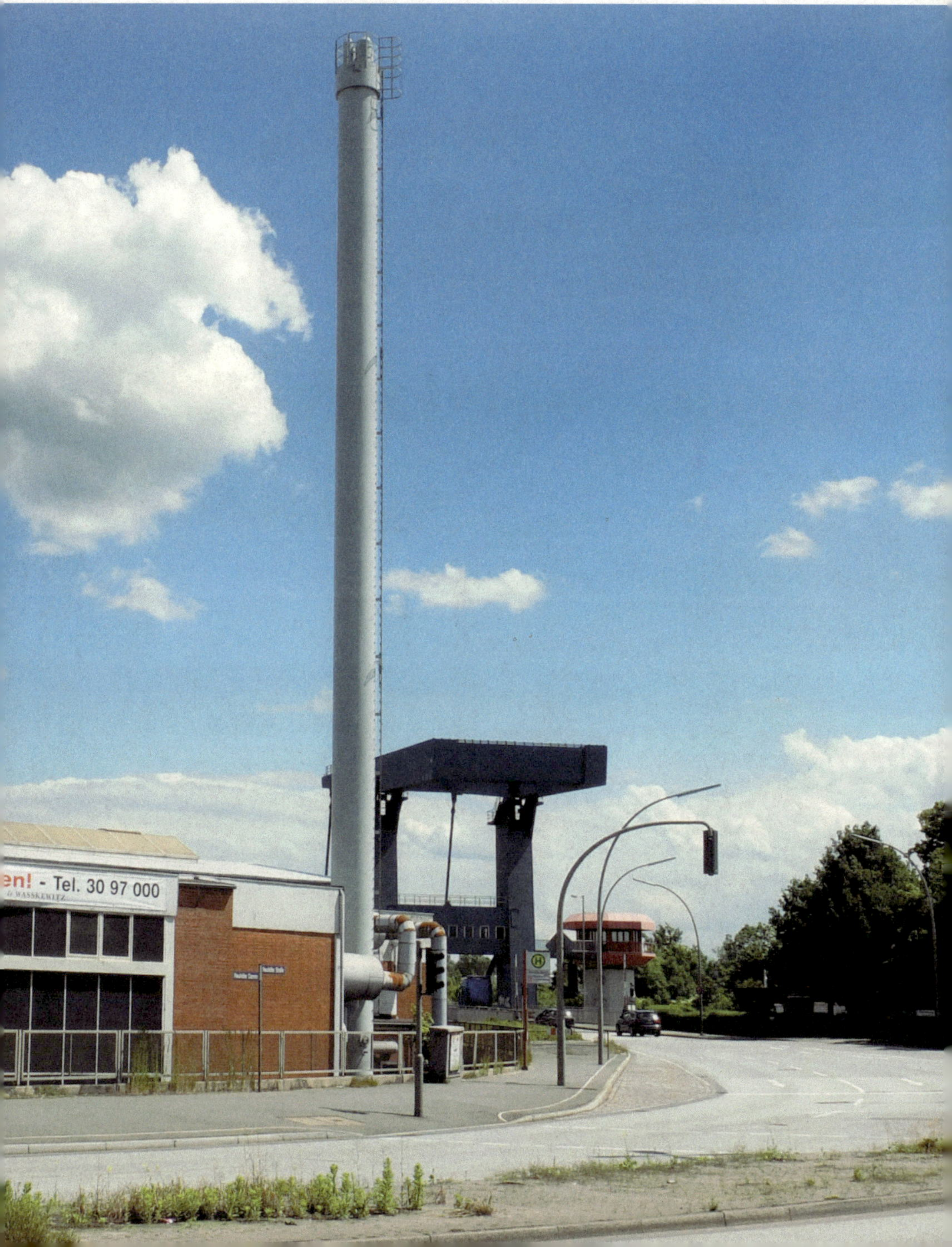

en! - Tel. 30 97 000
& WASSKEMITZ
H

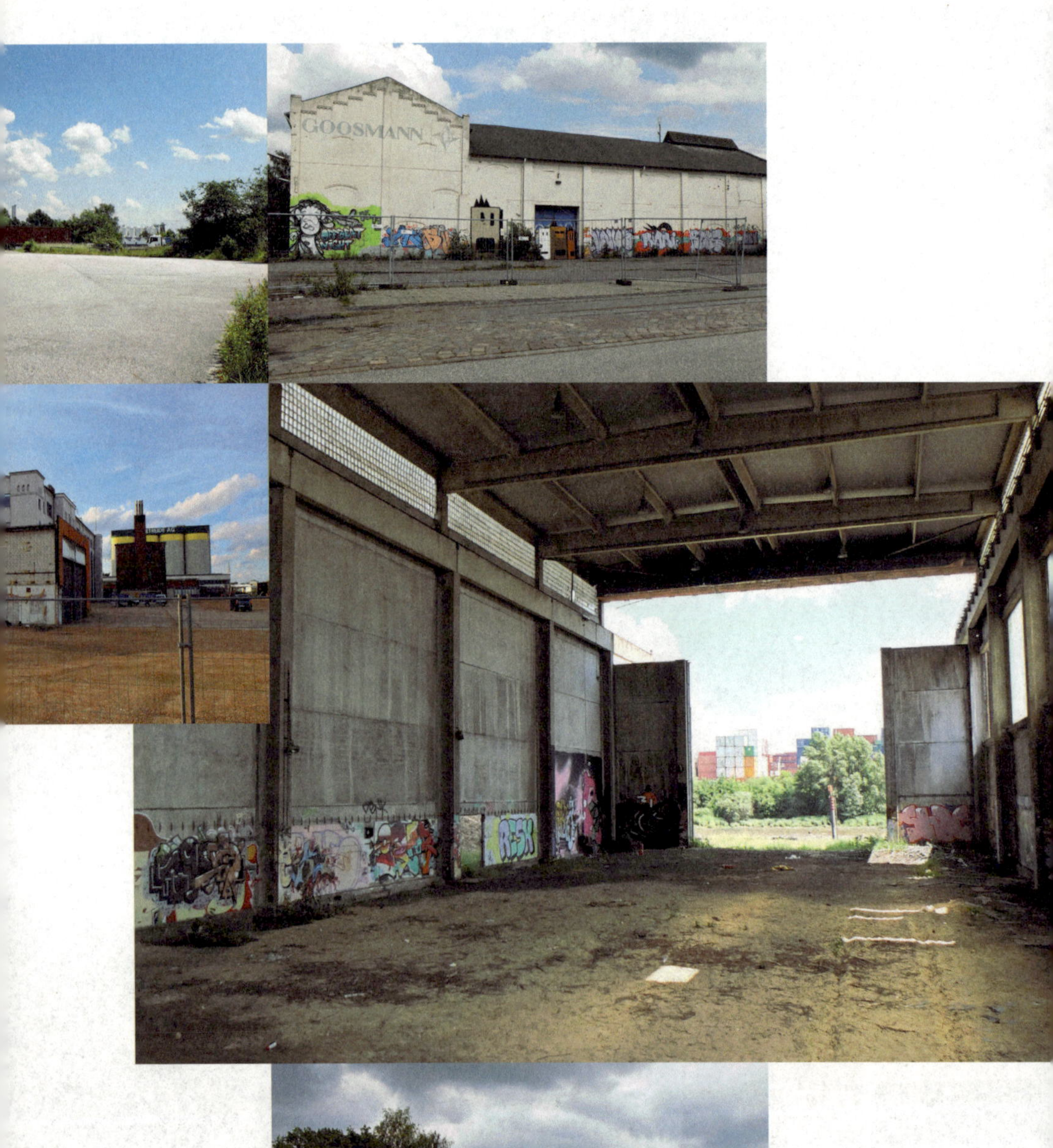

GOOSMANN

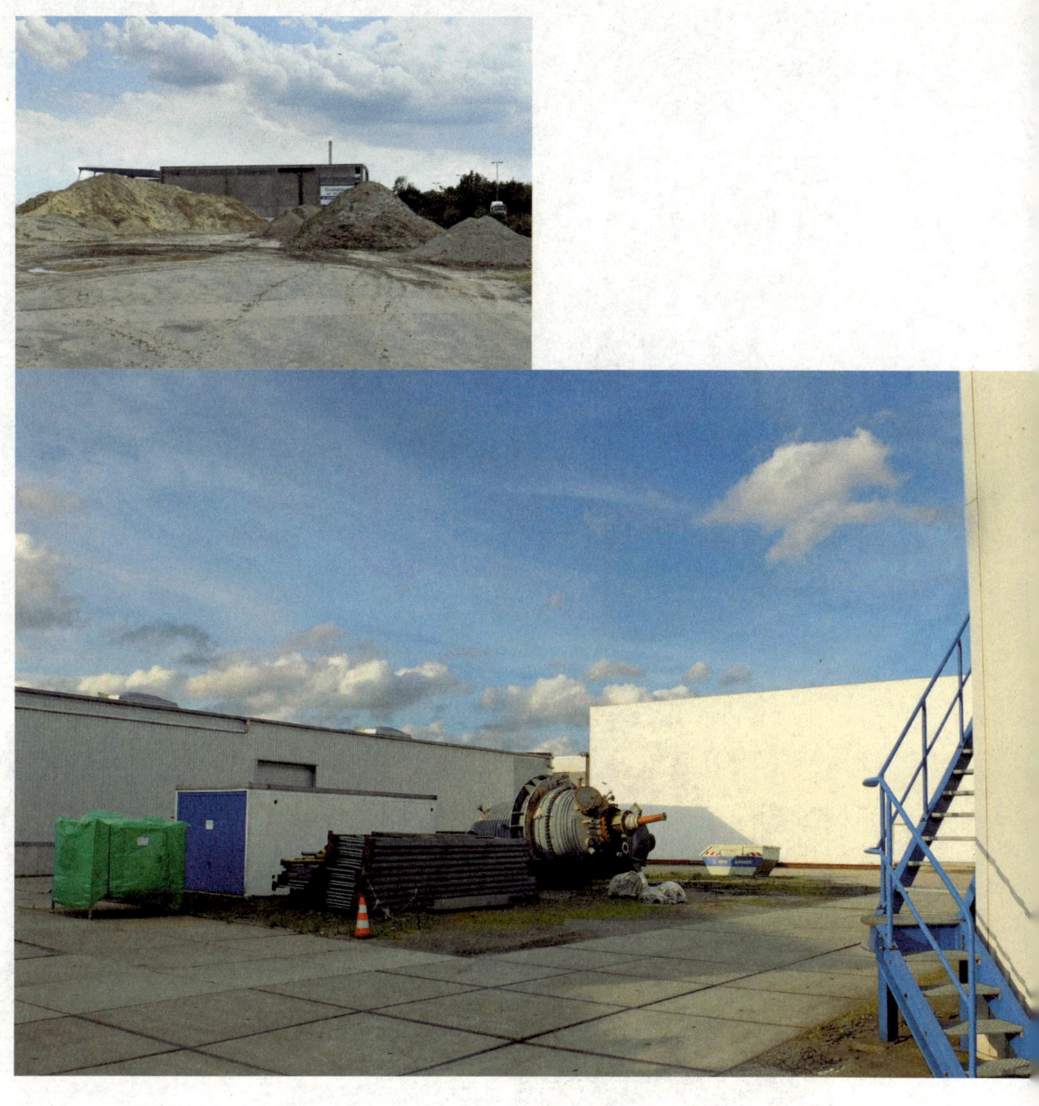

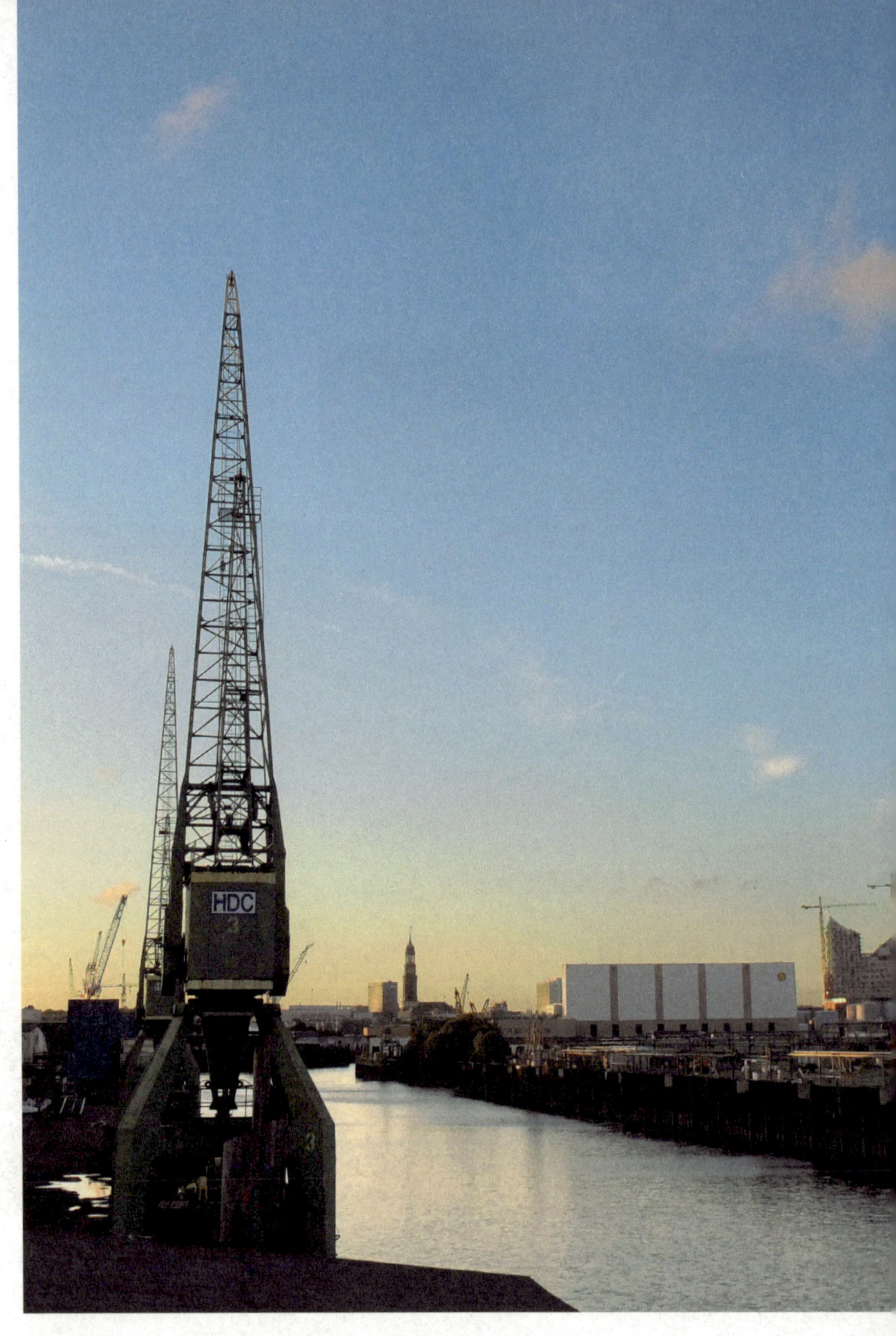

HDC

The Elbe Islands never sleep. The low hum is always audible. It is the unmistakable underlying island tone that fills everything and everyone. Stretches out in space. Audibly expands the space. Motor, heartbeat, and pulse. Above it fly higher, faster sounds. They mingle with the soothing underlying tone. It shrieks, pounds, beats, rattles, squeaks, pops, grinds, strikes, honks, and roars. A rhythm of its own. A 3/4 beat in a 24-hour rhythm. The Elbe Islands work incessantly, always audible. I only have to close my eyes and I can already hear it. So it is still there. Good! I rush through the machine room and move around between the assemblage of various apparatus, pipes, cables, ducts, screws, and nuts. It smells of engine oil, diesel, and petrol. We (I and the other actants and actors) intervene repeatedly, check, supplement, repair, isolate, explore, connect, grow, forward or back, adapt, modify, replace, fiddle, study, program ... everyday life and the Elbe Islands never sleep. They keep going. They keep going, on and on and on ...

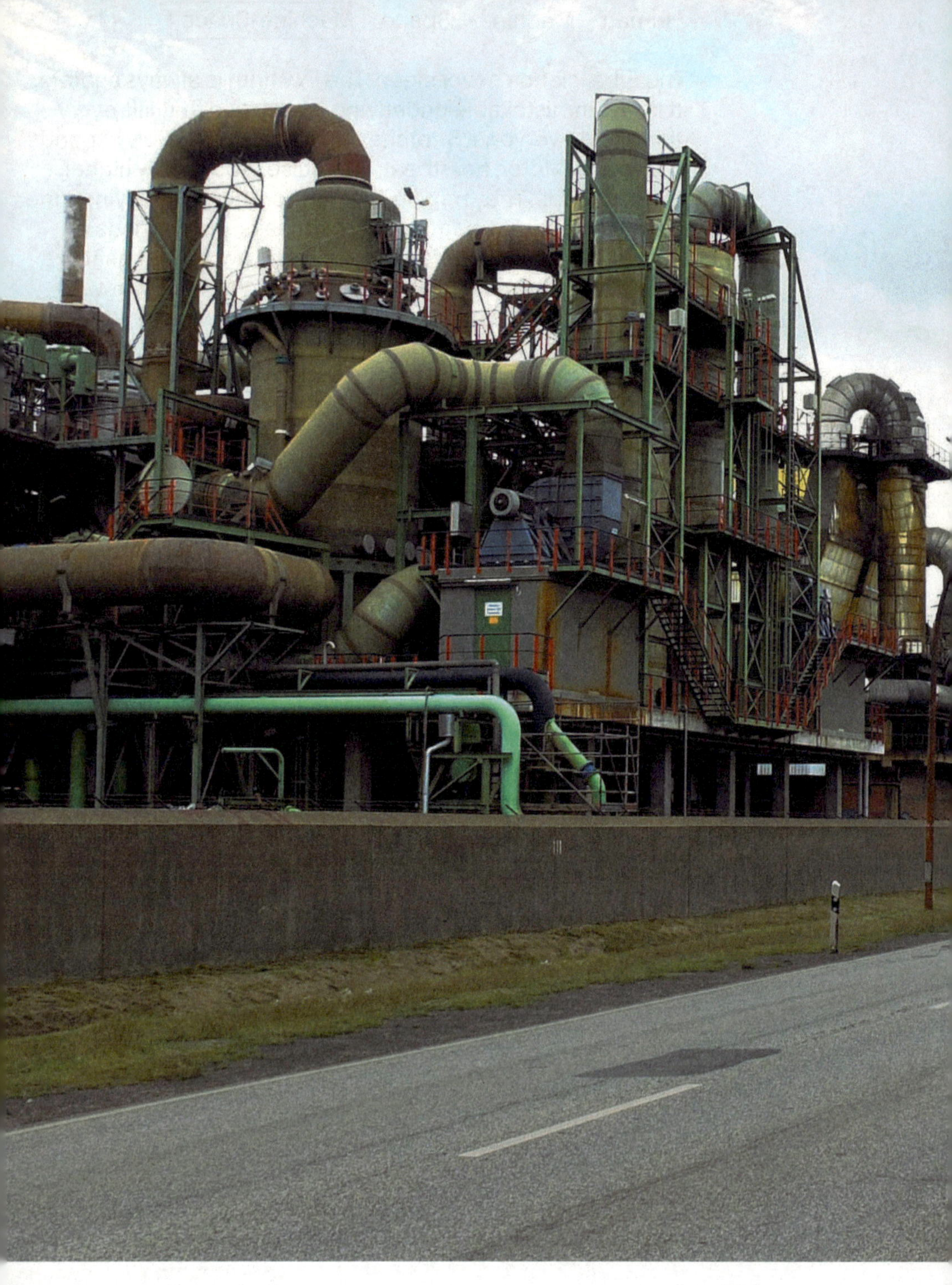

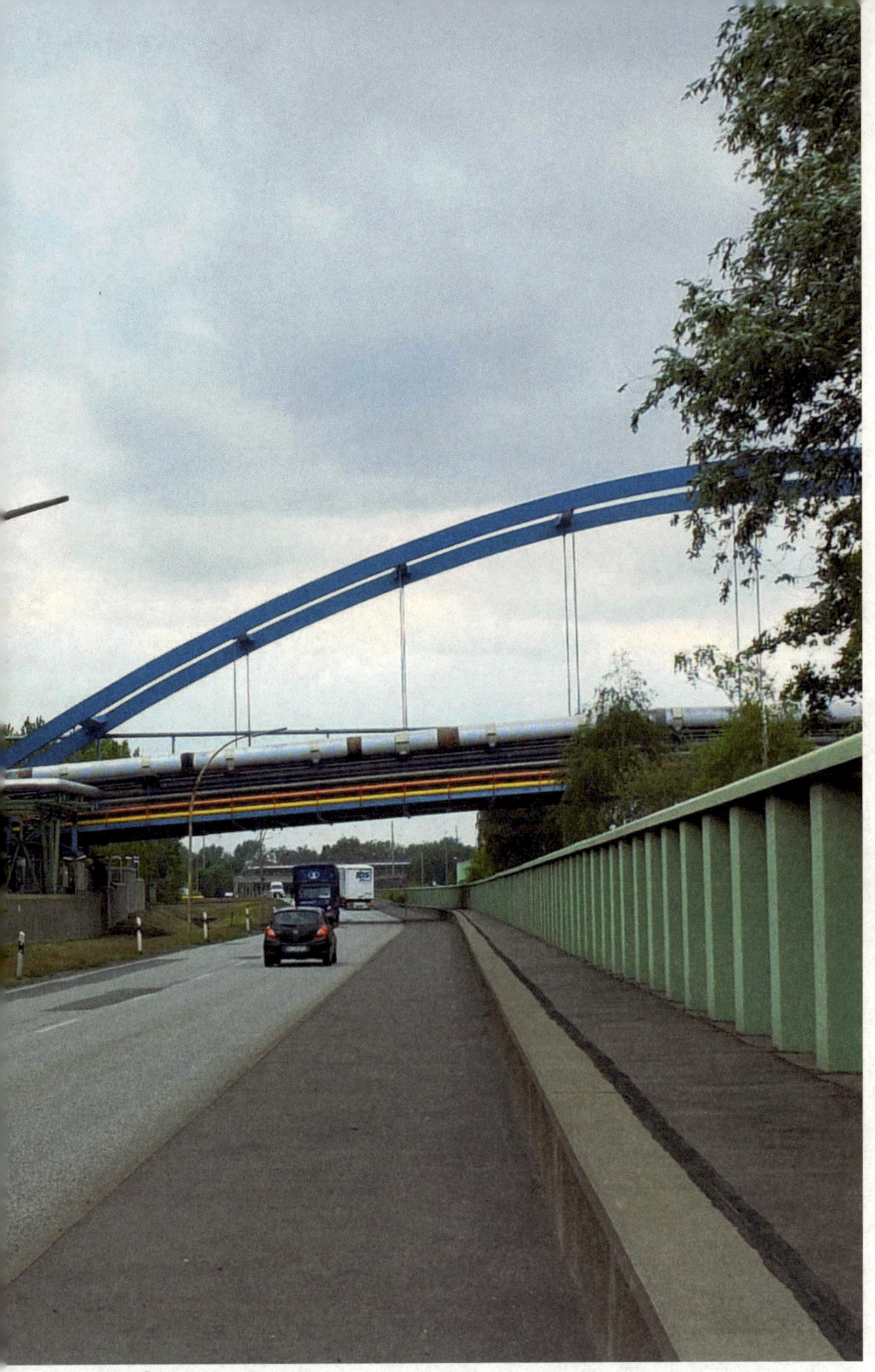

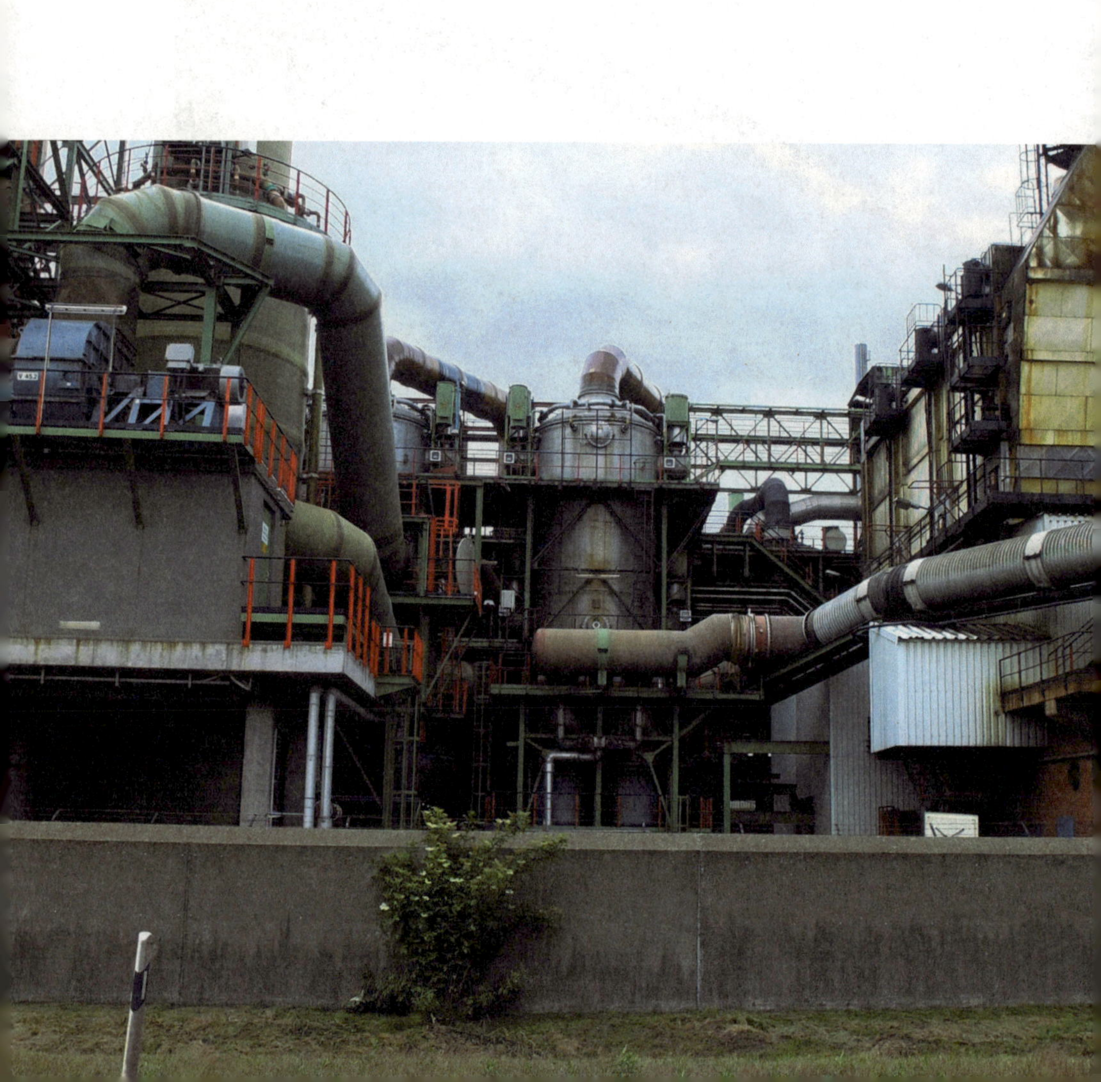

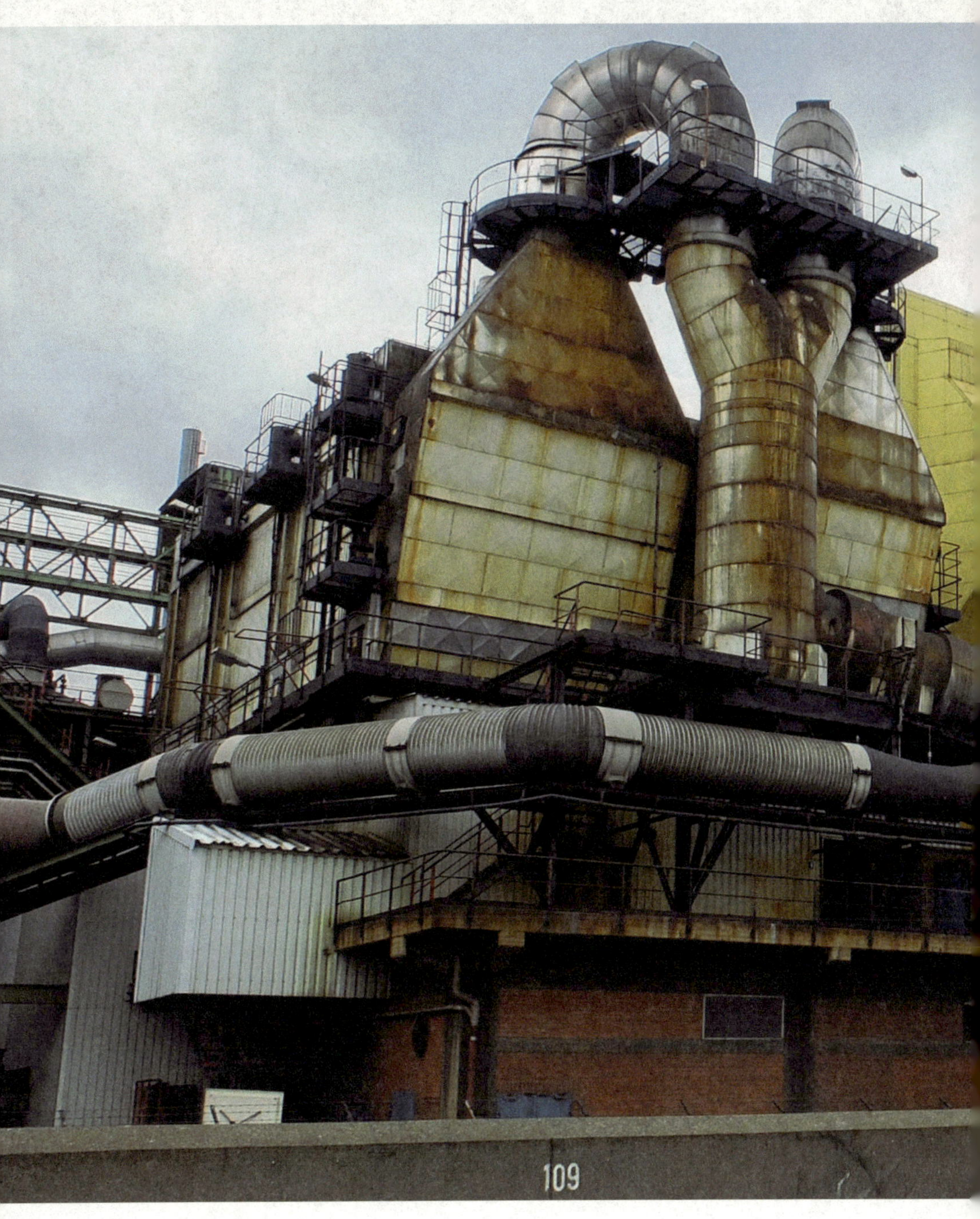
109

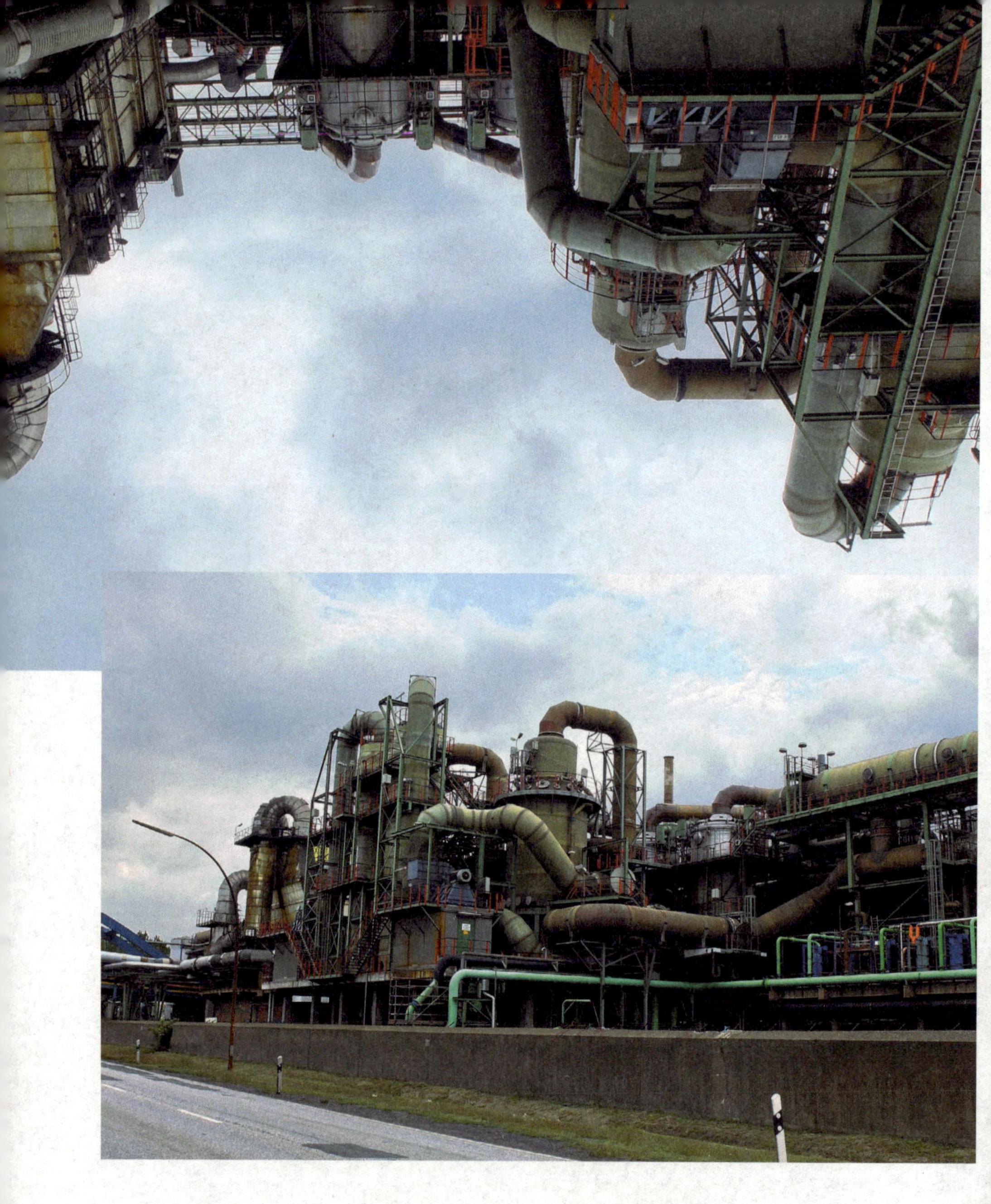

"Received a letter, written in the bunker, who would have thought! ..."

Daylight has only recently begun to fall into the interior. Through the immense opening on the west side, the bulldozer hauls concrete parts of the bunker, concrete hanging on bent rebar.

"... But you should be glad to have such a safe refuge nearby. We, unfortunately, have no protection at all. ..."

The heap of waste noisily grows under the wheels of the agile vehicle.

"... Who knows what will happen; can you understand the whole thing?"

Meanwhile the old black paint is overwritten by a concrete gray plaster on the façade.

"... Not me."[1]

1
Meine liebe E.,
Letter dated
23.6.1944;
see page: 124f

It is Wednesday. Following a particular flow, I have signed up for the seniors' breakfast in the morning. The doors are closed when I walk towards the pavilion-like building in Rotenhäuser Feld, which is surrounded by trees and shrubs. I ring. After a short time someone opens the door, I write my name in a book and pay the small five Euro voluntary contribution. The large room is already well filled, which you would never have guessed from outside. Older people talking excitedly are sitting at a long table with starched white tablecloths. Laughter. I am offered a place at the end of the table. For a moment I'm not sure what I'm doing here. What is the point of all this! The lady who opened the door for me disappears into the kitchen and comes back with two white thermos cans. She pours coffee into everyone's cups at regular intervals. My coffee turns chestnut brown with the cream. The first cup is amazingly strong. The pensioners

look at me with curiosity again and again, I nod to them,
and responding to multiple inviting gazes, I take a few of the
sandwiches garnished with parsley or cucumber. Classic.
The sunlight falls through the open-mesh curtain. A discreet
pattern is visible on the parquet floor; the radio is playing softly in the background. The dishes rattle intermittently.
Unframed photographs hanging on the walls: a group
of seniors bowling, doing gymnastic exercises or sitting in
front of huge gray computer screens. From my seat, I look
at these photographs and try to identify the people on
them with those in the room. Difficult. My seatmate follows
my gaze and tells me what used to be on offer here before.
I notice her bright and youthful laughter. Beside me the
breakfast lady sets a boiled egg in a pastel-colored plastic
eggcup by my plate for me. Without being asked, my
neighbor passes me the salt shaker, filled with salt and rice.
Thanking her, I take it from her. We talk for a while. She re-
sponds to my spontaneous question as I say goodbye,
asking whether she could tell me something about the Elbe
Islands with a yes. However she says that she does not have
time today, but does in the next few days. I jot down the
address of this—as she puts it—"real Wilhelmsburg woman."
A few days later, a bunch of letters, newspaper articles,
textbooks, and black-and-white photographs are lying on
the table at our first meeting. It is very bright and warm.
It is late May. It is just a few steps from my University of the
Neighborhoods (UdN) research station to her house.
She opens the door; her short gray hair is combed neatly
and makes her look very youthful. Smiling, she accepts the
pink peonies. Following her through to the kitchen, I sit
on the padded corner seat in the glass annex. Around us
is the garden of her parents' house. She puts the vase of
flowers and white coffee cups with matching saucers on the
beige tablecloth. I explain why I am interested in the Elbe
Islands and their stories. She pours the coffee carefully into
the two cups. She hands me the thick liquid creamer in
a small jug as I continue to explain about my forays on the
Elbe Islands. I tell her that I stumbled on street names like
An der Wollkämmerei (At the Wool Combing Works) or
Im Busch (In the Bushes), but so far have found no clues that
could tell me something about what those names mean.
At this point I have a break, take a sip of the filter coffee and

look at her quizzically. The Wilhelmsburg woman nods and leafs through her memories, beginning in 1926. The image of her grandfather appears; he had a steel factory, located at Im Busch (later renamed Vogelhüttendeich (Bird Hut Dike).[2] He produced metal window frames for industrial buildings and greenhouses. She pulls a faded company catalogue out of the stack. We look at the different products. Then. Shows me pictures of her mother in her youth as a cook and a seamstress. These two postcards were addressed to a soldier stationed in Jüterbog. Mail sent via the army's postal service for the man who would later become her father. Then. She remembers the accordion her little sister played in the garden. On the frozen canals in winter they ice-skated for hours. It was a popular diversion after school. Then. Her weekend trips with her parents to the cottage in the Harburg Heide. Back then it was unusual to have a holiday home. To this day, she heads to the heathland in her red sports car. Then. She talks about their helpful neighbor who drives her car to the garage. Then. The construction of the flak bunker in Rotenhäuser Feld. Her relatives often came to visit after it was completed. They slept in the living room on the floor. With the memory of the botched attempt to blow up the bunker after the Second World War, the image of football players on Rotenhäuser Feld. Before the war, football was unknown in Wilhelmsburg. Then. She got to know her first husband. They married. He worked as a teacher while she was still in training. Then. Her husband died suddenly. Later, she married her second husband, a friend of the family. The first son is born. They move into her parents' home. The husband is interested in the history of World War II, right up until his death. She shows me his notes, bound volumes in the living room closet. Then the image of the flood of the century and the furniture floating around on the ground floor. Around us. High tide. I've scarcely closed the garden gate behind me again when I find myself back in the present with the bundle of countless voices under my arm:

"... You want to risk it too, and take a trip? I'm going. We wanted to get away for a few days too, H. and me anyway. P. will not be going this year, unfortunately because he already has to travel so much because of all those work trips. I'm so afraid. ..."

I look from the people passing by with their various
companions to the displays in the shop windows up to
the balconies back to the clothes lines in the backyards.

"... When I think about the journey, trains getting
bombed or what those tank guys might dream up.
We better take our guardian angels along."[3]

The increasingly familiar, reciprocal dialogue with my
surroundings arises almost in passing, with a time lag too,
sometimes quite directly. There are short (fragmentary)
moments of a glance.

"How about Tuesday afternoon? ..."

A nod, a smile on the street or on the bus.

"... We would be delighted. ..."

These are signs of belonging.

"... Let's see if we can sort it out. ..."

Waves from window-sills. Trust that
is built up by repetitive gestures.

"... Then you can even have a real good blather."[4]

Step by step.

"I document your existence."

I encounter these and other
messages, short marginal notes:

"Consultation on Monday's in the caretaker's
office. For your feet, we are here."

The field communicates with me.

"Katarakt nedir? Integration through sport."

Non-stop.

"Here Heisswachs. Im Auftrag der Deutschen Post."

I move on, searching, waiting for the next impetus
which will push my randonnée in another direction.

"HOSGELDIN YA SEHR-I RAMAZAN!"

3
Meine liebe E.,
Letter dated
23.6.1944;
see page: 124f

4
ibid.

I notice the smell of roasted cocoa
beans wafting in from the east.

"Temporary help for cocktail bar wanted!
Your contact person in the vicinity."

I steer a course toward one of the many
Elbe Islands. So it's Peute Island today.

"Cyclist, please dismount."

The rhythm and the direction of my movements
are constantly influenced by clear instructions.

"Enter at your own risk."

I pursue these purposefully. Paying
attention to the ensuing (re)actions.

"Video Surveillance."

Then. Then I can already hear the loud honking of a small van
driving toward me in a decommissioned industrial complex
with the unequivocal message that I have to delete my photographs immediately.

"No picture, sie ist meine Schwester!"

Now I recognize the driver.

"It is forbidden to enter the exhibition."

The Wilhelmsburg icecream man in his icecream-van.
Aren't we welcome? The signs are clear and unambiguous

"Private property; no trespassing!"

There is a recurring sense that some sites in the everyday
program want to remain invisible, or rather must do so
to maintain their fragile existence.

"Pay attention when traffic lights change."

These and similar situations arise in particular
at the frayed edges of the island.

"Alight only at Kirchdorf Süd."

Dogs barking. The roads are very busy,
the sidewalks largely deserted.

"So you do not want to cooperate with me?"
"Débrouillez-vous."[5]

At the edge are two porta-potties standing next to a green trash can. Wait. Wait until …

"the removal van [back then] pulls up: Since the weekend Neuhof has become ever more become a ghost town.…"

Es ist staubig. Es ist laut.

"… For dozens of families April 1st means moving into a new apartment. The family of Turkish guest workers loading the rented removal van on our photo will live in Altona from now on.…"

Large warehouses and vacant building complexes, one after another, and in between the odd house or two, surrounded by high fences. From one of the halls the smell of fried chops floats by.

"… Just like them, on Saturdays in particular many other people who also lived in Neuhof would be hauling household goods and furniture.…"

Silent signs such as a low picnic table, a basketball hoop mounted askew by the gate or, between the battered chassis, the vectors of the clothes lines indicate that some-one is living there.

"… Whereas the migrant families in particular are sad to move because they lose very cheap housing, the few Germans who leave Neuhof at the weekend tend to heave a sigh of relief.…"

Some properties for sale. Also. In the immediate vicinity blackberry bushes are taking possession of the disused track, making it harder for everyone to make their way along it. These are inconspicuous places, seemingly timeless, their expression characterized by a degree of uncertainty and indecisiveness.

"… In recent weeks the dying district has grown in-creasingly unsightly; it has became more and more unpleasant to live there."[6]

5
Serres 2009/1998: 271

6
Wilhelmsburger Zeitung, 1979, "Die Möbelwagen fuhren vor";
see page: 248

Time out or a new awakening? Disintegration or retreat? Step by step I perceive the differences, the many moods and subtle fluctuations of the Elbe Islands. Differentiate their locally-specific languages which for me are articulated in the ephemeral vocabulary of empty sunflower seed shells beneath a bench, a melon cut in half by the trodden-down area along the canal, a gold-rimmed tea glass outside the mosque, a pair of men's shoes on the windowsill, a dark Persian rug on the balcony railing, the tattooed sports car in front of the local pub, empty Yum Yum bags near the kiosks, the winter tires put out on the balcony for storage. Questioning, I walk on to decode the signs and symbols of various different realities: What memories connects the carpet to those who live with it? What do the sports cars know about nightlife in Wilhelmsburg and beyond? What shared journeys do the shoes share with their wearer? Why are pawnshops found close to betting parlors? Whom or what is the white sofa waiting for by the roadside? Where do those blue overalls usually work when they are not just drying on the clothes line in the backyard? What do the men talk about all day in the tearooms? Who is transported in vans with darkened windows? Who eats the peppers that grow under the kitchen window? Are the anglers fishing because it is their hobby? What do they catch? Where do the Roma and Sinti girls go with their long skirts? Why do our paths cross several times a day? How many years has the Turkish couple been jogging together at Rotenhäuser Feld? Who buys and wears the wigs from the showcase next to the Kismet Bakery? What news from home do the satellite dishes report? What kinds of lives are to be found behind the doorbells at each front door? I ring the bell.

"Despite many hard blows of fate, August Chor remained a helpful neighbor, always ready to lend a hand when the need arose; he is always ready for a little chinwag too. That stayed just the same after he retired. He is especially involved with the Wilhelmsburger local history museum, always ready to do a shift when it is open and to keep things tidy. So his life is still defined by being ready to help his neighbors and the general public."[7]

And ring.

7
Wilhelmsburger
Zeitung, 1976,
"Greunhöker Cohr";
see page: 156

"We are not moving back in there again! On Monday, some thirty tenants of the houses met at Wilhelmsburg District Office on Ernst-August-Deich. These were people who live in the ground floor flats of the block on Ernst-August-Deich and who got the worst of this year's flooding: they cannot use their apartment at all right now ..."[8]

And ring. We sit in the garden on two white plastic garden chairs with pink cushions. It smells of freshly mown grass. My new acquaintance—a "real Wilhelmsburg woman," as she puts it—hands me a glass of mineral water. She was busy working in the garden when I rang. Yesterday she actually visited the bunker. Taking a sip of water I listen, fascinated as she talks. A long line was waiting in front of the huge opening on the west side. When she entered the bunker, it was very oppressive and gloomy, even though for a short while now the interior has been getting some natural light. Moved, she tells me that she had never seen it from the inside. She has clear memories of the construction phase. Yes, that she remembers. Her mother, sister, and other family members often sought refuge in it. She was stationed in a Bavarian orphanage as a caregiver and was rarely at home. We look at each other, eavesdropping in silence on the progressive transformation of the flak bunker into the Energy Bunker as part of the International Building Exhibition (IBA). I ring again.

"Non-nationals will soon participate in an advisory capacity in Wilhelmsburg Local Council meetings. The relevant provisions are stipulated in a Harburg District Assembly resolution. In addition, non-nationals shall be represented in the Committee on Education and Culture, in the Social Affairs and Youth Committee, and in the Economic and Building Committee. A CDU amendment that envisaged appointing non-nationals to the local committee in Süderelbe too came as such a surprise to the SPD and FDP that they rejected it. Socialist MEP Harald Muras considers participation of non-nationals in the technical committees as the first step towards granting tax-paying non-nationals the right to vote and stand in municipal elections."[9]

8
Wilhelmsburger Zeitung, 1976, "Wir ziehen da nicht wieder ein!"; see page: 364

9
Wilhelmsburger Zeitung, 1979, "Bald Ausländer im Ortsausschuß"; see page: 134

My enduring state is akin to simultaneously reading, translating, and connecting everyday practices envisaged in the program, never stopping for a moment. Various associations take me to places, near or far, in my everyday island life. The out-of-service bus line takes me to the Norwegian terminus Osterøy. China Town is located diagonally opposite. "The Caribbean is on the program for the next container link."[10] With the American Line we make a brief stopover by Argentina Bridge. It is drizzling in the realm of "King Ferdinand"[11]. At dusk I take a panoramic picture of Kassel as a memento. The whole scene looks uninviting until a vegetable boat passing along the Reiherstieg.[12] Otherwise, the British fishing village at the port of Rotterdam looks rather deserted. I buy a bowl of red strawberries in Las Vegas and finally end up at the single women's hostel on Rotenhäuser Damm. The lawn outside the single-storey building is dotted with daisies; a flagpole without a flag is the prelude.[13] The plaster on the façade is virtually flawless. The anti-aircraft bunker is visible in the background. There is nothing to suggest that the single women's hostel will one day be surrounded by a dense green jungle. I enter the building sometime in the nineteen fifties. A celebration is just beginning. In the large hall, young women are sitting at a long, festively decorated table. They are watching someone, appearing thoughtful and attentive at the same time. A woman with short hair is smoking.[14] Through the narrow hallway, gloomy even during the day, I finally arrive in my studio, here I live, work, sleep, and research for several weeks, a bed, a shelf, a desk, two chairs. A few personal things lined up on the windowsill. Found good luck charms, collected souvenirs. Variously dimensioned images of a heart-throb, cut from magazines, used to hang above the bed years ago. Perhaps Marlon Brando.[15] There are no curtains hanging over the window. I open the window. There is a heavy rain and warm air pours into the room. My computer starts up from sleep mode. I will spread out my material in the desk lamp's diffuse light. It is a disjointed assembly and interconnection of a plethora of spaces and moments. Zooming, sharpening, individualizing. Circulating and getting lost in the material. An adventure and a labyrinth at the same time. Nothing is linear. My perception grows more keen to the subtle and acute. Perspectives changed by

10
Wilhelmsburger Zeitung, 1976, "Containerverkehr nach Südafrika wird aufgenommen"; see page: 270

11
Elbe Wochenblatt, 1995

12
Wilhelmsburger Zeitung, 1979, "Wooden sailing boats on the Reiherstieg"; see page: 155

13
Single women's hostel, Rotenhäuser Damm, c. 1950; see page: 126

14
Large hall, Christmas, single women's hostel, Rotenhäuser Damm, c. 1950; see page: 122

15
Private bedroom, single women's hostel, Rotenhäuser Damm, c. 1950; see page: 127

the polyphony. I read, understanding repetitions or changes
in the everyday patterns of Wilhelmsburg. Slowly. By brows-
ing back and forth between times and pages, I develop
my reading of the everyday program. But. Do the Elbe Islands
actually never sleep? I close my eyes. Their deep hum is
audible. So it is still there. Before soaring lighter, higher and
faster sounds. "Please enter," the typical UdN sound filters
through to me. The doors are wide open. People coming and
going. Housing. Research. Studying. Samples. Build.
Back and forth. I get up, open the door, walking through the
flickering glare of the neon strip-lighting in the hallway.
Arriving at the end, I am dazzled for a moment by the unusu-
ally bright daylight, which passes through the translucent
roof and the large wall opening. Gradually my eyes get used
to it. Around me: high tide. In the large hall, students, along
with children from the neighborhood, are stitching together
white truck tarpaulins. Next to them, the oversized knitting,
Jenny is joining up oversized knotted strips to make an
open-mesh tree house hose. Others are still building minia-
ture tree house models. In the background a dishwasher
program is running; from time to time, sounds come from the
coffee machine. These are very familiar scenes. Seamlessly
everyday interactions continue outside on Rotenhäuser Feld.
Through the large opening in the kitchen / foyer I step out
into the open. Around me it is Sunday. Maybe Monday.
It is a late summer afternoon. The first wisps of smoke rise up
between the leaves. There is a smell of grilled meat and
vegetables. Children chase a ball. A large blanket is spread
on the ground, and others join onto the airy outdoor room.
Nearby someone is reading a book on the grass. A couple
is jogging along the gravel path. Two elderly ladies are talking on the park bench opposite. Their two walkers are parked
next to them. Teens gesticulating in the air. A mother calls
her child's name. Again and again. The cyclist rummages in
the trash with one hand, looking for returnable bottles. Children with white hard hats race past me with their plans.
Our neighbor starts his evening stroll with his dog. Leisurely.
Continuously. My vocabulary grows ever denser and denser.

Salut — You Elbe Islands

I would like to thank Professor Bernd Kniess for our intensive, critical, and open dialogue over the last five years. I am particularly grateful to him for giving me such enormous support to continue pursuing this work and to publish it in the UD series. Last but not least, he has enabled me to develop a complex and relational understanding of the city and landscape through the University of the Neighborhoods research project and the Urban Design Master's Program.

My heartfelt thanks goes to Professor Alexa Färber for her focused questions and the illuminating references she pointed out, which again and again have sharpened my sense of the new in my methodology and theoretical engagement in this work.

I am very grateful to Katrin Klitzke and Katja Heinecke for their intensive ethnographic-methodological training, and their precise appraisal of the intermediate stages of my work.

I would also like to say a special word of thanks to Professor Christopher Dell for his theory-rich lecture-performances at Urban Design Meta Lab. These extended my attentiveness to urban connections and emboldened me to develop my own reading mode for the urban realm.

My thanks also goes to the University of the Neighborhoods and its countless actors for the unique opportunity to research, work, and live in this context. I would especially like to thank Stefanie Gernert, Benjamin Becker, Immanuel Mihm, and Max Müller for that.

I would like to express my heartfelt gratitude to Doris Tausendpfund, Eva-Maria Würth, Franziska Wodicka, Gabi Lerch, Imke Plinta, Philippe Sablonier, and Sophie Staub for their friendly solidarity and for our on-going exchange of ideas; their conceptual and analytic input have accompanied me throughout this lengthy process.

My thanks to graphic designer Claudia Stöckli, who was involved in re-working one of my first versions.

I would like to thank Jan Wenzel and Wolfgang Schwärzler for their creative design solutions in every conceivable aspect of this publication and for their relational transposition of my work into a "Spector book."

Thank you to Helen Ferguson for her sensitive translation into English and a thank you to Ames Gerould for his precise proofreading.

Many warm thanks to you, Ben Pohl, for our inspiring dialogues during countless walks.

I would like to express my most heartfelt thanks to my family for their marvelous trust. They have supported me lovingly at all the crucial moments.

Thanks to my small black FUJI X 10 camera for being such a faithful companion.

And my warmest thanks to my island-friend Friedel, whom I have grown so very fond of. Last but not least, let me thank the Elbe Islands and their human and non-human inhabitants for the spontaneous encounters, the diverse panoramas, shifting perspectives—the unexpected possibilities.

—Merci à tous!

Imperceptibly, we have not only followed Michaelis'
randonnée; we have let her spur us to leave our own paths
and to follow the flows. Unintentionally, our experiences
have become part of this rambling. This dérive-like movement of the randonnée thematizes the placing of its own
intrinsic mediality; it leads us both around the Elbe Islands
and through the book, through our experiences and our
conceptions concerning the program of what we might call
the 'space of possibilities'.
How to begin? Something catches Michaelis' attention, at first
just for a moment, but then it will not let go of her. The force
that drives her is in the first instance her unstinting interest:
in the urban situation as-it-is, and in the program of the space
of possibilities that is contained within that urban realm
however yet is not quite realized—Michaelis is aware that it
is an impossible undertaking. The Elbe Islands are her case
study and empirical field. She has embarked on a journey
to explore the islands, armed with the inquisitive gaze of the
researcher, subjective, searching, and approachable.
The landscape dimension is familiar to her in all of this; her
own academic training is the backdrop that allows her to
understand it. It is just that her 'new' landscape is a cityscape,
which she reads like an open book, a book whose pages she
seeks to open even wider.
What though do we mean when we talk about the city?
The images and conceptions associated with the term could
not be more different than the cities themselves are. Just as
the realities of how cities are constituted today differ dra-
matically, there is huge variation in the circumstances in which
they came into being and in their inhabitants' expectations
and hopes for the future. It is a truism: cities grow and shrink,
they never stand still—even if we might wish for that—
but instead are constantly evolving.

'City' cannot be subsumed into an unambiguous image or
a generally valid description. For example, when people refer
to the European city, it is often associated with the notion
of a centralized city, even if the picture conveyed by noctur-
nal satellite images makes clear to us that urban reality in

413

Europe has long been woven into the sprawling amorphous constellation they depict. Thomas Sieverts used the term "Zwischenstadt" (literally "in-between city") to describe this state of affairs, which he describes as being made up "of more or less dense areas of activities, characteristics, appeals, signs, messages and recollections, of stable and elusive elements" (Sieverts 2003/1997: 91). Like other influential studies on decentralized and suburbanized forms of the city, for example Edward Soja's "Thirdspace" or Joel Gareau's "Edge City," Sieverts also refers to "Learning from Las Vegas," the seminal text by Venturi, Scott-Brown, and Izenour. Other studies too, such as Koolhaas' Delirious New York or "Project on the City" or Atelier Bow-Wow's "Made in Tokyo" also take the methodology and approach of 'Learning from' as their point of departure. Although they focus on another form of the city, generally summed up as the centralized city, these approaches nonetheless extract decentralized, fragmenting and polycentral dimensions and procedures from it. It is striking here that research on cities with an urban or suburban focus shares the same attitude to the object studied: both in the first instance posit the city as a given. "In both cases the architects envisioned themselves primarily in the role of a reader or interpreter of an existing cultural and urban aggregate, which was defined 'retroactively' as the starting point for a theory of urbanism" (Stierli 2013/2010: 318).

What however does 'given' mean in this context? Its starting point is not—and this is the decisive issue—a realism that is rooted in a pre-existing world that simply needs to be represented and that views knowledge as the best possible representation. This kind of realism can no longer function if we consider the city as action, as a "set of intertwined activities" (Venturi et al. 1972: 76), as 'Learning from' asserts. We ask instead how a phenomenal reality comes into being as an urban action and, over and above this, how knowledge about this is presented, produced, and becomes a subject for attention.

Insight into a possible change of direction is provided here by the short term 'retroactive,' which Koolhaas introduced into discourse on the city. Koolhaas' 'Retroactive Form' and his thesis of the city as a sociological happening fundamentally displace the perspective: moving away from pure conception, over-planning, and concentration on the built object and toward the performative actions of the users. That does not mean though that space (and thus the city) are performative merely by virtue of being produced through speech acts of social constructions, or rather through conventions or theatrical acts. Instead "social aggregates must always be produced, bargained for anew through the activity of collecting" (Dell 2014: 217). That also displaces the focus onto the subject-matter of the city as a thing: it can be programmed and can, in performative utilization, program itself. The city as grid, in contrast, is elevated to an exemplary collective "laboratory of [...] man-made experience" (Koolhaas 1999/1978: 10), in which planners must also subject themselves in a transformational process. Rather than struggling against alienation, a critical affirmation comes into play here, seeking, through an analysis of the city, to tease out possibilities of emergence 'in' the grid, as Koolhaas demonstrates by way of example using the concept of the skyscraper as machine. The skyscraper affords scope to a multitude of possible worlds, enables them but does not impose them. One of its structural characteristics — in interaction with the minimal structure of the Zoning Law — is that it is a thoroughly simple mathematical construction, provoking, through this very simplicity, a plethora of diagrammatic interconnection options. Considerations of this kind zero in on the point we made above with reference to the space of possibilities: the virtuality comprised within it is not a surface or illusory world (as a virtual imitation of the real), but rather the essence of the diagrammatic realm (as the virtual dimension of the real) that is situated between representation and non-representation, the intelligible and sensible world and that awaits with aspects to be updated if we manage, through discourse, to unveil specific situations, de-construct these and, in the Latourian sense, to rearrange them.

This turns the spotlight on the kind of idea of design that forms the yardstick for the Urban Design degree course: design here is neither pure craftsmanship nor autonomous art but instead a political working through of a vector field of the conditions determining possibility. Structure is understood in this context not as an impediment but rather as a constructive parameter that forms the basis for action.

That gives rise to a diagrammatic variant of Structuralism
(as shown by Deleuze too), which makes structure the
productive tool of programming and connects design with
cultural practices of everyday life. Design and research
converge, by invoking not only the performative but by becoming—as the randonnée demonstrates—performative
themselves, i.e. mobile: form comes into being on the basis
of movement, not vice-versa. The competence of the
design therefore lies in the re-designing of resources and
options, which, through diagrammatic procedures, identify
new contexts of references and connections and make
it possible to update these.

This book is therefore entirely a product of the Urban Design
Master's course. That makes it a rather special publication
that looks at the fundamental issue of how the process
vanishes behind the product. Conceived as a designed form,
it does not supply a blueprint, a plan, or a rendering as a
pre-emptive simulation of what is possible. The product is
the book.
Turning its attention to what Lefebvre dubbed the virtual
object of the urban, in which "the encounter and assembly
of all objects and subjects, existing or possible" comes into
effect (Lefebvre 2003/1970: 122), this book by no manner
of means intends to adhere to the tenuous notion of emulat-
ing urban reality. Instead Michaelis seeks to encompass
the virtual dimension of the city into terms of what could be
described as potentialities of the future, which only become
accessible through precise observation of those very encounters and assemblies and through devising and filling
prototypes with life on the virtual plane. That is representative of the methodological thrust of our work in Urban Design,
which seeks to extend the classical design as understood
in urban planning and the closed form associated with it
into an open form. Rooted in an interest of epistemological
processes, we no longer play off design against research,
or substitute one for the other, but instead seek through
(inter)relation to elevate research to the status of design too.
Research is not understood here to mean providing information about a given reality, of which it provides a representation. The focus is more on reflective confrontation with
the perspectives, lenses, and foils of one's own discipline

and subjective viewpoint, with which we encounter the city as the subject of research. Text and image, or the object examined and the knowledge gleaned, cannot be made to coincide within one meaning. Instead, as recipients of the book, we can generate connections, relational urban reference systems by raising our own questions and conducting our own research, tapping into the examples examined and the in-depth exploration that Michaelis has undertaken based on Wilhelmsburg's specific situation. It is not so much about looking for answers to given or identified problems; instead, new arrangements should come into being that will allow questions to be generated.

Ultimately, continuing to view the city today as a closed object would be an overly restricted way of looking at the urban realm. It would mean considering it as demarcated from a before or in-between, not recognizing that the city has broken free of its form. The city is constantly renewed in the connections between the everyday practices of its human and non-human actors. It is no longer an object but instead an open process or form, which can only be grasped structurally. The question of how and whether the 'inside' can still be distinguished from the 'outside' becomes superfluous.

• Dell, Christopher (2014): Das Urbane Wohnen. Leben. Produzieren, Berlin.
• Koolhaas, Rem (1978): Delirious New York. A Retroactive Manifesto for Manhattan, New York, Oxford, Paris (page references here from 1994 edition).
• Lefebvre, Henri (2003/1970): The Urban Revolution, Minneapolis / La révolution urbaine, Paris.
• Sieverts, Thomas; (2003/1997): Cities Without Cities. An Interpretation of the Zwischenstadt. London, New York / Zwischenstadt: Zwischen Ort und Welt, Raum und Zeit, Stadt und Land, Berlin.
• Stierli, Martino; (2010/2013): Las Vegas im Rückspiegel. Die Stadt in Theorie, Fotografie und Film / Las Vegas in the Rearview Mirror: The City in Theory, Photography and Film, Los Angeles.
• Venturi, Robert; Scott Brown, Denise; Izenour, Steven (1972): Learning from Las Vegas: The Forgotten Symbolism of Architectural Form, Cambridge, Massachusetts and London.

Bibliography

- Brandes, Uta; Erlhoff, Michael; Schemmann, Nadine (2009): "Design und Forschung," in: Designtheorie und Designforschung, Paderborn, pp. 63–100.
- Brands, Bart; Broekman, Marco (2010): "This is not a Plan!", in: International New Town Institute of Planners (ed.), New Towns for the 21st Century. Amsterdam, SUN architecture, pp. 271–79.
- Certeau, Michel de (1988): "Walking in the City," in: Practice of the Everyday Life, University of California, p. 91–111.
- Dell, Christopher (2009/10): "Editorial," in: Kniess, Bernd; Dell, Christopher (eds.), Kunst der Funktion, UD Metalab—Studio für angewandte Theorie, Hamburg, pp. 6–8.
- Dell, Christopher (2009/10): "Taktiken strategisch machen. Performative Politiken der Stadtuntersuchung," in: Kniess, Bernd; Dell, Christopher (eds.), Kunst der Funktion, UD Metalab—Studio für angewandte Theorie, Hamburg, pp. 11–29.
- Dell, Christopher (2011): Replay City: Improvisation als urbane Praxis, Berlin, pp. 151–56.
- Durot, Frédéeric; Lacaton, Anne; Vassal, Jean-Philippe (2007): Plus, large scale housing development: An exceptional case, Barcelona.
- Easterling, Keller (2010): "The Action is the Form," in: Dérive N° 40/41, Understanding Stadtforschung, Vienna, pp. 29–31.
- Färber, Alexa (2010): "Greifbarkeit der Stadt: Überlegungen zu einer stadt- und wissensanthropologischen Erforschung stadträumlicher Aneignungspraktiken," in: Dérive N° 40/41, Understanding Stadtforschung, Vienna, pp. 100–05.
- Glaser, Barney; Strauss, Anselm L. (2008): "Die Entdeckung der Grounded Theory," in: Grounded Theory. Strategien, qualitativer Forschung, Bern, pp. 19–27.
- Glaser, Barney; Strauss, Anselm L. (1967): "The Discovery of Grounded Theory," in: The Discovery of Grounded Theory: Strategies for Qualitative Research, Chicago, Chapter I, pp. 10–21.
- Gans, Herbert J. (1962): "Appendix: The Types and Problems of Participant-Observation," in: The Urban Villagers—Group and Class in the Life of Italian-Americans, New York, pp. 338–46.
- Geschichtswerkstatt Wilhelmsburg Honigfabrik e.V.; Museum Elbinsel Wilhelmsburg e.V. (eds.) (2008): Wilhelmsburg, Hamburgs große Elbinsel, Hamburg.
- Girtler, Roland (2004): "10 Gebote der Feldforschung," in: Forum Qualitative Sozialforschung, Vienna, pp. 3–13.
- Handke, Peter (1996/1984): Walk about the Villages. A Dramatic Poem, Goins Court Riverside, CA.
- Handelskammer Hamburg (2004): Leben und Arbeiten im Herzen Hamburgs—Die Entwicklungsperspektive der Elbinsel, Hamburg.
- Innhofer, Roland; Rothe, Katja; Harrasser, Karin (eds.) (2011): "Einleitung," in: Das Mögliche regieren. Gouvernementalität in der Literatur- und Kulturanalyse, Bielefeld, pp. 9–19.
- Internationale Bauausstellung (IBA) Hamburg GmbH (ed.) (2008):

Wasseratlas; Wasser Land-Topologien für die Hamburger Elbinsel, Hamburg.
• Kaijima, Momoyo; Kuroda, Junzo; Tsukamoto, Yoshiharu (2010): "Methods," in: Made in Tokyo, Tokyo, pp. 18–21.
• Koolhaas, Rem; Mau, Bruce (1995): "Nothingness," in: O.M.A., S, M, L, XL, New York.
• Latour, Bruno (1999): "Glossary," in: Pandora's Hope: An Essay on the Reality of Science Studies, Harvard University Press, pp. 303–12.
• Latour, Bruno (2006/1986): "Die Macht der Assoziationen," in: Belliger, Andrea; Krieger, David. J. (eds.), ANThology. Ein einführendes Handbuch zur Akteur-Netzwerk-Theorie, Bielefeld, pp. 195–212.
• Latour, Bruno (1986): "The Powers of Association," in: John Law (ed.): Power, Action and Belief. A New Sociology of Knowledge?, Sociological Review Monograph, Keele University, pp. 261–77.
• Latour, Bruno (2005): "Third Move: Connecting Sites," in: Reassembling the Social: An Introduction to Actor-Network-Theory. Clarendon Lectures in Management Studies, New York, pp. 219–46.
• Law, John (2009): "Actor-Network-Theory and Material Semiotics," in: Bryan S. Turner (ed.), Oxford, Malden, The New Blackwell Companion to Social Theory, pp. 141–58.
• Lefebvre, Henri (1991/1974): "Die Produktion des Raums," in: Günzel, Stephan; Dünne, Jörg (eds.), Raumtheorie, Frankfurt a.M., pp. 330–42.
• Lefebvre, Henri (1974): The Production of Space, Oxford, pp. 1–67.
• Lindner, Rolf (1981): "Die Angst des Forschers vor dem Feld: Überlegungen zur teilnehmenden Beobachtung als Interaktionsprozeß," in: Zeitschrift für Volkskunde 77, Berlin, pp. 51–66.
• Löw, Martina (2001): "Raumsoziologie," in: Günzel, Stephan; Dünne, Jörg (eds.), Raumtheorie, Frankfurt a.M., pp. 158–72.
• Michaelis, Tabea; Pohl, Ben (2010): Towards a Landscape of Possibilities. Urban Design Project 2, HafenCity Universität, Hamburg.
• Oertzen, Jürgen (2006): "Grounded Theory," in: Behnke, J., Gschwend, T., Schindler, D., & Schnapp, K.U. (eds.), Methoden der Politikwissenschaft. Neuere qualitative und quantitative Analyseverfahren, Baden-Baden, pp. 145–54.
• Saunders, Doug von (2012): Arrival City: How the largest migration in history is reshaping our world, New York.
• Schneider, Jochem; Baumgärtner, Christine (2000): Offene Räume, Open Spaces, Stuttgart.
• Serres, Michel (2009/1998): "(Local) Landscape," in: The Five Senses: A Philosophy of Mingled Bodies, London, New York, Chapter Visit, pp. 236–310.
• Serres, Michel (2009/1998): "Method and Rambling (The Global and the Local)," in: The Five Senses: A Philosophy of Mingled Bodies, London, New York, Chapter Visit, pp. 236–310.
• Sieweke, Jorg; Schultz Joachim (2007): Atlas Wilhelmsburg: Die Insel neu vermessen, Hamburg.
• Situationtische Internationale (2011/1958): Definitions, Paris.

- Spradley, James P. (1980): Participant Observation, New York, pp. 3–35.
- Strauss, Anselm L.; Corbin, Juliet M. (1990): "Kodier-Verfahren," in: Grounded Theory: Grundlagen qualitativer Sozialforschung, Weinheim, Chapter II, pp. 39–58.
- Strauss, Anselm L.; Corbin, Juliet M. (2015/1990): "Theoretical Foundations," in: Basics of Qualitative Research: Grounded Theory Procedures and Techniques, Thousand Oaks, pp. 17–31.
- Strauss, Anselm L. (1994/1987): Grundlagen qualitativer Sozialforschung. Datenanalyse und Theoriebildung in der empirischen soziologischen Forschung, Munich, pp. 44–51 and pp. 172–73.
- Strauss, Anselm L. (1987): "Qualitative analysis of data: an introduction," in: Qualitative Analysis for Social Scientists, University of Cambridge, pp. 10–21.
- Venturi, Robert; Scott Brown, Denise; Izenour, Steven (1972): Learning from Las Vegas: The Forgotten Symbolism of Architectural Form, Cambridge, Massachusetts and London.
- Yaneva, Albena (2013): "Actor-Network-Theory: Approach to the archaeology of contemporary architecture.", in: Paul Graves-Brown, Rodney Harrison and Angela Piccini (eds.), Oxford Handbook of the Archaeology of the Contemporary World, Oxford University Press, pp. 121–35.
- Yaneva, Albena (2009): Made by the Office for Metropolitan Architecture: An Ethnography of Design, Rotterdam.
- Wolff, Stephan (2008): "Wege ins Feld und ihre Varianten," in: Ernst von Kardorff; Ines Steinke; Uwe Flick (eds.), Qualitative Forschung. Ein Handbuch, Reinbek bei Hamburg, pp. 334–49.

Further Sources

- Geschichte Alt-Wilhelmsburg. www.alt-wilhelmsburg.de/geschichte.htm, consulted on 19.4.2015.
- Gezer, Özlem (2011): "Die Hoffnungsreisenden," in: Spiegel: 16/2011: www.spiegel.de/spiegel/print/d-78076145.html, consulted on 19.4.2015.
- IBA Energiebunker — Verwandlung in ein Öko-Kraftwerk: www.iba-hamburg.de/fileadmin/Projekte/00_Projekte_Infografiken-Lageplaene/infografik_bunker_de.gif, consulted on 19.04.2015.
- Internationale Bauausstellung IBA Hamburg 2013: www.iba-hamburg.de/, consulted on 19.4.2015.
- Lost Places — Orte der Fotografie: Kunsthalle Hamburg. www.hamburger-kunsthalle.de/index.php/lostplaces/articles/lostplaces.html, consulted on 19.4.2015.
- Statistisches Amt für Hamburg und Schleswig-Holstein, December 2011.
- Urban Design (UD), Project; University of the Neighborhoods (UdN), HafenCity University, Hamburg. www.ud.hcu-hamburg.de/77-1-UdN.html, udn.hcu-hamburg.de/de/, consulted on 19.4.2015.
- "Wilhelmsburger Straßennamen erzählen," in: Elbe Wochenblatt, January 1995.

Illustrations

All photographs taken by the author from May to August 2012 on the Wilhelmsburg Elbe Islands, Hamburg, with the exception of images from the following sources:

• p.123: Wilhelmsburg Labor: "Made in … Lokale Praktiken urbaner Produktion," Ben Pohl, March 2011.
• p. 338: Documenta Kassel 13, July 19 2012.

Private collection of the E.S. family (as letter, postcards, newspaper cuttings, or photographs) with the kind permission of E.R-S. Early photographs of the single women's hostel (now University of the Neighborhoods): Archiv Lehrstuhl Urban Design; with the kind permission of Urban Design, Prof. Bernd Kniess.

• Wittkohl house, date unknown, in: Wilhelmsburger Zeitung, 1965.
• "Zum Fährhaus," date unknown, in: Wilhelmsburger Zeitung, 1972.
• "Vogelschießen schon 1680," in: Wilhelmsburger Zeitung, 1972.
• Meine liebe E. [Letter], 14.1.1944.
• Anti-aircraft bunker VI, Floor plan, 1940.
• Meine liebe E. [Letter], 29.5.1944.
• "Das Buch war ein Spiegel," in: Wilhelmsburger Zeitung, 1972
• The rest and nursing home by the town hall, in: Wilhelmsburger Zeitung, 1967.
• Large hall, Christmas, single women's hostel, Rotenhäuser Damm, c.1950.
• Single women's hostel, Rotenhäuser Damm, c.1950.
• Private bedroom, single women's hostel, Rotenhäuser Damm, c.1950
• Meine liebe E. [Letter], 23.6.1944.
• "Bald Ausländer im Ortsausschuß," in: Wilhelmsburger Zeitung, 1979.
• Dr. Reinhold Gräßner, as very many still remember him, in: Wilhelmsburger Zeitung, 1970.
• "Wiedersehen nach 20 Jahren," in: Wilhelmsburger Zeitung, 1979.
• Wooden sailing boats on the Reiherstieg, date unknown, in: Wilhelmsburger Zeitung, 1979.
• "Greunhöker Cohr," in: Wilhelmsburger Zeitung, 1976.
• Vegetable stands on Veringplatz, date unknown, in: Wilhelmsburger Zeitung, 1972.
• Portrait of Father S. with daughter, c.1930.
• Seamstresses in Wilhelmsburg, c.1920.
• Garment clinic advert, in: Wilhelmsburger Zeitung, 1979.
• Kirchdorf school class in 1908, in: Wilhelmsburger Zeitung, 1979.
• Reinhold/Nippold children, date unknown, in: Wilhelmsburger Zeitung, 1970.
• Portrait of E.S., c.1920.
• The doctor and his spouse in elegant bathing suits, date unknown, in: Wilhelmsburger Zeitung, 1970.
• Advert for the barbershop Frisör-Wolfgang, in: Elbe Wochenblatt, January 1995.
• Bush of the Pioneer, 1908, in: Wilhelmsburger Zeitung, 1976.
• Kitchen maids, c.1920.
• "Die Möbelwagen fuhren vor," in: Wilhelmsburger Zeitung, 1979.
• Soldiers, date unknown
• "Wasser wird teurer," in: Wilhelmsburger Zeitung, 1979.

• "Ist ein Geschäfts-
zentrum drin?",
in: Wilhelmsburger
Zeitung, 1967.
• "Containerverkehr
nach Südafrika wird auf-
genommen," in: Wilhelms-
burger Zeitung, 1976.
• The famous old Opel,
date unknown,
in: Wilhelmsburger
Zeitung, 1970.
• The Number 2 tram /
Elbbrücken, in: Wilhelms-
burger Zeitung, 1974.
• Reiherstieg ferry, date
unknown, in: Wilhelms-
burger Zeitung, 1974.
• "Wir ziehen da nicht
wieder ein!", in: Wilhelmsburger Zeitung, 1976.
• The repurposed
motorbike, date unknown,
in: Wilhelmsburger
Zeitung, 1970.
• Sievers farmhouse,
date unknown,
in: Wilhelmsburger
Zeitung, 1965.
• "Die schwerste Sturmflut
seit Menschengedenken,"
in: Wilhelmsburger
Zeitung, 1976.
• "Ratten hatten den Deich
unterwühlt," in: Wilhelmsburger Zeitung, 1954.
• A much-admired
excursion, in: Wilhelms-
burger Zeitung, 1974.
• Rethe warehouse,
in: Wilhelmsburger
Zeitung, 1979.

License-free historical
map material:
• Source: Open Source
database of Christian
Terstegge, www.christian-
terstegge.de;
consulted on 19.4.2015,
Map, Elbe Islands in 1071,
Map, Elbe Islands in 1600,
Map, Elbe Islands in 1903.
• Topographic and histori-
cal maps: Cartographic
Collection, HafenCity
University Hamburg;
Map, Elbe Islands in 1789,
Map, Elbe Islands in 1867,
Map, Elbe Islands in 1978,
Map, Elbe Islands in 2004.

Imprint

The series UD is edited by
• Bernd Kniess
Urban Design
HafenCity Universität Hamburg

Research and Design
• Tabea Michaelis

Editing
• Bernd Kniess, Tabea Michaelis

Translation
• Helen Ferguson

Copy-editing and Proofreading
• Jan Wenzel, Ames Gerould

Graphic Design
• Wolfgang Schwärzler

Paper
• Munken Print White, 80 g/m^2
• Colorplan Factory Yellow,
Fabric, 270 g/m^2

Printing
• Druckhaus Köthen

Binding
• Buchbinderei Stein+Lehmann

Published by
Spector Books Leipzig
Harkortstraße 10
04107 Leipzig
www.spectorbooks.com

Distribution
• Germany, Austria: GVA,
Gemeinsame Verlagsauslieferung
Göttingen GmbH&Co. KG
www.gva-verlage.de
• Switzerland: AVA Verlagsaus-
lieferung AG, www.ava.ch
• France, Belgium: Interart Paris,
www.interart.fr
• UK: Central Books Ltd,
www.centralbooks.com
• USA, Canada: RAM
Publications+Distribution Inc.,
www.rampub.com
• Australia, New Zealand:
Perimeter Distribution,
www.perimeterdistribution.com
• Other Countries: Motto Distribution,
www.mottodistribution.com

© 2015 The editor, the author
and Spector Books, Leipzig

First edition
Printed in Germany

ISBN 978-3-95905-060-9

Made possible by Urban Design
HafenCity University and
Lawaetzstiftung as part of the
EU funding program SEEDS.

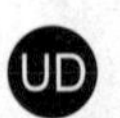
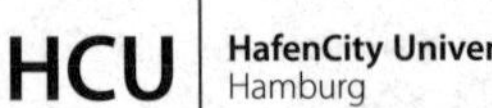
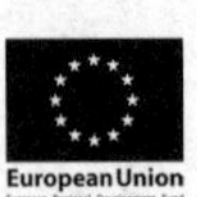
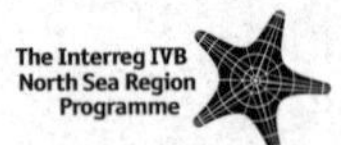
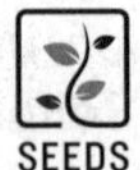